Wild Bill Elliott

Wild Bill Elliott

A Complete Filmography

GENE BLOTTNER

McFarland & Company, Inc., Publishers

Jefferson, North Carolina, and London

LIBRARY OF CONGRESS CATALOGUING-IN-PUBLICATION DATA

Blottner, Gene, 1938–
Wild Bill Elliott : a complete filmography / Gene Blottner.
p.   cm.
Includes bibliographical references and index.

ISBN-13: 978-0-7864-2986-8 (illustrated case binding : 50# alkaline paper)

1. Elliot, Gordon, 1905–1965.   I. Title.

PN2287.E44B56   2007   791.4302'8092 — dc22   2007007484
[B]

British Library cataloguing data are available

On the cover: Wild Bill Elliott comic book cover,
issue #9, July–September, 1952

Manufactured in the United States of America

*McFarland & Company, Inc., Publishers
Box 611, Jefferson, North Carolina 28640
www.mcfarlandpub.com*

To my good friends
Bill Sasser and Larry Floyd

Acknowledgments

Many people assisted me in obtaining information for this book. I would like to thank the stars who had the patience to allow me to interview them either by phone, in person or via correspondence through the mail: Claudia Barrett, Dale Berry, Adrian Booth Brian, Joe Canutt, John Crawford, Phyllis Coates, Johnny Duncan, Barbra Fuller, Anne Jeffreys, Dick Jones, Kay Linaker, Marjorie Lord, Jimmy Lydon, House Peters Jr., Paul Picerni, Elaine Riley, Peggy Stewart, Neil Summers and Helen Talbot.

A special thanks to those who willingly shared their knowledge, memorabilia and information, or who helped me with my research: Larry Blanks, Catherine Blottner, Charles Blottner, Minna Blottner, Judge Hal Bonney, Jack Borden (Parker County Sheriff's Posse), Gene Carpenter, Becky Coleman (Boulder City Library, Boulder City, NV), Dr. Lang Elliott, Carrie Farriss, Larry Floyd, Penn Genthner (Pasadena Community Playhouse), Tom Goldrup, Josie Walters Johnson (Motion Picture Reading Room of the Library of Congress), Shane Joiner (Turner Classic Movies), Alun Jones, Boyd Magers, Bob Neuman, Anita Palmer (National Cutting Horse Association), Cindy Peery, Bill Sasser, Buddy Saunders (Lone Star Comics), Decla Simpson (Alumni Affairs at Rockhurst University), Kenny Stier, John Struchtemeyer (Kansas City Missouri School District), Jenny Stuerzl (American Royal Museum), Mary Anne Vandivort and staff (Kirn Memorial Library, Norfolk, VA), Mitch Weisberg and Don Young.

Contents

Preface

Although this is a filmography of western star Wild Bill Elliott, a biographical sketch begins the book.

His film appearances are then divided into two sections— starring and supporting roles. His guest appearance in *Bells of Rosarita* (Republic, 1945) and his television pilot *Marshal of Trail City* (Century Television, 1950) are included in the section devoted to his starring roles.

Other Elliott appearances in feature films, serials and documentaries through archive footage have been listed.

Illustrations in the biographical sketch are courtesy of Bill Sasser and the author. Unless otherwise acknowledged, illustrations in the filmographic sections on Elliott's starring and supporting roles are from the author's collection.

About the Entries

Advertising Blurb: Above the title of almost every film covered, there is an example of a "blurb" used in the advertising copy for the film.

Release Dates: All release dates of Elliott's western films were taken from Les Adams and Buck Rainey's *The Shoot-'Em-Ups*. The release dates of Elliott's non-western films came from various sources.

Alternate Title: If a film used a title other than that given on initial release, this title is listed.

Color/B&W: Few of Elliott's films were shot in color and the designation "B&W" (black and white) is accordingly not supplied. If a film is in color, this is, however, noted.

Cast: All cast members listed before the designation "//" were identified in either the beginning or end credits or both. All cast members listed after that designation were identified by the author.

Credits: Each person listed received on-screen billing.

Songs: All identifiable songs have been named, along with composers and artists, if known.

Location Filming: Locations are given only for Elliott's westerns. Kenneth Stier provided information for those sites not identified by the author.

Running Time: All running times of western films were obtained from Adams and Rainey's *The Shoot-'Em-Ups*. Other running times were obtained from various sources, primarily critical reviews.

Source: If a film was derived from a published work, this is stated, along with the name(s) of the author(s).

Story: This is an encapsulation of the happenings on the silver screen and not an attempt to describe every scene in detail. All of Elliott's starring films were viewed by the author. Of the 158 pictures in the section on Elliott supporting roles, the author was unable to view 18.

Notes and Commentary: This is information obtained from stars who graciously allowed me to interview them, and from many other sources.

Reviews: To give the reader a flavor of how critics received the film, reviews at the time of release or retrospective views are presented.

Summation: My overall appraisal of the film, with which I can only hope the reader might concur.

Appendices

The appendices cover Elliott's comic books with story titles; Elliott's Las Vegas television programs; western star polls; and alphabetical and chronological listings of Elliott's feature films. A selected bibliography is included. The work concludes with an index.

Wild Bill Elliott: His Life

Wild Bill Elliott hung up his spurs over fifty years ago with the release of his last starring western, *The Forty-Niners* (Allied Artists), on May 9, 1954. His screen career would last three more years as he portrayed a police lieutenant in five detective films, ending with *Footsteps in the Night* (Allied Artists, 1957). In these last films, Elliott was billed simply as Bill Elliott. He had come full circle: with his second starring venture the studios dubbed him Bill; Republic starred him as Wild Bill and William; Monogram/Allied Artists went back to Wild Bill for his western series and then to Bill for his final starring films.

Wild Bill Elliott was a major western star for over fifteen years. Known, and proclaimed by himself and others, as a "peaceable" man, his screen persona met evil head-on and emerged victorious. Though a second definition of peaceable is "at peace or peaceful," Websters' primary definition is "fond of, inclined toward or promoting peace." Elliott's gunplay and unusual style of fisticuffs brought cheers from millions of Saturday moviegoers. In *Hollywood Corral* (Popular Library, 1976), author Don Miller stated Elliott exuded a "steely, reassuring calm." From 1940 through 1954, Elliott was listed as a top moneymaking western star in the *Motion Picture Herald* poll of exhibitors and the *Boxoffice* magazine poll from 1945 through 1953. In addition, Wild Bill ranked 18th in Boyd Magers' list of the top 100 cowboys of the 20th century.

Gordon Nance, 1904–1925

Elliott was born Gordon Ami Nance in Pattonsburg, Missouri, on October 16, 1904, to

William Elliott, Republic Studios, late 1940s (courtesy Bill Sasser).

LeRoy (Roy) Whitfield and Maude Myrtle Auldridge Nance. Gordon had two siblings, a sister, Carmen, and a younger brother, Dale. The Nances lived on a ranch in Pattonsburg where Gordon began riding at the age of five. While Gordon was still a youngster, the Nance family moved to Kansas City where Roy was a stockman at the Kansas City stockyards. Some references indicate that Roy was a commissioner, but listings of commissioners in the Kansas City newspapers in 1919 and 1920 fail to include his name. About this time, Gordon became interested in the West through the movies of William S. Hart and, later, Tom Mix. Maude Nance supposedly predicted that Gordon would one day become a western star in the movies. In Kansas City, Gordon lived at 3226 Charlotte, 6020 Main Street and 228 West 62nd Street, attending Hyde Park Grade School in 1916–1917 and Bryant Grade School from 1917 through 1920, graduating from grade school on June 11, 1920. Interested in livestock, at age sixteen, Gordon won a first place award at the American Royal, a prestigious livestock show, where Hertford, shorthorn and Angus cattle were judged and sold. Neither local newspaper, the *Kansas City Star* or the *Kansas City Times* listed Gordon as a winner. Owners' names were listed in 1919, but only the animal's name received recognition in 1920. Gordon attended Westport High School in 1920 but dropped out on February 22, 1921. By some reports, Roy took Gordon to the stockyards where he met actual cowboys. Learning primarily from the cowboys, especially brothers Grover, Sylvan and Lester Metzger, Gordon, by age sixteen, learned to ride by controlling his horse with his knees instead of jerking the reins or using his spurs. Later Roy and Maude decided to get a divorce. Gordon moved to the West Coast on the heels of this development.

Gordon Elliott, 1925–1938

In Hollywood, Nance had signed with a talent scout, who changed his name to Gordon Elliott. He appeared in his first motion picture, *The Plastic Age* (Commonwealth Pictures, 1925), starring the "It Girl," Clara Bow, which was released in December. Gordon appeared in two more productions, a short comedy, *Napoleon, Jr.* (Fox, 1925), and director John Ford's *Shamrock Handicap* (Fox, 1926). In *Handicap*, Gordon was no more than a fleeting face in a crowd of villagers at the picture's end. Gordon returned to Kansas City, where he obtained a job as a "soda jerk" at the Crown Drug Store at 39th and Main. Actor Johnny Duncan, best known for his role of Robin in the serial *Batman and Robin* (Columbia, 1949), remembered that at around age 4 he used to buy cherry phosphate sodas from Gordon. Duncan's father started a barbershop in the hotel next door and would cut Gordon's hair. Johnny was present in his father's shop on the Saturday night when Gordon had his shoes shined and then put on his spats. Duncan's father asked Gordon, "What are you getting all ready for?" Gordon replied, "I'm going to Hollywood. I'm going to be a cowboy extra." Johnny was sitting in a barber chair when the conversation took place. Then Gordon turned to Johnny and said, "J.B., I won't be able to make you any more cherry phosphate sodas. So you'll have to tell them what you want at the drug store." Duncan couldn't remember if Gordon was known as Elliott or Nance at that time. Duncan's father used Brillantine in Gordon's hair, slick in the back, and Johnny said, "He looked really spiffy." Johnny added, "Elliott played himself. That's what he was like off the screen. He didn't act, he played himself."

Returning to California, Elliott received a good part in a Tom Mix western, *Arizona Wildcat* (Fox, 1927), receiving 4th billing as heroine Dorothy Sebastian's brother. But Elliott's comment noted above about a cowboy extra might have been in reference to an unbilled role in *Valley of Hunted Men* (Pathe, 1928), with Buffalo Bill, Jr., which was released after the Mix vehicle.

In the waning days of silent films, Elliott had good roles in small productions and small roles in the bigger features. On February 6, 1927, Elliott married Helen Josephine Meyer, a marriage that would last for 34 years. Helen was working at I. Magnin's, a high fashion woman's store, when Elliott met her. Elliott was immediately attracted to Helen and pursued her until she caught him. They would have one daughter, Barbara.

To gain acting experience, Elliott auditioned for a part in the Pasadena Playhouse production of *Wind Mills*, a three-act play by Lee Arms. He won and played the part of Larry Foster. The play was presented on December 15 and 22, 1928. Also in the cast was Robert Young as Paul Clarke.

The introduction of sound to motion pictures slowed Elliott's screen career. From substantial supporting roles, Elliott's parts now were fleeting walk-ons. From late 1929 through the end of 1931, Elliott appeared in almost 3 dozen feature films and 3 comedy short subjects. He had one line of dialog in *Sunny* (First National, 1930), *City Streets* (Paramount, 1931), *Woman Between* (Radio, 1931), *Magnificent Lie* (Paramount, 1931) and *Delicious* (Fox, 1931)— in which he delivers a line that would prove prophetic of his screen career: looking at a photograph of his polo team, Elliott states, "It would look better if I had my horse." His best role of that period was as a flyer who attempts to romance Jean Harlow in *Platinum Blonde* (Columbia, 1931). Elliott also shared the screen with other favorites of that time: Eddie Cantor, Charles Farrell, Ruth Chatterton, Marion Davies and Marilyn Miller.

In 1932, Elliott was busy in motion pictures, appearing in 20 feature films. In addition, Elliott again appeared at the Pasadena Playhouse in Noel Coward's *The Young Idea*, which was presented March 17–26, 1932. Elliott assayed the role of Rodney Masters. In the *Pasadena Community*

Playhouse News, it was stated that Elliott returned after a long absence, and while rehearsing, completed a part in a motion picture with Constance Bennett. The article mentioned that Elliott was now under contract to both Warner Bros. and Hal Roach studios. The star of the play was Addison Richards, who would team up with Elliott to menace Dick Foran in *Trailin' West* (Warner Bros., 1936). Elliott received dialog in a few of his films, usually only one line. He spoke

---

PASADENA COMMUNITY   PLAYHOUSE NEWS

PASADENA COMMUNITY PLAYHOUSE ASSOCIATION

PRESENTS

"The Young Idea"

By NOEL COWARD

MARCH 17 to 26, 1932

331st regular production of the Pasadena Community Playhouse, now in its 15th year.

CURRENTLY, Noel Coward's play, "Cavalcade," is scoring a tremendous hit in London. "Private Lives," his earlier play, achieved wide popularity and his performance in it won the unanimous praise of critics. Play right, actor and composer, the versatile Mr. Coward, now in Hollywood, is justly rated a leading exponent of England's theatre. "The Young Idea," first produced in 1923, was revived last year in London with greater success than the original production. Both "The Young Idea" and "Hay Fever," another of his plays, were written when the author was twenty-one . . . or younger.

GILMOR BROWN, *Director*	ADDISON RICHARDS, *Associate Director*
CORLISS McGEE, *Art Director*	MURRAY YEATS, *General Production Mgr.*

CHARACTERS

GEORGE BRENT ....ADDISON RICHARDS
GERDA ------} (His Children) ....{ DOLLY GRAVES
SHOLTO ----}   { ALEX COURTNEY
JENNIFER (His First Wife, Divorced) ....MARTHA DEANE
CICELY (His Second Wife) ....LOIS CORBET
PRISCILLA HARTLEBERRY ....CONSTANCE DEIGHTON SIMPSON
CLAUD ECCLES ....C. GLENNON HARDY
JULIA CRAGWORTHY ....LYSBETH ALLISON
EUSTACE DABBIT ....MURRAY YEATS
SIBYL BLAITH ....EVELYN KNOWLES
RODNEY MASTERS ....GORDON ELLIOTT
HUDDLE ....JOHN BLAGDEN
HIRAM J. WALKIN ....HOWARD HARDING
MARIA ....MARIA BONZI

SCENES

ACT I—Hall of George Brent's house, in England.
ACT II—The same. A week later.
ACT III—Jennifer Brent's villa, in Italy. Three weeks later.

LIGHTING, CONSTRUCTION and STAGE MANAGEMENT under the supervision of FRED C. HUXLEY.
SETTINGS CONSTRUCTED by JAMES CALLAHAN.
ARTIST'S ASSISTANT, DWIGHT COYE.
STAGE MANAGER, GENEVIEVE THAYER.
PRODUCTION CHAIRMAN, ROMENIA ELLIS LOXLEY.
PROPERTY COMMITTEE—Mrs. F. H. Parke, Miss Theodosia Parke.
COSTUME COMMITTEE—Mrs. E. B. Thompson, Miss Caroline Coulter.
Furniture in first two acts courtesy of THE CHEESEWRIGHT STUDIOS.
Furniture in third act courtesy of GEORGE HUNT.
Luggage courtesy of HERBOLD'S.

Ben Hur Drip Coffee and Chesterfield Cigarettes served during the intermission

Playbill, *The Young Idea* (Pasadena Playhouse, 1932)— Gordon Elliott played Rodney Masters.

in *Lady with a Past* (RKO, 1932), *Final Edition* (Columbia, 1932), *Vanity Fair* (Allied, 1932), *Two Against the World* (Warner Bros., 1932), *Jewel Robbery* (Warner Bros., 1932), *Week-End Marriage* (First National, 1932), *The Rich Are Always with Us* (First National, 1932) and *Forbidden* (Columbia, 1932). He shared the screen with Edward G. Robinson, Mae West and Constance Bennett.

The low point in Elliott's career was 1933, as he appeared in only 10 feature films and 2 comedy shorts. Elliott's performances still did not warrant billing, but he did receive dialog scenes in *Cocktail Hour* (Columbia, 1933), *Dancing Lady* (Metro-Goldwyn-Mayer, 1933) and *Little Giant* (First National, 1933). The only star of magnitude that he appeared with in 1933 was Edward G. Robinson.

The year 1934 showed an upswing in Elliott's career. He appeared in 20 feature films and one short subject. His role in *Friends of Mr. Sweeney* (Warner Bros., 1934), however, ended up on the cutting room floor. To his credit, Elliott finally received on-screen billing in a sound film, this for *Registered Nurse* (First National, 1934). Elliott had dialog sequences in ten additional feature films plus the comedy short, *Good Morning, Eve!* (Warner Bros., 1934), which starred Leon Errol. Elliott played in scenes with such stars as James Cagney, George Brent, Ricardo Cortez, Richard Barthelmess, Lyle Talbot and Pat O'Brien.

The year 1935 was a busy year for Elliott, as he showed up in 28 feature films plus one short subject. He would receive his best supporting role in Dick Foran's *Moonlight on the Prairie* (Warner Bros., 1935), in which he played an undercover lawman who is murdered by the outlaws, leaving it up to Foran to bring the killers to justice. Elliott also received billing in *Girl from 10th Avenue* (Warner Bros., 1935), *Goose and the Gander* (Warner Bros., 1935), *Man of Iron* (Warner Bros., 1935), *Personal Maid's Secret* (Warner Bros., 1935) and *The Traveling Saleslady* (Warner Bros., 1935). Elliott worked with Joe E. Brown, Pat O'Brien, Paul Muni, Bette Davis, James Cagney, George Brent, Kay Francis, Margaret Lindsay, Gene Raymond and

Anita Louise, with whom Elliott shared a screen kiss.

Elliott continued to stay busy in 1936 with 18 feature films (in two of these, *King of Hockey* [Warner Bros., 1936] and *Two Against the World* [Warner Bros., 1936], only his voice was heard), one short subject and one part that was cut from the final print. He received billing in 8 films: *Case of the Black Cat* (Warner Bros., 1936), where he had a great role as a murder suspect; *Case of the Velvet Claws* (Warner Bros., 1936), in which Warren William denounced him as the murderer; *Down the Stretch* (Warner Bros., 1936); *Fugitive in the Sky* (Warner Bros., 1936); *Murder by an Aristocrat* (Warner Bros., 1936); *Murder of Dr. Harrigan* (Warner Bros., 1936); *Polo Joe* (Warner Bros., 1936), which had Elliott as Joe E. Brown's rival for Carol Hughes' affections; and finally *Travelin' West* (Warner Bros., 1936), in which Elliott was the bad guy against hero Dick Foran in this Civil War western. Elliott worked with such stars as Edward G. Robinson, Ricardo Cortez, Warren William, Pat O'Brien, Bette Davis, Lyle Talbot, Joe E. Brown and Dick Foran.

The year 1937 showed Elliott parting company with Warner Bros. and beginning to freelance, appearing in films from 20th Century–Fox and Columbia to Republic and Grand National. What a range of studios! Elliott appeared in only 11 films and received billing in 8: *Boots and Saddles* (Republic, 1937), as the bad guy in this Gene Autry western; *Guns of the Pecos* (Warner Bros., 1937); *Love Takes Flight* (Grand National, 1937); *Melody for Two* (Warner Bros., 1937); *Midnight Court* (Warner Bros., 1937); *Roll Along Cowboy* (20th Century–Fox, 1937), providing the villainy for Smith Ballew; *Swing It, Professor* (Ambassador, 1937), in which Elliott plays a crime boss brought to justice by Pinky Tomlin; and *Wife, Doctor and Nurse* (20th Century–Fox, 1937). Elliott worked with Gene Autry, Dick Foran, Ann Dvorak, Smith Ballew and Louise Hovick, who was better known as burlesque queen Gypsy Rose Lee.

The turning point for Elliott was 1938. He began the year with film releases from 20th

Century–Fox, Monogram and Universal. Elliott received billing in *Boy of the Streets* (Monogram, 1938) and *Lady in the Morgue* (Universal, 1938). Sources have indicated that Elliott had a small part in *Letter of Introduction* (Universal, 1938), but in viewing the film three times, the author could not see Elliott. Reportedly, Columbia Pictures was impressed with Elliott's performance in *Moonlight on the Prairie* and signed him for their fourth serial production, *The Great Adventures of Wild Bill Hickok* (1938). Both Elliott and the chapter-play were hits with the Saturday matinee crowd. Columbia was looking for a second cowboy to complement Charles Starrett's popular series. Series with Ken Maynard, Bob Allen and Jack Luden had all failed to generate the necessary appeal. Elliott was signed for four films, to be produced by Larry Darmour and released by Columbia. Elliott's first starring western would be *In Early Arizona*. Initially Elliott would be billed as Gordon, but suddenly, because of the popularity of his serial, he was renamed Bill. Some of the advertising material, however, still called him Gordon.

Bill (Wild Bill, William) Elliott 1938–1965

Elliott's independently produced series was a success. Columbia placed Elliott in his second serial, *Overland with Kit Carson* (1939), and decided to produce his next season in-house. Elliot would play Wild Bill Saunders in four entries and would be proclaimed "a peaceable man." As he did in the *Hickok* serial, Elliott would now wear his guns butt forward. Elliott copied this fashion in wearing his guns after Gary Cooper, who portrayed Wild Bill Hickok in *The Plainsman* (Paramount, 1936).

With *Frontiers of '49* (Columbia, 1939), Elliott began to supply his own mounts. He used a horse named Sonny. In fact, Elliott had at least three other Sonnys that he used in his westerns. He had a fourth Sonny that he sold to actress/horsewoman Betty Miles.

In the 1940-41 season, Elliott played Hickok in six of eight films. In the other two, he played Wild Bill Boone and Davy Crockett. It didn't matter; he was still Wild Bill to his fans.

From 1935, there were two phenomena in series westerns—the singing cowboy and the trio westerns. Studios gave the public either music or two western stars for the price of one. With Elliott's series, Columbia decided to cover both with the addition of Tex Ritter. Ritter had been a top-ten cowboy in the *Motion Picture Herald* poll with his Grand National and Monogram Studios features. Both stars liked each other, but Elliott advised Ritter that he wasn't happy with the arrangement and would be looking for a solo starring series. (In fact, Elliott and Ritter became close friends; they would go hunting together once or twice a year for many years.) Ritter said he felt the same. There would be no hard feelings if either could manage to find one. There would be eight entries in the series. Even though Elliott would be the primary lead, Ritter had plenty of screen footage. Elliott would play Wild Bill Hickok in six of the features. With the possible exception of Ken Maynard and Hoot Gibson's Trail Blazers series at Monogram, the Elliott-Ritter films were probably the most equitable in terms of screen time of all the series with two western stars.

Elliott's popularity was ascending. For instance, his likeness appeared on Dixie Cup Ice Cream lids. Only Roy Rogers equaled Elliott's appearances, but Elliott sometimes was paired with other cowboys. Roy was the solo champion. Elliott could also be seen on Dixie premiums. The premium consisted of a star's color 8 × 10 photograph on the front, with a biographical sketch, some black and white photographs and a plug for the star's latest movie on the back.

In 1942, Republic Studios was looking for a western star to replace Gene Autry. Autry, against Republic President Herbert Yates' entreaties, joined the Air Force. Yates courted Elliott, and Elliott was convinced to join Republic. Columbia gave Elliott his release after placing him in his third serial, *Valley of Vanishing Men* (1942). In his initial contract with

Dixie Premiums with Bill Elliott, 1940s–1950s (courtesy Bill Sasser).

Republic, Elliott would make eight westerns and would be paid $2750 for each. It was further stipulated that Elliott would always receive top billing and would be excluded from appearing in serials. In addition, Elliott would furnish his own horses and would be paid the going rate charged by the rental stables. To give his series an extra lift, George "Gabby" Hayes was transferred from the Roy Rogers entries. Smiley Burnette, at large with Autry's departure, was assigned to work with Rogers.

Elliott's first Republic starring film would be titled *Calling Wild Bill Elliott* (1943). Only Gene Autry, with his *Gene Autry and the Mounties* (Columbia, 1951), and Sunset Carson, with *Sunset Carson Rides Again* (Astor, 1948) would also have their full names in the film's title. By Elliott's third entry, on-screen credits, ads and posters would proclaim Wild Bill Elliott as the star.

Republic was pleased to have their stars participate in the war effort. Dale Evans worked with the Victory Committee, and Ray Middleton did the same with the Hollywood Victory Caravan. Don Barry, Gabby Hayes and Ruth Terry displayed their talents for USO camp shows. Bill Elliott went on tours on behalf of War Bonds, while Smiley Burnette and Peggy Stewart made personal appearances to boost morale.

By 1943, Elliott began to purchase cutting horses. Doc Van Horn was instrumental in teaching Elliott everything about horses so Elliott could recognize excellence. One horse Elliott purchased was a bay gelding, Rey Boy, foaled at Swenson Brothers' SMS Ranch in Stamford, Texas. Another was a Morgan horse, Andy Pershing 8390. This horse was best known as Thunder in the Red Ryder series at Republic. Elliott sold Thunder to Allan Lane in 1946. When the Red Ryder series was cancelled, Thunder became Black Jack in the Allan "Rocky" Lane films.

Republic had been looking for a western star to play Fred Harman's comic strip character Red Ryder in a series. The Ryder character had been brought to the screen in a serial, *Adventures of Red Ryder* (Republic, 1940), with Don Barry in the lead. Barry's diminutive stature, however, didn't measure up to the tall, lanky presence of Harman's creation. Elliott fit the bill physically, but he turned the character into his own creation, with two guns butt forward and his "peaceable man" persona. But who cared — Elliott was Elliott, and he brought action and acting together in an impressive manner. Hayes co-starred in the first two films and then left the series to rejoin Rogers.

With the Ryder series, Elliott's contract was renegotiated. Elliott would receive $3750 each for eight features the first year, and then $4750 each for eight entries the second year.

Sixteen Ryders were made with Elliott in

Wild Bill Elliott in *Sheriff of Las Vegas* at the Capitol Theater, Richmond, VA, in early 1945 (courtesy Bill Sasser).

the lead. Bobby Blake, former Our Gang member and future top-flight actor, would portray Ryder's Indian companion, Little Beaver, and Alice Fleming played Ryder's aunt, the Duchess. After the first season, Elliott was seen as himself as a guest star in Roy Rogers' *Bells of Rosarita* (Republic, 1945). Elliott waived the top billing condition in his contract, with the stipulation he would be first billed of the other western stars and would be paid $2000. Elliott and the other Republic western stars, Sunset Carson, Allan Lane, Robert Livingston and Don "Red" Barry, helped Rogers bring Grant Withers, Roy Barcroft and three other bad guys to justice. It is interesting to note that when this film was released, both Livingston and Barry were now starring in non-westerns at the studio.

Randolph Scott had been announced as the star of Republic's big-budget production *In Old Sacramento* in 1946. Scott backed out, not wanting to make a picture at Republic. Elliott was assigned to replace Scott. Elliott accepted with some misgivings, feeling he would lose his Saturday matinee audience. In the 1946 *Motion Picture Herald* poll, Elliott had placed second to Roy Rogers. It has been noted that Elliott had been impressed with the austere westerns of William S. Hart. Elliott thought that this change could bring a heightened realism to his features. Republic would release two big-budgeted Elliott features a year through 1950. In the 1946–47 film schedule, as listed in *Boxoffice*, it was announced that Elliott would star in *The Old Spanish Trail* and *Pike's Peak*. Neither film was made.

Elliott made an appearance on Bing Crosby's *Philco Radio Time*, which aired Wednesday, March 24, 1948, on the ABC network. In between some humorous repartee with host Bing, Elliott plugged his latest Republic release, *Old Los Angeles*. Elliott joked about his name change from Wild Bill to William, simply stating, "Wild Bill Elliott sounds like a used car dealer." This became a fact in his later life in Las Vegas. Afterwards, Elliott and Crosby engaged in a short western skit in which Wild Bill Elliott and his sidekick, Gabby Crosby, trailed after rustler Rattlesnake Carpenter, played by Bing's announcer, Ken Carpenter. This was probably the only time that Elliott could demonstrate to his fans his fine sense of humor that for the most part was absent in his western features. As the show went off the air, it was mentioned that Elliott could be seen in person with his rodeo in Baton Rouge, Louisiana, that upcoming Saturday.

Elliott's *"Wild" Bill Elliott Bar Bar A Ranch Rodeo* opened Saturday, March 27, at the L.S.U. Agricultural Center for eight performances over a seven day run. This was the rodeo's world premier. Appearing with Elliott was his horse, Stormy Knight, as well as Doye O'Dell and His Radio Rangers (Frank Buckley, Buddy Ray and Jim Widimer). O'Dell and Elliott were good friends. Thanks to Elliott's influence, O'Dell was signed to a contract with Republic Pictures.   Nothing major came of the affiliation, with O'Dell receiving minor roles in *Man from Rainbow Valley* (1946), *Heldorado* (1946), and *Last Frontier Uprising* (1947). O'Dell appeared in three additional films, *Hit Parade of 1947* (1947), *The Gay Ranchero* (1948) and *Under California Stars* (1948), in which he did not receive billing.

Elliott did not forget his youthful audience. One hundred seventy-five news carriers for *Morning Advocate* and *Sun Times* newspapers were guests at the rodeo's Friday performance. One of the lucky paperboys was given the opportunity to ride Stormy Knight.

To help maintain his base of juvenile support, Elliott starred in his own radio program. After an audition program on July 3, 1948, the show was picked up on the ABC network. It ran five days a week, Mondays through Fridays, and was sponsored by

L.S.U. Rodeo and Livestock Show, March 27–April 2, 1948.

Quaker Puffed Wheat and Rice cereals. This was the first time a western star was featured in a 15-minute children's radio serial. The show began with the announcer shouting, "Look at him rope! Look at him ride!" Elliott then said, "Up there, boy. Let's ride, Stormy." He was Wild Bill Elliott, the peaceable man, who ran the Double Bar A Ranch (note: this was the actual name of Elliott's ranch, named after his daughter, Barbara) for his grandfather, Major Elliott, and was the head of the Cattleman's Association. The Major was the newspaper editor of the *Frontier Times* in the town of Rimhorn in El Dorado County. Helping Wild Bill run down outlaws were the youthful Buddy Fillmore, who lived on the ranch, and Range Inspector Longhorn Jones. Elliott rode Stormy Knight, and Buddy rode a horse named Sonny. These were the actual names of horses Elliott used in his motion pictures. In the first continued story, Elliott was challenged to unravel the mystery of the vanishing stagecoaches.

Leading lady Peggy Stewart has been asked at film festivals about her favorite western stars, and she has responded with two names—Wild Bill Elliott and Sunset Carson. Elliott was like a father figure to her. When Stewart asked to be released from her Republic contract, the studio responded that it would be fine but she would owe them money. Stewart went to Elliott for advice. Elliott remembered the times she had worked overtime in some of the Red Ryder pictures and figured Republic actually owed *her* money. Stewart quickly received her release.

Bill Elliott asked Stewart to be the Queen of the Rodeo at a rodeo to be held in Newhall. Elliott provided a mare for Stewart to ride. Stewart noted to Elliott that the mare seemed to be sluggish and was disappointed. Elliott told her not to worry, that the horse would perk up when the music started. The time came for Stewart to come galloping to the center of the arena. The mare wouldn't move. Stewart looked puzzled. Elliott, standing to one side, was laughing. With no Stewart coming forward, Elliott was announced and he

Quaker Puffed Rice ad, 1948.

rode out. About this time, Stewart realized why the mare didn't move — and the cause of Elliott's laughter: the mare was quietly relieving herself.

According to the Parker County Sheriff's Posse web site, Elliott became a member of the Parker County Sheriff's Posse in the late 1940s or early 1950s. The organization was formed in 1947 to preserve the southwestern traditions of the 140-year-old Parker County. In 1948, the organization could be seen at various rodeos and at the movie premier of *Red River* (United Artists, 1948). In 1949, the Posse formed an affiliation with the National Cutting Horse Association and was invited to attend the Lions Club International convention at Madison Square Garden, New York.

In a conversation with Jack Borden, one of the original members of the Posse, in 1952, Elliott received a gold badge and certificate of honorary membership at the 3rd Frontier Days Rodeo. Elliott, in partnership with rodeo stock contractor Tommy Steiner of Austin, Texas, produced this rodeo event in 1951 and 1952. Elliot and Steiner became partners in the summer of 1950. Elliott's last starring rodeo with Steiner was in September 1952. It was about this time that Elliott sold his interest to Steiner.

In 1950, Republic and Elliott parted company. It has been reported that Republic didn't think the Elliott films grossed as much as they felt they should. With Elliott's departure, Forrest Tucker was elevated to leading man for two features. Crooner Vaughn Monroe was signed as a singing cowboy in two big-budget westerns. Neither man filled the bill.

Helping to fill the void, Elliott signed with Dell Publishing Company to have his own comic book. The first issue appeared in May 1950 and soon would be published quarterly. His series came to an end in July 1955. Elliott was added to Dell's *Western Roundup* magazine in June 1952 and would appear until the Jan–Mar 1957 edition.

Elliott made a pilot film for a television series, *Marshal of Trail City* (Century Television Production, 1950), that didn't sell. But Monogram and Elliott came to terms for a new series of western features. In the smaller markets, most of Elliott's big-budget pictures played the top half of double bills. With his move to Monogram, Elliott's westerns sometimes found themselves on the lower half of the bill, usually paired with a Bowery Boys episode. Again Elliott was billed as Wild Bill, but now his films had an adult slant. His character would smoke and drink. In some instances, Elliott would play an outlaw who would reform over the course of the screenplay, in the tradition of William S. Hart. With *The Maverick* (1952), Elliott's features would be released by Monogram's parent company, Allied Artists. Two years later, Elliott's starring western career would come to an end. With five feature films left on his contract, Elliott would become a police lieutenant in an above-average mystery series. In 1957, with *Footsteps in the Night*, Elliott's thirty-two-year screen career came to an end.

Through the mid to late 1950s, Elliott became a spokesman for Viceroy cigarettes on the television detective program *The Lineup* (CBS). In later years, Elliott regretted this decision and hoped he wasn't responsible for enticing young people to become smokers.

At the Knoxville Western Caravan in 1990, Rex Allen commented on Elliott: "Bill Elliott was a perfectionist, a very personable guy. He lived not far from me out in Woodland Hills. He owned 60 acres. If Bill was alive and owned that 60 acres, he could buy out Trump. He became a cowboy. He wasn't a cowboy when he came there. Bill worked at it. He had good horses, good saddles, good equipment. He had one of the greatest spur collections that I've ever seen in my life. Bill, also, owned the world champion cutting horse for several years; a horse named Red Man. He used to show him. If you can sit a cutting horse, you can ride a horse. Bill was a good horseman."

Elliott was a member of the National Cutting Horse Association and entered Red Man in events during 1954–55. Red Man won $2058.78 during this time. This was a good, but certainly not outstanding, sum even for that time. The NCHA does not have Red Man listed as a world's champion.

In cutting horse competition, the rider is judged by the agility and athleticism of his horse, and his ability to walk his horse through the herd quietly without disturbing the rest of the cattle. Prior to separating a cow from the herd, the rider holds the reins in one hand, with the other hand on the saddle horn. After a cow has been separated from the herd, the reins must remain down on the horse's neck while the rider guides his horse with leg pressure. There are two sources of danger in this event: first, the horse may move in one direction while the rider goes in another, causing the rider to fall off; and second, on occasion a cow might try to rejoin the herd and charge directly at the horse and rider.

In the 1950s Elliott would perform at various movie theaters. On May 31, 1953, billed as "The Greatest of All Western Stars," Elliott brought his show to the Autoport Drive-In in Portsmouth, Virginia, for a 3:30 afternoon performance. Admission was only $1.50 per carload. The ad promised that Elliott would come to the concession stand after the show and shake hands with every fan. Assisting Elliott was Jack Sparks, who had appeared with Elliott in six of his western features at Republic.

Elliott retired to his ranch with his wife Helen. The ranch at this time was probably the former "Baby J" Ranch, which had been owned by Betty Grable and Harry James. It has been reported that Helen tried to control Elliott's life, being jealous of any time Elliott spent with his rodeo buddies, and of any woman who cast a romantic eye Elliott's way, probably with some justification. Peggy Stewart remarked, "He was very subtle. He didn't push it. I never saw it. He was discreet about it."

Elliott had a parcel of land to sell. He wanted to bring prospective buyers to a property at the top of a hill which looked down on this land. Elliott contacted owner Dolly Moore to see if he could bring people on her property. She agreed, and within a few weeks Elliott sold the land. Elliott wanted to take Dolly and her husband,

"Wild Bill" Elliott at the Autoport Drive-In, May 31, 1953.

Terrible's Gas Station, 2004.

Terrible's Casino, 2004.

William, to dinner to thank them for the favor. Dolly and William weren't getting along. William was upset with Dolly for leaving their children, at times, to pursue a modeling career. Also, William was jealous of Elliott, believing he spent too much time with Dolly. William abandoned Dolly and the children, leaving her without enough money to pay the expenses. Elliott helped Dolly with her bills and was not discreet about their relationship. Helen found out about Dolly and left Elliott. Elliott turned to Dolly and they began to live together.

Dolly Moore was the daughter of Edward and Lorraine Herbst. Herbst founded the successful Terrible Herbst Oil Company in Las Vegas, Nevada. Initially the company's primary thrust was gas stations and car wash operations. In later years, casinos were added. Dolly was a graduate of Northwestern University, where she earned an associate's degree in art and music. Later, when she moved to California, Dolly became a fashion model with other ladies. They called their group the Gold Diggers.

Elliott and Dolly moved to Wells (Elko), Nevada, and bought a ranch owned by Joel McCrea. While waiting for their divorces to be finalized, William and Helen got together to plot to have the custody of the children go to William. William and Dolly had two children, William (Corky) Jr. and Deborah (Debbie). In the custody battle, Dolly was asked by Acting Superior Judge Victor J. Hayek if she believed in the Seventh Commandment, "Thou shall not commit adultery." Dolly responded, "It was not as bad as abandoning my children." Elliott was asked the same question and said, "I do not." Elliott said he read the Bible to the children every night, but when he

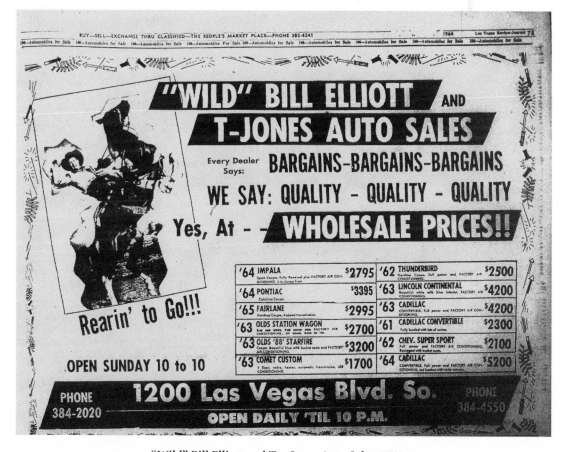

"Wild" Bill Elliott and T — Jones Auto Sales, 1964.

read the Ten Commandments, he always omitted the seventh. William initially was awarded custody of the children. When Elliott's divorce was finalized, he married Dolly in 1962 and they were able to regain custody of Corky and Debbie.

Elliott had a problem with the purchase of McCrea's ranch. Helen Elliott had emptied the account before Elliott could write a check to settle with McCrea. The deal fell through. Bill and Dolly moved to Las Vegas in September 1963 where Dolly's parents purchased a condominium for the couple.

In Las Vegas, Elliott became involved with various car dealerships in the sales and promotion division, first with Biddulph Rambler and then T. Jones. Additionally, Elliott was the vice president of Kem Plastics, an officer in the International Mining Corporation, and was to be a goodwill ambassador and spokesman for the Thunderbird Lounge. The company "Wild Bill" Elliott Enterprises, developers of the Aqua Tia Estates, had been

formed. Elliott spent some of his leisure time in the desert rock hunting and just enjoying the outdoors. He was also an excellent furniture maker.

He hosted a television show, *The Wild Bill Elliott Show*, on KSHO–TV for an eleven-week run in which he usually showed a western. In most, Elliott was himself the star. The show then moved to KORK–TV, where Elliott would introduce western films on both Saturday and Sunday morning or afternoon. None of Elliott's westerns would be shown. The program lasted until December 3, 1965, eight days after Elliott's death. *The Dolly Elliott Show* made its debut on December 11, 1965, and the title was changed after one program. Westerns continued to be shown, but now under the new title *Western Movie Time*. Dolly would host the program until 1967.

In 1965, Elliott was diagnosed with cancer; he passed away on November 26, 1965, at 7:15 p.m. in his home at 3030 El Camino Drive. Elliot was 61. He had been hospitalized

Palm Mausoleum, Palm Memorial Park, Las Vegas, Nevada.

at Sunrise Hospital for about four weeks prior to his discharge in October. Listed as survivors were his wife Dolly; his daughter Barbara Weeden of Largemont, N.Y.; grandchildren, Rue, Don and Honeybear Weeden; his brother Dale Nance of Hollywood, California; and two stepchildren, Corky and Debbie Elliott. There was no mention of Elliott's first wife, Helen.

The funeral service was tinged with additional sadness. Elliott's daughter, Barbara, sided with her mother after the divorce. She came to the funeral home only because it may have been expected of her but did not attend the service. Her mother, Helen, refused to demonstrate any form of sympathy.

The funeral services were held at Christ Church Episcopal on Maryland Parkway, with Rev. Tally Jarrett officiating. Elliott's pallbearers were E.B. Herbst, Jerry Herbst, Sam Sams, Jack Sparks, Bill Cramer, Mel Rapley, John Cronen, Buzz Floyd and Woody Cole. Sparks was the only pallbearer from Elliott's Hollywood days. Elliott was cremated and his remains were placed at Palm Memorial Park (Eternity Mausoleum, Row E, Niche 2011) in Las Vegas.

Fame is fleeting. It was disconcerting to the author to visit the Cowboy Walk of Fame at CBS Studios, formerly the home of Republic Pictures, in Hollywood to find the actor's last name misspelled as "Elliot." Needless to say, Wild Bill will be remembered as the "peaceable man," a no-nonsense range rider who righted countless wrongs, to the many fans who still remember and watch those wonderful westerns of yesterday.

Left: The author at Elliott's plot. *Right:* Plot — Eternity Mausoleum, Row E, Niche 2011.

Elliott's Starring Roles

"Outlaws, My Six-Guns Are Beggin' for a Red Hot Chat with You...!"
The Hardest Ridin', Toughest Fightin' Hombre in the West Hits the Thrill Trail!

Across the Sierras

Columbia (February, 1941)
A Wild Bill Hickok Adventure
ALTERNATE TITLE: *Welcome Stranger.*
CAST: Wild Bill Hickok, **Bill Elliott**; Larry Armstrong, **Richard Fiske**; Anne, **Luana Walters**; Cannonball, **Dub Taylor**; Mitch Carew, **Dick Curtis**; Stringer, **LeRoy Mason**; Lu Woodworth, **Ruth Robinson**; Dan Woodworth, **John Dilson**; Sheriff, **Milton Kibbee**; Hobie, **Ralph Peters**// "Sonny"; Townsman with baton, **Tex Cooper**; Wagon Driver, **Tom London**; Man on Wagon, **James Pierce**; Fawcett, **Edmund Cobb**; Ed, Cobb's cowhand, **Eddie Laughton**; Bartender, **Lew Meehan**; Ed, stage driver, **Art Mix**; Doctor, **Edward Coxen**; Blackjack, **Blackjack Ward**.
CREDITS: Director, **D. Ross Lederman**; Screenwriter, **Paul Franklin**; Editor, **James Sweeney**; Cinematographer, **George Meehan**.
SONGS: "Star Spangled Prairie" (Drake)— sung by **Dub Taylor**; "I Gotta Make Music" (Drake)— sung by **Dub Taylor**; and "Honeymoon Ranch" (Drake)— sung by **Dub Taylor**.
LOCATION FILMING: Iverson, California.
RUNNING TIME: 59 min.
STORY: After saving Richard Fiske from being lynched, Bill Elliott brings Fiske to Arroyo, where Elliott plans to settle down and begin a life as a rancher. Waiting in Arroyo is an old enemy of Elliott's, Dick Curtis, who plans to kill him. Elliott had arrested Curtis on a rob-

bery charge six years earlier. Curtis' terrifying presence forced John Dilson, whose testimony convicted Curtis, to draw first, only to be shot down in self defense. In Arroyo, Elliott meets Dilson's niece, Luana Walters, from Boston, and the two quickly fall in love. Fiske, looking to get rich quick, joins up with Curtis and participates in a stage holdup. During the robbery, Fiske is called by his first name, and Elliott seeks Fiske to persuade him to leave the country. Elliott finds Fiske. The two men talk, with Elliott unaware that Curtis and henchman LeRoy Mason are in the rocks close by. Fiske refuses Elliott's advice and Elliott turns his back to leave. Mason, seizing the opportunity, takes a shot at Elliott, which misses. Elliot turns and, thinking his friend had turned on him, fires a shot that mortally wounds Fiske. Fiske's death shakes Elliott, and he decides to give up his guns, buy a ranch and marry Walters. Curtis sends word by Elliott's pal, Dub Taylor, that he's waiting to shoot it out. Elliott refuses to leave town in disgrace and be thought of as a coward. He straps on his guns for what he hopes will be the last time. Elliott and Curtis meet, with Elliott ending Curtis' criminal career with a well placed bullet. Because of their different attitudes towards violence, Elliott knows he can never make Walters happy and rides away.
NOTES AND COMMENTARY: Stage driver Art

Across the Sierras (Columbia, 1941) movie still — Bill Elliott (left) gets the drop on Leroy Mason (center) and Dick Curtis (right).

Mix is called "Obie" by Dub Taylor, but a few scenes later he is called "Ed" by Milton Kibbee and Bill Elliott.

REVIEWS: "A concoction with average chances in the action bracket." *Variety*, 4/16/41; "Surprisingly austere 'Wild Bill Hickok' entry, a very good programmer." *Western Movies*, Pitts.

SUMMATION: *Across the Sierras* is an adult "B" western in the William S. Hart or Buck Jones tradition. Bill Elliott and Dick Curtis make worthy adversaries, and both acquit themselves well. The film is well directed by D. Ross Lederman, who uses George Meehan's excellent cinematography to fine advantage. Note the unusual but effective camera angles when Elliott and Curtis exchange words in the saloon. Elliott's performance is one of his best, as he portrays a man who wants to give up his guns for the woman he loves, with circumstances not permitting him to fully renounce his old life. A must see picture. With the adult slant, it makes one wonder if the juvenile trade bought into this one.

Like Your Action Fast? Thrills Pounding? Adventure Stirring?
See This Western Hit of All Hits ... Featuring All the Really Great Rangeland Stars!

Bells of Rosarita

Republic Pictures (June, 1945)

CAST: Roy Rogers, **Roy Rogers**; "Trigger"; Gabby Whittaker, **George "Gabby" Hayes**; Sue Farnum, **Dale Evans**; Patty Phillips, **Adele Mara**; Bill Ripley, **Grant Withers**; Slim Phillips, **Addison Richards**; Maxwell, **Roy Barcroft**; Rosarita, **Janet Martin**; the **Robert Mitchell Boy Choir**; Bob, **Bob Nolan**; Sons of the Pioneers (Tim Spencer, Ken Carson, Hugh Farr, Karl Farr, Shug Fisher); Republic Guest Stars, **Wild Bill Elliott, Allan Lane, Donald Barry, Robert Livingston** and **Sunset Carson**// "Thunder"; "Silver"; "Cyclone"; "Shamrock"; "Banner"; Circus Barker, **Earle Hodgins**; Roy's Director, **Frank McDonald**; Charlie, **Syd Saylor**; Sheriff, **Ed Cassidy**; Deputies, **Bob Wilke** and **Rex Lease**; Kidnappers, **Kenne Duncan** and **Charles Sullivan**; Telephone Operator, **Rosemonde James**; Barry's Director, **Eddie Kane**; Carson's heavies, **Frank McCarroll** and **Dale Van Sickel**; Studio Gate Guard, **Tom London**; Farmer, **Hank Bell**.

CREDITS: Director, **Frank McDonald**; Associate Producer, **Eddy White**; Screenwriter, **Jack Townley**; Editor, **Arthur Roberts**; Art Director, **Hilyard Brown**; Set Decorator, **Earl B. Wooden**; Cinematographer, **Ernest Miller**; Costumes, **Adele Palmer**; Makeup, **Bob Mark**; Sound, **Fred Stahl**; Special Effects, **Howard** and **Theodore Lydecker**; Musical Director, **Morton Scott**; Music Score, **Joseph Dubin**; Dance Director, **Larry Ceballos**.

SONGS: "Aloha"—danced by **Adele Mara**; "Bugler's Lullaby" (Mitchell and Best)—sung by **the Robert Mitchell Boys' Choir**; "Bells of Rosarita" (J. Elliott)—sung by **the Robert Mitchell Boys' Choir, Roy Rogers** and **Janet Martin**; "Under a Blanket of Blue"—sung by **Dale Evans**; "Singin' Down the Road"—sung by **Roy Rogers**; "I'm Gonna Build a Fence Around Texas" (Phillips and Friend)—sung by **Roy Rogers and the Robert Mitchell Boys Choir**; "Michael Finnegan"—sung by **the** Robert Mitchell Boys' Choir; "When the Circus Comes to Town"—sung by **the Sons of the Pioneers**; "Trail Herdin' Cowboy" (Nolan)—sung by **Roy Rogers, Bob Nolan** and **the Sons of the Pioneers**; "When the Circus Comes to Town" (reprise)—sung by **the Sons of the Pioneers**; "Bells of Rosarita" (reprise)—sung by **the Robert Mitchell Boys' Choir, Roy Rogers** and **Dale Evans**.

LOCATION FILMING: Iverson, California.

RUNNING TIME: 68 min.

STORY: Grant Withers plans to gain control of Dale Evans' ranch and circus because she cannot produce proof the debt has been paid. Evans brings her father's former partner, Addison Richards, to the ranch to help find the receipt. Withers has Richards kidnapped, and western star Roy Rogers is persuaded to help locate Richards. Rogers gets Evans and her foreman, George "Gabby" Hayes, to put on a show to raise money, and Rogers calls on fellow western stars Wild Bill Elliott, Allan Lane, Donald Barry, Robert Livingston and Sunset Carson to headline the show. With help from Hayes, Rogers frees Richards from his kidnappers. Withers' henchman, Roy Barcroft, overhears Richards tell Evans the receipt is in a safe deposit box in the bank. Withers breaks into the bank and steals the receipt. Rogers and the Republic stars round up the bank robbers and the receipt is recovered. Evans retains possession of her ranch and circus.

NOTES AND COMMENTARY: Wild Bill Elliott is one of the five "Republic Guest Stars" in this Roy Rogers western. Elliott is first seen training Thunder at his ranch when he's called by Rogers to appear in Dale Evans' circus. This scene can be seen in *Meanwhile, Back at the Ranch* (Curtco & RCR Productions, 1977). Next, Elliott is with Rogers at the circus when the bank is robbed and the western stars are called into action. Elliott, with Rogers and the others, race after the bank robbers. Each west-

Bells of Rosarita (Republic, 1945), starring Roy Rogers, scene card — Roy Rogers (center), Dale Evans (third right) and Adele Mara (second right) talk to members of the Robert Mitchell Boy Choir; climbing off the wagon are Bob Nolan and the Sons of the Pioneers; "Gabby" Hayes is standing behind Mara; Sheriff Edward Cassidy is standing outside the police car, with deputies Bob Wilke and Rex Lease inside. (Note: Elliott's name can be partially seen on the circus wagon.)

ern star has a man to capture. After a bullet from Barcroft's pistol just misses Elliott, Elliott captures Barcroft following a short fight. This latter scene is also used in *Meanwhile, Back at the Ranch*. Finally, Elliott joins Rogers and the other Republic guest stars at the circus finale.

A nice piece by Livingston as Lane, with all seriousness, fires at two bank robbers: "You're going to do a lot of damage with those blanks."

REVIEW: "Well-produced western." *Variety*, 5/16/45; "Interesting Roy Rogers outing with too much music." *Western Movies*, Pitts.

SUMMATION: This is a good Roy Rogers western featuring a number of Republic western stars — Wild Bill Elliott, Allan Lane, Donald Barry, Robert Livingston and Sunset Carson. Heavily loaded with songs, there is still enough action and comedy to deliver a solid audience pleaser. Elliott's role is just a cameo, but he handles it in fine style, capturing the last bank robber, Roy Barcroft.

A Frontier Threatened by Trigger Treachery!

Beyond the Sacramento

Columbia (November, 1940)
A Wild Bill Hickok Adventure
ALTERNATE TITLE: *Power of Justice.*
CAST: Wild Bill Hickok, **Bill Elliott**; Lynn Perry, **Evelyn Keyes**; Cannonball, **Dub Taylor**; Jason Perry, **John Dilson**; Cord Crowley, **Bradley Page**; Jeff Adams, **Frank LaRue**; Nelson, **Norman Willis**; Curly, **Steve Clark**; Sheriff, **Jack Clifford**; Warden McKay, **Don Beddoe**; Storekeeper, **Harry Bailey**// "Sonny"; "Lightning"; Joe, **Bud Osborne**; Henchman, **Art Mix**; Tom Jimson, **Olin Francis**; George (Bartender), **George McKay**; Tex/ Townsman, **Tex Cooper**; George (Bank Teller), **Ned Glass**.

CREDITS: Director, **Lambert Hillyer**; Screenwriter, **Luci Ward**; Editor, **James Sweeney**; Cinematographer, **George Meehan**.

SONGS: "Riding for the Law"—sung by **Dub Taylor**; "The West Gets Under My Skin"—sung by **Dub Taylor**.

LOCATION FILMING: Iverson and Corriganville, California.

RUNNING TIME: 58 min.

STORY: In Lodestone, Dub Taylor learns two confidence men, saloon owner Bradley Page and newspaper editor Frank LaRue, are masquerading as leading citizens, and sends for Bill Elliott. Page, LaRue and banker John Dilson

Beyond the Sacramento (Columbia, 1940) title card — Evelyn Keyes (left), Norman Willis (left center) and Bill Elliott (right center, struggling with Willis); Bill Elliott on Sonny (far right).

are promoting a phony bond issue. Elliott has been looking for Page and LaRue since he spoiled their scheme to defraud citizens of Albuquerque. Unaware of Dilson's involvement with Page, Elliott tries to convince Dilson that Page and LaRue are crooks. Dilson's daughter, Evelyn Keyes, thinks that Elliott may be right. Elliott and Taylor break into LaRue's newspaper office and reprint the front page, indicting LaRue as a crook. With the townspeople wanting an explanation from LaRue, Elliott offers him a way out by turning state's evidence. LaRue refuses and Elliott leaves him locked in his office. Not seeing any other way out, LaRue commits suicide. Dilson goes to Page, and Page gets Dilson to stall Elliott. Page has his men hold up Dilson's bank. Thanks to Keyes' quick action, the holdup is thwarted, but Keyes is shot. Dilson goes to Page's saloon for vengeance and is promptly shot down by Page. In a blazing gunfight, Elliot dispatches Page and two henchmen. Keyes recovers from her wound and wants Elliott to work in the bank with her. Although tempted, Elliott has to leave when he learns his brother needs his help.

NOTES AND COMMENTARY: The post card Bill Elliott receives at the story's end is the outline of the plot for *Wildcat of Tucson* (Columbia, 1940). This would be the next Wild Bill Hickok adventure to be released.

Evelyn Keyes, known for her role as Scarlet O'Hara's sister, Suellen, in *Gone with the Wind* (Selznick–Metro-Goldwyn-Mayer, 1939), is Bill Elliott's leading lady in this episode. It has been reported that the kiss Keyes gives Elliott, as he prepares to leave at the end of the film, was not in the script. Look at Elliott's stunned reaction. This would be Keyes' only appearance in a "B" western, but she would star in two big-budget color westerns, *The Desperadoes* (Columbia, 1943), with Randolph Scott and Glenn Ford, and *Renegades* (Columbia, 1946), with Willard Parker and Larry Parks.

Stage driver Tex Cooper is handed a bundle of newspapers to deliver as he drives the stage out of town. A few scenes later, Cooper is seen standing around as one of the townsmen.

REVIEWS: "A standard giddyapper boasting one unique twist. This will get by for satisfactory results with cowhand and junior trade. Elliott makes the proper and omniscient and omnipotent hero. *Variety*, 5/7/41; "Fast paced Bill Elliott vehicle." *Western Movies*, Pitts.

SUMMATION: Bill Elliott is handed a basically town-bound western, and his forceful personality makes this picture work. Elliott is only given three action sequences, and he carries them off in fine style. The rest of the time, Elliott's acting and personality keeps the audience interested. Sidekick Dub Taylor is given a neat running gag with a flea-infested cowhide vest. Evelyn Keyes does a nice job as Elliott's leading lady.

A Stranger Marked for Murder in a Lawless Stronghold of Desperate Men

Bitter Creek

Allied Artists (February, 1954)

A Westwood Production

CAST: Clay Tindal, **Wild Bill Elliott**; Quentin Allen, **Carleton Young**; Gail Bonner, **Beverly Garland**; Vance Morgan, **Claude Akins**; Dr. Prentiss, **Jim Hayward**; A.Z. Platte, **John Harmon**; Jerry Bonner, **Dan Mummert**; Oak Mason, **John Pickard**; Whitey, **Veda Ann Borg**; Harley Pruitt, **Forrest Taylor**; Sheriff, **Dabs Greer**; Joe Venango, **Mike Ragan**; 2nd Rider, **Zon Murray**; Gunman, **John Larch**; Pat Cleary, **Joe Devlin**; Charles Hammond, **Earl Hodgins**; Mrs. Hammond, **Florence Lake**; Oak's Girl, **Jane Easton**// Lazy Q Ranch Hand, **Stanley Price**.

CREDITS: Director, **Thomas Carr**; Assistant Director, **Melville Shyer**; Producer, **Vincent M. Fennelly**; Screenwriter, **George Waggner**; Editor, **Sam Fields**; Art Director, **James West**; Set Decorator, **Vincent A. Taylor**; Cinematographer, **Ernest Miller**; Special Effects, **Ray Mercer**; Sound, **Charles Cooper**; Music,

Raoul Kraushaar; Set Continuity, **Donna Nor-ridge**; Dialogue Supervisor, **Stanley Price**.

LOCATION FILMING: Iverson and Corrig-anville, California.

RUNNING TIME: 74 min.

STORY: Wild Bill Elliott comes to Bitter Creek to find the murderer of his brother. Beverly Garland also arrives to marry rancher Carleton Young. Young has taken over Elliott's brother's ranch, but Elliott takes it back. Young wants to wait until he's married Garland before allowing his foreman, Claude Akins, to deal with Elliott. Elliott and Garland meet and become fond of each other. Young sees Elliott and Garland together and hires gunman John Larch to murder Elliott. The plot fails when stage driver John Harmon shouts a warning to Elliott. Larch kills Harmon, and Akins shoots Larch to prevent him from talking to Elliott. This incident prompts Young's cook, Forrest Taylor, to go to work for Elliott. Young has

John Pickard give Taylor a severe beating, which is witnessed by Garland. Garland breaks her engagement to Young. Taylor is dumped on Elliott's doorstep. Doctor Jim Hayward, Elliott's only friend, is able to minister to Taylor's wounds. Elliott erects a grave marker to make Young believe Taylor has died. Elliott gets the drop on Pickard and gives him a beating that makes him finally reveal that Akins killed Elliott's brother on Young's order. Elliott tries to get to Young but is chased by Young's ranch hands. During the chase, Young wounds Elliott. Elliott takes refuge in Garland's hotel room. Akins and some of the ranch hands close in. Elliott and Akins meet, resulting in Akins' death. Elliott sees Young ride out of town and decides the death of Young is no longer important. Returning to his ranch, Young is waiting for Elliott. Hayward is also at the ranch. He pretends to be drunk and passed out, and is able to distract Young so that Elliott can shoot

Bitter Creek (Allied Artists, 1954) scene card — Bill Elliott (left) manhandles John Pickard (right).

Young. Elliott decides to remain in Bitter Creek with Garland at his side.

NOTES AND COMMENTARY: In an interesting script development, Wild Bill Elliott confronts John Pickard to find who murdered his brother. Elliott disarms Pickard, who says, "My hands against your guns?" Elliott replies, "Sure. This is a fixed fight." He then proceeds to beat Pickard into submission and get the information he needs. In most "B" westerns, the hero would also throw down his gun to beat his opponent in a fair fight.

In *Who's Who in Western Stars* (Dell, 1954), it's noted that Elliott has wanted to make a western in which proper motivation for the villain is stated. Elliott is pleased that *Bitter Creek* offers that explanation.

REVIEWS: "Action-packed Wild Bill Elliott western, best for the star in years. This is a good example of a western feature turned out on a moderate budget. Logical story motivations and action, excellent performance by an above-average cast and expert direction give familiar ingredients the punch needed for its market. It's Wild Bill Elliott's best in a long time." *Variety*, 3/17/54; "One of the better Elliott westerns, and it's due, in great part, to a fine script. The action never stops in the picture, except for some telling dialog. A fine example of how to make a good picture for little money." *Motion Picture Guide*, Nash and Ross.

SUMMATION: This is one of Elliott's best. Buoyed by a good script by veteran George Waggner, fine direction by Thomas Carr, and a top supporting cast, Elliott delivers the goods in convincing style. Elliott shows toughness as well as compassion as he finally realizes that more killing is not always the answer. His westerner will smoke, take a drink and, faced with a stronger man, refuse to throw down his gun in a physical fight. Don't miss this one.

... Two-Fisted Elliott Rides to His Greatest Adventure!... Hot on the Trail of a Scheming Gang of Killers!

Bordertown Gun Fighters

Republic (July, 1943)

CAST: Wild Bill Elliott, **Wild Bill Elliott**; Gabby Hayes, **George "Gabby" Hayes**; Anita Shelby, **Anne Jeffreys**; Cameo Shelby, **Ian Keith**; Dave Strickland, **Harry Woods**; Daniel Forrester, **Edward Earle**; Frank Holden, **Karl Hackett**; Jack Gattling, **Roy Barcroft**; Buck Newcombe, **Bud Geary**; Red Daily, **Carl Sepulveda**// "Sonny"; Henchman, **Frank McCarroll**; Roland Clark, **Wheaton Chambers**; Sheriff Barnes, **Charles King**; Train Conductor, **Jack Kinney**; Train tough, **Ken Terrell**; Brady, **Charles Sullivan**; Casino Patron and Messenger, **Ben Johnson**.

CREDITS: Director, **Howard Bretherton**; Associate Producer, **Eddy White**; Screenplay, **Norman S. Hall**; Editor, **Richard Van Enger**; Art Director, **Russell Kimball**; Set Decorator, **Charles Thompson**; Cinematographer, **Jack Marta**; Sound, **Dick Tyler**; Musical Score, **Mort Glickman**.

SONG: "Gwine to Run All Night (De Camptown Races)" (Foster)—sung by **Anne Jeffreys**.

LOCATION FILMING: Iverson and Walker Ranches, California.

RUNNING TIME: 56 min.

STORY: Wild Bill Elliott and his sidekick George "Gabby" Hayes are assigned to break up a crooked lottery racket in the New Mexico Territory. Elliott believes casino owner Ian Keith is the gang leader but has no proof. In time, Elliott first intercepts lottery tickets being transported to New Mexico and then obtains incriminating documents revealing Keith's involvement. Keith makes an unsuccessful attempt to have Elliott and Hayes killed. Keith tries to escape on horseback but is followed by Elliott and Hayes. In the chase, Keith rides into an overhanging tree branch, knocking him from his horse and leaving him bloody and blind. Still trying to get away, Keith falls to his

Bordertown Gun Fighters (Republic, 1943) scene card — Bill Elliott on Sonny is chasing villain Ian Keith.

death from a bluff onto a riverbank. Elliott and Hayes are praised for their efforts.

NOTES AND COMMENTARY: Republic's proofreaders fell down on the job by allowing a tag line for this film to go out as "hot on the trial of a scheming gang of killers" instead of "hot on the trail."

Pierre Watkin was scheduled to appear in this picture, and Edward Keane has been credited as appearing by some sources. Neither is in the final product.

Future cowboy great Ben Johnson was Wild Bill Elliott's double.

REVIEWS: "Typically fast moving Bill Elliott Republic entry." *Western Movies*, Pitts; "Run-of-the-mill B western." *The Motion Picture Guide*, Nash and Ross.

SUMMATION: This is another good Wild Bill Elliott "B" western. Elliot displays his riding, fighting and shooting skills while capably handling the dialogue sequences.

Thrill as These Two Top Western Stars Rock the Screen with Stirring Adventure and Song!

Bullets for Bandits

Columbia (February, 1942)
CAST: Wild Bill Hickok, **Bill Elliott**; Tex

Martin, **Tex Ritter**; Cannonball, **Frank Mitchell**; Dakota Brown, **Dorothy Short**; Clem

Jeeter, **Ralph Theodore**; Queen Katey, **Edythe Elliott**; Bert Brown, **Forrest Taylor**// "Sonny"; "White Flash"; Prince Katey, **Bill Elliott**; Cowboy who manhandles Cannonball, **Bud Osborne**; Croupier, **Hal Taliaferro**; Cheated Gambler, **Harry Harvey**; Beetle, **Joe McGuinn**; Whit, **Art Mix**.

CREDITS: Director, **Wallace W. Fox**; Producer, **Leon Barsha**; Screenwriter, **Robert Lee Johnson**; Editor, **Mel Thorsen**; Cinematographer, **George Meehan**.

SONGS: "Want My Boots on When I Die"— sung by **Tex Ritter**; "Reelin' Rockin' Rollin' Down the Trail"— sung by **Tex Ritter**; "Somewhere on the Lone Prairie"— sung by **Tex Ritter**.

LOCATION FILMING: Agoura, Corriganville and Iverson, California.

RUNNING TIME: 55 min.

STORY: Stopping off in a town in the Bad-lands, Bill Elliott sees a gunman who is his exact double. When gunman Elliott attempts to cheat another player at roulette, Elliott steps in and the two exchange shots. Gunman Elliott falls dead, but from a shot in the back from Joe McGuinn. McGuinn murdered gunman Elliott, at Ralph Theodore's direction, so Edythe Elliott's foreman, Frank Mitchell, can't bring him back to prevent Theodore from taking over E. Elliott's ranch. Mitchell mistakes Elliott for the man he was sent to get and persuades Elliott to come to E. Elliott's aid. Sheriff Tex Ritter goes after Elliott, thinking him involved in the killing. Elliott arrives in time to prevent Theodore's first attempt to grab E. Elliott's ranch. Theodore also is stirring up trouble between the homesteaders and E. Elliott. Ritter arrives and determines that Elliott is not the guilty party. The two men decide to work together. Theodore decides to lynch Elliott and

Bullets for Bandits (Columbia, 1942) scene card — Ralph Theodore (left) is about to hit Bill Elliott (right).

brand him the guilty party. Theodore and his henchmen lay siege to E. Elliott's ranch, with Elliott holding them at bay. Mitchell rides for Ritter's help. Ritter arrives and, with Elliott's help, arrests Theodore and McGuinn. E. Elliott and the homesteaders can now live as peaceful neighbors.

NOTES AND COMMENTARY: Bill Elliott here has his one and only turn at a double role, playing hero Wild Bill Hickok and notorious gunman Prince Katey. The shared screen time is brief, as they have an early shoot out, with Katey being shot in the back by Joe McGuinn and Elliott thinking it was *his* bullet that ended Katey's life.

Famed badman of westerns and serials Lane Bradford doubles Bill Elliott in this production.

REVIEW: "Somewhat uneven entry in the Bill Elliott-Tex Ritter starring series." *Western Movies*, Pitts.

SUMMATION: Okay entry in the Bill Elliott-Tex Ritter series due to Elliott's presence and some good running inserts. The slight story line does give Elliott a chance to show his acting prowess, especially in his scenes with Edythe Elliott. Ritter chips in with some good songs, but the script doesn't allow him to participate much in the action department this time out.

Thrill to the Action Adventures of Your Favorite Comic Strip Hero as He Dashes into Danger in His Greatest Western Triumph!

California Gold Rush

Republic Pictures (February, 1946)
CAST: Red Ryder, **Wild Bill Elliott**; Little Beaver, **Bobby Blake**; the Duchess, **Alice Fleming**; Hazel Parker, **Peggy Stewart**; Colonel Parker, **Russell Simpson**; Chopin, **Dick Curtis**; Murphy, **Joel Friedkin**; Felton, **Kenne Duncan**; Sheriff, **Tom London**; Pete, **Monte Hale**; the Idaho Kid, **Wen Wright**; Broken Arrow, **Dickie Dillon**; Stage Passenger, **Mary Arden**; Zack, **Jack Kirk**// "Thunder"; Frank, **Bud Osborne**; Townsman, **Nolan Leary**; Man in hotel lobby, **Frank Ellis**; Messenger Boy, **Freddie Chapman**; Deputy, **Pascale Perry**; Desk Clerk, **Budd Buster**.

CREDITS: Director, **R.G. Springsteen**; Associate Producer, **Sidney Picker**; Screenwriter, **Bob Williams**; Editor, **Charles Craft**; Art Director, **Frank Hotaling**; Cinematographer, **William Bradford**; Makeup, **Bob Mark**; Sound, **Earl Crain, Sr.**; Musical Director, **Richard Cherwin**.

LOCATION FILMING: Iverson, California.
RUNNING TIME: 56 min.
SOURCE: Based on Fred Harman's famous NEA Comic — by special arrangement with Stephen Slesinger.

STORY: When Alice Fleming sees that all of stageline owner Russell Simpson's drivers have quit because of holdups and the subsequent murders of the drivers, she sends for Wild Bill Elliott and his Indian pal, Bobby Blake. Hotel owner and outlaw boss Joel Friedkin, who wants to take over the line, intercepts the letter. Friedkin arranges for the notorious killer Wen Wright to ambush Elliott and assume Elliott's identity. The ambush fails, and in the exchange of shots, Elliott shoots Wright. Learning that Wright was to impersonate him, Elliott decides to impersonate Wright. The ruse works, until Wright's brother, Kenne Duncan, spots Elliott. Friedkin has his henchman, Dick Curtis, kidnap Fleming and then proceeds to have Elliott framed for gold robbery. Arrested by Sheriff Tom London, Elliott gains his freedom with the help of Blake. Elliott trails Duncan to the outlaw hideout and has Blake ride for London and his posse. Elliott gains entrance to the hideout just as Friedkin orders Curtis to murder Fleming. A fight breaks out between Elliott and henchmen Curtis and Duncan. As Elliott gains the upper hand, Friedkin takes aim at Elliott, but his bullet strikes Curtis instead. Elliott chases after Friedkin and shoots him after a short gunfight. Simpson's stageline troubles are now over.

California Gold Rush (Republic, 1946) scene card — Bobby Blake, Bill Elliott and Alice Fleming (left to right) in a humorous moment.

NOTES AND COMMENTARY: Ben Johnson was Wild Bill Elliott's double in this film.

Monte Hale has a small role in this feature. Even though he would be seen in Elliott's *Sun Valley Cyclone* (Republic, 1946), Hale's first starring venture, *Home on the Range* (Republic, 1946), would already have been released.

REVIEW: "Pretty good outing in the 'Red Ryder' series." *Western Movies*, Pitts.

SUMMATION: This is another good Red Ryder western, filled with excitement and fine action sequences. Again, Wild Bill Elliott is perfect as Ryder, showing his acting ability as well as deftly handling the action demands. Villains Dick Curtis and Joel Friedkin head the fine supporting cast. Both play their parts to perfection, Curtis as a wisecracking, harmonica-playing killer, and Friedkin as a seemingly mild-mannered individual who will stop at nothing to achieve his ends. William Bradford's cinematography adds luster to Bob Williams' well-crafted script (the scene in which Curtis and his men chase Simpson's stage coach, with Elliott in pursuit, being a prime example). R.G. Springsteen's direction is on target and keeps the story moving at a fast pace.

The Chiller with the Shocking Clue!

Calling Homicide

Allied Artists (June, 1956)

CAST: Lieutenant Andy Doyle, **Bill Elliott**; Sergeant Mike Duncan, **Don Haggerty**; Donna Graham, **Kathleen Case**; Jim Haddix, **Myron Healey**; Darlene Adams, **Jeanne Cooper**; Allen Gilmore, **Thomas B. Henry**; Tony Fuller, **Lyle Talbot**; Mrs. Dunsetter, **Almira Sessons**; Ray Engel, **Herb Vigran**; Detective Arnie Arnhoff, **James Best**; Benny Bendowski, **John Dennis**//Detective Johnny Phipps, **Robert Bice**; Flo Burton, **Mary Treen**; Peter von Elda, **Stanley Adams**.

CREDITS: Director/Screenwriter, **Edward Bernds**; Assistant Director, **Edward Morey, Jr.**;

Producer, **Ben Schwalb**; Editor, **William Austin**; Art Director, **Dave Milton**; Set Decorator, **Joseph Kish**; Cinematographer, **Harry Neumann**; Makeup, **Emile LaVigne**; Wardrobe, **Bert Henrikson**; Sound, **Ralph Butler**; Music, **Marlin Skiles**; Property, **Ted Mossman**; Production Manager, **Allen K. Wood**; Dialogue Supervisor, **Herman Rotsten**; Set Continuity, **John Dutton**; Construction Supervisor, **James West**.

RUNNING TIME: 61 min.

STORY: Police Lieutenant Bill Elliott is in charge of two tough murder cases, one victim being a police detective and the other a beau-

Calling Homicide (Allied Artists, June, 1956) scene card — Don Haggerty (left) and Bill Elliott (center) arrest John Dennis; the left border shows Bill Elliott, Kathleen Case and Don Haggerty (left to right).

tiful woman who owned a school for models. When Elliott tells the school's employees of the owner's death, only janitor John Dennis shows any emotion. Manager Jeanne Cooper and her associates, Lyle Talbot and Thomas B. Henry, refuse to cooperate with the police. Thinking the legitimate business is a cover-up for illegal activities, Elliott requests a court order to open the school's files. Elliott finds a former lover of the murdered woman, Stanley Adams, who tells Elliott she was a blackmailer. A mysterious intruder destroys the files. While drinking in a bar, Talbot boasts that he knows who the murderer is. Elliott goes to the scene but Talbot is murdered before he can reveal the killer's identity. After further investigation, Elliott finds the school was a front for an adoption racket. Models would become pregnant and their babies would be sold to those couples who refused to go through regular adoption channels. The buyers who came into money would be blackmailed. Remembering that Dennis was present when he left to meet Talbot, Elliott investigates him and finds evidence that he is the murderer. Elliott and his partner, Police Sergeant Don Haggerty, go to Dennis' apartment to arrest him. Dennis reaches for a gun and is cut down in a hail of bullets. Elliott surmises that Dennis murdered the police detective to stop his investigation, and the owner of the school when she laughed at him.

NOTES AND COMMENTARY: Down in the cast listing a familiar name would appear, James Best. Although an excellent dramatic actor, Best will forever remain in television viewers' memory as Roscoe P. Coltrane in the popular television program *The Dukes of Hazzard* (CBS, January 1979–February 1985).

REVIEWS: "Well-motivated detective yarn. Elliott shows to good advantage in this Ben Schwalb production." *Variety*, 10/17/56; "Well done, considering the tiny budget." *Motion Picture Guide*, Nash and Ross.

SUMMATION: This is a solid detective story on a small budget that plays fair with the audience. The dialog is crisp and the story is well-acted, especially by Bill Elliott, who registers strongly as the police lieutenant, Lyle Talbot, playing a drunken former movie actor, and murder suspects Myron Healey and Jeanne Cooper. Edward Bernds' direction shows a love of film noir. This is one of the best in Elliott's detective series.

A Two-Fisted Buckaroo Ready for Action in His Greatest Film!...

Calling Wild Bill Elliott

Republic (April, 1943)

CAST: Wild Bill Elliott, **Bill Elliott**; Gabby, **George "Gabby" Hayes**; Edith Richards, **Anne Jeffreys**; Governor Steve Nicholls, **Herbert Heyes**; Demijohn, **"Buzzy" Dee Henry**; John Culver, **Fred Kohler**; Captain Carson, **Roy Barcroft**; Mary Culver, **Eve March**; Cactus Jim Culver, **Burr Caruth**; Dean, **Bud Geary**; Ranch hand, **Lynton Brent**// **"Sonny"**; Rancher, Horace B. Carpenter; Saloon Henchman, **Frank Hagney**; Ace, **Charles King**; Saloon Tough with Cigar, **Bill Nestell**; Townsman, **Frank McCarroll**; Militiaman, **Yakima Canutt**; Judge Richards, **Forbes Murray**.

CREDITS: Director, **Spencer Bennet**; Associate Producer, **Harry Grey**; Story, **Luci Ward**; Screenplay, **Anthony Coldewey**; Editor, **Edward Schroeder**; Art Director, **Russell Kimball**; Set Decorator, **Charles Thompson**; Cinematographer, **Ernest Miller**; Musical Score, **Mort Glickman**.

SONG: "Long Long Ago" (Bayly)— sung by **Anne Jeffreys**.

LOCATION FILMING: Iverson, Corriganville and Burro Flats, California.

STORY: Fred Kohler's ranch is to be sold for back taxes by ruthless Governor Herbert Heyes. Kohler's foreman, George "Gabby" Hayes, and his father, Burr Caruth, travel to Eagle City to meet with Judge Forbes Murray and register complaints about Heyes. Heyes sends henchmen Roy Barcroft and Bud Geary

Calling Wild Bill Elliott (Republic, 1943) scene card — Bill Elliott (center) and "Gabby" Hayes (center right) look for trouble, with onlookers watching closely.

to prevent this meeting. The first attempt to kill Hayes and Caruth is foiled by Bill Elliott. In a second attempt, Barcroft murders Caruth. Elliott rides to see Heyes and finds himself arrested for Caruth's death. Kohler decides to take matters into his own hands and lynch Elliott. Elliott is saved by Hayes' timely intervention. Murray and his daughter, Anne Jeffreys, arrives at Heyes' hacienda. Elliott arranges to see Murray, and Murray plans to take action against Heyes. Heyes murders Murray and frames Elliott for the crime. Kohler meets Jeffreys and is taken into custody by Heyes. Elliott is finally able to convince Jeffreys of Heyes's duplicity. When Jeffreys attempts to contact Federal authorities, she is arrested by Heyes. Heyes decides to hang Kohler. Elliott rescues Kohler and the two, greatly outnumbered, barricade themselves in Heyes's hacienda. Things look grim until Hayes arrives

with Army troops. Elliott ends Heyes' dreams of his personal empire with victory in a short fistfight. With peace restored, Elliott rides off to new adventures with Hayes at his side.

NOTES AND COMMENTARY: This was Bill Elliott's Republic feature film debut, replacing Gene Autry, who was now in the Air Force. To further promote this series, Elliott's name was incorporated into the title. Later western stars who had this honor bestowed upon them were Sunset Carson in *Sunset Carson Rides Again* (Yucca Pictures/Astor, 1948) and Gene Autry in *Gene Autry and the Mounties* (Columbia, 1951).

With Autry in the service, Smiley Burnette needed a new series. Gabby Hayes was Roy Rogers' current sidekick, but Republic felt Hayes was a better fit than Burnette for the Elliott series. Burnette had worked successfully with Rogers earlier in his career.

At one point in the story, Bill Elliott, to escape capture, runs across the roof of Herbert Heyes' hacienda and drops onto the back of his pinto, Sonny. Stuntman Yakima Canutt and director Spencer Bennet constructed a platform behind an arch, out of camera range. Elliott ran across the roof and jumped from the arch to the platform. Before Elliott could land on the platform, Canutt dropped onto the back of the horse. To the viewer's eyes, this was a stunt performed in one continuous motion.

Two scenes from *Calling Wild Bill Elliott* were used for *Meanwhile, Back at the Ranch* (Curtco & RCR Productions, 1977): first, when Buzzy Henry brings word to Elliott that two ladies are held captive, and then as Elliott and some ranchers ride to the rescue.

When Metro-Goldwyn-Mayer refused to offer Anne Jeffreys a contract, her agent took her to Republic Studios where she immediately received one. After playing gangster molls and cheap chorus girls, Jeffreys asked to play a nice girl. She was told the only nice girl parts were in westerns. Asked to be placed in one, Jeffreys ended up in a series of eight with Gabby Hayes and Wild Bill Elliott. Jeffreys commented on Elliott: "Wild Bill was very staid but wild. I found that out on a tour when we were selling war bonds."

Calling Wild Bill Elliott was a remake of *The Kansas Terrors* (Republic, 1939), a Three Mesquiteers entry with Bob Livingston, Raymond Hatton and Duncan Renaldo.

REVIEWS: "Above average B western is allegedly the first talkie to incorporate the name of the star in the title." *Motion Picture Guide*, Nash and Ross; "Bennet's direction is faced paced and the script has more than enough brawls and chases." *The Western*, Hardy.

SUMMATION: Though *Calling Wild Bill Elliott* is strong on action and light on story, Bill Elliott brings this actioner through in fine style. Elliott reprises his Wild Bill Hickok persona in this, his Republic feature film debut, and is in fine fettle. Adding George "Gabby" Hayes to Elliott's series worked perfectly, as the chemistry between them is on target. Veteran director Spencer Bennet paces this story at a breakneck pace, which will more than satisfy action lovers.

The Hunted Man Who Lost His Mind... The Fingerprints That Lie...
The Dead Man with the Shocking Clue!

Chain of Evidence

Allied Artists (January, 1957)

CAST: Lieutenant Andy Doyle, **Bill Elliott**; Steve Nordstrom, **James Lydon**; Sergeant Mike Duncan, **Don Haggerty**; Harriet Owens, **Claudia Barrett**; Claire Ramsey, **Tina Carver**; Bob Bradfield, **Ross Elliot**; Polly, **Meg Randall**; Fowler, **Timothy Carey**; Jake Habermann, **John Bleifer**; Psychiatrist, **Dabbs Greer**; State Trooper, **John Close**// Morton Ramsey, **Hugh Sanders**; Jim Miller, **Donald Kerr**; Felipe Rodriguez, **Francis McDonald**.

CREDITS: Director, **Paul Landres**; Assistant Director, **Don Torpin**; Producer, **Ben Schwalb**; Screenwriter, **Elwood Ullman**; Editor, **Neil Brunnenkant**; Art Director, **Dave Milton**; Set Decorator, **Joseph Kish**; Cinematographer, **Harry Neumann**; Makeup, **Emile LaVigne**; Wardrobe, **Bert Henrickson**; Sound, **Ralph Butler**; Music, **Marlin Skiles**; Property, **Ted Mossman**; Production Manager, **Allen K. Wood**; Dialogue Supervisor, **Herman Rotsten**; Set Continuity, **Richard M. Chaffee**; Construction Supervisor, **James West**.

RUNNING TIME: 64 min.

STORY: James Lydon is released from an honor farm on probation. Lydon had assaulted Timothy Carey after Carey had accosted his girlfriend, Claudia Barrett. Carey attacks Lydon, who doesn't want to fight, and hits him with his fists and a board, leaving him unconscious. Lydon, with a total loss of memory, wanders from the scene. With Lydon now reported missing, his mentor, Lt. Bill Elliott, tries to locate Lydon. Lydon meets Hugh Saunders, who hires him as a handyman. Sanders' wife, Tina Carver, is having an affair with Ross Elliot. Because Lydon gets upset whenever anyone mentions him seeing a physician, Carver sees this as an opportunity for R. Elliot to murder Sanders and place the blame on Lydon. Lydon is arrested, and Elliott has no choice but to book him, although he believes Lydon is innocent. Elliott continues his investigation. Lydon finally regains his memory when Elliott has Lydon confront Carey. From information received from Lydon, Elliott begins to suspect Carver and R. Elliot of the murder. Elliott questions R. Elliot in such a way that R. Elliot calls Carver. With the connection between Carver and R. Elliot established, both suspects are arrested. Elliott directs Lydon and Barrett to a nearby wedding chapel.

NOTES AND COMMENTARY: Claudia Barrett said she enjoyed the film. She didn't like her role of Harriet, however, stating, "I thought she was rather whiney. I was rather disappointed in myself." She then said, "It was a very low budget film that showed in the technical aspects of the film. The actors were all good except myself. I really didn't like my performance in that particular picture. I just seemed to be one-dimensional, I think. I think Bill Elliott did excellent." Barrett commented that perhaps director Paul Landres could have helped in making her part more three-dimensional. She did like Landres as a director and found him easy to work with and a very nice man.

Barrett mentioned that "William Elliott was really a nice fellow. I've always been a Bill Elliott fan. I really like him and used to love

Chain of Evidence (Allied Artists, 1957) scene card — John Bleifer (left) gives Don Haggerty (center) and Bill Elliott (right) information; the extreme left border shows Meg Randall, Tina Carver and Bill Elliott (top to bottom), while the right side of the border shows James Lydon (right) attacking Hugh Sanders (center).

him in his westerns. So when I got this part, I was really surprised that it was a detective story. I thought he did very well as a detective. He's got a wonderful speaking voice, I just love it." Barrett also commented that Elliott was always on time, knew his lines and was very professional. She added, "He was a perfect gentleman, he was so polite and so nice that it made it easy to work with him."

Jimmy Lydon remembered: "Bill Elliott was one of the few western stars who was a superb horseman. He was also a fine gentleman — a far cry from the badly-schooled, knockabout western stars of that era."

Of the film itself, Lydon said, "I don't remember anything about making it except we shot it in 12 days. We all worked long and hard to finish on time and on schedule and within its limited budget."

REVIEWS: "Very routine with signals-ahead plotline. Elliott in his comparatively brief footage handles himself with his customary authority." *Variety*, 5/8/57; "A routine murder mystery with substandard script." *Motion Picture Guide*, Nash and Ross.

SUMMATION: This is another good entry in the Bill Elliott detective series. Elliott gives a nice performance as a tough police officer who can have sympathetic feelings for those he likes. James Lydon is outstanding as the young man who becomes an amnesiac suspected of murder. Director Paul Landres does a nice job with Elwood Ullman's highly competent script.

Your Ace Trouble-Shooter of Comic Strip Fame in an Adventure Packed with Tense, Throbbing Thrills!

Cheyenne Wildcat

Republic (September, 1944)

CAST: Red Ryder, **Wild Bill Elliott**; Little Beaver, **Bobby Blake**; the Duchess, **Alice Fleming**; Betty Lou Hopkins, **Peggy Stewart**; Jim Douglas, **Francis McDonald**; Meeker, **Roy Barcroft**; Colby, **Tom London**; Jason Hopkins, **Tom Chatterton**; Pete, **Kenne Duncan**; Henchman, **Bud Geary**; Sheriff, **Jack Kirk**; Bank Examiner, **Sam Burton**// "Thunder"; Clem, **Bob Burns**; Station Agent, **Steve Clark**; Deputy, **Frank Ellis**; Doctor, **Forrest Taylor**; Irate Townsman, **Franklyn Farnum**; Dryculcher, **Tom Steele**; Dusty, **Bud Osborne**; Charlie, **Robert J. Wilke**; Lynch Mob Leader, **Rex Lease**; Townsman, **Horace B. Carpenter**.

CREDITS: Director, **Lesley Selander**; Associate Producer, **Louis Gray**; Screenwriter, **Randall Faye**; Editor, **Charles Craft**; Art Director, **Fred Ritter**; Set Decorator, **Otto Siegel**; Cinematography, **Bud Thackery**; Sound, **Tom Carman**; Musical Score, **Joseph Dubin**.

LOCATION FILMING: Iverson, California.

RUNNING TIME: 56 min.

SOURCE: Based on Fred Harman's famous NEA Comic — by special arrangement with Stephen Slesinger.

STORY: Years previously, forger Tom London and his accomplice Roy Barcroft stole gold certificates and framed Francis McDonald. As they plan to do the same to McDonald's former partner, Tom Chatterton, he gets wise and catches London as he switches forged certificates for the real ones. McDonald has been released from prison, and Chatterton plans to meet him and tell how he was framed. Barcroft sends henchman Kenne Duncan to murder Chatterton and frame McDonald. Wild Bill Elliott and his Indian pal, Bobby Blake, witness the murder. Elliott captures Duncan and exonerates McDonald. Barcroft murders Duncan before he can talk. London gives McDonald a job as bank guard so he can be near Peggy Stewart. Stewart thinks Chatterton was her father, but McDonald is her actual father. London tells Elliott and Stewart that the bank is $60,000 short. Elliott, Stewart and Elliott's aunt, Alice Flemming, decide to cover the shortage. Barcroft instigates a run on the bank, which is thwarted by Elliott and Blake. Next, the bank is robbed, with suspicion thrown on McDonald. Elliott believes McDonald is innocent and finds evidence pointing to Barcroft and London.

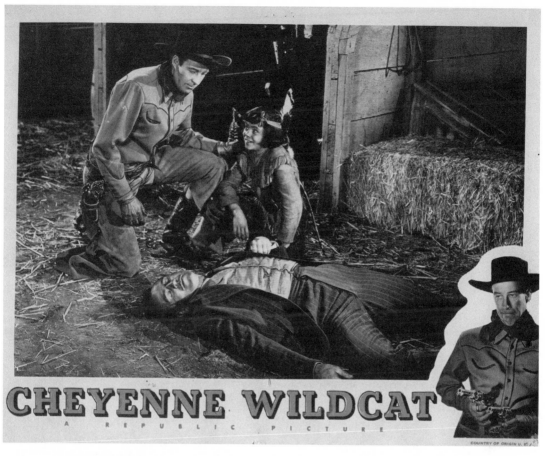

Cheyenne Wildcat (Republic, 1944) scene card — Bobby Blake (center) is pleased that Bill Elliott (left) has bested Roy Barcroft (on ground) in a fist fight.

Barcroft and London attempt to escape but are stopped by Elliott's fists. In the fight, Barcroft is killed with his own knife and London is brought to justice. McDonald and Stewart are reunited and plan to run the bank together.

NOTES AND COMMENTARY: In the fight sequences, Tom Steele doubled Bill Elliott and Fred Graham doubled Roy Barcroft.

REVIEWS: "Nicely done entry in the 'Red Ryder' series." *Western Movies*, Pitts; "Fair outing for Elliott in the popular Red Ryder series. Some good writing and stunts raise the level of this production." *Motion Picture Guide*, Nash and Ross.

SUMMATION: This is a good Red Ryder vehicle, with a fine story and fast action. Wild Bill Elliott is on target as Ryder. As well as showing he can handle the action heroics, Elliott displays the right emotion in poignant scenes with Peggy Stewart. Elliott also capably appears in some comedy scenes with Bobby Blake. Roy Barcroft matches Elliott as a clever villain with a penchant for using knives to kill his victims. Lesley Selander's direction is on target.

Punch Packed Adventure!
as Red Ryder Combats Old Tricks with New Methods to Beat Ruthless Cattle Rustlers!

Colorado Pioneers

Republic Pictures (November, 1945)

CAST: Red Ryder, **Wild Bill Elliott**; Little Beaver, **Bobby Blake**; the Duchess, **Alice Fleming**; Bull Reagan, **Roy Barcroft**; Bill Slade, **Bud Geary**; Joe, **Billy Cummings**; Skinny, **Freddie Chapman**; Dave Wyatt, **Frank Jaquet**; Sand Snipe, **Tom London**; Chuck, **Monte Hale**; Smokey, **Buckwheat Thomas**; Hank Disher, **George Chesebro**; Judge, **Emmett Vogan**; Father Marion; **Tom Chatterton**// "Thunder"; Ramsey, **Ed Cassidy**; Reagan's Henchman, **Fred Graham**; Wagon Owner, **Jack Kirk**; Chicago Policeman, **Frank O'Connor**; Parish Boys, **Robert Anderson, Gary Armstrong, Romey Foley, Robert Goldschmidt** and **Richard Lydon**; Sheriff, **Jack Rockwell**.

CREDITS: Director, **R.G. Springsteen**; Associate Producer, **Sidney Picker**; Story, **Peter Whitehead**; Screenwriter, **Earle Snell**; Editor, **Charles Craft**; Art Director, **Frank Hotaling**; Set Decorator, **Otto Siegel**; Cinematography, **Bud Thackery**; Special Effects, **Howard** and **Theodore Lydecker**; Makeup, **Bob Mark**; Sound, **Earl Crain, Jr.**; Musical Director, **Richard Cherwin**.

LOCATION FILMING: Iverson, California.

Colorado Pioneers (Republic, 1945) scene card — Edward Cassidy, Tom Chatterton, Frank O'Conner, Bill Elliott and Bobby Blake (standing left to right), and Emmett Vogan, Freddie Chapman and Billy Cummings (seated left to right).

RUNNING TIME: 55 min.

SOURCE: Based on Fred Harman's famous NEA Comic — by special arrangement with Stephen Slesinger.

STORY: Chicago hoodlum Roy Barcroft uses youngsters Billy Cummings and Freddie Chapman in his criminal activities. Wild Bill Elliott, aided by his pal Bobby Blake's keen observation, retrieves money stolen from cattle buyer Ed Cassidy and has Barcroft arrested. Elliott believes the boys can be rehabilitated if they will be allowed to spend the summer on his Aunt Alice Fleming's ranch. In addition to Cummings and Chapman, Father Tom Chatterton sends all the boys in the parish. Back in Blue Springs, Wyoming, Elliott and Fleming need to start a cattle drive but are plagued with arson and the loss of their cowhands to rival rancher Frank Jaquet. Jaquet is behind Elliott's problems. As Elliott looks for cowhands, Blake trains the Chicago youngsters to be good cowboys. Barcroft shows up and convinces Cummings to steal money from Fleming's ranch. Elliott wins top prize money in the annual buckboard race. Jaquet's henchman, Bud Geary, attempts to steal the prize money. Elliott defeats Geary in a rugged fistfight, which causes Geary to tell Elliot about Jaquet's du-plicity. Barcroft and Cummings steal the money but are arrested before they can leave town. Cummings finally realizes that Elliott's ways are right. The boys will be coming back next year.

NOTES AND COMMENTARY: Future western star and Academy Award winner Ben Johnson doubled for Wild Bill Elliott in this feature.

Footage from the buckboard race surfaced again in Monte Hale's *Outcasts of the Trail* (Republic, 1949).

REVIEWS: "Good outing for Elliott in the exciting Red Ryder series." *Motion Picture Guide*, Nash and Ross; "An out-of-the-ordinary plot gives some zest to this 'Red Ryder' segment." *Western Movies*, Pitts.

SUMMATION: This is a better than average western. Wild Bill Elliott does his usual good job as Red Ryder, both in the acting and action departments. Director R. G. Springsteen keeps the story moving and gets good performances from the supporting cast, especially Roy Barcroft as a Chicago hoodlum. Peter Whitehead's story and Earle Snell's screenplay concept of using children to round up cattle and go on a cattle drive predate John Wayne's *The Cowboys* (Warner Bros., 1972) by 27 years.

Blazing Oil ... Roaring Guns

Conquest of Cheyenne

Republic Pictures (July, 1946)

CAST: Red Ryder, **Wild Bill Elliott**; Little Beaver, **Bobby Blake**; the Duchess, **Alice Fleming**; Cheyenne Jackson, **Peggy Stewart**; Tom Dean, **Jay Kirby**; Tuttle, **Milton Kibbee**; Sheriff, **Tom London**; Daffy, **Emmett Lynn**; McBride, **Kenne Duncan**; Murdo, **George Sherwood**; Long, **Frank McCarroll**; Blake, **Jack Kirk**; Rancher Jones, **Tom Chatterton**// "Thunder"; Townsman (voice only), **LeRoy Mason**.

CREDITS: Director, **R.G. Springsteen**; Associate Director, **Sidney Picker**; Story, **Bert Horswell** and **Joseph Poland**; Screenwriter, **Earle Snell**; Editor, **Charles Craft**; Art Director, **Fred A. Ritter**; Set Decorators, **John Mc-Carthy, Jr.** and **Ralph Zakoura**; Cinematography, **William Bradford**; Makeup, **Bob Mark**; Sound, **Fred Stahl**; Musical Director, **Richard Cherwin**; Special Effects, **Howard** and **Theodore Lydecker**.

LOCATION FILMING: Iverson, California.

RUNNING TIME: 56 min.

SOURCE: Based on Fred Harman's Famous NEA Comic — by special arrangement with Stephen Slesinger.

STORY: Jay Kirby discovers oil on Peggy Stewart's ranch. Banker Milton Kibbee, who plans to foreclose on the ranch to capitalize on the discovery, knows this fact. Kirby tells Stewart and Alice Fleming that he had been framed and then served a prison term for oil fraud. Stewart, sweet on Kirby, wants him to begin drilling. Kibbee plans to allow Stewart and Kirby to set up an oil well derrick to pinpoint the location of the oil, then use sabotage to put Stewart further in debt so he can foreclose. Fleming's nephew, Wild Bill Elliott, captures George Sherwood, Kibbee's henchman, after he sets fire to the derrick. As Elliott forces Sherwood to talk, Kibbee shoots Sherwood and makes good his escape. Kibbee first convinces the ranchers and townspeople that Kirby plans to defraud them and that Elliott murdered Sherwood. Elliott takes matters into his own hands, and proves his innocence and Kibbee's guilt. Kirby brings in a gusher. Elliott tells Fleming that it looks like Stewart and Kirby will get married soon.

NOTES AND COMMENTARY: This would be Wild Bill Elliott's last appearance as Red Ryder. Elliott's first big-budget western, *In Old Sacra-* *mento*, was already on theater screens when this film was released.

Allan Lane would assume the role of Ryder for seven entries in the 1946–47 season.

At the Knoxville Film Festival in 1989, director R.G. Springsteen was asked to compare Bill Elliott and Allan Lane as Red Ryder. He stated, "I knew both of them very well. Bill Elliott was much better. He [Lane] was a little tough."

Peggy Stewart remembers the final scene in the picture as the gusher comes in. A black, synthetic oil would be sprayed over the cast members. Stewart was wearing an outfit she liked and planned to move out of harm's way. Bobby Blake had other ideas and tripped Stewart up so she would be soaked with the rest of the cast.

REVIEW: "Another well-made entry in the Red Ryder series, handled well by director R.G. Springsteen." *Western Movies*, Pitts.

Conquest of Cheyenne (Republic, 1946) movie still — Peggy Stewart (left) and Bill Elliott (right).

SUMMATION: Although somewhat enjoyable, this was probably the weakest entry in Wild Bill Elliott's Red Ryder series. Most of the blame can be laid on the story and screenwriter Earle Snell, who left more holes in the story than R.G. Springsteen's direction could cover. Elliott was off-screen too much, possibly working on *In Old Sacramento*, which didn't help matters either. Elliott gave his usual capable tight-lipped performance, but no more. Jay Kirby is more than adequate with the large amount of screen time given him.

Power-Packed Western Adventure Featuring the Action Hero Who's Fast Becoming a Favorite of the American Public!

Death Valley Manhunt

Republic (September, 1943)

CAST: Wild Bill Elliott, **Wild Bill Elliott**; Gabby Hayes, **George "Gabby" Hayes**; Nicky Hobart, **Anne Jeffreys**; Quinn, **Weldon Heyburn**; Judge Hobart, **Herbert Heyes**; Tex Benson, **Davison Clark**; Clayton, **Pierce Lyden**; Danny, **Charlie Murray, Jr.**; Marshal Hugh Ward, **Jack Kirk**; Blaine, **Eddie Phillips**; Roberts, **Bud Geary**; Lawson, **Al Taylor**// "Sonny"; Frank, **Franklyn Farnum**; Neal, **Neal Hart**; Ed, **Charles Sullivan**; Townsman, **Curley Dresden**; Ross, **Edward Keane**; Oil Drillers, **Marshall Reed** and **Kansas Moering**.

CREDITS: Director, **John English**; Associate Producer, **Eddy White**; Story, **Fred Myton** and **Eddy White**; Screenwriters, **Norman S. Hall** and **Anthony Coldewey**; Editor, **Harry Keller**; Art Director, **Russell Kimball**; Set Decorator, **Otto Siegel**; Cinematography, **Ernest Miller**; Sound, **Howard Wilson**; Music Score, **Mort Glickman**.

SONG: "Carry Me Back to Old Virginny" (Bland) — sung by **Anne Jeffreys**.

LOCATION FILMING: Iverson and Walker Ranch, California.

RUNNING TIME: 55 min.

STORY: Retired lawman Wild Bill Elliott is asked by Edward Keane to investigate the problems between his petroleum company and the wildcatters in the Death Valley area. Company representative Weldon Heyburn blames all the problems on the wildcatters. Actually, Heyburn, with Judge Herbert Heyes, plans to swindle both the company and the wildcatters. In Death Valley, Elliott, with help from an old friend, George "Gabby" Hayes, arranges to have the company lend the wildcatters money and supplies to bring in a promising oil well. Also, Elliott meets Heyes' niece, Anne Jeffreys, and the two begin to fall in love. Quickly, Elliott and the wildcatters learn that Heyburn has no intention of honoring the agreement, and is determined to take over the wildcatters' holdings. Hayes obtains the supplies and starts transporting them to the oil well. Heyburn sends men to intercept Hayes. Hayes's wagon crashes, but Hayes and the equipment are unharmed. Elliott's arrival prevents the henchmen from filling Hayes's body with bullets. As the wildcatters begin to strike oil, Elliott obtains proof of Heyburn and Heyes's duplicity. Heyburn and henchman Bud Geary ride to blow up the well. Elliott convinces Heyes to turn state's evidence, and the men ride to stop Heyburn. At the oil field, Heyburn is poised to dynamite the well when Elliott and Heyes arrive. Bullets from Heyburn's gun kill Heyes and Geary. Elliott and Heyburn engage in a terrific fistfight as the two men climb to the top of the derrick. Elliott avoids Heyburn's desperate lunge and Heyburn falls to his death, pushing down the plunger of the detonator. The dynamite causes a gusher, and the wildcatters are rich. Elliott and Jeffreys plan to marry.

NOTES AND COMMENTARY: Around 1878 James Bland, an African-American minstrel, wrote "Carry Me Back to Old Virginny." It became Virginia's state song in 1940. In 1997, because of lyrics that could be offensive to African-Americans, the Virginia Senate voted to make the song the state song emeritus, and a committee was directed to find a new state

Death Valley Manhunt (Republic, 1943) scene card — Bill Elliott (left) and Weldon Heyburn (right) fight on the top of an oil derrick.

song. To date, a replacement song has not been found.

There is an interesting early scene in which Bill Elliott decides to forsake law enforcement for ranch life. Two of the townsmen wishing Elliott good luck in his new endeavor are silent screen western heroes, Franklyn Farnum and Neal Hart. A neat touch.

REVIEWS: "It's all standard gunplay stuff." *Variety*, 11/17/43; "Highly competent Bill Elliott vehicle with lots of action and a good script." *Western Movies*, Pitts.

SUMMATION: This is a great "B" western. Bill Elliott is in top form as a lawman whose hands are tied until he can obtain proof of wrongdoing. George "Gabby" Hayes gives one of his best performances. Just look at the scene when he discovers his little dog has been killed. Try to watch it without a lump forming in your throat. Director John English does a fine job of deftly balancing action and story.

Hit the High Road to Thrills with Two Top Stars!

The Devil's Trail

Columbia (May, 1942)

ALTERNATE TITLES: *Rogue's Gallery* and *Devil's Canyon.*

CAST: Wild Bill Hickok, **Bill Elliott**; Tex Martin, **Tex Ritter**; Myra, **Eileen O'Hearn**; Cannonball, **Frank Mitchell**; Bull McQuade, **Noah Beery**; Ella, **Ruth Ford**; Dr. Willowby, **Joel Friedkin**; Jim Randall, **Joe McGuinn**; Sid Howland, **Edmund Cobb**; Ed Scott, **Tristram Coffin**; Blacksmith, **Paul Newlan**// "Sonny"; "White Flash"; Harris, **Bud Osborne**; Henchmen, **Buck Moulton, Stanley Brown, Steve Clark** and **Art Mix.**

CREDITS: Director, **Lambert Hillyer**; Pro-ducer, **Leon Barsha**; Screenwriter, **Philip Ketchum**; Editor, **Charles Nelson**; Art Directors, **Lionel Banks** and **Perry Smith**; Cinematographer, **George Meehan.**

SONGS: "When the Sun Goes Down"—sung by **Tex Ritter**; "Hi, Diddle Lum, Diddle Lum"—sung by **Tex Ritter.**

LOCATION FILMING: Iverson, California.

SOURCE: The story "The Town in Hell's Backyard," by **Robert Lee Johnson.**

STORY: Bill Elliott is hiding out in Tiburon until he can clear himself of a murder charge. Tiburon is under control of Noah Beery, who is plotting to have Kansas secede from the

The Devil's Trail (Columbia, 1942) scene card — Frank Mitchell (left) watches a discussion between Bill Elliott (center) and Noah Beery (right).

Union. Beery is holding Dr. Joel Friedkin and his daughter, Eileen O'Hearn, hostage. Marshal Tex Ritter arrives in Tiburon to arrest Elliott. Frank Mitchell, who is being held prisoner, helps Elliott escape. When Beery sends his henchmen after Elliott, O'Hearn takes the opportunity to escape on foot. Beery's henchmen attempt to murder Ritter, but O'Hearn's intervention saves his life. O'Hearn convinces Ritter to join forces with Elliott and Mitchell. Elliott proves he's innocent of the murder charge. Elliott and Ritter return to Tiburon to rescue Friedkin and are trapped in the blacksmith shop. After a gunfight, Elliott and Ritter get the drop on Beery and his men.

NOTES AND COMMENTARY: Here Bill Elliott and Noah Beery were reunited in pictures (as antagonists) after 13 years. Elliott and Beery were rivals in the silent film *Passion Song* (Excellent Pictures, 1928). They both appeared in *Big Boy* (Warner Bros., 1930) as well, but had no scenes together.

REVIEWS: "Top notch effort in the Bill Elliott-Tex Ritter series." *Western Movies*, Pitts; "Even the considerable talents of Elliott and Ritter can't prevent this tepid oater from boring." *Motion Picture Guide*, Nash and Ross.

SUMMATION: *The Devil's Trail* is a good Bill Elliott-Tex Ritter western, with plenty of action but a story marred by a mild windup in the capture of Noah Beery and his gang. Elliott and Ritter deliver fine performances in the action and dialog sequences. Director Lambert Hillyer is able to generate good suspense, especially in the scene where Edmund Cobb is forcing Ritter to fall from a cliff to his death.

Dial Red 0 ... for a Direct Line to Murder!

Dial Red 0

Allied Artists (March, 1955)

CAST: Lt. Andy Flynn, **Bill Elliott**; Connie Wyatt, **Helene Stanley**; Ralph Wyatt, **Keith Larsen**; Norman Roper, **Paul Picerni**; Lloyd Lavalle, **Jack Kruschen**; Gloria, **Elaine Riley**; Sgt. Tony Columbo, **Robert Bice**; Deputy Clark, **Rick Vallin**; Major Sutter, **George Eldredge**; Deputy Morgan, **John Phillips**; Mrs. Roper, **Regina Gleason**; Coroner, **Rankin Mansfield**; Photographer, **Mort Mills**; Devon, **William J. Tannen**// Motorcycle Policeman, **Holly Bane**; Policeman at Crime Scene, **John Hart**; Mr. Wayne, **Larry Blake**; Police Captain, **Forrest Lewis**; Hamburger Stand Proprietor, **Sam Peckinpah**.

CREDITS: Director/Screenwriter, **Daniel B. Ullman**; Assistant Director, **Edward Morey, Jr.**; Producer, **Vincent M. Fennelly**; Film Editor Supervisor, **Lester A. Sansom**; Editor, **William Austin**; Art Director, **David Milton**; Set Decorator, **Joseph Kish**; Cinematography, **Ellsworth Fredericks**; Special Effects, **Milt Rice**; Photographic Effects, **Ray Mercer**; Sound, **Charles Schelling** and **Ralph Butler**; Makeup, **Paul Malcolm**; Hair Stylist, **Mary Smith**; Music, **Marlin Skiles**; Jazz Sequences, **Shorty Rogers and His Giants**; Production Manager, **Allen K. Wood**; Property, **Sam Gordon**; Construction Supervisor, **James West**; Dialogue Supervisor, **Sam Peckinpah**; Set Continuity, **Mary Chaffee**; Wardrobe Supervisor, **Bert Henrikson**.

RUNNING TIME: 63 min.

STORY: After receiving final divorce papers from Helene Stanley, Keith Larsen, a patient in a VA Hospital for psychiatric evaluation, goes "over the fence." Fearing that Larsen's violent tendencies will emerge upon meeting Stanley, Police Lieutenant Bill Elliott is notified. Elliott begins a search for Larsen. Stanley has begun an affair with Paul Picerni, an old friend of Larsen's. Stanley begins pressuring Picerni to divorce his wife and marry her, and tells Picerni she's pregnant with his child. In a rage, Picerni, using judo, murders Stanley. Larsen is the obvious suspect and is arrested by Elliott. Larsen, learning how Stanley was murdered, immediately suspects Picerni and breaks out of jail and steals a revolver. Elliott, with some good police work, also begins to suspect Picerni. Elliott

Dial Red 0 (Allied Artists, 1955) scene card — Bill Elliott (right) arrests Keith Larsen (left).

alerts Picerni that Larsen might come to see him since they're old army buddies. Picerni decides to shoot Larsen when he arrives. Elliott arrives at Picerni's estate as Larsen and Picerni are exchanging shots. Elliott prevents Larsen from shooting Picerni and arrests Picerni for Stanley's murder.

NOTES AND COMMENTARY: *Dial Red 0* marks Bill Elliott's first leading role in a nonwestern. Elliott would go on to star in four more detective dramas. Elliott's character underwent a last-name change from "Flynn" in this film to "Doyle" in succeeding films. It seems that there was an Andy Flynn working in law enforcement in the Los Angeles area.

Paul Picerni remembered he had only one scene with Elliott, and remarked, "I was the killer in *Dial Red 0*. He [Elliott] was the detective. He was a great guy. It was kind of strange to see him — not in a cowboy outfit. I was always a big fan of his. I was honored to work with him."

Future director Sam Peckinpah had dual responsibilities in the production of *Dial Red 0*, as Dialogue Supervisor and as an actor in an unbilled role. Peckinpah would go on to become a top action director with such films as *Ride the High Country* (Metro-Goldwyn-Mayer, 1962), *The Wild Bunch* (Warner Bros., 1969) and *The Getaway* (Warner Bros., 1972). Peckinpah specialized in violent and bloody scenes, often employing slow motion to enhance the effect.

REVIEW: "Lightweight but passable for lower case bookings. Elliott is his customary taciturn self as the sheriff, doing okay without his horse and chaps." *Variety*, 4/13/55.

SUMMATION: In this taut, well-acted and directed police drama, Bill Elliott does a nice job as the detective, but acting honors go to Keith Larsen as the accused and Paul Picerni as the murderer.

*Out of the Lusty Days when Texas Was Young Comes
Fierce... Flaming... Furious... Fabulous Adventure!
Drama as Great as the Lone Star State ...
Romance as Big as the Heart of Texas!*

The Fabulous Texan

Republic (November, 1947)

ALTERNATE TITLE: *The Texas Uprising.*

CAST: Jim McWade, **William Elliott**; John Wesley Barker, **John Carroll**; Alice Sharp, **Catherine McLeod**; Gibson Hart, **Albert Dekker**; Elihu Mills, **Andy Devine**; Josie Allen, **Patricia Knight**; Utopia Mills, **Ruth Donnelly**; Bud Clayton, **Johnny Sands**; Reverend Barker, **Harry Davenport**; Doctor Sharp, **Robert H. Barrat**; Luke Roland, **Douglass Dumbrille**; Captain Jessup, **Reed Hadley**; Standifer, **Roy Barcroft**; Wade Clayton, **Russell Simpson**; Shep Clayton, **James Brown**; Sam Bass, **Jim Davis**; Dick Clayton, **George Beban**; Sim Clayton, **John Miles**// McGinn, **Olin Howland**; Telegraph Operator, **Eddie Acuff**; Owens, **Glenn Strange**; Zebrina, **Dick Elliott**; Andy Renfro, **Frank Ferguson**; Mrs. Renfro, **Helen Brown**; State Policemen, **Harry Woods** and **Jack Ingram**; Townsman, **Tom Chatterton**; Rancher, **Al Ferguson**; Tax Collector, **George Eldredge**; President Ulysses S. Grant, **John Hamilton**; Texas Senator, **Addison Richards**; Bass Gang Member, **Kenneth MacDonald**; Morbid Citizen, **George Lloyd**; General Sheridan, **Russell Hicks**; Judge Gavin, **Harry Cheshire**; Trooper, **Wade Crosby**; Mr. Killraine (Vigilante Leader), **Stanley Andrews**; Vigilante Member, **Ed Cassidy**; Wesley, **Gregory Marshall**; Visitor at McWade Memorial, **Pierre Watkin**.

CREDITS: Director, **Edward Ludwig**; Associate Producer, **Edmund Grainger**; Story, **Hal Long**; Screenwriters, **Lawrence Hazard** and **Horace McCoy**; Editor, **Richard L. Van Enger**; Art Director, **James Sullivan**; Set Decorators, **John McCarthy, Jr.** and **George Milo**; Cinematographer, **Reggie Lanning**; Costumes, **Adele Palmer**; Makeup, **Bob Mark**; Hair Stylist, **Peggy Gray**; Sound, **Earl Crain, Sr.**; Music, **Anthony Collins**; Special Effects, **Howard** and **Theodore Lydecker**.

LOCATION FILMING: Flagstaff and Sedona, Arizona, and Iverson, California.

RUNNING TIME: 95 min.

STORY: William Elliott and John Carroll return to Millsford, Texas, after fighting for the Confederacy. Elliott can't wait to be reunited with his fiancée, Catherine McLeod, who is really in love with Carroll. Elliott and Carroll discover Texas is overrun with corrupt politicians and their state police force. In an altercation with the State Police, Captain Reed Hadley shoots Harry Davenport, Carroll's father. Carroll faces Hadley in a gun duel and Hadley is killed, making Carroll an outlaw. Elliott obtains State Police Captain Albert Dekker's word that Carroll will receive a fair trial. Elliott and Carroll can't decide if Dekker will keep his word, but Carroll surrenders anyway. Before Carroll can go to trial, Dekker declares Millsford under martial law. Elliott breaks Carroll out of jail. The two men begin stealing State Police money and give it to ranchers to pay their taxes. The State Police begin a reign of terror to force Texans to tell where Carroll is hiding. McLeod arranges to have Elliott meet with General Russell Hicks to discuss the lawlessness of the State Police. Elliott also discovers that McLeod is really in love with Carroll. Elliott is sworn in as a U.S. Marshal to bring in Dekker. Carroll listens to outlaw Jim Davis and leads a robbery on a Federal Bank, now making him an outlaw in the eyes of the U.S. Government. The people of Texas now turn against Carroll and form a band of vigilantes, who ambush Carroll and his men. All the men are killed except a wounded Carroll who manages to escape. Carroll learns of a plot by Dekker to kill Elliott. In a blaze of gunfire, Carroll guns down Dekker and two henchmen, but in turn is mortally wounded. In later years, after his death, Elliott is recognized as a "fabulous Texan," but his widow, McLeod, notes there were others who did as much for Texas.

The Fabulous Texan (Republic, 1947) scene card — Bill Elliott (left) gets the drop on Albert Dekker (center) and Roy Barcroft (right).

NOTES AND COMMENTARY: Catherine McLeod developed a distaste for William Elliott after he wiped his mouth with the back of his hand following a romantic scene in which they kissed.

Patricia Knight was married to actor Cornel Wilde when she made this film. Wilde was attempting to control her career, which made Knight extremely nervous. In a scene where Catherine McLeod had to grasp Knight's hands, Knight's hands were badly shaking due to Wilde's presence on the set.

The Fabulous Texan was re-released in 1953 as *The Texas Uprising*. The film was edited to a 60 minute running time.

On a panel at the Western Film Fair in Charlotte, N.C., James Brown commented on Elliott: " Bill was great to work with, very cooperative. I put him at the very top. Bill was a very quiet person. You'd have to drag him into a conversation. Bill was a very quiet man, very reserved, very sophisticated type of guy. A clean, nice human being. I enjoyed working with him very, very much. Some I don't like to work with."

REVIEWS: "William Elliott, John Carroll, Catherine McLeod in super-western, good b.o. [box office]. On the credit side of the ledger is the fine work turned in by Elliott and Carroll. Former is a western star in the best William S. Hart tradition, even slightly resembling the old master. He's got plenty of opportunity to demonstrate his thesping, as well as riding and shooting ability in this one, and emerges on top in all three departments." *Variety*, 11/12/47; "Very well done William Elliott film, with a top notch cast of character actors." *Western Movies*, Pitts.

SUMMATION: This is a strong, well-directed and acted western. William Elliott received top billing and assays his part in good stead, but John Carroll steals acting honors portraying a decent but hotheaded individual who drifts over to the wrong side of the law. A good supporting cast is headed by Catherine McLeod as the woman loved by both Elliott and Carroll, and Albert Dekker who wants to rule Texas through the corrupt State Police. Edward Ludwig's direction is masterful, keeping the interest at a high level, and Reggie Lanning's cinematography is first rate, bringing a depth to night scenes not usually seen in films at the budget level. One minor misstep is the tacked-on ending in which McLeod, now Elliott's widow, expresses concern that others did as much for Texas, and perhaps even more. And why did McLeod marry Elliott anyway?

The Town the Law Forgot!
Rough, Tough Fargo Took the Best That Badmen Offered … and Paid Them Back — Bullet for Bullet!

Fargo

Monogram Pictures (September, 1952)

A Silvermine Production

CAST: Bill Martin, **Wild Bill Elliott**; Kathy MacKenzie, **Phyllis Coates**; Red Olsen, **Myron Healy**; Tad Sloan, **Fuzzy Knight**; Loren MacKenzie, **Jack Ingram**; Austin, **Arthur Space**; Link, **Robert Wilke**; Alvord, **Terry Frost**; Murdock, **Robert Bray**; Carey, **Denver Pyle**; Sam, **Tim Ryan**; Maggie, **Florence Lake**; Judge, **Stanley Andrews**; Bartender, **Richard Reeves**; Blacksmith, **Eugene Roth**// Farmer, **Stanley Price**; Rancher, **House Peters, Jr.**; Joe Hankins, **Bud Osborne**.

CREDITS: Director, **Lewis Collins**; Assistant Director, **Melville Shyer**; Producer, **Vincent M. Fennelly**; Screenwriters, **Jack DeWitt** and **Joseph Poland**; Editor, **Sam Fields**; Art Director, **Dave Milton**; Set Decorator, **Robert Priestley**; Cinematographer, **Ernest Miller**; Special Effects, **Ray Mercer**; Sound, **John Kean**; Music, **Raoul Kraushaar**; Continuity, **Emilie Ehrlich**; Dialogue Supervisor, **Stanley Price**; Color by **Sepiatone**.

LOCATION FILMING: Iverson and Corriganville, California.

RUNNING TIME: 69 min.

STORY: Informed of his brother's death, Wild Bill Elliott comes to Fargo, where he learns it was murder. Elliott decides to take over his brother's farm and follow his dream of having good land to grow crops. Unfortunately, the farm is located in the middle of cattle country. Land agent Arthur Space and Myron Healey, rancher Jack Ingram's foreman, want all the farmers' lands to sell to the cattlemen at a huge profit. Elliott decides to string barbed wire to keep cattle from grazing and trampling his crops. Healey begins a reign of terror against those who use the wire. Elliot is captured by Healey and his henchmen, and is beaten and wrapped in the wire, then delivered to the cattlemen's dance. The atrocity enrages the cattlemen, as Ingram has convinced the ranchers that they can co-exist with the farmers to raise grain-fed cattle, which will bring higher prices. Elliott begins a personal vendetta against Healey. Space has Healey lead his henchmen to burn out all the farmers. Ingram and his daughter, Phyllis Coates, who is sweet on Elliott, form a posse to help Elliott. Ingram catches up with Elliott and convinces him to first protect the homesteaders and then, at daybreak, go after Healey. Elliott learns where Healey is camped. Space meets Healey to pay off the henchmen, not knowing Elliott and the posse have sealed off all exits from the outlaw camp. In the gunfight that follows, Space is killed and the henchmen are either killed or captured. Healey is the sole surviving outlaw, and Elliott goes after him. The two men meet and shoot it out, with Elliott victorious. Elliott proves to all the cattlemen that barbed wire is no threat to the cattle. Elliott plans to settle down in Fargo with Coates.

NOTES AND COMMENTARY: This was Wild Bill Elliott's last picture under the Monogram

Fargo (Monogram, 1952) scene card — Bill Elliott (left) and Phyllis Coates (right) share a pleasant moment.

banner. His future starring films would be released by Monogram's parent company, Allied Artists.

REVIEWS: "Nicely done tale of barbed wire being introduced on the range." *Western Movies*, Pitts; "Well-made oater." *Motion Picture Guide*, Nash and Ross.

SUMMATION: This is an excellent adult "B"

western. *Fargo* offers a strong, violent story, with a literate script by Jack DeWitt and Joseph Poland, crisp direction by Lewis Collins, fine acting by Bill Elliott, Jack Ingram, Myron Healy and Phyllis Coates, and tough action from start to finish. Elliott, in particular, is excellent, totally believable as a man with a mission. This is a western not to be missed.

Terror Mounts with Every Strangling Second!

Footsteps in the Night

Allied Artists (March, 1957)

CAST: Lt. Andy Doyle, **Bill Elliott**; Sgt. Mike Duncan, **Don Haggerty**; Mary Raiken, **Eleanore Tanin**; Henry Johnson, **Douglas Dick**; Mr. Bradbury, **James Flavin**; Tony Reed (Orvello), **Gregg Palmer**; Dick Harris, **Harry Tyler**; Secretary, **Ann Griffith**; Fred Horner, **Robert Shayne**// Bartender, **Ralph Sanford**; Shaw, **Forrest Taylor**.

CREDITS: Director, **Jean Yarbrough**;

Footsteps in the Night (Allied Artists, 1957) movie still — Bill Elliott (right) pushes James Flavin (left) out of the line of fire.

Assistant Director, **Edward Morley, Jr.**; Producer, **Ben Schwalb**; Story, **Albert Band**; Screenwriters, **Albert Band** and **Elwood Ullman**; Dialogue Supervisor, **Herman Rotsten**; Editor, **Neil Brunnenkant**; Art Director, **Dave Milton**; Cinematographer, **Harry Neumann**; Production Manager, **Allan K. Wood**; Construction Supervisor, **James West**; Set Decorator, **Joseph Kish**; Property, **Ted Mossman**; Set Continuity, **Richard M. Chaffee**; Makeup, **Emile LaVigne**; Wardrobe, **Bert Henrikson**; Sound, **Ralph Butler**; Music, **Marlin Skiles**.

RUNNING TIME: 62 min.

STORY: Police Lieutenant Bill Elliott is in charge of the investigation of Robert Shayne's murder in a small Hollywood motel. Shayne was found in Douglas Dick's room, and Dick is on the run from the police. Prior to the murder, Dick and Shayne had been heard arguing. Dick meets his sweetheart, Eleanor Tanin, and tells her he's innocent and planning to find the killer. Following Tanin, Elliott arrests Dick. After interrogating Dick, Elliott comes to the conclusion that the wrong man was killed. Continuing his investigation, Elliott believes James Flavin, who is staying in a similar looking and adjacent motel, was the intended victim. Elliott has Dick released from jail and has Flavin tell everyone he plans to leave town. The murderer, gasoline station manager Gregg Palmer, enters Flavin's bungalow to rob and murder him. Elliott prevents the murder and, in a blaze of gunfire, captures Palmer.

NOTES AND COMMENTARY: James Flavin had finished his last scene midday on a Wednesday. Director Jean Yarbrough told Flavin to go home. Before Flavin could leave the set, however, assistant director Edward Morley, Jr. told Flavin he couldn't go home because some of his scenes might need to be re-shot. So Flavin stayed the rest of the day. He was on the set Thursday and Friday when the movie was completed. Friday evening the security guard found Flavin still on the set. Flavin told the guard Morley had not told him he could go home. Saturday morning Flavin was still on the set. The guard called Morley and Morley told Flavin he could go home. Flavin responded that he couldn't be sure that it was Morley on the other end of the line and refused to go home. Morley finally had to come to the studio to tell Flavin he could go home. Not only did Flavin get even with assistant director Morley, he earned some significant overtime salary.

Footsteps in the Night was Bill Elliott's last starring film. He would go on to appear in commercials and his own television show in Las Vegas, but he never again starred in a motion picture.

REVIEWS: "Run-of-the-mill mystery, a short and routine meller. Elliott has the majority of the footage and his underplaying goes with the role. Producer Ben Schwalb used his Allied Artists bungalow as the setting for a goodly portion of the action." *Variety*, 7/24/57; "Stock whodunnit." *Motion Picture Guide*, Nash and Ross.

SUMMATION: Though an interesting murder mystery/crime story, *Footsteps in the Night* closes with a too-pat ending. Bill Elliott is properly authoritative, and displays a good sense of humor. Marlin Skiles' nice jazz score enhances the proceedings.

He Had the Slowest Temper ... and the Fastest Guns in All the West!

The Forty-Niners

Allied Artists (May, 1954)
A Westwood Production
CAST: Marshal Sam Nelson, **Wild Bill Elliott**; Stella Walker, **Virginia Grey**; Alf Billings, **Henry Morgan**; Ernie Walker, **John Doucette**; Bill Norris, **Lane Bradford**; Everett, **Stanford Jolley**; Gambler with Derringer, **Harry Lauter**; Hotel Clerk, **Earle Hodgins**; Chief Marshal Sloan, **Dean Cromer**; Joe, **Ralph Sanford**// Guard, **Artie Ortego**; Desk Clerk, **Jack O'Shea**; Saloon Patron, **Stanley Price**.
CREDITS: Director, **Thomas Carr**; Assistant Director, **Melville Shyer**; Producer, **Vincent M. Fennelly**; Story, **Dan Ullman**; Editor, **Sam Fields**; Art Director, **James West**; Set Decorator, **Vincent A. Taylor**; Cinematographer, **Ernest Miller**; Special Effects, **Ray Mercer**; Sound, **Charles Cooper**; Music, **Raoul Kraushaar**; Dialogue Supervisor, **Stanley Price**; Set Continuity, **Mary Chaffee**.
LOCATION FILMING: Iverson and Corriganville, California.
RUNNING TIME: 71 min.
STORY: Marshal Wild Bill Elliott is assigned to find the murderers of a U.S. Marshal. His only clue is a small-time criminal, Henry Morgan, who arranged the murder. Elliott locates Morgan in a California gold camp and saves him from being tarred-and-feathered for cheating at cards. Elliott and Morgan decide to team up. In Cold Water, Morgan discovers John Doucette and Lane Bradford, who are the murderers for whom Elliott is looking. Blackmailing Doucette, Morgan becomes half owner of his saloon. Only a letter detailing Doucette and Bradford's crimes stop them from getting rid of Morgan. Doucette gets his wife, Virginia Grey, a former lover of Morgan's, to find where the letter is hidden. Elliott believes Doucette and Bradford are the men he seeks and writes a letter to have a witness brought to Cold Water. Bradford intercepts the letter, and he and Doucette tell Morgan he's to get rid of Elliott. Morgan is not a murderer and convinces Elliott to let him go back to town. Morgan will tell Doucette and Bradford that Elliott's dead and that they have to dispose of the body. Then Elliott can capture the murderers. On his way to town, Morgan meets Bradford, who realizes Morgan had not fired his gun. The two men struggle over a gun, which discharges, wounding Morgan. Morgan is able to get away and

The Forty-Niners (Allied Artists, 1954) scene card — Bill Elliott (right) has knocked Lane Bradford (left) down; the left border shows Bill Elliott.

ride to town. Elliott comes upon Bradford, but their confrontation ends in a stalemate. Bradford offers to shoot it out with Elliott. Elliott agrees and is too fast for Bradford. Elliott arrives in town to find Morgan has taken refuge in Grey's house. Morgan has sent Grey to retrieve the letter from the hotel safe. Morgan's wound proves fatal. Elliott takes the letter from Grey. Doucette comes home and attempts to kill Elliott, but Elliott disables Doucette with well-placed shots to both arms. Doucette is arrested, and following a trial is sentenced to hang.

NOTES AND COMMENTARY: This was Wild Bill Elliott's last starring western feature. Elliott's career as a western star lasted 16 years and covered appearances in 70 features and three serials. Elliott would next be seen in five detective entries over the next three years before retiring from the silver screen.

Bill Elliott's character in his final feature

would take a drink and smoke — a far cry from most of the roles he had prior to his big-budget films at Republic in 1946.

REVIEWS: "Over-plottage and too many story gaps without the star reduce this latest Wild Bill Elliott entry to an also-ran category. Star needs better material than this. Elliott is persuasive enough as he scouts the gold camps in search of crooked gambler Henry Morgan. Star makes a pitch for a good performance but doesn't stand any too much chance with material offered him." *Variety*, 4/28/54; "Well done Bill Elliott film." *Western Movies*, Pitts; "Almost film noir western." *Motion Picture Guide*, Nash and Ross.

SUMMATION: Wild Bill Elliott's final starring western is a winner. The action is secondary to the story and the fine acting of the principals. Elliott gives his customary fine performance. But acting honors go to Henry

Morgan as a man who'll do anything for money except murder, and Virginia Grey, who scores as a woman who has turned to alcohol to comfort her in a loveless marriage, and who sees hope in the presence of former lover Morgan. Kudos to Dan Ullman's literate script and Thomas Carr's steady direction.

---

*The West's Newest Star Scores Another Hit with Bullet, Fist and Lariat...
Amidst the Tumult and Terror of Early Pioneer Days!*

Frontiers of '49

Columbia (January, 1939)

CAST: John Freeman, **Bill Elliott**; Dolores de Cervantes, **Luana de Alcaniz**; Howard Brunton, **Charles King**; Kit, **Hal Taliaferro**; Brad, **Charles Whittaker**; Don Miguel, **Octavio Giraud**; Padre, **Carlos Villarias**; Romero, **Joe de la Cruz**; Pete, **Jack Walters**; Red, **Al Ferguson**// Bidder at Auction, **Lee Shumway**; Johnson, **Edward Cassidy**, Bank Teller, **Fred Parker**; Tex, **Tex Palmer**; Luke, **Frank Ellis**; Bert, **Kit Guard**; Judge Scott, **Bud Osborne**; Captain Beatty, **Jack Ingram**.

CREDITS: Director, **Joseph Levering**; Screenwriter, **Nate Gatzert**; Editor, **Dwight Caldwell**; Cinematographer, **James S. Brown, Jr.**; Original Music, **Lee Zahler**.

Frontiers of '49 (Columbia, 1939) scene card — upper left has Bill Elliott (left) getting the drop on Slim Whittaker (right); lower right shows Slim Whittaker (left) in a headlock from Bill Elliott (right).

LOCATION FILMING: Iverson, California.

RUNNING TIME: 54 min.

STORY: The Lower California Company, headed by Charles King, is extorting and grabbing lands from the citizens of lower California. A plan to auction the ranch belonging to Octavio Giraud and his daughter Luana de Alcaniz is stopped by the interference of Bill Elliott. Elliott, a captain in the Army, is investigating lawless activity in the area. Elliott knows King is behind the Californians' troubles but has no evidence to arrest him. Finally Elliott finds the evidence he needs. King learns Elliott is an Army officer and captures him. Realizing his time is short, King and his men plan to loot the town and head for Mexico. Elliott escapes and rides for Army troops. As King is looting the town, Elliott and the soldiers arrive. King attempts to escape but Elliott quickly brings him to justice. With lawlessness at an end, Elliott has time for romance with de Cervantes.

NOTES AND COMMENTARY: Some advertising material continued to bill Elliott as "Bill ('Wild Bill Hickok') Elliott."

REVIEWS: "Vehicle shapes into a very modest western. Play is all very slow, not too much action at climax times and Elliott is easily the outstanding performer." *Variety*, 12/22/39; "The film is routine." *The Western*, Hardy.

SUMMATION: This Larry Darmour production released by Columbia is an okay effort for Bill Elliott. Although Elliott handles himself nicely, he had not yet added the subtle nuances that would define his character and elevate him to the top tier of western stars.

The West's Greatest Man-Hunters.... They Were the Law!

The Gallant Legion

Republic Pictures (May, 1948)

CAST: Gary Conway, **William Elliott**; Connie Faulkner, **Adrian Booth**; Clarke Faulkner, **Joseph Shildkraut**; Beau Leroux, **Bruce Cabot**; Windy Hornblower, **Andy Devine**; Captain Banner, **Jack Holt**; Wesley Hardin, **Grant Withers**; Catalina, **Adele Mara**; Tom Banner, **James Brown**; Chuck Conway, **Hal Landon**; Sgt. Clint Mason, **Tex Terry**; Matt Kirby, **Lester Sharpe**; Billy Smith, **Hal Taliaferro**; Senator Beale, **Russell Hicks**; Major Grant, **Herbert Rawlinson**; Bowling, **Marshall Reed**; Dispatch Rider, **Steve Drake**; Lang, **Harry Woods**// Newspaper Correspondent with Fort Worth Democrat, **Emmett Vogan**; George Trent, **Joseph Crehan**; Saloon Patron, **Gene Roth**; Texas Ranger, **Ben Johnson**; Indian Spokesman, **Trevor Bardette**; Indian, **Iron Eyes Cody**; Renegades, **George Chesebro** and **John Cason**.

CREDITS: Director/Associate Producer, **Joe Kane**; Story, **John K. Butler** and **Gerald Geraghty**; Screenwriter, **Gerald Drayson Adams**; Editor, **Richard L. Van Enger**; Art Director, **James Sullivan**; Set Decorators, **John McCarthy, Jr.** and **George Milo**; Cinematographer, **Jack Marta**; Costumes, **Adele Palmer**; Makeup, **Bob Mark**; Hair Stylist, **Peggy Gray**; Sound, **Victor B. Appel**; Musical Director, **Morton Scott**; Special Effects, **Howard** and **Theodore Lydecker**.

SONGS: "Lady from Monterey"—sung by **Adele Mara**; "A Kiss or Two"—sung by **Adele Mara**; "A Gambler's Life"—sung by **Adele Mara**.

LOCATION FILMING: Iverson, Vasquez Rocks and Bronson Canyon, California.

RUNNING TIME: 88 min.

STORY: Bruce Cabot, with state senator Joseph Schildkraut and henchman Grant Withers as allies, wants to make West Texas a separate state of the Union — with Cabot in charge. To further his end, Cabot begins a wave of terror to discredit the Texas Rangers. Soldier of fortune William Elliott returns to Texas to take up ranching with his brother, Hal Landon. Unknown to Elliott, Landon is a member of Cabot's renegades. The renegades attempt to hold up a bank, but Ranger Captain Jack Holt and his men foil the attempt. As the renegades

The Gallant Legion (Republic, 1948) movie still — Bill Elliott, Adrian Booth, James Brown (left to right, standing) and Jack Holt (seated) (courtesy of Adrian Booth Brian).

make their escape, Holt's son, Texas Ranger James Brown, mortally wounds Landon. Landon is able to meet Elliott in El Paso, where he dies in Elliott's arms. Realizing Landon had been working with the renegades, Elliott decides to join the Texas Rangers. Schildkraut's niece, Adrian Booth, a field correspondent for a number of newspapers, is assigned to cover the lawlessness in West Texas. Cabot tells Schildkraut to edit and change Booth's reports, making them detrimental to the Rangers. Elliott and the Rangers confront a group of renegades led by henchman Hal Taliaferro. In the battle, Elliott mortally wounds Taliaferro, who lives long enough to tell Elliott that Brown shot his brother. Holt learns about Booth's reports in the newspapers and is prepared to banish her from the Ranger post. Elliott intervenes and sets a trap that reveals Schildkraut as the guilty party. Cabot murders Schildkraut and makes

the death look like suicide. Cabot plans to start an Indian war against the Rangers and even steals a Gatling gun for their use. The Rangers learn of Cabot's plan and ride to stop him. Elliott, Brown and Ranger Andy Devine are sent to scout ahead. They locate the renegades. Devine alerts Holt and his men. Elliott and Brown spot Cabot and ride after him. From an ambush, Cabot kills Brown, but his shots miss Elliott. Elliott gives chase, but Cabot eludes him. Holt finds his son's body, and his men convince him that Elliott murdered Brown. Elliott comes back to Brown's body and Booth tells him of Holt's thoughts. Elliott knows the only way he can clear himself is to bring Cabot to justice. Cabot decides to hold the Rangers back with the Gatling gun while Withers and his men arm the Indians. Elliott circles around behind Cabot. Holt sees Elliott and has him in his rifle sights but decides not to pull the trigger.

Elliott and Cabot engage in a brutal fight. As they break, Cabot grabs a rifle but Elliott uses the Gatling gun to end Cabot's dream of power. Elliott remains in the Rangers, with Booth a part of his life.

NOTES AND COMMENTARY: Adrian Booth had this to say about *The Gallant Legion*: "This was the first big-budgeted picture that Republic put me in. I was very thrilled at the part. It was a very good part. I played with Joseph Schildkraut, a classic actor." And about Bill Elliott: "I think I enjoyed playing with him as much as anyone."

Booth continued: "My very first scene was on the back lot. My boss [Herbert Yates] and his girl, Vera Ralston, were watching, I played the scene with Bruce Cabot. I think they printed the second take. Then I went back to my dressing room. I had this wonderful wardrobe woman, just an absolute darling. I was crying. I didn't move my face because I didn't want to spoil my makeup. She said something rather vulgar, 'Adrian, you're crying tears that are full of turds and you're just beautiful.'"

Booth talked about Elliott: "I think he was a real professional. He really loved to act. You wouldn't think that because he was real casual about it. He was always there right on time. He always knew his lines. He had a presence that you don't realize right away. Very few actors have it. Spencer Tracy had it. After you shot the scene and got it up on the screen, you would see the depth of it. He had an authority. He had a quietness. He had a believability that came out on the screen. It was wonderful."

Booth added more about Elliott: "I never knew him socially except one time. After we finished *The Gallant Legion*, I was so thrilled to have been in it. There was a beautiful restaurant [Eaton's] not far from the studio on Ventura Boulevard that everybody always went to. I wanted to give a cocktail party for everybody, which I did. I invited the cast and crew. There were rounds of drinks and I had hors d'oeuvres served. Then everybody left. I asked for the check and was told the bill was $10. I said. 'You must mean $100.' Bill Elliott, Joe Kane and others, as the rounds came, would pay for it."

Booth, asked if she had any knowledge of Elliott as a womanizer, responded, "Not at all. He was a perfect gentleman. I don't believe it."

Scenes from *Dark Command* (Republic, 1940) were used in the opening montage sequence.

Ben Johnson was Wild Bill Elliott's double in this big-budget western.

REVIEWS: "A strong western for all patrons who buy brawling outdoor action. Its basic story is a familiar one but is sold with a wallop that keeps it constantly on the move. They [Elliott and Cabot] make expert antagonists." *Variety*, 5/26/48; "A very fine William Elliott vehicle, strong in story, action and cast." *Western Movies*, Pitts.

SUMMATION: This is a great Western film and a rousing tribute to the Texas Rangers. William Elliott heads an impressive cast. Elliott makes a good impression as a soldier of fortune who finally finds a just cause for which to fight. Elliott gives one of his best performances; he is highly convincing in showing sorrow at his brother's death and then a grim determination to see justice prevail. Bruce Cabot makes a worthy adversary for Elliott, both in verbal and physical arguments. Andy Devine adds some subtle comedy without straying into "B" western buffoonery. Adrian Booth makes a fetching heroine and does a fine job in the acting department. Joe Kane's direction is on target, interspersing dialog with action to good advantage. Cinematographer Jack Marta uses familiar western locales to add luster to the picture.

America's Mightiest Hero Crashes to the Screen in a Blaze of Gun-Fire and Glory!
All Your Dreams of Adventure Come True ... in Columbia's Mammoth
Chapter-Play of the Old Wild West!...

The Great Adventures of Wild Bill Hickok

Columbia (June, 1938)
ALTERNATE TITLE: *Wild Bill Hickok.*
CAST: Wild Bill Hickok, **Gordon Elliott;** Cameron, **Monte Blue;** Ruth Cameron, **Carole Wayne;** Jerry, **Frankie Darro;** Bud, **Dickie Jones;** Boots, **Sammy McKim;** Kit Lawson, **Kermit Maynard;** Snake Eyes, **Roscoe Ates;** Danny, **Monte Collins;** Blakely, **Reed Hadley;** Little Elk, **Mala;** Morrell, **Robert Fiske;** Bruce, **Walter Wills;** Scudder, **J.P. McGowan;** Stone, **Eddie Waller**// Pinto (Elliott's horse), **Dice;** Blackie, **Al Bridge;** Cactus/Keno, **Slim Whitaker;** the Parson, **Buck Connors;** Kimball, **Earle Hodgins;** Wilson, **Edward Brady;** Sam, **Edmund Cobb;** Carter, **Frank Ellis;** Buck, **Curley Dresden;** Williams, **Ethan Laidlaw;** Phantom Raiders, **Francis Walker** and **Joe McGuinn;** Dolan, **Art Mix;** Kilgore, **Tom London;** Gally, **Lee Phelps;** Wilson, **Edward Brady;** Townsman, **Wally Wales;** Moran, **Blackie Whiteford;** Store Clerk, **Hank Bell;** the Apache Killer, **Richard Cramer;** Tom Stedman,

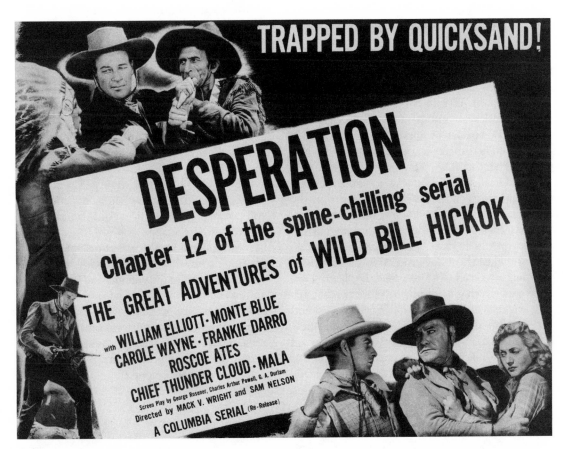

The Great Adventures of Wild Bill Hickok (Columbia, 1938) title card — the upper left shows unidentified actor, Bill Elliott and Frank Lacteen (left to right); the lower left features Bill Elliott with guns drawn; the lower right shows Reed Hadley, J. P. McGowan and Carole Wayne (left to right).

Edward Hearn; the Vulture, **Frank Lackteen**; Silver Cloud, **Artie Ortego**; Billy, **David McKim**; Blacksmith, **Kenne Duncan**.

CREDITS: Directors, **Mack V. Wright** and **Sam Nelson**; Supervisor, **Harry Webb**; Story, **John Peere Miles**; Screenwriters, **George Rosener, Charles Arthur Powell** and **G.A. Durlam**; Editor, **Richard Fantl**; Cinematographers, **Benjamine H. Kline** and **George Meehan**.

SONG: "Dixie" (Emmett)—instrumental.

LOCATION FILMING: Eagle Gate, Cave Lake, Three Lakes and Kanab, Utah; Bronson Canyon and Big Bear, California.

CHAPTER TITLES: Chapter 1, "Law of the Gun"; Chapter 2, "Stampede"; Chapter 3, "Blazing Terror"; Chapter 4, "Mystery Canyon"; Chapter 5, "Flaming Brands"; Chapter 6, "The Apache Killer"; Chapter 7, "Prowling Wolves"; Chapter 8, "The Pit"; Chapter 9, "Ambushed"; Chapter 10, "Savage Vengeance"; Chapter 11, "Burning Waters"; Chapter 12, "Desperation"; Chapter 13, "Phantom Bullets"; Chapter 14, "The Lure"; Chapter 15, "Trail's End."

RUNNING TIME: 270 min.

STORY: To gain possession of Texas lands and cattle, a notorious outlaw group, the Phantom Raiders, led by Robert Fiske, plots to stop all trail herds from leaving Texas. In addition, the Phantom Raiders attempt to stop the railroad from reaching Abilene, Kansas. U.S. Marshal Gordon Elliott is assigned to thwart the Raiders' efforts, as well as stop the rampart lawlessness in Abilene. Elliott has many narrow escapes as he battles the Phantom Raiders. With the help of allies from the Texas trail herd, the railroad and a group called the Flaming Arrows, which is made up of children in the Abilene area, Elliott is successful in bringing law and order to Abilene and bringing Fiske to justice.

NOTES AND COMMENTARY: This serial marked Bill Elliott's first starring appearance. Elliott would go on to star in 69 western features, 2 more serials and five detective films.

When Elliott finally makes his appearance in Chapter 1, it doesn't take him long to proclaim that he's a peaceable man before throwing down on outlaw Edmund Cobb.

The scene in which Gordon Elliott leads the Flaming Arrows in the recitation of the Pledge of Allegiance can be seen in *Brother, Can You Spare a Dime* (Goodtimes Enterprise, 1975), a documentary of the depression era.

A sign is hung proclaiming "William Hickok" as Marshal of Abilene. In real life, Hickok's first and middle names were James Butler.

Look closely at the fight between Elliott and a Phantom Raider on top of a stagecoach in Chapter 1. Elliott knocks the outlaw off the coach, and the outlaw's head strikes the left rear wheel as he falls to the ground.

When the serial was re-released in 1948, Elliott was then billed as William.

Slim Whitaker has two roles in the film — as an outlaw henchman, Keno, and a saloon owner catering to the outlaws, Cactus.

REVIEWS: "Well made and exciting cliffhanger which launched Bill Elliott to genre stardom." *Western Movies*, Pitts; "Like many of the players, the script is childish, but Wright and Nelson's energetic direction papers over the story's flaws efficiently enough." *The Western*, Hardy.

SUMMATION: On the whole this is a good serial. If the final chapter had been actionful and not just pleasant, the serial would have ranked among the upper echelon. Gordon Elliott as Wild Bill Hickok is in fine style in his starring debut, displaying his horsemanship and easily handling the action and acting requirements. Elliott is quite natural and looks as if he had been a leading western actor in films for years. The supporting cast is first rate, and cinematographers Benjamin H. Kline and George Meehan capture the vistas of Kanab and Red Rock Canyon to good effect.

Range War ... Spread by Cunning Outlaws Who Use It to Cloak Plans for the
Most Spectacular Robbery in Western History!

Great Stagecoach Robbery

Republic Pictures (February, 1945)

CAST: Red Ryder, **Wild Bill Elliott**; Little Beaver, **Bobby Blake**; the Duchess, **Alice Fleming**; Jed Quinlan, **Don Costello**; Con Hollister, **Francis McDonald**; Billy Hollister, **John James**; "Boots" Hollister, **Sylvia Arslan**; Joe Slade, **Bud Geary**; Tattletale Student, **Leon Tyler**; Freddie, **Freddie Chapman**// "Thunder"; Stagecoach Driver, **Hank Bell**; Stagecoach Guard, **Bob Wilke**; Jake, **Henry Wills**; Mrs. Goodbody, **Grace Cunard**; Goodbody Boy, **Dickie Dillon**; Goodbody Girl, **Patsy May**; Bank Customer, **Fred Graham**; Townsman, **Horace B. Carpenter**.

CREDITS: Director, **Lesley Selander**; 2nd Unit Director, **Yakima Canutt**; Associate Producer, **Louis Gray**; Screenwriter, **Randall Faye**; Editor, **Charles Craft**; Art Director, **Fred A. Ritter**; Set Decorator, **Charles Thompson**; Cinematography, **Bud Thackery**; Sound, **Ed Borschell**; Musical Director, **Richard Cherwin**.

LOCATION FILMING: Iverson, California.
RUNNING TIME: 56 min.

The Great Stagecoach Robbery (Republic, 1945) scene card — Bill Elliott (left) and Fred Graham (right) in a fist fight; lower border left shows Bobby Blake; right border shows Bill Elliott.

SOURCE: Based on Fred Harman's famous NEA comic, by special arrangement with Stephen Slesinger.

STORY: Francis McDonald, released from prison, plans to return the $150,000 he stole from Alice Fleming's stage line. Schoolmaster Don Costello, actually the head of an outlaw gang, with henchman Bud Geary and McDonald's son, John James, plan to steal the money as it is being transported to Blue Springs. Fleming's nephew, Wild Bill Elliott, thwarts the holdup. McDonald recognizes James as a member of the holdup gang and tries to make James break from the outlaws. After the money has been deposited in the bank, Costello and his gang blow up the bank vault and make off with the money. Elliott gives chase and sends a bullet through the saddlebags into Costello's shoulder. Costello gives Elliott the slip, but Elliott's Indian pal, Bobby Blake, sees where Costello went. Costello takes refuge in McDonald's barn and hides when McDonald and his daughter, Sylvia Arslan, enter. McDonald finds the money as Elliott enters the barn. Elliott plans to take McDonald into custody, but McDonald turns the tables and locks Elliott in a closet. McDonald leaves with the money to find James. Blake, who had followed Elliott, frees him and they ride after McDonald. Arslan goes into the barn and finds Costello. Costello murders Arslan and tells McDonald that Elliott killed his daughter. McDonald holds Blake hostage to make Elliott come to his ranch. El-liott proves Costello murdered Arslan and brings him to justice. Costello is sentenced to hang, and McDonald becomes a welcome member of the community.

NOTES AND COMMENTARY: An amusing dialogue exchange between schoolmaster Don Costello and Grace Cunard saw Cunard, talking about her two children who have just played a practical joke on Costello, opine "You'll learn to love them," to which Costello replies, "If they live that long." Shades of W.C. Fields!

Tom Steele doubled Wild Bill Elliott in this film.

REVIEWS: "Only average." *Western Movies*, Pitts; "A twist to the usual oater theme throws in an element of humanity." *Motion Picture Guide*, Nash and Ross.

SUMMATION: This is a superior "B" western from a good script by Randall Faye. In addition to some fine action scenes, it offers some excellent acting by the principals. Wild Bill Elliott displays strength and compassion, and is excellent in the scene in which he's trying to convince Francis McDonald that he didn't murder Sylvia Arslan. McDonald is first-rate as a man trying to leave his crooked past behind. Villain Don Costello, Elliott's pal Bobby Blake and child actress Arslan bring distinction to their roles. The scene in which Costello stalks Arslan is suspenseful and chilling. Lesley Selander directs capably.

See Him Out-Shoot an Outlaw Band ... to Outdo All His Past Hits for Thrills!

Hands Across the Rockies

Columia (June, 1941)

A Wild Bill Hickok Adventure

CAST: Wild Bill Hickok, **Bill Elliott**; Marsha, **Mary Daily**; Cannonball, **Dub Taylor**; "Juneau" Jessup, **Kenneth MacDonald**; Rufe Crawley, **Frank LaRue**; Dade Crawley, **Donald Curtis**; Hi Crawley, **Tom Moray**; Johnny Peale, **Stanley Brown**; Marshal Bemis, **Slim Whitaker**; Abel Finney, **Harrison Greene**; Red, **Art Mix**; Judge Plunkett, **Eddy Waller**; Cash Jennings, **Hugh Prosser**// Stage Passenger, **John Tyrell**; Ranger, **Edmund Cobb**; Bartender, **Ethan Laidlaw**; Court Clerk, **Eddie Laughton**; Jury Foreman, **George Morrell**; Jurors, **Buck Moulton**, **George Chesebro** and **Tex Cooper**; Callie, **Kathryn Bates**.

CREDITS: Director, **Lambert Hillyer**; Producer, **Leon Barsha**; Screenwriter, **Paul Franklin**; Editor, **Mel Thorson**; Cinematographer, **Benjamine Kline**.

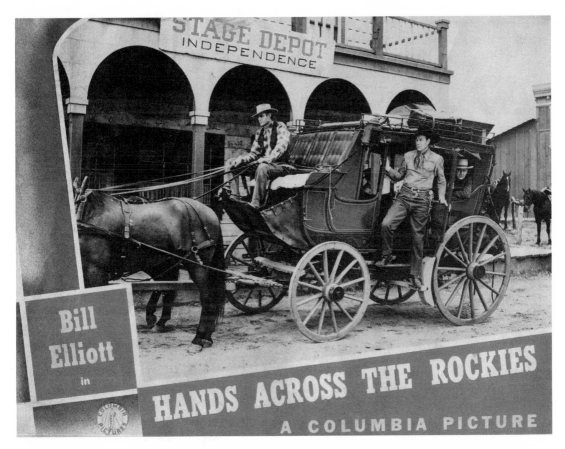

Hands Across the Rockies (Columbia, 1941) scene card — Bill Elliott steps down from the stagecoach while two unidentified actors look on.

SONGS: "The Stage Went Bumping Along" — sung by **Dub Taylor**; "A Cowboy Goes Rollin'" — sung by **Dub Taylor**.

LOCATION FILMING: Iverson, California.

RUNNING TIME: 56 min.

SOURCE: story by **Norbert Davis**.

STORY: Frank LaRue warns Stanley Brown to stay away from his niece, Mary Daily. Brown and Daily are in love and want to get married. Town boss Kenneth MacDonald wants to marry Daily so she can't be forced to testify she saw him murder Dub Taylor's father. Taylor arrives in Independence with his pal, Bill Elliott, to find his father's killer. Brown tries to run away with Daily but is stopped by LaRue and arrested for kidnapping. Elliott feels that Daily holds the key to uncovering the murderer and appoints himself Brown's lawyer. Elliott uncovers evidence to prove Brown innocent and announces Daily can prove MacDonald murdered Taylor's father. MacDonald attempts to escape but falls before Elliott's guns in a blazing gunfight. As Brown and Taylor plan to marry, Elliott receives word his services are needed elsewhere, and he and Taylor ride off to new adventures.

NOTES AND COMMENTARY: Eddy Waller is best known to western fans as Nugget Clark, sidekick to Allan "Rocky" Lane in 32 western features for Republic (1947–1950, 1952–1953).

REVIEW: "Pretty actionful Bill Elliott film." *Western Movies*, Pitts.

SUMMATION: This is one of the best and most enjoyable entries in Bill Elliott's Wild Bill Hickok series. Elliott's and Eddy Waller's performances, with able assistance from Dub Taylor and Kenneth MacDonald, bring first rate entertainment to the screen. Elliott gives a fine performance as the tight-lipped agent of justice, delivering his lines forcefully or with compassion to meet the demands of the script. Waller matches Elliott as a cantankerous judge who will not stand for any nonsense in his courtroom. Taylor adds some nice comedic touches while being quite efficient as Elliott's sidekick. Don't miss this one.

Roarin'! Ridin'! Shootin'!
William Elliott in a New Kind of Role!
In a New Kind of Adventure!

Hellfire

Republic (June, 1949)
An Elliott-McGowan Production
CAST: Zeb Smith, **William Elliott**; Doll Brown, **Marie Windsor**; Bucky McLean, **Forrest Tucker**; Gyp Stoner, **Jim Davis**; Brother Joseph, **H. B. Warner**; Dusty Stoner, **Paul Fix**; Sheriff Martin, **Grant Withers**; Sheriff Duffy, **Emory Parnell**; Birdie, **Esther Howard**; Full Moon, **Jody Gilbert**; Red Stoner, **Louis R. Faust**; Lew Stoner, **Harry Woods**; Rex, **Denver Pyle**; Wilson, **Trevor Bardette**; Cheyenne Bartender, **Dewey Robinson**; No Man's Land Bartender, **Harry Tyler**// Blacksmith, **Richard Alexander**; Card Players in Livery Stable, **Stanley Price** and **Fred Kohler, Jr.**; Dry Springs Bartender, **Olin Howland**; Dry Springs Townsman, **Hank Worden**; Saloon Girl, **Paula Hill**; Townsman with Warning, **Kenneth MacDonald**.

CREDITS: Director, **R.G. Springsteen**; 2nd Unit Director, **Yakima Canutt**; Screenwriters/Executive Producers, **Dorrell** and **Stuart McGowan**; Producer, **William J. O'Sullivan**; Editor, **Tony Martinelli**; Art Director, **James Sullivan**; Set Decorators, **John McCarthy, Jr.** and **Charles Thompson**; Cinematographer, **Jack Marta**; Makeup, **Bob Mark**; Costumes, **Adele Palmer**; Hair Stylist, **Peggy Gray**; Sound, **T.A. Carman** and **Howard Wilson**; Music Score, **Dale Butts**; Orchestrator, **Stanley Wilson**; Special Effects, **Howard** and **Theodore Lydecker**; Color by **Trucolor**.

SONGS: "Shoo Fly, Don't Bother Me" (unknown) — sung by **Marie Windsor**; "Bringing in the Sheaves" (Shaw and Minor) — sung by **Marie Windsor** and **chorus** (note: Virginia Rees provided the singing voice for Marie Windsor).

LOCATION FILMING: Sedona, Arizona, and Iverson, California.

RUNNING TIME: 90 min.

STORY: Preacher H.B. Warner takes a bullet meant for crooked gambler William Elliott. Elliott promises the dying Warner that he'll build a church according to the rules of the Bible. Marie Windsor is wanted for an express robbery. Elliott, Marshal Forrest Tucker and Jim Davis and his brothers want the $5000 reward for her capture. Windsor was separated from her sister when Davis' brother, Harry Woods, sent her sister west on a wagon train. While searching for her, Windsor and Woods meet, and Windsor kills Woods in a gun duel. Elliott wants Windsor to turn herself in so he can collect the reward money to build a church. Elliott finds that Tucker is married to Windsor's sister and wants to bring Windsor to justice to prevent the siblings from reuniting. Elliott begins to travel with Windsor, and his influence begins to soften her. Elliott tells Windsor that Tucker knows where her sister is living. Windsor gets a job singing in a saloon and makes a play for Tucker. Davis and his brothers arrive in town, accost Elliott, and torture him to make him tell where they could find Windsor. Sheriff Grant Withers rescues Elliott, but Elliott refuses to press charges. Withers makes Elliott his deputy. Elliott then prevents Tucker from succumbing to Windsor's charms by arresting her. Elliott learns that Davis and his brothers have returned to town and want to kill Windsor. Elliott wants to take Windsor to another county, but Windsor tricks Elliott and locks him in a jail cell. Windsor and Elliott are in a standoff when Tucker gets the drop on Windsor. Elliott prevents Tucker from

Hellfire (Republic, 1949) portrait card — Forrest Tucker, Marie Windsor and Bill Elliott (left to right).

shooting Windsor, but Windsor shoots Tucker. Elliott tells Windsor that Tucker is married to her sister. Elliott has Windsor apply pressure to Tucker's wound while he goes for a doctor. Windsor begins to pray for God's help in saving Tucker. Davis and his brothers break into the jail. Davis puts bullets in Windsor's arms but she refuses to relinquish pressure on Tucker's wound. Elliott shows up with a doctor and shoots Davis and his brothers. The doctor begins working on Tucker as Elliott cradles Windsor in his arms.

NOTES AND COMMENTARY: From 1934 until the release of *Hellfire*, the word hell, through censorship from the Johnston office, had not been used in the title of a motion picture. Prior to the ban, movies using "hell," such as *Hell Divers* and *Hell's Angels*, had been moneymakers. When the Johnston Office began putting pressure on William Elliott and co-producers Stuart and Dorrell McGowan to change the title, Elliott argued that the title was chosen from the Biblical quotation "Man by his misdeeds kindles his own hellfire," which inspired the screenplay. The Johnston Office agreed to consider Elliott's plea and eventually allowed the film to be released as *Hellfire*.

At the Knoxville Film Festival in 1989, director R.G. Springsteen commented: "Actually, I never saw it. Somebody complained about it and Bill Elliott said [to Springsteen], 'Don't you touch that picture. I don't want you to see it again. It can't be better. It's the best picture I've ever done.' This was Bill Elliott. So I never got to see it."

Bill Elliott insisted that Republic hire Marie Windsor as his leading lady for *Hellfire*. Elliott had seen a test Windsor had made, as well as *Outpost in Morocco* (United Artists, 1949), and was favorably impressed. When he learned she was a horsewoman, that clinched his resolve to have her as his leading lady. Elliott taught Windsor how to twirl her pistols. Windsor performed a lot of her own stunts in the film, far more than most actresses would do.

REVIEWS: "As kingpin of more than sixty westerns and as star and co-producer of *Hellfire*, William Elliott is obviously comfortable in his surroundings and he does nobly by himself and his property. But aside from one plot twist, this number hardly is different from the countless sagebrush sagas which have been clattering into theaters since the admission price was a nickel." *New York Times*, 5/30/49; "A slambang actioner with a religioso motif and a helping of s.a. [sex appeal]. Well-paced blend of hoss-opery and a Sadie Thompsonish romance. Elliott, hero of some 60 oaters and co-producer of 'Hellfire,' makes the role of the converted gambler believable." *Variety*, 6/1/49; "Exceeding good William Elliott vehicle." *Western Movies*, Pitts.

SUMMATION: This is a different, delightful, and emotional western film. Like a number of projects by the McGowens, this picture has a religious theme. William Elliott plays to perfection an unscrupulous gambler who completely changes his life, becoming a man guided by the principles sent down in the Bible. Co-star Marie Windsor turns in a beautiful performance as a woman pushed to the wrong side of the law in her quest to find her lost sister. Watch Windsor's scene as she portrays, with honest emotion, a woman determined to save Forrest Tucker's life at the possible cost of her own, and her final resolution to prayer to guide her. R.G. Sprinsteen, usually noted as a director of "B" films, capably guides the story to its satisfactory conclusion.

Wild Bill's Six-Guns Speak Again!

Hidden Valley Outlaws

Republic (April, 1944)

CAST: Wild Bill Elliott, **Wild Bill Elliott**; Gabby Hayes, **George "Gabby" Hayes**; June Clark, **Anne Jeffreys**; Gilbert Leland, **Roy Barcroft**; Bannon, **Kenne Duncan**; Clark, **Charles Miller**; Danny Clark, **John James**; Snowflake, **Fred Toones**; Ned Murphy, **Budd Buster**; Sheriff McBride, **Tom London**; Canary, **LeRoy Mason**; Hamlet (Eddie Percel), **Earle Hodgins**, Tracy, **Yakima Canutt**// "Sonny"; Colter, **Frank McCarroll**; Gridley, **Charles Morton**; Art, **Tom Steele**; Vigilante, **Robert Wilke**; Governor Walker, **Forbes Murray**; Jackson, **Bud Geary**; Marshal Bud Masterson, **Edward Cassidy**.

CREDITS: Director, **Howard Bretherton**; Associate Producer, **Louis Gray**; Story, **John K. Butler**; Screenwriters, **John K. Butler** and **Bob Williams**; Editor, **Tony Martinelli**; Art Director, **Fred Ritter**; Set Decorator, **Charles Thompson**; Cinematographer, **Reggie Lanning**; Sound, **Dick Tyler**; Music, **Mort Glickman**.

SONG: "Oh! Susanna" (Foster)—whistled by **LeRoy Mason** and **John James**.

LOCATION FILMING: Iverson and Corriganville, California.

RUNNING TIME: 55 min.

STORY: Respected lawyer Roy Barcroft is actually the brains behind an outlaw gang using "head rights" to take all the desirable property in the area. Rancher Charles Miller is murdered by henchman LeRoy Mason when Miller tries to prevent his property from being taken. When Mason and his men are acquitted, Miller's son, John James, swears vengeance and kills two of the men in fair gunfights. James is now branded a murderer, and Barcroft sends for Wild Bill Elliott and his pal, George "Gabby" Hayes. Barcroft has actor Earle Hodgins impersonate the sheriff and sends Elliott and Hayes to capture James. Unknown to the lawmen, Mason is following them. Elliott and Hayes locate James. Hayes fires shots to distract James while Elliott closes in, but Mason fires a shot that kills James. Elliott and Hayes, thinking they were responsible for James' death, bring the body in to the real sheriff, Tom London,

Hidden Valley Outlaws (Republic, 1944) scene card — Bill Elliott (right) gets the drop on Kenne Duncan (left); the lower left border shows Bill Elliott, Anne Jeffreys and "Gabby" Hayes (left to right).

and find themselves arrested for murder. Elliott and Hayes break jail and join the ranchers in the fight to keep their ranches. Elliott finds Hodgins, who tells him Barcroft is behind the ranchers' troubles. Barcroft leaves town by train with all the deeds to the ranches in the guise of helping the ranchers with the government authorities. Barcroft plans to use the deeds for his own gain and in the process double-cross Mason and other gang members. Elliott and Hayes cut across country and board the train. Mason, fearing that Barcroft would try to keep the deeds for himself, had boarded the train and takes the deeds. Elliott and Hayes, in a wild free-for-all, capture Mason and Barcroft. The ranchers secure clear titles to their property, and Elliott and Hayes ride off to new adventures.

NOTES AND COMMENTARY: Even though, at picture's end, Edward Cassidy sends Wild Bill Elliott and George "Gabby" Hayes off to new adventures, the Wild Bill Elliott series came to an end with this feature. In the next season, Elliott would become Fred Harman's comic character, Red Ryder, a part he would play in sixteen feature films. Hayes would join him for the first two before moving back to Roy Rogers' western films.

The working title for *Hidden Valley Outlaws* was *The Outlaw Buster*.

Tom Steele doubles Bill Elliott in the film.

REVIEW: "Fast moving and highly entertaining 'Wild Bill' Elliott vehicle." *Western Movies*, Pitts.

SUMMATION: In this swift, above average Wild Bill Elliott adventure, Elliott delivers his usual impressive performance. George "Gabby" Hayes is a little too silly at times, especially for a sidekick of his statue. Roy Barcroft takes acting honors, playing a timid, well-educated outlaw boss who collects insects to perfection. Howard Bretherton's direction is on target.

Toughest of the Trail Bosses!
Roughest of the Cattle Kings!
... Most Daring of the Early West's Adventure-Blazing Breed!

The Homesteaders

Allied Artists (March, 1953)

A Silvermine Production

CAST: Mace Corbin, **Wild Bill Elliott**; Clyde Moss, **Robert Lowery**; Grimer, **Emmett Lynn**; Meade, **George Wallace**; Charlie, **Buzz Henry**; Van, **Stanley Price**; Slim, **Rick Vallin**; Hector, **William Fawcett**; Kroger, **James Seay**; Jake, **Tom Monroe**; Jenny, **Barbara Allen**; Colonel Peterson, **Ray Walker**.

CREDITS: Director, **Lewis Collins**; Assistant Director, **Melville Shyer**; Producer, **Vincent M. Fennelly**; Screenwriters, **Sid Theil** and **Milton Raison**; Editor, **Sam Fields**; Art Direc-

tor, **Dave Milton**; Set Decorator, **Theodore F. Offenbecker**; Cinematographer, **Ernest Miller**; Sound, **Frank Webster**; Music, **Raoul Kraushaar**; Special Effects, **Ray Mercer**; Set Continuity, **Mary Chaffee**; Dialogue Supervisor, **Stanley Price**; Color by **Sepiatone**.

LOCATION FILMING: Corriganville, Burro Flats and Iverson, California.

RUNNING TIME: 62 min.

STORY: The Army is willing to sell dynamite to Wild Bill Elliott. Elliott needs the dynamite so he and his fellow ranchers and farmers can clear their fields of unwanted rocks and

The Homesteaders (Allied Artists, 1953) portrait card — Bill Elliott.

tree stumps. Elliott and his best friend, Robert Lowery, ride to bring the dynamite back to Oregon. Unknown to Elliott, Lowery has decided to double-cross him and allow the crooked James Seay and his henchman to steal the shipment. Elliott finds the dynamite is defective, but Lowery persuades him to purchase it anyway. Needing a trail crew, Elliott is able to hire men that are scheduled to be released from the Army jail. Old-timer Emmett Lynn is made trail boss. On the arduous trek, Elliott has to face dissension from a few of the men and an Indian attack. With only days before their journey ends, Elliott offers Lowery an equal partnership in their venture. Lowery tries to dissuade Seay from attacking the wagon train and tells Elliott about his agreement with Seay. Seay and his men attack. The outlaws are driven off, primarily by a well-placed bullet from Lowery that ends Seay's criminal career. Lowery rides away only to be stopped by Elliott, who tells him he still wants to go through with the partnership agreement.

NOTES AND COMMENTARY: *The Homesteaders* owes more than a little to Elliott's first Monogram western, *The Longhorn* (1950). In both, Elliott has to make an arduous trek; he has a best friend who sells Elliott out to an outlaw boss; he has to obtain a trail crew from men who have had problems with the authorities; one of the trail crew will be fired for drinking; and Elliott offers the best friend a partnership, which makes the best friend back out of his agreement with the outlaw boss. The plots differ in that the best friend dies in *The Longhorn*, and lives to be Elliott's partner in *The Homesteaders*. Also, the love interest was excised for *The Homesteaders*.

REVIEWS: "Wild Bill Elliott in slow-paced program oater. A routine program western that doesn't hit a hard enough action pace to satisfy the regular followers of this type of secondary oater." *Variety*, 3/25/53; "There is relatively little action in this slow-paced western." *The Western*, Hardy.

SUMMATION: *The Homesteaders* receives a passing grade thanks to the performances of Wild Bill Elliott and Emmett Lynn. Elliott brings the right balance of reasonableness and toughness to his part of a rancher trying to deliver dynamite to the Oregon territory against all odds. Emmett Lynn, usually thought of as a bumbling comic sidekick, brings a freshness to his role as an Army prisoner who wants the chance to start a new life and will fight to make it happen. Too bad the screenwriters couldn't come up with a fresh script (see notes and commentary), and the usually reliable director Lewis Collins couldn't give it the pace it sorely needed.

Bandit-Blasting Cyclone of Thrills!
Bill Elliott of "Wild Bill Hickok" Wins Stardom in a Thriller from Columbia!

In Early Arizona

Columbia (November, 1938)

ALTERNATE TITLE: *Unwelcome Visitors.*

CAST: Whit Gordon, **Bill Elliott**; Alice Weldon, **Dorothy Gulliver**; Bull, **Harry Woods**; Marshal, **Jack Ingram**; Spike, **Franklyn Farnum**; Ben, **Frank Ellis**; Art, **Art Davis**; Kaintuck, **Charles King**; Tom Weldon, **Edward Cassidy**; Sheriff, **Charles Whitaker**.

CREDITS: Director, **Joseph Levering**; Screenwriter, **Nate Gatzert**; Editor, **Dwight Caldwell**; Cinematographer, **James S. Brown, Jr.**; Musical Director, **Lee Zahler**.

LOCATION FILMING: Iverson and the Monogram Ranch, California.

RUNNING TIME: 53 min.

STORY: Bill Elliott and his pals, Art Davis and Charles King, are summoned to lawless Tombstone, Arizona. Initially refusing to help clean up the town, Elliott changes his mind when he hears that badman Harry Woods said the town would be too tough for him. Elliott suspects a higher-up is giving orders to Woods and his gang. Elliott runs for sheriff, and Woods receives orders to kill him. Woods' attempt

In Early Arizona (Columbia, 1938) title card — lower left shows Bill Elliott (right) hitting Harry Woods (or his double); the right side shows Bill Elliott with gun drawn, protecting Dorothy Gulliver.

fails. On election night, the outlaws exchange ballot boxes. Elliott foils the plot to stuff the ballot boxes, and in the process exposes respected citizen Edward Cassidy as the outlaw leader. Elliott is elected sheriff. Woods decides to take the fight to Elliott. Elliott and his pals take care of the lawless element, with Elliott besting Woods in a rugged fistfight. Elliott is appointed Federal Marshal and rides off to new adventures.

NOTES AND COMMENTARY: This was Bill Elliott's first starring feature film. As production began, Elliott was to be billed as "Gordon," but the success of his serial, *The Great Adventures of Wild Bill Hickok*, led to the name change to "Bill."

This was a Larry Darmour production. Two previous stars for Darmour, Bob Allen and Jack Luden, had not proved satisfactory, which led to Elliott's chance for stardom.

REVIEWS: "The film version is quiet in comparison to the story told by Walter Noble Burns in his book. Full quota of riding, shooting, a little brawling, practically no romance, and a string of expected sequences which shorten suspense possibilities, kills the story." *Variety*, 12/28/38; "Bill Elliott's first starring series oater is a corker, with plenty of action and a good script and one of the best roundup of genre bad guys in the history of the 'B' western." *Western Movies*, Pitts.

SUMMATION: This is a good, fast-moving "B" western. The story is all action, but that's enough, with director Joseph Levering generating some welcome suspense in the final confrontation. Scriptwriter Nate Gatzert eschewed character development and romance for Bill Elliott and Dorothy Gulliver, but the fans were cheering Elliott at the end. Elliott showed the stuff that would make him one of the all-time western greats, with his tight-lipped acting and adroit handling of the action.

Where Gold Was King ... and Love Was Queen
Excitement and Romance Culled from the Turbulent Era When the Dangerous West Was Coming of Age.

In Old Sacramento

Republic Pictures (May, 1946)

ALTERNATE TITLE: *Flame of Sacramento*.

CAST: Johnny Barrett (Spanish Jack), **William Elliott**; Belle Malone, **Constance Moore**; Sam Chase, **Hank Daniels**; Zebby Booker, **Ruth Donnelly**; Jim Wales, **Eugene Paulette**; Eddie Dodge, **Lionel Stander**; Laramie, **Jack LaRue**; Mark Slayter, **Grant Withers**; Marchetti, **Charles Judels**; Stagecoach Driver, **Paul Hurst**; Ma Dodge, **Victoria Horne**; Newsboy, **Bobby Blake**; Oscar, **Dick Wessel**// Bud Barrett, **Marshall Reed**; Claim Jumper, **William Haade**; Wagon Driver, **Eddy Waller**; Card Player, **LeRoy Mason**; Stagecoach Passenger, **Jack O'Shea**; Doctor, **Hal Taliaferro**; Barber, **Lucien Littlefield**; Ling, **H. T. Tsiang**; Bartender, **Tom London**; Scrubwoman, **Ellen Corby**; Deputy, **Kenne Duncan**.

CREDITS: Director/Associate Producer, **Joe Kane**; Story, **Jerome Odlum**; Adaptation, **Frank Gruber**; Screenwriter, **Frances Hyland**; Editor, **Fred Allen**; Art Director, **James Sullivan**; Set Decorators, **John McCarthy, Jr.** and **Earl Wooden**; Cinematographer, **Jack Marta**; Costumes, **Adele Palmer**; Makeup, **Bob Mark**; Hair Stylist, **Peggy Gray**; Sound, **Bill Clark**; Musical Director, **Morton Scott**; Orchestrator, **Dale Butts**; Musical Numbers Stager, **Fanchon**; Special Effects, **Howard** and **Theodore Lydecker**.

LOCATION FILMING: Iverson, Kernville, Tuolumme County and Kennedy Meadow, California.

SONGS: "Banks of Sacramento"—sung by male chorus; "Strike Up the Band" (Sterling and Ward)—sung by female chorus; "Speak to Me of Love" (Lenoir and Sieveier)—sung by **Constance Moore**; "Man Who Broke the Bank at Monte Carlo" (Gilbert)—sung by **Constance Moore**; "Gwine to Run All Night (De Camptown Races)" (Foster)—sung by **Constance Moore** and **chorus**; "My Gal's a High Born Lady" (Fagan)—sung by male quartet; "Can't Tell Why I Love You, but I Do" (Cobb and Edwards)—sung by **Constance Moore**; "Speak to Me of Love" (reprise)—sung by **Constance Moore**.

RUNNING TIME: 89 min.

STORY: Years before, William Elliott had his claim jumped, and in the process his brother, Marshall Reed, was killed. Now Elliott poses as a gambler while living a double life as the notorious stagecoach bandit Spanish Jack. Elliott is in love with entertainer Constance Moore. Moore won't marry Elliott unless he gives up his outlaw ways. Sheriff Eugene Paulette plans to set a trap for Elliott. Elliot eludes the trap and steals the gold shipment. Paulette suspects that vigilante Jack LaRue works with Elliott. Elliott decides to help LaRue escape capture. They stop at miner Hank Daniels' cabin for breakfast. Daniels has stuck it rich, and LaRue tries to rob him. LaRue and Daniels fight, and Daniels emerges victorious. Leaving Daniels' cabin, Elliott and LaRue are spotted by Paulette and his posse. LaRue is captured but Elliott escapes capture. Daniels comes to Sacramento and becomes Elliott's rival for Moore's affections. Moore introduces Daniels to gambler Grant Withers. Withers gets Daniels in a card game and wins all his money. Elliott tells Daniels that Withers is a crooked gambler. Daniels disguises himself as Spanish Jack and robs Withers, taking his money back. Paulette arrests Daniels and brings LaRue to face him. LaRue, still smarting from the beating from Daniels, identifies him as Spanish Jack. Moore has promised Elliott she will go away with him if he prevents Daniels being hanged. Elliott shows up as Spanish Jack. LaRue and Elliott trade shots, with Elliott's proving fatal. Elliott attempts an escape, but an accurate shot by Paulette mortally wounds him. In the muddy streets of Sacramento, Elliott dies in Moore's arms. Paulette tells Daniels that he

In Old Sacramento (Republic, 1946) scene card — Bill Elliott (left) holds up a stagecoach, with passengers Constance Moore (center) and Ruth Donnelly (in coach) concerned about a wounded Eugene Paulette (on ground).

knows he robbed Withers, but tells him to leave on the stagecoach to San Francisco with Moore. Daniels hopes he can start a new life with Moore by his side.

NOTES AND COMMENTARY: *In Old Sacramento* was reissued in 1952 as *Flame of Sacramento*. The film was re-edited to a running time of 60 minutes.

The roots of this film reach back into the twenties when Joe Kane's story came to the screen as *Diamond Carlisle* (1922) with future "B" villain George Chesebro. Then the story was resurrected for Roy Rogers' *The Carson City Kid* (Republic, 1940) before being rewritten for the screenplay of *In Old Sacramento*.

Randolph Scott was the first choice for the role of Johnny Barrett, but Scott ultimately decided he didn't want to work at Republic. Ann Dvorak was Republic's first choice to play Belle

Malone. Dvorak wanted her co-star to be a bigger name than she was, and suggested John Wayne, Randolph Scott or George Raft. Constance Moore was then given the role.

REVIEWS: "Handsomely mounted western with songs. William Elliott, who was featured in the Red Ryder western series, made his bow as a more substantial romantic figure in the role of 'Spanish Jack.' The physical equipment is perfect, Elliott being tall and lean, with a strong chin and voice of deep masculine timbre. Thesping is a bit uncertain, however, with a stiffness visible in the trying spots." *Variety*, 5/1/46; "Going all out on this one, and lavishing every attention on fast-moving pace, superior photography and elaborate settings, the studio [Republic] has managed to produce a Western considerably above the usual. It will please all Western fans and a lot of other people too. As the strong silent hero, William Elliott is a bit on the wooden side." *New York Times*, 4/29/46; "Elliott is Spanish Jack, a masked bandit with a way with the ladies who finally dies in the arms of songstress Moore. He [Elliott] made the change from series to A grade productions effortlessly but refused to move outside the genre. Kane's direction is action-packed, as ever." *The Western*, Hardy.

SUMMATION: This is a good, well-acted and well-scripted western. William Elliott's measured performance easily shows why he was elevated to big-budget features. Elliott is even handed a death scene and does well by it. Co-star Constance Moore is lovely, showing in fine style her singing and acting ability. The chemistry is there between Elliott and Moore, and they work well together. Eugene Paulette, as a sheriff who trusts no one, and Ruth Donnelly, Moore's closest friend, head a sterling supporting cast. Kane works in a neat touch by including a scene with Elliott and Bobby Blake, his co-star from the Red Ryder series, that shows the duo's mutual admiration and friendship. Joe Kane directs effectively and keeps the action flowing.

Out of the Lead-Splattered Pages of Kansas' Wildest Days...
... When the Roaring Plains Ran Red from Dodge City to Eldorado!

Kansas Territory

Monogram Pictures (May, 1952)

A Frontier Pictures Production

CAST: Joe Daniels, **Wild Bill Elliott**; Carruthers, **House Peters, Jr.**; Kay Collins, **Peggy Stewart**; Fred Jethro, **Lane Bradford**; Slater, **Stan Jolley**; Cap, **Fuzzy Knight**; Governor, **Stan Andrews**; Bob Jethro, **Marshall Reed**; Stark, **Terry Frost**; Marshall Matt Furness, **John Hart**; Weatherbee, **William Fawcett**; Arthur Larkin, **Lee Roberts**; Doctor Johnson, **Pierce Lyden**; Ed Rank, **Ted Adams**// Mac, **George Eldredge**; Cowboys from Redding, **Dale Van Sickel** and **Rory Mallinson**; Redding Bartender, **Roy Butler**; Clark, **Stanley Price**; Sam Collins, **Lyle Talbot**.

CREDITS: Director, **Lewis Collins**; Assistant Director, **Melville Shyer**; Producer, **Vincent M. Fennelly**; Story/Screenplay, **Dan Ullman**; Editor, **Richard Heermance**; Art Director, **David Milton**; Settings, **Vincent Taylor**; Cinematographer, **Ernest Miller**; Sound, **Charles Cooper**; Original Music, **Raoul Kraushaar**; Set Continuity, **Mary Chafee**; Dialogue Director, **Stanley Price**; Color by **Sepiatone**.

LOCATION FILMING: Jack Ingram Ranch, Iverson and Red Rock Canyon, California.

RUNNING TIME: 65 min.

STORY: Wild Bill Elliott receives word that his brother has been killed and rides to Redding, Kansas, to find his murderer, even though he still has to clear up charges of being an outlaw during the Civil War. On the trail Deputy Marshal Marshall Reed tries to outdraw Elliott and receives a bullet in the shoulder. Another attempt to ambush Elliott by Reed's brother, Lane Bradford, and henchmen Terry Frost and Stanley Price, fails when Peggy Stewart intervenes. Stewart and Elliott's brother had been engaged to be married. From the townspeople of Redding, Elliott learns his brother had an unsavory reputation, which Elliott refuses to believe. Lawyer House Peters, Jr. befriends Elliott and persuades the Town Council to offer Elliott the job of Sheriff. Elliott refuses and the council nominates Peters. Marshal John Hart, an old friend of Elliott's, has obtained a pardon absolving him of all charges of outlawry. Reed ambushes Hart in a failed attempt to steal the document. Elliott chases Reed and brings him to justice. Peters and the council members arrive and take Reed into custody. On the way to town, Reed tries to escape and is shot by Peters. Peters tells Elliott that Reed implicated saloon keeper Stan Jolley as his brother's murderer. Before Elliott and Jolley can engage in a gun duel, Stewart intervenes. Stewart tells Elliott that his brother shot

Kansas Territory (Monogram, 1952) scene card — Peggy Stewart and Bill Elliott look for danger.

and crippled her father when she broke their engagement. Bradford learns that Reed is dead, shot by Peters. Bradford then tells Elliott that Peters killed his brother. Elliott, realizing that his way of revenge is wrong, allows the Town Council to arrest Peters and walks away. Gunshots are heard. Bradford shot Peters to avenge Reed's death. Elliott and Stewart realize they love each other.

NOTES AND COMMENTARY: House Peters, Jr. talked about his role in *Kansas Territory*: "I played the heavy in it. I played the good guy all the way through and I turned out to be the heavy at the end. They put me in a dress suit. I looked very prosperous and I looked liked the nice guy. I was neither a heavy nor a leading man. That was part of my problem in the business but I sure played a variety of roles. There was one type of role I played, usually at the end I'd end up being the heavy and somebody'd shoot me. And sure enough it did. I believe

it happened in that one. What's his name, he [Lane Bradford] died on a ship, his yacht in Hawaii, he walked right up to me. Lyle Talbot is standing there. I guess Lee Roberts and so forth, the old gang, and pumps me full of lead."

Long-time comic sidekick Fuzzy Knight here made his first of four appearances in Bill Elliott's Monogram/Allied Artists series. Knight was asked to emphasize characters with a touch of humor.

REVIEWS: "Wild Bill Elliott acquits himself with his usual flourish as an avenger. This Monogram release gives western audiences a good run for their money. Elliott is up to his usual excellence, handling both his fists and guns with equal facility." *Variety*, 5/28/52; "Another intriguing Ullman-scripted, Collins-directed Western starring Elliott; it is one of the most adult of B westerns of the period." *The Western*, Hardy.

SUMMATION: This is a first-rate "B" western with a decided adult slant. Wild Bill Elliott is totally believable as a man intent on vengeance who finally realizes he's embarked on a misguided cause. The supporting cast, especially Peggy Stewart and Lyle Talbot, deliver fine performances.

Your Two Favorite Western Stars
in One Terrific Blast of Thrills and Range Melodies!

King of Dodge City

Columbia (August, 1941)

CAST: Wild Bill Hickok, **Bill Elliott**; Tex Rawlings, **Tex Ritter**; Janice Blair, **Judith Linden**; Cannonball, **Dub Taylor**; Morgan King, **Guy Usher**; Judge Lynch, **Rick Anderson**; Jeff Carruthers, **Kenneth Harlan**; Reynolds, **Pierce Lyden**; Carney, **Francis Walker**; Stephen Kimball, **Harrison Greene**; Martin, **Jack Rockwell**// "Sonny"; "White Flash"; Sheriff Daniels, **Edward Coxen**; Crooked Gambler, **Tristram Coffin**; Gamblers, **Edmund Cobb** and **George Chesebro**; Bill Lang, **Jack Ingram**; Samuels, **Steve Clark**.

CREDITS: Director, **Lambert Hillyer**; Producer, **Leon Barsha**; Screenwriter, **Gerald Geraghty**; Editor, **Jerome Thoms**; Cinematography, **Benjamine Kline**.

SONGS: "There's an Empty Cot in the Bunkhouse Tonight"—sung by **Tex Ritter**; "To Shoot a Low Down Skunk"—sung by **Tex Ritter**; "Riding the Trail to Home"—sung by **Tex Ritter**; "Riding the Trail to Home" (reprise)—sung by **Tex Ritter**.

LOCATION FILMING: Iverson and Monogram Ranch, California.

RUNNING TIME: 63 min.

STORY: Wanted for the murder of a crooked gambler in a lawless community, Bill Elliott is asked by government official Harrison Greene to break up the lawlessness in Kansas and bring Guy Usher to justice. In Abilene, Tex Ritter is the sheriff, and his actions lead Elliott to suspect he is in league with Usher. Elliott suspects Usher is misappropriating bank funds for his own purposes. Elliott is framed for murder. Ritter finds proof that Elliott is working for the state government. The two men join forces to bring Usher to justice. When Eliott and Ritter return to Abilene, they are met by a hail of bullets from Usher and his henchmen. Joined by the honest citizens, Elliot and Ritter begin to get the upper hand. Usher tries to escape but is shot down in a gunfight with Elliott. With Usher's reign of terror ended, Elliott and Ritter ride off to new adventures.

NOTES AND COMMENTARY: Bill Elliott utters an interesting bit of dialogue when, as henchmen Francis Walker and Pierce Lyden level their guns at Tex Ritter, Elliott steps into the picture and says, "I'm superstitious. I hate to see anyone shot in the back."

Tex Ritter sports a bruise on his cheek after being hit by Bill Elliott.

REVIEWS: "Picture is an average shoots-and-saddles actioner. Lambert Hillyer's direction maintains a good tempo for an action western. Ritter suffers by comparison in the acting against the better performance by Elliott." *Variety*, 8/13/41; "Steady Bill Elliott-Tex Ritter outing but not one of their better vehicles." *Western Movies*, Pitts.

SUMMATION: This initial teaming of Bill Elliott and Tex Ritter is a sturdy western. Elliott is convincing as a man willing to take the law into his own hands where there is no law, even if it means being branded an outlaw. Ritter capably handles the action sequences. The movie moves well, but, like most in this series, has the two leads at odds until the final wrap-up, which in this case is too quickly accomplished.

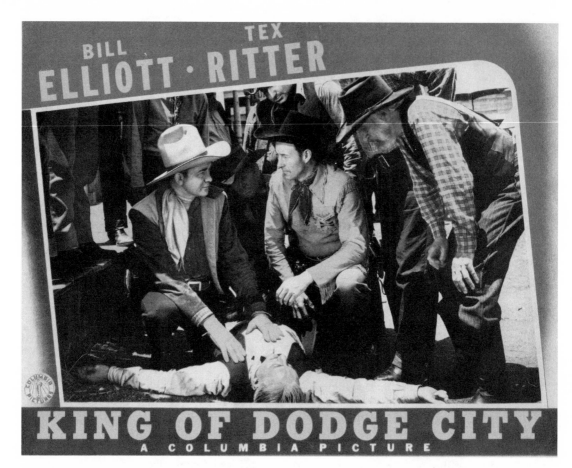

King of Dodge City (Columbia, 1941) scene card — Tex Ritter (left) and Bill Elliott (center) discuss the latest killing.

— *A Carload of Gold ... and the Men Who Vowed to Steal It!*

The Last Bandit

Republic (February, 1949)

CAST: Frank Norris (Frank Plummer), **William Elliott**; Kate Foley (Kate Sampson), **Adrian Booth**; Jim Plummer, **Forrest Tucker**; Casey Brown, **Andy Devine**; Mort Pemberton, **Jack Holt**; Winnie McPhail, **Minna Gombell**; Ed Bagley, **Grant Withers**; Kate's Mother, **Virginia Brissac**; Hank Morse, **Louis R. Faust**; Jeff Baldwin, **Stanley Andrews**; Patrick Moreno, **Martin Garralaga**; Engineer of Local no. 44, **Joseph Crehan**; Circuit Rider, **Charles Middleton**// Dancer at Wedding, **Buster West**; Rolley, **George Chesebro**; Pete, **Tex Terry**; Blonde Saloon Girl, **Vera Marshe**; Stage Driver, **Rex Lease**; Stage Passenger, **Gene Roth**; Traveling Salesman, **Rodney Bell**; Sheriff, **Hank Bell**; Drunk, **Emmett Lynn**; Chaw, **Len Torrey**; Bank Teller, **George Eldredge**; Sid Walker, **David Williams**; Smitty, **Jack O'Shea**.

CREDITS: Director/Associate Producer, **Joe Kane**; Story, **Luci Ward** and **Jack Natteford**; Screenwriter, **Thames Williamson**; Editor, **Arthur Roberts**; Art Director, **Frank Arrigo**; Set Decorators, **John McCarthy, Jr.** and **George Milo**; Cinematography, **Jack Marta**; Costumes, **Adele Palmer**; Makeup, **Bob Mark**; Hair

Stylist, **Peggy Gray**; Sound, **Dick Tyler** and **Howard Wilson**; Music, **Dale Butts**; Orchestrator, **Stanley Wilson**; Special Effects, **Howard** and **Theodore Lydecker**; Color by **Trucolor**.

SONGS: "Billy Boy" (unknown)—sung by unidentified actor; "Skip to My Lou" (traditional)—sung by **Forrest Tucker**; "Blue Tail Fly" (traditional)—instrumental; "Love Is Such a Funny Thing"—sung by **Adrian Booth**; "Skip to My Lou" (reprise)—instrumental.

LOCATION FILMING: Iverson, Vasquez, Red Rock Canyon, Brandais, Soledad Canyon and Fillmore & Western Railroad, California.

RUNNING TIME: 80 min.

STORY: Grant Withers convinces Adrian Booth not to marry Forrest Tucker but to travel to Bannock City, Nevada, to convince Tucker's brother, William Elliott, to participate in a gold-train robbery. Elliott, under an assumed name, works for the railroad. Tucker finds out about the caper and takes his gang to Nevada. Booth gets acquainted with Elliott so she can talk him into returning to outlaw life, but instead the two fall in love. Tucker arrives and can't persuade Elliott to help them. Elliott gives Tucker money to leave the area. Tucker agrees but uses the money to finance the robbery. Elliott learns that Tucker is going to try to steal $1,000,000 in gold bullion. Booth's intervention prevents railroad owner Jack Holt from arresting Elliott. Elliott is unable to prevent Tucker's theft when he's knocked from the train in a struggle with Tucker. Tucker takes the train, with Booth aboard, to an old mine tunnel over an abandoned spur line. Tucker ties up Booth to take her with him when he makes his escape. When the safe is blasted, the explosion causes a small rockslide that shows Elliott the location of the gold train. Elliott gets to the train, frees Booth and drives the train

The Last Bandit (Republic, 1949) movie still—Bill Elliott, Adrian Booth, Jack Holt, Hank Bell and Andy Devine (left to right) (courtesy of Adrian Booth Brian).

into the rocks in an attempt to break free. The impact knocks both Elliott and Booth unconscious. Tucker takes Booth with him as the outlaws make their escape. The crash causes steam to rise and alerts a posse, led by Holt, who finds Elliott. Elliott leads the posse in the pursuit of Tucker and his gang. Seeing the posse closing in, Tucker abandons the wagon with Booth and the gold. Elliott rescues Booth from the runaway wagon just before it overturns. Tucker is trailed into the rocks and is shot by Holt as Elliott watches helplessly. Elliott decides to answer the charges of outlawry in Missouri. Elliott then plans to return to Nevada to marry Booth and resume his job with the railroad.

NOTES AND COMMENTARY: *The Last Bandit* is a remake of *The Great Train Robbery* (Republic, 1941), with Bob Steele and Milburn Stone as brothers on the opposite sides of the law. Elements of *The Last Bandit*, primarily the diversion of a gold train into an abandoned mine tunnel, were incorporated into the Rex Allen western *South Pacific Trail* (Republic, 1952).

Adrian Booth remembered *The Last Bandit* fondly: "I loved *The Last Bandit*. I wore a kind of silky outfit. I was a singer in a saloon. I had to get out through a window. Then I had to get on a horse. There was no way I could stay on a horse because the saddle, silk and me didn't do very well together. *The Last Bandit* was wonderful. Bill Elliott was always marvelous to work with. He was such a gentleman. He was a businessman. Actually, it's one of my favorite movies. Didn't I take a bath in that? My director was Joe Kane. He never had a lady take a bath in any one of his movies he made in his whole put-together. Everyone was happy about my taking a bath."

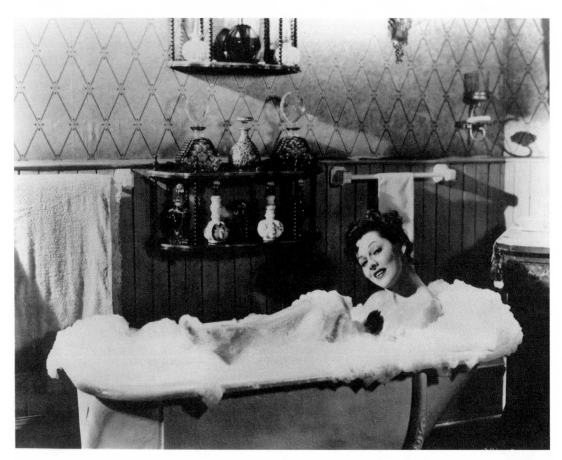

The Last Bandit (Republic, 1949) movie still — Adrian Booth in her bath scene (courtesy of Adrian Booth Brian).

After Jack Holt jumps from a moving train and has the telegrapher wire ahead to stop the train, he wants William Elliott and Adrian Booth arrested. Holt calls Booth by her correct character name, Kate Foley, but Booth has been using an alias, Kate Sampson.

When William Elliott is wounded by Grant Withers, Withers takes Elliott's pistol. Later in the film, when Elliott tells Holt and the posse the direction Forrest Tucker rode, Elliott retrieves his weapon from a posse member. One can only suppose the posse rode by Withers' corpse before reaching Elliott, and the cowboy picked up the pistol.

REVIEWS: "Off beaten path western for hefty returns. Under his [Kane's] helming, Elliott and Tucker turn in capital performances." *Variety*, 2/23/49; "Pretty good William Elliott action film; quite colorful." *Western Movies*, Pitts.

SUMMATION: This is another good William Elliott big-budget western. Elliott displays his fine acting ability as a former outlaw trying to go straight while dealing with emotional issues, as he has to fight his brother, Forrest Tucker, to do so. Look at Elliott's inner torment as he reaches to prevent Jack Holt from shooting Tucker and then draws his hand back. Nice performances by Tucker, love interest Adrian Booth, good friend Andy Devine and saloon owner Minna Gombell bolster the good script. Joe Kane's direction is on-target.

Texas Tolerates No More Bandits ...
Watch My Fists and Six-Guns Prove It!

The Law Comes to Texas

Columbia (April, 1939)

CAST: John Haynes, **Bill Elliott**; Dora Lewis, **Veda Ann Borg**; Judge Dean, **Bud Osborne**; Barney, **Charles Whittaker**; Jeff, **Leon Beaumon**; Governor, **Paul Everton**; Kaintuck, **Charles King**// Sheriff Ben Lorimer, **Edmund Cobb**; Duke, **Tex Palmer**; Sheriff Amos Barlow, **Jack Ingram**; Monk, **Frank Ellis**; Mr. Childers, **Frank LaRue**; Lt. Governor Fenton, **Lee Shumway**; Al, **David Sharpe**; Buzz, **Buzz Barton**; Fenton's secretary, **Forrest Taylor**; Henchmen, **Francis Walker** and **Jim Corey**; Court Clerk, **Budd Buster**; Captain, **Lane Chandler**; Scout, **Dan White**.

CREDITS: Director, **Joseph Levering**; Screenwriter, **Nate Gatzert**; Editor, **Dwight Caldwell**; Cinematographer, **James S. Brown**; Music, **Lee Zahler**.

LOCATION FILMING: Iverson, California.

RUNNING TIME: 61 min.

STORY: Bailey County, under the control of Judge Bud Osborne, is a hotbed of lawlessness. Governor Paul Everton sends Bill Elliott and his sidekick Charles King to bring law and order. Elliott gets proof that Osborne is the outlaw leader. Under Texas law, Osborne must be tried in Bailey County, where Elliott knows he will never be convicted. Elliott convinces everyone that he has given up, letting only King know that this is a ruse. Using a disguise, Elliott is able to work his way into Osborne's gang. Lt. Governor Lee Shumway, Osborne's confederate, arranges to have $100,000 sent to Bailey County. Shumway tells Osborne to steal the money in a neighboring county. Elliott arranges to have the money guarded by troops. Shumway orders the troops to return to Austin, but Elliott interferes and the troops ride to protect the money shipment. Elliott sends King to capture Shumway. The troops round up the henchmen. Osborne and henchman Charles Whittaker try to escape but are easily brought to justice by Elliott. Elliott is appointed head of the newly formed Texas Rangers.

NOTES AND COMMENTARY: This was the last of Bill Elliott's Larry Darmour–produced westerns. Elliott would star in the serial *Overland with Kit Carson* (Columbia, 1939) before embarking on his four Wild Bill Saunders adventures produced by Columbia.

Veda Ann Borg, Elliott's love interest, would have a role of greater substance in Elliott's

The Law Comes to Texas (Columbia, 1939) scene card — Bill Elliott (right) tells an unidentified actor (left) and Dan White (center) that it is all right to go to Baileyville; the left border shows Bill Elliott.

next to last western, *Bitter Creek* (Allied Artists, 1954). Borg would show her acting talent as a woman in love with ruthless Carlton Young, who plans to wed Beverly Garland, a lady from a prominent Eastern family.

REVIEWS: "Bill Elliott is a new western star who has come to the fore in no uncertain manner. He chalks up a perfect score in this saga of lawless days in Texas. He is rugged and personable in the best William S. Hart tradition, riding, shooting and fighting desperadoes single-handed. Western fans can't help liking Elliott and his loyal partner, 'Kaintuck.' Picture has been spiritly directed by Joseph Levering. It has pace, an interesting story, a credible cast and the thrills one expects in an outdoor action film. Osborne, as the crooked judge, shares

honors with Elliott." *Variety*, 5/17/39; "Hand to hand battles in the climax lend spirit to the rugged drama of the cleaning up of some lawless elements plaguing Texas." *Motion Picture Guide*, Nash and Ross.

SUMMATION: In this highly entertaining "B" western, Bill Elliott is perfect both in the acting and action departments as the heroic figure who brings an end to lawlessness in one Texas county. Elliott is given a fine supporting cast, though the usually reliable Bud Osborne turns in an unexpectedly poor performance. A very mild windup involving Elliott's capture of Osborne and henchman Charles Whitaker keeps the film from earning even higher acclaim.

Thrill as Two-Gun Justice Hits the Texas Badlands!

Lone Star Pioneers

Columbia (March, 1939)

ALTERNATE TITLE: *Unwelcome Visitors.*

CAST: Pat Barrett, **Bill Elliott**; Virginia Crittenden, **Dorothy Gulliver**; Bill Ruphy, **Lee Shumway**; Buck Bally, **Charles Whittaker**; Pike, **Charles King**; John Coe, **Jack Ingram**; Eph Brown, **Harry Harvey**; Chuck, **Buzz Barton**; Joe Cribben, **Frank LaRue**// "**Sonny**"; Ranger Williams, **Jack Rockwell**; Mike, **Kit Guard**; Henchman, **Merrill McCormick**; Kate, **Marin Sais**; Singing Outlaw, **Art Davis**; Barlow, **Frank Ellis**; Crittenden, **Budd Buster**; Bud Crittenden, **David Sharpe**.

CREDITS: Director, **Joseph Levering**; Screenwriter, **Nate Gatzert**; Editor, **Dwight Caldwell**; Cinematographer, **James S. Brown, Jr.**; Music, **Lee Zahler**.

LOCATION FILMING: Iverson, California.

RUNNING TIME: 56 min.

STORY: A guerrilla band is terrorizing the citizens of west Texas and intercepts a wagon train bringing necessary supplies. U.S. Marshal Bill Elliott arrives to help Ranger Captain Jack Ingram stop the lawlessness. Elliott masquerades as a wanted man and infiltrates the gang. The gang is using Budd Buster's ranch as their headquarters. Elliott tells Buster and his children, Dorothy Gulliver and David Sharpe, that

Lone Star Pioneers (Columbia, 1939) scene card — Bill Elliott (left) pummels Charlie King (right); the left border shows Bill Elliott manhandling an unidentified actor.

he is a lawman. Outlaw boss and respected citizen Lee Shumway arranges to have his right hand man, Charles Whittaker, substitute gang members for a ranger company requested by Ingram. Elliott is able to alert Ingram, and the lawmen arrest the fake rangers. Whittaker and his men ride out to raid another wagon train. Elliott gathers the townsmen and has Shumway lead the posse. Whittaker spots Shumway and, thinking he's double-crossed him, shoots him. Elliott and the posse quickly round up Whittaker and his men. The wagon train reaches the town safely. A budding romance begins to form between Elliott and Gulliver.

NOTES AND COMMENTARY: Bill Elliott here introduces his horse, Sonny, to movie audiences. He even shows Sonny off to good advantage by letting him perform a couple of tricks. During a chase, a remark is made on how fast Sonny runs.

There has been some discussion of Budd Buster's family name in this film. In the credits, Dorothy Gulliver is listed as "Crittenden," and Bill Elliott calls Buster "Crittenden." It has been said on some sound tracks the name

sounds like "Fettington." I'll stick with Crittenden.

Singing cowboy Art Davis is seen briefly as the outlaw warbling a few lines of a western tune. Davis was Tim McCoy's sidekick in McCoy's final PRC western, *The Texas Marshal* (1941). Advertising material for the film promoted Davis's singing of the song, "Ridin' Down the Texas Trail." Shortly after, Davis joined Bill "Cowboy Rambler" Boyd and the original screen Lone Ranger, Lee Powell, in the short-lived Frontier Marshals series for PRC in 1942.

REVIEWS: "Strictly a cheap western, Elliott is gaining ease in chaps and spurs. The days of drawing room parts now probably seeming far behind." *Variety*, 3/22/39; "Okay Bill Elliott vehicle, which tends to be a bit draggy." *Western Movies*, Pitts.

SUMMATION: Another winning outing for Bill Elliott, *Lone Star Pioneers* possesses a good script and fast-paced direction. Elliott is quite good as the stalwart hero, fighting, riding and shooting in fine style. A somewhat mild windup is the only negative factor with this one.

A Roaring Blast of Blazing Action!

Lone Star Vigilantes

Columbia (January, 1942)
ALTERNATE TITLE: *The Devil's Price.*
CAST: Wild Bill Hickok, **Bill Elliott**; Tex Martin, **Tex Ritter**; Cannonball, **Frank Mitchell**; Shary Monroe, **Virginia Carpenter**; Marcia Banning, **Luana Walters**; Colonel Monroe, **Budd Buster**; Dr. Banning, **Forrest Taylor**; Major Clark, **Gavin Gordon**; Peabody, **Lowell Drew**; Charlie Cobb, **Edmund Cobb**; Benson, **Ethan Laidlaw**; Lige Miller, **Rick Anderson**// "Sonny"; "White Flash"; Kellogg, **Francis Walker**; Pedro, **Dick Botiller**; Manton, **Eddie Laughton**; Jones, **Steve Clark**; Soldier, **John Cason**.
CREDITS: Director, **Wallace W. Fox**; Producer, **Leon Barsha**; Screenwriter, **Luci Ward**; Editor, **Mel Thorson**; Cinematography, **Benjamine Kline**.

SONGS: "Headin' Home to Texas" — sung by **Tex Ritter** and **Frank Mitchell**; "When the Moon Is Shining on the Old Corral" — sung by **Tex Ritter**; "Goin' to Join the Rangers" — sung by **Tex Ritter**.
LOCATION FILMING: Corriganville, Burro Flats, Agoura and Iverson, California.
RUNNING TIME: 58 min.
STORY: Civil War veterans Bill Elliott, Tex Ritter and Frank Mitchell return to Texas. Even though they fought on the side of the Confederacy, the men realize it's now important to have but one nation. As wounds between neighbors are beginning to heal, Union Major Gavin Gordon announces that Winchester County is under martial law and confiscates all weapons. Gordon plans to loot and gain control of all properties. Elliott and Ritter recognize one of Gordon's

Lone Star Vigilantes (Columbia, 1942) scene card — Gavin Gordon (second right) and unidentified actor (right) get the drop on Bill Elliott (left) and Tex Ritter (second left), as Virginia Carpenter (left center) and Frank Mitchell (right center) watch.

soldiers as a horse thief, and they have their doubts about his intentions. Luana Walters, who was treated badly by Confederate sympathizers prior to the war, wants revenge and decides to work with Gordon. Elliott plans to expose Gordon as an impostor. Ritter decides to join vigilantes to fight Gordon with guns stolen from the Army. Walters informs Gordon about the vigilantes, and Ritter is arrested and sentenced to hang. Figuring Walters is an informant, Elliott gives her false information to draw Gordon and his men out of town. Elliott breaks Ritter out of jail and obtains proof that Gordon is an impostor and not an Army officer. Walters brings Gordon back in time to begin a gunfight with Ritter, Elliott, Mitchell and the Texans. A bullet takes Walters' life, and Ritter captures Gordon. With peace restored, Elliott, Ritter and Mitchell ride to join the Texas Rangers.

NOTES AND COMMENTARY: Even though Frank Mitchell was listed as playing "Cannonball" in the credits of the previous film, *Roaring Frontiers* (Columbia, 1941), he was never called by name in the film. In *The Lone Star Vigilantes*, Mitchell was introduced as Cannonball Q. Boggs.

REVIEWS: "*Lone Star Vigilantes* is the best of the first three Bill Elliott-Tex Ritter western series. Full of action, with plenty of gun-pumping and heroics, picture is a good entry in the western field. Good western-type script accentuating action and excitement combined with fast-paced direction. Elliott is most prominent for heroics." *Variety*, 9/24/41; "Plenty of gun-fighting action." *Motion Picture Guide*, Nash and Ross.

SUMMATION: A strong story highlights this superior entry in the Bill Elliott-Tex Ritter series.

The story spends little time with Elliott and Ritter on opposite sides of the fence. The stars complement each other well, and the story benefits greatly. Elliott, again, is the stronger of the two in the acting category, but both overshadow a more than adequate supporting cast. Luana Walters gives a nifty performance as a Northern sympathizer who can't let old hurts heal. Wallace W. Fox's direction is up to the story's demands.

Dangerous Criminals on the Loose...
Thrill to the Excitement!... The Actions!... The Pulse-Pounding Adventure!...
When Red Ryder Takes to Their Trail!

Lone Texas Ranger

Republic Pictures (May, 1945)

CAST: Red Ryder, **Wild Bill Elliott**; Little Beaver, **Bobby Blake**; the Duchess, **Alice Fleming**; "Hands" Weber, **Roy Barcroft**; Sheriff "Iron Mike" Haines, **Tom Chatterton**; Tommy Haines, **Jack McClendon**; Sally Carter, **Helen Talbot**; Betcha, **Bud Geary**; F.E., **Budd Buster**; Henry Grimm, **Nelson McDowell**; Payne, **Larry Olsen**; Whitey, **Rex Lease**; Bill Bradley, **Jack Kirk**// "Thunder"; Art Carter, **Frank O'-Connor**; Hill, **Horace B. Carpenter**; Baker, **Dale Van Sickel**; Mine Watchman, **Hal Price**; Outlaws, **Bob Wilke** and **Frederick Howard**.

CREDITS: Director, **Spencer Bennett**; Associate Producer, **Louis Gray**; Screenwriter, **Bob Williams**; Editor, **Charles Craft**; Art Director, **Russell Kimball**; Set Decorator, **George Milo**; Cinematography, **Bud Thackery**; Makeup, **Bob Mark**; Sound, **Ed Borschell**; Musical Director, **Richard Cherwin**.

LOCATION FILMING: Iverson, California.

RUNNING TIME: 56 min.

SOURCE: Based on Fred Harman's famous NEA comic, by special arrangement with Stephen Slesinger.

STORY: Wild Bill Elliott discovers that famous lawman Tom Chatterton is in league with the outlaw gang that's terrorizing the area. In a gunfight, Elliott mortally wounds Chatterton. As Chatterton dies, he asks Elliott not to tell the town and spare his son, Jack McClendon, the disgrace. Elliott tells the town that Chatterton was killed by the outlaws, and has the town appoint McClendon the new sheriff. Elliott keeps interfering with the lawless plans of blacksmith — and outlaw leader — Roy Barcroft. When henchman Bud Geary informs Barcroft that Elliott shot Chatterton, Barcroft figures if he tells McClendon, McClendon will engage Elliott in a gunfight. Elliott refuses to fight and goes looking for Geary, finding him at Barcroft's blacksmith shop. Elliott is in the process of arresting both Geary and Barcroft when McClendon bursts in. The outlaws get the drop on Elliott and McClendon, but Elliott's Indian pal, Bobby Blake, causes a diversion. A fistfight and a gunfight erupt, leaving Geary and Barcroft dead. Elliott convinces McClendon not to tell the truth about his father.

NOTES AND COMMENTARY: At the Knoxville Film Caravan, Helen Talbot commented about Bill Elliott: "Bill Elliott was very much of a gentleman. He liked William Hart, was his hero. He patterned himself, in a way, about William Hart. He was curious and knowledgeable about what he was doing."

Ms. Talbot once came to Bill Elliott's rescue. Elliott was shopping for a dress for his daughter, Barbara. He found one he liked but wasn't certain if it would fit correctly. Talbot was shopping at the same time. Elliott noticed that Talbot and his daughter were about the same size and asked Talbot if she would try it on for him. She did. Elliott was satisfied and bought the dress.

Jack McClendon was usually billed as Robert Grady in his brief career in motion pictures.

Tom Steele doubled Wild Bill Elliott in this feature.

REVIEW: "A strong script highlights this actionful 'Red Ryder' entry." *Western Movies*, Pitts.

Lone Texas Ranger (Republic, 1945) scene card — Bill Elliott (left) questions his prisoner, Rex Lease (right).

SUMMATION: This is an excellent "B" western. Will Bill Elliott is given some dramatic scenes in which he decides whether or not to destroy the reputation of lawman Tom Chatterton, and then in his confrontation scenes with Chatterton's son, Jack McClendon, which he handles well. Elliott receives fine support from Bobby Blake, villain Roy Barcroft, Tom Chatterton and Jack McClendon. Bob Williams delivers a superior script, and Spencer Bennett's direction is on target.

Toughest of the Cattle Kings!
He Staked Out an Empire Along the Wyoming Line ...
and Blazed Law and Order Every Bitter Mile!

The Longhorn

Monogram Pictures (November, 1951)
A Frontier Pictures Production
CAST: Jim Kirk, **Wild Bill Elliott**; Andy, **Myron Healey**; Gail, **Phyllis Coates**; Charley, **Stanford Jolley**; Purdy, **Lane Bradford**; Moresby, **John Hart**; Latimer, **Marshall Reed**; Bartender, **William Fawcett**; Clark, **Lee Roberts**; Henchman, **Carol Henry**; Tyler, **Zon Murray**// Doctor, **Marshall Bradford**; Oregon Rancher, **Steve Clark**; Henchman, **Carl Mathews**.

CREDITS: Director, **Lewis Collins**; Assistant Director, **Melville Shyer**; Producer, **Vincent M. Fennelly**; Screenwriter, **Dan Ullman**; Editor, **Richard Heermance**; Art Director, **David Milton**; Set Decorator, **Vincent Taylor**; Cinematographer, **Ernest Miller**; Sound, **George Cooper**; Musical Director, **Raoul Kraushaar**; Set Continuity, **Mary Chaffee**; Dialogue Director, **Stanley Price**; Color by **Sepiatone**.

LOCATION FILMING: Iverson, California.

RUNNING TIME: 70 min.

STORY: With longhorn beef prices at their lowest, Wild Bill Elliott plans to improve his stock by breeding longhorn bulls with Hereford cows. Elliott and his friend Myron Healey begin a journey from Wyoming to Oregon, where Herefords are available. Unknown to Elliott, Healey is working with saloon owner John Hart and his henchmen to steal Elliott's herd and murder him on his return from Oregon. As Elliott and Healey near Oregon, Indians attack them, their horses are stolen and Healey is wounded. Walking for help, Elliott meets Phyllis Coates, who, with her father Stanford Jolley, renders aid. The only cowhands Elliott can hire are former outlaws and convicts, promising them jobs when they reach his ranch. Jolley signs on as cook, with Coates helping him. Both Elliott and Healey fall in love with Coates, but Coates favors Elliott. As they near Elliott's ranch, Healey tells Hart and chief henchman Marshall Reed how to steal the cattle. Hart plans to take the cattle and kill both Healey and Elliott. As Healey prepares to set the rustling scheme in motion, Elliott tells him that he will be his foreman and will own a share in the cattle. Healey tries to prevent the theft, but a shot stampedes the cattle. Healey helps Elliott, and the cowhands bring the cattle under control.

The Longhorn (Monogram, 1951) scene card — Bill Elliott (left) requests help from Phyllis Coates (right).

Furious at his plans being thwarted, Hart mortally wounds Healey and attempts to escape. Elliott chases after Hart. The two men meet and shots are exchanged. Elliott's shot finds its mark, killing Hart. Elliott and Coates plan to wed.

NOTES AND COMMENTARY: With *The Longhorn*, Bill Elliott moves from his big-budget series for Republic to a smaller-budgeted group of westerns for Monogram. To Elliott's credit, these films had an adult slant, and his hero was of a more realistic bent.

Phyllis Coates remarked, "I will say Bill was probably the only real cowboy. When he wasn't shooting, he was 'rodeoing.' Very professional. We did those cheapies for Vince Fennelly and Monogram back to back. Six days shooting, low pay—oh! God!"

The Longhorn was remade as *Canyon River* (Allied Artists, 1956), with George Montgomery, in Deluxe Color and Cinemascope, and with a longer running time. As in most cases with remakes, the original remains the superior product.

REVIEWS: "Satisfactory Wild Bill Elliott western for the lesser action market. Film is a cut above the regular oater programmer both in its 70 minute running time and production values. Elliott is a realistic saddle hero who looks the part and gives considerably to the picture." *Variety*, 10/10/51; "Very fine Bill Elliott vehicle with a good script, cast and fast action; recommended." *Western Movies*, Pitts.

SUMMATION: In his first series western at Monogram, Wild Bill Elliott has a real winner, bolstered by a first rate script by Dan Ullman, steady direction by Lewis Collins, and a fine supporting cast headed by Myron Healey as Elliott's friend who plans to betray him, Phyllis Coates, the girl both Elliott and Healey love, and Stanford Jolley, a farmer who wants to return to working on a cattle ranch. Elliott delivers the best performance, realistically portraying a tough rancher who exhibits compassion and sorrow.

Wild Bill Elliott Rides Again!
Action ... Adventure!
Where Gun-Law Is the Only Law!

The Man from Thunder River

Republic (June, 1943)

CAST: Wild Bill Elliott, **Wild Bill Elliott**; Gabby Whittaker, **George "Gabby" Hayes**; Nancy Ferguson, **Anne Jeffreys**; Henry Stevens, **Ian Keith**; Jack Ferguson, **John James**; Aunt Beth, **Georgie Cooper**; Ed Foster, **Jack Ingram**; Wong, **Eddie Lee**; Main Henchman, **Charles King**; Sheriff, **Jack Rockwell**// "Sonny"; Prospector, **Al Bridge**; Bates, **Edward Cassidy**; Deputies, **Roy Brent** and **Al Taylor**; Jim, **Edmund Cobb**; Lynch Leader, **Bud Geary**; Henchmen, **Curley Dresden** and **Jack O'Shea**; Store Clerk, **Robert Barron**.

CREDITS: Director, **John English**; Associate Producer, **Harry Grey**; Screenwriter, **J. Benton Cheney**; Editor, **Harry Keller**; Art Director, **Russell Kimball**; Set Decorator, **Charles Thompson**; Cinematographer, **Bud Thackery**; Sound, **Earl Crain, Sr.**; Music, **Mort Glickman**.

SONG: "Kiss Me Quick (and Go)" (Traditional)—sung by **Anne Jeffreys**.

LOCATION FILMING: Iverson and Corriganville, California.

RUNNING TIME: 55 min.

STORY: Wild Bill Elliott and his pal George "Gabby" Hayes visit Georgie Cooper's ranch, primarily so Elliott can visit with Cooper's niece, Anne Jeffreys. Elliott learns that Jeffreys' brother, John James, wants to reopen the Big Hope mine, to the objections of family friend Ian Keith. Keith knows there is a rich gold strike in the mine and plans to steal the ore to meets commitments from his own mine. When

The Man from Thunder River (Republic, 1943) title card — upper left shows Bill Elliott on Sonny; lower left shows unidentified actor, Bud Geary, Jack Ingram, unidentified actor, Ian Keith and Charles King (left to right); lower right shows Bill Elliott, Georgie Cooper, Eddie Lee, Anne Jeffreys, "Gabby" Hayes and John James (left to right).

James arranges financing to reopen the mine, Keith frames him for murder. Elliott and Hayes hide James from the law. When Keith's offer to help James results in another narrow escape from the law, Elliott begins to suspect Keith of being behind James' troubles. Elliott and Hayes investigate the Big Hope mine. They find that Keith has made a concealed passageway between the two mines and is taking gold ore from the Big Hope. At peril to their lives, Elliott and Hayes round up Keith's henchmen, and Elliott brings Keith to justice after a rugged fistfight. James is cleared, the Big Hope mine is reopened, and Elliott and Hayes ride off to new adventures, with Elliott promising to come back to see Jeffreys soon.

NOTES AND COMMENTARY: This was the first film to bill Elliott as "Wild Bill," even though the title card still listed Elliott as just plain "Bill."

Footage from *Man from Thunder River* was utilized in *Prince of the Plains* (Republic, 1949) for the scene in which Monte Hale prevents the lynching of Harry Lauter.

Early in the film, it is evident that Jack Ingram's character name is "Les Foster." Later in the film Ian Keith calls Ingram "Ed."

REVIEWS: "Strong Bill Elliott series entry at Republic, well written and directed." *Western Movies*, Pitts; "Rip-snorting western, the action rarely lets up in this entertaining, action-packed outing." *Motion Picture Guide*, Nash and Ross.

SUMMATION: This is a top flight "B" western. Wild Bill Elliott is at his best handling the action and acting chores. Elliott is a delight in his mild flirtation scenes with Anne Jeffreys, and the chemistry between Elliott and sidekick George "Gabby" Hayes is on-target. Director John English paces the film adroitly, stressing the well-done action sequences. Badman Ian Keith and young-man-in-trouble John James add excellent support.

He's Satan Himself ... Throwing Crimson Streaks of Death from His Two Blazing Six-Guns ... Blasting a Bandit's Reign of Terror from the Old West's Wildest Range!

The Man from Tumbleweeds

Columbia (May, 1940)

A Wild Bill Saunders Adventure

CAST: Wild Bill Saunders, **Bill Elliott**; "Spunky" Cameron, **Iris Meredith**; Cannonball, **Dub Taylor**; Powder Kilgore, **Raphael Bennett**; Lightning Barloe, **Francis Walker**; Shifty Sheldon, **Ernie Adams**; Honest John, **Al Hill**; Slash, **Stanley Brown**; Dixon, **Richard Fiske**; Jeff Cameron, **Edward LeSaint**; Governor Dawson, **Don Beddoe**// "**Sonny**"; Jackson, **Eddie Laughton**; Bank Robbers, **Olin Francis** and **George Chesebro**; Marshal of Tumbleweeds, **Steve Clark**; Wilson, **Edward Cecil**; Prison Warden, **Bruce Bennett**; Stage Driver, **Hank Bell**; Henchman, **Blackie Whiteford**.

CREDITS: Director, **Joseph H. Lewis**; Screenwriter, **Charles Francis Royal**; Editor, **Charles Nelson**; Cinematographer, **George Meehan**.

LOCATION FILMING: Iverson, California.

RUNNING TIME: 59 min.

STORY: Raphael Bennett is behind the lawless activity in Gunsight. Bill Elliott is asked to help, but he realizes one man can't stop Bennett and his gang. With backing from Governor Don Beddoe, Elliott is given a group of hardened convicts to become state rangers. One of the convicts, Al Hill, becomes Elliott's chief lieutenant. Elliott asks another convict, Ernie Adams, to infiltrate Bennett's gang, not knowing Adams is in league with Bennett. Bennett and Adams set a trap to murder Elliott. Hill and fellow convict Stanley Brown realize Elliott is riding into a trap, and ride to prevent Elliott from being ambushed. From a note sent to Adams, Elliott knows the location of Bennett's hideout. Elliott and Hill arrive at the hideout, and a suspenseful gunfight ensues, resulting in Elliott bringing Bennett and his gang to justice. Elliott turns down the commission of Commander-in-Chief of the state rangers and recommends Hill instead. Elliott rides off to new adventures.

NOTES AND COMMENTARY: Joseph H. Lewis was noted for his edgy direction and unusual camera angles to enhance a story (e.g., shooting scenes through wagon wheels and windows). In his "B" western career, Lewis directed four Bob Bakers at Universal before moving to Columbia. At Columbia, he directed three Charles Starretts and two Bill Elliotts. He then moved back to Universal to directed three Johnny Mack Brown vehicles.

In an interesting scene from *The Man from Tumbleweeds*, chief villain Raphael Bennett tells one of his minions to climb up a ladder into a tree to draw a bead on Bill Elliott. Bennett asks, "Can you get him?" A shot rings out and the henchman's lifeless body falls to the ground.

REVIEWS: "This opus is a good one in its field. Elliott fits well into the leading role, a cool, slow-forming-opinion, fast on the draw individual. Bill Elliott finally hits his stride, coming up with a hard-shooting action pic." *Variety*, 5/29/40; "Speedy and entertaining Bill Elliott oater." *Western Movies*, Pitts.

SUMMATION: This is a forerunner of *The Dirty Dozen* (Metro-Goldwyn-Mayer, 1967), as Bill Elliott recruits convicts to fight lawlessness in this top-flight "B" western. Elliott brings some fine shading to his heroic characterization, which makes his performance all the more enjoyable. Al Hill, the leader of the convicts picked to be state rangers, leads the competent supporting cast. The chemistry between

ASTOR PICTURES *Presents*
Blazing Guns
Fighting Courage
"Wild Bill" ELLIOTT

THE MAN FROM TUMBLEWEEDS

RELEASED THRU ASTOR PICTURES CORP.

The Man from Tumbleweeds (Columbia, 1940) scene card — Raphael Bennett (left) takes the pistol out of Bill Elliott's holster (center) as Elliott struggles with Francis Walker (right); the left border shows Bill Elliott and Iris Meredith.

Elliott and Hill is perfect and natural. Joseph H. Lewis' edgy direction is on-target. Lewis has a number of scenes enhanced by innovative camera angles, including the fistfight between Elliott and Francis Walker, and the gunfight between Elliott and Walker.

Thrills Up and Down Your Spine When Red Ryder and Little Beaver
Smoke Out a Band of Prairie Racketeers.

Marshal of Laredo

Republic Pictures (October, 1945)

CAST: Red Ryder, **Wild Bill Elliott**; Little Beaver, **Bobby Blake**; the Duchess, **Alice Fleming**; Judy Bowers, **Peggy Stewart**; Larry Randall, **Robert Grady**; Denver Jack, **Roy Barcroft**; Pretty Boy Murphy, **Don Costello**; Ferguson, **Bud Geary**; Mrs. Randall, **Sarah Padden**; Barton, **Tom London**; Reverend Parker, **Tom** Chatterton; Dr. Allen, **Wheaton Chambers**; Deputy, **George Cheseboro**; Mel Bowers, **George Carleton**// "Thunder"; Spud, **Jack O'Shea**; Suzanne, **Dorothy Granger**.

CREDITS: Director, **R.G. Springsteen**; Associate Producer, **Sidney Picker**; Screenwriter, **Bob Williams**; Editor, **Charles Craft**; Art Director, **Hilyard Brown**; Set Decorator, **George**

Milo; Cinematographer, **Bud Thackery**; Sound, **Earl Crain, Sr.**; Makeup, **Bob Mark**; Musical Director, **Richard Cherwin**.

LOCATION FILMING: Iverson, California.

RUNNING TIME: 56 min.

SOURCE: Based on Fred Harman's famous NEA comic, by special arrangement with Stephen Slesinger.

STORY: Saloon owner Roy Barcroft is the brains behind a wave of lawlessness. He forces his gang members to blindly following him via blackmail and intimidation. His way of keeping henchman Don Costello in line is to strike matches close to his face. Young lawyer Robert Grady, fearful of losing fiancée Peggy Stewart, decides to break with Barcroft. Barcroft arranges to have Grady framed for murder. Though Grady has been sentenced to hang, Marshal Wild Bill Elliott and his Indian pal, Bobby Blake, believe him to be innocent of the charges. Elliott allows Grady to escape from jail, and his suspicions are confirmed. Elliott searches Barcroft's office for evidence to clear Grady but is taken captive. Grady and Blake come back to town looking for Elliott. Grady is apprehended and readied for the gallows. Blake goes looking for Elliott and is grabbed by Barcroft. Elliott sees that Costello is afraid of fire when Barcroft strikes a match near Costello. Though tied up, Elliott is able to toss a lighted match, which starts a fire in Barcroft's office. Frightened, Costello unties Elliott, who extinguishes the flames and then forces Costello to write a confession clearing Grady of murder. Before Elliott can save Grady, he is forced to best both Barcroft and Costello in a rugged fistfight. Now cleared of all charges, Grady and Stewart can be married.

Marshal of Laredo (Republic, 1945) scene card — Bill Elliott (right) and Bobby Blake (second right) discover the dead body of George Carlton, while Robert Grady (left) looks at the window and sees a hand holding a gun.

NOTES AND COMMENTARY: It is not my usual custom to relate personal anecdotes, but in this instance, I'm making an exception. Moviegoers of the last forty or so years have become fairly accustomed to the level of violence and gore found in some films. When I was eight years old, my mother took my brother and myself to our neighborhood theater one Friday night, and the preview for the Saturday western *Marshal of Laredo* was shown. When my mother saw Roy Barcroft striking matches near the face of Don Costello to intimidate him, she commented that she didn't know if she should let us see the film. I quickly commented, "Mom, it's only a movie," and she relented. If scenes like that bothered her, what would she have thought of some of today's fare?

In his brief career, Robert Grady was also billed as Jack McClendon.

Fred Graham doubled Roy Barcroft in his fight with Wild Bill Elliott at the film's finale.

REVIEW: "Actionful entry in the popular Red Ryder series." *Western Movies*, Pitts.

SUMMATION: This is a top-flight Red Ryder saga boasting fine acting, a solid script, good action and surehanded direction. The script allows both Wild Bill Elliott and Peggy Stewart to show their acting range, rather than just effectively deliver their lines. The film has a stellar supporting cast, headed by villain Roy Barcroft, his henchman Don Costello, Stewart's fiancée Robert Grady and Elliott's Indian pal Bobby Blake. R.G. Springsteen, by his adroit pacing, is able to generate some genuine suspense as Elliott has to overcome many obstacles to set matters right. A neat touch in Bob Williams' script is Barcroft's way of keeping Costello in line by striking matches near his burn-scarred face.

Your Comic Strip Comet, Rip-Snortin' Red Ryder!...
in His Most Dangerous Two-Fisted Adventure!

Marshal of Reno

Republic (July, 1944)

CAST: Red Ryder, **Wild Bill Elliott**; Gabby, **George "Gabby" Hayes**; Little Beaver, **Bobby Blake**; the Duchess, **Alice Fleming**; John Palmer, **Herbert Rawlinson**; Danny Boyd, **Jay Kirby**; Faro Carson, **LeRoy Mason**; Lee, **Blake Edwards**; Drake, **Fred Graham**; Kellogg, **Jack Kirk**; Adams, **Kenne Duncan**; Ward, **Bud Geary**; Stage Robber, **Tom Steele**; Sheriff, **Tom London**; Judge, **Tom Chatterton**// "Thunder"; Stage Driver, **Carl Sepulveda**; Townsman, **Horace B. Carpenter**; Stage Robber, **Charles King**; Joe Richards, **Hal Price**; Bob Wendell, **Edmund Cobb**; Brownie, **Al Taylor**; Henchman, **Marshall Reed**; Deputy, **Bob Wilke**; Waiter, **Ken Terrell**; Saloon Patron, **Jack O'Shea**.

CREDITS: Director, **Wallace Grissell**; Associate Producer, **Louis Gray**; Story, **Anthony Coldewey** and **Taylor Caven**; Screenwriter, **Anthony Coldewey**; Editor, **Charles Craft**; Art

Director, **Gano Chittenden**; Set Decorator, **George Milo**; Cinematographer, **Reggie Lanning**; Sound, **Tom Carman**; Musical Score, **Joseph Dubin**.

LOCATION FILMING: Iverson and Corriganville, California.

RUNNING TIME: 54 min.

SOURCE: Based on Fred Harman's famous NEA comic, by special arrangement with Stephen Slesinger.

STORY: Tenderfeet Jay Kirby and Blake Edwards are mistaken for stage robbers by a posse led by Sheriff Tom London. Outlaw gang member Jack Kirk murders Edwards. Wild Bill Elliott, who had recovered the money, arrives in time to prevent Kirby from being lynched. Elliott can't understand why there is a wave of lawlessness in Blue Springs but none in the neighboring town of Rockland. Elliott persuades Kirby not to avenge Edwards' murder but leave it up to him to find the guilty party.

Marshal of Reno (Republic, 1944) scene card — Bill Elliott (left) and "Gabby" Hayes (right) discuss strategy after the death of Charles King (on ground).

Kirby relocates to Rockland. Newspaper editor Herbert Rawlinson and Rockland saloon owner LeRoy Mason are behind the outlawry, intending that Rockland be chosen as the county seat. Another murder occurs, with Kirk blaming the crime on Kirby. Elliott knows Kirby is innocent and works his way into Mason's gang. Unknowingly, Elliott confides in Rawlinson, who tells Mason that Elliott is trying to uncover the gang leader's identity. After Elliott has sent Kirby back to Blue Springs, Mason captures Elliott and his sidekick, George "Gabby" Hayes. Elliott's Indian pal, Bobby Blake, helps free the captives. Kirby stops Mason and his gang from stealing money from London. In doing so, Rawlinson and Kirk lead a posse to gun down Kirby, saying he stole the money. Kirby holes up among some rocks as Elliott, Hayes and Blake ride up. Elliott walks up to talk with Kirby, knowing he's not a killer. Rawlinson

sends Kirk to murder Kirby so that Kirby and Elliott cannot talk to each other. Kirk wounds Kirby. Elliott faces Rawlinson and Kirk, and forces them to admit their guilt. Elliott brings Kirk to justice after a short fistfight, and Blake and Hayes stop Rawlinson from getting away. Blue Springs become the county seat.

NOTES AND COMMENTARY: This would be Wild Bill Elliott's last Republic "B" western with George "Gabby" Hayes as his sidekick. Hayes would move back to Roy Rogers' series with *Lights of Old Santa Fe* (Republic, 1944), and would stay with Rogers for thirteen more features, ending with *Heldorado* (Republic, 1946). Hayes subsequently made only big-budget westerns, primarily with Randolph Scott. Elliott and Hayes would appear twice more together, first in *Bells of Rosarita* (Republic, 1945) and then *Wyoming* (Republic, 1947).

Blake Edwards, who played the part of

Lee, Jay Kirby's friend, would appear in one more western. He was a gunman shot down by Rod Cameron in *Panhandle* (Allied Artists, 1948), a film Edwards also co-produced. Edwards then became a screenwriter and director, helming such box office hits as *Operation Petticoat* (Universal-International, 1959), *Breakfast at Tiffany's* (Paramount, 1961), *The Pink Panther* (United Artists, 1963) and *Victor/Victoria* (Metro-Goldwyn-Mayer, 1982). Edwards married celebrated singer-actress Julie Andrews in 1969.

Set decorator George Milo would be nominated for Academy Awards for his work on Alfred Hitchcock's *Psycho* (Paramount, 1960), *Judgment at Nuremberg* (United Artists, 1961) and *That Touch of Mink* (Universal-International, 1962).

Tom Steele doubled Wild Bill Elliott in his *Marshal of Reno* fight scenes.

REVIEW: "Fast moving adventure in the 'Red Ryder' series with a top notch genre cast." *Western Movies*, Pitts.

SUMMATION: Wild Bill Elliott again shows why he's one of the top western stars as he takes charge in this episode. Elliott demonstrates his no-nonsense acting style while easily handling the required action scenes. Out of a fine supporting cast, Jay Kirby delivers a good performance as a tenderfoot who quickly learns the ways of the west. The story is just okay, but good acting and performances elevate this feature to an above-average entry.

The Marshal of Trail City

Century Television Productions (1950)

CAST: Wild Bill Elliott, **"Wild" Bill Elliott**; Cannonball, **Dub "Cannonball" Taylor**; Valley Keene, **Valley Keene**; Timmy, **Timmy Tate**; Red, **Bill Kennedy**; Mr. Phillips, **Tom Hubbard**; Pioneer Woman, **Mildred Huntley**; Burt Kennedy, **Bob Clark**// Town Council Member, **Richard Alexander**.

CREDITS: Director/Producer, **Richard C. Kahn**; Production Associates, **Norman K. Doyle** and **Edward C. Simme**; Screenwriter, **Harold Shumate**; Editor, **William Faris**; Art Director, **Frank Tipper**; Production Manager, **Burnet Lamont**; Cinematographer, **Andy McIntyre**; Sound, **Glen Glenn**.

RUNNING TIME: 26 min.

STORY: Wild Bill Elliott turns down the offer of marshal of Trail City, primarily because of his childhood friendship with Bill Kennedy, who has become a train robber. Later, Elliott takes the marshal's job as a joke and then has to go after outlaw Bob Clark. After a short fight and exchange of shots, Elliott kills Clark. Kennedy likes the idea of Elliott being marshal to protect him after his crimes. Kennedy's latest robbery forces Elliott to arrest him.

NOTES AND COMMENTARY: While riding into Trail City, Elliott notes that he owns the Double Bar A ranch. This was the name of Elliott's actual ranch. "Double Bar A" was a tribute to his daughter, Barbara.

The author was told that Century Television Productions was unhappy with Elliott signing a contract with Monogram Pictures and initiated a lawsuit. The author was unable to find the outcome of the suit, but in any event, Elliott continued his career with Monogram/Allied Artists until 1957.

The most interesting aspect of this television pilot is the opportunity to watch Elliott demonstrate his skill with a cutting horse. In later years, Elliott and his horse, Red Man, would compete for prize money in cutting horse competitions.

SUMMATION: Wild Bill Elliott makes a stalwart hero in this television pilot, but the slight story and poor production values do him in. Elliott possesses a nice screen presence but offers nothing new to his character. The pacing is too slow, as the screenplay takes too much time in introducing regulars Valley Keene, Timmy Tate and Dub Taylor. Richard C. Kahn's direction adds little to the proceedings. It's evident why this pilot didn't sell.

Cavalry Rough-Rider vs. Renegade Gunslinger!

The Maverick

Allied Artists (December, 1952)

A Silvermine Production

CAST: Lieutenant Pete Devlin, **Wild Bill Elliott**; Sergeant Frick, **Myron Healey**; Della Watson, **Phyllis Coates**; Frank Bullit, **Richard Reeves**; Trooper Westman, **Terry Frost**; Trooper Barnham, **Rand Brooks**; Major Hook, **Russell Hicks**; Corporal Johnson, **Robert Bray**; Grandma Watson, **Florence Lake**; George Fane, **Gregg Barton**; Bud Karnes, **Denver Pyle**; William Massey, **Robert Wilke**; Fred Nixon, **Eugene Roth**; John Rowe, **Joel Allen**// Rancher Who Refuses to Fight the Army, **Stanley Price**.

CREDITS: Director, **Thomas Carr**; Assistant Director, **Melville Shyer**; Producer, **Vincent M. Fennelly**; Story and Screenwriter, **Sid Thiel**; Editor, **Sam Fields**; Art Director, **David Milton**; Set Decorator, **Robert Priestley**; Cinematographer; **Ernest Miller**; Special Effects, **Ray Mercer**; Sound, **John Kean**; Music, **Raoul Krushaar**; Set Continuity, **Emile Ehrlich**; Dialogue Supervisor, **Stanley Price**; Color by **Sepiatone**.

LOCATION FILMING: Iverson, California.

RUNNING TIME: 71 min.

STORY: Lt. Wild Bill Elliott, Sgt. Myron Healey and Cpl. Robert Bray are assigned to take unscrupulous rancher Richard Reeves and

The Maverick (Allied Artists, 1952) scene card — Bill Elliott (right) delivers a right to the jaw of Myron Healey (left) as Eugene Roth (center) looks on.

three outlaws to Fort Jeffrey to stand trial for murder and terrorism. Elliott is told the prisoners must arrive at their destination alive. Reeves' cohort, Robert Wilke, is determined to prevent Elliott from completing his mission. On the trail, Elliott encounters a wagon with Phyllis Coates and Florence Lake. Elliott refuses to allow them to accompany the detail. Coates decides to join them anyway, citing freedom to travel the same road. Reeves feigns illness and Coates volunteers to take care of him, against Elliott's wishes. Reeves make an escape attempt, which is stopped by a well-thrown knife into his back by Healey. Elliott's emergency treatment saves Reeves' life. Elliott demotes Healey to Trooper and places Coates under arrest. One of the outlaws, Denver Pyle, offers Healey a large sum of money to help them escape when Wilke and his men attack. Healey accepts Pyle's offer. Wilke and his men attack. Elliott prevents Healey from freeing the prisoners and places him under arrest. Coates joins Elliott in repulsing the outlaws. Wilke sneaks in close, sees Healey with the outlaws, thinks he's guarding them and guns him down. Elliott shoots Wilke and then gets behind the outlaws. Caught in a crossfire, the outlaws surrender. Because of Coates' actions in the gunfight, Elliott drops all charges against her.

Elliott gets his detail safely to Fort Jeffrey, where it looks like a romance is blooming between him and Coates.

NOTES AND COMMENTARY: When Wild Bill Elliott attempts to mount his horse after leaving Phyllis Coates' wagon, watch as his foot slips out of the stirrup. The viewer can take this as a sign of Elliott's fatigue, as well as a cost-saving decision not to shoot the scene over.

Wild Bill Elliott's character name is misspelled as "Delvin" instead of "Devlin" in the closing credits.

REVIEWS: "Routine Wild Bill Elliott western." *Variety*, 12/24/52; "Another good entry in Bill Elliott's final starring western series." *Western Movies*, Pitts.

SUMMATION: In this good Wild Bill Elliott western, Elliott gives a solid performance as a stick-by-the-rules, no-nonsense Army officer who finally learns that there are times when rules can be bent. Phyllis Coates scores in her role as the young lady who humanizes Elliott. Myron Healey's role is written and played in a way that the audience knows that he'll be trouble for Elliott from the moment he appears on-screen. Unfortunately, this tips off the direction the story is headed too soon. Thomas Carr's capable direction is able to generate some suspense.

A Town Mad with Terror ... with Lawlessness Unchecked Until ... Wild Bill Rides Into the Thick of the Trouble!

Mojave Firebrand

Republic (March, 1944)

CAST: Wild Bill Elliott, **Wild Bill Elliott**; Gabby Hayes, **George "Gabby" Hayes**; Abigail Holmes, **Anne Jeffreys**; Tracy Dalton, **LeRoy Mason**; Matt Ganton, **Jack Ingram**; Johnny Taylor, **Harry McKim**; Luke Reed, **Karl Hackett**; Sheriff Barker, **Forrest Taylor**; Mayor Frisbie, **Hal Price**; Nate Bigelow, **Marshall Reed**; Tony Webb, **Kenne Duncan**; Red Collins, **Bud Geary**; Jeff Butler, **Jack Kirk**// "**Sonny**"; Frank Brady, **Fred Graham**; Saloon Patron, **Frank Ellis**; Miners, **Tom London** and **Bob Burns**; Marshal Tom Scott, **Larry Steers**.

CREDITS: Director, **Spencer Bennett**; Associate Producer, **Eddy White**; Screenwriter, **Norman S. Hall**; Editor, **Harry Keller**; Art Director, **Fred Ritter**; Set Decorator, **George Milo**; Cinematographer, **Ernest Miller**; Sound, **Fred Stahl**; Musical Score, **Mort Glickman**.

SONG: "Ring, Ring the Banjo" (Foster)— sung by **George "Gabby" Hayes** and **Anne Jeffreys**, and danced by **Hayes**.

LOCATION FILMING: Iverson and Corriganville, California.

RUNNING TIME: 55 min.

STORY: George "Gabby" Hayes discovers

Mojave Firebrand (Republic, 1944) scene card — Bill Elliott (center) and "Gabby" Hayes (right) look for trouble.

silver and establishes a town devoted to honesty and justice. Instead, Hayes's town becomes a haven for the lawless, led by gambler LeRoy Mason. Wild Bill Elliott rides through town and is asked by Hayes to stay and combat the lawless element. Elliott decides to stay after a failed attempt on his life, and finding out that Mason, who he recognizes as a wanted criminal, is behind the nefarious activities. Mason forms the Miners Protective Association to extort money from the miners and to find out when the richest shipments are being transported so his gang can seize them. Elliott gets proof that Mason is behind the protection racket. Since Hayes is Elliott's only witness, Mason dry-gulches Hayes. Hayes is saved when the bullet hits a Bible in Hayes' pocket. Knowing that it's only a matter of time before Elliott arrests him, Mason and his gang decide to rob

the bank and leave the area. Elliott and Hayes foil the holdup attempt, but a gunfight ensues. The gang is rounded up and Mason's criminal career comes to an end when he tries to outdraw Elliott.

NOTES AND COMMENTARY: Stuntman Tom Steele doubled Wild Bill Elliott in this feature.

REVIEW: "Well made and fast moving Bill Elliott vehicle." *Western Movies*, Pitts.

SUMMATION: This is one of the best entries in the Wild Bill Elliott series, with good acting from the principals, especially Wild Bill Elliott, sidekick George "Gabby" Hayes and villain LeRoy Mason. Director Spencer Bennett paces the film at breakneck speed. Cinematographer Ernest Miller chips in with some excellent camerawork, primarily in the chase sequences and the brawl in Mason's saloon.

Watch Bandits Run to Cover ... When "Wild Bill" Starts Taking Over!

North from the Lone Star

Columbia (March, 1941)

CAST: Wild Bill Hickok, **Bill Elliott**; Clint Wilson, **Richard Fiske**; Madge Wilson, **Dorothy Fay**; Cannonball, **Dub Taylor**; "Flash" Kirby, **Arthur Loft**; "Rawhide" Fenton, **Jack Roper**; Spike, **Chuck Morrison**; Lucy Belle, **Claire Rochelle**; Slats, **Al Rhein**; Dusty Daggett, **Edmund Cobb**// "Sonny"; Saloon Patron, **Lane Bradford**; Bartender, **Hank Bell**; Henchmen, **Steve Clark** and **Art Mix**; Saloon Brawler, **Francis Walker**.

CREDITS: Director, **Lambert Hillyer**; Pro-
ducer, **Leon Barsha**; Screenwriter, **Charles Francis Royal**; Editor, **Mel Thorsen**; Cinematography, **Benjamine Kline**.

SONGS: "Home on the Range" (Traditional)—played by **Dub Taylor**; "Of Course, It's Your Horse" (M. Drake)—sung and played by **Dub Taylor**; "Saturday Night in San Antone" (M. Drake)—sung and played by **Dub Taylor**.

LOCATION FILMING: Iverson, California.

RUNNING TIME: 58 min.

STORY: Bill Elliott arrives in Deadwood to

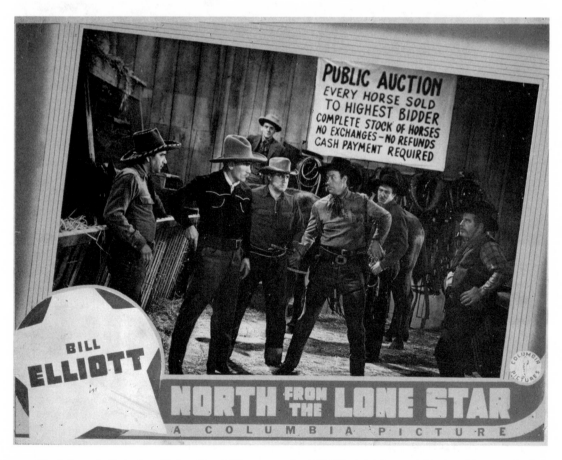

North from the Lone Star (Columbia, 1941) scene card — Bill Elliott (right center) points his gun at Jack Roper (left center) as Chuck Morrison (center), Richard Fiske (center back) and unidentified actors look on.

settle down. He finds an old nemesis, Arthur Loft, taking over all the businesses. When Loft tries to gain control of Richard Fiske's livery stable, Elliott steps in and stops Loft's henchmen. Loft offers Elliott the marshal's job and Elliott finally accepts. When Elliott arrests Fiske for shooting one of Loft's henchmen, Loft believes Elliott is working with him. Actually, Elliott jailed Fiske to prevent him from being lynched. Fiske's sister, Dorothy Fay, tries to break Fiske out of jail, but Elliott had him removed to a neighboring county. With Loft out of town, Elliott finds the gambling in Loft's saloon is crooked and closes the saloon down. Elliott and Loft give each other thirty minutes to leave town. Elliott and his deputy, Dub Taylor, go to Fiske's livery stable where Fay is being held prisoner. A gunfight ensues and Loft is about to get Elliott under his gunsight. Fiske, who has escaped from the neighboring county's jail, returns in time to help Elliott. Loft and Fiske exchange shots, killing each other. Realizing he cannot settle down in Deadwood, Elliott rides off to new adventures.

NOTES AND COMMENTARY: Dorothy Fay would become the wife of the great western star Tex Ritter.

REVIEWS: "Nicely made western, chuckful of swift action, nicely compact script job. Besides Bill Elliott's neat portrayal of the Wild Bill Hickok role, Dub Taylor provides essential comic relief as Cannonball, his sidekick." *Variety*, 6/25/41; "Actionful Bill Elliott vehicle with a well staged saloon fight sequence." *Western Movies*, Pitts.

SUMMATION: This is another good Wild Bill Hickok adventure. Bill Elliott carries off the action and acting capably, having to fend off two lovely ladies, Dorothy Fay and Claire Rochelle, in this one. A nicely crafted gunfight in the final reel greatly enhances this western. *North from the Lone Star* is a town-bound western, which director Lambert Hillyer paces adroitly.

Bill and Tex Give You Top Thrills and Action!

North of the Rockies

Columbia (April, 1942)

ALTERNATE TITLES: *False Clues, Royal Canadians* and *Roundup Time in the Rockies*.

CAST: Sergeant Wild Bill Cameron, **Bill Elliott**; Tex Martin, **Tex Ritter**; Cannonball Rideaux, **Frank Mitchell**; Lydia Rogers, **Shirley Patterson**; Jim Bailey, **Larry Parks**; Lionel Morgan, **John Miljan**; Lazare, **Ian MacDonald**; Constable McDowell, **Lloyd Bridges**; Flora Bailey, **Gertrude Hoffman**; John Callan, **Earl Gunn**; Captain Adams, **Boyd Irwin**// "White Flash"; "Sonny"; George, **George Morrell**.

CREDITS: Director, **Lambert Hillyer**; Producer, **Leon Barsha**; Screenwriter, **Herbert Dalmas**; Editor, **Mel Thorsen**; Art Directors, **Lionel Banks** and **Perry Smith**; Cinematography, **George Meehan**.

SONGS: "Jog, Jog, Jogging Along" — sung by **Tex Ritter**; "Get Your Man, Mountie Boy, Get Your Man" — sung by **Tex Ritter**; "Ninety Nine Days" — sung by **Tex Ritter**.

LOCATION FILMING: Iverson, Lake Arrowhead, Big Bear and Baldwin Dry Lake, California.

RUNNING TIME: 60 min.

STORY: Mounted Police Sergeant Bill Elliott is trying to run down thieves who have been stealing furs in Canada and smuggling them into the United States. The fur thieves, led by John Miljan, are using Gertrude Hoffman's ranch in the United States as a base of operations. Hoffman's grandson, Larry Parks, has become a member of the gang. Foreman Tex Ritter wants to stop the gang's activities and break Parks from Miljan's influence. Ritter refuses to cooperate with Elliott until he can accomplish his mission. Miljan makes one last big robbery before leaving the area. Ritter has a chance to free Parks from Miljan's influence and rides to round up the fur thieves. A gunfight between Ritter and the fur thieves ensues. Elliott follows and arrives in time to

North of the Rockies (Columbia, 1942) scene card — Mountie Bill Elliott (right) questions John Miljan (center) and Ian MacDonald (left) about a recent fur robbery.

prevent Miljan's henchman, Ian MacDonald, from ambushing Ritter. In the fight, Parks tries to stop Miljan from resisting arrest and is killed. Elliott and Ritter band together to bring Miljan and his men into custody and recover the stolen furs.

NOTES AND COMMENTARY: In the credits, Bill Elliott's screen name is "Wild Bill Cameron." At no time is Elliott called Wild Bill, nor does he declare himself to be a peaceable man.

There is a nice bit of dialogue between Frank Mitchell and Boyd Irwin after Mitchell tells of trouble at the trading post and Irwin sends Elliott to take care of the situation:

Mitchell: "You're sending only one man!"

Irwin: "There's only one riot, Cannonball."

REVIEW: Well-made actioner that is somewhat hurt by having its two stars spending most of their screen time as opponents." *Western Movies*, Pitts.

SUMMATION: This is a very good Bill Elliott-Tex Ritter adventure. Both Elliott and Ritter perform the heroics admirably, even though they spend too much time battling each other, both verbally and physically. Lambert Hillyer directs at a breakneck pace, even generating some suspense in the process.

Crossroads of Adventure ... Highroad to Romance!

Old Los Angeles

Republc (April, 1948)

ALTERNATE TITLES: *California Outpost* and *In Old Los Angeles.*

CAST: Bill Stockton, **William Elliott**; Johnny Morrell, **John Carroll**; Marie Marlowe, **Catherine McLeod**; Luis Savarin, **Joseph Schildkraut**; Sam Bowie, **Andy Devine**; Estelita Del Rey, **Estelita Rodriguez**; Senora Del Rey, **Virginia Brissac**; Marshal Luckner, **Grant Withers**; Tonio Del Rey, **Tito Renaldo**; Clyborne, **Roy Barcroft**; Larry Stockton, **Henry Brandon**; Diego, **Julian Rivero**; Horatius P. Gassoway, **Earle Hodgins**; Miguel, **Augie Gomez**// "Stormy Knight"; Waiter, **Chris-Pin Martin**; Rancher, **Sam Flint**; Del Ray Housekeeper, **Rosa Turich**; Stage Passenger, **Paul Hurst**.

CREDITS: Director/Associate Producer, **Joe Kane**; Story, **Clements Ripley**; Screenwriters, **Gerald Adams** and **Clements Ripley**; Editor, **Richard L. Van Enger**; Art Director, **James Sullivan**; Set Decorators, **John McCarthy, Jr.** and **Charles Thompson**; Cinematographer, **William Bradford**; Costumes, **Adele Palmer**; Hair Stylist, **Peggy Gray**; Makeup, **Bob Mark**; Sound, **Fred Stahl** and **Howard Wilson**; Musical Director, **Morton Scott**; Musical Score, **Nathan Scott** and **Ernest Gold**; Special Effects, **Howard** and **Theodore Lydecker**.

SONGS: "Eres Tan Fina" (Gonzales and Scott)—sung by **Estelita Rodriguez**; "On the Boulevard (Jesuita En Chihuahua)" (Mendoza and Elliott)—sung by **Catherine McLeod**; "Jarabe Tapatio" (Traditional)—sung by **Estelita Rodriguez**; "Ever Faithful" (Traditional)—English version sung by **Catherine McLeod**, and Spanish version sung by **Estelita Rodriguez**; "Tus Ojos" (Traditional)—sung by **John Carroll**.

LOCATION FILMING: Iverson, California.

RUNNING TIME: 88 min.

STORY: William Elliott and his pal Andy Devine come to Los Angeles to prospect for gold with Elliott's brother, Henry Brandon. Saloon owner Joseph Schildkraut, the secret leader of the renegades plaguing the area, tells Elliott that Brandon has been murdered. Elliott swears vengeance but at the same time falls in love with singer Catherine McLeod. Elliott believes that Marshal Grant Withers and cowboy John Carroll are members of the outlaw gang. Carroll and rancher Virginia Brissac's daughter, Estelita Rodriguez, are in love. Elliott asks McLeod to marry him, but she turns him down for Schildkraut and his money. Now Elliott thinks Schildkraut, Withers or McLeod could be the gang leader. Brissac believes either Schildkraut or McLeod could be a friend. Elliott tells McLeod where the ranchers have been smelting gold. Carroll leads a raid on the ranchers but is captured by Elliott. Withers breaks Carroll free, intending to shoot him, but Carroll reverses the situation and kills Withers. Carroll tells the renegades he's the new leader, but Schildkraut shows up to give him orders. Carroll then kills Schildkraut and begins a reign of terror. Elliott finds that McLeod is a government agent working undercover. Elliott gathers Devine and the ranchers, and attacks the outlaws. All the renegades are killed or captured except Carroll. Carroll follows Elliott into Los Angeles and the two men begin to stalk each other. Rodriguez tries to get Carroll to go away with her. This gives Carroll's position away to Elliott. Elliott's bullet hits Carroll. Carroll returns fire but his bullet hits Rodriguez, who was running to his side. Two more shots from Elliott's pistol end Carroll's outlaw career. Rodriguez is taken to a nearby doctor, while, outside, Elliott and McLeod contemplate life together.

NOTES AND COMMENTARY: William Elliott appeared on Bing Crosby's *Philco Radio Time* to plug *Old Los Angeles* on March 24, 1948.

In April, a Quaker Puffed Rice cartoon ad appeared in the Sunday comics sections plugging *Old Los Angeles*, starring not "William" or "Wild Bill," but simply "Bill Elliott." In the ad,

WILLIAM
ELLIOTT
JOHN
CARROLL
CATHERINE
McLEOD
JOSEPH
SCHILDKRAUT

OLD LOS ANGELES

A Republic Picture

Old Los Angeles (Republic, 1948) scene card — Bill Elliott (center) is poised to hit John Carroll (right) as Estelita Rodriguez watches in horror.

Elliott takes two youngsters, a boy and a girl, to the set of *Old Los Angeles*, where they watch Elliott in action. As they leave, Elliott stresses the importance of a breakfast of Puffed Rice cereal.

Old Los Angeles was reissued in 1953 as *California Outpost*. The film had been re-edited to a 60 min. running time.

Catherine McLeod agreed to appear in *Old Los Angeles* if Republic would release her from her contract with the studio. McLeod, who didn't care for William Elliott, was happy to work again with John Carroll but was unhappy with his harsh treatment of Estelita Rodriguez during the production of the film.

House Peters, Jr. commented about his part in the film: "A minor role. *Old Los Angeles* was the first thing I did after I came out of the service." The author couldn't spot Peters behind all the masked renegades.

Footage from *The Dark Command* (Republic, 1940) was used in the opening montage sequence.

REVIEWS: "An overlong oatuner with a story that could have been told in a breezy 60 minutes. Film shapes up as only fair entertainment. William Elliott plays a Sir Galahad–like warrior, handy with his dukes and six-guns, who makes a fearsome nemesis for renegades to face." *Variety*, 4/7/48; "Fast paced and quite entertaining Bill Elliott 'A' effort." *Western Movies*, Pitts.

SUMMATION: This is a good, fast-moving action western. William Elliott is perfect as a man of vengeance seeking his brother's murderer. Elliott gets to show emotion as he learns of his brother's death, and also at the shooting of Estelita Rodriguez. To the film's betterment, Elliott is given two fine villains to fight — John Carroll as a reckless, overly ambitious killer, and Joseph Schildkraut as a man who wants control of all the land in the Los Angeles area. Catherine McLeod gives a good performance as the woman Elliott loves but doesn't know if he can trust. Joe Kane's direction is on-target.

His Courage Was Challenged!!!
Turning His Fear and Timidity to Ferocious Fighting Ability!!!

Overland Mail Robbery

Republic (November, 1943)

CAST: Wild Bill Elliott, **Wild Bill Elliott**; Gabby, **George "Gabby" Hayes**; Judy Goodrich, **Anne Jeffreys**; Ma Patterson, **Alice Fleming**; John Patterson, **Weldon Heyburn**; Tom Hartley, **Kirk Alyn**; David Patterson, **Roy Barcroft**; Lola Patterson, **Nancy Gay**; Jimmy Hartley, **Peter Michael**; Slade, **Bud Geary**; Sheriff, **Tom London**// "**Sonny**"; Townsmen, **LeRoy Mason** and **Frank Ellis**; Stage Driver, **Hank Bell**; Mrs. Bradley, **Maxine Doyle**; Stage-line Employees, **Jack Rockwell, Jack O'Shea** and **Frank McCarroll**; Hank, **Kenne Duncan**; Henchman, **Bob Wilke**.

CREDITS: Director, **John English**; Associate Producer, **Louis Gray**; Story, **Robert Yost**; Screenwriters, **Bob Williams** and **Robert Yost**; Editor, **Charles Craft**; Art Director, **Fred Ritter**; Set Decorator, **Charles Thompson**; Cinematography, **John MacBurnie**; Sound, **Earl Crain, Sr.**; Original Music, **Mort Glickman**.

SONG: "Coming Home" — sung by **Anne Jeffreys**.

LOCATION FILMING: Iverson and Corriganville, California.

RUNNING TIME: 56 min.

STORY: Alice Fleming and her sons, Weldon Heyburn and Roy Barcroft, want control of the local stage line, even resorting to murder to obtain it. Learning that the last heir, co-owner Kirk Alyn, is bringing money to keep the stage line going, Barcroft holds up the coach and is about to shoot Alyn when Texas Ranger Wild Bill Elliott interferes. Elliott is investigating the death of Alyn's brother, Peter Michael. Since Alyn is a tenderfoot and not known, Elliott decides to impersonate Alyn. Elliott proves to be an obstacle to Fleming's plans. When an attempt on Elliott's life fails, Fleming is determined to find out who he is. Fleming's niece, Nancy Gay, learns that Alyn is the real heir, and Alyn is kidnapped. Barcroft frames Elliott for murder. Stageline manager George "Gabby" Hayes discovers Elliott is a Texas Ranger and helps him escape. Fleming convinces the other co-owner, Anne Jeffreys, to sell her share of the stage line. Elliott and Hayes find where Alyn is being held. Alyn is rescued and all the gang members captured except Heyburn. Elliott gives chase and corners Heyburn. The two men fight; in the struggle, Heyburn falls from a high precipice to his death. Alyn and Jeffreys have fallen in love and they get married.

NOTES AND COMMENTARY: Alice Fleming would join Wild Bill Elliott in his Red Ryder series for the 1944–45 season. Fleming would portray the Duchess in 16 episodes.

Footage was lifted from *Overland Mail Robbery* to aid Monte Hale in his chase and fight with Rory Mallinson in *Prince of the Plains* (Republic, 1949).

Kirk Alyn would later become a major serial hero at both Republic and Columbia studios, turning out 6 cliffhangers, three for Columbia and three for Republic. He was best known as Superman/Clark Kent in *Superman* (Columbia, 1948) and *Atom Man vs. Superman* (Columbia, 1950), although he didn't receive billing in either serial. Producer Sam Katzman wanted the audience to believe that it was really Superman on the silver screen. Okay, how did he explain all the flying sequences being animation?

Look closely and you can see stuntman Tom Steele doubling for Elliott in the *Overland Mail Robbery* fight scenes.

REVIEWS: "This is a standard addition to

Overland Mail Robbery (Republic, 1943) scene card — Kirk Alyn, Anne Jeffreys, Tom London, Bill Elliott and an unhappy "Gabby" Hayes (left to right).

the Wild Bill Elliott series. Difficulties with the plot might have been overcome with more paceful direction and less standard action shots." *Variety*, 12/22/43; "Standard but fast paced and actionful Republic entry." *Western Movies*, Pitts.

SUMMATION: This is a good, fast-moving Wild Bill Elliott western. Elliott is perfect as the stalwart hero, looking and acting the part in fine style. Kirk Alyn, Alice Fleming and George "Gabby" Hayes lend worthy support. John English's direction is noteworthy, making good use of an excellent screenplay by Bob Williams and Robert Yost, and assisted by the fine cinematography by John MacBurnie, especially in the action sequences.

Overland with Kit, Peerless Frontier Fighter!
Mighty Saga of the Winning of the West in the Year's Top Chapter Play!

Overland with Kit Carson

Columbia (August, 1939)

CAST: Kit Carson, **Bill Elliott**; Carmelita, **Iris Meredith**; David Brent, **Richard Fiske**; Andy, **Bobby Clack**; Arthur Mitchell, **Trevor Bardette**; John Baxter, **LeRoy Mason**; Pierre, **Olin Francis**; Tennessee, **James Craig**; Dr. Parker, **Francis Sayles**; Winchester, **Kenneth MacDonald**; Drake, **Dick Curtis**; Natchez, **Dick Botiller**; Jim Stewart, **Hal Taliaferro**; Ma Stewart, **Flo Campbell**; Captain Gilbert, **John Tyrrell**; Don Jose, **Francisco Moran**; Broken-Hand Fitzpatrick, **Hank Bell**; Juanita, **Irene Herndon**; Thor, **Ernie Adams**; Red, **Jack Rockwell**; Tom, **Stanley Brown**; Bill Cooper, **Art Mix**// "Pinto"; Midnight, **Blackie**; White Eagle, **Lee Prather**; Vice-President, **Edward LeSaint**; Henry Clay, **Robert Fiske**; Colonel Marino, **Martin Garralaga**; Running Wolf, **Iron Eyes Cody**; Stevens, **Carl Stockdale**.

CREDITS: Directors, **Sam Nelson** and **Norman Deming**; Screenwriters, **Joseph F. Poland**, **Morgan B. Cox** and **Ned Dandy**; Editors, **Richard Fantl** and **Jerry Thoms**; Cinematographers, **Benjamin Kline** and **George Meehan**.

LOCATION FILMING: Cave Lake, Zion National Park, Kaibab Forest and Kanab, Utah, and Red Rock Canyon, California.

RUNNING TIME: 258 min.

CHAPTER TITLES: Chapter 1, "Doomed Men"; Chapter 2, "Condemned to Die"; Chapter 3, "The Flight for Life"; Chapter 4, "The Ride of Terror"; Chapter 5, "The Path of Doom"; Chapter 6, "Rendezvous with Death"; Chapter 7, "The Killer Stallion"; Chapter 8, "The Devil's Nest"; Chapter 9, "Blazing Peril"; Chapter 10, "The Black Raiders"; Chapter 11, "Foiled"; Chapter 12, "The Warning"; Chapter 13, "Terror in the Night"; Chapter 14, "Crumbling Walls"; Chapter 15, "Unmasked."

STORY: The mysterious Pegleg, with his army of Black Raiders, plans to take over a western territory for his own personal empire. Pegleg uses his black stallion, Blackie, to trample anyone who disobeys his orders. Army scout Bill Elliott and Lt. Richard Fiske are assigned to stop Pegleg's scheme. Elliott, at his own peril, begins to rebuff Pegleg's plans. At Stewart's Post, the Raiders are terrorizing the trappers. Thanks to Iris Meredith, Elliott soon suspects one of the trappers is masquerading as Pegleg. Finally, Elliott is able to infiltrate Pegleg's stronghold. Elliott is discovered and, after a fight, almost killed in an explosion. Thought to be dead, Elliott overhears Pegleg's plans to wipe out the trappers and gets a clue to Pegleg's identity. Elliott rides to warn the trappers on Pegleg's horse. Elliott tricks Trevor Bardette into revealing he is the leader of the Black Raiders. Bardette attempts to escape but is bulldogged from his saddle by Elliott. An exchange of punches leaves Elliott dazed. Before Bardette can kill Elliott, his stallion turns on him and tramples him to death. Elliott and Meredith ride to Meredith's home in Santa Fe, with the promise he will bring her back to Stewart's Post.

NOTES AND COMMENTARY: The serial utilized two production units. Directors Sam Nelson and Norman Deming each led one. In each episode, one would direct Bill Elliott and his followers, while the other would follow Trevor Bardette and his men.

Trevor Bardette undertook physical hardships to appear in this serial. When on-camera as Pegleg, Bardette had to be fitted with a harness that had a strap running from his boot to his belt. The right foot was pulled upward and forward. Then the pegleg was strapped to Bardette's knee and around the thigh and calf. Bardette would be in pain and his leg would go to sleep after an hour. Ingenious camera angles were used to heighten the effect. Bardette's double was Earl Bund, a stunt man who only had one leg. Bund also doubled other cast members, while John Daheim doubled Elliott.

Footage from *Overland with Kit Carson* was used in Columbia's final serial, *Blazing the Overland Trail* (Columbia, 1956), with Dennis

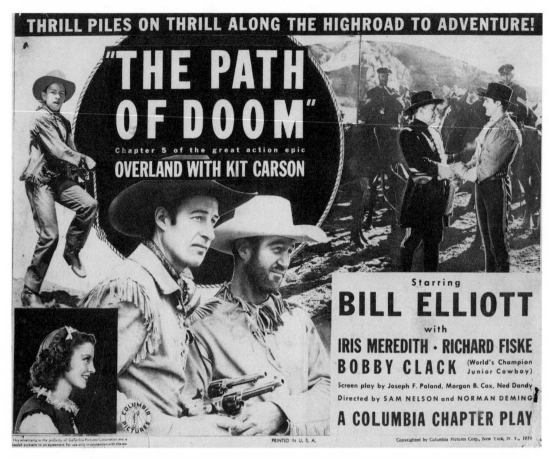

Overland with Kit Carson (Columbia, 1939) title card — upper left shows Bobby Clack; lower left shows Iris Meredith; left center shows Bill Elliott (left) and unidentified actor; upper right shows John Tyrrell and Richard Fiske.

Moore and Lee Roberts dressed to match Bill Elliott and Richard Fiske, respectively. Twelve of the chapter endings were utilized as cliffhangers or other action sequences.

Overland with Kit Carson's ending for chapter 2 was later recycled to unspool behind the opening titles for *Massacre Canyon* (Columbia, 1954).

REVIEWS: "Bill Elliott in a lame script filled with Indians, renegades and gun runners 'somewhere in the west.' For the juvs, 14 and under." *Variety*, 10/11/39; "There is nothing really special about this cliffhanger other than Bill Elliott holds it all together in good fashion as he essays the title role." *Western Movies*, Pitts.

SUMMATION: Given that one of the screenwriters was Ned Dandy, it would have been a pleasure to state that the serial had a "dandy" script, but it just wasn't to be. Bill Elliott was the hero and he handles the role in proper serial hero fashion, without time for the little nuances that made him a top western star. In addition to Elliott, the serial had a great mystery villain, a fine supporting cast and a lickety-split pace. But to its detriment, the cliffhanger endings were too standard, and offered totally unbelievable resolutions in most instances. The serial was loud, with major gunfights in almost every chapter; thousands of bullets were fired, sometimes at close range, but there were very few casualties. In chapter 12, both Elliott and heroine Iris Meredith are shot — with no resulting sign of injury. Even when co-hero Richard Fiske is shot, he remarks to Elliott that he was only stunned. This could have been one of the great serials, but instead comes in only as average (and that only because of Elliott's presence and the strong performance by Trevor Bardette as Pegleg). Elliott overcomes the bad guys but can't overcome the script given him here.

When Red's Away the Rats Will Play ...
But He Has an Uncanny Knack for Showing Up at the Right Place at the Wrong Time ... for the Outlaws!

Phantom of the Plains

Republic Pictures (September, 1945)

CAST: Red Ryder, **Wild Bill Elliott**; Little Beaver, **Bobby Blake**; the Duchess, **Alice Fleming**; Fancy Charlie (Talbot Champneys), **Ian Keith**; Ace Hanlon, **William Haade**; Celeste, **Virginia Christine**; Pete Burdett, **Bud Geary**; Banker, **Henry Hall**; Chuck, **Fred Graham**; Sheriff, **Jack Kirk**; Buck, **Jack Rockwell**// "Thunder"; the Duchess' Suitors, **Tom London** and **Earle Hodgins**.

CREDITS: Director, **Lesley Selander**; Associate Producer, **R.G. Springsteen**; Screenwriters, **Charles Kenyon** and **Earle Snell**; Editor, **Charles Craft**; Art Director, **Hilyard Brown**; Set Decorator, **Charles Thompson**; Cinematographer, **William Bradford**; Sound, **Ed Borschell**; Makeup, **Bob Mark**; Musical Director, **Richard Cherwin**.

LOCATION FILMING: Iverson, California.

RUNNING TIME: 55 min.

SOURCE: Based on Fred Harman's famous NEA comic, by special arrangement with Stephen Slesinger.

STORY: Wild Bill Elliott and his pal Bobby Blake return to Blue Springs to find that Alice Fleming, Elliott's aunt, is engaged to marry a titled Englishman, Ian Keith. Keith has convinced Fleming to liquidate all her assets and move with him to England. Keith, with his associate, Virginia Christine, plans to murder Fleming and escape with Fleming's money. Keith is recognized by Bud Geary; Geary and Keith had been cellmates in prison. Geary and his partner, William Haade, plan to cut themselves in on Keith's scheme. When Keith attempts to abuse Thunder, Elliott begins to have doubts about Keith's authenticity and starts checking into his past. Knowing Elliott could upset his plans, Keith tells Haade and Geary that they will be cut in on the scheme if they will take care of Elliott. As Fleming prepares to leave Blue Springs with Keith and Christine, Elliott and Blake are captured and held captive in Haade's saloon. Not trusting Keith, Haade rides after the stagecoach to make certain Keith splits the money as promised. Elliott and Blake are able to free themselves and ride to the rescue. Haade reaches the stage as Keith prepares to murder Fleming, and hears that Keith plans to double-cross him. Elliott arrives on the scene. Keith and Haade try to escape on the stagecoach. Elliott boards the coach and begins fighting with the two men. Keith falls from the coach. Elliott and Haade engage in a terrific struggle. Meanwhile, in the coach, Fleming and Christine begin fighting over a pistol. Before Fleming gains the upper hand, the pistol discharges, with the bullet going through the roof of the coach, killing Haade. Elliott stops the runaway coach to find Blake and Sheriff Jack Kirk coming toward them, with Keith under arrest.

NOTES AND COMMENTARY: *Texas Manhunt* was the intended release title for this film. Posters and ads had been prepared. The change was precipitated by the realization that PRC released the Bill Boyd-Art Davis-Lee Powell series western, *Texas Manhunt*, in January 1942.

This was the third appearance of Red Ryder's arch enemy, Ace Hanlon. The character had been played previously by Noah Beery in the serial *The Adventures of Red Ryder* (Republic, 1940), and by Glenn Strange in *The San Antonio Kid* (Republic, 1944). Ace Hanlon's final screen appearance was in Jim Bannon's *Roll, Thunder, Roll* (Eagle-Lion, 1949), portrayed again by Glenn Strange. Interestingly enough, the Hanlon character is killed off in each of the Republic productions.

Phantom of the Plains (Republic, 1945) scene card — Bill Elliott (left) and William Haade (center) in a hand-to-hand struggle.

Phantom of the Plains sports two glaring production gaffs. For the first, Ian Keith asks, "When's the next stage to Blue Springs?"— while he is *in* Blue Springs. For the second, while riding to Alice Fleming's rescue, Wild Bill Elliott's gun falls out of his holster — but in the next scene the pistol has miraculously returned to his holster.

REVIEW: "So-so 'Red Ryder' episode." *Western Movies*, Pitts.

SUMMATION: *Phantom of the Plains* is a fast-moving, exciting "B" western. Wild Bill Elliott is in good form as Red Ryder, both in acting and action. William Haade and Bud Geary make good adversaries. Keith is adequate but has a tendency to overact. Alice Fleming, Bobby Blake and Virginia Christine add good support. Director Lesley Selander keeps things moving briskly.

Defying Death ... to Wipe Out a Swindling Gang of Cut-Throats!

Pioneers of the Frontier

Columbia (February, 1940)
A Wild Bill Saunders Adventure
ALTERNATE TITLE: *The Anchor.*

CAST: Wild Bill Saunders, **Bill Elliott**; Joan Darcey, **Linda Winters**; Matt Brawley, **Dick Curtis**; Cannonball, **Dub Taylor**; Dave, **Stanley Brown**; Bart, **Richard Fiske**; Jim Darcey, **Carl Stockdale**; Mort Saunders, **Lafe McKee**; Lem Wilkins, **Ralph McCullough**; Marshal Larsen, **Al Bridge**// Settler, **Hank Bell**; Appleby, **George Chesebro**; Ed Carter, **Edmund Cobb**; Tommy, **Buddy Cox**; Stagecoach Agent, **Ralph Peters**; Henchmen, **Francis Walker** and Black-jack Ward; Rancher, **Jack Kirk**, Townsmen, **Jim Corey** and **Kenne Duncan**.

CREDITS: Director, **Sam Nelson**; Screenwriter, **Fred Myton**; Editor, **James Sweeney**; Cinematographer, **George Meehan**.

LOCATION FILMING: Iverson, California.

RUNNING TIME: 58 min.

STORY: Dick Curtis murders Bill Elliott's uncle, Lafe McKee. Curtis then takes over McKee's lands and plans to extort money from the ranchers who work on McKee's spread. Linda Winters sends Elliott a letter asking him to come home at once. Elliott finds that Curtis

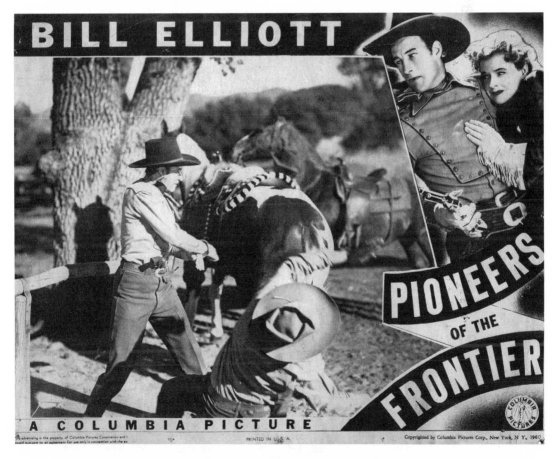

Pioneers of the Frontier (Columbia, 1940) scene card — Bill Elliott (left) knocks an unidentified actor to the ground; the right border shows Bill Elliott and Linda Winters.

wants to be king of the vast area. With help from Winters and rancher Dub Taylor, Elliott sets a trap to catch Curtis and his men. Curtis is informed of the trap. He and his men trap Winters and the ranchers. Curtis and a few henchmen go after Elliott. Taylor warns Elliott. Elliott's quick thinking and his ability with his six-guns brings an end to Curtis' dream of power. Elliott rides off to new adventures.

NOTES AND COMMENTARY: Columbia's continuity lapsed as Stanley Brown is shown with his arm in a sling *before* Bill Elliott wounds him.

Linda Winters was billed as Dorothy Comingore in the classic film *Citizen Kane* (RKO, 1941). Winters played Susan Alexander, an aspiring opera singer with no great talent, and Orson Welles's mistress.

REVIEWS: "Very good Bill Elliott actioner." *Western Movies*, Pitts; "Action-packed Elliott entry." *The Western*, Hardy.

SUMMATION: This is a good, fast-moving action western bolstered by solid performances from Bill Elliott, Dick Curtis and Dub Taylor. Elliott is convincing as the stalwart hero, easily handling the action elements while delivering his lines in a convincing manner. Curtis is a strong adversary, and Taylor does a nice turn as Elliott's sidekick.

The Thrilling Story of the Building of the Pony Express.

Plainsman and the Lady

Republic (November, 1946)

ALTERNATE TITLE: *Drumbeats Over Wyoming.*

CAST: Sam Cotton, **William Elliott**; Ann Arnesen, **Vera Ralston**; Cathy Arnesen, **Gail Patrick**; Peter Marquette, **Joseph Schildkraut**; Dringo, **Andy Clyde**; Feisty, **Donald Barry**; Judge Wynters, **Raymond Walburn**; Michael Arnesen, **Reinhold Schunzel**; Senator Twin, **Russell Hicks**; Mr. Russell, **William B. Davidson**; Al, **Paul Hurst**; Manuel, **Charles Judels**; Mr. Sommons, **Byron Foulger**; Sival, **Jack Lambert**; Pete, **Hal Taliaferro**; Matt, **Stuart Hamblin**; Wassac, **Noble Johnson**; Anita Lopez, **Eva Puig**// D.A., **Hank Bell**; Cowboy at the Bar, **Roy Barcroft**; Bartender, **Jack O'Shea**; Deputies, **Tex Terry**, **Chuck Roberson** and **Norman Willis**; Dancers, **Fernando** and **Lola**; Postmaster General, **Joseph Crehan**; Male Secretary, **Grady Sutton**; Doctor, **Charles Morton**; Alvarades, **Martin Garralaga**; Fred Willats, **Eddy Waller**.

CREDITS: Director/Associate Producer, **Joe Kane**; Story, **Michael Uris** and **Ralph Spence**; Screenwriter, **Richard Wormser**; Editor, **Fred Allen**; Art Director, **Gano Chittenden**; Set Decorators, **John McCarthy, Jr.** and **George Milo**; Cinematographer, **Reggie Lanning**; Makeup, **Bob Mark**; Costumes, **Adele Palmer**; Hair Stylist, **Peggy Gray**; Sound, **Richard Tyler**; Original Music, **George Antheil**; Musical Director, **Cy Feuer**; Choreographer, **Fanchon**; Special Effects, **Howard** and **Theodore Lydecker**.

LOCATION FILMING: Mammoth Lakes, Iverson and Lone Pine, California; House Rock Valley and Monument Valley, Utah.

STORY: Adventurer William Elliott decides to join Reinholt Schunzel, William B. Davidson and Russell Hicks in a venture to establish the Pony Express. Elliott's interest is prompted by his affection for Schunzel's daughter, Vera Ralston. Elliott's rival, Joseph Schildkraut, wants the project to fail so he won't lose a valuable mail contract. Gail Patrick, Schunzul's young wife and Schildkraut's mistress, is in league with Schildkraut. As Elliott is scouting for relay stations, Schildkraut's chief henchman, Donald Barry, makes a failed attempt to kill Elliott. Patrick, tired of being married to Schunzel, tells him of her relationship with Schildkraut. This revelation causes Schunzel to have a fatal heart attack. Patrick plans to take over Schunzel's bank and deny funds to start the Pony Express. Elliott blocks Patrick with his threat to reveal Patrick's affair with Schildkraut.

Schildkraut vows to destroy the Pony Express. Schildkraut's renegades attack a relay station. Elliott and his sidekick, Andy Clyde, discover a murdered son of Indian chief Noble Johnson, and that the renegades are dressed as Indians. Elliott sends Clyde to defend the next relay station while he takes the murdered Indian to his tribe. Elliott convinces Johnson that Schildkraut is an enemy of both himself and the Indian tribe. Elliott and the Indians arrive in time to save Clyde from an attack by Schildkraut and his men. Schildkraut attempts to escape. Elliott and Schildkraut trade shots. A Schildkraut bullet wounds Elliott, but Elliott's bullets mortally wound Schildkraut. Schildkraut begs Elliott to rescue a stranded Patrick. Elliott backtracks along Schildkraut's trail and finds the cabin. Elliott realizes that Patrick is not alone, and that Barry is present. Barry fires at Elliott, but his bullet kills Patrick. Elliott's bullets end Barry's murderous career. Elliott and Ralston plan to marry.

NOTES AND COMMENTARY: *Plainsman and the Lady* was re-released in 1954 as *Drumbeats Over Wyoming*. The film was re-edited to a 60-minute running time.

REVIEWS: "William Elliott, Vera Ralston in OK pony express opus. Elliott is very good as the courageous westerner." *Variety*, 11/6/46; "Slick Bill Elliott 'A' vehicle which benefits from good production values and nice support from Don Barry and Gail Patrick." *Western Movies*, Pitts.

SUMMATION: This is a very exciting and basically well-done western feature. William Elliott is perfect as the stalwart hero, handling the action and acting responsibilities nicely, except when enacting a poorly written scene he has with Vera Ralston. The screenplay has Elliott bumbling around trying to kiss Ralston —

Plainsman and the Lady (Republic, 1946) scene card — Bill Elliott; the right border shows Bill Elliott and Vera Ralston.

even burrowing his head in a throw pillow as Ralston evades his advances. The scene was probably meant to be funny, but poor Elliott cannot carry it off, (such a sequence is better suited to the talents of a Bob Hope or Don Knotts). The supporting players are well cast, with accolades going to Andy Clyde and Gail Patrick. Clyde is Elliott's sidekick — this time offering intelligence rather than the bumbling found in the Hopalong Cassidy series. A neat touch is the scene in which Elliott begins to give Clyde advice on how to hand a potential raid on a Pony Express station and suddenly realizes his advice is not necessary. Patrick is a scheming villainess. Watch her performance as she tells her bedridden husband, Reinhold Schunzel, who has a weak heart, that she is involved in an adulteress affair with Joseph Schildkraut. This knowledge causes Schunzel to have a fatal heart attack. Joe Kane directs competently from a good script by Richard Wormser. Reggie Lanning's superior cinematography optimally utilizes the beautiful scenic locations.

Two Famous Stars Keep the Range Hummin' with Bullets and Songs!
Fists Crash ... Hoofs Thunder ... Guns Blaze ... in a Hair-Raising Saga of the West!

Prairie Gunsmoke

Columbia (July, 1942)

CAST: Wild Bill Hickok, **Bill Elliott**; Tex Terrell, **Tex Ritter**; Cannonball, **Frank Mitchell**; Lucy Wade, **Virginia Carroll**; Henry Wade, **Hal Price**; Jim Kelton, **Tristram Coffin**; Spike Allen, **Joe McGuinn**; Sam, **Frosty Royce**; Dan Whipple, **Rick Anderson**// "Sonny"; "White Flash"; Buck Garrick, **Steve Clark**; Ranchers, **Milburn Morante** and **Horace B. Carpenter**; Henchmen, **Art Mix** and **Francis Walker**.

CREDITS: Director, **Lambert Hillyer**; Producer, **Leon Barsha**; Story, **Jack Ganzhorn**; Screenwriter, **Fred Myton**; Editor, **Arthur Seid**; Cinematographer, **Benjamin Kline**.

SONGS: "Where the Buffalo Roam" — sung by **Tex Ritter**; "Someone" — sung by **Tex Ritter**.

LOCATION FILMING: Iverson, California.

RUNNING TIME: 56 min.

STORY: Tristram Coffin wants to control the rangeland because of valuable ore deposits. The only rancher with this knowledge is Rick Anderson, who is murdered by Coffin's henchman Joe McGuinn. Rancher Tex Ritter plans to fight to keep his property. Bill Elliott rides in and is branded one of Coffin's hired gunmen by Ritter, rancher Hal Price and Virginia Carroll, Price's daughter and Ritter's sweetheart. When he's not given a chance to explain, Elliott decides to see Coffin. Coffin offers Elliott the job of running Ritter off his ranch, which Elliott says he'll consider. In an abandoned tunnel on Ritter's ranch, Elliott finds some of the valuable ore. Elliott tells Coffin he wants to be a partner in his scheme. Coffin decides to move fast by ordering the destruction of Ritter's cattle and the kidnapping of both Price and Carroll. Elliott finds proof implicating Coffin in Anderson's murder. Elliott tells Ritter that Anderson was his uncle, and the two men decide to work together. Elliott rescues Price while Ritter goes to Carroll's aid. Ritter and Carroll are pinned down in Anderson's cabin by Coffin and his men. Elliott arrives and the tide is turned. Elliott and Coffin fight. A blow by Elliott knocks Coffin down a mineshaft to his death. Elliott rides on, while Ritter and Carroll now have time for romance.

NOTES AND COMMENTARY: Hal Price's character name is Bill Wade in the cast listing, but in the film, Price is referred to as Henry.

REVIEW: "Pretty good actioner in the Bill Elliott-Tex Ritter series." *Western Movies*, Pitts.

SUMMATION: This is an action-packed, fast-paced, superior western that effectively spotlights the talents of its stars, Bill Elliott and Tex Ritter. Elliott has the better of Ritter in the acting department, especially as he has to react to unfounded accusations about the type of

Prairie Gunsmoke (Columbia, 1942) title card — Bill Elliott (left), Tris Coffin (center, taking a solid left) and Tex Ritter (right).

person he really is. Branded a gunman by Ritter, Hal Price and Virginia Carroll, Elliott's disappointment in being unable to explain himself properly is evident in his reactions, both verbally and in his facial expressions. If you like fisticuffs, there is an abundance, making the film reminiscent of a Charles Starrett-Russell Hayden saga, in addition to plenty of gunplay and hard riding.

Hot Lead Flies ... on the Bullet-Riddled Plain!

Prairie Schooners

Columbia (September, 1940)

A Wild Bill Hickok Adventure

CAST: Wild Bill Hickok, **Bill Elliott**; Virginia Benton, **Evelyn Young**; Cannonball, **Dub Taylor**; Dalton Stull, **Kenneth Harlan**; Wolf Tanner, **Ray Teal**; Jim Gibbs, **Bob Burns**; Cora Gibbs, **Neta Packer**; Adams, **Richard Fiske**; Rusty, **Edmund Cobb**; Chief Sanche, **Jim Thorpe**// "Sonny"; Farmer, **Jim Corey**; Dude Geeter, **Sammy Stein**; Skinny Hutch, **Ned Glass**; Mack, **Merrill McCormick**; Pawnee Boy, **Lucien Maxell**.

CREDITS: Director, **Sam Nelson**; Story, **George Cory Franklin**; Screenwriters, **Robert Lee Johnson** and **Fred Myton**; Editor, **Al Clark**; Cinematography, **George Meehan**.

LOCATION FILMING: Iverson and Lone Pine, California.

RUNNING TIME: 56 min.

STORY: The Kansas farmers have their backs to the wall, given a severe drought and their debt to Kenneth Harlan. Harlan wants the land, knowing it will be valuable in the future. Bill Elliott, spokesman for the farmers, is unable to work out a settlement with Harlan. Elliott persuades the farmers to pull up stakes and relocate to Colorado. Rancher Evelyn Young gives the farmers money to pay their debts on all supplies. Harlan is happy to see the farmers leave until he learns they're heading for Colorado. Harlan's partner Ray Teal has been supplying guns to the Sioux, enemy of the Pawnees, and buying valuable furs from the Pawnees for less than their true value. Settlers in Colorado will ruin this lucrative business. Elliott leads the farmers through perils until they arrive in Pawnee country. Harlan entices Pawnee Chief Jim Thorpe to attack the settlers. The attack is called off when Young is kidnapped. Elliott follows and is captured also. Harlan tells Elliott that Young will be released if the farmers return to Kansas. Elliott agrees but changes his mind when he learns Teal is a blood brother of the Sioux. Harlan and Teal try to escape but are stopped by the Pawnees. The settlers continue on their trek. Elliott decides to settle down, but Young tells him he never will as long as he can throw a leg over a saddle.

NOTES AND COMMENTARY: Footage from *End of the Trail* (Columbia, 1933) can be viewed as the Indians leave their village.

Jim Thorpe, a Native-American who played the part of Chief Sanche, was a 1912 Olympic Champion. He was a major league

Prairie Schooners (Columbia, 1940) scene card — a grim Bill Elliott (right) and his sidekick Dub Taylor (second right) talk with the settlers as Evelyn Young (left) watches; the left border shows Bill Elliott on Sonny.

outfielder for 7 years, playing for the New York Giants, Cincinnati Reds and the Boston Braves. He also played halfback for 14 years with the Canton Bulldogs, Cleveland Indians, Oorang Indians, Rock Island Independent, New York Giants and Chicago Cardinals. In 1963, Thorpe was a charter member of the Pro Football Hall of Fame. In 1931, he began a 20-year career in films, usually playing an Indian in "B" westerns. Because Thorpe played in a professional sport prior to his appearance in the Olympics, he was stripped of his medals, which were later returned to his family in the early 1990s. Thorpe was named America's greatest athlete of the first half of the 20th Century.

REVIEWS: "Latest Wild Bill Hickok thriller gives Bill Elliott a break showing him a comer in the horse opera rank. As much can't be said for the rambling, implausible yarn. Bill Elliott again as Wild Bill Hickok besides looking like a cowboy, he is also a first-rate thespian." *Variety*, 11/13/40; "Actionful Bill Elliott vehicle." *Western Movies*, Pitts.

SUMMATION: This is a better than average western with a weak ending. Bill Elliott is perfect as the hero in his first Wild Bill Hickok adventure. The chemistry between Elliott and leading lady Evelyn Young is right on target. Just look at the way Young touches Elliott's arm as he rides to talk with Kenneth Harlan, and the way she looks at him when the wagon train rolls through Lone Pine, adding to the enjoyment of the picture. Stock footage makes the film more impressive, even though at times it doesn't match too well. Dub Taylor does well after some unfunny slapstick in his first few scenes. The film would receive a higher rating if there had been a final confrontation between Elliott and villains Harlan and Ray Teal.

His Guns Were Loaded for One Town ... One Man ... One Roaring Moment of Revenge!

Rebel City

Allied Artists (May, 1953)
A Silvermine Production
CAST: Frank Graham, **Wild Bill Elliott**; Jane Dudley, **Marjorie Lord**; Captain Ramsey, **Robert Kent**; Temple, **Keith Richards**; Perry, **Stanford Jolley**; Greeley, **Denver Pyle**; Hardy, **Henry Rowland**; Spencer, **John Crawford**; Spain, **Otto Waldis**; Herb, **Stanley Price**; Colonel Barnes, **Ray Walker**; Sam, **Michael Vallon**; William, **Bill Walker**// Henchman, **Gregg Barton**; Junction City Sheriff, **Pierce Lyden**.
CREDITS: Director, **Thomas Carr**; Assistant Director, **Melville Shyer**; Producer, **Vincent M. Fennelly**; Screenwriter, **Sid Theil**; Editor, **Sam Fields**; Art Director, **David Milton**; Set Decorator, **Theodore Offenbecker**; Cinematographer, **Ernest Miller**; Special Effects, **Ray Mercer**; Sound, **Frank Webster**; Music, **Raoul Kraushaar**; Dialogue Supervisor, **Stanley Price**; Set Continuity, **Mary Chaffee**; Color by **Sepiatone**.
LOCATION FILMING: Iverson, California.
RUNNING TIME: 62 min.

STORY: Gambler Wild Bill Elliott returns to Kansas seeking his father's murderer. Elliot finds that his father's freight business has been taken over by the U.S. Army and his father's wagons are missing. His only clue is counterfeit money his father was holding after being knifed in the back. Elliott soon learns that the Army, led by Colonel Ray Walker and Captain Robert Kent, have no interest in solving his father's murder, so Elliott decides to conduct his own investigation. Elliott is suspicious of the merchants in Belfrey, Kansas, but has no proof. Elliott gets a job hauling freight for Marjorie Lord. On his first day, Elliott is beaten up, has the counterfeit money stolen from him and is framed for murder. Elliott is arrested but released into Lord's custody. All freight going in and out of Belfry is inspected due to suspected Copperhead activity in the area. On one delivery into Belfrey, three riders trail Elliott and Lord. As they near the inspection station, the riders charge and fire at the wagon. Kent, on duty at the station, waves the wagon through.

Rebel City (Allied Artists, 1953) scene card — Marjorie Lord (left) and Bill Elliott (right) watch for trouble.

Elliott, suspicious of why the riders didn't act sooner, inspects the wagon and finds stolen Army rifles. Elliott sets a trap and, with Lord and Walker's help, corrals the Copperhead members and exposes Kent as the leader. Elliott decides to settle down in the freight business, and he and Lord plan to marry.

NOTES AND COMMENTARY: Asked about *Rebel City*, Marjorie Lord responded, "I saw it recently and don't like myself in it too much."

John Crawford commented, "It was a thousand years ago. I remember I had a Polaroid camera, which was a new thing in those days. I remember taking a picture of Bill Elliott. Later I blew it up. I don't remember what happened to it. That's about all I remember of it."

REVIEWS: "Compact and entertaining Bill Elliott vehicle." *Western Movies*, Pitts; "Weak story, Elliott's performance is unconvincing and the direction and other facets of production are far below par." *Motion Picture Guide*, Nash and Ross.

SUMMATION: This is a taut, suspenseful western drama with a nicely turned performance by Wild Bill Elliott. Thanks to Sid Theil's fine script, Elliott effectively registers pain at his father's death, and then strength and determination in pressing forward to find his father's killer.

Gun-Flaming Fury Blasts Bandits to Their Doom!

Return of Daniel Boone

Columbia (May, 1941)

ALTERNATE TITLE: *The Mayor's Nest.*

CAST: Wild Bill Boone, **Bill Elliott**; Ellen Brandon, **Betty Miles**; Cannonball, **Dub Taylor**; Leach Kilgrain, **Ray Bennett**; Mayor Elwell, **Walter Soderling**; Jeb Brandon, **Carl Stockdale**; Red, **Bud Osborne**; Bowers, **Francis Walker**; Tax Collector Fuller, **Lee Powell**; Wagner, **Tom Carter**; Henderson, **Edmund Cobb**; Melinda and Matilda, **the Rodik Twins//** "**Sonny**"; Lash Flanders, **Buel Bryant**; Eddie Flanders, **Edwin Bryant**; Sheriff of Bisbee, **Steve Clark**; Telegrapher, **Murdock Mac-** Quarrie; Wagon Driver, **Hank Bell**; Townsman, **Tex Cooper.**

CREDITS: Director, **Lambert Hillyer**; Story, **Paul Franklin**; Screenwriters, **Paul Franklin** and **Joseph Hoffman**; Editor, **Mel Thorsen**; Cinematographer, **Philip Tannura.**

SONGS: "Golden Days and Silvery Nights"—sung by **Dub Taylor** and **Verda Rodik**; "A Cowboy's a Man for Me"—sung by **Verda Rodik**; "Beware of the Company You Keep"—sung by **Dub Taylor**; "When It's Hitchin' Time in the Chapel"—sung by **the Rodik Twins.**

Return of Daniel Boone (Columbia, 1941) scene card—Betty Miles (right) exchanges horses with Bill Elliott (left) at gunpoint.

LOCATION FILMING: Corriganville, California.

RUNNING TIME: 61 min.

STORY: In Pecos, ranchers, led by Carl Stockdale's daughter Betty Miles, are complaining about the unjust tax increases instigated by saloon owner Ray Bennett. Tax collector Lee Powell, attempting to collect taxes from Stockdale, struggles over a gun and is killed by Miles. Miles, in her escape, needs a fresh horse and forces Bill Elliott, at gunpoint, to swap horses. Riding into Pecos on Miles' horse, Elliott gets into a fight with two of Bennett's henchmen and whips both. Bennett offers Elliott the job of tax collector. Elliott believes Bennett and Mayor Walter Soderling are working together to get the ranches and sell them for a huge profit. Elliott runs a bluff and sees Bennett open Soderling's safe. This proves that Bennett and Soderling are working together to defraud the ranchers. Bennett attempts to escape but Elliott brings him to justice. Elliott leaves for new adventures—to the obvious displeasure of Miles.

NOTES AND COMMENTARY: In the early scenes of the film, Betty Miles is riding Bill Elliott's horse, Sonny. At the point of a gun, Miles forces Elliott to swap horses. Elliott then rides Sonny for the rest of the film. It is now believed Elliott, who had multiple horses named Sonny, sold one of his horses to Miles. Miles' Sonny received billing in *Lone Star Law Man* (Monogram, 1941) and in programs during her brief circus career.

In a continuity lapse, Bill Elliott can be seen losing his hat when he bulldogs Ray Bennett from his horse, but as they rise from the ground, Elliott's hat is firmly on his head when the two men begin a rugged fistfight.

Is this a case of ménage á trois? As the film ends, Dub Taylor is seen arm in arm with the Rodik Twins, both of whom have professed undying love for him.

REVIEWS: "Okay Bill Elliott western." *Western Movies*, Pitts; "One of the weaker westerns, whose situations by now have become so standard as to be recognized in advance by even the most puerile intellects. Elliott does as well as can be expected." *Variety*, 9/10/41.

SUMMATION: Some unusual touches lift this western to a higher level. To save his sidekick Cannonball Taylor's life, Bill Elliott has to beat him up; Elliott and villain Ray Bennett engage in a particularly rugged fistfight at the film's end; and the director and screenwriters have Taylor end up with both Rodik Twins. Bill Elliott and Betty Miles exhibit the right chemistry between them; too bad the screenwriters had Elliott ride away at the fade. Elliott gets to demonstrate some acting range, especially in scenes with Miles and Taylor. Miles plays a pretty and determined girl, not afraid to use a gun. Veteran director Lambert Hillyer puts this all together nicely for an enjoyable time for action fans.

The Most Feared Gunman in the West Adds Plenty to His Reputation ... in the Most Exciting Gunfight in History!

The Return of Wild Bill

Columbia (June, 1940)

A Wild Bill Saunders Adventure

ALTERNATE TITLES: *False Evidence* and *Block K Rides Tonight*.

CAST: Wild Bill Saunders, **Bill Elliott**; Sammy Lou Griffin, **Iris Meredith**; Matt Kilgore, **George Lloyd**; Kate Kilgore, **Luana Walters**; Lige Saunders, **Edward LeSaint**; Ole Mitch, **Frank LaRue**; Jake Kilgore, **Francis Walker**; Bart, **Chuck Morrison**; Cannonball, **Dub Taylor**; Mike, **Buel Bryant**; Hep, **William Kellogg**// "Sonny"; Sam Griffin, **John Ince**; Sheriff, **Jack Rockwell**; Townsman, **Tex Cooper**; Dusty Donahue, **John Merton**; Blacksmith, **Bill Nestell**.

CREDITS: Director, **Joseph H. Lewis**;

Producer, **Leo Barsha**; Story, **Walt Coburn**; Screenwriters, **Robert Lee Johnson** and **Fred Myton**; Editor, **Richard Fantl**; Cinematographer, **George Meehan**.

LOCATION FILMING: Iverson, California.

RUNNING TIME: 60 min.

STORY: George Lloyd and his gang, ruthless outlaws posing as vigilantes, hang an innocent John Ince for rustling Edward LeSaint's cattle, hoping to start a range war between Ince's daughter, Iris Meredith, and LeSaint. Warned of trouble by Lloyd's sister, Luana Walters, LeSaint sends for his son, Bill Elliott. Lloyd wants LeSaint's ranch and sends his brother, Francis Walker, to either buy the ranch or murder LeSaint. When LeSaint won't sell, Walker shoots him. Elliott arrives moments after the shooting and in time for LeSaint to tell who shot him and what Lloyd's up to. Elliott catches up to Walker. The two men fight and then struggle over Elliott's pistol. The gun discharges, killing Walker. Elliott teams up with Meredith and an old family friend, Frank LaRue, to organize the ranchers against Lloyd. Lloyd sends fake lawmen to arrest Elliot and bring Elliott to Lloyd to be lynched. Walters reaches Meredith, LaRue and the ranchers, and takes them to Elliott in time to prevent the hanging. Lloyd attempts to shoot Elliott. Walters intervenes. In a tussle with Lloyd, the trigger is pulled and Walters is killed. Elliott goes after Lloyd and two henchmen, bringing all three down in a gunfight. Elliott receives word that he's needed desperately in Kansas. He tells Meredith that he'll return one day to "hang lace curtains."

NOTES AND COMMENTARY: At the end, as Bill Elliott is about to settle down with Iris

The Return of Wild Bill (Columbia, 1940) scene card — Luana Walters (center, on ground) dies in the arms of Bill Elliott (center right) as Iris Meredith, unidentified actor and Frank La Rue (left to right) look on.

Meredith, Dub Taylor arrives to tell Bill that he's needed in Kansas because a lot of farmers and ranchers are in trouble. This sets the stage for Elliott's next release, *Prairie Schooners* (Columbia, 1940). There would be one significant change: Elliott begins his journey as Wild Bill Saunders, and when he arrives in Kansas he's now Wild Bill Hickok.

The fight scene between Bill Elliott and Francis Walker is utilized in *Meanwhile, Back at the Ranch* (Curtco & RCR Productions, 1977).

REVIEWS: "Lewis' edgy direction is absolutely the best thing about this film." *The Western*, Hardy; "Well made Bill Elliott vehicle." *Western Movies*, Pitts.

SUMMATION: This is one of the best "B" westerns, featuring good acting, directing, writing and cinematography. Bill Elliott is allowed to act. Look at Elliott as he realizes his father, Edward LeSaint, has died. Elliott captures the pain and sadness in his eyes and face. Both leading ladies, Iris Meredith and Luana Walters, turn in fetching performances. They vividly portray jealous women who both love Elliott. Joseph H. Lewis' edgy direction works. His pacing is impeccable and his interesting use of the camera gives the story added punch.

Bad News for Bandits ... but Good News for All Lovers of Rhythm and Thrills!

Roaring Frontiers

Columbia (October, 1941)

ALTERNATE TITLE: *Frontier*.

CAST: Wild Bill Hickok, **Bill Elliott**; Tex Martin, **Tex Ritter**; Reba Bailey, **Ruth Ford**; Cannonball, **Frank Mitchell**; Hawk Hammond, **Bradley Page**; Flint Adams, **Tristam Coffin**; Link Twiddle, **Hal Taliaferro**; Boot Hill, **Francis Walker**; Knuckles, **Joe McGuinn**; Red Thompson, **George Chesebro**; Moccasin, **Charles Stevens**// "Sonny"; "White Flash"; Sheriff, **George Eldredge**; Henchman, **Jim Corey**; Old Timer, **Rick Anderson**; Jailer, **Ernie Adams**; Hank, the Stage Driver, **Hank Bell**; Stage Guard, **Steve Clark**.

CREDITS: Director, **Lambert Hillyer**; Producer, **Leon Barsha**; Screenwriter, **Robert Lee Johnson**; Editor, **Mel Thorsen**; Cinematographer, **Benjamin Kline**.

SONGS: "You've Got to Come and Get Me Boys"—sung by **Tex Ritter**; "Judge Morrow Will Find the Truth and Set Me Free"—sung by **Tex Ritter**; "Then You're a Part of the West"—sung by **Tex Ritter**.

LOCATION FILMING: Iverson, California.

RUNNING TIME: 60 min.

STORY: Trying to find the killer of his father, Tex Ritter goes to see saloon owner Bradley Page. Page is talking with a stranger when Ritter enters Page's office. Sheriff George Eldredge, fearing trouble, comes into the room. The stranger breaks the solitary lamp, plunging the room into darkness, and fires a shot meant for Ritter but kills Eldredge instead. Page then blames Ritter for the crime, forcing Ritter to flee. Ritter's horse goes lame and he has to hole up in a blind canyon. Page's men bottle up Ritter. Marshal Bill Elliott arrives in Goldfield, and Page asks Elliott to bring in Ritter. Through a ruse, Elliott is successful in arresting Ritter. In Goldfield, Elliott realizes Ritter will not receive a fair trial and grants Ritter's request to have his case heard at the county seat. Page sends men to kill Ritter, but Elliott intervenes. In the struggle, Ritter is shot in the leg, but Elliott and Ritter are able to get to the stagecoach traveling to the county seat. On the stage are three men and a woman. The woman, Ruth Ford, is a transplanted Easterner who can't understand the violence of the West. The other passengers are Frank Mitchell, a prospector, Hal Taliaferro, a barber, and Tristam Coffin, a gambler. Forced to stop at a way station to rest the horses, Ritter's wound is cared for by Ford. Elliott learns there was another person in the room besides Page when Eldredge was killed and surmises Coffin was that man. Knowing

Roaring Frontiers (Columbia, 1941) scene card — Bill Elliott and Ruth Ford watch for trouble.

he's suspected by Elliott, Coffin steals a horse and rides to warn Page. Elliott and Ritter return to Goldfield and shoot it out with Page and his men. Ritter corners Page and Coffin in Page's office. The two men try to outgun Ritter but are unsuccessful. Ritter becomes mayor of Goldfield, and Elliott rides off to new adventures.

NOTES AND COMMENTARY: In the cast listings, Tex Ritter's character name is given as Rawlings, but in the film he plays Tex Martin.

Frank Mitchell replaced Dub Taylor in this film. Mitchell played his character straight until the final scene in which he and Tex Ritter staged a fake fight in an attempt to convince Bill Elliott to settle down. In the next six entries, Mitchell would demonstrate his acrobatic talents via many pratfalls— to the delight of the younger members of the audience.

Ritter's song, "Judge Morrow Will Find the Truth and Set Me Free," was deleted from many TV prints.

REVIEW: "Solid entertainment in the Bill Elliott-Tex Ritter series." *Western Movies*, Pitts.

SUMMATION: This is a superior "B" western. Bill Elliott and Tex Ritter are handed a good script and make the most of it, both in the acting and action departments. Of particular note, the songs sung by Ritter reflect his thoughts at the time, and the dialogue is superior to that found in most "B's" of the time. *Roaring Frontiers* is well directed by veteran director Lambert Hillyer.

Danger Is His Hobby...
and Justice Is His Trademark! He's the Living Spirit of the Raw, Rough, Exciting West ...
Red Ryder!

The San Antonio Kid

Republic (August, 1944)

CAST: Red Ryder, **Wild Bill Elliott**; Little Beaver, **Bobby Blake**; the Duchess, **Alice Fleming**; Ann Taylor, **Linda Stirling**; Happy Jack, **Earle Hodgins**; Ace Hanlon, **Glenn Strange**; Walter Garfield, **LeRoy Mason**; Johnny Bennett (the San Antonio Kid), **Duncan Renaldo**; Lon, **Tom London**; Ben Taylor, **Jack Kirk**; Henchman, **Bob Wilke**; Ed, **Cliff Parkinson**; Nick, **Jack O'Shea**// "Thunder."

CREDITS: Director, **Howard Bretherton**; 2nd Unit Director, **Yakima Canutt**; Associate Producer, **Stephen Auer**; Screenwriter, **Norman S. Hall**; Editor, **Tony Martinelli**; Art Director, **Gano Chittenden**; Set Decorator, **Charles Thompson**; Cinematographer, **William Bradford**; Sound, **Earl Crain, Sr.**; Musical Score, **Joseph Dubin**.

LOCATION FILMING: Iverson and Vasquez Rocks, California.

RUNNING TIME: 59 min.

SOURCE: Based on Fred Harman's famous NEA comic, by special arrangement with Stephen Slesinger.

STORY: Crooked geologist LeRoy Mason and saloon keeper Glenn Strange plan to drive all the ranchers out of Painted Valley to buy lands containing a huge oil deposit. Raiders kill Linda Stirling's father, and Wild Bill Elliott brings her to Alice Fleming's ranch to live. Elliott surmises the raiders want the land and believes Strange is behind the lawlessness. Elliott accuses Strange, and the two men fight, with Elliott the victor. Strange realizes Elliott is the one man who can stop his scheme and sends for gunman Duncan Renaldo to kill him. Elliott finds oil on Stirling's ranch and buys her ranch, with the proviso that she can have the ranch back anytime she wants it. Mason offers to buy the ranch, but Elliott refuses to sell. Elliott tells Stirling about the oil deposit and that she's a rich young lady. On his way to meet Strange, Renaldo's horse is spooked and Renaldo is thrown over a cliff. Renaldo grabs some brush and is hanging on when Elliott pulls him to safety. Elliott takes Renaldo to Fleming's ranch, where he meets Stirling. Renaldo and Stirling are immediately attracted to each other. Renaldo meets Strange and learns that Strange wants him to gun down Elliott. At first Renaldo refuses, but changes his mind when Strange tells him that he'll send for another gunfighter. Renaldo tells Elliott of Strange's duplicity. With Renaldo's help, Elliott discovers that Mason is Strange's partner. Elliott declares a showdown with Strange and Mason. In a blazing gunfight Renaldo is wounded, and Strange's henchmen are killed or captured. Renaldo tells Elliott where he can find Mason and Strange. Elliott engages the two in a rugged fistfight in which Strange is killed and Mason is brought to justice. Stirling and Renaldo plan to wed.

NOTES AND COMMENTARY: After *The San Antonio Kid*, Duncan Renaldo appeared with Allan Lane and Max Terhune in *Sheriff of Sundown* (Republic, 1944), before starring as the Cisco Kid in *The Cisco Kid Returns* (Monogram, 1945). After two more entries, *The Cisco Kid in Old New Mexico* (Monogram, 1945) and *South of the Rio Grande* (Monogram, 1945), Renaldo became involved in government work and had to leave the series, to be replaced by Gilbert Roland. After Monogram dropped the Cisco Kid series, Philip Krasne obtained the rights, and the Cisco Company was formed with Frederick Ziv as president, Krasne as producer and Renaldo as associate producer, who would also star as Cisco. United Artists released five feature films for the 1949–50 season before the company turned to television for one hundred-and-sixty-five half-hour episodes.

REVIEWS: "Average outing in the popular 'Red Ryder' series." *Western Movies*, Pitts; "A routine entry in Republic's popular Red Ryder series." *Motion Picture Guide*, Nash and Ross.

The San Antonio Kid (Republic, 1944) title card — three unknown actors, Bill Elliott, Bobby Blake and Tom London (left to right).

SUMMATION: This is an entertaining Red Ryder adventure, thanks to a commanding performance by Wild Bill Elliott in the lead. Elliott is authoritative and convincing as the man who is going to get to the bottom of the lawless activity. Duncan Renaldo adds fine support as the gunfighter who is finally able to leave his troubled past behind. Howard Bretherton directs briskly, but a couple of "funny" bits between Bobby Blake and Earle Hodgins slow the proceedings. Linda Stirling looks lovely, as usual, but is given little to do in the acting department.

Get "Ringo!" He's Gun-Mad ...

The Savage Horde

Republic (May, 1950)

CAST: Ringo (John Baker), **William Elliott**; Livvy Weston, **Adrian Booth**; Wade Proctor, **Grant Withers**; Louise Cole, **Barbra Fuller**; Glenn Larrabee, **Noah Beery**; Lt. Mike Baker, **Jim Davis**; Dancer, **Bob Steele**; Col. Price, **Douglass Dumbrille**; Judge Cole, **Will Wright**; Fergus, **Roy Barcroft**; Buck Yallop, **Earle Hodgins**; Stuart, **Stuart Hamblen**; Sgt. Gowdy, **Hal Taliaferro**; Sam Jeffries, **Lloyd Ingraham**; Polk, **Marshall Reed**; Greb, **Crane Whitley**; Morellis, **Charles Stevens**; Army

Guard, **James Flavin**// Army Officer, **Reed Howes**; Town Marshal, **Jack O'Shea**; Ranchers, **Ed Cassidy**, **Bud Osborne** and **Monte Montague**; Al, **George Chesebro**; Pete, **Kermit Maynard**.

CREDITS: Director/Associate Producer, **Joseph Kane**; Story, **Thames Williamson** and **Gerald Geraghty**; Screenplay, **Kenneth Gamet**; Editor, **Arthur Roberts**; Art Director, **Frank Arrigo**; Set Decorators, **John McCarthy, Jr.** and **George Milo**; Cinematographer, **Reggie Lanning**; Costumes, **Adele Palmer**; Makeup, **Bob Mark**; Hair Stylist, **Peggy Gray**; Sound, **Dick Tyler** and **Howard Wilson**; Special Effects, **Howard** and **Theodore Lydecker**; Music, **Dale Butts**; Orchestrator, **Stanley Wilson**; Optical Effects, **Consolidated Film Industries**.

SONGS: "Riding Old Paint and Leading Old Bald" (Hamblen)— sung by **Stuart Hamblen**; "Sheepskin Corn" (Hamblen)— sung by **Stuart Hamblen**; "Ten Thousand Cattle Gone Astray" (traditional)— sung by **Stuart Hamblen**.

LOCATION FILMING: Sedona, Arizona; Red Rock Canyon, Iverson and Agoura, California.

RUNNING TIME: 90 min.

STORY: Gunman William Elliott is wanted for the murder of an Army officer that he killed in self-defense. As the Army closes in on Elliott, he fires, wounding his own brother, Jim Davis. The incident prompts Elliott to discard his guns. Elliott rides to Gunlock, Utah, to see a former sweetheart, Adrian Booth. Elliott finds that Booth is engaged to rancher Grant Withers, who is trying to drive the small ranchers off their lands. Rancher Noah Beery offers Elliott an equal partnership in his ranch, which he accepts. After Elliott proposes that the small ranchers band together to meet this threat, Withers has his gunmen, Bob Steele, Roy Barcroft and Marshall Reed, lead attacks on the small ranchers. Next, Withers has Judge Will Wright draft a range restriction notice giving all government lands to him. In a raid on the small ranchers' cattle, Steele guns down cowhand Stuart Hamblen. This act brings Wright over to Elliott and the ranchers' side. The Army comes to the Gunlock area looking for Elliott. Booth warns Elliott, and he plans to leave before Withers is defeated. Elliott sees his brother,

and Withers overhears enough of the conversation to realize Elliott is wanted by the Army. Withers' men capture Elliott and bring him to Army headquarters. With the Army leaving the area, Withers plans to drive all the ranchers out. In town, Beery is almost goaded into a gunfight with Steele. When Booth sees that Withers refuses to stop the fight, she steps in and prevents Steele from drawing his gun. Wright has Beery arrested. Booth breaks off her engagement to Withers. Withers orders his men to fire on the occupants in the jail. As Withers' men gain the upper hand, Elliott, who has escaped from the Army, returns to Gunlock. Elliott bests Steele in a gunfight. In the battle Withers is fatally wounded. The Army returns to recapture Elliott, who promises to return to Booth.

NOTES AND COMMENTARY: Barbra Fuller commented about William Elliott: "Bill Elliott was wonderful to work with. There was one scene in there, near the end, when I ride in and had to get off the horse in a hurry to be with Adrian Booth. When the scene was over, the makeup man said, 'Did you notice Mr. Elliott while you were doing that?' I said, 'No, all I was thinking was to get off the horse all right.' He said, 'He was standing right behind the cameraman ready to grab the horse if he gave you trouble.' I thought that was pretty doggone nice. He could have been sitting back in his dressing room, instead of being concerned about a young actress, who didn't know what she was doing on a horse."

Fuller then mentioned that Elliott was more of a natural, rather than trained, actor, stating, "I don't think he was much of an actor. He just trained himself and it came off beautifully. He had a strength about him, a masculinity about him. Of course, that's attractive to women. He had a calm masculinity, the same as he had in this picture. He had a certain animal magnetism. I think he was playing Bill Elliott very often. Most of the big stars were. Gary Cooper. John Wayne. That's what makes them a star."

Elliott took Fuller to dinner one of the first nights on the picture. Fuller commented, "I was very thrilled to have the star of the movie ask me to have dinner with him."

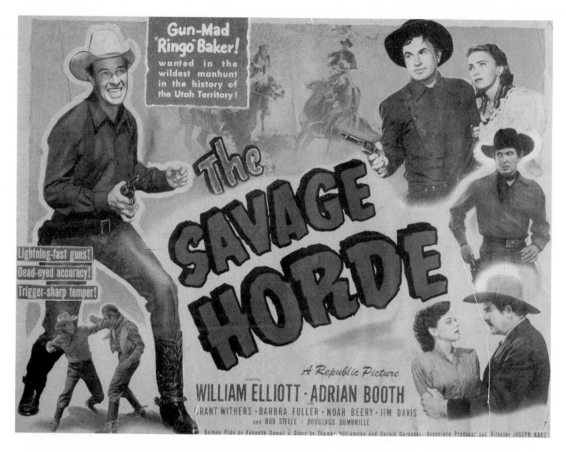

The Savage Horde (Republic, 1950) title card — upper left shows Bill Elliott; lower left shows Bill Elliott (left) and Roy Barcroft (right); upper right shows Noah Beery, Jr. (left) and Barbra Fuller (right); center right shows Bob Steele; lower right shows Adrian Booth (left) and Grant Withers (right).

The author asked Barbra Fuller to comment on a claim made in the book *Ladies of the Western* (McFarland, 2002) that Elliott was "wolfish." Fuller was quick to respond: "He wasn't wolfish with me. Some people thought he was wolfish but he figured I was somebody he needed to protect. I can't think of anything detrimental in that fashion to say about him, I'm happy to say."

Fuller called *The Savage Horde* "my favorite picture of everything I did." She particularly remembered one scene with Noah Beery, Jr. as being "cute." In the scene, Beery had been taking an outdoor shower, and runs into the ranch house with a towel around him when Fuller rides up. "I thought it was cute in the movie, too," recalled the actress. "I laughed about it."

In talking about what she did between

takes, Fuller recollected, "I was knitting on the set. I don't like to read. I want to concentrate on what's going on on the set. I can knit and still be conscious of what's going on. I was knitting a sweater, a white and gold sweater. Bill Elliott had said he named his ranch the 'Double Bar A' because he had a daughter named Barbara." Fuller thought it was a great idea, so she put two bars of gold and a big gold "A" on her sweater. Unfortunately, Elliott never saw the sweater because it wasn't finished until well after the picture.

Adrian Booth commented, "I didn't do much in that one. Little Barbra Fuller had a better part than I did. She was very cute in it, very sweet little girl." Talking about her role, Booth continued, "There was one scene in the kitchen that was kind of a good scene. I expressed that even though I love him I just can't follow him and be followed. I wanted a more comfortable life. It turns out he was the stalwart person. A responsible person."

Booth added, "I had that wonderful scene where I call Grant Withers a murderer. They used that scene when they gave me the Golden Boot [award] two or three years ago."

Stuart Hamblen, a prolific songwriter who wrote "This Ole House" and "It Is No Secret," ran for the office of President of the United States on the Prohibition ticket in 1952.

REVIEWS: "William Elliott's final big budget Western is a fine action drama." *Western Movies*, Pitts; "Could have been better had the script stressed action more and talk less.

Okay William Elliott feature. Elliott is a good, tight-lipped western hero and will be liked." *Variety*, 7/5/50.

SUMMATION: This is a top-rated minor "A" western led by the steady direction of Joseph Kane and the fine performance of William Elliott. Elliott is quite believable as a man who has lived by the gun and now wants nothing to do with them, but then realizes that only his gun will bring peace. The supporting cast is first rate, with a nod to Bob Steele's role as a slimy gunman with a bloodlust for killing. Stuart Hamblen's songs and singing help raise this film to its high level.

Gun-Slingin'
Rip-Roarin'
Thrills and Action!

Sheriff of Las Vegas

Republic Pictures (December, 1944)

CAST: Red Ryder, **Wild Bill Elliott**; Little Beaver, **Bobby Blake**; the Duchess, **Alice Fleming**; Ann Carter, **Peggy Stewart**; Arthur Stanton, **Selmer Jackson**; Dan Sedley, **William Haade**; Tom Blackwell, **Jay Kirby**; Judge Blackwell, **John Hamilton**; Henchmen, **Kenne Duncan** and **Bud Geary**; Buck, **Jack Kirk**; Oliver, **Dickie Dillon** // "Thunder"; Cowboy in Saloon, **Robert J. Wilke**; Sheriff Lonegan, **Frank McCarroll**; Ulysses Botts, **Freddie Chapman**.

CREDITS: Director, **Lesley Selander**; Associate Producer, **Stephen Auer**: Screenwriter, **Norman S. Hall**; Editor, **Charles Craft**; Art Director, **Fred A. Ritter**; Set Decorator, **Earl Wooden**; Cinematographer, **Bud Thackery**; Sound, **Ed Borschell**; Musical Director, **Richard Cherwin**.

LOCATION FILMING: Iverson and Corriganville, California.

RUNNING TIME: 55 min.

SOURCE: Based on Fred Harman's famous NEA comic — by special arrangement with Stephen Slesinger.

STORY: Wild Bill Elliott stops a drunken Jay Kirby, son of Judge John Hamilton, from shooting up a saloon, and gives Kirby a stern lecture. Selmer Jackson's bank is held up and Sheriff Frank McCarroll is killed. Elliott retrieves the stolen money, and Hamilton appoints Wild Bill Elliott as temporary sheriff. Hamilton, upset because of his son Jay Kirby's irresponsible behavior, decides to cut Kirby out of his will. Jackson and saloon owner William Haade convince Kirby to meet with Hamilton. Kirby and Hamilton meet and argue. An angry Kirby storms out of Hamilton's office. Haade then murders Hamilton and frames Kirby for the crime. Elliott arrests Kirby but realizes he is innocent (Hamilton was killed by a derringer, and Kirby carries a forty-five). Elliott then hides Kirby in the schoolhouse. Haade and henchmen Bud Geary and Kenne Duncan go to the schoolhouse to kill Kirby but find Elliott waiting. A battle royale ensues and the outlaws are killed. Kirby enters Jackson's office and tells him he has the gun that killed Hamilton, and that Haade's boss is behind the crime. Jackson admits he was Haade's boss and plans to kill Kirby. Elliott, standing outside Jackson's window, shoots the gun from his hand. Jackson is found to be an embezzler who needed Hamilton's estate to cover the loss.

Sheriff of Las Vegas (Republic, 1944) scene card — Bobby Blake, Bill Elliott, Alice Fleming and Peggy Stewart (left to right) in a lighter moment.

NOTES AND COMMENTARY: Some film historians claim scenes were filmed at various Nevada location sites. It is obvious, however, that the filmmakers didn't venture far from the greater Los Angeles area.

The scene in which Elliott comes out of the saloon to open fire on outlaws is used in *Meanwhile, Back at the Ranch* (Curtco & RCR Productions, 1977).

Sheriff of Las Vegas was remade as *Beyond the Purple Hills* (Columbia, 1950), with Gene Autry in the lead.

REVIEWS: "Well written 'Red Ryder' series entry with a bang-up finale." *Western Movies*, Pitts; "Another solid entry in the popular series." *Motion Picture Guide*, Nash and Ross.

SUMMATION: *Sheriff of Las Vegas* is an above-average "B" western. Elliott capably handles both action and acting. Some good comedy enhances the story.

He's TNT on the Screen! Dynamic, Two-Gun Hero of Millions ... Leaping from the Pages of Your Newspaper ... Blazing into Action in a Brand New Adventure!

Sheriff of Redwood Valley

Republic Pictures (March, 1946)
CAST: Red Ryder, **Wild Bill Elliott**; Little

Beaver, **Bobby Blake**; the Reno Kid, **Bob Steele**; the Duchess, **Alice Fleming**; Molly,

Peggy Stewart; Harvey Martin, **Arthur Loft**; Bidwell, **James Craven**; Sheriff, **Tom London**; Jackson, **Kenne Duncan**; Strong, **Bud Geary**; Johnny, **John Wayne Wright**; Doc Ellis, **Tom Chatterton**; Crump, **Budd Buster**; Pete, **Frank McCarroll**// "Thunder"; Stage Driver, **Jack Kirk**; Clem, **James Linn**.

CREDITS: Director, **R.G. Springsteen**; Associate Producer, **Sidney Picker**; Screenwriter, **Earle Snell**; Editor, **Ralph Dixon**; Art Direction, **Fred A. Ritter**; Set Decorators, **John McCarthy, Jr.** and **Allen Alperin**; Cinematographer, **Reggie Lanning**; Sound, **Fred Stahl**; Makeup, **Bob Mark**; Musical Director, **Richard Cherwin**.

LOCATION FILMING: Iverson, California.

RUNNING TIME: 56 min.

SOURCE: Based on Fred Harman's famous NEA comic — by special arrangement with Stephen Slesinger.

STORY: Redwood Valley and Indian Gap are vying for the railroad right-of-way. James Craven has $50,000 to finance a tunnel through a mountain to allow the railroad access to Redwood Valley. With the escape from prison of a notorious outlaw, Bob Steele, Craven and Sheriff Tom London try to secretly deliver the money to the railroad. Craven has henchmen Kenne Duncan and Bud Greary shoot London and take the money. Craven identifies Steele as one of the robbers. Wild Bill Elliott is appointed temporary sheriff and starts after the bandits. Elliott catches up with Duncan and Geary, and is wounded in a gunfight. Elliott's pal, Bobby Blake, takes Elliott to a nearby cabin, inhabited by Steele, his wife Peggy Stewart, and their baby boy, John Wayne Wright. Steele and Stewart minister to Elliott. Steele talks about himself in the third person and tells Elliott his lawyer, Arthur Loft, poorly represented the

Sheriff of Redwood Valley (Republic, 1946) scene card — Bill Elliott (left) is poised to jump on Tom London (center) and James Craven (right).

outlaw. Loft, working with Craven, has purchased most of the land around Indian Gap and stands to make a fortune if the railroad comes there. Loft had Steele framed so he could gain control of his ranch. Little by little, Elliott realizes Steele is innocent. Elliott confronts Loft and forces him to admit his guilt. A masked man enters the room; Loft thinks it's Steele and shoots the masked man. The dead man turns out to be Craven. Realizing all is lost, Loft attempts to escape but is captured by Steele. Elliott tells Steele that he's now a free man.

NOTES AND COMMENTARY: Western great Bob Steele was beginning a new career as a supporting performer in westerns. With the release of *Sheriff of Redwood Valley*, Steele would have only one more starring western film, *Thunder*

Town (PRC, 1946). In addition to Elliott, Steele would be featured with three other Republic western stars in the next 15 months: Sunset Carson (*Rio Grande Raiders*, September, 1946), Gene Autry (*Twilight on the Rio Grande*, April, 1947) and Allan "Rocky" Lane (*Bandits of Dark Canyon*, December, 1947).

REVIEW: "More than competent 'Red Ryder' series film greatly aided by Bob Steele in the supporting cast." *Western Movies*, Pitts.

SUMMATION: This is a nice Red Ryder series entry with good performances by Elliott and Steele. The script has Elliott realistically feel severe pain when creased by a bullet. Elliott essays his part competently and is perfectly matched by Bob Steele.

Thrills! Adventure!! Romance!!!
A Screenful of Entertainment That's Sure to Satisfy Everyone!...

The Showdown

Republic (August, 1950)

CAST: Shadrach Jones, **William Elliott**; Cap MacKellar, **Walter Brennan**; Adelaide, **Marie Windsor**; Rod Main, **Henry Morgan**; Chokecherry, **Rhys Williams**; Cochran, **Jim Davis**; Mike Shattay, **William Ching**; Gonzales, **Nacho Galindo**; Big Mart, **Leif Erickson**; Dutch, **Henry Rowland**; Indian Joe, **Charles Stevens**; Hemp, **Victor Kilian**; Davis, **Yakima Canutt**; Pickney, **Guy Teague**; Terry, **William Steele**; Bartender, **Jack Sparks**// Cowhand, **Harry Lauter**.

CREDITS: Directors/Screenwriters, **Dorrell** and **Stuart McGowan**; Producer, **William J. O'Sullivan**; Editor, **Harry Keller**; Art Director, **Frank Arrigo**; Set Decorators, **John McCarthy, Jr.** and **Charles Thompson**; Cinematographer, **Reggie Lanning**; Costumes, **Adele Palmer**; Makeup, **Bob Mark**, Hair Stylist, **Peggy Gray**; Sound, **Earl Crain, Sr.** and **Howard Wilson**; Music, **Stanley Wilson**; Special Effects, **Howard** and **Theodore Lydecker**.

LOCATION FILMING: Gates Pass (Tucson area), Arizona, and Iverson, California.

RUNNING TIME: 86 min.

SOURCE: *Esquire* magazine story by **Richard Wormser** and **Dan Gordon**.

STORY: Former Texas State Policeman William Elliott is seeking his brother's murderer. Elliott discovers his brother was staying at the Halfway House, run by Marie Windsor, at the time he was killed. When Elliott realizes a member of Walter Brennan's outfit killed his brother, he takes Brennan's offer of trail boss. Windsor buys a third interest in Brennan's herd and goes on the drive. Brennan asks Elliott to give up his quest for revenge, but Elliott refuses to listen. Knowing that winter weather is about to close in, Elliott drives the men and cattle unmercifully. Tried of Elliott's harsh treatment, cowhand Henry Morgan wants to face Elliott in a gun duel. As the two men begin the duel, a shot from the darkness ends Morgan's life. Elliott announces that the same caliber bullet that killed Morgan killed his brother. As the drive nears its conclusion, Elliott and Windsor begin to fall in love. A swollen river needs to be forded, and Elliott tells the cowboys to take their pants and boots off. All comply except cowhand William Ching, who refuses to remove his boots. Thinking the murder weapon may be concealed in his boots, Elliot removes them to discover Ching was hiding the fact he was a cripple. Humbled by this incident, Elliott decides to abandon his quest for revenge and tells Brennan he's riding on after the herd is safely across the river. Dismounting to help a calf, Brennan is gored by an angry bull. As he's dying, Brennan admits to Elliott that *he* murdered Elliott's brother and Morgan. Elliott, again becoming ruthless, plans to let Brennan die alone and in agony. Then Elliott relents and has Ching stay with Brennan until he dies. Windsor brings Brennan's thanks to Elliott.

NOTES AND COMMENTARY: This was William Elliott's last film for Republic Pictures. After a failed attempt at a television series, Elliott signed on with Monogram Pictures. Elliott would make eleven western features under the Monogram, and later the Allied Artists,

banner before starring in five detective films for Allied Artists to round out his big-screen career in 1957.

REVIEWS: "Strong program western. Showdown injects some fresh twists in displaying western adventure and dramatics during a cattle drive from Arizona to Montana. William Elliott shows to excellent advantage in the lead spot with a particularly forceful part." *Variety*, 8/30/50; "Elliott gives a fine performance under an intelligent suspenseful direction." *Motion Picture Guide*, Nash and Ross; "The direction is as eloquent as the screenplay, and Elliott plays his forceful role to the hilt." *The Western*, Hardy.

SUMMATION: This is a very fine western, with a different William Elliott. Elliott is allowed to extend his acting range in his role of a revenge-seeking individual who finally realizes that vengeance is eating his soul, bringing

The Showdown (Republic, 1950) movie still — Marie Windsor, Walter Brennan and Bill Elliott (left to right).

him sorrow instead of happiness. Elliott plays his part to perfection, never striking a false note. Walter Brennan scores well as a peaceful, supposedly religious man who in reality is a cold-blooded murderer. Marie Windsor adds charm and beauty to her characterization of a greedy, calculating woman. R. G. Springsteen's direction captures the somber mood perfectly. The film's one false note is sounded by the fact that all the major scenes take place on a sound stage rather than on actual locations, but the dramatic impact of the story is able to overcome this deficiency.

The West at Its Wildest!

Son of Davy Crockett

Columbia (July, 1941)

ALTERNATE TITLE: *Blue Clay*.

CAST: Dave Crockett, **Bill Elliott**; Doris Mathews, **Iris Meredith**; Cannonball, **Dub Taylor**; King Canfield, **Kenneth MacDonald**; Jesse Gordon, **Richard Fiske**; Grandpa Mathews, **Eddy Waller**; Jack Ringe, **Donald Curtis**; Zeke, **Paul Scardon**; Lance, **Edmund Cobb**; Curly, **Steve Clark**; President Grant, **Harrison Greene**// "**Sonny**"; Doctor Banks, **Francis Sayles**; Bartender, **Hank Bell**; Poisoners, **Jack Ingram** and **Jim Corey**; Marshal, **Frank LaRue**; Saloon Patron, **Jack Kirk**; Ranger Logan, **Tom London**; Rancher, **Horace B. Carpenter**; Clint, **Stanley Brown**; Sammy, **Lloyd Bridges**; Lopez, **Martin Garralaga**; Hank, **Russ Powell**; Swede, **Sven Hugo Borg**.

CREDITS: Director/Screenwriter, **Lambert Hillyer**; Producer, **Leon Barsha**; Editor, **Mel Thorsen**; Cinematographer, **Benjamin Kline**.

SONGS: "Columbia, the Gem of the Ocean" (Shaw)—played by **Dub Taylor**; "Oh, Susanna" (Foster)—played by **Dub Taylor**.

LOCATION FILMING: Iverson, California.

RUNNING TIME: 55 min.

STORY: Bill Elliott is sent to the Yucca Valley strip, an area not under United States authority because of an error in surveying, to help the ranchers get rid of dictator Kenneth MacDonald and allow the citizens to vote to become part of the United States. Elliott and MacDonald meet, and both know this will be a fight to the finish. Rancher Eddy Waller sets the date for the election to decide if the area joins the United States. MacDonald allows the election because be believes a campaign of intimidation will ensure victory for him. On Election Day, Elliott prevents MacDonald's henchmen from tampering with the ballots. Now facing the possibility of defeat, MacDonald plans to have his henchmen burn the voting building and all the ballots therein. With minutes to go, enough citizens find the nerve to cast the deciding votes. Before MacDonald can signal his henchmen, Elliott faces him down and, in a gun duel, ends MacDonald's reign of terror. With the area now a part of the Union, MacDonald's minions leave Yucca Valley and Elliott rides on to new adventures.

NOTES AND COMMENTARY: *Son of Davy Crockett* is the last solo starring western feature for Bill Elliott at Columbia. In his next feature, *King of Dodge City* (Columbia, 1941), western great Tex Ritter becomes Elliott's co-star. Elliott would have the solo lead in his final Columbia serial, *The Valley of Vanishing Men*, in 1942. His next solo starring feature film would be *Calling Wild Bill Elliott* (Republic, 1943).

Dub Taylor receives one particularly clever line of dialogue: "A politician is a man who shakes hands with you and then you go count your fingers."

Son of Davy Crockett was revived in 1955 and paired with George Montgomery's *Davy Crockett, Indian Scout* (United Artists, 1950) to cash in on the Davy Crockett craze generated by Walt Disney's series with Fess Parker as Crockett.

REVIEWS: "Actionless Bill Elliott western," *Variety*, 7/9/41; "Well written and directed segment in the pseudo-historical series of films Bill Elliott did for Columbia." *Western Movies*, Pitts.

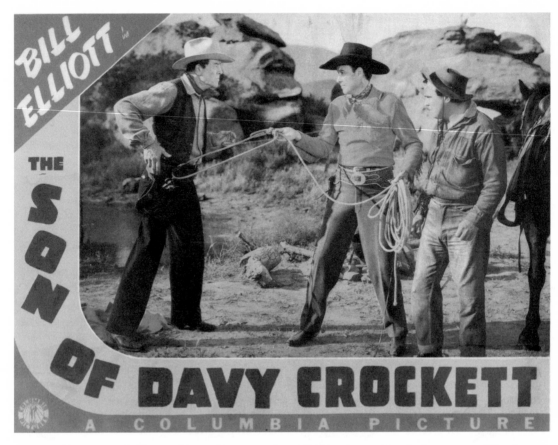

Son of Davy Crockett (Columbia, 1941) scene card — Bill Elliott (center) lassos the gun out of Tom London's (left) holster as Dub Taylor (right) looks on.

SUMMATION: A cursory glance at the script might indicate that this film would be a disaster. It is very talky, and offers only two fistfights (in which the hero dispatches his adversaries without really being touched), no hard riding and very little gunplay; but, surprisingly, the film works. Credit must go to the very effective performances by hero Bill Elliott and villain Kenneth MacDonald. Both actors play strong men, very much in the habit of having things their own way. Elliott becomes both judge and jury when dealing with evil. MacDonald is evil incarnate, who believes everyone should obey him. Their scenes together are highlights of the film. In the large supporting cast, Eddy Waller stands out as an elderly rancher who believes in justice and will risk his life for it. Without the benefit of fast, hell-bent-for-leather action, Lambert Hillyer directs with confidence and creates a film best enjoyed by older audiences.

It Lures You Up a Blind Alley of Crime!

Sudden Danger

Allied Artists (December, 1955)
ALTERNATE TITLE: *Calculated Risk*.
CAST: Lt. Andy Doyle, **Bill Elliott**; Wally Curtis, **Tom Drake**; Phyllis Baxter, **Beverly Garland**; Raymond Wilkins, **Dayton Lummis**; Harry Woodruff, **Lyle Talbot**; Vera, **Helene**

Stanton; Bartender, **Frank Jenks**; Dave Glennon, **Lucien Littlefield**; George Caldwell, **Pierre Watkin**; Mrs. Kelly, **Minerva Urecal**; Sgt. Mike Duncan, **John Close**; Dr. Hastings, **Ralph Gamble**// Caldwell's Secretary, **Dorothy Neumann**.

CREDITS: Director, **Hubert Cornfield**; Assistant Director, **Austen Jewell**; Producer, **Ben Schwalb**; Story, **Daniel B. Ullman**; Screenwriters, **Daniel B. Ullman** and **Elwood Ullman**; Editor, **William Austin**; Art Director, **Dave Milton**; Set Decorator, **Clarence Steensen**; Cinematography, **Ellsworth Fredericks**; Makeup, **Paul Malcolm**; Wardrobe Supervisor, **Bert Henrikson**; Sound, **Charles Schelling** and **Ralph Butler**; Music, **Marlin Skiles**; Production Manager, **Allen K. Wood**; Set Continuity, **Kathleen Fagan**.

RUNNING TIME: 65 min.

STORY: A blind Tom Drake returns home to find his mother asphyxiated by gas. Lt. Bill Elliott is assigned to investigate the case and finds a typewritten suicide note. Landlady Minerva Urecal alludes to Elliott that Drake might have murdered his mother to obtain money for an eye operation. Dayton Lummis, Drake's mother's business partner, tells Elliott the company is not doing well. Elliott thinks Drake could have been the murderer. The suicide note was written on his girlfriend Beverly Garland's typewriter. Drake has his operation. When the bandages are removed, Drake only tells Garland he can see so he can investigate his mother's death. Drake finds that Lummis is bestowing lavish gifts on model Helene Stanton and believes Lummis murdered his mother. Elliott has already learned that Lummis has been embezzling from his firm. Elliott has

Sudden Danger (Allied Artists, 1955) scene card — Bill Elliott (left) and John Close (right) arrest Dayton Lummis (center); the upper left border shows Tom Drake; the lower left border features Dayton Lummis (left) and Beverly Garland (right).

Drake and Garland gather evidence at the firm's office. Elliott investigates the warehouse and finds it empty. Lummis discovers Garland and Drake at the office and attempts to kill them. Elliott's intervention prevents this, and Lummis is arrested. Drake and Garland are now free to marry.

NOTES AND COMMENTARY: Beverly Garland had this to say about Bill Elliott: "I do know I liked Bill as a cowboy instead of a detective. I just could not make the transfer in my mind of him in city clothes as opposed to cowboy clothes. I will say he was one of the nicest actors that I worked for."

REVIEWS: "Bill Elliott proves suicide was really murder in good meller. Good performances, direction and writing do a better job of meeting entertainment than the average supporting film fair." *Variety*, 12/21/55; "Strong efforts in all production areas make for an entertaining production." *Motion Picture Guide*, Nash and Ross.

SUMMATION: This is a good crime drama with solid writing, acting and directing. Bill Elliott is believable and properly authoritative as the police lieutenant. Tom Drake shines as the murder suspect, and Beverly Garland stands out as Drake's girlfriend. Hubert Cornfield's firm directorial hand brings the fine script by Daniel and Elwood Ullman to life.

More Glorious Adventure Than Before...
as Red Ryder Battles to Save Thunder ... His Wonder Horse!

Sun Valley Cyclone

Republic Pictures (May, 1946)

CAST: Red Ryder, **Wild Bill Elliott**; Little Beaver, **Bobby Blake**; the Duchess, **Alice Fleming**; Blackie Blake, **Roy Barcroft**; Dow, **Kenne Duncan**; Major Harding, **Eddy Waller**; Sheriff, **Tom London**; Luce, **Edmund Cobb**; Theodore Roosevelt, **Ed Cassidy**; Jeff, **Monte Hale**; Shorty, **George Chesebro**; Army Sergeant, **Rex Lease**; "Thunder"// Deputy Marshall, **Jack Rockwell**; Marshal Henry McGaw, **Hal Price**; Townsman, **Horace B. Carpenter**; Doctor, **Frank O'Connor**; Wagon Driver, **Jack Kirk**.

CREDITS: Director, **R. G. Springsteen**; 2nd Unit Director, **Yakima Canutt**; Associate Producer, **Sidney Picker**; Screenwriter, **Earle Snell**; Editors, **Harry Keller** and **Charles Craft**; Art Director, **James Sullivan**; Set Decorators, **John McCarthy, Jr.** and **Marie Arthur**; Cinematographer, **Bud Thackery**; Sound, **Victor Appel**; Musical Director, **Richard Cherwin**.

LOCATION FILMING: Iverson, California.

RUNNING TIME: 56 min.

SOURCE: Based on Fred Harman's famous NEA Comic — by special arrangement with Stephen Slesinger.

STORY: Wild Bill Elliott and Bobby Blake ride from Wyoming to Arizona to bring horse thief Roy Barcroft to justice. In Los Altos, a disguised Barcroft spots Elliott and attempts to shoot him from an ambush. Elliott's horse, Thunder, charges at Barcroft, spoiling his plan. Quickly branded as an outlaw horse, Thunder is to be destroyed. Elliott demands a trial, with Marshal Hal Price as judge. Elliott explains that he obtained Thunder in a horse trade with Ed Cassidy (playing Theodore Roosevelt) when Elliott tried to join the Rough Riders. Cassidy told Elliott that he would be of greater service if he stopped the horse rustling in Wyoming. In Wyoming, Barcroft was stirring up trouble between neighboring ranch owners Alice Fleming and Eddy Waller to make it easier for his gang to rustle horses. Horses are rustled from Waller's ranch. Thunder follows to be with a mare owned by Waller, and is captured by the outlaw gang. Barcroft unsuccessfully attempts to ride Thunder. In anger, Barcroft takes a whip to Thunder, but Thunder is able to break away and escape with an expensive saddle on his back. Henchman Kenne Duncan tries to retrieve the saddle but is trampled by Thunder when he stops to take a shot at Elliott. Duncan is badly injured and taken to jail. Barcroft and his men break Duncan out of jail. Alerted by

Sun Valley Cyclone (Republic, 1946) scene card — Sheriff Hal Price (second left) restrains Bill Elliott (center) from hitting a disguised Roy Barcroft (right) as Bobby Blake (left) watches.

Blake, Elliott and his cowhands arrive in town and the two sides open fire. Thunder has found the stolen horses and leads them into town, which helps Elliott round up all the gang members except Barcroft. As Elliott ends his story, he sees through Barcroft's disguise and Barcroft is quickly arrested.

NOTES AND COMMENTARY: This was the only entry in the Red Ryder series in which Thunder received on-screen billing. It was also the one feature in which a horse ridden by Wild Bill Elliott was billed.

REVIEW: "Well written and paced 'Red Ryder' series entry." *Western Movies*, Pitts.

SUMMATION: This is a good Red Ryder adventure in which the emphasis is on Wild Bill Elliott's horse, Thunder. Thunder saves Elliott's life twice, rescues a stolen herd of horses, is responsible for the capture of badman Roy Barcroft and defeats a rival stallion for the attentions of a beautiful mare. Elliott is effective in the role of Ryder, especially in the scenes involving Thunder. The film is nicely photographed by Bud Thackery and briskly directed by R. G. Springsteen.

The Law Reached Only as Far as His Guns Could Shoot!

Taming of the West

Columbia (October, 1939)
A Wild Bill Saunders Adventure

CAST: Wild Bill Saunders, **Bill Elliott**; Pepper, **Iris Meredith**; Rawhide, **Dick Curtis**; Cannonball, **Dub Taylor**; Handy, **James Craig**; Slim, **Stanley Brown**; Judge Bailey, **Ethan Allen**; Blaisdale, **Kenneth MacDonald**; Cholly Wong, **Victor Wong**; Jackson, **Charles King**// "**Sonny**"; Blake, **Richard Fiske**; Blackie Gilbert, **Art Mix**; Townsman, **Horace B. Carpenter**; Turkey, **Lane Chandler**; Marshal, **Hank Bell**; Cheated Gambler, **John Tyrell**; Mary Jenkins, **Irene Herndon**; Gun Checker, Jack Kirk; Mrs. Gardner, **Stella LeSaint**; Shifty, **Bob Woodward**.

CREDITS: Director, **Norman Deming**; Story, **Robert Lee Johnson**; Screenwriters, **Charles Francis Royal** and **Robert Lee Johnson**; Editor, **Otto Meyer**; Cinematographer, **George Meehan**.

LOCATION FILMING: Iverson and Burro Flats, California.

RUNNING TIME: 55 min.

STORY: Bill Elliott rides into the town of Prairie Port. When gambler Lane Chandler murders Marshal Hank Bell, Elliott gives chase.

Taming of the West (Columbia, 1939) scene card — Bill Elliott (left) and Dick Curtis (right); the left border shows Iris Meredith (left) and Bill Elliott (right).

The two men fight, and in the struggle Chandler falls to his death. Elliott takes the job of marshal when outlaws Dick Curtis and James Craig kill restaurant owner Iris Meredith's sister, Irene Herndon. Elliott arrests gang members for various crimes. Banker Kenneth Mac-Donald, the outlaw leader, starts a wave of intimidation that gains freedom for his henchmen. Through a ruse, Elliott determines that MacDonald is the outlaw leader. Elliott quickly brings MacDonald and his men to justice before heading to new adventures.

NOTES AND COMMENTARY: After four features produced by Larry Darmour, Columbia now took over production of Bill Elliott's westerns. *Taming of the West* was the first in the series of four Wild Bill Saunders adventures.

At the picture's end, Bill Elliott receives a letter informing him that he has inherited a ranch, which is now an outlaw's headquarters. This sets the stage for the plot of Elliott's next Wild Bill Saunders adventure, *Pioneers of the Frontier* (Columbia, 1940).

Kenneth MacDonald would provide the villainy in four more Columbia entries, *Wildcat of Tucson* (1941), *Hands Across the Rockies* (1941), *Son of Davy Crockett* (1941) and *The Valley of Vanishing Men* (1942). MacDonald was most impressive in the latter two films. He had already appeared with Elliott in *Overland with Kit Carson* (Columbia, 1939), and would be featured in two Elliott big-budget films at Republic, *The Fabulous Texan* (1947) and *Hellfire* (1949).

REVIEWS: "*Taming of the West* is an above average horse opera. Bill Elliott, on top, is a type likely to become quite popular. He's more along the line of William S. Hart and somewhat of a slugger with punches not always pulled." *Variety*, 10/11/39; "Bill Elliott fans will enjoy this actionful outing." *Western Movies*, Pitts.

SUMMATION: This was the first of the Columbia-produced Bill Elliott series westerns, and it is a winner. The film starts on a high note, which, unfortunately, the movie cannot sustain, with Elliott bringing Lane Chandler to justice. It then reverts to the standard plot of cleaning up the town, but it's put over with style thanks to Elliott's presence and the fine supporting cast, led by Iris Meredith. Elliott gets a chance to show his acting ability most convincingly in the scene in which he learns of the shooting of a courageous rancher. Look at Elliott reveal and then quickly suppress his anger over the incident. A tip of the hat goes to George Meehan's cinematography, especially in the chase sequences, and to Norman Demming's efficient directorial effort.

A Trail of Gunsmoke Drew Him to Topeka!

Topeka

Allied Artists (August, 1953)
A Westwood Production

CAST: Jim Levering, **Wild Bill Elliott**; Marian Harrison, **Phyllis Coates**; Ray, **Rick Vallin**; Pop Harrison, **Fuzzy Knight**; Marv, **John James**; Jonas, **Denver Pyle**; Peters, **Dick Crockett**; Mack Wilson, **Harry Lauter**; Jake Manning, **Dale Van Sickel**; Cully, **Ted Mapes**; Rancher, **Henry Rowland**; Corley, **Edward Clark**; Doc Mason, **Stanford Jolley**// Guthrie Bank Teller, **Stanley Price**; Bartender, **Michael Vallon**.

CREDITS: Director, **Thomas Carr**; Assistant Director, **Melville Shyer**; Producer, **Vincent M. Fennelly**; Screenwriter, **Milton M. Raison**; Editor, **Sam Fields**; Set Decorator, **Theodore Offenbecker**; Cinematography, **Ernest Miller**; Special Effects, **Ray Mercer**; Sound, **Thomas Lambert**; Music, **Raoul Kraushaar**; Set Continuity, **Emilie Ehrlich**; Dialogue Supervisor, **Stanley Price**; Color by **Sepiatone**.

LOCATION FILMING: Iverson and Corriganville, California.

RUNNING TIME: 69 min.

STORY: In Iowa, bank robber Wild Bill Elliott's luck with easy bank robberies comes to an end when his gang's attempt to rob the

Guthrie bank is foiled by alert bank teller Stanley Price. Elliott and gang members Rick Vallin, John James, Denver Pyle and Dick Crockett decide to travel to Kansas. In Topeka, Elliott finds that saloon owner Harry Lauter controls the town and is extorting all businessmen. Seeing that Elliott and his men are not afraid of Lauter, prominent businessmen, led by Fuzzy Knight, persuade Elliott to take the job of sheriff. Elliott takes the job with the idea of replacing Lauter as town boss so he and his gang can loot the town for themselves. As Topeka becomes a friendly town, Knight's daughter, Phyllis Coates, tells Elliott the town council knows all about Elliott's background but believes he and his men are serious about making a new start. Elliott and Vallin decide they welcome the opportunity to live an honest life, but the rest of the gang members want to proceed with the original plan. James, Pyle and Crockett join

Lauter and decide to loot the town and place the blame on Elliott. When Lauter leads a posse to lynch Elliott, Knight is able to warn Elliott. When Lauter returns to town, Elliott forces him to lead him to his henchmen's hideout. At the hideout there is a gunfight in which Lauter and the gang members are either killed or captured. Elliott and Vallin are planning to leave town, but Coates and the town council persuade Elliott to stay. A petition has been sent to the Governor for a pardon for Elliott and Vallin. It looks like romance will blossom between Elliott and Coates.

NOTES AND COMMENTARY: With *Topeka*, director Thomas Carr really made use of camera movement to enhance the story. This experimentation would aid Carr in future, both for feature films and television.

REVIEWS: "Well done little actioner with a strong script and performances." *Western*

Topeka (Allied Artists, 1953) scene card — Fuzzy Knight (left) and Bill Elliott (right); the left border shows Bill Elliott on horseback.

Movies, Pitts; "A gripping western tale." *Motion Picture Guide*, Nash and Ross.

SUMMATION: This is a very good adult "B" western in which Bill Elliott is an outlaw, not a lawman masquerading as one, who will take a drink and smoke. Elliott's transformation from outlaw to honest citizen is believable, showing the inner conflict as he makes his decision. Thomas Carr's direction is exceptional, making use of unusual camera angles and movement to enhance the story.

Red Ryder ... No. 1 Comic Strip Hero of Fans from Coast-to-Coast!
Dashing, Fearless, Exciting ... Riding to His Most Amazing Action Adventure on the Trail of
Desperate Killers Who Terrorize the West!...

Tucson Raiders

Republic (May, 1944)

CAST: Red Ryder, **Wild Bill Elliott**; Gabby Hopkins, **George "Gabby" Hayes**; Little Beaver, **Bobby Blake**; the Duchess, **Alice Fleming**; Hannah Rogers, **Ruth Lee**; Beth Rogers, **Peggy Stewart**; Jeff Stark, **LeRoy Mason**; Governor York, **Stanley Andrews**; Tom Hamilton, **John Whitney**; One Eye, **Bud Geary**; Rev. George Allen, **Karl Hackett**; 1st Deputy, **Tom Steele**; 2nd Deputy, **Marshall Reed**; Judge James Wayne, **Tom Chatterton**; Sheriff Kirk, **Edward Cassidy**// "**Thunder**"; Logan, **Edward Howard**; Henchmen, **Fred Graham** and **Frank McCarroll**; Voice of Matthews, **Tom London**.

CREDITS: Director, **Spencer Bennett**; 2nd Unit Director, **Yakima Canutt**; Associate Producer, **Eddy White**; Story, **Jack O'Donnell**; Screenwriter, **Anthony Coldewey**; Editor, **Harry Keller**; Art Director, **Gano Chittenden**; Set Decorator, **Otto Siegel**; Cinematographer, **Reggie Lanning**; Sound, **Tom Carman**; Musical Score, **Joseph Dubin**.

LOCATION FILMING: Iverson, California.

RUNNING TIME: 55 min.

SOURCE: Based on Fred Harman's famous NEA comic, by special arrangement with Stephen Slesinger.

STORY: Summoned to Painted Valley by his aunt, Alice Fleming, Wild Bill Elliott and his Indian pal, Bobby Blake, return to find the area under the brutal control of Governor Stanley Andrews. Andrews' secret partner is respected banker LeRoy Mason. Fleming also sends for Federal Judge Tom Chatterton to bring law and order to Painted Valley. The unscrupulous Mason has as his ally Ruth Lee, a friend of Fleming's. Lee tells Mason that Chatterton is on the way to Painted Springs. Mason tells his henchmen to kill Chatterton, but they kill an innocent man instead. Elliot is framed for the murder and jailed. Realizing a trial will clear Elliott, Mason plans to allow Elliott to escape and subsequently be killed. Blake foils the plan and helps Elliott escape. Elliott realizes Lee is in league with the outlaws, and when Blake is kidnapped, has Fleming force Lee to tell him where Blake is being held. Lee also reveals that Mason is behind the lawlessness. Elliott frees Blake and a gun battle starts between Elliott and Mason and the outlaws. Elliott tells Mason that he has booby-trapped the strong box his men have stolen with explosives. Mason believes Elliott is running a bluff and tries to escape with the box. Outlaw Bud Geary sees Mason running out on his men with the strong box and shoots him. The box falls from Mason's grasp and explodes when it hits the ground, killing Mason and his gang. Andrews is removed from office, to be replaced by Chatterton. Elliott and Blake ride off to new adventures.

NOTES AND COMMENTARY: This was the first of eight westerns that Peggy Stewart would make with Bill Elliott. As the Red Ryder series progressed, Stewart, Elliott and Bobby Blake became close friends. Stewart noted that Elliott had a fine sense of humor and loved to kid cast members. Elliott loved to laugh, but Stewart said he had a funny sort of laugh. Instead of laughing outwardly, Stewart said he seemed to inhale his laughter.

Tucson Raiders (Republic, 1944) scene card — Bill Elliott (left) captures Edward Cassidy (right).

In the Red Ryder series, Elliott wore a hair piece designed to make him look more like the comic strip cowpoke. Don "Red" Barry wore a hair piece in the serial *Adventures of Red Ryder* (Republic, 1940), as well, but Peggy Stewart didn't think Allan Lane needed one for his turn as Red Ryder.

When Red Ryder returns to Painted Valley, he introduces Little Beaver to both the Duchess and Gabby. Little Beaver explains that a dam broke and drowned his people, but he was saved by Red, who took him under his wing.

The barn explosion at the end can be seen in many westerns and serials, both by Republic and Universal.

Two scenes found their way into *Meanwhile, Back at the Ranch* (Curtco & RCR Productions, 1977): first, Elliott goes to Bobby

Blake's rescue when Blake tries to stop Edward Cassidy from taking a shot at Elliott; then Elliott deciphers a code in an otherwise harmless looking note.

REVIEWS: "Mediocre plot, but lots of action in this 'Red Ryder' series entry." *Western Movies*, Pitts; "The new Red Ryder was a success." *Motion Picture Guide*, Nash and Ross.

SUMMATION: This is a good, fast-moving series entry, a solid start for Wild Bill Elliott's popular Red Ryder westerns. Elliott molds Fred Harman's famous comic strip character in his own image, which was still good news for western fans. Elliott makes a dynamic hero, and has able support from sidekicks George "Gabby" Hayes and Bobby Blake. A special nod goes to the fine cinematography of Reggie Lanning and steady direction of Spencer Bennett.

Something New in Western Serials!
Hair-Trigger, Hair-Raising Adventure Thundering to Rib-Tickling Hilarity!

The Valley of Vanishing Men

Columbia (December, 1942)

CAST: Wild Bill Tolliver, **Bill Elliott**; Missouri Benson, **Slim Summerville**; Consuelo Ramirez, **Carmen Morales**// "Sonny"; Jonathan Kincaid, **Kenneth MacDonald**; Major Stacy Roberts, **Lane Chandler**; Canyon City Marshal, **Michael Vallon**; Carter, **Stanley Price**; Butler, **Jack Ingram**; Taggart/Miner, **George Chesebro**; Mullins, **John Shay**; Slater, **Tom London**; Jose, **Julian Rivero**; General Garcia, **Martin Garralaga**; Luke, **Roy Barcroft**; Carl Enger, **Arno Frey**; Henry Tolliver, **Frank Shannon**; Stubby, **Ernie Adams**; Logan, **Kenne Duncan**; Harvey Cole, **Robert Fiske**; Ben Rutledge, **Davidson Clark**; Jim, **Karl Hackett**; Dr. Williams, **Forrest Taylor**; Henchmen, **Lane Bradford** and **Carl Mathews**; Townsman, **Blackie Whiteford**; Town Businessman, **Nolan Leary**; Cave Entrance Guard, **Ted Mapes**; Cave Prisoner's Guard, **Nick Thompson**; Raiders Cook, **Horace B. Carpenter**; Townsman, **Tex Cooper**; Chief Tall Tree, **Chief Thundercloud**; Miners, **Fred Burns**, **Hank Bell** and **John L. Cason**; Torrance, **I. Stanford Jolley**; Cave Prisoner, **Milburn Morante**; Raider with whip, **Constantine Romanoff**.

CREDITS: Director, **Spencer Bennet**; Screenwriters, **Harry Fraser**, **Lewis Clay** and **George Gray**; Editors, **Dwight Caldwell** and **Earl Turner**; Cinematographer, **James S. Brown, Jr.**

LOCATION FILMING: Iverson and Monogram Ranch, California.

RUNNING TIME: 279 min.

CHAPTER TITLES: Chapter 1, "Trouble in Canyon City"; Chapter 2, "The Mystery of the Ghost Town"; Chapter 3, "Danger Walks by Night"; Chapter 4, "Hillside Horror"; Chapter 5, "Guns in the Night"; Chapter 6, "The Bottomless Well"; Chapter 7, "The Man in the Gold Mask"; Chapter 8, "When the Devil Drives"; Chapter 9, "The Traitor's Shroud"; Chapter 10, "Death Strikes at Seven"; Chapter 11, "Satan in the Saddle"; Chapter 12, "The Mine of Missing Men"; Chapter 13, "Danger on Dome Rock"; Chapter 14, "The Door That Has No Key"; Chapter 15, "Empire's End."

STORY: Bill Elliott and his pal Slim Summerville travel to Canyon City to find his father, Rick Anderson, who has mysteriously disappeared. Kenneth MacDonald and his marauders are terrorizing the region and have imprisoned Anderson in an underground mine. As Elliott attempts to locate his father, he helps the lovely Carmen Morales in her fight against MacDonald. Morales and MacDonald are backing different factions in Mexico. After many harrowing adventures, Elliott and Summerville gain entrance to MacDonald's hideout. Elliott defeats MacDonald in a rugged fist fight. An explosion set by one of MacDonald's men causes a massive stone statue to fall on MacDonald, killing him. Elliott is reunited with Anderson. It looks like a romance is blooming between Elliott and Morales until Summerville breaks up a clinch.

NOTES AND COMMENTARY: *The Valley of Vanishing Men* was Bill Elliott's final effort for Columbia. Columbia's contract with Elliott called for one more serial. After completing the cliffhanger, Elliott moved over to Republic. His term-picture contract called for eight features at $2750 each. The contract also stipulated, at Elliott's request, that he was not to appear in serials.

Bill Elliott was the last major western performer to star in a serial. Clayton Moore and Jock Mahoney starred in serials prior to achieving major stardom in television and the silver screen, but not afterwards.

Copious footage from *The Valley of Vanishing Men* would be used in the serial *Riding with Buffalo Bill* (Columbia, 1954). Cliffhanger endings from eight chapters could be seen, plus footage from other chapters.

Wagner's "Ride of the Valkyries" was used

Valley of Vanishing Men (Columbia, 1942) title card — upper left shows Bill Elliott; lower left shows Slim Summerville (left) and Carmen Morales (right).

under the opening credits of each serial chapter.

REVIEW: "Bill Elliott's final Columbia assignment is a sadly cheap and dull cliffhanger." *Western Movies*, Pitts.

SUMMATION: Bill Elliott's third serial is a solid effort, thanks to Elliott's presence and performance, a good supporting cast headed by badman Kenneth MacDonald and Roy Barcroft, and some exciting cliffhanger endings and resolutions. On the minus side is some bumbling comedy sequences with sidekick Slim Summerville. Spencer Bennet directs at a fast clip.

A Double Dose of Hot Lead for Outlaws!

Vengeance of the West

Columbia (August, 1942)
ALTERNATE TITLE: *The Black Shadow*.
CAST: Joaquin Murietta, **Bill Elliott**; Captain "Tex" Lake, **Tex Ritter**; Cannonball Boggs, **Frank Mitchell**; Anita Morell, **Adele Mara**; Jeff Gorman, **Dick Curtis**; Gil Kirby, **Robert Fiske**; Mason, **Ted Mapes**; Maria, **Eva Puig**; Florencio, **Jose Tortosa**; Long John, **Guy Wilkerson**//

Vengeance of the West (Columbia, 1942) title card — lower left shows Adele Mara (left) and Tex Ritter (right); center shows Bill Elliott on Sonny; upper right shows a grim Bill Elliott (left) and Dick Curtis (right).

"Sonny"; "White Flash"; Henchman, **Steve Clark**; Carlos Murietta, **Stanley Brown**; Bartender, **John Tyrell**.

CREDITS: Director, **Lambert Hillyer**; Producer, **Leon Barsha**; Story, **Jack Townley**; Screenwriter, **Luci Ward**; Editor, **Burton Kramer**; Art Directors, **Lionel Banks** and **Perry Smith**; Cinematographer, **George Meehan**.

SONGS: "Along the Trail Somewhere"—sung by **Tex Ritter** and "Only Yesterday"—sung by **Tex Ritter**.

LOCATION FILMING: Iverson, California.

RUNNING TIME: 61 min.

STORY: Marshal Tex Ritter is summoned by Dick Curtis and Robert Fiske to bring the outlaw The Black Shadow to justice. Bill Elliott plays the role of The Black Shadow, a notorious outlaw thought to be dead but who is exacting revenge on Curtis and Fiske for crimes committed against him and his brother, Stanley Brown. Curtis and Fiske had jumped Elliott and Brown's gold claim, killing Brown and leaving Elliott for dead. As Curtis attempts to steal a deed to a gold mine owned by Adele Mara, Ritter soon learns where the real villainy lies. Elliott exacts a confession from Fiske, which implicates Curtis. Curtis kills Fiske believing him to be The Black Shadow. Finally, Elliott captures Curtis and gives him a chance to save himself by escaping from a posse while dressed as The Black Shadow. Curtis is unable to outrace a posse member's bullet and his evil career is finished. Ritter reports that Curtis was The Black Shadow, who robbed his own gold shipments. Elliott sails for South America with Mara at his side.

NOTES AND COMMENTARY: This was the last teaming of Bill Elliott and Tex Ritter. Elliott would star in his third serial, *Valley of Vanishing Men* (Columbia, 1942), before replacing Gene Autry at Republic. Ritter would appear in Charles Starrett's *Cowboy Canteen* (Columbia, 1942) before joining Johnny Mack Brown at Universal.

Vengeance of the West was a remake of Buck Jones' *The Avenger* (Columbia, 1931) with Jones as Murietta and Edward Hearn as Captain Lake.

To effect the role of a man of Hispanic descent, Elliott has a mustache, reminding viewers with long memories of his drawing room days in pictures.

REVIEW: "Fair entry in the Bill Elliott-Tex Ritter Columbia series which treads very lightly on history." *Western Movies*, Pitts.

SUMMATION: This is another good "B" western, with good acting, action and a strong story. Bill Elliott in particular shines as a man set upon vengeance, forsaking his peaceable man persona. Elliott shows both toughness and tenderness in his role, adding much to the proceedings. Also, look at the scene in which he's whipped by Dick Curtis, which focuses on Elliott's facial reactions to good effect. In support, Tex Ritter, Adele Mara and Curtis give able performances. Robert Fiske can be singled out portraying a greedy man, now afraid for his life. Frank Mitchell's dialog primarily consists of the line, "I never miss." And after some initial buffoonery, his character proves to be a capable ally of Elliott's. Lambert Hillyer's direction holds all the ingredients together for a proper finale to the Elliott-Ritter series.

Blazing Guns Were Their Badges
as They Struck in the Night!

Vigilante Terror

Allied Artists (November, 1953)

A Westwood Production

CAST: Tack Hamlin, **Wild Bill Elliott**; Lucy Taylor, **Mary Ellen Kay**; Gene Smith, **Robert Bray**; Matt Taylor, **Stanford Jolley**; Mayor Winch, **Henry Rowland**; Brett, **Myron Healey**; Brewer, **George Wallace**; Strummer, **Fuzzy Knight**; Bill, **Zon Murray**; Artie, **Richard Avonde**; Jamison, **Michael Colgan**; Sperry, **Denver Pyle**; Wilson, **Lee Roberts**; Jed, **John James**// Townsmen, **Stanley Price** and **Edward Cassidy**; Shotgun Guard, **Ted Mapes**.

CREDITS: Director, **Lewis Collins**; Producer, **Vincent M. Fennelly**; Assistant Director, **Melville Shyer**; Screenwriter, **Sid Theil**; Editor, **Sam Fields**; Set Decorator, **Theodore Offenbecker**; Cinematographer, **Ernest Miller**; Special Effects, **Ray Mercer**; Sound, **Thomas Lambert**; Music, **Raoul Kraushaar**; Set Continuity, **Emilie Ehrlich**; Dialogue Supervisor, **Stanley Price**.

LOCATION FILMING: Iverson and Corriganville, California.

RUNNING TIME: 70 min.

STORY: The Pinetop area is beset by outlaws and vigilante justice, with both groups headed by saloonkeeper Myron Healey. Wild Bill Elliott arrives to break his brother, John James, away from George Wallace's outlaw gang. Elliott and James see a sample of vigilante justice when innocent storekeeper Stanford Jolley is about to be hanged. Elliott stops the hanging and sends Jolley to his cabin for safekeeping. Then Elliott is shot and left for dead, and James is hanged. Elliott becomes marshal of Pinetop and, with deputy Fuzzy Knight, begins to bring law and order to the community. Healey and Wallace plan to frame Elliott for a stagecoach holdup. Wallace finds Jolley in Elliott's cabin. Healey incites the townspeople to lynch Elliott, Jolley and Knight. Jolley's daughter, Mary Ellen Kay, steps in and helps the men escape. Elliott knows where the outlaws are heading, and he and his group ride to catch up with them. Healey heads a posse to find Elliott and inadvertently leads them to

Vigilante Terror (Allied Artists, 1953) lobby card — Myron Healey (left) grabs the arm of Bill Elliott (center) as Fuzzy Knight (right) looks on.

Wallace and his gang. Wallace thinks Healy has double-crossed him, and he and his men open fire. Elliott and his group catch the outlaw gang in a crossfire. Elliott captures Wallace. Healey attempts to shoot Elliott but is wounded by Jolley. Still believing Healey to be a traitor, Wallace shots him. With the outlaw gang and the vigilante organization eliminated, law and order comes to Pinetop.

NOTES AND COMMENTARY: Mary Ellen Kay had a harrowing moment during the filming of *Vigilante Terror*. Bill Elliott had advised Kay that an upcoming scene involved some possibly perilous riding and wanted to know if she wanted a stuntwoman. Kay declined. As the shot progressed, the riders rode faster and faster. As the scene ended, all the riders brought their horses to a standstill except Kay. Her horse continued to race. Suddenly, Elliott came to her side, grabbed her horse's reins and brought her horse to a stop. Kay later remarked that this was exactly what the hero would do.

In an interview, Mary Ellen Kay remarked about Bill Elliott: "Bill Elliott was like a father figure to me. Being away from home, I felt he brought out some daughter-like feelings in me."

REVIEW: "The plot is nothing new, but good acting and production values makes this Bill Elliott vehicle a pleasing one." *Western Movies*, Pitts.

SUMMATION: *Vigilante Terror* is a strong, suspenseful, well-acted and directed "B" western. Wild Bill Elliott is in good form as a man driven to avenge his brother's death and bring law and order to the community. Fuzzy Knight chips in with a fine performance as Elliot's sidekick, eschewing the silliness he brought to some of his earlier works.

If It's Western Thrills You Crave....
Ride on Down to Dodge City with "Red." ... But We Warn You ... Don't Complain If You Run
into Trouble on the Trail ... There Are Desperate Killers on the Loose!

Vigilantes of Dodge City

Republic (November, 1944)

CAST: Red Ryder, **Wild Bill Elliott**; Little Beaver, **Bobby Blake**, the Duchess, **Alice Fleming**; Carol Franklin, **Linda Stirling**; Luther Jennings, **LeRoy Mason**; Bishop, **Hal Taliaferro**; Denver, **Tom London**; Captain Glover, **Stephen Barclay**; Benteen, **Bud Geary**; Dave Brewster, **Kenne Duncan**; Bill, **Bob Wilke**// "**Thunder**"; Jim Evans, **Post Parks**; Jeff Moore, **Horace B. Carpenter**; General Wingate, **Stanley Andrews**; Henchmen, **Ralph Bucko** and **Dale Van Sickel.**

CREDITS: Director, **Wallace Grissell**; 2nd Unit Director, **Yakima Canutt**; Associate Producer, **Stephen Auer**; Editor, **Charles Craft**; Art Director, **Fred A. Ritter**; Set Decorator, **Earl Wooden**; Cinematographer, **William Bradford**; Sound, **Ed Borschell**; Musical Director, **Joseph Dubin.**

LOCATION FILMING: Iverson, California.

RUNNING TIME: 54 min.

SOURCE: Based on Fred Harman's famous NEA comic, by special arrangement with Stephen Slesinger.

STORY: Banker LeRoy Mason and Insurance agent Hal Taliaferro want control of Alice

Vigilantes of Dodge City (Republic, 1944) scene card — Bill Elliott (left) and Bobby Blake (right) are ready for action.

Fleming's freight and stage line. Mason has outlaw Bud Geary and his men hold up Fleming's wagons. Realizing Fleming's nephew, Wild Bill Elliott, will make trouble, Mason has Geary rustle the horses meant to fulfill a government contract. Elliott is accused of defrauding the Army and is arrested by Captain Stephen Barclay. A plan to murder Barclay and frame Elliott is thwarted by Elliott's quick action. Believing Elliott to be innocent, Barclay allows Elliott to return to Dodge City and find the guilty party. Elliott's Indian pal, Bobby Blake, locates the stolen horses and learns that Mason and Taliaferro are behind the lawlessness. Both are killed when Elliott tries to bring the men to justice. Elliott receives another Army contract for horses.

NOTES AND COMMENTARY: In this Red Ryder entry, the Duchess is known as "Miss Ryder." In earlier episodes, her name was given as Martha Wentworth.

The chase sequence at the climax of the film was borrowed for the finale in the Monte Hale western, *Outcasts of the Trail* (Republic, 1949).

Tom Steele doubled Wild Bill Elliott in *Vigilantes of Dodge City*.

REVIEW: "Fast paced and actionful 'Red Ryder' series entry." *Western Movies*, Pitts.

SUMMATION: This is an exciting, well-done Red Ryder adventure. Wild Bill Elliott doesn't get a chance to show his acting range, but does deliver his lines convincingly, as well as excelling in the action department. The supporting cast chips in with good performances, even though Linda Stirling has little to do but look beautiful. Wallace Grissell directs briskly, utilizing a good script from Norman S. Hall and Anthony Coldewey, and exceptional cinematography from William Bradford, especially in the chase sequences.

Wild, Wide Open...
Its Bitter Brawls Blazed from Dusk to Dawn!
Its Roaring Guns Echoed from the Pecos to the Panhandle!

Waco

Monogram (February, 1952)
A Silvermine Production
ALTERNATE TITLE: *The Outlaw and the Lady*.

CAST: Matt Boone, **Wild Bill Elliott**; Curly Ivers, **Stanford Jolley**; Kathy Clark, **Pamela Blake**; Lou Garcia, **Paul Fierro**; Al, **Rand Brooks**; Pedro, **Richard Avonde**; Farley, **Pierce Lydon**; Wallace, **Lane Bradford**; Richards, **Terry Frost**; Waco Sheriff, **Stanley Price**; Judge, **Stanley Andrews**; Barnes, **Michael Whalen**; Bull Clark, **Ray Bennett**; Crawford, **Rory Mallinson**; Logan, **Richard Paxton**; Pecos Sheriff, **Russ Whitman**; Doctor, **House Peters, Jr.**// Bank Guard, **Ed Cassidy**; Waco Bartender, **Michael Vallon**; Stage Driver, **George Sowards**; Stage Guard, **Ted Mapes**; Ranger Carmody, **John Hart**.

CREDITS: Director, **Lewis Collins**; Assistant Director, **Melville Shyer**; Producer, Vin-cent M. Fennelly; Screenwriter, **Dan Ullman**; Editor, **Sam Fields**; Art Director, **Martin Obzina**; Set Decorator, **Theo Offenbecker**; Cinematographer, **Ernest Miller**; Sound, **John Kean**; Music, **Raoul Kraushaar**; Dialogue Director, **Stanley Price**; Set Continuity, **Emilie Ehrlich**; Color by **Sepiatone**.

LOCATION FILMING: Iverson and Corriganville, California.

RUNNING TIME: 68 min.

STORY: In a crooked card game in Waco, Wild Bill Elliott outdraws and kills leading rancher Ray Bennett. Branded an outlaw, and with a price on his head (courtesy of Bennett's daughter, Pamela Blake), Elliott finds refuge with Stanford Jolley's outlaw gang. Realizing he has no other course of action, Elliott begins taking part in the gang's holdups. During a bank holdup, Elliott is wounded and captured. Two leading Waco citizens, Terry Frost and

Pierce Lyden, bring Elliott back for trial. Elliott is found not guilty and is made sheriff of Waco. Jolley tells Elliott his gang will stay out of Elliott's jurisdiction. Slowly, Elliott begins to bring law and order to the community. Pamela Blake is opposed to Elliott receiving a pardon for his past crimes. Blake is kidnapped by Paul Fierro, Jolley gang member, and is rescued by Elliott. When Elliott tells Fierro to stay out of his way instead of shooting him down in cold blood, Blake begins to respect and then fall in love with Elliott. Jolley is captured and brought to Waco for trial. Jolley tells Elliott that Fierro is coming in to shoot Elliott. Elliott, unable to stand to see his friend executed, releases Jolley. Jolley stays in town to meet Fierro but is no match for Fiero's speed and accuracy with a gun. Elliott arrives, and he and Fierro exchange shots. Elliott is wounded, but Elliott's bullets prove fatal. Elliott and Blake now plan to marry.

NOTES AND COMMENTARY: House Peters, Jr. commented about Bill Elliott: "Bill Elliott was a very congenial gentleman on the set. He was a very friendly guy, but he was the star of the picture. I wasn't as close to him as Roy [Rogers] or even Gene [Autry], for that matter."

REVIEWS: "An acceptable blend of western action. Elliott paces himself excellently through the Dan Ullman plot that finds the hero turned outlaw after killing a man in self defense and then is hired as sheriff to clean up the town of Waco." *Variety*, 2/27/52; "Sturdy Bill Elliott vehicle with an entertaining and literate script." *Western Movies*, Pitts.

SUMMATION: This is a terrific adult "B" western with an introspective and thoughtful performance by Wild Bill Elliott. Elliott is excellent as an innocent man driven outside the law who is given a second chance to live an honest life.

Waco (Monogram, 1952) scene card — Bill Elliott (second right) grabs the vest of Rory Mallinson (left) as cowboy Dale Van Sickel (second left) and bartender George Eldredge (right) look on. Note: Though this is a great card, the scene is actually from Elliott's *next* release, *Kansas Territory*.

The Peak of Thrill-Packed Adventure with Your Action Ace, "Wild Bill" Elliott!...

Wagon Tracks West

Republic (August, 1943)

CAST: Wild Bill Elliott, **Wild Bill Elliott**; Gabby Whittaker, **George "Gabby" Hayes**; Clawtooth, **Tom Tyler**; Moonhush, **Anne Jeffreys**; Fleetwing, **Rick Vallin**; Robert Warren, **Robert Frazier**; Laird, **Roy Barcroft**; Brown Bear, **Charles Miller**; Lem Martin, **Tom London**; Matt, **Cliff Lyons**; Sheriff Summers, **Jack Rockwell**// "**Sonny**"; Professor at Medical School, **Bryant Washburn**; Townsmen, **Jack O'Shea** and **Marshall Reed**; Blacksmith, **Curley Dresden**; Saloon Patrons, **Hank Bell, Roy Butler, Kenne Duncan** and **Frank McCarroll**; Nurse, **Minerva Urecal**; Henchman, **Jack Ingram**.

CREDITS: Director, **Howard Bretherton**; Associate Producer, **Louis Gray**; Screenwriter, **William Lively**; Editor, **Charles Craft**; Art Director, **Russell Kimball**; Set Decorator, **Charles Thompson**; Cinematography, **Reggie Lanning**; Sound, **Tom Carman**; Original Music, **Mort Glickman**.

LOCATION FILMING: Bronson Canyon, Iverson and Lake Sherwood, California.

RUNNING TIME: 55 min.

STORY: Wild Bill Elliott and his sidekick George "Gabby" Hayes make a narrow escape from a band of Indians by jumping into a contaminated lake. Only Hayes swallows some of

Wagon Tracks West (Republic, 1943) scene card — Bill Elliott, Anne Jeffreys (notice her black wig), Tom Tyler and unidentified actor (left to right, standing) watch as Rick Vallin ministers to the tribal chief.

the water, and he becomes ill. Rick Vallin, the first Indian physician to graduate from medical school, successfully treats Hayes. The trouble between the Indians and the settlers stems from the faulty irrigation system installed by the cattlemen. Indian agent Robert Frazier, and his assistant Roy Barcroft, are working with medicine man Tom Tyler to have the Indians relocated so that Frazier can start a cattle empire. To further his plans, Frazier murders cattleman Tom London and has the crime blamed on Vallin. Elliott and Hayes hide Vallin so they can uncover the culprits. Tyler leads a posse to Vallin, who is captured and sentenced to hang. Elliott gets both Tyler and Barcroft to confess their part in Frazier's scheme. Elliott then brings Frazier to justice. The cattlemen plan to clean up the contaminated lake and open an office for Vallin.

NOTES AND COMMENTARY: Tom Tyler had just completed the Three Mesquiteers series, and Republic had Tyler for this last western before he left the studio. Tyler's starring career was almost over. He was the lead in the serial *The Phantom* (Columbia, 1943) and the western musical *Sing Me a Song of Texas* (Columbia, 1945), and co-starred with Rod Cameron in *Boss of Boomtown* (Universal, 1944). Tyler was then relegated to villain and support roles for the rest of his career.

Anne Jeffreys, a blonde, had to wear a black wig with pigtails in the film. Darker makeup was applied. She was costumed in a buckskin outfit and moccasins. In this attire, Jeffreys went to the Republic commissary for lunch and sat at the counter. Her agent sat down in a seat next to Jeffreys. She could tell he didn't recognize her. Jeffreys asked him,

"You makeup pictures?" Her agent ignored her. Jeffreys started laughing. Her agent finally realized who she was. Jeffreys reminded him that he was her agent and got her the part of the Indian maiden, Moonhush.

On the set, the crew was always playing tricks on each other. One day Anne Jeffreys was sitting in her chair studying her script. Quietly, the crew tied her fringe to the chair. Jeffreys had removed her moccasins, and the practical jokers had filled them with talcum powder. Called to the set, Jeffreys found that she was dragging the chair, and with every step a white cloud of smoke would rise from her feet. Jeffreys decided to get even. On location she took some smoked salmon used for a scene in the picture and put it in the prop box. An unpleasant smell resulted, and it took three days for the crew to locate the fish. No more tricks were played on Jeffreys.

In watching *Wagon Tracks West*, to this author's eyes it looks more like Bill Hazlett (Chief Many Treaties) playing Brown Bear than the credited Charles Miller.

REVIEWS: "Standard western dualer featuring Bill Elliott and 'Gabby' Hayes." *Variety*, 10/27/43; "A superb supporting cast is one of the many plus factors in this good Bill Elliott vehicle." *Western Movies*, Pitts.

SUMMATION: This is a good Wild Bill Elliott adventure, with a strong story line. Elliott delivers a tough but sensitive performance. Look at his reaction when he realizes George "Gabby" Hayes is sick. Hayes does well in his role, except for the few minutes he's asked to play the buffoon. Howard Bretherton directs in a workmanlike manner.

Ride the Adventure Trail with Red Ryder...
The Fast-Shootin,' Hard Ridin' Hero of Millions. A Pulse-Pounding Action Thrill You'll Never Forget!

Wagon Wheels Westward

Republic Pictures (December, 1945)
CAST: Red Ryder, **Wild Bill Elliott**; Little Beaver, **Bobby Blake**; the Duchess, **Alice Fleming**; Arlie, **Linda Stirling**; McKean, **Roy Bar**croft; Pop Dale, **Emmett Lynn**; Tuttle, **Dick Curtis**; Bob Adams, **Jay Kirby**; Lunsford, **George J. Lewis**; Fake Sheriff Brown, **Bud Geary**; Fake Judge Worth, **Tom London**; Joe,

Kenne Duncan; Butch, **George Chesebro**// "Thunder"; Henchman at stable, **Jack Kirk**; John Larkin, **Robert McKenzie**.

CREDITS: Director, **R.G. Springsteen**; Associate Producer, **Sidney Picker**; Story, **Gerald Geraghty**; Screenwriter, **Earle Snell**; Editor, **Fred Allen**; Art Director, **Frank Hotaling**; Cinematographer, **William Bradford**; Makeup, **Bob Mark**; Sound, **Earl Crain**; Musical Director, **Richard Cherwin**.

LOCATION FILMING: Iverson and Bronson Canyon, California.

RUNNING TIME: 56 min.

SOURCE: Based on Fred Harman's Famous NEA Comic — by special arrangement with Stephen Slesinger.

STORY: Outlaw leader Roy Barcroft intercepts mail telling of a wagon train, led by Wild Bill Elliott, that is heading for Desert Springs. The settlers plan to buy businesses and prop-

erty. Barcroft and his men arrive in Desert Springs first and find the town deserted. Barcroft decides to have himself and his men pose as town inhabitants, and collect the money for whatever property the wagon train members wish to purchase. George J. Lewis had joined the wagon train to blackmail newlywed Linda Stirling, wife of Jay Kirby. Lewis and Kirby argue when Kirby believes Lewis is trying to force his attentions on Stirling. In Desert Springs, Lewis recognizes one of Barcroft's men and wants to be cut in on the deal. Barcroft's henchman, Dick Curtis, murders Lewis, and Kirby is accused of the crime. Elliott believes Kirby is innocent, and he and his Indian pal Bobby Blake search for clues. Blake finds the murder bullet that proves Kirby is not guilty. But fake Sheriff Bud Geary wants to keep Kirby in jail. Elliott senses something is wrong and has the wagon train leave town. Elliott, with

Wagon Wheels Westward (Republic, 1945) scene card — Bill Elliott (center) and Emmett Lynn (right) get the drop on Bud Geary (left).

Blake and scout Emmett Lynn, returns to town to free Kirby. At the same time, Barcroft and most of his henchmen ambush the wagon train. After a gunfight with the henchmen left to guard the town, Elliott frees Kirby. Elliott, Blake, Lynn and Kirby ride to help the wagon train. With the outlaws caught in a crossfire, Barcroft sees that his plan is doomed and tries to escape. Elliott gives chase and whips Barcroft in a short fight. The wagon train returns to Desert Springs, to be greeted by land agent Robert MacKenzie. News of a gold strike stampeded the whole town. The wagon train members are now able to settle in Desert Springs.

NOTES AND COMMENTARY: Roy Barcroft would reprise his role of McKean against Allan Lane's Red Ryder in *Vigilantes of Boom Town* (Republic, 1947). He would be the only actor to play the same role in two different entries of Republic's Red Ryder series. Although Ace Hanlon would appear in two Republic Red Ryders, *The San Antonio Kid* (Republic, 1944) and *Phantom of the Plains* (Republic, 1945), two different actors would essay the role, Glenn Strange in *Kid* and William Haade in *Phantom*.

Strange would get a second shot at playing Hanlon in Jim Bannon's *Roll, Thunder, Roll* (Eagle Lion, 1949).

In the rugged fistfight between Wild Bill Elliott and Dick Curtis, Tom Steele doubled Elliott, while Fred Graham stood in for Curtis.

When Elliott is registering the wagon train members at the hotel in Desert Springs, the Duchess' name is seen on the register as Martha Wentworth.

REVIEW: "Well written 'Red Ryder' series vehicle." *Western Movies*, Pitts.

SUMMATION: This is a fast moving, highly entertaining Red Ryder entry, despite it being a trifle illogical. Once you suspend your disbelief that one incident could vacate an entire community, the story becomes very enjoyable, thanks to Wild Bill Elliott's ability as both an actor and action star. The film boasts a fine supporting cast of genre performers, with special mention going to Roy Barcroft's fine performance as the boss heavy. Listen to Barcroft address his gang of roughnecks as "my children" before outlining his latest villainous scheme.

It's Show-Down Time ... Out Where the West Begins!

The Wildcat of Tucson

Columbia (December, 1940)
A Wild Bill Hickok Adventure
ALTERNATE TITLE: *Promise Fulfilled*.
CAST: Wild Bill Hickok, **Bill Elliott**; Vivian Barlow, **Evelyn Young**; Dave Hickok, **Stanley Brown**; Cannonball, **Dub Taylor**; Rance McKee, **Kenneth MacDonald**; Judge Barlow, **Ben Taggart**; Seth Harper, **Edmund Cobb**; U.S. Marshal, **George Lloyd**; Gus Logan, **Sammy Stein**// "**Sonny**"; Bobby, **Robert Winkler**; Tough in Newspaper Office, **Francis Walker**; Charlie (Newspaper Editor), **Forrest Taylor**; Henchman, **George Chesboro**; Doctor, **Murdock MacQuarrie**; Vigilantes, **Steve Clark** and **Jim Corey**.
CREDITS: Director, **Lambert Hillyer**; Screenwriter, **Fred Myton**; Editor, **Charles Nelson**; Cinematography, **George Meehan**.

SONGS: "Wild Bill and Me"— sung by **Dub Taylor**; "Looking Out and Looking In"— sung by **Dub Taylor**.
LOCATION FILMING: Iverson, California.
RUNNING TIME: 59 min.
STORY: Kenneth MacDonald is systematically taking ranches from their lawful owners, with help from Judge Ben Taggart and U.S. Marshal George Lloyd. In preventing Lloyd and MacDonald's henchman Sammy Stein from taking possession of Edmund Cobb's ranch, Stanley Brown is arrested and convicted of attempted murder. Brown's partner, Dub Taylor, gets Brown's brother, Bill Elliott, to take a hand. Elliott surmises that MacDonald is behind Brown's problems. Brown escapes from jail, making him an outlaw. Finding where Brown is hiding, Elliott and Brown's sweetheart, Eve-

Wildcat of Tucson (Columbia, 1941) scene card — Bill Elliott (center) gets the drop on Sammy Stein (second left), as an unidentified actor (left), Kenneth MacDonald (second right) and George Chesebro (right) look on; the left border shows Bill Elliott and Evelyn Young.

lyn Young, ride to convince him to turn himself in. Brown refuses, accusing Elliott of wanting him in jail so that Elliott can romance Young. In truth, Young fleetingly has romantic designs on Elliott, but Elliott isn't interested. Elliott discovers Taggart is in league with MacDonald and makes him sign a document to that effect. MacDonald decides to have Taggart killed by Stein. Brown comes to town and Stein shoots Brown, only wounding him. Taylor returns fire, killing Stein. Taggart tells Elliott all charges will be dropped against Brown. Elliott meets MacDonald in his office. In a gun duel, Elliott is the victor. Brown recovers, soon to be married to Young. Elliott rides off to new adventures.

NOTES AND COMMENTARY: Newt Kirby doubled Bill Elliott; Dorothy Andre doubled Evelyn Young; John Daheim doubled Stanley Brown; and Bert Young doubled Dub Taylor.

REVIEWS: "Fairly actionful Bill Elliott vehicle." *Western Movies*, Pitts; "An indifferent series entry for Elliott, distinguished only by his final exciting showdown with MacDonald." *The Western*, Hardy.

SUMMATION: Bill Elliott's presence, with a matching performance by Kenneth MacDonald, brings this western saga satisfactorily to the screen. Elliott, tight lipped and grim, but with a touch of humor towards youngsters and friends, is in fine form as Wild Bill Hickok. MacDonald, almost as equally tight lipped, makes a worthy villain. The final confrontation between the two adversaries is beautifully constructed. An interesting subplot has heroine Evelyn Young momentarily switching her affection from Stanley Brown to his brother, Elliott. Lambert Hillyer's direction is first rate.

Thrilling Wyoming *Is a Great Outdoor Drama!*

Wyoming

Republic (July, 1947)

CAST: Charles Alderson, **William Elliott**; Karen Alderson (Elliott's wife), **Vera Ralston**; Karen Alderson (Elliott's daughter), **Vera Ralston**; Glenn Forrester, **John Carroll**; Windy Gibson, **George "Gabby" Hayes**; Duke Lassiter, **Albert Dekker**; Lila Regan, **Virginia Grey**; Maria, **Mme. Maria Ouspenskaya**; Joe Sublette, **Grant Withers**; Ben Jackson, **Harry Woods**; Queenie, **Minna Gombell**; Ed Lassiter, **Dick Curtis**; Sheriff Niles, **Roy Barcroft**; Timmons, **Trevor Bardette**; Judge Sheridan, **Paul Harvey**; Karen (age 9), **Louise Kane**; Will Jennings, **Tom London**; Jackson Henchman, **George Chesebro**; Karen (age 3), **Linda Green**; Steve, **Jack O'Shea**// Jennings Ranch Hand, **Glenn Strange**; Townsmen, **Tex Cooper** and **Marshall Reed**; Alderson Ranch Hands, **Ben Johnson** and **Olin Howlin**; Grub Line Rider, **Eddy Waller**; Court Clerk, **Rex Lease**; Reverend, **Charles Middleton**; Homesteaders, **Eddie Acuff** and **Edward Piel, Sr.**; Morrison, **Tex Terry**.

CREDITS: Director/Associate Producer, **Joe Kane**; Second Unit Director, **Yakima Canutt**; Screenwriters, **Lawrence Hazard** and **Gerald Geraghty**; Editor, **Arthur Roberts**; Art Director, **Frank Hotaling**; Set Decorators, **John McCarthy, Jr.** and **George Suhr**; Cinematographer, **John Alton**; Costumes, **Adele Palmer**; Makeup, **Bob Mark**; Hair Stylist, **Peggy Gray**; Sound, **Herbert Norsch**; Musical Director, **Cy Fruer**; Original Music, **Nathan G. Scott** and **Ernest Gold**; Special Effects, **Howard** and **Theodore Lydecker**.

SONGS: "Get Along Little Doggie" (traditional) — sung by **George "Gabby" Hayes**, **John Carroll**, **William Elliott**, **Vera Ralston** and **chorus**.

LOCATION FILMING: Iverson, Kernville and Bronson Canyon, California.

RUNNING TIME: 84 min.

STORY: William Elliott brings his wife, Vera Ralston, and Maria Ouspenskaya to settle in Wyoming. Elliott teams up with George "Gabby" Hayes to build a cattle empire. With the death of his wife in childbirth, Elliott's daughter, Vera Ralston, will benefit from his vast holdings. On her return from school in Europe, Ralston, now a young lady, meets Elliott's foreman and best friend, John Carroll. Ralston and Carroll quickly fall in love. The Homestead Act allows nesters to claim land, to which Elliott is opposed. Albert Dekker plots to cause a range war between the ranchers and nesters to cover up his cattle rustling activities. Dekker's chief henchman, Grant Withers, murders Hayes. Elliott wants to take revenge by wiping out all the homesteaders. Elliott is encouraged by the small ranchers to hire outlaw Harry Woods to gun down the nesters, not realizing Woods is really in the employ of Dekker. Elliott's determination to rid the area of homesteaders causes a rift between him and Carroll. Dekker arranges to have the homesteaders bottled up in a blind canyon so Woods and his men can slaughter them. Ralston tells Elliott she has to be with Carroll. As Woods and his men are about to fire on the homesteaders, Elliott allows the homesteaders to ride out of the canyon. Carroll and the homesteaders ride down on Woods and his gang. A shot from Carroll's pistol ends Woods' outlaw career, and the homesteaders easily scatter the gang. Elliott decides to settle things with Dekker, and they meet out on the plains. Withers attempts to cut down Elliott from ambush, but Carroll shoots him. In a gun duel, Elliott outdraws Dekker and kills him. Carroll and Ralston rush to Elliott's side. Elliott tells Carroll the ranchers and homesteaders have to find a common ground and work together. Ralston is happy, since Elliott and Carroll have patched up their differences and now she can marry Carroll.

NOTES AND COMMENTARY: *Wyoming* was originally scheduled to be filmed in Technicolor. William Marshall was assigned to the role of Glenn Forrester, which eventually went to John Carroll. The screenplay was to be writ-

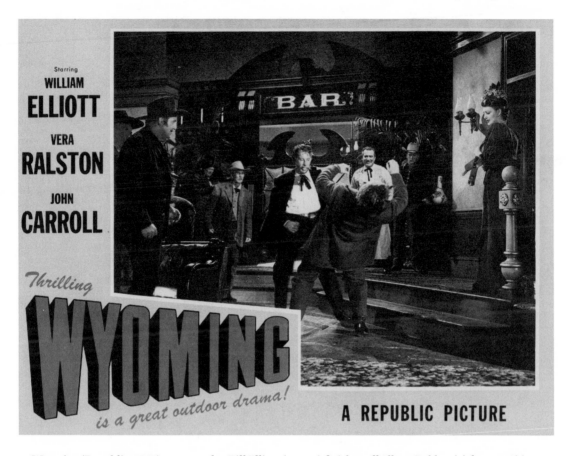

Starring
WILLIAM
ELLIOTT

VERA
RALSTON

JOHN
CARROLL

Thrilling

WYOMING
is a great outdoor drama!

A REPUBLIC PICTURE

Wyoming (Republic, 1947) scene card — Bill Elliott (center) finishes off Albert Dekker (right center) in a great screen fistfight as Roy Barcroft (left), Jack O'Shea (over Dekker's head) and Virginia Gray (right) watch.

ten by Richard Wormser, Mary Loos and Richard Sale, from an original story by Wormser, but Lawrence Hazard and Gerald Geraghty penned the final script.

In the fight between William Elliott and Albert Dekker, Ben Johnson doubles Elliott and Fred Graham stands in for Dekker.

REVIEWS: "There is plenty of six-gun shooting, hard riding and a pip of a knockdown and drag-out Donnybrook between the boss (Elliott) and Dekker. Everything, in fact, is plausible and exciting, providing one is fiendishly addicted to saddle sagas. Mr. Elliott, a cowpoke opera veteran, is at home in the saddle and handling his twin Colts." *New York Times*, 7/25/47; "Beautifully lit by Alton with a vividness that was unusual for the period and energetically directed by Kane, this one of Elliott's prestige Westerns." *The Western*, Hardy.

SUMMATION: *Wyoming* is a very good western. William Elliott believably portrays a man first bent on establishing a cattle empire and then obsessed with keeping the power he's attained — before realizing his ambitions will estrange him from the daughter he loves. Elliott's performance is outstanding. Elliott is backed by an impressive supporting cast, notably George "Gabby" Hayes as the old-timer who shows Elliott the ropes; Albert Dekker as the man who tries to bring Elliott's empire crashing down; John Carroll as Elliott's best friend, now at odds with Elliott; and Virginia Gray as the woman who loves Elliott through all adversity. The fistfight between Elliott and Dekker is well choreographed and one of the finest to be brought to the screen. Joe Kane smartly directs the film, with cinematographer John Alton beautifully utilizing the impressive locations to great advantage.

Elliott's Supporting Roles

*Batter Up! ... and the Battier the Better ... as the Iron Man
of the Diamond Is Struck Dumb by a Dame's Curves!*

Alibi Ike

Warner Bros. (June, 1935)

CAST: Frank X. Farrell, **Joe E. Brown**; Dolly Stevens, **Olivia de Havilland**; Bess, **Ruth Donnelly**; Carey, **Roscoe Karns**; Cap, **William Frawley**; Mack, **Eddie Shubert**; Crawford, **Paul Harvey**; Mr. Johnson, **Joseph King**; Conductor, **Joseph Crehan**; Lieutenant, **G. Pat Collins**; Minister, **Spencer Charters**; Smitty, **Gene Morgan**// Baseball Game Spectator, **Gordon Elliott**.

CREDITS: Director, **Ray Enright**; Screenwriter, **William Wister Haines**; Editor, **Thomas Pratt**; Art Director, **Esdras Hartley**; Cinematographer, **Arthur L. Todd**; Musical Director, **Leo F. Forbstein**; Dialogue Director, **Gene Lewis**.

RUNNING TIME: 73 min.

SOURCE: Story, "Alibi Ike" by **Ring Lardner**.

STORY: Joe E. Brown, rookie pitching sensation for the Chicago Cubs, meets manager William Frawley's sister-in-law, Olivia de Havilland. The two immediately fall in love. Their engagement falls through when Brown, known for making excuses for anything he does, downplays his romantic attentions to de Havilland. Brown, love-sick, begins to pitch badly — to delight of gangsters who previously had tried to intimidate him. De Havilland, told of Brown's tendency to "alibi," comes to Chicago to see Brown pitch the crucial game that would get the Cubs into the World Series. The gangsters kidnap Brown. Brown gets free and races to the stadium. Even though Brown allows the tying runs to score in the top of the ninth inning, Brown hits an inside-the-park home run to win the game. Brown and de Havilland tie the knot.

NOTES AND COMMENTARY: In a brief scene, Gordon Elliott plays a spectator at the Chicago Cubs' crucial baseball game. Learning that Joe E. Brown won't play, Elliott remarks to a fellow spectator, "They better, if they want to win this game."

REVIEWS: "A genuinely amusing little comedy." *New York Times*, 7/17/35; "One of the more substantial Joe E. Brown comedies." *The Warner Bros. Story*, Hirshhorn.

SUMMATION: Joe E. Brown is at his best in this hilarious baseball comedy.

Never So Many Different Kinds of Thrills — Crammed into One Picture Before.

Arizona Wildcat

Fox (November, 1927) A R. William Neill production

CAST: Tom Phelan, **Tom Mix**; Regina Schyler, **Dorothy Sebastian**; Wallace Van Acker, **Ben Bard**; Roy Schyler, **Gordon Elliott**; Low Jack Wilkins, **Monte Collins**; Mother Schyler, **Cissy Fitzgerald**; Marie, **Doris Dawson**; Helen Van Acker, **Marcella Daly**; "Tony."

CREDITS: Director, **R. William Neill**; Assistant Director, **Wynn Mace**; Story, **Adele Rogers St. Johns**; Screenwriter, **John Stone**; Cinematography, **Dan Clark**.

RUNNING TIME: 56 min.

STORY: Tom Mix meets his childhood sweetheart, Dorothy Sebastian, after a number of years and finds her being maneuvered by two Eastern crooks. One of the crooks attempts to cause Gordon Elliott's (Sebastian's brother) polo team to lose an important match by disabling a key player. Although the crooks try to stop him, Mix, riding Tony, enters the match and secures victory for Elliott. The crooks kidnap Sebastian but Mix rescues her and brings them to justice.

NOTES AND COMMENTARY: Gordon Elliott receives fourth billing in this Tom Mix western.

REVIEW: "Nicely played with good comedy values. Picture has ingenuity and a certain elegance that raises it above the typical western to a punch melodramatic subject." *Variety*, 1/25/28.

SUMMATION: This film was not available for viewing by the author.

There Wasn't a Kick in a Carload of His Kisses ... but His Bankroll Packed a Wallop.

Bachelor's Affairs

Fox (June, 1932)

CAST: Andrew Hoyt, **Adolphe Menjou**; Sheila Peck, **Minna Gombell**; Oliver Denton, **Arthur Pierson**; Eva, **Joan Marsh**; Luke Radcliff, **Alan Dinehart**; Jane, **Irene Purcell**; Ramon, **Don Alverado**; Jepson, **Herbert Mundin**; Mrs. Oliver Denton, **Rita La Roy**// Ship's Passenger, **Gordon Elliott**.

CREDITS: Director, **Alfred L. Werker**; Producer, **Edmund Grainger**; Screenwriters, **Barry Conners** and **Philip Klein**; Editor, **Alfred De-Gaetano**; Cinematographer, **Norbert Brodine**; Costumes, **David Cox**.

SOURCE: play, *Precious* by **James Forbes**.

RUNNING TIME: 64 min.

STORY: Adolphe Menjou falls for Joan Marsh, a much younger but not-so-bright woman. Marsh pretends not to like men her own age. To please Marsh, Menjou begins to act like a younger man. Marsh falls for Arthur Pierson, which means the end of her marriage with Menjou. Pierson's divorced wife, Rita La Roy, demands $5000 from Menjou, which he happily gives her.

NOTES AND COMMENTARY: One source states that Gordon Elliott appears as a ship's passenger.

REVIEWS: "A rather obvious but nevertheless frequently amusing screen contribution." *New York Times*, 6/25/32; "Predictable comedy." *Motion Picture Guide*, Nash and Ross.

SUMMATION: This film was not available for viewing by the author.

Beyond London's Lights

FBO Pictures (March, 1928)

CAST: Kitty Carstairs, **Adrienne Dore**; John Risk, **Lee Shumway**; Colin Drummond, **Gordon Elliott**; Symington, **Herbert Evans**; Lady Dorothy, **Jacqueline Gadsden**; Mrs. Drummond, **Florence Wix**; Stephen Carstairs, **Templar Saxe**; Mrs. Bundle, **Blanche Craig**; Landlady, **Katherine Ward**.

CREDITS: Director, **Tom Terris**; Assistant Director, **Ray McCarey**; Screenwriter, **Jean DuPont**; Titles, **George Arthur**; Adaptation, **Beatrice Burton**; Editor, **Pandro S. Berman**; Cinematographer, **Robert De Grasse**.

RUNNING TIME: 55 min.

SOURCE: *Kitty Carstairs* by **John Joy Bell**.

STORY: Gordon Elliott is engaged to marry Adrienne Dore. Disapproving of the romance, Elliott's mother, Florence Wix, hires Dore as a maid. Also, Wix invites the wealthy and beautiful Jacqueline Gadsden to visit, hoping to entice Elliott to show interest in her. With Wix' animosity against her, Dore leaves and become acquainted with artist Lee Shumway. Dore becomes a model in a modiste shop. Elliott realizes that he's still in love with Dore and breaks his engagement to Gadsden. But it's too late, as Dore and Shumway have fallen in love.

NOTES AND COMMENTARY: Gordon Elliott receives third billing and loses out to Lee Shumway for Adrienne Dore's affections. Elliott's name was listed first in *Variety*'s review.

REVIEW: "A light but nicely put together melodrama." *Variety*, 4/11/28.

SUMMATION: This film was not available for viewing by the author.

Comedy Classic of the Year
Jolson Songs, Jolson Gags and Jolson Personality Is the Greatest Entertainment Yet.

Big Boy

Warner Bros. (September, 1930)

CAST: Gus, **Al Jolson**; Annabel, **Claudia Dell**; Mother, **Louise Closser Hale**; Jack, **Lloyd Hughes**; Coley Reed, **Eddie Phillips**; Doc Wilbur, **Lew Harvey**; Jim, **Franklin Batie**; Joe, **John Harron**; Tucker, **Tom Wilson**; Steve Leslie, **Colin Campbell**; Bagby, **Noah Beery**// Race Track Fan, **Gordon Elliott**.

CREDITS: Director, **Alan Crosland**; Screenwriters, **William K. Wells** and **Rex Taylor**; Editor, **Ralph Dawson**; Cinematographer, **Hal Mohr**; Costumes, **Earl Luick**; General Musical Director, **Erno Rapee**; Musical Conductor, **Louis Silvers**.

SONGS: "Liza Lee" (Burke)— sung by **Al Jolson** and **chorus**; "Little Starshine" (Burke)— sung by **Al Jolson**; "Dixie" (Emmett)— sung by **chorus**; "Walk All Over God's Heaven" (spiritual)— sung by **Al Jolson** and **chorus**; "Let My People Go" (spiritual)— sung by **Al Jolson** and **chorus**; "Tomorrow Is Another Day" (Burke)— sung by **Al Jolson**, reprised twice by **Jolson**; "Hooray for Baby and Me" (Burke)— sung by **Al Jolson**; "Sonny Boy" (Jolson, De Sylva, Brown and Henderson)— sung by **Al Jolson**.

RUNNING TIME: 70 min.

SOURCE: Play by **Harold Atteridge**.

STORY: Horse trainer Al Jolson is scheduled to ride Big Boy in the Kentucky Derby. Eddie Phillips and Lew Harvey, agents for a syndicate that want Big Boy to lose the race, arrange for Jolson to be fired. Jolson is able to turn the tables and rides Big Boy to victory. The movie turns out to be just a stage play.

NOTES AND COMMENTARY: Gordon Elliott can be seen in the climactic horse race sequence. Elliott, between two women, is standing behind principles Louise Closser Hale, Lloyd Hughes, John Harron and Claudia Dell. Elliott obviously picked the winning horse and can be seen happily leaving the stands.

REVIEWS: "Comedy entertaining in hoke way, but inferior to previous Jolson features." *Variety*, 9/17/30; "Jolson's singing was the main attraction in this routine musical." *The Warner Bros. Story*, Hirshhorn.

SUMMATION: Entertaining Al Jolson musical—comedy.

Danger— Man Working! And Working Overtime to Bring You New Laughs and Thrills! Come Today and Meet a Swell Guy in

The Big Noise

Warner Bros. (June, 1936)
ALTERNATE TITLE: *Modern Madness.*
CAST: Julius Trent, **Guy Kibbee**; Ken Mitchell, **Warren Hull**; Betty Trent, **Alma Lloyd**; Don Andrews, **Dick Foran**; Daisy, **Marie Wilson**; Charlie Caldwell, **Henry O'Neill**; Harrison, **Olin Howlin**; Mrs. Trent, **Virginia Brissac**; Welford Andrews, **William Davidson**; Rosewater, **Andre Berenger**; Aldrich, **Robert Emmett Keane**; Machine Gun Nolan, **Eddie Shubert**// Sharp, **Gordon Elliott**.
CREDITS: Director, **Frank McDonald**; Story, **Edward Hartman**; Screenwriters, **George Bricker** and **William Jacobs**; Editor, **Terry Morse**; Art Director, **Carl Jules Weyl**; Cinematographer, **L. Wm. O'Connell**.
RUNNING TIME: 57 min.
STORY: Guy Kibbee is replaced as the president of his textile company when he fails to adopt new technology. Scorning retirement, he becomes co-owner of a dry cleaners with Warren Hull. Hull meets Kibbee's daughter, Alma

Lloyd, and the two fall in love. Gangsters try to extort money from Kibbee and Hull. Kibbee causes a gun battle between two rival gangs, resulting in the death of its leaders. The new technology of his textile company proves to be flawed, and Kibbee is reinstated as president, with Hull his chief chemist and son-in-law.

NOTES AND COMMENTARY: In a small role, Gordon Elliott, representing the Traders Exchange, is a board member of Guy Kibbee's textile company. He recommends that Kibbee should be replaced as president by William Davidson.

REVIEWS: "The film moves with a mechanical briskness under Frank McDonald's direction." *New York Times*, 7/4/36; "Ridiculous premise with a few laughs provided by a talking parrot." *Motion Picture Guide*, Nash and Ross.

SUMMATION: Very amusing comedy with a deft performance by Guy Kibbee.

He Races for Glory and Romance ... and Comes Thru with Flying Colors!

Boots and Saddles

Republic (October, 1937)
CAST: Gene Autry, **Gene Autry**; Frog Milhouse, **Smiley Burnette**; Bernice Allen, **Judith Allen**; Spud, **Ra Hould**; Colonel Allen, **Guy Usher**; Jim Neale, **Gordon Elliott**; Wyndham, **John Ward**; Shorty, **Frankie Marvin**; Juan, **Chris Martin**; Sergeant, **Stanley Blystone**; Larkins, **Bud Osborne, "Champion."**

CREDITS: Director, **Joe Kane**; Associate Producer, **Sol C. Siegel**; Story, **Jack Natteford**; Screenwriters, **Jack Natteford** and **Oliver Drake**; Editor, **Lester Orlebeck**; Cinematographer, **William Nobles**; Musical Director, **Raoul Kraushaar**.
SONGS: "(Take Me Back To My) Boots and Saddles" (Samuels, Whitecup and Powell)—

Boots and Saddles (Republic, 1937). Smiley Burnette (second right) brings in henchman Bud Osborne (right center) as Gene Autry (third left), Gordon Elliott (left center) and Guy Usher (center) watch.

sung by **Gene Autry** and **chorus**; "Riding the Range" (Allan, Autry and Shawn)— sung by **Gene Autry** and **chorus**; "Dusty Roads" (Burnette)— sung by **Smiley Burnette**; "Celito Lindo" (traditional)— sung by **female chorus**; "The One Rose (That's Left in My Heart)" (McIntire and Lyons)—**sung by Gene Autry** and **chorus**; "Why Did He Get Married"— sung by **Gene Autry**; "Boots and Saddles" (refrain)— sung by **Gene Autry, Smiley Burnette, Ra Hould** and **chorus**.

LOCATION FILMING: Lone Pine and Iverson, California.

STORY: Gene Autry convinces teenager Ra Hould not to sell his ranch, but he needs to sell horses to the Army to pay off all debts. Autry and rival rancher Gordon Elliott both submit identical bids. Army Colonel Guy Usher proposes a race to determine the winner. Elliott plans to win at any cost, including burning

down the stable housing Autry's horses. Autry, riding Champion, comes in first. Autry's pal, Smiley Burnette, provides proof of Elliott's duplicity and Elliott is arrested.

NOTES AND COMMENTARY: Gordon Elliott has a good role as the primary villain in this Gene Autry feature. Elliott comes to Ra Hould's ranch to purchase it and gets angry when Hould refuses to sell; Elliott helps Judith Allen get the dust out of her clothes; Allen tells Elliott that Autry has come to sell horses to the Army; Elliott and henchman Bud Osborne come to the cantina to spy on Autry and Allen; Elliott is present at the opening of the bids to sell horses to the Army; Elliott sends Merrill McCormick and Al Taylor to ambush Autry; Elliott tells Osborne to make sure that Autry's horses won't be ready for the race; Elliott interrupts Autry romancing Allen; Elliott becomes angry and Autry knocks him down; Elliott tells his men to win the race at any cost; Elliott and Autry race to the finish line; Elliott is accused of arson by Osborne and is arrested by Army soldiers.

REVIEWS: "Another of those convey-nothing titles which hides a good picture, westernly speaking." *Variety*, 10/13/37; "Although actionful, this Gene Autry opus is somewhat hampered by a complicated plot." *Western Movies*, Pitts.

SUMMATION: Some exciting action scenes are offset by too many unfunny comedy sequences, resulting in a barely passable Western feature. Gordon Elliott is very effective as the main villain, showing strength and determination in his scenes plotting against Gene Autry.

Love's Precious Moments Seized and Enjoyed, for Tomorrow Might Never Come!
But Tomorrow Did Come, Bringing Peace to the World but Turmoil to Her Heart!

Born to Love

RKO (April, 1931)

CAST: Doris Kendall, **Constance Bennett**; Barry Craig, **Joel McCrea**; Sir Wilfred Drake, **Paul Cavanaugh**; Lord Ponsonby, **Frederick Kerr**; Lady Ponsonby, **Louise Closser Hale**; Leslie Darrow, **Anthony Bushell**// Hotel guest, **Gordon Elliott**.

CREDITS: Director, **Paul L. Stein**; Screenwriter, **Ernest Pascal**; Editor, **Claude Berkeley**; Art Director, **Carroll Clark**; Cinematography, **John Mexcall**; Costumes, **Gwen Wakeling**; Sound, **Charles O'Loughlin** and **Ben Winkler**; Musical Director, **Francis Gromon**.

SONGS: "There Are Smiles" (Roberts)— played by an orchestra; "Pack Up Your Troubles in Your Old Kit Bag and Smile, Smile, Smile" (Powell and Asaf)— played by an orchestra; "The Darktown Strutters Ball" (Brooks)— played by an orchestra; "Rule Britannia" (Arne and Thomson)— played by a band; "Over There" (Cohan)— played by a band.

RUNNING TIME: 81 min.

STORY: American nurse Constance Bennett meets Captain Joel McCrea during a London air raid. The couple fall in love. Bennett receives word that McCrea was killed in action, then finds she's pregnant with their child. Paul Cavanaugh, who's always loved Bennett, marries her and accepts the baby as his own. McCrea, who was only wounded, returns to Lon-

don. Bennett goes to McCrea's hotel room to tell him that she must stay with Cavanaugh even though she loves McCrea. Cavanaugh assumes Bennett was unfaithful and grants her a divorce but, out of spite, takes custody of the baby. Bennett refuses to go with McCrea to America, preferring to stay close to her baby. After two years, Cavanaugh relents and Bennett is granted permission to see her child. McCrea has finally located Bennett, but again she chooses her baby over McCrea. Arriving at Cavanaugh's residence, she learns that the baby had died that afternoon. In shock, Bennett returns to her apartment and finds McCrea waiting for her.

NOTES AND COMMENTARY: Gordon Elliot makes a fleeting appearance in a London hotel lobby scene. Elliott can be seen in the background with a young lady at the hotel desk as Anthony Bushell is reunited with his comrade Joel McCrea.

REVIEWS: "*Born to Love* was picture born to draw the women. For men it's a pain in the neck." *Variety*, 4/29/31; "Mauldin tear jerker, designed for female audiences." *The Motion Picture Guide*, Nash and Ross.

SUMMATION: Constance Bennett's beauty can't save this soap opera melodrama, marred by a predictable story line and stilted direction and acting.

Thrills and Heart-Throbs of the World's Biggest City!

Boy of the Streets

Monogram (January, 1938)

CAST: Chuck, **Jackie Cooper**; Norah, **Maureen O'Connor**; Julie, **Kathleen Burke**; Rourke, **Robert Emmett O'Connor**; Mrs. Brennan, **Marjorie Main**; Blackie, **Matty Fain**; Farley, **George Cleveland**; Dr. Alben, **Gordon Elliott**; Brennan, **Guy Usher**; Spike, **Paul White**.

CREDITS: Director, **William Nigh**; Assistant Director, **W.B. Eason**; Story, **Rowland Brown**; Screenwriters, **Gilson Brown** and **Scott Darling**; Editor, **Russell Schoengarth**; Cinematographer, **Gilbert Warrenton**; Sound, **W.C. Smith**; Production Manager, **George E. Kann**; Technical Director, **E.R. Hickson**.

SONGS: "When Your Mother Comes from Ireland"—sung by **Maureen O'Connor**; "Carelessly"—sung by **Maureen O'Connor**; "These Foolish Things (Remind Me of You)" (Strarhey, Marvell and Link)—sung by **Maureen O'Connor**; "Swing Low, Sweet Chariot" (African-American spiritual/ melody–Burleigh)—sung by **Maureen O'Connor**.

RUNNING TIME: 76 min.

STORY: Jackie Cooper wants to be a big shot like his father, Guy Usher. Cooper is devastated when he sees that Usher is just a stooge for local politicians. Filled with disappointment, Cooper becomes a protégé of gangster Matty Fain. When a warehouse robbery goes wrong, Fain shoots policeman Robert Emmett O'Connor. Cooper rushes to O'Connor's aid and is also shot by Fain. Cooper informs on Fain and, after fully recovering from his wound, joins the Navy to make something of himself.

NOTES AND COMMENTARY: Gordon Elliott receives eighth billing but has more screen time in this than most of his fellow actors. After Maureen O'Connor finishes singing her first number, Dr. Elliott drops in to see her mother, Marjorie Main, and tell her she is going to a sanitarium. Then he tells Kathleen Burke, owner of the tenement slum apartment house, that he would like to talk with her. Elliott tells Burke off for keeping the building in such a deplorable condition. Elliott is on hand to see Main placed in an ambulance. After a neighborhood brawl between two gangs, Elliott tends to bruises sustained by Jackie Cooper and Burke. Elliott learns that Burke inherited the building that morning, and he promises to help her make necessary improvements. The two begin to fall in love. Elliott returns to the tenement house as Burke begins to make improvements. To keep O'Connor from becoming a ward of the courts, Burke sends her to a private school, and Elliott tells Burke she's swell for doing this. Elliott and Burke bring O'Connor to Marjorie Main's apartment. In his last scene, Elliott is at the hospital with a wounded Jackie Cooper.

REVIEWS: "The best scenes are glimpses of gang rituals and interpolated battles royal, having little or nothing to do with the story. The characters are about as real as the virtuous folk in a comic strip (examples include the roles of Maureen O'Connor, Kathleen Burke, Gordon Elliott and Robert Emmett). *New York Times*, 1/24/38; "Monogram's most ambitious production effort to date. It's Jackie Cooper's picture all the way. Gordon Elliott is poor as the doctor." *Variety*, 12/1/37.

SUMMATION: The scenes of the day-to-day activities of tenement slum life are compelling, but the primary story less so, even though Jackie Cooper gives it a good try. Gordon Elliott is adequate as the liberal doctor, considering the unwieldy dialogue he's forced to deliver.

With His Mouth Wide Open — He's Dan-cing ...
and You've Never Seen Anyone Dance, Sing and Make Merry the Way Joe Does in His Big Show!

Bright Lights

Warner Bros. (July, 1935)

A First National Picture

ALTERNATE TITLE: *Funny Face.*

CAST: Joe Wilson, **Joe E. Brown**; Fay Wilson, **Ann Dvorak**; Claire Whitmore, **Patricia Ellis**; Dan Wheeler, **William Gargan**; Oscar Schlemmer, **Joseph Cawthorn**; Anderson, **Henry O'Neill**; Wilbur, **Arthur Treacher**; Wellington, **Gordon Westcott**; Postal Official, **Joseph Crehan**; Detective, **William Demarest**; Nightclub Acrobatic Team, **the Maxellos**// Actor Dressed in Armor, **Gordon Elliott**.

CREDITS: Director, **Busby Berkeley**; Story, **Lois Leeson**; Screenwriters, **Bert Kalmar** and **Harry Rubin**; Adaptation, **Ben Markson** and **Benny Rubin**; Editor, **Bert L'Orle**; Art Direction, **Anton Grot**; Cinematography, **Sid Hickox**; Gowns, **Orry-Kelly**; Musical Direction, **Leo F. Forbstein**.

SONGS: "She Was an Acrobat's Daughter"— sung by **Joe E. Brown**; "Powder My Back for Me"— sung by unknown female singer and chorus; "Love Must Have Sunny Weather"— sung by **Ann Dvorak**, and danced by **Joe E. Brown** and **Ann Dvorak**; "You and I Are Full of Heaven"— sung by **Patricia Ellis**, and danced by **Joe E. Brown**.

RUNNING TIME: 83 min.

STORY: Socialite Patricia Ellis, running away from home, joins a burlesque show headlined by Joe E. Brown and his wife, Ann Dvorak. Press agent William Gargan signs all three to appear in a lavish Broadway show. Producer Henry O'Neill wants Brown to team with Ellis. Brown and Ellis are a smash hit. Dvorak, thinking Brown might be falling in love with Ellis, decides to go back to burlesque. Brown does fall in love with Ellis, but Ellis loves Gargan and they plan to marry. Brown's valet, Arthur Treacher, mails a letter from Brown to Dvorak in which Brown tells of his love for Ellis. The letter reaches Dvorak before Brown can retrieve it. In tears, Dvorak goes on stage, only to have Brown show up and tell her that he loves only her. Dvorak pretends she had never read the letter, and the two are reunited.

NOTES AND COMMENTARY: Gordon Elliott plays an actor, dressed in armor, from whom Joe E. Brown tries to get a cigarette. Elliott speaks first, "Hello, Wilson, good luck to you." Elliott can't supply a cigarette but finds gum for Brown. He then inquires if Brown is nervous, which upsets Brown because he is.

REVIEWS: "Enough entertainment in it to bring fair attention." *Variety*, 8/21/35; "Brisk pace with a close eye for detail from Berkeley." *Motion Picture Guide*, Nash and Ross.

SUMMATION: A bright, funny Joe E. Brown musical comedy.

Packed with Pep! Jammed with Joy! All Steamed Up! And Raring to Go!

Broadway Gondolier

Warner Bros. (July, 1935)

CAST: Dick Purcell, **Dick Powell**; Alice Hughes, **Joan Blondell**; Professor de Vinci, **Adolphe Menjou**; Mrs. Flaggenheim, **Louise Fazenda**; Cliff Stanley, **William Gargan**; Hayward, **George Barbier**; Richards, **Grant Mitchell**; Ted Fio Rito and His Band; the Four Mills Bros.; Gilmore, **Hobart Cavanaugh**; Red, **Joseph Sauers**; Ramon, **Rafael Storm**; Irish Policeman, **Bob Murphy**; Uncle Andy, James Burke// Reporter, **Gordon Elliott**.

CREDITS: Director, **Lloyd Bacon**; Story, **Sig Herzig**, **E.Y. Harburg** and **Hanns Kraly**; Screenplay, **Warren Duff** and **Sig Herzig**; Editor, **George Amy**; Art Director, **Anton Grot**; Cinematography, **George Barnes**; Gowns, **Orry-Kelly**; Musical Director, **Leo F. Forbstein**.

SONGS: "The Pig and the Cow (and the Dog and Cat)" (Dubin and Warren)— sung by **Joan Blondell** and **Dick Powell**; "Flagenheim's Odorless Cheese" (Dubin and Warren)— sung by **Dick Powell**; "Outside of You" (Dubin and Warren)— sung by **Dick Powell**; "Lonely Gondolier (Il Gondoliere)" (Dubin and Warren; Italian lyrics by Emanuel)— sung by **Dick Powell** and **chorus**; "The Rose in Her Hair (Rosa D'Amor)" (Dubin and Warren; Italian lyrics by Emanuel)— sung by **Dick Powell**; "Outside of You" (reprise)— played by **Ted Fio Rito and His Band**, with **vocal chorus**; "Lulu's Back in Town" (Dubin and Warren)— sung by **Dick Powell** and **the Four Mills Bros.**; "You Can Be Kissed" (Dubin and Warren)— played by **Ted Fio Rito**, with **vocal chorus**; "Lonely Gondolier" (reprise)— sung by **Dick Powell**; "Outside of You" (reprise)— sung by **Dick Powell**; "Flagenheim's Odorless Cheese" (reprise)— sung by **unknown singer**, **Dick Powell** and **Joan Blondell**.

RUNNING TIME: 100 min.

STORY: Singing cab driver Dick Powell is unable to make it big in radio in New York. Powell travels to Italy where he's discovered by Joan Blondell, who's looking for a singer for a prominent radio program. Powell and Blondell begin to fall in love. Powell's ruse as an Italian singer is exposed and he leaves the show. Public outcry forces radio executive Grant Mitchell to give Powell his job back. Powell and Blondell plan to marry.

NOTES AND COMMENTARY: Gordon Elliott plays a reporter at Dick Powell's introduction to the press as the new radio sensation. He is in a second scene when Grant Richards tells reporters that Powell is definitely Italian.

Joseph Sauers, better known as Joe Sawyer, shoots Gordon Elliott down in cold blood in Dick Foran's first starring western, *Moonlight on the Prairie* (Warner Bros., 1935).

REVIEWS: "Silly but entertaining minor musical." *The Motion Picture Guide*, Nash and Ross; "*Broadway Gondolier* rates no better than fair." *The New York Times*, 7/18/35.

SUMMATION: This is a bright, tuneful musical, perhaps a shade too long but still quite satisfactory.

She Is the Gay New Star Our Electric Lights Fea-ture!
Take Our Word, She's the Zippiest Crea-ture!

Broadway Hostess

Warner Bros. (December, 1935)
A First National Picture

CAST: Winnie, **Winifred Shaw**; Iris, **Genevieve Tobin**; Lucky, **Lyle Talbot**; Fishcake, **Allen Jenkins**; Tommy, **Phil Regan**; Dorothy, **Marie Wilson**; Mrs. Duncan-Griswald-Wembly-Smythe, **Spring Byington**; Big Joe, **Joseph King**; Ronnie, **Donald Ross**; Morse, **Frank Dawson**; Emcee at Club Intime, **Harry Seymour**// Playboy in "Playboy of Paree" Number, **Gordon Elliott**.

CREDITS: Director, **Frank McDonald**; Screenwriter, **George Bricker**; Editor, **Jack Killifer**; Art Director, **Esdras Hartley**; Cinematographer, **Arthur L. Todd**; Gowns, Orry-Kelly; Musical Director, **Leo F. Forbstein**; Song and Dance Director, **Bobby Connolly**.

SONGS: "Dancing with Tears in My Eyes" (Dubin and Burke)— sung by **Winifred Shaw**; "Weary" (Wrubel and Dixon)— sung by **Winifred Shaw**; "He Was Her Man" (Wrubel and Dixon)— sung by **Winifred Shaw**; "Weary" (reprise)— sung by **Winifred Shaw**; "Who but You" (Wrubel and Dixon)— sung by **Winifred Shaw**, **Phil Regan** and **others**; "Let It Be Me" (Wrubel and Dixon)— sung by **Phil Regan**; "Playboy of Paree" (Wrubel and Dixon)— sung by **Winifred Shaw**; "Let It Be Me" (reprise)— sung by **Winifred Shaw** and **Phil Regan**; "He Was Her Man" (reprise)— sung by **Winifred Shaw**.

RUNNING TIME: 68 min.

STORY: Small-town girl Winifred Shaw, due to Lyle Talbot's influence, makes it big on Broadway. Shaw falls in love with Talbot, but Talbot loves socialite Genevieve Tobin. Tobin refuses Talbot's marriage proposal because she wants to marry a man with money. Talbot decides to go back to gambling to make the money he needs. Tobin's brother, Donald Ross, loses a significant sum of money to Talbot. To pay his debt, Ross steals jewels from Tobin's safe. Talbot is arrested for the robbery. Shaw uses all her money to bail Talbot from jail. Tobin learns Ross took the jewelry and charges are dropped. Shaw's money is stolen by her lawyer, leaving her broke. Talbot and Tobin marry. Shaw's piano player, Phil Regan, tells Talbot of Shaw's plight. Talbot arranges for Shaw to headline a new Broadway show. At intermission, Ross shoots Talbot. Shaw races to the hospital and learns that Tobin and Talbot love each other. Talbot recovers from his wound, and Shaw accepts a marriage proposal from Regan.

NOTES AND COMMENTARY: Winifred Shaw sings to Gordon Elliott throughout the "Playboy of Paree" number. In the number, Elliott, while listening to Shaw, first presents himself as a penniless drunk, and then cuddles Shaw in a garden scene before they leave the restaurant.

REVIEWS: "Sitting through the film is like having to be polite to the boss while he tells an old story badly." *New York Times*, 12/16/35; "Only the staging is well done in this lackluster production." *Motion Picture Guide*, Nash and Ross.

SUMMATION: This musical drama tries to tell too many stories, and not too well, in its limited running time.

All-Talking, Dancing, Singing Musical Comedy Hit

Broadway Scandals

Columbia (November, 1929)

CAST: Mary, **Sally O'Neil**; Ted Howard, **Jack Egan**; Valeska, **Carmel Myers**; Bill Gray, **Tom O'Brien**; Le Claire, **J. Barney Sherry**; Pringle, **John Hyams**; Jack Lane, **Charles C. Wilson**; George Halloway, **Gordon Elliott**; Bobby, **Doris Dawson**; **Charles Lane**.

CREDITS: Director, **George Archainbaud**; Assistant Director, **C.C. Coleman**; Producer, **Harry Cohn**; Screenwriters, **Howard J. Green**, **Norman Houston** and **Gladys Lehman**; Editors, **Leon Barsha** and **Ben Pivar**; Art Director, **Harrison Wiley**; Cinematographer, **Harry Jackson**; Sound, **W. Hancock** and **John P. Livadary**; Dialogue Directors, **Rufus Le Maire** and **James Seymour**.

SONGS: "What Is Life Without Love" (Thompson, Franklin and Stone) — sung by **Jack Egan**; "Does the Elephant Love Peanuts" (Hanly) — sung by **Jack Egan** and **Sally O'Neill**; "Can You Read in My Eyes" (Coslow) — sung by **Carmel Myers**; "Would I Love to Love You" (Dryer and Clare) — sung by **Jack Egan** and **Carmel Myers**; "Love Is the Cause of All My Blues" (Trent and Daniels) — sung by **Jack Egan**; "Rhythm of the Tambourine" (Franklin); "Kickin' the Blues Away" (Franklin).

RUNNING TIME: 73 min.

STORY: Stranded in a small town, vaudeville performer Jack Egan meets Sally O'Neil. With O'Neil's money, Egan and O'Neil start a new act that proves very successful. Broadway star Carmel Myers sees the act and wants Egan to team up with her in a Broadway production. O'Neil agrees to accept a lesser role in the show. O'Neil wows the audience — to Myers' displeasure. Myers wants O'Neil fired. Egan leaves the show to again team up with O'Neil. O'Neil and Egan marry.

NOTES AND COMMENTARY: Gordon Elliott receives eighth billing in the *New York Times* review, playing the part of George Halloway.

REVIEWS: "They can't make a hit musical show of an opus which solely depends upon its chorus to get it over. The feature unwinds as if Columbia couldn't make up its mind to do a revue or a book musical. Consequently it's overboard on numbers and shy on script." *Variety*, 10/30/29; "So long as the narrative does not intrude too impudently, one can be mildly entertained by some of the passages in the production." *New York Times*, 10/29/29.

SUMMATION: This film was not available for viewing by the author.

Little Caesar Blasts His Way Back to the Dictatorship of Modern Gangdom as Warner Bros. "New and Different" Underworld Expose Explodes on the Screen — to Smash a $15,000,000,000 Secret Syndicate of Crime!

Bullets or Ballots

Warner Bros. (June, 1936)

CAST: Johnny Blake, **Edward G. Robinson**; Lee Morgan, **Joan Blondell**; Al Kruger, **Barton MacLane**; "Bugs" Fenner, **Humphrey Bogart**; Herman, **Frank McHugh**; Dan McLaren, **Joseph King**; Driscoll, **Richard Purcell**; Wires, **George E. Stone**; Johnson, **Joseph Crehan**; Ward Bryant, **Henry O'Neill**; Hollister, **Henry Kolker**; Thorndyke, **Gilbert Emery**; Caldwell, **Herbert Rawlinson**; Nellie, **Louise Beavers**; Vinci, **Norman Willis**// Hunter, **Gordon Elliott**.

CREDITS: Director, **William Keighley**; Story, **Seton I. Miller**; Screenwriters, **Martin Mooney** and **Seton I. Miller**; Editor, **Jack Killifer**; Art Director, **Carl Jules Weyl**; Cinematographer, **Hal Mohr**.

SONG: "The Lady in Red" (Dixon and Wrubel) — whistled by **Edward G. Robinson**.

RUNNING TIME: 82 min.

STORY: The city is in the grip of racketeers ostensibly led by Barton MacLane and Humphrey Bogart, but actually bossed by three respected businessmen, Henry Kolker, Gilbert Emery and Herbert Rawlinson. When police captain Joseph King is promoted to commissioner, he fires a number of policemen, including tough detective Edward G. Robinson. MacLane hires Robinson to make sure all facets of the rackets are working perfectly. In actuality, Robinson is working undercover to break up the rackets and uncover the real bosses. Bogart kills MacLane in hopes of replacing MacLane, but the bosses pick Robinson instead. With the identity of the bosses revealed to him, Robinson sets things in motion for mass arrests, but Bogart evades the trap. Bogart and Robinson shoot it out; Bogart is killed and Robinson mortally wounded. Robinson stays alive long enough to have the police arrest Kolker, Emery and Rawlinson.

NOTES AND COMMENTARY: Gordon Elliott works for crime boss Henry Kolker and is seen in four scenes. First, Gordon Elliott telephones Edward G. Robinson to meet with Henry Kolker. Second, when Robinson arrives at Kolker's office, Elliott tells Robinson to go right in to meet Kolker. Third, Elliott lets Robinson in the office to bring racket proceeds to the gang leader. And fourth, Elliott is arrested with gang leaders Kolker, Emery and Rawlinson.

Norman Willis would appear with Bill Elliott in *Beyond the Sacramento* (Columbia, 1940) and *Plainsman and the Lady* (Republic, 1946).

REVIEWS: "The Brothers Warner have turned out another crackling underworld melodrama." *The New York Times*, 5/27/36; "A tough, hard-hitting, well-scripted, well-acted, tautly directed melodrama that certainly makes the most of its 81 action-packed minutes." *The Warner Bros. Story*, Hirshhorn.

SUMMATION: Top flight crime melodrama with an outstanding performance by Edward G. Robinson.

He Wanted to Be Good — But the Flesh Is Weak!
When He Told 'Em the Truth, They Wouldn't Believe Him!

—But the Flesh Is Weak

Metro-Goldwyn-Mayer (April, 1932)
ALTERNATE TITLE: *But the Flesh Is Weak.*
CAST: Max, **Robert Montgomery**; Rosine, **Nora Gregor**; Lady Joan, **Heather Thatcher**; Sir George, **Everett Edward Horton**; Florian, **C. Aubrey Smith**; Prince Paul, **Nils Asther**; Duke of Hampshire, **Frederick Kerr**; Lady Ridgway, **Eva Moore**; Gooch, **Forrester Harvey**; Findley, **Desmond Roberts**// Guest at Lady Joan's Party, **Gordon Elliott**.
CREDITS: Director, **Jack Conway**; Screenwriter, **Ivor Norvello**; Editor, **Tom Held**; Art Director, **Cedric Gibbons**; Cinematographer, **Oliver T. Marsh**; Gowns, **Adrian**; Sound, **Douglas Shearer**.
RUNNING TIME: 77 min.
SOURCE: Play, *Truth Game* by **Ivor Novello**.
STORY: C. Aubrey Smith and his son, Robert Montgomery, make their way through life by romancing rich women. Montgomery meets the beautiful but impoverished Nora Gregor and they fall in love. Smith loses a large sum of money while gambling and contemplates suicide. To save Smith from disgrace and imprisonment, Montgomery obtains the necessary funds by becoming engaged to wealthy Heather Thatcher. Montgomery confesses his love of Gregor to Thatcher, and Thatcher breaks the engagement. Montgomery and Gregor decide to marry. Smith marries a wealthy woman and will be able to support Montgomery.

NOTES AND COMMENTARY: Look closely, and Gordon Elliott can be seen dancing behind Nora Gregor's head as she talks to Robert Montgomery at Heather Thatcher's party.

REVIEWS: "Weak programmer, tale is actionless, improbable and generally inept in almost every department." *Variety*, 4/19/32; "Unappealing adaptation of Ivor Novello's less-than-classic play, *The Truth Game*." *Motion Picture Guide*, Nash and Ross.

SUMMATION: There is an occasional amusing moment, but ultimately the story is boring and predictable, and the audience can hardly wait for things to end.

A Murderous Cat His Client! A Dead Man His Star Witness! Poor Perry Mason's Got His Hands
Full Again in Erle Stanley Gardner's Most Thrilling Story! And There'll Be a New Thrill for You as
Perry Lets the Cat Out of the Bag!

Case of the Black Cat

Warner Bros. (October, 1936)
A First National Production
ALTERNATE TITLE: *Curse of the Black Cat.*
CAST: Perry Mason, **Ricardo Cortez**; Della Street, **June Travis**; Wilma Laxter, **Jane Bryan**; Frank Oafley, **Craig Reynolds**; Douglas Keene, **Carlyle Moore, Jr.**; Sam Laxter, **Gordon Elliott**; Louise DeVoe, **Nedda Harrington**; Paul Drake, **Garry Owen**; Peter Laxter, **Harry Davenport**; Ashton, **George Rosener**; Dr. Jacobs, **Gordon Hart**; Shuster, **Clarence Wilson**; Hamilton Burger, **Guy Usher**; Mrs. Pixley, **Lottie Williams**; Reverend Stillwell, **Harry Hayden**.
CREDITS: Director, **William C. McGann**; Screenwriter, **F. Hugh Herbert**; Editor, **Frank Magee**; Art Director, **Hugh Reticker**; Cinematographer, **Allen G. Siegler**; Gowns, **Milo Anderson**; Dialogue Director, **Frank Beckwith**.
RUNNING TIME: 65 min.
SOURCE: Novel, *The Case of the Caretaker's Cat* by **Erle Stanley Gardner**.

Case of the Black Cat (Warner Bros., 1936). Elliott received sixth billing in the ad.

STORY: Millionaire Harry Davenport calls lawyer Ricardo Cortez to come to his mansion in the middle of the night to make changes in his will. Jane Bryan is cut out of his will, with his fortune to be divided between Craig Reynolds and Gordon Elliott. Davenport dies in a mysterious fire. Cortez suspects foul play. In his investigation, two more murders are committed. Mason reveals that Davenport faked his death upon realizing Reynolds was plotting to murder him. Reynolds committed one murder, and the second death is attributed to Davenport in a self-defense struggle.

NOTES AND COMMENTARY: Gordon Elliott has one of his best early sound roles here. He is seen in twelve scenes: Elliott throws a shoe at the caretaker's cat; Elliott complains to Davenport about the cat's noise; Elliott greets Cortez when he arrives at the Davenport mansion and states he wishes Davenport would die; the nervous Elliott warns caretaker George Rosener that if the cat bothers him any more, he will kill it; after Elliott scares the cat, he puts his golf clubs in a car and drives off; Elliott brings his lawyer, Clarence Wilson, to Cortez' office to find why the cat has to stay at Davenport's estate; Elliott is in the library searching for missing diamonds and then eavesdrops on Cortez' phone call to Rosener; a disheveled El-liott comes into the mansion, only to be questioned by D.A. Guy Usher; Elliott and Reynolds argue in Cortez' office after Elliott claims Cortez is trying to name him as Davenport's murderer; Elliott is present in court at Carlyle Moore, Jr.'s hearing; Elliott is present in court when Cortez reveals Davenport faked his death; in Cortez's denouncement, a flashback sequence, Elliott finds one of the murder victims and sees Moore enter; Elliott manufactures evidence to frame Moore and then rams a truck into a fire hydrant to cover an injury to himself.

REVIEWS: "Film version of Erle Stanley Gardner's whodunit is nice entertainment. Rest of the cast members are all heavies, or portrayed as such till the finale, with all of them okay as menaces. These include Nedda Harrigan, Gordon Elliott, Craig Reynolds and George Rosener." *Variety*, 12/30/36; "Suspense and action are ample in the fine, technically satisfying production." *The Motion Picture Guide*, Nash and Ross.

SUMMATION: Ricardo Cortez is tops as the fictional lawyer in this excellent Perry Mason mystery. The supporting cast is first rate, with Gordon Elliott registering strongly as a nervous, neurotic murder suspect.

Meet Perry Mason, New King of Crime Hunters

Case of the Howling Dog

Warner Bros. (September, 1934)

CAST: Perry Mason, **Warren William**; Bessie Foley, **Mary Astor**; Sgt. Holcomb, **Allen Jenkins**; Claude Drumm, **Grant Mitchell**; Della Street, **Helen Trenholme**; Elizabeth Walker, **Helen Lowell**; Lucy Benton, **Dorothy Tree**; Arthur Cartwright, **Gordon Wescott**; Sam Martin, **Harry Tyler**; Bill Pemberton, **Arthur Aylesworth**; Clinton Foley, **Russell Hicks**; Dr. Cooper, **Frank Reicher**; Judge Markham, **Addison Richards**; Dobbs, **James Burtis**; Wheeler, **Eddie Shubert**; David Clark, **Harry Seymour**// Courtroom Reporter, **Gordon Elliott**.

CREDITS: Director, **Alan Crosland**; Screenwriter, **Ben Markson**; Editor, **James Gibbon**; Art Director, **John Hughes**; Cinematographer, **William Rees**; Gowns, **Orry-Kelly**; Musical Conductor, **Leo F. Forbstein**; Dialogue Director, **Arthur Greville Collins**.

RUNNING TIME: 75 min.

SOURCE: Novel, *Case of the Howling Dog* by **Erle Stanley Gardner**.

STORY: A dog's incessant barking brings Gordon Wescott to Warren William's office, as Wescott believes the howls to be an omen of death. In a web of marital infidelity, Mary Astor returns to confront her husband, Russell

Hicks. A few years earlier, Hicks had run off with Wescott's wife. In Astor's encounter with Hicks, Hicks and his dog are murdered. Astor is arrested for the crime. The police believe that Wescott and his wife could also be suspects. Astor goes on trial, and William proves that Hicks murdered Wescott and Wescott's wife because of his love for his housekeeper, Dorothy Tree. Williams gains an acquittal for Astor, knowing that Astor shot Hicks and his dog in self-defense.

NOTES AND COMMENTARY: Gordon Elliott plays a reporter assigned to cover Mary Astor's murder trial. Elliott is first seen as the camera pans the courtroom at the trial's beginning. Later, when William has the trial moved to the scene of the crime, Elliott tells his fellow reporters, "Aw, that's just a grandstand play."

REVIEWS: "A well-knit story, swiftly paced, dramatically punctuated and, above all, honest with its audience." *The New York Times*, 10/18/34; "It has some new angles on handling the mystery element, some good acting, plenty of suspense and sufficient action." *Variety*, 10/23/34.

SUMMATION: This is neat, fast-moving murder mystery, well acted by the principals.

Cocktails, Corpses, Kisses and Killings! A Very Merry Perry and a Very Mirthful Provide the Season's Most Mysterical Hit! Don't Miss It!

Case of the Velvet Claws

Warner Bros. (August, 1936)

A First National Picture; A Clue Club Selection

CAST: Perry Mason, **Warren William**; Della, **Claire Dodd**; Eva Belter, **Winifred Shaw**; Carl Griffin, **Gordon Elliott**; George C. Belter, **Joseph King**; Frank Locke, **Addison Richards**; Spudsy Drake, **Eddie Acuff**; Wilbur Strong, **Olin Howlin**; Crandal, **Dick Purcell**; Peter Milner, **Kenneth Harlan**; Judge Mary O'Daugherty, **Clara Blandick**; Mrs. Veite, **Ruth Robinson**; Norma Veite, **Paula Stone**; Sergeant Hoffman, **Robert Middlemass**; Digley, **Stuart Holmes**; Esther Linton, **Carol Hughes**; Detective Jones, **Eddie Shubert**; Kickopopolos, **Harry Semels**.

CREDITS: Director, **William Clemens**; Screenwriter, **Tom Reed**; Editor, **Jack Saper**; Art Director, **Esdras Hartley**; Cinematographer, **Sid Hickox**.

RUNNING TIME: 63 min.

SOURCE: Novel, *Case of the Velvet Claws* by **Erle Stanley Gardner**.

STORY: After Warren William's marriage to his secretary, Claire Dodd, Winifred Shaw kidnaps William at gunpoint. Shaw involves William in a blackmail plot involving herself and Kenneth Harlan. Shaw's husband, Joseph King, is subsequently murdered. Shaw implicates William as the killer. William proves Gordon Elliott, heir to King's fortune, is the murderer.

NOTES AND COMMENTARY: While Gordon Elliott receives fourth billing, Elliott is only in five scenes. Elliott meets Warren William when William enters King's mansion through the kitchen; Elliott, while drunk, implicates Winifred Shaw as a murderess; Elliott, still showing the effects of alcohol, recants his accusation; in a Chinatown den, Elliott refuses to agree to Ruth Robinson's request to marry Paula Stone; in William's denouncement, William shows how Elliott murdered Joseph King, and as Elliott is arrested, he knocks Eddie Acuff to the ground.

REVIEWS: "A murky mélange of malefic and murder." *The New York Times*, 8/29/36; "Pace is so fast that the audience has no time to dwell on the incredibility of all that happens." *The Motion Picture Guide*, Nash and Ross.

SUMMATION: This is an entertaining but average whodunit with an interesting story. Elliott capably handles the role of the murderer, with a nifty drunk sequence.

Tears Will Choke Back Your Cheers for the Greatest Air Drama Since "Hell's Angels"

Ceiling Zero

Warner Bros. (January, 1936)

A Cosmopolitan Production; A Howard Hawks Production

CAST: Dizzy Davis, **James Cagney**; Jake Lee, **Pat O'Brien**; Tommy Thomas, **June Travis**; Texas Clarke, **Stuart Erwin**; Al Stone, **Barton MacLane**; Tay, **Henry Wadsworth**; Mary Lee, **Martha Tibbetts**; Lou Clarke, **Isabel Jewell**; Joe Allen, **Craig Reynolds**; Smiley, **Richard Purcell**; Eddie Payson, **Carlyle Moore, Jr.**; Fred, **Addison Richards**; Mike Owens, **Garry Owen**; Doc Wilson, **Edward Gargan**; Les Bogan, **Robert Light**; Buzz, **James Bush**; Baldy, **Pat West**// Transportation Agent, **Gordon Elliott.**

CREDITS: Director, **Howard Hawks**; Screenwriter, **Frank Wead**; Editor, **William Holmes**; Art Director, **John Hughes**; Cinematographer, **Arthur Edeson**; Musical Director, **Leo F. Forbstein**; Technical Advisor, **Paul Mantz.**

RUNNING TIME: 95 min.

SOURCE: Play by **Frank Wead.**

STORY: Hotshot pilot James Cagney is reunited with his old pal, Pat O'Brien, at Federal Airlines at Newark Airport. In order to keep a date with June Travis, Cagney feigns illness and Stuart Erwin takes his run. On his return trip, Erwin runs into ceiling zero weather, the plane crashes, and Erwin perishes. Erwin's wife, Isabel Jewell, tells Cagney that he's no good and he hurts everyone with whom he comes in contact. Cagney's pilot's license is not renewed for repeated violations of air regulations. Without permission, Cagney makes a dangerous flight with ceiling zero weather and dangerous ice conditions. The de-icer mechanism is not effective and the plane ices up. Before the plane crashes and Cagney goes to his death, he gives O'Brien the information needed to correct the problem.

NOTES AND COMMENTARY: Gordon Elliott plays a transportation agent. In the opening scene, Elliott is concerned when James Bush cannot contact pilot Carlyle Moore, Jr. Elliott then has Bush call manager Pat O'Brien. Elliott is present when Moore finally calls in and O'Brien arrives at the control room. O'Brien tells Elliott to cancel all passenger runs for the following day. Elliott is effective in his role.

REVIEWS: "A rugged and virile screenplay." *New York Times*, 1/20/36; "Hawks redeemed himself, not at the end but in the middle, with a series of brilliantly directed action sequences." *Warner Bros. Story*, Hirshhorn.

SUMMATION: Too stagey and predictable to be truly effective. The actors try hard but to no avail.

Parents! Divorce Is a Way Out for You! But It Is a Way into Scandal for Your Children!

Children of Divorce

Paramount (April, 1927)

CAST: Kitty Flanders, **Clara Bow**; Jean Waddington, **Esther Ralston**; Ted Larrabee, **Gary Cooper**; Prince Ludovico de Sfax, **Einar Hanson**; Duke de Gondreville, **Norman Trevor**; Katherine Flanders, **Hedda Hopper**; Tom Larrabee, **Edward Martindel**; Princess de Sfax, **Julia Swayne Gordon**; the Secretary, **Tom Ricketts.**

CREDITS: Director, **Frank Lloyd**; Screenwriters, **Hope Loring** and **Louis D. Lighton**; Cinematographer, **Victor Milner.**

RUNNING TIME: 72 min.

SOURCE: Novel, *Children of Divorce* by **Owen McMahon Johnson.**

STORY: Esther Ralston and Gary Cooper, both children of divorce, fall in love. Ralston wants Cooper to become successful in business before they marry. Clara Bow, a mutual friend, gives a wild party and Cooper forgets his promise to Ralston. When intoxicated, Bow and Cooper marry. Even though they have a child, Bow realizes there is no love between her and Cooper, and she commits suicide. Cooper and Ralston are reunited.

NOTES AND COMMENTARY: One source states that Gordon Elliott had a bit part in the film.

REVIEWS: "In spite of its tendency to ramble this film succeeds in holding the attention, thanks to the excellent lighting effects and to the presence of Esther Ralston and Clara Bow." *New York Times*, 4/26/27; "Good program material because it has been technically well treated." *Variety*, 4/20/27.

SUMMATION: This film was not available for viewing by the author.

The Heroic Climax of All Aviation Triumphs Becomes the Thundering Climax to All Air Dramas!

China Clipper

Warner Bros. (August, 1936)

A First National Picture

CAST: Dave Logan, **Pat O'Brien**; Jean Logan, **Beverly Roberts**; Tom Collins, **Ross Alexander**; Hap Stuart, **Humphrey Bogart**; Sunny Avery, **Marie Wilson**; Jim Horn, **Joseph Crehan**; Mr. Pierson, **Joseph King**; B.C. Hill, **Addison Richards**; Mother Brunn, **Ruth Robinson**; Dad Brunn, **Henry B. Walthall**; Radio Operator on Clipper, **Carlyle Moore, Jr.**; Co-Pilot on Clipper, **Lyle Moraine**; Engineer on Clipper, **Dennis Moore**; Navigator on Clipper, **Wayne Morris**; Bill Andrews, **Alexander Cross**; Pilot, **William Wright**; Department of Commerce Inspector, **Kenneth Harlan**; Secretary, **Anne Nagel**; Secretary, **Marjorie Weaver**; Radio Operator, **Milburn Stone**; Radio Operator, **Owen King** // Pilot, **Gordon Elliott**. (Note: Warner Bros. slipped up on the end credits; the parts played by Lyle Moraine and Dennis Moore should be switched, and Anne Nagel is more properly a receptionist than a secretary.)

CREDITS: Director, **Ray Enright**; Screenwriter, **Frank Wead**; Art Director, **Max Parker**; Cinematographer, **Arthur Edeson**; Special Photographic Effects, **Fred Jackman**; Gowns, **Orry-Kelly**; Musical Director, **Leo F. Forbstein**; Dialogue Director, **Gene Lewis**.

RUNNING TIME: 88 min.

STORY: Visionary Pat O'Brien believes transoceanic flights can be made over the Pacific Ocean. O'Brien proves flights can be made over the Caribbean and throughout South America. O'Brien's wife, Beverly Roberts, does not share his dreams and leaves him. O'Brien begins to drive both himself and his men relentlessly. Still, the men remain loyal. Henry B. Walthall designs the revolutionary China Clipper, and pilot Humphrey Bogart makes a successful flight across the Pacific to China. Roberts now believes in O'Brien, and the two reunite.

NOTES AND COMMENTARY: This is a thankless role in Gordon Elliott's career. Elliott has a non-speaking part as a pilot first seen in class as one of Pat O'Brien's students. Then Elliott can be seen in the background tinkering with an airplane engine as O'Brien comes into the room.

REVIEWS: "A fascinating and surprisingly literal dramatization of the China Clipper's transpacific flight." *New York Times*, 8/12/36; "The plot had O'Brien navigating the usual clichés with everything tying itself into a neat little bow at the fade." *Warner Bros. Story*, Hirshhorn.

SUMMATION: Almost devoid of suspense, the film succeeds in entertaining due to the good performances of the cast and the picture's feel-good atmosphere.

"The Kid" a Crackshot Who Became a Big Shot — As Quick on the Trigger as He Is on the Smile!

City Streets

Paramount (April, 1931)

CAST: The Kid, **Gary Cooper**; Nan, **Sylvia Sidney**; Big Fellow, **Paul Lukas**; McCoy, **William Boyd**; Agnes, **Wynne Gibson**; Pop Cooley, **Guy Kibbee**; Blackie, **Stanley Fields**; Pansy, **Betty Sinclair**; Police Inspector, **Robert Homans**; Esther, **Barbara Leonard**// Speakeasy Patron, **Gordon Elliott**.

CREDITS: Director, **Rouben Mamoulian**; Story, **Dashiell Hammett**; Screenwriters, **Max Marcin** and **Oliver H.P. Garrett**; Editor, **William Shea**; Cinematographer, **Lee Garmes**.

RUNNING TIME: 83 min.

STORY: Sylvia Sidney, daughter of racketeer Guy Kibbee, falls in love with stranded rodeo cowboy Gary Cooper. To further himself in the beer rackets, Kibbee murders Stanley Fields and passes the gun off to Sidney. Sidney is arrested, refuses to talk, and is sent to prison. Kibbee then persuades Cooper to join him in the rackets. Upon her release, Sidney begs Cooper, unsuccessfully, to leave the mob. Gang leader Paul Lucas wants Sidney as his mistress and sends men to murder Cooper.

Cooper outsmarts the gunmen and decides to settle affairs with Lucas. Sidney arranges to meet Lucas at his house and plans to stay with Lucas if Cooper is allowed to leave the gang. Lucas' ex-mistress, Wynne Gibson, murders Lucas and frames Sidney. With Lucas's death, Cooper takes over as leader. Cooper thwarts plans to murder Sidney and then leaves the rackets with Sidney at his side.

NOTES AND COMMENTARY: After Guy Kibbee murders Stanley Fields, patrons run out of a speakeasy, led by Gordon Elliott, who reaches the murdered man first. Elliott remarks, "I don't know what happened."

REVIEWS: "It's all melodramatic and incredible. The production, however, is quite entertaining." *New York Times*, 4/18/31; "Picture is lifted from mediocrity through the intelligent acting and appeal of Sylvia Sidney." *Variety*, 4/22/31.

SUMMATION: A suspenseful, first-rate crime drama with a sparkling performance by Sylvia Sidney.

She Drank Too Deeply of the Cup of Life!

Cocktail Hour

Columbia (June, 1933)

CAST: Cynthia, **Bebe Daniels**; Morgan, **Randolph Scott**; Lawton, **Sidney Blackmer**; Olga, **Muriel Kirkland**; Princess, **Jessie Ralph**; Philippe, **Barry Norton**; Alvarez, **George Nardelli**; Mrs. Lawton, **Marjorie Gateson**// Mr. Gordon, **Gordon Elliott**.

CREDITS: Director/Music, **Victor Schertzinger**; Screenwriter, **Richard Schayer**; Editor, **Jack Dennis**; Cinematographer, **Joseph August**.

SONG: "Listen, Heart of Mine" (Schertzinger) — sung by **Bebe Daniels**.

RUNNING TIME: 73 min.

SOURCE: Story, "Pearls and Emeralds" by James K. McGuinness.

STORY: Advertising manager Randolph Scott wants his top artist Bebe Daniels to stop working and marry him. On vacation, Daniels sails for Europe. On board are a young suitor, Barry Norton, and his mother Jessie Ralph. Daniels avoids Norton by beginning a shipboard romance with another passenger, Sidney Blackmer. Having fallen in love, Daniels is devastated when Blackmer tells Daniels he's married. Scott comes to Europe pretending to ask Daniels to work on her vacation but actually to play hard-to-get so she will accept his marriage proposal. After a party at Norton's estate, Blackmer follows Daniels to her hotel and tries to resume their romance. Daniels orders Blackmer to leave. Norton arrives to defend Daniels' honor, and the two men fight. In the struggle, Blackmer loses his balance and falls to the street below. Daniels sends Norton home before the police arrive, and she is taken to the police station for questioning. Scott intercedes and brings Norton to the station to tell what happened. A telephone call from the hospital reveals Blackmer will recover, and he refuses to press charges. After this harrowing experience, Daniels finally quits her job to marry Scott.

NOTES AND COMMENTARY: Gordon Elliott is the first party guest seen, and remarks to another guest, "I think I'll stay cockeyed all the time she's in Europe," referring to Bebe Daniels' impending trip abroad. Later, Elliott is talking with Jessie Ralph, who refers to Elliott as Mr. Gordon. When Ralph requests a drink, Elliott says, "Never mind, Frank. Allow me." Finally, Elliott is briefly seen as one of the well-wishers as Daniels prepares to sail to Europe.

REVIEWS: "It's only when the picture takes itself seriously that it becomes ludicrous, particularly in a melodramatic sequence just before the finish." *The New York Times*, 6/2/33; "Amusing mostly for limited big town audiences." *Variety*, 6/6/33.

SUMMATION: So-so melodrama of a career woman who finds happiness in marriage.

A Sensational Mystery at Sea.

Convicted

Weiss Bros. Artclass Pictures Corp. (November, 1931)

Produced by Supreme Features, Inc. LTD, Alfred T. Mannon, president

ALTERNATE TITLES: *Convicto* and *El Misterio Del Mar.*

CAST: Claire Norville, **Aileen Pringle**; Bruce Allan, **Jameson Thomas**; Constance Forbes, **Dorthy Christy**; Tony Blair, **Richard Tucker**; Sturgeon, **Harry Myers**; Roy Fenton, **Niles Welch**; Weldon, **John Vosburgh**; Henderson, **Jack Mower**; Captain Hammond, **Wilfred Lucas**// Passenger, **Gordon Elliott**.

CREDITS: Director, **Christy Cabanne**; Assistant Director, **William McGaugh**; Screenwriters, **Jo Van Ronkel** and **Barry Barringer**; Editors, **Thomas Persons** and **Don Lindberg**; Cinematographer, **Sidney Hickox**; Production Manager, **Geo. M. Merrick**; Sound, **L.E. Tope**.

RUNNING TIME: 55 min.

SOURCE: Story by **Ed Barry**.

STORY: Richard Tucker, an embezzler, takes an ocean voyage to try to get actress Ailene Pringle to accept his romantic overtures. Tucker makes enemies aboard ship and is found murdered. Clues point to Pringle as the guilty person. Criminologist Jameson Thomas is able to prove that ship's officer John Vosburgh was the murderer and wins the hand of Pringle.

NOTES AND COMMENTARY: Gordon Elliott can be seen briefly as a passenger in the closing scene.

REVIEWS: "Nicely developed murder mystery." *Motion Picture Guide*, Nash and Ross.

SUMMATION: *Convicted* is an adequate but undistinguished low-budget murder mystery.

The Truth About Radio!

Crooner

First National Pictures (August, 1932)

CAST: Teddy Taylor, **David Manners**; Judy Mason, **Ann Dvorak**; Peter Sturgis, **Ken Murray**; Nick Meyer, **J. Carrol Naish**; Mike, **Guy Kibbee**; Mrs. Brown, **Claire Dodd**; Ralph, **Allen Vincent**; Henry, **Edward J. Nugent**; Pat, **William Janney**; Mack, **Teddy Joyce**// Night Club Patrons, **Gordon Elliott** and **Allan Lane**.

CREDITS: Director, **Lloyd Bacon**; Story, **Alan James**; Screenwriter, **Charles Kenyon**; Editor, **Howard Bretherton**; Art Director, **Robert Haas**; Cinematographer, **Robert Kurrle**; Costumes, **Orry-Kelly**; Musical Conductor, **Leo F. Forbstein**.

SONGS: "In a Shanty in Old Shanty Town" (Young and Siras) — played by David Manner's orchestra, and sung by unknown singer; "Sweethearts Forever" (Friend and Caesar) — sung by **David Manners**; "Three's a Crowd" (Dubin, Kahal and Warren) — sung by **David Manners**; "I Send My Love with the Roses" (Dubin and Berke) — sung by **David Manners**.

RUNNING TIME: 64 min.

STORY: Musician David Manners becomes an overnight singing sensation. Success goes to Manners' head. Believing he can do no wrong, Manners alienates his fans and is reduced to being a member of a small band.

NOTES AND COMMENTARY: Gordon Elliott can be seen on the dance floor during the first two songs sung by David Manners through a megaphone.

Allan Lane plays another nightclub patron. This is the second of three films in which both Elliott and Lane would appear. The others were *Week-End Marriage* (First National Pictures, 1932) and *Bells of Rosarita* (Republic, 1945).

Editor Howard Bretherton would later direct Wild Bill Elliott in a quartet of westerns, *Wagon Tracks West* (Republic, 1943), *Bordertown Gunfighters* (Republic, 1944), *Hidden Valley Outlaws* (Republic, 1944) and *San Antonio Kid* (Republic, 1944).

REVIEWS: "A slick script and well-honed direction give this one its strength." *The Motion Picture Guide*, Nash and Ross; "Its intent is malicious, the story by Alan James is almost too authentic, and it makes a shrewdly amusing comedy of what a national radio idol is like behind the scenes." *The New York Times*, 8/20/32.

SUMMATION: Well directed, written and acted, *Crooner* was a good interpretation of a musician's inability to handle success.

The Funniest Bird in the World!
The Nit-Wit Kings of Hilarious Hokum, Comedy Stars of Rio Rita *in the Greatest Carnival of Fun and Foolishness That Ever Cracked the Lips of the Cockeyed World!*

The Cuckoos

Radio Pictures (April, 1930)

A RKO Production

CAST: Sparrow, **Bert Wheeler**; Professor Bird, **Robert Woolsey**; Anita, **Dorothy Lee**; Fannie Furst, **Jobyna Howland**; Billy, **Hugh Trevor**; Ruth, **June Clyde**; the Baron, **Ivan Lebedeff**; Gypsy Queen, **Marguerita Padula**; Julius, **Mitchell Lewis**; Singing Gypsy, Raymond Maurel // Party Guest, **Gordon Elliott**.

CREDITS: Director, **Paul Sloane**; Producer, **William LeBaron**; Associate Producer, **Louis Sarecky**; Screenwriter, **Cyrus Wood**; Editor, **Arthur Roberts**; Art Director and Costumes, **Max Ree**; Cinematographer, **Nick Musuraca**; Photographic Effects, **Lloyd Knechtel**; Sound, **John Tribby**; Choreographer, **Pearl Eaton**.

SONGS: "Down in Mexico" (Ruby and Kalmar)—sung by chorus; "Oh! How We Love Our Alma Mater" (Ruby and Kalmar)—sung by Bert Wheeler and Robert Woolsey, with chorus; "All Alone Monday" (Ruby and Kalmar)—sung by June Clyde and Hugh Trevor; "California Skies" (Ruby and Kalmar)—sung by chorus; "Wherever You Are" (Tobias and Friend)—sung by June Clyde, Hugh Trevor and chorus; "I'm a Gypsy" (Ruby and Kalmar)—sung by Robert Woolsey and Jobyna Howland; "Good Bye" (Ruby and Kalmar)—sung by Bert Wheeler, Robert Woolsey, Jobyna Howland and chorus; "Tomorrow Never Comes" (Ruby and Kalmar)—sung by Raymond Maurel, with chorus; "I Love You So Much" (Ruby and Kalmar)—sung by Dorothy Lee and Bert Wheeler; "Dancing the Devil Away" (Ruby, Kalmar and Harbach)—sung by Marguerita Padua, danced by Dorothy Lee and chorus; "Wherever You Are" (reprise)—sung by Hugh Trevor and June Clyde; "I Love You So Much" (reprise)—sung by Dorothy Lee, Bert Wheeler, Jobyna Howland, Robert Woolsey, June Clyde, Hugh Trevor and chorus.

SOURCE: Play, *The Ramblers* by Guy Bolton, Bert Kalmar and Harry Ruby.

COLOR: The "Good Bye" and "Dancing the Devil Away" musical numbers, and the finale scenes, were filmed in Two-Strip Technicolor.

RUNNING TIME: 90 min.

STORY: Phony fortune teller Robert Woolsey and his assistant, Bert Wheeler, are stranded at a Mexican border resort. Wheeler falls in love with Dorothy Lee, who has been living with Mitchell Lewis and his band of Gypsies. Lewis disapproves of the romance and threatens Wheeler. Jobyna Howland brings her daughter June Clyde to the resort to get her away from Hugh Trevor. Trevor and Clyde are in love. Howland wants Clyde to marry Baron Ivan Lebedeff. Lebedeff hires Lewis to kidnap Clyde. Trevor, with help from Wheeler and Woolsey, rescues Clyde. Trevor, Clyde, Lee, Wheeler and Woolsey then fly to San Diego.

NOTES AND COMMENTARY: Gordon Elliott played a guest at Jobyna Howland's party. First Elliott can be seen at the left of the screen at the start of the "Good Bye" number. Then Elliott can be seen flashing his patented smile in the middle of the scene as Howland gives her blessings to June Clyde's romance with Hugh Trevor.

REVIEWS: "A rip-roaring farce." *The RKO Story*, Jewell and Harbin; "A pleasantly irrational screen comedy with sequences in color and riotous and, at times, ribald buffoonery, which manages to live up to its title and provides tuneful music and good dancing as well as spirited slapstick." *New York Times*, 4/26/30.

SUMMATION: Engaging musical comedy due principally to the sparkling musical numbers.

The Dreams of Youth
A Romance You'll Adore—Problems You'll Understand—Courage You'll Applaud ...
The Sweethearts of "Bad Girl" Will Captivate You.
She Thought He Was Marvelous. He Thought She Was Perfect. And Broadway Believed Them.

Dance Team

Fox (January, 1932)

CAST: Jimmy Mulligan, James Dunn; Poppy Kirk, Sally Eilers; Cora Stuart, Minna Gombell; Fred Penworthy, Edward Crandall; Jane Boyden, Nora Lane; Alec Prentice, Ralph Morgan; Herbert Wilson, Harry Beresford; Benny Weber, Charles Williams// Nightclub Patron, Gordon Elliott.

CREDITS: Director, Sidney Lanfield;

Screenwriter, Edwin J. Burke; Editor, Margaret Chancey; Cinematographer, James Wong Howe.

RUNNING TIME: 76 min.

SOURCE: Novel by Sarah Addington.

STORY: Dancers James Dunn and Sally Eilers decide to enter show business as a team. They finally make it big, but the team dissolves when Dunn believes Eilers is interested in well-to-do Edward Crandall. Dunn flops in his attempt to perform solo. Dunn returns to Eilers, who has always loved him.

NOTES AND COMMENTARY: One source indicates Gordon Elliott was a patron in a nightclub scene.

REVIEWS: "It's a combination of sentiment, hokum, bright lines and clever acting." *New York Times*, 1/16/32; "Nice program material with Dunn and Eilers." *Variety*, 1/19/32.

SUMMATION: This film was not available for review by the author.

Tops Any Musical Picture Ever Made!

Dancing Lady

Metro-Goldwyn-Mayer   (November, 1933)

CAST: Jamie Barlow, **Joan Crawford**; Patch Gallagher, **Clark Gable**; Tod Newton, **Franchot Tone**; Dolly Todhunter, **May Robson**; Rosette LaRue, **Winnie Lightner**; Fred Astaire, **Fred Astaire**; Ward King, **Robert Benchley**; Steve, **Ted Healy**; Art Jarrett, **Art Jarrett**; Jasper Bradley, Sr., **Grant Mitchell**; Nelson Eddy, **Nelson Eddy**; Jasper Bradley, Jr., **Maynard Holmes**; Pinky, **Sterling Holloway**; Vivian Warner, **Gloria Foy**; Stage Hand, **Moe Howard**; Curly, **Jerry Howard**; Larry, **Larry Fine**// Café Patron, **Gordon Elliott**.

CREDITS: Director, **Robert Z. Leonard**; Executive Producer, **David O. Selznick**; Associate Producer, **John W. Considine, Jr.**; Screenwriters, **Allen Rivkin** and **P.J. Wolfson**; Editor, **Margaret Booth**; Art Director, **Merrill Pye**; Interior Decorator, **Edwin B. Willis**; Cinematographer, **Oliver T. Marsh**; Gowns, **Adrian**; Sound, **Douglas Shearer**; Special Effects, **Slavko Vorkapich**; Choreographers, **Sammy Lee** and **Eddie Prinz**; Musical Conductor, **Lou Silvers**.

SONGS: "Hold Your Man" (Brown and Freed)— sung by **Winnie Lightner** and chorus; "Alabama Swing" (Johnson)— danced by **Joan Crawford**; "Everything I Have Is Yours" (Lane and Adamson)— sung by **Art Jarrett**; "My Dancing Lady" (McHugh and Fields)— sung by **Art Jarrett**, and danced by **Joan Crawford**; "Heigh Ho" (Lane and Adamson)— sung and danced by **Fred Astaire**, **Joan Crawford** and **chorus**; "Let's Go Bavarian" (Lane and Adamson)— sung and danced by **Fred Astaire**, **Joan Crawford** and **chorus**; "That's the Rhythm of the Day" (Rogers and Hart)— sung by **Nelson Eddy**, **Joan Crawford** and **Art Jarrett**, and danced by **chorus**.

RUNNING TIME: 92 min.

SOURCE: Novel by **James Warren Bellah**.

STORY: Showgirl Joan Crawford wants a career on Broadway as a dancer. Wealthy Franchot Tone asks Crawford to give up show business and marry him. Crawford agrees to marry Tone if she gets a part in a show and she and the show are a flop. Tone arranges to have Crawford hired for a part in Clark Gable's new production. Gable sees Crawford's talent and makes her the star of the show. Before the show opens, Tone has the backers withdraw their money from the show, forcing it to close. Gable decides to carry on, using his own money. Crawford learns of Tone's duplicity and returns to star in the show. The show is a hit. Crawford and Gable realize they love each other.

NOTES AND COMMENTARY: Gordon Elliott has a small part as a café patron playing a slot machine. As the slot machine finally pays off, his distinctive voice can be heard saying, "Oh boy, I won!"

REVIEWS: "A lively affair, nevertheless one constructed along familiar lines." *The New York Times*, 12/1/33; "A strong backstage story with musical trimmings on a lavish scale." *The MGM Story*, Eames.

SUMMATION: A sparkling and highly entertaining musical with lavish production numbers.

*Warning Inflammable Mixture! When Man-Wrecking Bette and Heart-Breaking Franchot
Start Playing with Fire, Get Set for a Bolt of Drama That Will Blow the Fuses!*

Dangerous

Warner Bros. (December, 1935)

ALTERNATE TITLE: *Hard Luck Dame.*

CAST: Joyce Heath, **Bette Davis**; Don Bellows, **Franchot Tone**; Gail Armitage, **Margaret Lindsay**; Mrs. Williams, **Alison Skipworth**; Gordon Heath, **John Eldredge**; Teddy, **Dick Foran**; Farnsworth, **Walter Walker**; Hanley, **Richard Carle**; Melton, **George Irving**; George Sheffield, **Pierre Watkin**; Elmont, **Douglas Wood**; Walsh, **William Davidson**// Charles (in play), **Gordon Elliott**.

CREDITS: Director, **Alfred E. Green**; Story/Screenwriter, **Laird Doyle**; Editor, **Thomas Richards**; Art Director, **Hugh Reticker**; Cinematographer, **Ernest Haller**; Gowns, **Orry-Kelly**; Musical Director, **Leo F. Forbstein**.

RUNNING TIME: 79 min.

STORY: Though a great actress, Bette Davis is thought to be a jinx to her leading men and the plays in which she appears. Davis has become dependent on alcohol when spotted by architect Franchot Tone. Tone takes Davis to his country house to rest. Tone falls under Davis' spell and breaks his engagement to socialite Margaret Lindsay. Using his own money, Tone backs a play for Davis. Knowing the play will be a big hit; Tone wants to marry Davis after opening night. Davis reluctantly agrees even though she is still married to John Eldredge. Eldredge refuses to grant Davis a divorce. Davis takes Eldredge on an automobile ride in which she deliberately crashes into a tree, hoping to kill one of them. Both Davis and Eldredge survive the impact. Finding that Davis is married, Tone refuses to have any more to do with her. The play opens without Davis and quickly closes. Davis decides to change her life. Davis persuades Pierre Watkin to reopen the play. The play is a hit. Davis repays Tone the money he lost. Tone marries Lindsay, while Davis finds happiness with Eldredge.

NOTES AND COMMENTARY: Gordon Elliott has one scene as the male lead in Bette Davis' play. He has one line during the rehearsal. Then Elliott begs off repeating the final scene and all go home. Elliott is effective in this small part.

REVIEW: "Except for a few scenes where the tension is convincing as well as deadly, she [Davis] fails." *New York Times*, 12/27/35; "Though the story was one prolonged melodramatic cliché, Davis' dogged determination not to allow Doyle's over-heated screenplay to sink her, paid off handsomely." *Warner Bros. Story*, Hirshhorn.

SUMMATION: Some good acting saves the film from being just another soap opera.

A Love Story Deliciously Different!

Delicious

Fox Film Corporation (December, 1931)

CAST: Heather, **Janet Gaynor**; Larry, **Charles Farrell**; Jansen, **El Brendel**; Sascha, **Raul Roulien**; O'Flynn, **Lawrence O'Sullivan**; Olga, **Manya Roberti**; Diana, **Virginia Cherrill**; Mrs. Van Bergh, **Olive Tell**; Mischa, **Mischa Auer**; Toscha, **Marvine Maazel**// Larry's Friend, **Gordon Elliott**.

CREDITS: Director, **David Butler**; Story, **Guy Bolton**; Screenwriters, **Guy Bolton** and **Sonya Levien**; Art Direction, **Joe Wright**; Cinematographer, **Ernest Palmer**; Sound, **Joseph E. Aiken**; Music, **George Gershwin**; Lyrics, **Ira Gershwin**.

SONGS: "Ochi Chyorniye" (traditional)— sung by **Manya Roberti**; "Delicious" (G.

Gershwin and I. Gershwin)—sung by **Paul Roulien**; "Welcome to the Melting Pot" (G. Gershwin and I. Gershwin)—sung by **male chorus**; "Somebody from Somewhere" (G. Gershwin and I. Gershwin)—sung by **Janet Gaynor**; "Katinkitsha" (G. Gershwin and I. Gershwin)—sung by **Mischa Auer** and **Manya Roberti**, and danced by **Janet Gaynor**; "Blah-Blah-Blah" (G. Gershwin and I. Gershwin)—sung by **El Brendel** and **Manya Roberti**; "Rhapsody in Rivets" (G. Gershwin)—played and narrated by **Raul Roulien**.

RUNNING TIME: 106 min.

STORY: Janet Gaynor is coming to America to live with her uncle, but her uncle refuses to make a home for her. Gaynor is faced with deportation. Wealthy sportsman Charles Farrell offers help and leaves a note for Gaynor. Wanting her daughter, Virginia Cherrill, to become Farrell's wife, Olive Tell destroys the letter. Gaynor is able to enter America illegally. Farrell and Gaynor meet and fall in love. Gaynor is devastated when she is told Farrell plans to marry Cherill. When Farrell is injured in an accident at a major polo match, Gaynor rushes to his side. Cherill phones the police to have Gaynor arrested. Gaynor eludes the police but finally gives herself up to be deported. Farrell finds out about Cherrill's duplicity and races to Gaynor's side just as the ship is leaving the dock. They plan to have the ship's captain marry them. The voyage will be their honeymoon.

NOTES AND COMMENTARY: Gordon Elliot is seen briefly as one of Charles Farrell's friends who come aboard the ship. As a photographer is taking a picture of the group with a trophy won in a polo contest, Elliott remarks, prophetically, "It would look better if I had my horse." Farrell then hands Elliott the trophy to take off the ship.

REVIEWS: "The strength of this talkie is in the title and its co-stars." *Variety*, 12/29/31; "A conventional piece of sentimentality with dialogue that is scarcely insipid." *New York Times*, 12/26/31.

SUMMATION: Infectious fun, very entertaining musical comedy.

Learn the Season's New Rules for Husband Hunting! It Will Open Your Eyes!

Desirable

Warner Bros. (September, 1934)

CAST: Lois, **Jean Muir**; McAllister, **George Brent**; Helen, **Verree Teasdale**; Austin, **John Halliday**; Russell, **Charles Starrett**; Chet, **Russell Hopton**; Barbara, **Joan Wheeler**; Margaret, **Barbara Leonard**; Mrs. Emily Gray, **Virginia Hammond**; McAllister's secretary, **Pauline True**// Guest at Lois' Party, **Gordon Elliott**.

CREDITS: Director, **Archie L. Mayo**; Story/Screenplay, **Mary McCall, Jr.**; Editor, **Thomas Pratt**; Art Director, **John Hughes**; Cinematographer, **Ernest Haller**; Gowns, **Orry-Kelly**; Musical Director, **Leo F. Forbstein**.

RUNNING TIME: 68 min.

STORY: Advertising executive George Brent is an admirer of Broadway actress Verree Teasdale. Teasdale gives Brent the key to her apartment, not knowing her daughter, Jean Muir, has returned from school. Brent is immediately captivated by Muir's charms, and Muir is more than fond of Brent. Teasdale engineers Muir's engagement to socialite Charles Starrett. Muir, realizing she's not in love with Starrett, breaks off the engagement. Muir and Brent, who love each other, finally get together.

NOTES AND COMMENTARY: An out-of-focus Gordon Elliott can be seen behind Verree Teasdale's right shoulder as she looks at a bewildered George Brent at a party given for Jean Muir.

REVIEWS: "The story in which she [Jean Muir] participates so eloquently, while it would diminish perceptibly in effectiveness without her, can claim some modest attention on its own merits." *New York Times*, 9/15/34; "Good entertainment, but lacks star power." *Variety*, 9/18/34.

SUMMATION: Sparkling drama, thanks to Muir, about a young girl's quest for true love.

All America Is Looking Up — as Jimmy and Pat Join the Air Marines!

Devil Dogs of the Air

Warner Bros. (February, 1935)

CAST: Tommy O'Toole, **James Cagney**; Lieut. Brannigan, **Pat O'Brien**; Betty Roberts, **Margaret Lindsay**; Crash Kelly, **Frank McHugh**; Mac, **John Arledge**; Ma Roberts, **Helen Lowell**; Commandant, **Robert Barrat**; Commanding General, **Russell Hicks**; Captain, **William Davidson**; Flight Instructor, **Ward Bond**// First Flight Instructor, **Gordon Elliott**.

CREDITS: Director, **Lloyd Bacon**; Story, **John Monk Saunders**; Screenwriters, **Malcolm Stuart Boylan**; Editor, **William Clements**; Art Director, **Arthur Jay Kooken**; Cinematographer, **Arthur Edeson**; Musical Conductor, **Leo F. Forbstein**; Technical Advisor, **Lt. Col. Ralph J. Mitchell**.

RUNNING TIME: 86 min.

STORY: New recruit James Cagney is assigned to the same naval station as his pal, Pat O'Brien. Brash and cocky, Cagney knows he's a good aviator and doesn't think the Navy can teach him anything about flying. Both Cagney and O'Brien are interested in the same girl, Margaret Lindsay. Cagney becomes a hero when he saves a disabled plane after O'Brien bailed out. Later, the positions are reversed when Cagney wants to jump from a disabled plane and O'Brien talks him into bringing it down. Both are heroes, and Lindsay kisses O'Brien. Lindsay really loves Cagney, however, and O'Brien gets himself transferred to another station. Cagney and Lindsay get together.

NOTES AND COMMENTARY: The fortunes of fame in Hollywood: Both Gordon Elliott and Ward Bond play flight instructors; Elliott has a larger part, but Bond receives billing and Elliott does not. First, Elliott is present when Pat O'Brien receives a telegram informing him that James Cagney will be stationed at the naval base with him. Elliott engages in a dialog exchange with O'Brien in this scene. Then Elliott is instructing new students about the operation of a plane — to Cagney's obvious boredom. Finally, Elliott takes Cagney up in a plane to test Cagney's flying ability. Cagney performs stunts — to Elliott's displeasure and Cagney's delight. Upon landing, Elliott tells O'Brien that *he'll* have to check flight Cagney because Elliott will have nothing more to do with Cagney.

REVIEWS: "A stirring melodrama of the Navy's Birdmen. The film is both amusing and exciting." *New York Times*, 2/7/35; "The story was hardly epoch-making, but the special effects were super." *The Warner Bros. Story*, Hirshhorn.

SUMMATION: First-rate aerial photography and the performances of Cagney and O'Brien raise this obvious plot to the status of a highly entertaining film.

Street Gang Leader Grown Up to City Boss ... But Never on the Up and Up!...
Until Childhood Loyalties Pricked the Bubble of His New Found Power!

Devil's Party

Universal (May, 1938)

CAST: Marty Malone; **Victor McLaglen**; Mike O'Mara, **William Gargan**; Jerry Donovan, **Paul Kelly**; Helen McCoy, **Beatrice Roberts**; Sam, **Frank Jenks**; Joe O'Mara, **John Gallaudet**; Judge Harrison, **Samuel S. Hinds**; Frank Diamond, **Joe Downing**; Webster, **Arthur Hoyt**// James Brewster, **Gordon Elliott**.

CREDITS: Director, **Ray McCarey**; Associate Producer, **Edmund Grainger**; Screenwriter, **Roy Chanslor**; Editor, **Philip Cahn**; Art Directors, **Jack Otterson** and **N.V. Timchenko**; Cinematography, **Milton Krasner**; Sound, **Charles Carroll** and **Edwin Wetzel**; Musical Director, **Charles Previn**.

SONGS: "Things Are Coming My Way" (McHugh and Adamson)— sung by **Beatrice Roberts**; "Old Lang Syne" (Burns and Thomson)— sung by **Paul Kelly**, **Victor McLaglen**, **John Gallaudet**, **Beatrice Roberts** and **William Gargan**.

RUNNING TIME: 65 min.

SOURCE: Novel, *Hells' Kitchen Has a Pantry* by **Borden Chase**.

STORY: Five childhood gang members from Hell's Kitchen— nightclub owner and gambler Victor McLaglan, brothers and now police officers William Gargan and John Gallaudet, priest Paul Kelly and nightclub singer Beatrice Roberts— meet annually at McLaglan's club. Both McLaglan and Gargan are sweet on Roberts. Two of McLaglan's henchmen, Frank Jenks and Joseph Downing, murder Gordon Elliott for welshing on a gambling debt. Gallaudet investigates but meets his death at the hands of the henchmen. Downing sends Gargan evidence that McLaglan is involved in his brother's death. Kelly prevents Gargan from killing McLaglan. McLaglan is charged with murder after he admits to Kelly that he was indirectly responsible. Fearing that McLaglan will inform on him, Downing wants to get rid of Gargan. Roberts is kidnapped in order to force McLaglan to participate in a robbery. Gargan is tipped off and arrives to arrest McLaglan, not realizing he's walking into a trap. McLaglan takes the bullet meant for Gargan, and in a final effort knocks out Downing with his strong right hand. Gargan and Roberts decide to marry.

NOTES AND COMMENTARY: Gordon Elliott has a small but critical role in the film. Elliott tells Victor McLaglan that he stopped payment on his check for a gambling debt, and that he refuses to pay. McLaglan's henchmen then murder Elliott.

REVIEW: "We are continually won by such harmless and richly improbable factions as *The Devil's Party*." *New York Times*, 5/31/38; "Not particularly compelling melodrama." *The Universal Story*, Hirshhorn.

SUMMATION: This an interesting crime story with good performances by the principals.

Only a Super-Woman Could Have Lived This Story ... Only a Super-Star Could Bring It to the Screen!

Dr. Monica

Warner Bros. (June, 1934)

ALTERNATE TITLE: *Doctor Monica*.

CAST: Dr. Monica, **Kay Francis**; John, **Warren William**; Mary, **Jean Muir**; Anna, **Verree Teasdale**; Mrs. Monahan, **Emma Dunn**; Bunny, **Phillip Reed**; Pettinghill, **Herbert Bunston**; Mrs. Hazlitt, **Ann Shoemaker**; Mrs. Chandor, **Virginia Hammond**; Dr. Brent, **Hale Hamilton**; Louise, **Virginia Pine**// Rutherford, **Gordon Elliott**.

CREDITS: Director, **William Keighley**; Screenwriter and Adapter, **Charles Kenyon**; English Adaptation, **Laura Walker Mayer**; Editor, **William Clemens**; Art Director, **Anton Grot**; Cinematography, **Sol Polito**; Gowns, **Orry-Kelly**; Musical Conductor, **Leo F. Forbstein**.

RUNNING TIME: 61 min.

SOURCE: A Polish play by **Marja Morozowicz Szczepkowska**.

STORY: To all appearances, Kay Frances, a noted OB physician, and writer Warren William are happily married. William, however, is having an affair with their mutual friend, Jean Muir. William does break off the romance when he takes a trip to Europe, not knowing Muir is pregnant with his child. Francis becomes her physician and overhears Muir desperately trying to reach William. William, upon his return and still not knowing of Muir's pregnancy, realizes Francis is the woman for him. Francis still attends to Muir, although jealous that Muir can bear William's child while she is unable to have children. Francis plans to leave William so he can marry Muir. Before she can do this, Muir, knowing William no longer loves her, leaves the child at Francis' apartment and then commits suicide. Francis decides to stay with William and adopt the baby.

NOTES AND COMMENTARY: Gordon Elliott can be seen in the horseback sequence. He remarks, "The same two held us up yesterday morning," as Kay Francis and Jean Muir are late for their morning ride.

REVIEWS: "If women go for it, it will be okay, but that seems doubtful." *Variety*, 6/26/34; "The ladies did their best is such lugubrious circumstances." *The Warner Bros. Story*, Hirshhorn.

SUMMATION: Pretty soggy going in this soap opera.

Muni as the "Scarface" of Medicine.
Terrific in His Unforgettable Characterization of the Outcast Doctor Who Fought Gangdom
with the Deadliest Weapons Known to Science!

Dr. Socrates

Warner Bros. (October, 1935)

ALTERNATE TITLE: *Doctor Socrates.*

CAST: Lee, **Paul Muni**; Josephine, **Ann Dvorak**; Red Bastian, **Barton MacLane**; Dr. Ginder, **Robert Barrat**; Dr. Burton, **John Eldredge**; Stevens, **Hobart Cavanaugh**; Ma Ganson, **Helen Lowell**; Muggsy, **Mayo Methot**; Greer, **Henry O'Neill**; Caroline, **Grace Stafford**; Dr. McClintock, **Samuel Hinds**; Dublin, **June Travis**; Ben Suggs, **Raymond Brown**; Catlett, **Olin Howland**; Cinq Laval, **Joseph Downing**// Collins, **Gordon Elliott**.

CREDITS: Director, **William Dieterle**; Story, **W.R. Burnett**; Adaptation, **Mary C. McCall, Jr.**; Screenwriter, **Robert Lord**; Editor, **Ralph Dawson**; Art Director, **Anton Grot**; Cinematographer, **Tony Gaudio**; Musical Director, **Leo F. Forbstein**; Dialogue Director, **Stanley Logan**.

RUNNING TIME: 71 min.

STORY: Feeling responsible for the death of the woman he loved, Doctor Paul Muni prefers to isolate himself in the small town of Big Bend. Public enemy Barton MacLane forces Muni to treat him for bullet wounds received in a bank robbery. MacLane then targets the Big Bend bank. On the way to the bank, MacLane picks up hitchhiker Ann Dvorak. During the robbery, Dvorak seizes the chance to escape. MacLane sees Dvorak and shoots her, wounding her slightly. Muni treats Dvorak and the two begin to fall in love. MacLane forces Muni to come to his hideout to further treat his wound. MacLane tells Muni that Dvorak will become his girl, and kidnaps her before Muni can return home. Muni gets word of MacLane's hideout to the law officers but asks them to give him a chance to get Dvorak out of the hideout before they close in. Muni convinces MacLane that the water they've been drinking is contaminated and they'll come down with typhoid. Muni vaccinates the gangsters with a narcotic that puts them to sleep. Muni becomes the town hero, with Dvorak at his side.

NOTES AND COMMENTARY: Gordon Elliott is seen prominently in his role of a Department of Justice operative, an assistant to Henry O'Neill. He asks the sheriff about Ann Dvorak and then comes up with a hundred-dollar bill from a bank robbery that was passed by Paul Muni. Elliott is present when Helen Lowell is questioned, and then leaves with O'Neill for Barton MacLane's hideout. Elliott is with O'Neill when the lawmen surround the hideout, then discusses Muni's request to give him a chance to rescue Dvorak with O'Neill, and finally moves in on the hideout with O'Neill and the other lawmen.

REVIEWS: "Entertaining." *Variety*, 10/9/35; "Enjoyable film." *1996 Movie and Video Guide*, Maltin.

SUMMATION: Good, well acted minor crime melodrama.

You Can Bet Your Bottom Dollar — It's a Winner!

Down the Stretch

Warner Bros. (September, 1936)

A First National Picture

CAST: Patricia Barrington, **Patricia Ellis**; Snapper Sinclair, **Mickey Rooney**; Cliff Barrington, **Dennis Moore**; Noah, **William Best**; Judge Adams, **Gordon Hart**; Robert Bates, **Gordon Elliott**; Aunt Julia, **Virginia Brissac**; Tex Reardon, **Charles Wilson**; C.D. Burch, **Joseph Crehan**; Nurse, **Mary Treen**; Nick, **Robert Emmett Keane**; Arnold Roach, **Charles Foy**; Sir Oliver Martin, **Crauford Kent**.

CREDITS: Director, **William Clemens**; Story/Screenwriter, **William Jacobs**; Editor, **Louis Hesse**; Art Director, **Ted Smith**; Cinematographer, **Arthur Todd**; Gowns, **Milo Anderson**; Dialogue Director, **Gus Shy**.

RUNNING TIME: 66 min.

STORY: Unable to find a job as a jockey because of his father's reputation, and facing a year in a reformatory, Mickey Rooney is given a job by horse breeder and racer Patricia Ellis. Rooney finally gets a chance to prove himself and becomes a top jockey. When he won't work with gambler Robert Emmett Keane, Rooney is framed and suspended from racing for a year. Rooney is able to go to England and continue his racing career. Rooney is asked to ride a top horse in the important race but wants to ride Ellis' horse. Rooney knows Ellis needs the winner's purse to continue her business. Ellis' husband, Dennis Moore, hears his offer but doesn't tell Ellis. When he finds out that Ellis would have let him ride her horse, Rooney causes a pileup on the track that allows Ellis' entry to win. Rooney is barred from racing in England, but Ellis has a job for him in America.

NOTES AND COMMENTARY: Gordon Elliott received sixth billing in a thankless, underdeveloped role. Elliott is first seen prior to Mickey Rooney's inaugural race for Patricia Ellis, inviting Ellis and her group to attend a party in honor of his horse's victory. Later, Elliott speaks to Rooney in a gambling casino. Lastly, Elliott overhears gambler Robert Emmett Keane talking to Rooney. By Elliott's facial reaction, the audience senses Elliott will play a critical part in the story. Alas, that's the end of Elliott's on-screen footage.

REVIEWS: "Another racetrack pic. Adds little that is new in faces, acting or plot." *Variety*, 11/11/36; "A well-made programmer with a racing background." *Warner Bros. Story*, Hirshhorn.

SUMMATION: Mickey Rooney shines in this above-average racing drama, with an unsatisfactory ending.

Score a Goal for Dick!

The Drop Kick

First National Pictures (September, 1927)

ALTERNATE TITLE: *Glitter.*

CAST: Jack Hamill, **Richard Barthelmess**; Cecily Graves, **Barbara Kent**; Eunice Hathaway, **Dorothy Revier**; Brad Hathaway, **Eugene Strong**; Molly, **Alberta Vaughn**; Ed Pemberton, **Brooks Benedict**; Mrs. Hamill, **Hedda Hopper**; Bones, **James Bradbury**; Dean Carson, **George Pearce**// Chump at Thanksgiving Prom, **Gordon Elliott**.

CREDITS: Director, **Millard Webb**; Producer, **Ray Rockett**; Cinematographers, **Arthur Edeson** and **Alvin Knechtel**.

COLOR: Tinted yellow.

RUNNING TIME: 65 min.

SOURCE: Novel, *Glitter* by **Katherine Brush**.

STORY: Reintroduced to Barbara Kent by his mother, Hedda Hopper, college football star Richard Barthelmess begins to fall in love with her. Complicating matters is Dorothy Revier, wife of Barthelmess' coach, Eugene Strong, who has romantic designs on Barthelmess. Faced with charges of embezzlement to support Revier's extravagant lifestyle, Strong commits suicide. Revier convinces Barthelmess that Strong killed himself because he believed they were in love. Hopper confronts Revier and learns the truth, relieving Barthelmess from his promise to wed Revier. Barthelmess and Kent plan to marry.

NOTES AND COMMENTARY: Although his part is brief, Gordon Elliott's role is key to the plot. To please his mother, Richard Barthelmess takes Barbara Kent to the Thanksgiving Prom, even though he's more interested in Dorothy Revier. When Barthelmess leaves Kent alone, Elliott moves in and attempts to romance her on the dance floor. Disgusted with Elliott's behavior, Kent leaves the dance, quickly to be followed by Barthelmess. Barthelmess catches up to Kent and soon realizes she is the girl for him.

As Kent flees the dance, Elliott flashes the smile known to his countless fans.

REVIEW: "The story is one wherein the producers and others have successfully dodged anything in the form of human psychology." *The New York Times*, 9/20/27.

SUMMATION: Though a minor melodrama, *The Drop Kick* succeeds in holding the audience's interest.

Love Not for Sale.
Charm and Enchantment When East Meets West!

East Is West

Universal (October, 1930)
A Monta Bell Production
CAST: Ming Toy, **Lupe Velez**; Billy Benson, **Lew Ayres**; Charlie Yong, **Edward G. Robinson**; Lo Sang Kee, **E. Allyn Warren**; Hop Toy, **Tetsu Komai**; Mrs. Benson, **Mary Forbes**; Mr. Benson, **Henry Kolker** // Party Guest, **Gordon Elliott**.

CREDITS: Director, **Monta Bell**; Producer, **Carl Laemmle, Jr.**; Associate Producer, **E.M. Asher**; Screenwriters, **Tom Reed** and **Winifred Eaton Reeve**; Supervising Film Editor, **Maurice Pivar**; Editor, **Fred Allen**; Art Director, **Herman Rosse**; Cinematographer, **Jerry Ash**; Sound, **C. Roy Hunter**; Musical Score, **Heinz Roemheld**.

SONG: "Love Boat"— sung by **Lupe Velez**.
RUNNING TIME: 74 min.
SOURCE: Play by **Samuel Shipman** and **John B. Hymer**.

STORY: Lew Ayres arrives in China to find the beautiful Lupe Velez being auctioned with a number of other women on the Love Boat. Through Ayres' efforts, E. Alyn Warren buys Velez and takes her to San Francisco. Warren sells Velez to the Chop Suey King, Edward G. Robinson, so she can stay in America. Ayres steps in again and takes Velez to live at his house. When Robinson comes to take Velez away, Ayres asks Velez to marry him. Ayres' family is against the marriage but relents when it is revealed that Velez is not of Chinese descent. A Chinese family raised Velez after her missionary parents were murdered.

NOTES AND COMMENTARY: At the party to announce Lew Ayres' engagement to Lupe Velez, Gordon Elliott can be seen sitting on a piano bench watching a female party guest play the piano.

REVIEWS: "Good daily change meller. Suspense better sustained than the average." *Variety*, 11/5/30; "An intricately plotted and quite implausible affair which runs its tedious length for an hour and twenty minutes." *New York Times*, 11/1/30.

SUMMATION: This is a sluggish melodrama, marred by Edward G. Robinson's overacting. Again, there is the inevitable copout when it's revealed at the last moment that Lupe Velez is not Chinese but white. Now her marriage to Lew Ayres is acceptable to San Francisco society.

The Crime That Shocked the City Lives Again.
Cyclonic Breath Taking Drama ... Your Blood Will Race ... Your Nerves Will Tingle. A Big Scoop!

Final Edition

Columbia (February, 1932)

ALTERNATE TITLE: *Determination.*

CAST: Brad, **Pat O'Brien**; Anne, **Mae Clarke**; Selby, **Morgan Wallace**; Malvern, **Bradley Page**; Patsy, **Mary Doran**; Freddie, **James Donlan**; Dan, **Phil Tead**; Conroy, **Robert Emmett O'Connor**; Mrs. Conroy, **Bertha Mann**// Reporter, **Gordon Elliott**.

CREDITS: Director, **Howard Higgin**; Story, **Roy Chanslor**; Screenwriter, **Dorothy Howell**; Editor, **Jack Dennis**; Cinematographer, **Joseph Walker**.

RUNNING TIME: 66 min.

STORY: Police Commissioner Robert Emmett O'Connor tells lawyer Morgan Wallace and his associates, Bradley Page and Mary Doran, that he has evidence they are behind the rackets, giving them 24 hours to leave town. In retaliation, Page murders O'Connor and steals his evidence. Newspaper reporter Mae Clarke gets an exclusive story on how and why O'Connor was murdered — to the consternation of her boss and boyfriend, Pat O'Brien. Clarke follows up on the story and finds where the evidence was hidden. Page kidnaps Clarke and retrieves the incriminating papers. Clarke leaves a message for O'Brien, telling him where she will be taken. O'Brien outsmarts Page, Wallace and Doran, whose escape attempt is thwarted by the police. Clarke decides to quit her job as reporter and accept O'Brien's marriage proposal.

NOTES AND COMMENTARY: In one brief scene, Gordon Elliott is heard and seen as one of the reporters trying to interview Bertha Mann following the death of Robert Emmett O'Connor.

REVIEWS: "Plenty of action and a generally good production with Mae Clarke scoring another hit." *Variety*, 3/1/32; "A completely effective and entertaining piece." *New York Times*, 2/22/32.

SUMMATION: Fast, suspenseful and well-done crime story.

A Woman Who Loved Him Killed Him (So It Might Be Any Woman in Europe).
He Wrecked the Lives of Many Women — Which One Was Desperate Enough to Kill Him.
A Great Story of Murder.

The Firebird

Warner Bros. (November, 1934)

CAST: Carola Pointer, **Verree Teasdale**; Herman Brandt, **Ricardo Cortez**; John Pointer, **Lionel Atwill**; Mariette, **Anita Louise**; Police Inspector, **C. Aubrey Smith**; Jolan, **Dorothy Tree**; Mlle. Mousquet, **Helen Trenholme**; Emile, **Hobart Cavanaugh**; Halasz, **Robert Barrat**; Assistant Stage Manager; **Hal K. Dawson**; Mr. Beyer, **Russell Hicks**; Max (the Porter), **Spencer Charters**; Professor Peterson, **Etienne Girardot**; Thelma, **Florence Fair**; Alice, **Nan Gray**// Jolan's Companion, **Gordon Elliott**.

CREDITS: Director: **William Dieterle**; Adaptation, **Jeffrey Dell**; Screenwriter, **Charles Kenyon**; Editor, **Ralph Dawson**; Art Direction, **Anton Grot**; Cinematographer, **Ernest Haller**; Gowns, **Orry-Kelly**; Music Director, **Leo F. Forbstein**; Dialogue Director, **Arthur Greville Collins**.

RUNNING TIME: 74 min.

SOURCE: Play by **Lajos Zilahy**; produced by **Gilbert Miller**.

STORY: Womanizer Ricardo Cortez, a noted actor, wants to have an affair with Verree Teasdale. His invitation is overheard by Teasdale's daughter, Anita Louise. Later that night a mysterious woman is seen entering Cortez' apartment. A few weeks later Cortez is murdered. Teasdale tells police inspector C. Aubrey Smith that she was the woman who went to the apartment, but she didn't kill Cortez. Teasdale is covering for Louise. Louise shot Cortez in a violent struggle for the gun. Smith believes a trial will clear Louise.

NOTES AND COMMENTARY: Gordon Elliott can be seen and heard in this film as Dorothy Tree's companion. First, Elliott is seen buying items for himself and Tree to take on their train trip from Vienna to Paris. Next, Elliott and Tree are in their compartment on the train when police officers barge in and take them to police headquarters.

REVIEWS: "The photoplay is professional rather than startling. An ordinary mystery melodrama." *New York Times*, 11/15/34; "A routine whodunnit with no startling surprises." *The Warner Bros. Story*, Hirshhorn.

SUMMATION: Interesting though fairly predictable mystery drama.

Was She Any Happier Than the Girls in Her Father's Store?
Every Girl Who Works (and Loves!) Must See It!

Five and Ten

Metro-Goldwyn-Mayer (June, 1931)

A Robert Z. Leonard Production; A Marion Davies Production

ALTERNATE TITLE: *Daughter of Luxury*.

CAST: Jennifer Rarick, **Marion Davies**; Berry Rhodes, **Leslie Howard**; John Rarick, **Richard Bennett**; Jenny Rarick, **Irene Rich**; Avery Rarick, **Kent Douglass**; Muriel Preston, **Mary Duncan**// Footman, **Gordon Elliott**; Wedding Guest, **Gordon Elliott**.

CREDITS: Director, **Robert Z. Leonard**; Screenplay, **Edith Fitzgerald**; Editor, **Margaret Booth**; Art Director, **Cedric Gibbons**; Cinematographer, **George Barnes**; Sound, **Douglas Shearer**; Gowns, **Adrian**.

SONGS: "Bury Me Not on the Lone Prairie" (traditional)— sung by **Kent Douglass**; "Rye Whiskey" (traditional)— sung by **Kent Douglass**.

RUNNING TIME: 88 min.

SOURCE: Novel, *Five and Ten* by **Fannie Hurst**.

STORY: Marion Davies, daughter of millionaire Richard Bennett, is snubbed by high society. Davies meets playboy Leslie Howard and decides they'll marry. Instead, Howard marries his fiancée, Mary Duncan, even though Howard really loves Davies. The accumulation of wealth begins the disintegration of Bennett's family. Bennett neglects his wife, Irene Rich, and she plans to leave him for a gigolo. Davies plans to run off with a married man. Bennett's son, Kent Douglass, feels helpless and decides to take his own life. This tragedy brings the family back together and they embark on a trip to Europe. Howard has obtained a divorce from Duncan and plans to follow Davies.

NOTES AND COMMENTARY: Gordon Elliott has two roles in this film. As a footman, Elliott is seen walking behind Marion Davies as he brings packages to the car. Next, Elliott takes luggage out of the car as Davies arrives at a weekend party. Elliott appears later as a guest at Leslie Howard's marriage to Mary Duncan. Elliott can be seen to the left of Davies' head.

REVIEWS: "Far beyond the glum outlook of the economic lords is the fact the picture is enjoyable." *New York Times*, 7/11/31; "Sumptuous production lacks a solid story, but Howard is a standout." *The Motion Picture Guide*, Nash and Ross.

SUMMATION: A good melodrama of the trials and tribulations of a wealthy family.

She Went to the Threshold of Hell for Happiness!

Forbidden

Columbia (January, 1932)

A Frank Capra Production

ALTERNATE TITLE: *Jane Doe.*

CAST: Lulu, **Barbara Stanwyck**; Bob, **Adolphe Menjou**; Holland, **Ralph Bellamy**; Helen, **Dorothy Peterson**; Wilkinson, **Thomas Jefferson**; Roberta (baby), **Myrna Fresholt**; Roberta (18), **Charlotte V. Henry**; Briggs, **Oliver Eckhardt** // Reporter, **Gordon Elliott**.

CREDITS: Director/Story, **Frank Capra**; Producer, **Harry Cohn**; Screenwriter, **Jo Swerling**; Editor, **Maurice Wright**; Cinematography, **Joseph Walker**.

SONG: "Cupid's Holiday" (Bebo and Fylling)—sung by unknown male trio.

RUNNING TIME: 83 min.

STORY: Spinster Barbara Stanwyck takes a vacation cruise to Havana where she meets lawyer Adolphe Menjou, who has political aspirations. The two fall in love, with Stanwyck unaware that Menjou is married to Dorothy Peterson. Peterson is an invalid because of an automobile accident in which Menjou was driving. The romance continues after they return to the States. Menjou finally confesses that he's a married man. Stanwyck orders him to leave without telling him she's pregnant with his child. Stanwyck and Menjou later reunite, with Menjou adopting their child and Stanwyck becoming Menjou's mistress. Newspaperman Ralph Bellamy, who wants to marry Stanwyck, hates Menjou and wants to destroy his political career. Menjou, on the threshold of becoming Governor, wants to run off with Stanwyck. To prevent this, Stanwyck finally accepts Bellamy's marriage proposal. Bellamy obtains proof of Menjou's affair with Stanwyck and plans to publish this information, not caring it will devastate Peterson and her daughter. Bellamy and Stanwyck fight, and Bellamy strikes Stanwyck. Stanwyck retrieves a gun and shoots Bellamy and then burns all the evidence. After a year in prison, Stanwyck receives a full pardon from Menjou. On his deathbed, Menjou has Stanwyck brought to him and gives her a note entitling her to half of his wealth. Menjou dies and Stanwyck destroys the note.

NOTES AND COMMENTARY: At the deathwatch at the Governor's mansion for Adolphe Menjou, Gordon Elliott is one of the reporters awaiting Menjou's demise. As the reporters wisecrack about Menjou's impending demise, Elliott remarks, "Yeah, they won't catch me laying any odds. He's the kind that's liable to hang on for another year." Then Elliott can be seen on the telephone as all the reporters phone in news of Menjou's death when Barbara Stanwyck comes through the room.

REVIEWS: "Good woman's picture having an involved, somewhat prolonged but good story." *Variety*, 1/12/32; "A weepy, implausible melodrama, the only redeeming feature here are professional performances by Menjou and Stanwyck and some very good photography by Walker." *Motion Picture Guide*, Nash and Ross.

SUMMATION: A good melodrama, with fine acting by Stanwyck and Menjou.

---

*A Timid Soul and a Tiger Woman Get Together ... on a Riotous Rampage on
His First Night Out in Twenty Years!*

Friends of Mr. Sweeney

Warner Bros. (July, 1934)

CAST: Asaph, **Charlie Ruggles**; Beulah, **Ann Dvorak**; Rixey, **Eugene Paulette**; Alex, **Robert Barrat**; Brumbaugh, **Berton Churchill**; Millie, **Dorothy Burgess**; Olga, **Dorothy Tree**; Mike, **Harry Tyler**; Claude, **Harry Beresford**; Stephen Prime, **William Davidson**.

CREDITS: Director, **Edward Ludwig**; Screenwriters, **Warren Duff** and **Sidney Sutherland**; Added Dialog, **F. Hugh Herbert** and **Erwin Gelsey**; Editor, **Thomas Pratt**; Art Direction, **Robert M. Haas**; Cinematographer, **Ira Morgan**; Gowns, **Orry-Kelly**; Musical Conductor, **Leo F. Forbstein**.

RUNNING TIME: 68 min.

SOURCE: Novel, *Friends of Mr. Sweeney* by **Elmer Davis**.

STORY: Meek Charlie Ruggles is ordered to write an article praising crooked politician William Davidson as the best choice for governor. With prodding from his secretary, Ann Dvorak, and college friend Eugene Paulette, Ruggles' article tells the truth about Davidson. Ruggles and Dvorak fall in love.

NOTES AND COMMENTARY: Gordon Elliott was to appear on-screen as a young man. His scenes were deleted, as were scenes with Milton Kibbee, Willis Marks, Tom Ricketts, Harry Seymour and Charles Williams.

Eugene Paulette would play the part of the sheriff in William Elliott's *In Old Sacramento* (Republic, 1946). Paulette would mortally wound Elliott as he tried to escape through the muddy Sacramento streets.

REVIEWS: "An unusually engaging comedy." *The New York Times*, 7/31/34; "An everything but the kitchen sink comedy in which Ruggles' unrestrained performance carries the day." *The Motion Picture Guide*, Nash and Ross.

SUMMATION: Okay comedy that underutilized the talents of Ruggles, Dvorak and Paulette.

---

*All the News Too Hot to Print
About That Notorious*

Front Page Woman

Warner Bros. (July, 1935)

CAST: Ellen Garfield, **Bette Davis**; Curt Devlin, **George Brent**; Toots, **Roscoe Karns**; Inez, **Winifred Shaw**; Judge Rickard, **Walter Walker**; Robert, **J. Carroll Naish**; Maitland Coulter, **Gordon Wescott**; Mae LaRue, **Dorothy Dare**; Olive, **June Martel**; Spike, **Joseph Crehan**; Hallohan, **J. Farrell MacDonald**; District Attorney, **Addison Richards**; Hartnett, **Joseph King**; Joe Davis, **Selmer Jackson**; Fuji, **Miki Morita**; Marvin Q. Stone, **Huntley Gordon**; Chinard, **Georges Renavent**// Pale Reporter, **Gordon Elliott**.

CREDITS: Director, **Michael Curtiz**; Screenwriters, **Laird Doyle, Lillie Hayward** and **Roy Chanslor**; Editor, **Terry Morse**; Art Director, **John Hughes**; Cinematographer, **Tony Gaudio**; Dialogue Director, **Frank McDonald**; Musical Director, **Leo F. Forbstein**.

RUNNING TIME: 82 min.

SOURCE: Novel, *Women Are Bum Newspapermen* by **Richard Macauley**.

STORY: Bette Davis is out to prove to her boyfriend George Brent that she is just as good a reporter as any man. Both Davis and Brent are out to uncover the murderer of tycoon Huntley Gordon. Brent plays a trick on Davis, whereby she reports that the jury declared Gordon Wescott, rival of Gordon for the affections of Winifred Shaw, guilty of Gordon's murder.

Davis gets fired and meets Shaw in a bar. After a few drinks, she gets Shaw to admit that Shaw is the actual killer. Davis proves she's a top reporter, and she and Brent plan to marry.

NOTES AND COMMENTARY: Gordon Elliott is briefly seen, but to good effect. Elliott plays a reporter looking sickly over the prospect of watching an execution of a former female Broadway star. First a fellow reporter comments that Elliott is looking pale, and Elliott retorts, "What's that on your forehead, dew?"

Then Elliott is seen walking through the door to the execution, at Bette Davis' side. Finally Elliott is later seen reporting the execution story.

REVIEWS: "Incredible newspaper yarn, nicely handled for laughs." *Variety*, 7/17/35; "It added up to pretty good entertainment." *The Warner Bros. Story*, Hirshhorn.

SUMMATION: Fairly entertaining newspaper comedy that should have been better, considering the stars involved.

A Modern Killer Takes to the Air ... as Warner Bros. Bring You Thrills and Chills in the Most Daring Madman Hunt in History!

Fugitive in the Sky

Warner Bros. (November, 1936)

CAST: Rita Moore, **Jean Muir**; Terry Brewer, **Warren Hull**; Bob White, **Gordon Oliver**; Johnny Martin, **Carlyle Moore, Jr.**; "Killer" Madsen, **Howard Phillips**; Autumn Day, **Winifred Shaw**; Agatha Ormsby, **Mary Treen**; Mike Phelan, **John Litel**; Ramon Duval, **Gordon Elliott**; Holmberg, **Gordon Hart**; Mrs. Tristo, **Nedda Harrigan**; Kid Gouch, **John Kelly**; Spike, **Joe Cunningham**; Ronald DeWitt, **Don Barclay**; Steve Fanning, **Charley Foy**; Henry, **Spencer Charters**; Martha, **Lillian Harmer**; Dave Brandon, **Tom Jackson**.

CREDITS: Director, **Nick Grinde**; Story/Screenplay, **George Bricker**; Editor, **Frank Dewar**; Art Direction, **Ted Smith**; Cinematography, **Ted McCord**; Special Photographic Effects, **Fred Jackman**; Gowns, **Milo Anderson**; Dialogue Director, **Harry Seymour**.

RUNNING TIME: 58 min.

STORY: Reporter Warren Hull, at the airport to see off his girlfriend, stewardess Jean Muir, spots federal agent John Litel boarding the plane under an alias. Hull senses a story and decides to follow. On the plane, passenger Gordon Elliott is murdered. When Litel takes charge, Howard Phillips, disguised as a woman, takes Litel's gun and hijacks the plane. When the plane flies through a dust storm, all engines fail and the plane makes an emergency landing. As the engines are being repaired, Hull, with Muir's help, captures Phillips. An eccentric passenger, Neda Harrigan, disguised as an older woman, murdered Elliott because he was double-crossing her. The adventure over, Hull and Muir finally decide to marry.

NOTES AND COMMENTARY: This time out, Gordon Elliott plays a murder victim. Elliott is first seen leaving the plane in Albuquerque with Winifred Shaw. Then, on the plane, Elliott comes on to Shaw. In his last scene, a shadowy figure plunges a knife into a sleeping Elliott's body.

REVIEWS: "The Warner raconteurs have spun this yarn excitedly and well, making it fairly interesting, if incredible, action picture." *New York Times*, 1/16/37; "A competent screenplay and acceptable direction made it all quite acceptable." *Warner Bros. Story*, Hirshhorn.

SUMMATION: Though it's an above-average action picture, the denouement of Elliott's murderer is weak and rushed. Elliott is effective in his brief role.

Hollywood's Most Famous Bad Man Joins the "G-MEN" and Halts the March of Crime!

"G" Men

Warner Brothers Pictures & Vitaphone Corporation (May, 1935)

CAST: "Brick" Davis, **James Cagney**; Kay McCord, **Margaret Lindsay**; Jean Morgan, **Ann Dvorak**; Jeff McCord, **Robert Armstrong**; Collins, **Barton MacLane**; Hugh Farrell, **Lloyd Nolan**; "Mac" McKay, **William Harrigan**; Gerard, **Russell Hopton**; Leggett, **Edward Pawley**; Durfee, **Noel Madison**; Fingerprint Expert, **Monte Blue**; Edward Buchanan, **Regis Toomey**; Gregory, **Addison Richards**; Venke, **Harold Huber**; Gangsters' Messenger, **Raymond Hatton**// Intern, **Gordon Elliott**.

CREDITS: Director, **William Keighley**; Story/Screenplay, **Seton I. Miller**; Art Director, **John Hughes**; Editor, **Jack Killifer**; Cinematographer, **Sol Polito**; Musical Director, **Leo F. Forbstein**.

SONG: "Lullaby of Broadway" (Dubin and Warren) — sung by chorus.

RUNNING TIME: 85 min.

SOURCE: Novel, *Public Enemy No.1* by Darryl F. Zanuck.

STORY: The death of former college classmate and G-man Regis Toomey inspires James Cagney to give up his struggling law practice and join the FBI. After training, Cagney is assigned to the Chicago office, headed by Robert Armstrong. The FBI's success in bringing a number of the top criminals to justice causes gangster Barton MacLane and his cohorts to hide out at former gang boss William Harrigan's lodge. Unknown to the agents, Harrigan is being held captive. Cagney discovers MacLane's whereabouts, and the lodge is raided. MacLane causes Harrigan to be killed in the raid, in which all gangsters except MacLane are either killed or captured. Harrigan was Cagney's mentor, and his death almost causes Cagney to resign from the service. MacLane returns to Chicago and kidnaps Armstrong's sister, Margaret Lindsay, as a hostage to allow him to escape to Canada. Cagney learns where Lindsay is being held and goes to her rescue. In an exchange of bullets, Cagney wounds MacLane and rescues Lindsay. The wounded MacLane tries to escape but is cut down in a hail of bullets from Armstrong's machine gun. Cagney and Lindsay, who had been falling in love with each other, decide to marry.

NOTES AND COMMENTARY: Elliott, as an intern, has a short scene with Cagney as he tries to prevent Cagney from leaving the hospital against medical advice.

REVIEWS: "Standard Warner pulp, ripped from the tabloid page and briskly told." *The Motion Picture Guide*, Nash and Ross; "*G Men*, despite its flaws, is a superior melodrama." *The New York Times*, 5/2/35.

SUMMATION: *"G" Men* is a top-notch, tough, fast-moving crime melodrama, with James Cagney in top form.

She Woke Up Married! But Her Husband Was Still in Love with the Other Girl!

Girl from 10th Avenue

Warner Bros. (May, 1935)

A First National Production

ALTERNATE TITLE: *Men on Her Mind.*

CAST: Miriam Brady, **Bette Davis**; Geoffrey Sherwood, **Ian Hunter**; Mr. Marland, **Colin Clive**; Mrs. Martin, **Alison Skipworth**; Hugh Brown, **John Eldredge**; Tony Hewlett, **Phillip Reed**; Valentine, **Katharine Alexander**; Miss Mansfield, **Helen Jerome Eddy**; James, **Gordon Elliott**; Art Shop Manager, **Edward McWade**; Marcel, **Adrian Rosley**; Max, **Andre Cheron**.

CREDITS: Director, **Alfred E. Green**; Screenwriter, **Charles Kenyon**; Editor, **Owen Marks**; Art Director, **John Hughes**; Cinematography, **James Van Trees**; Gowns, **Orry-Kelly**; Musical Director, **Leo F. Forbstein**.

RUNNING TIME: 69 min.

SOURCE: Play by **Hubert Henry Davies**.

STORY: Thrown over by socialite Katharine Alexander for another man, Ian Hunter goes on an extended drinking spree. Hunter meets working girl Bette Davis in front of the church on the day of Alexander's wedding. Davis becomes Hunter's nursemaid, and when both of them are drunk, they get married. Alexander is still interested in Hunter. Davis decides to fight for Hunter. Hunter declares his marriage with Davis is over. Davis moves out first, to the consternation of Hunter. With Davis gone, Hunter finally realizes he really loves her. Hunter wants Davis to be his wife, and she agrees.

NOTES AND COMMENTARY: Gordon Elliott plays James, an employee at the College Club. Elliott is seen in four scenes. First, Elliott talks on the phone to John Eldredge, who is looking for Ian Hunter. Next, Elliott talks to Bette Davis over the phone about Hunter. Then Elliott greets Hunter when he moves into the club; and in a follow up scene, Elliott arranges for Hunter to have his old room back.

REVIEWS: "Bette Davis' trouping saves this one from the triteness of the story." *Variety*, 5/29/35; "By energetically skirting the clichés of writing which are implicit in its theme, *The Girl from 10th Avenue* is able to lift itself into a semblance of intelligent social comedy." *New York Times*, 5/27/35.

SUMMATION: A well done but highly predictable drama with good performances, especially by Bette Davis.

Here They Are — In Their First Great Hit Together!

Go Into Your Dance

Warner Bros. (March, 1935) A First National Picture

ALTERNATE TITLE: *Casino de Paree.*

CAST: Al, **Al Jolson**; Dorothy, **Ruby Keeler**; Molly, **Glenda Farrell**; Duke, **Barton MacLane**; Toledo, **Patsy Kelly**; Mexican in Cantina, **Akim Tamiroff**; Luana Wells, **Helen Morgan**; Chorus Girl, **Sharon Lynn**; Drunk in Cantina, **Benny Rubin**; Eddie Rio, **Phil Regan**; Fred, **Gordon Wescott**; McGee, **William B. Davidson**; Chorus Girl, **Joyce Compton**; Jackson, **Joseph Crehan**// Jackson's secretary, **Gordon Elliott**.

CREDITS: Director, **Archie Mayo**; Story, **Bradford Ropes**; Screenwriter, **Earl Baldwin**; Editor, **Harold McLernon**; Art Director, **John Hughes**; Cinematographer, **Tony Gaudio**; Gowns, **Orry-Kelly**; Choreographer, **Bobby Connolly**; Orchestral Arrangements, **Ray Heindorf**; Musical Director, **Leo F. Forbstein**.

SONGS: "Cielito Lindo" (traditional)— sung by **Al Jolson** and **chorus**; "A Good Old Fashioned Cocktail (with a Good Old Fashioned Gal)" (Dubin and Warren)— sung and danced by **Ruby Keeler** and **chorus**; "Mammy, I'll Sing About You" (Dubin and Warren)— sung by **Al Jolson**; "About a Quarter to Nine" (Dubin and Warren)— sung by **Al Jolson** and **chorus**, and danced by **Ruby Keeler**; "The Little Things You Used to Do" (Dubin and Warren)— sung by **Helen Morgan**; "Casino de Paree" (Dubin and Warren)— sung by **Al Jolson**; "Spain" (Warren)— danced by **Ruby Keeler**; "She's a Latin from Manhattan"— sung by **Al Jolson**; "Go Into Your Dance" (Dubin and Warren)— sung by **Al Jolson**.

RUNNING TIME: 92 min.

STORY: Broadway star Al Jolson makes a habit of walking out on hit shows. Producers decide to boycott Jolson from appearing in any future productions. Jolson's sister, Glenda Farrell, arranges to have Jolson team with dancer Ruby Keeler and star in Chicago. Then Farrell convinces gangster Barton MacLane to back

Jolson's show and café in New York. Believing the show won't open, MacLane sends hit men to shoot Jolson. The murder attempt fails, but a bullet meant for Jolson wounds Keeler. The show is a success and Jolson realizes he and Keeler love each other.

NOTES AND COMMENTARY: Gordon Elliott plays Joseph Crehan's secretary. He announces to Crehan that Glenda Farrell, Al Jolson's sister, wants to see him. Then he asks Farrell to go into Crehan's office.

REVIEWS: "The film had the authentic Warner Bros. look about it plus a crackling score by songwriters Dubin and Warren." *The Warner Bros. Story*, Hirshhorn; "All told, *Go Into Your Dance* is not the best, not the worst, but generally above average for its type." *The New York Times*, 5/4/35.

SUMMATION: *Go Into Your Dance* is a very good musical drama with a dynamic performance by Al Jolson.

Frank Fay 1932 Model Lover! Built for Speed, Style and Endurance!

God's Gift to Women

Warner Bros. (April, 1931)

ALTERNATE TITLES: *The Devil Was Sick* and *Too Many Women*.

CAST: Toto, **Frank Fay**; Diane, **Laura La Plante**; Fifi, **Joan Blondell**; Mr. Churchill, **Charles Winniger**; Auguste, **Alan Mowbray**; Dr. Dumont, **Arthur Edmund Carewe**; Cesare, **Billy House**; Dagmar, **Yola d'Avril**; Chaumier, **John T. Murray**; Florine, **Louise Brooks**; Tania Donaliff, **Margaret Livingston**; Rancour, **Armand Kaliz**; Undertaker, **Charles Judels**; Basil, **Tyrell Davis**; Maybelle and Marie, **Sisters G//** Nightclub patron, **Gordon Elliott**.

CREDITS: Director, **Michael Curtiz**; Screenwriters, **Frederick Hazlitt Brennan, Joseph Jackson** and **Raymond Griffith**; Editor, **James Gibbon**; Art Director, **Robert Haas**; Cinematographer, **Robert Kurrle**; Costumes, **Earl Luick**; Musical Conductor, **Leo F. Forbstein**.

RUNNING TIME: 72 min.

SOURCE: Play, *The Devil Was Sick* by **Jane Hinton**.

STORY: In Paris, philanderer Frank Fay, a descendant of Don Juan, falls in love with Laura La Plante. Charles Winniger, La Plante's father, knows La Plante is in love with Fay. Winniger tells Fay he'll consent to the marriage if Fay refrains from drinking, partying and womanizing for six months. Fay tells Winniger that he loves La Plante more than life itself. Winniger arranges for Dr. Arthur Edmund Carewe to examine Fay. Carewe tells Fay that his heart has been so severely damaged that to kiss even one woman would result in his immediate death. La Plante is returning to the United States and wants to see Fay. Fay decides he wants to kiss La Plante, regardless of the consequences. Fay and La Plante kiss, but nothing happens to Fay. It turns out that it was a hoax concocted by Winniger to see how much Fay really loved La Plante. Winniger gives his blessing and the couple wed.

NOTES AND COMMENTARY: Gordon Elliott's role is extremely brief. As Laura La Plante and Billy House step on the dance floor of a Parisian nightclub, Elliott and his partner can be seen dancing across the screen from left to right.

REVIEWS: "A French bedroom farce, which is just mild when it isn't mildly risqué, is raised to the dignity of agreeable light comedy by its leading player, Frank Fay." *The New York Times*, 4/18/31; "Frank Fay did an impressive salvage job on *God's Gift to Women* and brought a lot of fun to the flimsy story." *The Warner Bros. Story*, Hirshhorn.

SUMMATION: A fairly amusing French bedroom farce.

Guy and Zasu Crashing Society — And Smashing All Laugh Records!

Going Highbrow

Warner Bros. (August, 1935)

CAST: Matt Upshaw, **Guy Kibbee**; Mrs. Upshaw, **Zasu Pitts**; Augie, **Edward Everett Horton**; Harley Marsh, **Ross Alexander**; Sandy, **June Martel**; Samuel Long, **Gordon Wescott**; Annie, **Judy Canova**; Mrs. Marsh, **Nella Walker**; Sinclair, **Jack Norton**; Waiter, **Arthur Treacher**// Reporter, **Gordon Elliott**.

CREDITS: Director, **Robert Florey**; Screenwriter, **Edward Kaufman** and **Sy Bartlett**; Additional Dialogue, **Ben Markson**; Editor, **Harold McLernon**; Art Direction, **Esdras Hartley**; Cinematographer, **William Rees**; Costumes, **Orry-Kelly**; Musical Director, **Leo F. Forbstein**.

SONG: "You're One in a Million" (Alter and Scholl) — sung by **Ross Alexander** and **Edward Everett Horton**.

RUNNING TIME: 68 min.

SOURCE: Story, "Social Pirates" by **Ralph Spence**.

STORY: To enter New York high society, millionaires Guy Kibbee and Zasu Pitts pay Edward Everett Horton fifty thousand dollars to have Nella Walker and her son, Ross Alexander, sponsor them. Kibbee and Pitts find the best route would be to have their daughter make her debut. Kibbee hires waitress June Martel to be their daughter. Martel and Alexander fall in love. Martel is in a dilemma because she's married to wastrel Gordon Wescott. Horton discovers that Wescott was already married when he wed Martel, so his marriage to Martel is not valid. Martel and Alexander can now get together.

NOTES AND COMMENTARY: Gordon Elliott is a reporter assigned to interview French actress Christine Gess and is able to ask two questions: "Ever break the bank at Monte Carlo?" and "Any grand dukes ever commit suicide over you?" Zasu Pitts then interrupts, demanding to be interviewed, and Elliott comments, "I'll take it you're in the social register." He then asks, "Husband living?" to which Pitts inquires if he knows where her husband might be. Elliott replies, "I'm sure I don't know."

REVIEWS: "So-so flick." *Variety*, 9/4/35; "It's all pretty routine material, with barely competent direction by Florey. Poor camera angles and pacing." *Motion Picture Guide*, Nash and Ross.

SUMMATION: This is a bright, sparkling comedy with good performances by all concerned.

Laughs — And Nothing Else But!

Going Wild

First National Pictures (December, 1930)
A William A. Seiter production

CAST: Rollo Smith, **Joe E. Brown**; Jack Lane, **Lawrence Gray**; Ruth Howard, **Ona Munson**; "Ace" Benton, **Walter Pidgeon**; Peggy Freeman, **Laura Lee**; Rickey Freeman, **Frank McHugh**; May Bunch, **May Boley**; Edward Howard, **Anders Randolf**; Robert Story, **Arthur Hoyt**; Simpkins, **Johnny Arthur**; the Conductor, **Fred Kelsey**; Herndon Reamer, **Harvey Clark**// Guest at Physical Exam, **Gordon Elliott**.

CREDITS: Screenwriters, **Humphrey Pearson** and **Henry McCarty**; Editor, **Pete Fritch**; Art Director, **Anton Grot**; Cinematographer, **Sol Polito**; General Musical Director, **Erno Rapee**; Conductor, **David Mendoza**.

SONG: "My Hero" — sung by **Joe E. Brown** and **Laura Lee**.

RUNNING TIME: 68 min.

SOURCE: Play, *The Aviator* by **James Montgomery**.

STORY: Down-at-the-heels newspaperman Joe E. Brown is mistaken for a famous aviator. Brown is persuaded to challenge veteran pilot Walter Pidgeon to an air race. Brown attempts to leave town but changes his mind when he realizes his absence will cost Laura Lee and her brother, Frank McHugh, all their savings. Brown's bizarre antics in the air forces Pidgeon to withdraw from the contest. Brown not only wins the race but the hand of Lee.

NOTES AND COMMENTARY: Look quickly for a glimpse of Gordon Elliott. As Joe E. Brown comes off the elevator for his physical examination, Elliott takes a look at Brown, then turns away.

REVIEWS: "Standard comedy fare of the period." *The Motion Picture Guide*, Nash and Ross; "A hilariously funny talking film." *New York Times*, 1/26/31.

SUMMATION: This tame Joe E. Brown comedy desperately needs more laughs.

The Show of the Century! Thrill to the Charms of 300 Beautiful Girls, 5 New Song Hits, 13 Famous Stars

Gold Diggers of 1933

Warner Bros. (September, 1933)
ALTERNATE TITLE: *High Life*.

CAST: Lawrence, **Warren William**; Carol, **Joan Blondell**; Trixie, **Aline MacMahon**; Polly, **Ruby Keeler**; Brad, **Dick Powell**; Peabody, **Guy Kibbee**; Barney, **Ned Sparks**; Fay, **Ginger Rogers**// Nightclub Patron, **Gordon Elliott**.

CREDITS: Director, **Mervyn LeRoy**; Screenplay, **Erwin Gelsey** and **James Seymour**; Dialogue, **David Boehm** and **Ben Markson**; Editor, **George Amy**; Art Direction, **Anton Grot**; Cinematography, **Sol Polito**; Costumes, **Orry-Kelly**; Dance Director, **Busby Berkeley**; Musical Director, **Leo F. Forbstein**.

SONGS: "The Gold Diggers Song (We're in the Money)" (Dubin and Warren)— sung by **Ginger Rogers** and **chorus**; "The Shadow Waltz" (Dubin and Warren)— sung by **Dick Powell**; "I've Got to Sing a Torch Song" (Dubin and Warren)— sung by **Dick Powell**; "Pettin' in the Park" (Dubin and Warren)— sung by **Dick Powell** and **Ruby Keeler**; "The Shadow Waltz" (reprise)— sung by **Dick Powell, Ruby Keeler** and **chorus**; "Remember My Forgotten Man" (Dubin and Warren)— sung by **Joan Blondell, Etta Moten** and **chorus**.

RUNNING TIME: 94 min.

SOURCE: Play, *The Gold Diggers* by **Avery Hopwood**.

STORY: Scion of a prominent family Dick Powell, living as a struggling young artist, agrees to back a Broadway play. Powell's one stipulation is that Ruby Keeler would have a prominent role. Powell and Keeler have fallen in love. Powell's show business life is revealed when he has to appear in the leading role in the hit production. Powell's brother, Warren William, makes a futile attempt to break up the romance as he falls in love with Keeler's roommate, Joan Blondell.

NOTES AND COMMENTARY: Again, look quickly for about a two-second sighting of Gordon Elliott. In the nightclub sequence, Dick Powell dances with Joan Blondell. As they dance away from Warren William, look over Powell's left shoulder to see Elliott on the dance floor.

REVIEWS: "To the accompaniment of tuneful melodies and flying sparks from the jokesmith's shop, Mammon apparently bows to Cupid in *Gold Diggers of 1933*. It is an imaginatively staged, breezy show, with a story of no greater consequences than is to be found in this type of picture." *The New York Times*, 6/8/33; "Directed by LeRoy with a pace and attack rare in musicals, and with a top-notch score by Dubin and Warren, *Gold Diggers of 1933* opened with the prophetic 'We're in the Money.'" *The Warner Bros. Story*, Hirshhorn.

SUMMATION: A wonderful, delightful musical comedy with a great cast.

Beauty! Brilliance! Immense Beauty in an All New 1935 Festival of Brilliance!

Gold Diggers of 1935

Warner Bros. (March, 1935)

A First National Picture

CAST: Dick Curtis, **Dick Powell**; Nicolai, **Adolphe Menjou**; Ann Prentiss, **Gloria Stuart**; Mrs. Prentiss; **Alice Brady**; T. Mosely Thorpe, **Hugh Herbert**; Betty Hawes, **Glenda Farrell**; Humbolt Prentiss, **Frank McHugh**; Schultz, **Joseph Cawthorn**; Louis Lampson, **Grant Mitchell**; Arline Davis, **Dorothy Dare**; Winny, **Winifred Shaw**// Martin, **Gordon Elliott**.

CREDITS: Director, **Busby Berkeley**; Story, **Robert Lord** and **Peter Milne**; Screenplay, **Peter Milne** and **Manuel Seff**; Editor, **George Amy**; Art Direction, **Anton Grot**; Cinematography, **George Barnes**; Gowns, **Orry-Kelly**; Choreographer, **Busby Berkeley**; Orchestral Arranger, **Ray Heindorf**; Musical Conductor, **Leo F. Forbstein**.

SONGS: "I'm Goin' Shoppin' with You" (Dubin and Warren) — sung by **Dick Powell** and **Gloria Stuart**; "The Words Are in My Heart" (Dubin and Warren) — sung by **Dick Powell**; "Dagger Dance" (Dubin and Warren) — sung by **chorus**; "The Gold Diggers' Song (We're in The Money)" — sung by **Glenda** Farrell; "The Words Are in My Heart" (reprise) — sung by **Dick Powell**, **Gloria Stuart**, **female vocal trio** and **chorus**; "Lullaby of Broadway" (Dubin and Warren) — sung by **Winifred Shaw**, **Dick Powell** and **chorus**.

RUNNING TIME: 95 min.

STORY: Dick Powell is paid by Alice Brady to be the escort for her daughter, Gloria Stuart. Over the objections of Brady, Powell and Stuart fall in love and plan to marry.

NOTES AND COMMENTARY: Gordon Elliott can easily be seen in three early sequences: first, during the employee meeting prior to the hotel opening; next, Elliott is asked about Brady's hotel reservations; and, finally, Elliott registers guest Hugh Herbert.

REVIEWS: "A silly story, its interest began and ended with Berkeley's three production numbers." *The Warner Bros. Story*, Hirshhorn; "A generally amusing screen comedy." *The New York Times*, 3/15/35.

SUMMATION: This is a sappy musical, with the "Lullaby of Broadway" number being its only redeeming feature.

The Most Eagerly Awaited Screen Event of the Year! The Winner of the Academy Award for 1935 in Her First Picture Since Capturing That Famous Prize!

The Golden Arrow

Warner Bros. (May, 1936)

A First National Picture

CAST: Daisy Appleby, **Bette Davis**; Johnny Jones, **George Brent**; Mr. Meyers, **Eugene Paulette**; Tommy Blake, **Dick Foran**; Hortense Burke-Meyers, **Carol Hughes**; Miss Pommesby, **Catherine Doucet**; Jorgenson, **Craig Reynolds**; Count Guilliano, **Ivan Lebedeff**; Aubrey Rutherford, **G.P. Huntley, Jr.**; DeWolfe, **Hobart Cavanaugh**; Mr. Appleby, **Henry O'Neill**; Davis, **Eddie Acuff**; Alfred Parker, **Earle Foxe**; Prince Peter, **Rafael Storm**; Walker, **E.E. Clive**; Mrs. Myers, **Sarah Edwards**// Dance Hall Ticket Taker, **Gordon Elliott**.

CREDITS: Director, **Alfred E. Green**; Story, **Michael Arlen**; Screenplay, **Charles Kenyon**; Editor, **Thomas Pratt**; Art Director, **Anton Grot**; Cinematographer, **Arthur Edeson**; Gowns, **Orry-Kelly**; Musical Conductor, **Leo F. Forbstein**.

RUNNING TIME: 68 min.

STORY: The public believes that Bette Davis is a rich socialite, but actually she is employed by a cosmetic company to play the part.

Tired of being chased by fortune seekers, Davis proposes a marriage of convenience to reporter George Brent. This will give Brent a chance to work on his novel. Davis falls in love with Brent and wishes he would fall in love with her. Brent resists because he thinks Davis has money. When Brent finds that Davis is penniless, he expresses his feelings to Davis' satisfaction.

NOTES AND COMMENTARY: Look quickly! Gordon Elliott can be seen for a few seconds taking tickets at a sleazy dance hall. Then the camera cuts to Bette Davis and George Brent dancing, thus ending Elliott's screen time.

REVIEWS: "Trivial tale." *The Warner Bros. Story*, Hirshhorn; "*The Golden Arrow* drifts rather pleasantly across the screen." *The New York Times*, 5/4/36.

SUMMATION: There's not much to this "B" comedy, but Davis and Brent at least make it watchable.

One Surprise After Another Keeps You Absorbed Every Minute!

Goose and the Gander

Warner Bros. (September, 1935)
A First National Picture
CAST: Georgiana, **Kay Francis**; Bob Mc-Near, **George Brent**; Betty, **Genevieve Tobin**; Lawrence, **John Eldredge**; Connie, **Claire Dodd**; Ralph Summers, **Ralph Forbes**; Aunt Julia, **Helen Lowell**; Wink, **Spencer Charters**; Arthur, **William Austin**; Sweeney, **Eddie Shubert**; Jones, **Charles Coleman**; Miriam Brent, **Olive Jones**; Teddy, **Gordon Elliott**; Murphy, **John Sheehan**; Sprague, **Wade Boteler**.

CREDITS: Director, **Alfred E. Green**; Story and Screenplay, **Charles Kenyon**; Editor, **Bert Lenard**; Art Direction, **Robert M. Haas**; Cinematographer, **Sid Hickox**; Gowns, **Orry-Kelly**; Musical Director, **Leo F. Forbstein**.

RUNNING TIME: 65 min.

STORY: Kay Francis, ex-wife of Ralph Forbes, arranges to have Forbes' current wife, Genevieve Tobin, and her boyfriend, George Brent, stay at her house. Francis plans to have Forbes arrive and see Tobin's infidelity, which will drive Forbes into her arms. Into this situation comes two jewel thieves, John Eldredge and Claire Dodd. Dodd impersonates Forbes' wife, but Tobin states she's Brent's wife. All ends happily: Francis and Brent fall in love, the two jewel thieves are arrested and Tobin goes back to Forbes.

NOTES AND COMMENTARY: Gordon Elliott receives on-screen billing in this film. He plays Kay Francis' date in several early scenes, one even with George Brent.

REVIEWS: "A well made minor farce." *The New York Times*, 9/12/35; "What was noteworthy about *The Goose and the Gander* was just how much plot writer Kenyon managed to pack into a mere 65 minutes of screenplay time." *The Warner Bros. Story*, Hirshhorn.

SUMMATION: Entertaining but undemanding comedy farce.

Vitaphone's Presentation of the Great American Stage Play.

The Great Divide

First National Pictures (September, 1929)
A First National Vitaphone Production
CAST: Ruth Jordan, **Dorothy Mackaill**; Stephen Ghent, **Ian Keith**; Manuella, **Myrna Loy**; Edgar Blossom, **Creighton Hale**; Texas Tommy, **Lucien Littlefield**; Dutch Romero, **Ben Hendricks, Jr.**; MacGregor, **George Fawcett**; Winthrop Amesbury, **Claude Gillingwater**; Joe Morgan, **Roy Stewart**; Verna, **Jean Laverty**; Wong, **Frank Tang** // Ruth's friend, **Gordon Elliott**.

CREDITS: Director, **Reginald Barker**;

Screenwriters, **Fred Myton** and **Paul Perez**; Musical Conductor, **Leo Forbstein**.

SONGS: "End of the Lonesome Trail" (Ruby and Perkins)— sung by **Ian Keith**; "Si Si Senor" (Ruby and Perkins)— sung by **Myrna Loy**; "La Golondrina" (traditional)— instrumental.

LOCATION FILMING: Grafton, Utah.

RUNNING TIME: 72 min.

SOURCE: Play, *The Great Divide* by **William Vaughn Moody**.

STORY: Ian Keith, part owner of a mine with his late partner's daughter, Dorothy Mackill, asks Mackill to come west. Keith discovers that Mackill is a frivolous party girl and, in disguise, kidnaps her. Keith takes Mackill to the Great Divide until she changes her life style. The two fall in love. Mackill disperses a lynch mob sent to lynch Keith for kidnapping her. Keith and Mackill decide to marry.

NOTES AND COMMENTARY: In his first sound feature, Gordon Elliott is initially seen strumming a banjo in a party sequence on a train carrying Dorothy Mackaill and her entourage to a fiesta out west. Elliott is present in the scenes in which Mackaill and her friends attend the fiesta and go into the cantina. It sounds like Elliott's voice in the background as Mackaill and Creighton Hale leave the cantina.

In later years, Lucien Littlefield would co-star as Elliott's sidekick in the serial *Valley of Vanishing Men* (Columbia, 1942). Keith would be Elliott's adversary in *Phantom of the Plains* (Republic, 1945).

REVIEWS: "There was little director Barker could do with *The Great Divide*, an antediluvian." *The Warner Bros. Story*, Hirshhorn; "An old-fashioned tale, popular when the untamed flapper vogue was rife in pictures." *The New York Times*, 2/17/30.

SUMMATION: This fairly interesting telling of the story of a high-living society girl who, under the hand of a strong leading man, becomes accustomed to the American West features a plot line, with action added, that would be the basis for many "B" westerns, primarily with Gene Autry.

Here's to Our Men! Long May They Give! A Riotous Story of Three Gold Diggers Who Came to Broadway to Have Their "Break" Relined!

Greeks Had a Word for Them

United Artists (February, 1932)

ALTERNATE TITLE: *Three Broadway Girls*.

CAST: Schatze, **Joan Blondell**; Jean, **Ina Claire**; Polaire, **Madge Evans**; Feldman, **Lowell Sherman**; Dey, **David Manners**; Justin Emery, **Phillips Smalley**; Herbert Scroggins, **Sidney Bracey**// Usher at Wedding, **Gordon Elliott**.

CREDITS: Director, **Lowell Sherman**; Screenwriter, **Sidney Howard**; Editor, **Stuart Heisler**; Cinematographer, **George Barnes**; Music Score, **Alfred Newman**.

RUNNING TIME: 79 min.

SOURCE: Play, *The Greeks Had a Word for Them* by Zoe Akins.

STORY: Gold diggers Joan Blondell and Madge Evans persuade Evans' boyfriend, David Manners, to give a party and bring a rich man, Lowell Sherman, to meet their friend Ina Claire. Sherman and Claire are immediately attracted to each other. Over the course of the evening, Sherman's attentions shift to Evans. Not to be outdone, Claire seduces Sherman, and the two have a brief affair. Meanwhile, Manners wants to marry Evans and introduce her to his father, Phillips Smalley. Claire manages to break up the impending engagement and gets herself engaged to Smalley. Just before the wedding, Blondell and Evans get Claire drunk and entice her to travel with them to France. Manners, realizing he's still in love with Evans, follows her. Aboard ship, Manners and Evans plan to marry, while Claire is still on the prowl for a handsome man with money.

NOTES AND COMMENTARY: Quick eyes can glimpse Gordon Elliott on three occasions as he ushers young ladies to their seats for the impending wedding between Ina Claire and Phillips Smalley.

REVIEWS: "Grand rowdy comedy that sustains itself for 75 minutes." *Variety*, 2/9/32;

"The trio [Madge Evans, Joan Blondell and Ina Claire] are well cast and provide many laughs." *Motion Picture Guide*, Nash and Ross.

SUMMATION: Okay comedy about gold diggers and their men.

Hell-Bent for Thrills!
Dick Foran Rides with the Lone Star Rangers to Bring Law and Order to the Bad Lands ...
New Spine-Tingling Action to You!

Guns of the Pecos

Warner Bros. (January, 1937)
A First National Production
CAST: Steve Ainslee, **Dick Foran** (the Singing Cowboy); Alice Burton, **Anne Nagel**; Major Burton, **Gordon Hart**; Captain Norris, **Joseph Crehan**; Jeff Carter, **Eddie Acuff**; Judge Blake, **Robert Middlemass**; "Smoke, the Wonder Horse"; Aunt Carrie, **Gaby Fay**; Wellman, **Gordon Elliott**; Luke, **Monte Montague**; Carlos, **Milton Kibbee**; Jake, **Bud Osborne**; Bartender, **Cliff Saum**; Hank Brady, **Henry Otho**; Jordan, **Bob Burns**; Governor, **Douglas Wood**.
CREDITS: Director, **Noel Smith**; Story, **Anthony Coldeway**; Screenwriter, **Harold Buckley**; Editor, **Frank DeWar**; Art Director, **Ted Smith**; Cinematography, **Ted McCord**; Dialogue Director, **Harry Seymour**.
SONGS: "When a Cowboy Takes a Wife" (Jerome and Scholl)—sung by **Dick Foran**; "The Prairie Is My Home" (Jerome and Scholl)—sung by **Dick Foran**; "When a Cowboy Takes a Wife" (reprise)—sung by **Dick Foran**.
LOCATION FILMING: Iverson and Andy Jauregui Ranch, California.
RUNNING TIME: 56 min.
STORY: Judge Robert Middlemass, leader of the lawless element in Pecos County, has his men rustle Gordon Hart's horses. During the raid, Hart is murdered. Texas Rangers Dick Foran and Eddie Acuff are assigned to bring Middlemass to justice. Middlemass' attempt to gain control of Hart's daughter's, Anne Nagel's, ranch is thwarted by Foran and Acuff. Foran and Acuff take refuge at Nagel's ranch. Middlemass and his henchmen attack the ranch. Foran brings a company of Texas Rangers to the ranch, and Middlemass and his gang are arrested. Foran and Nagel fall in love and get married.

NOTES AND COMMENTARY: In a small role, Gordon Elliott plays a tenderfoot who, after having too much to drink, states he will recommend that his company *not* invest money in Texas. Crooked Judge Robert Middlemass takes exception and accuses Elliott of saying there is no law in the territory. Elliott is fined all the cash he has in his possession and then thrown out into the street against a hitch rail.

REVIEWS: "There's enough nose flattening material and gunfire to make it ideal action fare." *Variety*, 3/23/37; "Fair entry in Dick Foran's Warner Brothers series." *Western Movies*, Pitts.

SUMMATION: Fast moving and entertaining "B" western. Gordon Elliott is fine as the Eastern dude who runs afoul of "justice" in Pecos City.

This Million Dollar Broadway Baby Can't Trust Herself with a Man ... and the Men Can't Trust Her with Each Other. So Even the Playboy Who Hires Her a Guard Can't See Her Alone.

Her Bodyguard

Paramount (July, 1933)

A B.P. Schulberg Production

CAST: Casey McCarthy, **Edmund Lowe**; Margot Brienne, **Wynne Gibson**; Orson Bitzer, **Edward Arnold**; Lester Cunningham, **Alan Dinehart**; Lita, **Marjorie White**; Ballyhoo, **Johnny Hines**; Bunny Dare, **Fuzzy Knight**// Speakeasy Patron, **Gordon Elliott**.

CREDITS: Director, **William Beaudine**; Adaptation, **Frank Partos** and **Francis Martin**; Screenwriters, **Ralph Spence** and **Walter DeLeon**; Cinematographer, **Harry Fischbeck**.

SONGS: "Good Evening, Dear People"— sung by **Wynne Gibson** and **Marjorie White**; "Shubert's Serenade" (Shubert)— played by **Fuzzy Knight**; "Where Have I Heard That Melody"— sung and played by **Fuzzy Knight**.

RUNNING TIME: 71 min.

SOURCE: Story by **Corey Ford**.

STORY: Millionaire Edward Arnold hires Edmund Lowe as actress Wynne Gibson's bodyguard, primarily to prevent Alan Dinehart from romancing her. Lowe threatens to quit, but Gibson persuades him to stay during the four weeks rehearsal for her latest play. This way neither Dinehart nor Arnold can bother her. Over time Lowe and Gibson fall in love.

NOTES AND COMMENTARY: Look closely and don't blink, or you'll miss Gordon Elliott in this one. Elliott can be seen on the speakeasy dance floor behind Alan Dinehart and Johnny Hines as they talk about Wynne Gibson.

Fuzzy Knight would appear in four westerns with Wild Bill Elliott: *Kansas Territory* (Monogram, 1952), *Fargo* (Monogram, 1952), *Topeka* (Allied Artists, 1953) and *Vigilante Terror* (Allied Artists, 1953).

REVIEW: "Dialog and pacing gives this trite story what moderate value it possesses as a picture." *Variety*, 8/8/33; "The actual plot may be shallow and unimportant, but the variety of cheery incidents make for a capital warm-weather entertainment." *New York Times*, 8/7/33.

SUMMATION: A mildly amusing screwball comedy.

What Thrills! What Action! What Romance!

Here Comes the Navy

Warner Bros. (July, 1934)

ALTERNATE TITLE: *Hey, Sailor!*

CAST: Chesty, **James Cagney**; Biff, **Pat O'Brien**; Dorothy, **Gloria Stuart**; Droopy, **Frank McHugh**; Gladys, **Dorothy Tree**; Commander Denny, **Robert Barrat**; Executive Officer, **Willard Robertson**; Dance Hall Manager, **Guinn Williams**; Captain, **Howard Hickman**; Droopy's Mother, **Maude Eburne**; Admiral, **George Irving**// Officer on USS Arizona, **Gordon Elliott**.

CREDITS: Director, **Lloyd Bacon**; Story, **Ben Markson**; Screenwriters, **Earl Baldwin** and **Ben Markson**; Editor, **George Amy**; Art Director, **Esdras Hartley**; Cinematographer, **Arthur Edeson**; Gowns, **Orry-Kelly**; Musical Director, **Leo F. Forbstein**.

RUNNING TIME: 87 min.

STORY: To get even with Naval Chief Pat O'Brien, who stole his girl at a dance, James Cagney joins the Navy. Cagney makes a play for Gloria Stuart, thinking she's O'Brien's girl, but it turns out she's his sister. O'Brien tries to keep the couple apart, but Cagney and Stuart have fallen in love. Cagney's disregard for Navy rules and regulations earns him a reputation as a troublemaker and alienates Stuart. Cagney shows his true self when he risks his life to save

O'Brien. Cagney and Stuart reunite and marry, with O'Brien's blessing.

NOTES AND COMMENTARY: In the man-overboard sequence with James Cagney, Gordon Elliott appears as a ship's officer. Elliott shouts, "Man overboard!" in answer to Cagney's cry for help. Then he asks O'Brien, "Who is it?" As Cagney is brought aboard, Elliott asks him, "What's your name?" and then confines Cagney to the ship.

REVIEWS: "A man's comedy picture." *Variety*, 7/24/34; "A fast-moving comedy enriched by authentic naval setting." *New York Times*, 7/21/34.

SUMMATION: This rousing and highly entertaining tribute to the Navy features fine performances by Cagney and O'Brien.

Ah! They're Cracked! Hot and Cold Chuckles in Every Room!

Hook, Line and Sinker

Radio Pictures (December, 1930)

CAST: Wilbur Boswell, **Bert Wheeler**; Addington Ganzy, **Robert Woolsey**; Mary Marsh, **Dorothy Lee**; John Blackwell, **Ralf Harolde**; Mrs. Marsh, **Jobyna Howland**; Duchess Bessie Von Essie, **Natalie Moorhead**; House Detective, **Hugh Herbert**; Bellboy, **George F. Marion**; McKay, **Stanley Fields**; Frank Dukette, **William Davidson**// Hotel Guest, **Gordon Elliott**.

CREDITS: Director, **Edward Cline**; Producer, **William Le Baron**; Associate Producer, **Myles Connolly**; Screenwriters, **Tim Whelan** and **Ralph Spence**; Editor, **Archie Marshek**; Art Director/ Costumes, **Max Ree**; Cinematographer, **Nick Musuraca**; Sound, **Hugh McDowell, Jr.**

SONG: "Three Little Words" (Kalmar and Ruby)—played by an orchestra.

RUNNING TIME: 75 min.

STORY: Dorothy Lee is running away from her mother, Jobyna Howland. Howland wants Lee to marry Ralf Harolde, not realizing he is really a gangster. Lee wants to operate a run-down hotel that she owns, and enlists Bert Wheeler and Robert Woolsey to help her. Lee and Wheeler fall in love. Harolde wants control of the hotel because it's the base for his smuggling operation. A rival gang wants to steal the valuables of the hotel guests. Wheeler and Woosley's interference cause all gang members to be captured or killed. Wheeler and Lee plan to marry, as do Woolsey and Howland.

NOTES AND COMMENTARY: No other film historian lists Gordon Elliott as a cast member in this film. Sharp eyes can spot Elliott on the dance floor in the upper right hand corner of the screen as the storm is about to hit the patio.

REVIEWS: "One of the best and most successful of the Bert Wheeler and Robert Woolsey pictures." *The RKO Story*, Jewell and Harbin; "A combination of gangster burlesque and vaudeville repartee which drew loud and fairly continuous laughter." *New York Times*, 12/25/30.

SUMMATION: Wheeler and Woolsey are very funny in this good comedy outing.

Can a Modern Wife Hold Her Own Against a Modern Bachelor Girl?

Housewife

Warner Bros. (August, 1934)

CAST: William Reynolds, **George Brent**; Patricia Berkeley, **Bette Davis**; Nan, **Ann Dvorak**; Paul, **John Halliday**; Dora, **Ruth Donnelly**; George, **Hobart Cavanaugh**; Sam Blake, **Robert Barrat**; Krueger, **Joe Cawthorne**; Mike Hathaway, **Phil Regan**; Judge Matthews, **Willard Robertson**; Buddy, **Ronnie Cosby**; Jenny, **Leila Bennett**; Mr. Simmons, **Harry Tyler**; Bolton, **Charles Coleman**// Hotel Desk Clerk, **Gordon Elliott**.

CREDITS: Director, **Alfred E. Green**; Story, **Robert Lord** and **Lillie Hayward**; Screenplay, **Lillie Hayward** and **Manuel Seff**; Editor, **James Gibbon**; Art Direction, **Robert M. Haas**; Cinematographer, **William Rees**; Gowns, **Orry-Kelly**; Musical Conductor, **Leo F. Forbstein**.

SONG: "Cosmetics by Dupree" (Dixon and Wrubel) — sung by **Phil Regan**.

RUNNING TIME: 69 min.

STORY: Housewife Ann Dvorak gives her husband, George Brent, the support and money to open his own advertising agency. As the business becomes a success, Brent begins an affair with co-worker and old friend Bette Davis. Dvorak finally grants Brent's request for a divorce. At the divorce proceedings, Brent and Dvorak realize they're still in love and reconcile.

NOTES AND COMMENTARY: Gordon Elliott is seen briefly as the desk clerk at the Savoy Hotel. George Brent insists Elliott ring John Halliday's room. Elliott is equally insistent that Halliday is not in his room. The scene ends when Brent sees Halliday come out of the elevator.

REVIEWS: "A characteristic of a poor boxer is that he telegraphs his punches. In *Housewife*, the dramatic punches are not merely telegraphed, but radioed." *The New York Times*, 8/10/34; "Little punch in story." *1996 Movie & Video Guide*, Maltin.

SUMMATION: Dreary soap opera of the eternal triangle caused by a husband not fully appreciating his wife.

The Story of a Beautiful Female Philo Vance ... in Love with a Man Who Brags He Is the World's Cleverest Thief!

I Am a Thief

Warner Bros. (November, 1934)

CAST: Odette, **Mary Astor**; Pierre, **Ricardo Cortez**; Col. Jackson, **Dudley Digges**; Baron Von Kampf, **Robert Barrat**; Count Trentini, **Irving Pichel**; Daudet, **Hobart Cavanaugh**; M. Cassiet, **Ferdinand Gottschalk**; Francois, **Arthur Aylesworth**; Mme. Cassiet, **Florence Fair**; Max Bolen, **Frank Reicher**; Borricci, **John Wray**; Auctioneer, **Oscar Apfel**// Auctioneer's Assistant, **Gordon Elliott**.

CREDITS: Director, **Robert Florey**; Story and Screenplay, **Ralph Block** and **Doris Malloy**; Dialog Director, **Frank McDonald**; Editor, **Terry Morse**; Art Director, **Jack Okey**; Cinematographer, **Sid Hickox**; Gowns, **Orry-Kelly**; Musical Director, **Leo F. Forbstein**.

RUNNING TIME: 64 min.

STORY: Paris is plagued by a series of unsolved jewel robberies, and authorities decide to bait a trap with the Karenina diamonds. Mary Astor, Ricardo Cortez, Dudley Digges, Robert Barrat and Irving Pichel show an interest in obtaining the jewels. At auction, Cortez purchases the diamonds for a buyer in Istanbul. On the train to Instanbul, Cortez sells the jewels to Digges. Astor steals the jewels and substitutes fakes. Astor is working with Pichel to expose the robbers. Cortez is working with Digges to defraud the insurance company. Barrat and his henchmen take over the train. Barrat plans to steal the diamonds and then cause an accident which will kill the others who were interested in the jewels. Cortez' fast action earns him a suspended sentence, and he's free to marry Astor.

NOTES AND COMMENTARY: Gordon Elliot can be seen in three scenes as auctioneer Oscar Apfel's assistant. In the first, Elliott is in the background when Cortez purchases the Karenina diamonds. Next, Elliott has an exchange of dialog with Cortez as Cortez is leaving for his hotel. Finally, Elliott has a scene with Cortez when he delivers the jewels to Cortez' hotel room.

Dialog Director Frank McDonald would become a director and would guide Wild Bill Elliott through his paces in his guest star appearance in Roy Rogers' *Bells of Rosarita* (Republic, 1945).

REVIEWS: "A routine-on-the-train film." *The Motion Picture Guide*, Nash and Ross; "This corner — with all the appreciation of the mystifying melodramatics of the film — ventures a timid plea to the film producers, won't you give up making any more 'Shanghai-Orient-Silk-I-Am-a-Thief Express' in 1935? We're tired of railroading." *The New York Times*, 1/1/35.

SUMMATION: A good murder mystery crime caper film.

The Story Nobody Knows About the Stage Star Everyone Knows...

I Found Stella Parish

Warner Bros. (November, 1935)
A First National Picture
ALTERNATE TITLE: *Stella Parish.*
CAST: Stella Parish, **Kay Francis**; Keith Lockridge, **Ian Hunter**; Stephen, **Paul Lukas**; Gloria, **Sybil Jason**; Nana, **Jessie Ralph**; Cliff Jeffords, **Barton MacLane**; Dimmy, **Eddie Acuff**; Chuck, **Joseph Sawyer**; Reeves, **Walter Kingsford**; James, **Harry Beresford**; Jed Duffy, **Robert Strange**// Reporter, **Gordon Elliott**.
CREDITS: Director, **Mervyn LeRoy**; Story, **John Monk Saunders**; Screenwriter, **Casey Robinson**; Editor, **William Clemens**; Art Director, **Robert M. Haas**; Cinematography, **Sid Hickox**; Gowns, **Orry-Kelly**; Musical Conductor, **Leo F. Forbstein**.
SONGS: "The Pig and the Cow (and the Dog and Cat)" (Dubin and Warren) — sung by **Sybil Jason**; "Powder My Back for Me" — sung by female chorus.
RUNNING TIME: 85 min.
STORY: Actress Kay Francis comes off the London stage on the opening night of her latest hit play to find Barton MacLane waiting in her dressing room. Francis has been living a life of mystery, refusing to reveal her past to outsiders. MacLane's appearance causes her to sail to New York, in disguise, with her daughter,

Sybil Jason, and her best friend, Jessie Ralph. Reporter Ian Hunter also sails on the same ship and realizes Francis is in disguise. Hunter gains Francis' confidence, not knowing Francis has fallen in love with him. Hunter discovers Francis had been wrongly convicted as an accessory to a murder MacLane committed, and sends the story to his paper in London. Francis, not knowing what Hunter has done, tells him all the details of her past. Hunter tries to stop publication but he's too late. Francis will have nothing more to do with Hunter and decides to exploit her past. To ensure that Jason will not find out about her past, she has Ralph take her out of the country. Hunter is able to bring Francis back to the London stage and reunite her with Jason. In the process, Francis and Hunter fall back in love.

NOTES AND COMMENTARY: Gordon Elliott plays one of the reporters interviewing Kay Francis after her past has been revealed. Elliott attempts to go into an adjoining room to take a picture of Sybil Jason, but Francis stops him.

REVIEWS: "Powerful story of an actress and mother love." *Variety*, 11/6/35; "A 40-carat weepie." *The Warner Bros. Story*, Hirshhorn.

SUMMATION: A tearjerker of the first rank, bolstered by fine acting.

The Whole World's on a Honeymoon when Everett Marshall Sings to Dolores Del Rio in I Live for Love.

I Live for Love

Warner Bros. (October, 1935)

ALTERNATE TITLES: *I Live for You* and *Romance in a Glass House*.

CAST: Roger, **Everett Marshall**; Donna, **Dolores del Rio**; Henderson, **Guy Kibbee**; Mac, **Allen Jenkins**; Fabian, **Berton Churchill**; Townsend, **Hobart Cavanaugh**; Street Musicians, **Eddie Conrad, Shaw and Lee**; Rico, **Don Alvarado**; Clementine, **Mary Treen**; Man at Nightclub, **Robert Greig**; Toyo, **Miki Morita**.

CREDITS: Director, **Busby Berkeley**; Screenwriters, **Jerry Wald, Julius J. Epstein** and **Robert Andrews**; Editor, **Terry Morse**; Art Director, **Esdras Hartley**; Cinematographer, **George Barnes**; Gowns, **Orry-Kelly**; Musical Director, **Leo F. Forbstein**.

SONGS: "Oh, Marie"—sung by **Everett Marshall, Eddie Conrad, Sam Shaw and Alan Lee**; "I Live for Love" (Dixon and Wrubel)—sung by **Everett Marshall**; "Mine Alone" (Dixon and Wrubel)—sung by **Everett Marshall**; "A Man Must Shave" (Dixon and Wrubel)—sung by **Everett Marshall, Eddie Conrad, Sam Shaw, Alan Lee** and **Allen Jenkins**; "Silver Wings" (Dixon and Wrubel)—sung by **Everett Marshall**.

RUNNING TIME: 64 min.

STORY: Everett Marshall walks out on a Broadway play when it becomes evident star Delores del Rio wants her lover, Don Alvarado, to play opposite her. Marshall is quickly signed to star in his own radio program. When del Rio's play folds, she is signed to appear on Marshall's program. Hate between them quickly grows into love, and they plan to marry and leave show business. Producer Berton Churchill wants del Rio to appear in a play. Marshall and del Rio quarrel. Churchill initially blocks efforts for the lovers to reconcile. When del Rio plans to wed Alvarado, Churchill tells her the truth. Marshall is waiting at the church, and del Rio decides she really wants to marry him.

NOTES AND COMMENTARY: Film historians and websites list Gordon Elliott as appearing in this film either as Friend or Alverez' (Dolores del Rio) Friend. In the 64-minute print that reached theaters and that survives today, Elliott cannot be seen. My conclusion is that all of his scenes ended up on the cutting room floor.

REVIEWS: "Obvious and pointed, tale creates no particular excitement, but it has been brought to the screen with competence." *Variety*, 10/23/35; "Competently directed, given the weak plot and poor script." *Motion Picture Guide*, Nash and Ross.

SUMMATION: This is an enjoyable show business romp of a singing star winning the love of an actress.

He Stole Her Jewels, but That Wasn't All!

Jewel Robbery

Warner Bros. (August, 1932)

CAST: Robber, **William Powell**; Teri, **Kay Francis**; Marianne, **Helen Vinson**; Paul, **Hardie Albright**; Fritz, **Alan Mowbray**; Andre, **Andre Luguet**; Von Hohenfels, **Henry Kolker**; Lenz, **Spencer Charters**; Hollander, **Lee** Kohlmar; President of Police, **Clarence Wilson**// Policeman Following Blonde, **Gordon Elliott**.

CREDITS: Director, **William Dieterle**; Associate Director, **William Keighley**; Screenwriter, **Erwin S. Gelsey**; Editor, **Ralph Daw-**

son; Art Director, **Robert Haas**; Cinematographer, **Robert Kurrle**; Musical Conductor, **Leo F. Forbstein**.

RUNNING TIME: 63 min.

SOURCE: Play, *Ekszarrablas a Vaciuccaban* by **Ladislas Fodor**; English version by **Bertram Bloch**.

STORY: Married to a multi-millionaire in Vienna, the bored Kay Francis is looking for an affair with a much younger man. Francis, present at a jewel robbery, falls in love with jewel thief William Powell. Powell eludes the police to meet Francis in Nice.

NOTES AND COMMENTARY: In an early scene, Gordon Elliott can be seen following a young blonde, a decoy who leads him away from the scene of a jewel robbery. Elliott shows up at the end of the film with other police officers to chase William Powell over the rooftops. Elliott has one line: "There he is."

REVIEWS: "Dieterle's direction gives this film a breakneck comic pace." *The Motion Picture Guide*, Nash and Ross; "*Jewel Robbery* is only mild. All this is nervous, brittle comedy of a sort that is sufficiently novel in the film to be stimulating." *The New York Times*, 7/23/32.

SUMMATION: *Jewel Robbery* begins as a delightful sophisticated comedy. The film is finally reduced to a broad farce, but it still holds audience interest as viewers wait to see if Francis will have an affair with Powell or stay with her husband.

Husbands Paid Him to Learn the Worst! He Ruined a Reputation for a Wage — But He Paid for It All When He Saw the One He Loved Through — The Keyhole.

The Keyhole

Warner Bros. (March, 1932)

CAST: Anne, **Kay Francis**; Neil, **George Brent**; Dot, **Glenda Farrell**; Maurice, **Monroe Owsley**; Hank, **Allen Jenkins**; Portia, **Helen Ware**; Schuyler, **Henry Kolker**; Brooks' Lawyer, **Ferdinand Gottschalk**// Ship's Passenger, **Gordon Elliott**.

CREDITS: Director, **Michael Curtiz**; Screenplay, **Robert Presnell**; Editor, **Ray Curtiss**; Art Director, **Anton Grot**; Cinematographer, **Barney McGill**; Gowns, **Orry-Kelly**; Dialogue Director, **Arthur Greville Collins**; Musical Conductor, **Leo F. Forbstein**.

RUNNING TIME: 70 min.

SOURCE: Story, "Adventuress" by **Alice D.G. Miller**.

STORY: Kay Francis married wealthy Henry Kolker, believing her first husband, Monroe Owlsby, had obtained a divorce. Owlsby is now blackmailing Francis. Confiding in Kolker's sister, Helen Ware, Francis hatches a plan to lure Owlsby out of the country so his visa can be terminated while annulment proceedings take place. Francis takes a cruise to Cuba. The jealous Kolker hires private detective George Brent to see if she can be tempted into an affair. With Owlsby onboard the ship, Francis allows Brent to escort her so Owlsby will keep his distance. Francis and Brent begin to fall in love, but Francis remains faithful to Kolker. Ware tells Kolker why Francis went to Cuba and Kolker flies to Cuba. Brent tells Francis why Kolker hired him. Furious, Francis wants nothing to do with Kolker. Owlsby dies in an accidental fall, but Brent makes it look like suicide so no suspicion will fall on Francis. Francis and Brent plan to marry.

NOTES AND COMMENTARY: Gordon Elliott makes a fleeting appearance in this film. Elliott can be seen dancing in the background on the ship's deck while George Brent and Kay Francis are talking at the rail.

REVIEWS: "It has many amusing moments." *The New York Times*, 3/31/32; "The film is little more than soap opera with some fine acting." *The Motion Picture Guide*, Nash and Ross.

SUMMATION: Though *The Keyhole* is a good, well acted melodrama with some welcome comedy, the quick, too convenient demise of blackmailer Monroe Owlsby hurts the otherwise sturdy screenplay.

The Real Lowdown on Big League Hockey!

King of Hockey

Warner Bros. (December, 1936)

ALTERNATE TITLE: *King of the Ice Rink.*

CAST: Gabby Dugan, **Dick Purcell**; Kathleen O'Rourke, **Anne Nagel**; Elsie, **Marie Wilson**; Jumbo Mullins, **Wayne Morris**; Nick Torga, **George E. Stone**; Mike Trotter, **Joseph Crehan**; Peggy O'Rourke, **Ann Gilles**; Dr. Noble, **Gordon Hart**; Mrs. O'Rourke, **Dora Clement**; Mr. O'Rourke, **Guy Usher**; Jitters McCarthy, **Garry Owen**; Torchy, **Max Hoffman, Jr.**; Evans, **André Beranger**; Swede, **Frank Faylen**; Loogan, **Frank Bruno**; Tom, **Harry Davenport**// Radio Broadcaster (voice only), **Gordon Elliott**.

CREDITS: Director, **Noel Smith**; Screenwriter, **George Bricker**; Editor, **Harold McLernon**; Art Director, **Carl Jules Weyl**; Cinematographer, **L.W. O'Connell**; Dialogue Director, **Gus Shy**.

RUNNING TIME: 55 min.

STORY: Believing that hockey star Dick Purcell has thrown in with gamblers, teammate Wayne Morris hits Purcell, affecting his vision.

Purcell is kicked off the hockey team. Faced with blindness, Purcell begins to lead a solitary life. Purcell's girl, Anne Nagel, makes him undergo an operation, which restores his sight. Purcell leads his team to victory and plans to marry Nagel.

NOTES AND COMMENTARY: Gordon Elliott is not seen but only heard in this film. Elliott gives the play-by-play description of the final moments of the Violets-Shamrocks hockey game over the radio to a group of passers-by, which includes Dick Purcell.

REVIEWS: "It's a run-of-the-mill yarn of the athlete accused of crooked work." *Variety*, 12/9/36; "Supervisor Foy's production was better than average for such programmer material, had little going for it except a series of ice-hockey sequences and even they weren't particularly exciting." *The Warner Bros. Story*, Hirshhorn.

SUMMATION: A minor sports film, *King of Hockey* is a little maudlin, but it holds the interest.

Detective Bill Crane Again! Too Busy with a Drinking Glass ... to Bother About a Magnifying Glass!

Lady in the Morgue

Universal (April, 1938)

A Crime Club Production

ALTERNATE TITLE: *The Case of the Missing Blonde.*

CAST: Bill Crane, **Preston Foster**; Mrs. Sam Taylor, **Patricia Ellis**; Doc Williams, **Frank Jenks**; Strom, **Thomas Jackson**; Chauncey Courtland, **Gordon Elliott**; Sam Taylor, **Roland Drew**; Kay Renshaw, **Barbara Pepper**; Steve Collins, **Joseph Downing**; Frankie French, **James Robbins**; Spitzy, **Al Hill**; Leyman, **Morgan Wallace**; Johnson, **Brian Burke**; Greening, **Donald Kerr**; Taxi Driver, **Don Brodie**; Coroner, **Rollo Lloyd**; Colonel Black, **Gordon Hart**.

CREDITS: Director, **Otis Garrett**; Producer, **Irving Starr**; Screenwriters, **Eric Taylor** and **Robertson White**; Editor, **Ted Kent**; Art Directors, **Jack Otterson** and **Charles H. Clarke**; Cinematographer, **Stanley Cortez**; Gowns, **Vera West**; Sound, **Charles Carroll** and **Edwin Wetzel**; Production Manager, **Ben Hersh**.

RUNNING TIME: 67 min.

SOURCE: Novel, *Lady in the Morgue* by **Jonathan Latimer**.

STORY: A dead woman is found in a hotel room. Two gangsters, Joseph Downing and James Robbins, and a young man, Gordon Elliott, want to identify the body. Before the dead woman can be identified, the body is stolen and the morgue attendant killed. Private detective Preston Foster is hired to find the corpse. Foster recovers the body and tells the police that musician Roland Drew murdered the dead woman because she would not give him a divorce. Drew wanted to marry Elliott's sister, Patricia Ellis. Elliott killed morgue attendant Byron Folger by accident when he stole the body to prevent identification. By cooperating with the police, Elliott is promised a light sentence.

NOTES AND COMMENTARY: Gordon Elliott has a substantial part, receiving fifth billing, in this film. His many scenes include giving a false name as he comes to the morgue to identify the dead woman; arriving at the dead woman's apartment with Police Inspector Thomas Jackson; and coming to Preston Foster's apartment where he reveals he's his client, provides an important clue, and offers to help Foster after his run-in with gangster Joseph Downing. Elliott also returns to Foster's apartment to tell him he's received word from his sister, and that the woman Foster is looking for will be at an exclusive party. Elliott meets Foster in a cemetery when the "lady in the morgue" is found. At the morgue, Elliott offers to stay with Foster to see who might try to take the body, but attempts to hit Foster with a blunt instrument. During the denouement, Elliott confesses he killed the morgue attendant by accident and stole the body to save the family name.

REVIEWS: "Crime Club whodunit is easily superior to the average run of films. Others who do well are Gordon Elliott and the two racketeers played by Joseph Downing and James Robbins. *Variety*, 5/11/38; "Overloaded with dialogue and other complicated factors and ending with explanations more baffling on the whole, than the original mystery." *New York Times*, 5/9/38.

SUMMATION: In this neat murder mystery with snappy dialogue, Gordon Elliott turns in a nice performance as a man trying to protect his sister's and family's name, which results in a man's death.

Sparkling! Dramatic! She Rises Resplendent Above Her Triumphs in "Bought"!

Lady with a Past

RKO (February, 1932)

ALTERNATE TITLE: *Reputation*.

CAST: Venice Muir, **Constance Bennett**; Guy Bryson, **Ben Lyon**; Donnie Wainwright, **David Manners**; Carlos Santiagos, **Don Alvarado**; Rene, **Albert Conti**; Ann, **Merna Kennedy**; Lola, **Astrid Allwyn**; Jerry, **Donald Dillaway**; Nora, **Blanche Frederici**; Karl, **John Roche**; Spaulding, **Cornelius Keefe**; Aunt Emma, **Nella Walker**// Alex Brown, **Gordon Elliott**.

CREDITS: Director, **Edward H. Griffith**; Associate Producer, **Harry Joe Brown**; Screenwriter, **Horace Jackson**; Editor, **Charles Craft**; Art Director, **Carroll Clark**; Cinematographer, **Hal Mohr**; Costumes, **Gwen Wakeling** of Lucinda, Inc.; Musical Director, **Max Steiner**.

RUNNING TIME: 80 min.

SOURCE: Novel by **Harriet Henry**.

STORY: Constance Bennett is something of a wallflower because all the eligible men, including David Manners, are looking at notorious but beautiful women. Bennett goes to Paris, where she meets the impoverished Ben Lyons. Lyons takes Bennett under his wing and makes her a woman of mystery who has all Paris at her feet. On a business trip to Paris, Manners is astounded and wants Bennett to return to New York and marry him. Manners changes his mind when Bennett is innocently involved in a scandal regarding a rejected suitor who commits suicide. Bennett becomes the toast of New York. Bennett and Manners love each other and finally decide to marry.

NOTES AND COMMENTARY: Gordon Elliott plays Alex Brown, one of the eligible men in New York. Elliott is introduced to Constance Bennett when she arrives at Astrid Allwyn's party. They carry on a short conversation before Elliott walks away. Then Elliott is seen trying to get Myrna Kennedy's phone number. Elliott is in the scene when Bennett is introduced to Kennedy, and stays until Bennett asks if anyone has read any good books. As he leaves Bennett, Elliott says simply, "Good afternoon, Miss Muir."

REVIEWS: "A bright and entertaining pro-duction, somewhat unconvincing at times, but nevertheless enjoyable." *New York Times*, 2/22/32; "A cosmopolitan comedy well handled by director Griffith." *The RKO Story*, Jewell and Harbin.

SUMMATION: Bright frothy comedy with a nice performance by Constance Bennett.

Ursula Parrott's Drama of Modern Woman's Freedom.

Leftover Ladies

Tiffany (October, 1931)
ALTERNATE TITLE: *Broken Links.*
CAST: Patricia, **Claudia Dell**; the Duchess, **Marjorie Rambeau**; Ronny, **Walter Byron**; Jerry, **Alan Mowbray**; Amy, **Dorothy Revier**; Vera, **Rita LaRoy**; "Scoop," **Roscoe Karns**; Churchill, **Selmer Jackson**; Buddy, **Buster Phelps**; Benson, **Franklyn Farnum**// Gigolo, **Gordon Elliott**.
CREDITS: Director, **Erle C. Kenton**; Screenwriter, **Robert Presnell, Sr.**; Editor, **Martin G. Cohn**; Cinematographer, **John Stumar**.
RUNNING TIME: 65 min.
SOURCE: Novel by **Ursula Parrott**.
STORY: Claudia Dell divorces her husband Alan Mowbray, while Dorothy Revier does the same with spouse Walter Byron. To spice up their lives, Dell marries Byron and Revier ties the knot with Mowbray. Having a child brings happiness to Dell and Byron, while alcohol and depression dooms the marriage of Revier and Mowbray.

NOTES AND COMMENTARY: Various sources state that Gordon Elliott has the role of a gigolo in this production.

REVIEWS: "The writing is too undistinguished to make their [Dell, Rambeau, Byron, Karns and Mowbray] performances either believable or interesting." *New York Times*, 11/9/31; "Unskilled handling, from the production to the writing, makes this one to avoid." *Motion Picture Guide*, Nash and Ross.

SUMMATION: The film was unavailable for viewing by the author.

Introducing You to a Truly Great Picture! A Drama of the Heart ... So Moving ... So Human ... Yet So Crackling with Laughter ... That Only a Master Cast Directed by a Master Could Do It Justice!

Letter of Introduction

Universal (August, 1938)
A John M. Stahl Production
CAST: John Mannering, **Adolphe Menjou**; Katherine Martin, **Andrea Leeds**; Barry Paige, **George Murphy**; Edgar Bergen, **Edgar Bergen**; "Charlie McCarthy"; Honey, **Rita Johnson**; Lydia Hoyt, **Ann Sheridan**; Andrews, **Ernest Cossart**; Joe, **Frank Jenks**; Cora Phelps, **Eve Arden**.
CREDITS: Director, **John M. Stahl**; Assistant Director, **Joseph A. McDonough**; Executive in Charge of Production, **Charles R. Rogers**; Story, **Bernice Boone**; Screenwriters, **Sheridan Gibney** and **Leonard Spigelgass**; Editors, **Ted Kent** and **Charles Maynard**; Art Directors, **Jack Otterson** and **John Ewing**; Set Decorator, **R.A. Gausman**; Cinematographer, **Karl Freund**; Gowns, **Vera West**; Sound, **Bernard B. Brown** and **Joe Lapis**.
SONG: "Auld Lang Syne" (Burns and

Thomson)—sung by **George Murphy**, **Andrea Leeds**, **Rita Johnson** and **chorus**.

RUNNING TIME: 104 min.

STORY: Andrea Leeds, who aspires to an acting career, has a letter of introduction to noted actor Adolphe Menjou. Unknown to Menjou, Leeds is his daughter from his first marriage. Leeds meets struggling performer George Murphy and the two fall in love. Murphy becomes jealous when Leeds spends time with Menjou. Thinking there is a romantic liaison between them, Murphy asks his dancing partner, Rita Johnson, to marry him. To further Leeds' acting career, Menjou agrees to star in a Broadway play with her. On opening night, Menjou collapses on stage. Then Menjou leaves the theater and walks in front of taxi, critically injuring himself. On his death bed, Menjou plans to tell the reporters that Leeds is his daughter, but dies before he can do so. Leeds decides to leave New York and go back to her home town. Murphy never married Johnson because he still loves Leeds. Leeds shows Murphy the letter of introduction, which explains her relationship with Menjou. Leeds and Murphy are free to marry.

NOTES AND COMMENTARY: Film historians list Gordon Elliott as the Backgammon Man. In viewing the film, this author found no sign of Elliott. In addition, other personnel listed as having supporting or bit parts did not appear in the final print. It looks like Elliott's role ended up on the cutting room floor.

REVIEWS: "A surprisingly frank, uncommonly diverting, remarkably well-done film." *New York Times*, 9/1/37; "Adept, imaginative direction, a very good story, a fine cast, effective comedy relief and competent acting." *Variety*, 8/3/37.

SUMMATION: A very good drama with some fine comedic interludes with Edgar Bergen and Charlie McCarthy.

Ex-Gangster Put on Spot by Society!

Little Giant

First National Picture (May, 1933)

CAST: Bugs Ahern, **Edward G. Robinson**; Ruth Wayburn, **Mary Astor**; Polly Cass, **Helen Vinson**; Al Daniels, **Russell Hopton**; John Stanley, **Kenneth Thomson**; Edith Merriam, **Shirley Grey**; Donald Hadley Cass, **Berton Churchill**; Gordon Cass, **Donald Dillaway**; Mrs. Cass, **Louise Mackintosh**// Cartwright, **Gordon Elliott**.

CREDITS: Director, **Roy Del Ruth**; Screenwriters, **Robert Lord** and **Wilson Mizner**; Editors, **George Marks** and **Ray Curtiss**; Art Director, **Robert M. Haas**; Cinematographer, **Sid Hickox**; Gowns, **Orry-Kelly**; Musical Conductor, **Leo F. Forbstein**.

SONGS: "Chicago" (Fisher)—played by the **Vitaphone Orchestra**; "How Dry I Am" (traditional)—played by the **Vitaphone Orchestra**; "Stars and Stripes Forever" (Sousa)—played by the **Vitaphone Orchestra**; "Pilgrim Chorus" from *Tannhauser* (Wagner)—hummed by **Edward G. Robinson**.

RUNNING TIME: 76 min.

STORY: With the end of Prohibition, beer baron Edward G. Robinson decides to quit the rackets, become a gentleman and mingle with the upper classes. Robinson and his pal, Russell Hopton, leave Chicago for California. Robinson becomes infatuated with socialite Ruth Vinson, not knowing she and her family are conniving crooks. Mary Astor, who has fallen on hard times, rents her estate to Robinson and is hired by Robinson to help him deal with society people. Robinson is scammed into purchasing a failing business from Vinson's father, Burton Churchill, and his associates. The company has been selling worthless stock. Using mob tactics, Robinson takes back his money, buys back all stock certificates and puts the company on a sound basis. Robinson and Astor realize they love each other.

NOTES AND COMMENTARY: Gordon Elliott appears as Cartwright, a guest at Helen Vinson's party. As the scene opens, Elliott can be seen with a coffee cup in his hands. A few moments later, Vinson introduces Edward G. Robinson to Elliott. Finally, Robinson passes Elliott, now seated with food in his hands, and remarks to Elliott, "Looks good. Just what I wanted, too."

REVIEWS: "Plenty of fun, boisterous though it is most of the time." *The New York Times*, 5/27/33; "Edward G. Robinson's first comedy success." *The Warner Bros. Story*, Hirshhorn.

SUMMATION: Entertaining comedy with Edward G. Robinson a standout as a mobster trying to break into high society.

The Glorious Mad Romance of Three People You'll Be Mad About!

Living on Velvet

Warner Bros. (March, 1935)

A First National Production; A Frank Borzage Production

CAST: Amy Prentiss, **Kay Francis**; Gibraltar, **Warren William**; Terry Parker, **George Brent**; Aunt Martha, **Helen Lowell**; Harold Thornton, **Henry O'Neill**; Major, **Russell Hicks**; Mrs. Parker, **Maude Turner Gordon**; Henry Parker, **Samuel Hinds**; Cynthia Parker, **Martha Merrill**; Counterman, **Edgar Kennedy**// Husband Kissing His Wife, **Gordon Elliott**.

CREDITS: Director, **Frank Borzage**; Story/Screenwriters, **Jerry Wald** and **Julius J. Epstein**; Editor, **William Holmes**; Art Director, **Robert M. Haas**; Cinematographer, **Sid Hickox**; Gowns, **Orry-Kelly**; Musical Conductor, **Leo F. Forbstein**.

RUNNING TIME: 75 min.

STORY: George Brent piloted a plane that crashed, killing his mother, father and sister, but leaving him with only minor scratches and bruises. The incident sends Brent down a daredevil path — until he meets Kay Francis. They immediately fall in love. They marry — over Brent's objections that he is still a will-o-the-wisp. Brent turns down all job offers, and he and Francis become financially strapped. Their good friend, Warren William, buys some of Brent's worthless stock, and Brent uses the money to start a small airline passenger service. This is the last straw for Francis, who loves Brent but decides to leave him. Brent, driving at excessive speed, suffers major injuries. Because they still love each other, the accident is the catalyst that brings Brent and Francis back together.

NOTES AND COMMENTARY: Gordon Elliott can be seen briefly as one of the husbands kissing their wives goodbye as he takes the train from a Long Island station into New York City. His dialogue consisted of saying, "Goodbye, dear."

REVIEWS: "With all the advantage of a neat plot situation, some brittle dialogue and the presence of Brent and Francis, the photoplay dwindles off to an unconvincing and rather meaningless ending, which does its best in one stroke, to destroy most of the interest which the picture had succeeded in arousing during the earlier scenes." *New York Times*, 3/8/35; "A soap-sod of a melodrama." *The Warner Bros. Story*, Hirshhorn.

SUMMATION: Interesting but not quite satisfying melodrama.

The Year's Biggest Musical Hit with a Great Cast.

Lord Byron of Broadway

Metro-Goldwyn-Mayer (February, 1930)
ALTERNATE TITLE: *What Price Melody?*
CAST: Roy, **Charles Kaley**; Ardis, **Ethelind Terry**; Nancy, **Marion Shilling**; Joe, **Cliff Edwards**; Bessie, **Gwen Lee**; Phil, **Benny Rubin**; Edwards, **Drew Demarest**; Mr. Millaire, **John Byron**; Redhead, **Rita Flynn**; Blondie, **Hazel Craven**; Riccardi, **Gino Corrado**; Marie, **Pauline Paquette**// Nightclub Patron, **Gordon Elliott**.

CREDITS: Directors, **William Nigh** and **Harry Beaumont**; Screenwriters, **Crane Wilbur** and **Willard Mack**; Editor, **Anne Bauchens**; Art Director, **Cedric Gibbons**; Cinematographer, **Henry Sharp**; Costumes, **David Cox**; Sound, **Douglas Shearer**; Choreographer (dances), **Sammy Lee**; Choreographer (ballet), **Madame Albertina Rasch**; Music Composer (ballet), **Dimitri Tiomkin**.

SONGS: "Japanese Sandman" (Egan and Whiting)— sung by **Cliff Edwards**; "Just a Bundle of Old Love Letters" (Brown and Freed)— sung by **Cliff Edwards**, **Charles Kaley** and **Marion Shilling**; "The Doll Dance" (Brown and Freed)— danced by **Rita Flynn** and **Hazel Craven**; "Blue Daughter of Heaven" (Egan and Tiomkin)— sung off-camera by **James Burroughs**, and danced by the **Albertina Rasch Ballet**; "Should I?" (Brown and Freed)— sung by **Charles Kaley**, reprised by **Ethelind Terry**; "The Woman in the Shoe" (Brown and Freed)— sung by **Ethelind Terry**, **offstage male singer** and **chorus**; "Old Pal, Why Did You Leave Me" (Brown and Freed)— sung by **Charles Kaley** and **Benny Rubin**; "The Woman in the Shoe" (reprise)— sung by **male trio**; "Only Love Is Real" (Brown and Freed)— sung by **Cliff Edwards**, reprised by **Ethelind Terry**; "You're the Bride and I'm the Groom" (Brown and Freed)— sung by **Charles Kaley**.

COLOR: Musical numbers "Blue Daughter of Heaven" and "The Woman in the Shoe" in 2-strip Technicolor.
RUNNING TIME: 78 min.
SOURCE: Novel by **Nell Martin**.
STORY: Lothario Charles Kaley uses the women he ultimately spurns as an inspiration for his songwriting. With his career at a standstill, he and pianist Marion Shilling join singer Cliff Edwards to form a smash Vaudeville act. Shilling falls in love with Kaley, but Kaley maintains his roving eye until he meets singer Ethelind Terry. Terry is still the wife of Edwards but, though separated, neither has followed through with divorce proceedings. Edwards' warning to Kaley about Terry falls on deaf ears. Despondent that Kaley will make the same mistake about Terry that he did, Edwards wanders into a busy street and is hit by a taxi. Edwards dies and Kaley, capitalizing on the tragedy, writes a song destined to be a hit. Shilling talks Kaley out of publishing the song. Kaley realizes that success at others' expense is wrong. Shilling and Kaley marry, as new songs have made him successful again.

NOTES AND COMMENTARY: Gordon Elliott can briefly be seen in the nightclub scene. Elliott, with three others, comes over to Charles Kaley's table to invite him to a party. Kaley accepts and leaves with them.

REVIEWS: "Entertainment is here, even if big names in the cast aren't." *Variety*, 3/12/30; "No go." *The MGM Story*, Eames.

SUMMATION: A good backstage musical drama with nice songs.

A Favorite Star — Fired by the Spark of an Electrifying Role — Flames with New Brilliance in Willa Cather's Throbbing Revelation of a Woman's Heart....

A Lost Lady

First National (September, 1934)
ALTERNATE TITLE: *Courageous.*

CAST: Marian, **Barbara Stanwyck**; Forrester, **Frank Morgan**; Ellinger, **Ricardo Cortez**; Neil, **Lyle Talbot**; Ned, **Phillip Reed**; Robert, **Hobart Cavanaugh**; Ormsby, **Henry Kolker**; Rosa, **Rafaela Ottiano**; Simpson, **Edward McWade**; Judge Hardy, **Walter Walker**; Sloane, **Samuel Hinds**; Forrester's Cook, **Willie Fung**; Lord Verrington, **Jameson Thomas**// Polo Match Spectator, **Gordon Elliott**.

CREDITS: Director, **Alfred E. Green**; Screenwriters, **Gene Markey** and **Kathryn Scola**; Editor, **Owen Marks**; Art Director, **Jack Okey**; Cinematographer, **Sid Hickox**; Gowns, **Orry-Kelly**; Musical Conductor, **Leo F. Forbstein**.

RUNNING TIME: 61 min.

SOURCE: Novel by **Willa Cather**.

STORY: Barbara Stanwyck's fiancé, Phillip Reed, is murdered on the eve of their wedding by an irate husband. Falling into a state of depression, Stanwyck meets an older man, Frank Morgan, who falls in love with her. Stanwyck agrees to marry Morgan, even though she's not in love with him. Ricardo Cortez comes into Stanwyck's life and they fall in love. As Stanwyck plans to leave Morgan, Morgan suffers a heart attack. Stanwyck decides to stay with Morgan and refuses to run away with Cortez. Over time, Stanwyck realizes she loves Morgan and they plan to face life together.

NOTES AND COMMENTARY: Look quickly at the spectators at the polo match to see Gordon Elliott. He's sitting behind Barbara Stanwyck and Frank Morgan, smiling and clapping.

REVIEWS: "A competent, unexciting and familiar movie." *New York Times*, 10/4/34; "Critics deployed what screenwriters Markey and Scola did to Willa Cather's Pulitzer-prize winning novel and audiences didn't approve either." *The Warner Bros. Story*, Hirshhorn.

SUMMATION: Barbara Stanwyck's dynamic performance lifts this maudlin tale out of the ordinary run.

*They Took Romance for a Ride
Air-Thrills! Air-Spills! Adventure! Romance! A Gripping Story of the Airways*

Love Takes Flight

Grand National (November, 1937)
A Condor Production

CAST: Neil Bradshaw, **Bruce Cabot**; Joan Lawson, **Beatrice Roberts**; Diane Audre, **Astrid Allwyn**; Dave Miller, **Edwin Maxwell**; Spud Johnson, **John Sheehan**; Grey, **Arthur Hoyt**; Donald, **Grady Sutton**; Stone, **Harry Tyler**; Bill Parker, **Gordon Elliott**; Mr. Parker, **William Thorne**; Tommy, **Elliot Fisher**; Rice, **William Moore**; Eddie, **Brooks Benedict**; Myrtle Johnson, **Carol Tevis**; Jack Duffy; News Commentator, **Reed Howes**; Bartender, **Henry Roquemore**.

CREDITS: Director, **Conrad Nagel**; Assistant Director, **Doc Merman**; Executive Producer, **Edward L. Alperson**; Producer, **George A. Hirliman**; Associate Producer, **Ben Pivar**; Story, **Anne Morrison Chapin**; Screenwriters, **Lionel Houser** and **Mervin J. Houser**; Supervising Editor, **Robert Crandall**; Editor, **Tony Martinelli**; Art Director, **F. Paul Sylos**; Cinematographer, **Mack Stengler**; Sound, **William Wilmarth**; Musical Supervisor, **Abe Meyer**; Production Manager, **Samuel Diege**; Aerial Technician; **Herb White**.

RUNNING TIME: 71 min.

STORY: Pilot Bruce Cabot and his girl-friend, air hostess Beatrice Roberts, plan to open an airline serving the United States to Manila. Cabot is assigned to fly actress Astrid Allwyn to New York. The plane develops trouble and is forced down. From their brief association, Allwyn persuades producer Edwin Maxwell to make Cabot her leading man in her latest film. Cabot becomes an instant star. Roberts decides to make news by making a solo flight from Los Angeles to Manila. Cabot, knowing Roberts is too inexperienced to make the flight, stows away on her plane. When Roberts gets into trouble, Cabot takes the controls. Cabot bails out so Roberts can take credit for a solo flight. Roberts refuses to take credit. Cabot realizes he loves Roberts.

NOTES AND COMMENTARY: Gordon Elliott receives ninth billing in this romantic drama. Elliott, as an airline passenger, has always wanted to date Beatrice Roberts and receives the chance when Roberts goes to work for Elliott's father, William Thorne. Next, Elliott watches Roberts win an air race. Later, at Thorne's estate, Elliott tries to talk Roberts out of making the solo flight to Manila, suggesting she accompany him on a six month cruise to Manila instead. After Roberts receives a phone call from Cabot advising her not to make the flight, Roberts tells Elliott she is determined to make the flight.

REVIEWS: "Poorly cast and loosely directed plane yarn is entirely too airy for discriminating patrons." *Variety*, 8/18/37; "Not a very nice maiden flight as a director for Nagel." *Motion Picture Guide*, Nash and Ross.

SUMMATION: In this pleasant but innocuous romantic drama, Elliott is quite satisfactory as a suitor for Roberts' affections.

Love Liar — Or Love-Saint? What Is the Secret of This Strange Woman?

Magnificent Lie

Paramount (July, 1931)

CAST: Poll, **Ruth Chatterton**; Bill, **Ralph Bellamy**; Elmer, **Stuart Erwin**; Rosa, **Francoise Rosay**; Larry, **Sam Hardy**; Jacques, **Charles Boyer**; Pierre, **Tyler Brooke**// Nightclub Patron, **Gordon Elliott**.

CREDITS: Director, **Berthold Viertel**; Screenwriters, **Samuel Raphaelson** and **Vincent Lawrence**; Cinematographer, **Charles Lang**.

SONG: "Just One More Chance" (Coslow and Johnston)— sung by **Ruth Chatterton**.

RUNNING TIME: 81 min.

SOURCE: Story, "Laurels and the Lady" by **Leonard Merrick**.

STORY: Ralph Bellamy, who met Parisian actress Francoise Rosay in a hospital during the World War, learns about her American tour and goes to the theater to meet her. During the performance, Bellamy, who had been having problems with his sight, goes blind. As a joke, two of Rosay's fellow performers arrange for nightclub singer Ruth Chatterton to impersonate Rosay and meet Bellamy. Chatterton begins to fall in love with Bellamy. Bellamy learns of the deception and wants nothing to do with Chatterton. Chatterton drives Bellamy to his home at a high rate of speed, but the car overturns, throwing them from the car. The accident restores Bellamy's eyesight. Bellamy decides he wants to see more of Chatterton, which is fine with her.

NOTES AND COMMENTARY: Gordon Elliott is seated at a table with friends when singer Ruth Chatterton joins them. Chatterton then sings "Just One More Chance," with Elliott visible over Chatterton's right shoulder. After the song, Chatterton is asked to go to another table. Chatterton gets up and says, "Excuse Me." Elliott replies, "Surely."

REVIEWS: "Well handled performance by Ruth Chatterton but a weak story unwinds at a slow pace." *Variety*, 7/28/31; "Overwrought melodrama." *The Motion Picture Guide*, Nash and Ross.

SUMMATION: A good woman's picture with a fine performance by Ruth Chatterton.

See What Happens When the Public Enemy of "G-Men" Tries to Swap His Gat for a Top-Hat!

Man of Iron

Warner Bros. (December 1935)
A First National Picture
CAST: Chris Bennett, **Barton MacLane**; Vida, **Mary Astor**; Tanahill, **John Eldredge**; Bessie, **Dorothy Peterson**; Tom Martin, **Joseph Crehan**; Harry Adams, **Craig Reynolds**; Crawford, **Joseph Sawyer**; Balding, **Joseph King**; Collins, **John Qualen**; Charlie Fagan, **Gordon Elliott**; Mrs. Balding, **Florence Fair**; Mortgage Man, **Edward Keane**.

CREDITS: Director, **William McGann**; Screenwriter, **William Wister Haines**; Editor, **Terry Morse**; Art Director, **Hugh Reticker**; Cinematographer, **L.W. O'Connell**; Musical Director, **Leo F. Forbstein**.

RUNNING TIME: 61 min.

SOURCE: Story by **Dawn Powell**.

STORY: Barton MacLane, foreman for Joseph King's machine works factory, is promoted to General Manager, which infuriates John Eldredge, who expected to get the position. Having trust in Eldredge, MacLane doesn't realize Eldredge's advice and schemes are primed to discredit him. MacLane lets success go to his head and thinks he belongs in high society. Eldredge's actions finally cause the workers to riot. MacLane tries to disperse the workers, but a fight breaks out and MacLane is knocked unconscious. The workers and MacLane find out that Eldredge is behind the factory's problems. MacLane wants to quit, but King wants him to remain as his second in command. MacLane returns to work, but in his old job of foreman, as he realizes his place is with the workers.

NOTES AND COMMENTARY: Gordon Elliott plays an architect who works with the upper class. John Eldredge introduces Barton MacLane to Elliott and Craig Reynolds at the country club. Elliott talks MacLane into building an estate from plans drawn by him.

REVIEWS: "He [MacLane] hasn't been given a strong enough story. Yarn fits MacLane well, but it won't suit the fans. An action programmer, it will just get by on double bills." *Variety*, 12/11/35; "A shoddily made, uninterestingly performed drama." *The Warner Bros. Story*, Hirshhorn.

SUMMATION: In this okay but unexceptional drama, Gordon Elliott is fine as an unscrupulous architect primed to take advantage of Barton MacLane.

If You Like Your Hey-De-Hay Served in Warners' Sure-Hit Way—
Crammed with Romance, Swing and Fun, Don't <u>Walk</u> to See This ... <u>Run</u>!

Melody for Two

Warner Bros. (May, 1937)
ALTERNATE TITLES: *King of Swing* and *Special Arrangements*.

CAST: Tod Weaver, **James Melton**; Gale Starr, **Patricia Ellis**; Camille Casey, **Marie Wilson**; "Remorse" Rumson, **Fred Keating**; Mel Lynch, **Dick Purcell**; Lorna Wray, **Winifred Shaw**; Bill Hallam, **Craig Reynolds**; "Scoop" Trotter, **Charles Foy**; Wilson, **Gordon Elliott**; Exodus Johnson, **Eddie Anderson**; Alex Montrose, **Eddie Kane**; Woodruff, **Gordon Hart**; Armstrong, **Harry Hayden**.

CREDITS: Director, **Louis King**; Screenwriters, **George Bricker**, **Luci Ward** and **Joseph K. Watson**; Editor, **Jack Saper**; Art Director, **Esdras Hartley**; Cinematographer, **Arthur Todd**; Gowns, **Milo Anderson**; Musical Director, **Leo F. Forbstein**; Production Numbers Director, **Robert Vreeland**; Dialogue Director, **Gene Lewis**.

SONGS: "A Flat in Manhattan" (Jerome and Scholl)—sung by **Patricia Ellis**; "Melody for Two" (Warren and Dubin)—sung by **James Melton**; "Macushula" (Macmurrough and Rowe)—sung by **James Melton**; "Dangerous Rhythm" (Jerome and Scholl)—sung by **Winifred Shaw**; "An Excuse for Dancing" (Jerome and Scholl)—sung by **Winifred Shaw**, and danced by **Eddie Anderson** and **Charles Foy**; "September in the Rain" (Warren and Dubin)—sung by **James Melton**; "Jose O'Neill, the Cuban Heel" (Jerome and Scholl)—sung by **Winifred Shaw**; "A Flat in Manhattan" (reprise)—sung by **Patricia Ellis**; "Melody for Two" (reprise)—sung by **James Melton**.

RUNNING TIME: 60 min.

STORY: Bandleader James Melton has a falling out with his arranger, Dick Purcell. Melton needs Purcell's arrangement for a nightclub opening. Melton's girlfriend, Patricia Ellis, is able to buy the arrangements from Purcell, with the provision that an assumed name be placed on them so no one will know they're his. Purcell breaks his word and tells the story to nightclub columnist Gordon Elliott. Melton becomes upset, walks out of his nightclub contract, and breaks up with Ellis. Ellis takes over as bandleader at the nightclub. Melton is finally able to land a job at a small club. When Melton changes his musical style to swing, the club becomes a success. Ellis soon follows suit, and the two have the most popular spots in town. Melton and Ellis have a chance to win a spot on a radio program. Purcell makes it impossible for Melton's singer, Winifred Shaw, to appear, and Ellis steps in. Both bands are hired, and Melton and Ellis resume their romance.

NOTES AND COMMENTARY: Gordon Elliott receives ninth billing in this feature. Elliott plays a noted nightclub columnist. He is first seen at a table commenting that Patricia Ellis is singing well. When Melton is singing, Dick Purcell tells Elliott that Melton unknowingly is using his arrangements under the name of joke-teller Joe Miller.

REVIEWS: "Nothing much ever happens—certainly nothing you can't afford to miss." *New York Times*, 5/21/37; "There isn't much fun to the story, but there's some tuneful music." *Variety*, 5/26/37.

SUMMATION: No more than a harmless diversion, with some good music.

In Her Innocence She Expected Days and Nights of Tender Love. What She Got Was a Bitter Shock!

Merrily We Go to Hell

Paramount Pictures (June, 1932)

ALTERNATE TITLE: *Merrily We Go to ___.*

CAST: Joan, **Sylvia Sidney**; Jerry, **Fredric March**; Clair, **Adrianne Allen**; Buck, **Skeets Gallagher**; Prentice, **George Irving**; Vi, **Esther Howard**; Charlie, **Florence Britton**; Damery, **Charles Coleman**; Charlie Baxter, **Cary Grant**; Greg, **Kent Taylor**// Party Guest, **Gordon Elliott**.

CREDITS: Director, **Dorothy Arzner**; Screenwriter, **Edwin Justus Mayer**; Cinematographer, **David Abel**.

RUNNING TIME: 78 min.

SOURCE: Story, "I, Jerry, Take Thee, Joan" by **Cleo Lucas**.

STORY: Alcoholic newsman and play-wright Fredric March, and socialite Sylvia Sidney, fall in love and marry. Alcoholism and infidelities cause a matrimonial split, but the death of their child brings the two lovers together again.

NOTES AND COMMENTARY: In the party sequence to announce Sylvia Sidney's engagement to Fredric March, Gordon Elliott can be seen dancing in the background.

REVIEW: "This production is another with excellent acting, especially by Sylvia Sidney and Fredric March, but the many scenes showing constant intoxication of a newspaperman who writes a successful play are not particularly interesting or edifying." *The New York Times*, 6/11/32; "The script made some good tries [for silliness] in that direction, always straining after modern sophistication which didn't often come off." *The Paramount Story*, Eames.

SUMMATION: This is a very good melodrama with comedic overtones, well acted by Sylvia Sidney and Fredric March.

When Smoke Gets in Your Eyes the Frinks Get in Your Hair!
There's No Sense to 'Em ... So What? So Whoop — eeeeeee.

Merry Frinks

First National Pictures (June 1934)
ALTERNATE TITLE: *Happy Family*.
CAST: Mom Frink, **Aline MacMahon**; Uncle Newt Frink, **Guy Kibbee**; Joe Frink, **Hugh Herbert**; Emmett Frink, **Allen Jenkins**; Grandma Frink, **Helen Lowell**; Norman Frink, **Frankie Darro**; Ramon, **Ivan Lebedeff**; Benny Lopez, **Harold Huber**; Camille, **Louise Beavers**; Mrs. Shinliver, **Maidel Turner**; Mr. Brumby, **Harry Beresford**; Dr. Shinliver, **Harry Bradley**; Oliver, **James Bush**; Witherspoon, **Charles Coleman**; Frieda, **Joan Sheldon**; United Charities Worker, **Ethel Wales**; Truant Officer, **Edward Keane**; Barkefky, **Ivan Linow**; Katzelmalov, **Michael Visaroff**// Nightclub Patron, **Gordon Elliott**.

CREDITS: Director, **Alfred E. Green**; Story and Screenplay, **Gene Markey** and **Kathryn Scola**; Editor, **James Gibbon**; Art Director, **Jack Okey**; Cinematographer, **Arthur Edeson**; Gowns, **Orry-Kelly**; Music Conductor, **Leo F. Forbstein**.

RUNNING TIME: 68 min.

STORY: Mom Aline MacMahon is the glue that holds her dysfunctional family together. Uncle Guy Kibbee comes to live with them, and the family believes he's a freeloader, despite his story of great wealth. Kibbee dies of acute gastritis. MacMahon's husband, Hugh Herbert, again is fired from his job. Finally MacMahon is fed up with her family taking advantage of her. She welcomes the opportunity to leave when she receives a large inheritance from Kibbee. After two months, MacMahon's family's fortune goes from bad to worse, and they realize they need her. MacMahon is happy to return to her family.

NOTES AND COMMENTARY: Again Gordon Elliott has only a brief appearance. As Aline MacMahon dances with Ivan Lebedeff, Elliott can be seen dancing in the background.

REVIEWS: "A felicitous combination of humor and pathos, emerging as light-hearted and entertaining." *The Warner Bros. Story*, Hirshhorn; "It's not especially funny, nor is the story-telling very polished, but it's certainly an oddity." *The Motion Picture Guide*, Nash and Ross.

SUMMATION: Entertaining and sometime hilariously funny comedy about a crazy dysfunctional family.

A Hilarious Tour of Reno's Matrimonial Battlefields!

Merry Wives of Reno

Warner Bros. (May, 1934)
CAST: Tom, **Guy Kibbee**; Bunny, **Glenda Farrell**; Frank, **Donald Woods**; Madge, **Margaret Lindsay**; Colonel Fitch, **Hugh Herbert**; Al, **Frank McHugh**; Lois, **Ruth Donnelly**; the Trapper, **Roscoe Ates**; Derwent, **Hobart Ca-** vanaugh// Man Leaving Train Station, **Gordon Elliott**.

CREDITS: Director, **H. Bruce Humberstone**; Story and Screenwriter, **Robert Lord**; Additional Dialogue, **Joe Traub**; Editor, **Thomas Pratt**; Art Director, **Jack Okey**; Cinematographer, **Ernest Haller**; Gowns, **Orry-Kelly**; Musical Conductor, **Leo F. Forbstein**.

RUNNING TIME: 64 min.

STORY: Through a mix-up in Glenda Farrell's apartment, Donald Woods' wife, Margaret Lindsay, and Guy Kibbee's spouse, Ruth Donnelly, are headed for Reno to obtain divorces. Farrell arranged to have salesman Woods come to her apartment on false pretenses so she could seduce him. Woods is prepared to leave when Kibbee comes on the scene and pretends to be Farrell's husband so he can be alone with her. Kibbee has to make a quick exit when Farrell's husband, Hugh Herbert, arrives unexpectedly. Woods and Kibbee arrive in Reno. Woods' attempts at reconciliation are unsuccessful. Bell-hop Frank McHugh arranges to have Herbert, Lindsay and Donnelly, in their bedclothes, caught in the same room by Farrell, Woods and Kibbee. Lindsay and Donnelly call off their divorce plans, but Farrell intends to divorce Herbert.

NOTES AND COMMENTARY: Gordon Elliott is briefly seen leaving the train station with a young lady on his arm.

REVIEWS: "Stylized farce with excellent cast and considerable humor." *Variety*, 6/12/34; "A fanciful comedy that made a few wry comments on the divorce facilities offered in Reno." *The Warner Bros. Story*, Hirshhorn.

SUMMATION: Mildly amusing farce about marital mix-ups in Reno.

"No One in the World Can Take You from Me." The Words "I Love You" Take on a New Meaning as This Unforgettable Drama of an Emotion Stronger Than a Mother's Love Burns Itself on Your Heart!

Michael O'Halloran

Republic (May, 1937)

ALTERNATE TITLE: *Any Man's Wife*.

CAST: Grace Mintum, **Wynne Gibson**; Dr. Douglas Bruce, **Warren Hull**; Michael O'Halloran, **Jackie Moran**; Lily O'Halloran, **Charlene Wyatt**; Jim Mintum, **Sidney Blackmer**; Leslie, **Hope Manning**; Ted Frost, **G. P. Huntley**; Craig, **Robert Greig**; Hettie, **Helen Lowell**; Mrs. Levinsky, **Vera Gordon**; Mark Grave, **Pierre Watkin**; Mrs. Tolliver, **Dorothy Vaughan**; Mrs. Polska, **Bodil Rosing**; Judge, **Guy Usher**// Fauntleroy, **Gordon Elliott**.

CREDITS: Director, **Karl Brown**; Producer, **Herman Schlom**; Screenwriter, **Adele S. Buffington**; Editor, **Edward Mann**; Cinematographer, **Jack A. Marta**; Music, **Alberto Columbo**.

RUNNING TIME: 68 min.

SOURCE: Novel, *Michael O'Halloran* by **Gene Stratton-Porter**.

STORY: After the death of their parents, Jackie Moran and his sister, Charlene Wyatt, go to live with Wynne Gibson. Gibson's husband, Sidney Blackmer, is in the process of divorcing her. Gibson tries hard to properly take care of Moran and Wyatt, and the three begin to care for and love each other. Blackmer notices what a good mother Gibson has become. Blackmer no longer wants a divorce and becomes part of the new family.

NOTES AND COMMENTARY: It has been noted that Gordon Elliott has the role of Fauntleroy in this production. *Republic Confidential, Volume 2: The Players* (Jack Mathis Advertising, 1992), by Jack Mathis, lists Elliott as appearing in the film, but he did not receive billing.

SUMMATION: The film was not available for viewing by the author.

All Mankind Provides the Thrills in Midnight Court.

Midnight Court

Warner Bros. (March, 1937)

CAST: Carol O'Neil, **Ann Dvorak**; Victor Shanley, **John Litel**; Bob Terrill, **Carlyle Moore, Jr.**; Judge Thompson, **Joseph Crehan**; Al Kruger, **William B. Davidson**; "Slim" Jacobs, **Stanley Fields**; Lt. Jerry Burke, **Walter Miller**; "Clouter" Hoag, **John Sheehan**; City Attorney Seabrook, **Gordon Elliott**; Superior Court Judge, **Gordon Hart**; Bailiff, **Harrison Greene**; Dutch, **Charles Foy**; Louie, **Eddie Foster**; Harry Jills, **Lyle Moraine**; Adolph Nodle, **George Offerman, Jr.**; Chiquita, **Joan Woodbury**; Car Thief, **Don Downen**.

CREDITS: Director, **Frank McDonald**; Story/Screenplay, **Don Ryan** and **Kenneth Gamet**; Editor, **Frank Magee**; Art Director, **Hugh Reticker**; Cinematographer, **Warren Lynch**; Gowns, **Milo Anderson**.

RUNNING TIME: 63 min.

STORY: Former D.A. John Litel goes to work for crime boss William B. Davidson, garnering the displeasure of his ex-wife, Ann Dvorak. As the greatest criminal attorney, Litel is highly successful in freeing Davidson's underlings. Litel wants a young gang member, Carlyle Moore, Jr., to quit the gang and attend college. Davidson, afraid Moore will talk, has henchman Stanley Fields murder him. This action causes Litel to split with Davidson. Litel is appointed special prosecutor to assist City Attorney Gordon Elliott in prosecuting Davidson and Fields. With Litel's switch back to law and order, he and Dvorak get back together.

NOTES AND COMMENTARY: Gordon Elliott is the attorney who prosecutes cases at night court. First he shows Judge Joseph Crehan an item an elderly woman shoplifted, and then reminds the judge about previous times she had been found guilty. At the climax, Elliott brings charges against crime boss William B. Davidson and his henchman Stanley Fields before giving way to special prosecutor John Litel. Finally, Elliott, Litel and Ann Dvorak face the guns of Davidson and Fields before the police round up the gangsters.

REVIEW: "*Midnight Court* is a B picture given A production. The story is backed by smooth direction and some able acting." *Variety*, 3/10/37.

SUMMATION: Speedy but predictable tale that produces sufficient entertainment. Gordon Elliott is very effective in the role of the City Attorney.

Midnight Mystery

A Radio Picture (June, 1930)

CAST: Sally Wayne, **Betty Compson**; Tom Austen, **Lowell Sherman**; Paul Cooper, **Raymond Hatton**; Gregory Sloan, **Hugh Trevor**; Louise Hollister, **June Clyde**; Mischa Kawelin, **Ivan Lebedeff**; Madeline Austen, **Rita LaRoy**; Harriet Cooper, **Marcelle Corday**; Barker, **Sidney D'Albrook**; Rogers, **William P. Burt**.

CREDITS: Director, **George B. Seitz**; Producer, **William Le Baron**; Associate Producer, **Bertram Millhauser**; Screenplay, **Beulah Marie Dix**; Editor, **Otto Ludwig**; Art Director, **Max Ree**; Cinematographer, **Joseph Walker**; Photographic Effects, **Lloyd Mitchell**; Sound, **Clem Portman**.

RUNNING TIME: 69 min.

SOURCE: Play, *Hawk Island* by **Howard Irving Young**.

STORY: On a stormy, windswept night on an isolated island off the Cuban coast, Lowell Sherman discovers his wife, Rita LaRoy, is having an affair with pianist Ivan Lebedeff. Lebedeff has a violent argument with the island's owner, Hugh Trevor. A shot is heard, and Trevor announces to his guest that he's killed Lebedeff and thrown his body into the ocean. Later Trevor tells his fiancée, mystery writer Betty Compson, that the murder was a hoax, and Lebedeff will appear at breakfast. Sherman discovers Lebedeff and shoots him, knowing Trevor will be blamed for the crime. Using trickery, Compson gets Sherman to confess. Compson and Trevor plan to marry.

NOTES AND COMMENTARY: One film historian lists Gordon Elliott as a cast member in *Midnight Mystery*. The film's cast listing indicates parts for only ten actors, and only ten actors appear on screen. All are accounted for, and there is no sign of Elliott.

REVIEW: Beulah Marie Dix' adaptation was hardly Hitchcock, but managed to tickle the fancy of sleuth addicts." *The RKO Story*, Jewell and Harbin.

SUMMATION: This is not a particularly well-acted or directed film. The film plods along to the expected happy conclusion.

She Gave Him One Shining Hour of Love Then Married Another Man!

Modern Hero

Warner Bros. (April, 1934)

CAST: Pierre, **Richard Barthelmess**; Joanna, **Jean Muir**; Mme. Azais, **Marjorie Rambeau**; Claire, **Verree Teasdale**; Leah, **Florence Eldredge**; Hazel, **Dorothy Burgess**; Mueller, **Hobart Cavanaugh**; Young Pierre, **William Janney**; Flint, **Arthur Hohl**; Elmer, **Theodore Newton**; Mr. Ryan, **J.M. Kerrigan**; Clara, **Maidel Turner**; Young Pierre (as a child), **Mickey Rentschler**; Mr. Eggelson, **Richard Tucker**; Mrs. Eggelson, **Judith Vosselli**// Bridge Player, **Gordon Elliott**.

CREDITS: Director, **G.W. Pabst**; Screenwriters, **Gene Markey** and **Kathryn Scola**; Editor, **James Gibbon**; Art Director, **Robert M. Haas**; Cinematographer, **William Rees**; Gowns, **Orry-Kelly**; Musical Director, **Leo F. Forbstein**; Dialogue Director, **Arthur Greville Collins**.

RUNNING TIME: 71 min.

SOURCE: Novel by **Louis Bromfield**.

STORY: Circus performer Richard Barthelmess has a brief liaison with small-town girl Jean Muir, resulting in pregnancy. Muir, knowing she would not be happy leaving town, refuses Barthelmess' offer of marriage. Barthelmess leaves the circus to attempt a career in business. Barthelmess' career receives a boost when he enters into business with Arthur Hohl and begins a loveless marriage with Dorothy Burgess. Barthelmess' greed induces him to enter into a business venture with an unscrupulous capitalist, Richard Tucker. Barthelmess becomes a part of his illegitimate son's, William Janney's, life. Janney is given the chance at a top education and a taste of the high life. Barthelmess' life comes crashing down when Tucker absconds with the money and Janney is killed in an automobile accident. Barthelmess finds his mother, Marjorie Rambeau, who tells him that he's free of the pursuit of greed and can now live a better life. Rambeau convinces Barthelmess they can start life over in Europe.

NOTES AND COMMENTARY: Gordon Elliott is seen at Richard Tucker's apartment playing bridge with Verre Teasdale and two other ladies. He remarks, "Hope you'll have better hands." When Richard Barthelmess enters the apartment, Elliott comments, "How are you, Radler?" Elliott and his partner lose at bridge and money passes hands from Elliott to Teasdale. Teasdale then looks for a ride to her apartment. Elliott is about to acquiesce when Barthelmess offers to escort her.

REVIEWS: "An earnest, sketchy and spiritless account of Pierre Radler's rise and fall." *New York Times*, 4/20/34; "A fine example of the trials and tribulations of the working man." *The Warner Bros. Story*, Hirshhorn.

SUMMATION: Good, well acted and directed drama of a man's rise to wealth and power, and his subsequent fall.

A New Star in the Saddle to Spur You to Cheers and Stir You to Song! ... Different! Dangerous! Quick on the Trigger! Ready with a Song! Six-Feet-Three of Hard-Galloping, Heart-Walloping Cowboy ... Riding High, Wide and Handsome to Stardom!

Moonlight on the Prairie

Warner Bros. (November, 1935)

CAST: Ace Andrews, **Dick Foran "The Singing Cowboy"**; "Smoky"; Barbara, **Sheila Mannors**; "Small Change," **George E. Stone**; Luke Thomas, **Joe Sawyer**; the Sheriff, **Joseph King**; Buck, **Robert Barrat**; Dickie Roberts, **Dickie Jones**; Jeff, **Gordon Elliott**; Pop Powell, **Herbert Heywood**; Stage Agent, **Raymond Brown**; Colonel Gowdy, **Richard Carle**; Pete, **Milton Kibbee**.

CREDITS: Director, **D. Ross Lederman**; Screenwriter, **William Jacobs**; Editor, **Thomas Pratt**; Art Direction, **Esdras Hartley**; Cinematography, **Fred Jackman, Jr.**; Musical Director, **Leo F. Forbstein**.

SONGS: "Covered Wagon Days" (Jasmyn and Jerome)—sung by **Dick Foran**; "Moonlight on the Prairie" (Nolan and Spencer)—sung by **Dick Foran**.

LOCATION FILMING: Lone Pine and June Lake, California.

RUNNING TIME: 63 min.

SOURCE: Story, "Boss of the Bar B Ranch" by **William Jacobs**.

STORY: Dick Foran returns to Wagon Wheel Gap to clear himself of a murder charge. Arriving at the same time are Sheila Bromley and her son, Dickie Jones. Bromley and Jones have to reach the Bar B Ranch by midnight or forfeit the ranch to Joe Sawyer. Foran decides to help them and gets Jones to the ranch with a minute to spare. Jones is the new owner, and he makes Foran his foreman. Foran fires all the hands except an old friend, Gordon Elliott. Elliott is working for the Cattleman's Association, trying to stop the rustling in the area. Sawyer is behind the rustling, and captures Foran and Elliott. Sawyer shoots Elliott down in cold blood. Foran is able to avenge Elliott's murder and bring Sawyer and his gang to justice. Now Foran has time to romance Bromley.

NOTES AND COMMENTARY: Director D. Ross Lederman would be reunited with Bill Elliott for *Across the Sierras* (Columbia, 1941). This would be Lederman's last feature film western. He would direct a couple of shorts in the forties and then some episodes of *The Gene Autry Show* and *Annie Oakley* in the fifties.

Dick Jones was asked to name the best riders of the western stars. He replied, "Ben Johnson, Gordon Elliott and Joel McCrea."

REVIEWS: "Dick Foran initial series film is a pleasant outing with a good script and cast and enhanced by Foran's brand of singing." *Western Movies*, Pitts; "Warners' strong production values and Lederman's efficient direction result in a pleasant musical outing." *The Western*, Hardy.

SUMMATION: This is a good "B" western. Gordon Elliott shows his potential as a leading man in his secondary role. His voice displays the authority that would mark him as one of the screen's top western stars.

A Red-Blooded Mystery of Blue-Blooded Killers!

Murder by an Aristocrat

Warner Bros. (June, 1936)

A First National Picture; A Clue Club Selection

CAST: Dr. Allen Carick, **Lyle Talbot**; Sally Keating, **Marguerite Churchill**; Janice Thatcher, **Claire Dodd**; John Tweed, **John Eldredge**; Dave Thatcher, **Gordon Elliott**; Adela Thatcher, **Virginia Brissac**; Bayard Thatcher,

William B, Davidson; Hilary Thatcher, **Joseph Crehan**; Evelyn Thatcher, **Florence Fair**; Higby, **Stuart Holmes**; Emeline, **Lottie Williams**; Florrie, **Mary Treen**; Cab Driver, **Milton Kibbee**; Sheriff Whiting, **Henry Otho**.

CREDITS: Director, **Frank McDonald**; Screenwriters, **Luci Ward** and **Roy Chanslor**; Editor, **Louis Hesse**; Art Director, **Hugh Reticker**; Cinematographer, **Arthur L. Todd**; Costumes, **Orry-Kelly**; Dialogue Director, **Irving Rapper**.

RUNNING TIME: 60 min.

SOURCE: Story by **Mignon G. Eberhart**.

STORY: William B. Davidson demands $25,000 to leave the family home. As spokesperson for the family, Virginia Brissac, tells Davidson she'll get him the money. Davidson is mysteriously shot, and Dr. Lyle Talbot and nurse Marguerite Churchill are called in to care for him. Davidson tells Churchill that someone tried to kill him. A second attempt to kill Davidson is successful. Churchill deduces that Brissac is the guilty party. As she tries to escape the villain's clutches, Brissac suffers a heart attack and dies.

NOTES AND COMMENTARY: Gordon Elliott received fifth billing in this murder mystery. Elliott is present when William B. Davidson demands $25,000 to leave the family home. Comments indicate that Elliott has been ill since Davidson has taken up residence. A tortured-looking Elliott throws a glass in the fireplace before Claire Dodd leads Elliott off to bed. Elliott, in his dressing gown, comes to Davidson's room after Davidson has been shot and asks, "He won't die?" Later, without a word, Elliott passes Marguerite Churchill on the stairs as he goes to Davidson's room; Elliott walks slowly down the stairs, speaks to Lyle Talbot and walks past Virginia Brissac to his study. Talbot remarks to Churchill that Elliott is either on liquor or drugs. Elliott leaves the house with John Eldredge to go fishing and is subsequently seen at the lake with him. Later, Elliott is seen leaving the house in a hurry and is called back to the lake. In response to Eldredge's query of where Elliott had been, Elliott responds, "I just sat back there out of the sun." Elliott and Eldredge enter the house after Davidson has been murdered. Elliott gets upset when he looks at the body, and leaves the room. Elliott tries to search Davidson's body but is stopped by Brissac. Elliott is present when the family learns that maid Mary Treen had suffered a drug overdose, and Elliott secretly empties the contents of a pill box into a drawer. Elliott attempts to propose a theory for Davidson's death, but is stopped by Eldredge. Dodd and Brissac then see Elliott to his room. Elliott enters Treen's room for the drugs he hid, and is discovered by Churchill. The two struggle, and Elliott runs across the rooftop to the attic, where he is found dead of a drug overdose.

REVIEWS: "A routine mediocrity obviously destined for duals and fill-ins." *Variety*, 6/17/36 "A dim murder mystery." *Motion Picture Guide*, Nash and Ross.

SUMMATION: In this decent but unremarkable murder mystery, Gordon Elliott does a good job as a weakling turned into a drug addict by William B. Davidson. Elliott effectively shows a man wracked with torment.

Mystery in the Air! Murder on Wing! You've Been Thrilled, Shocked, Terrorized Before — But Save Your Shrieks for the Moment You Meet This Human Vulture Whose Passion Is Murder in the Clouds.

Murder in the Clouds

Warner Bros. (December, 1934)
A First National Picture

CAST: "Three Star" Bob Halsey, **Lyle Talbot**; Judy, **Ann Dvorak**; George, **Gordon Westcott**; Tom, **Robert Light**; Wings, **George Cooper**; Lackey, **Charles Wilson**; Brownell, **Henry O'Neill**; Taggart, **Russell Hicks**; Jason, **Arthur Pierson**; Williams, **Edward McWade**; Flight Commander, **Clay Clement**; Pat, **Eddie Shubert**; Joe, **Wheeler Oakman**; Henchman, **Nick Copeland**// Saunders, **Gordon Elliott**.

CREDITS: Director, **D. Ross Lederman**;

Murder in the Clouds (Warner Bros., 1934). Gordon Elliott, Clay Clement, Wheeler Oakman, George Cooper, Nick Copeland, Lyle Talbot and Arthur Pierson (left to right).

Story and Screenplay, **Roy Chanslor** and **Dore Schary**; Editor, **Thomas Pratt**; Art Direction, **Jack Holden**; Cinematography, **Warren Lynch**; Aerial Photographer, **Elmer Dyer**; Gowns, **Orry-Kelly**; Musical Conductor, **Leo F. Forbstein**.

RUNNING TIME: 60 min.

STORY: A plane blows up in mid-air; Ann Dvorak's brother, Robert Light, is killed and a revolutionary new explosive is stolen by traitors who plan to sell it to a foreign nation. In attempting to reach the crash site, Dvorak falls into the traitor's hands. Ace pilot Lyle Talbot rescues Dvorak and helps bring the villains to justice.

NOTES AND COMMENTARY: Gordon Elliott plays a lieutenant in the Aero Patrol. Elliott is first seen, in his plane, waving off George Cooper, who is trying to have the Aero Patrol follow him. Upon landing, Elliott helps catch Wheeler Oakman and the other henchmen. Next he has a scene with Lyle Talbot and Clay Clement in which he is told to broadcast the alarm to shoot down the plane with the escaping gang leaders. Elliott has a final scene in which he sounds the alarm.

REVIEWS: "A dynamic little melodrama, the film story races to a climax at a pace calculated to render its audience breathless, speechless and thoughtless. An out-and-out thriller." *The New York Times*, 12/26/34; "Fast paced, entertaining programmer." *The Motion Picture Guide*, Nash and Ross.

SUMMATION: This is a good, speedy action melodrama with a solid mystery angle.

Murder with a Surgeon's Scalpel! A Dead Doctor Reveals What Nurses Won't Tell!

Murder of Dr. Harrigan

Warner Bros. (January, 1936)

A First National Picture; A Clue Club Picture

CAST: George Lambert, **Ricardo Cortez**; Sally Keating, **Kay Linaker**; Dr. Harrigan, **John Eldredge**; Lillian Cooper, **Mary Astor**; Lieut. Lamb, **Joseph Crehan**; Dr. Coate; **Frank Reicher**; Agnes Melady; **Anita Kerry**; Doctor Simon, **Phillip Reed**; Peter Melady, **Robert Strange**; Margaret Brody, **Mary Treen**; Kenneth Martin, **Gordon Elliott**; Jackson, **Don Barclay**; Wentworth, **Johnny Arthur**; Ina Harrigan, **Joan Blair**.

CREDITS: Director, **Frank McDonald**; Screenwriters, **Peter Milne** and **Sy Bartlett**; Dialogue, **Charles Belden**; Editor, **William Clemens**; Art Director, **Robert M. Haas**; Cinematographer, **Arthur L. Todd**; Musical Director, **Leo F. Forbstein**.

RUNNING TIME: 66 min.

SOURCE: Novel, *From This Dark Stairway* by **Mignon G. Eberhart**.

STORY: Robert Strange is in the hospital for a major surgical procedure. Instead of ether, a new anesthetic, owned by Strange, will be used. Dr. John Eldredge, Strange's bitter enemy, will perform the operation. Eldredge is murdered before the operation can be performed, and Strange goes missing, his dead body later discovered in the city morgue. Nurse Kay Linaker is accused of the murders. With her boyfriend Ricardo Cortez' help, the murderer is revealed to be intern Philip Reed.

NOTES AND COMMENTARY: In this film Gordon Elliott is romancing a married woman and becomes a murder suspect. He can be seen in four scenes. First, Elliott is visiting Joan Blair, wife of noted physician John Eldredge, in her hospital room. Then Eldredge catches Elliott in the hospital room with Blair. Next, Elliott is brought back to the hospital in handcuffs and accused of Eldredge's murder by Police Lieutenant Joseph Crehan. Finally, still in handcuffs, Elliott tries to go to Anita Kerry's hospital room, but is restrained.

REVIEWS: "A murder mystery that's too routine to inspire more than casual audience interest." *Variety*, 1/22/36; "Routine murder-in-a-hospital story." *The Motion Picture Guide*, Nash and Ross.

SUMMATION: This is an okay murder mystery marred by some unfunny comedy scenes with Don Barclay and Johnny Arthur. Gordon Elliott is adequate in the role of Joan Blair's boyfriend.

The Star of My Weakness *in Her Second Great Cinema Triumph!*

My Lips Betray

Fox (November, 1933)

ALTERNATE TITLE: *His Majesty's Car*.

CAST: Lili, **Lilian Harvey**; King Rupert, **John Boles**; Stigmat, **El Brendel**; Queen Mother, **Irene Browne**; Mamma Watscheck, **Maude Eburne**; De Conti, **Henry Stephenson**; Weininger, **Herman Bing**// Auto Showroom Spectator, **Gordon Elliott**.

CREDITS: Director, **John Blystone**; Screenwriters, **S.N. Behrman**, **Hanns Kraly**, and **Jane Storm**; Editor, **Alex Troffey**; Cinematographer, **Lee Garmes**; Costumes, **Joe Strassner**; Music, **Hugo Friedhofer**; Choreographer, **Sammy Lee**.

SONGS: "I'll Build a Nest" (Kernell); "His Majesty's Car" (Kernell); "The Band Is Gaily Playing" (Kernell); "To Romance" (Kernell); "Why Am I Happy" (Kernell).

SOURCE: Play, *Der Komet* by **Attila Orbok**.
RUNNING TIME: 70 min.

STORY: Commoner Lilian Harvey becomes Ruthania's favorite singer because she's supposed to be the girlfriend of King John Boles. Boles, who would rather be a songwriter, disguises himself as a songwriter and meets Harvey. The two fall in love and, overcoming obstacles, finally marry.

NOTES AND COMMENTARY: Film historians state Gordon Elliott plays a spectator in an automobile showroom.

REVIEWS: "As a romantic comedy, this new film has an unhappy talent for seeming slightly fly blown on the first count and a good deal less than hilarious on the second." *New York Times*, 11/4/33; "The film's plot smacks of operetta yet doesn't quite have the charm needed to pull it off successfully. The dialog is witless and overly cute." *Motion Picture Guide*, Nash and Ross.

SUMMATION: The film was unavailable for viewing by the author.

The Story Was Too Beautiful for Words ... So They Set It to Music.

My Weakness

Fox (September, 1933)

ALTERNATE TITLE: *That's My Weakness.*

CAST: Looloo Blake, **Lilian Harvey**; Ronnie Gregory, **Lew Ayres**; Gerald Gregory, **Charles Butterworth**; Dan Cupid, **Harry Langdon**; Maxie, **Sid Silvers**; Jane Holman, **Irene Bentley**; Ellery Gregory, **Henry Travers**; Baptiste, **Adrian Rosley**; Diana Griffith, **Mary Rogers**; Eve Millstead, **Irene Ware**; Lois Crowley, **Barbara Weeks**; Jacqueline Wood, **Susan Fleming**; Marion, **Marcelle Edwards**; Lillian, **Marjorie King**; Consuello, **Jean Allen**; Mitzi, **Gladys Blake**; Dixie, **Dixie Francis**// Spectator, **Gordon Elliott**.

CREDITS: Director, **David Butler**; Producer, **Buddy G. DeSylva**; Screenwriters, **David Butler**, **Buddy G. DeSylva** and **Bert Hanlon**; Editor, **Irene Morra**; Cinematographer, **Arthur C. Miller**; Costumes, **Rita Kaufman** and **Joe Strassner**.

SONG: "Gather Lip Rough While You May" (DeSylva, Robin and Whiting).

RUNNING TIME: 73 min.

STORY: Lilian Harvey is a hotel clerk who falls for the sophisticated Lew Ayers. In two weeks, Harvey's girlfriends transform Harvey into the cream of society. Harvey ends up with Ayers.

NOTES AND COMMENTARY: According to one source, Gordon Elliott appears as a spectator in this film.

REVIEWS: "She [Harvey] is an ethereal presence, making the fantasy work with her charm and grace." *Motion Picture Guide*, Nash and Ross; "A fluffy piece of work with no more of a story than most musical comedies." *New York Times*, 9/22/33.

SUMMATION: This film was not available for viewing by the author.

Love Sways Them — Passion Strikes Them — Danger Surrounds Them — in Joe Anton's Place.

Night After Night

Paramount (October, 1932)

CAST: Joe Anton, **George Raft**; Miss Healey, **Constance Cummings**; Iris Dawn, **Wynne Gibson**; Maudie Triplett, **Mae West**; Miss Mabel Jellyman, **Alison Skipworth**; Leo, **Roscoe Karns**; Dick Bolton, **Louis Calhern**; Frankie Guard, **Bradley Page**; Blainey, **Al Hill**; Jerky, **Harry Wallace**; Patsy, **Dink Templeton**;

Malloy, **Marty Martyn**; Tom, **Tom Kennedy**// One of Maudie's Escorts, **Gordon Elliott**.

CREDITS: Director, **Archie Mayo**; Screenwriter, **Vincent Lawrence**; Continuity, **Kathryn Scola**; Cinematographer, **Ernest Haller**.

RUNNING TIME: 76 min.

SOURCE: Story, "Single Night" by **Louis Bromfield**.

STORY: Speakeasy owner George Raft falls for Constance Cummings, incurring the wrath of Raft's current girlfriend, Wynne Gibson. Wynne makes a failed attempt to shoot Raft, inspiring Cummings to kiss Raft. Raft believes Cummings loves him and reveals his feelings for her. Cummings lets Raft know she's marrying Louis Calhern for his money. Raft tells Cummings off. In a rage, Cummings goes to Raft's speakeasy to get revenge but soon realizes she really loves Raft.

NOTES AND COMMENTARY: Gordon Elliott is seen briefly as one of three escorts who bring Mae West to George Raft's speakeasy.

Bradley Page would play villainous roles with Bill Elliott in *Beyond the Sacramento* (Columbia, 1940), and with Bill Elliott and Tex Ritter in *Roaring Frontiers* (Columbia, 1941).

REVIEWS: "It does succeed in being virile and interesting." *The New York Times*, 10/31/32; "The film caught the bold, pleasure-loving Prohibition era's atmosphere with style, and smart dialogue put over by an excellent cast." *The Paramount Story*, Eames.

SUMMATION: This is an entertaining Prohibition-era melodrama, with a stunning film debut by Mae West.

They're Raising the Roof of the World's Swankiest Hotel to Give You a Look at What Goes on When Boys and Girls Step Out For...

A Night at the Ritz

Warner Bros. (February, 1935)

ALTERNATE TITLE: *King of the Ritz*.

CAST: Duke Regan, **William Gargan**; Marcia, **Patricia Ellis**; Gyp, **Allen Jenkins**; Kiki, **Dorothy Tree**; Leopold, **Erik Rhodes**; Mr. Vincent, **Berton Churchill**; Scurvin, **Gordon Westcott**; Mama, **Bodil Rosing**; Mr. Hassler, **Arthur Hoyt**; Henri, **Paul Porcasi**; Connolly, **William Davidson**; Isabelle, **Mary Treen**; Miss Barry, **Mary Russell**// Vincent's Assistant, **Gordon Elliott**.

CREDITS: Director, **William H. McGann**; Story/Screenplay, **Albert J. Cohen** and **Robert T. Shannon**; Additional Dialogue, **Manuel Seff**; Editor, **Jack Killifer**; Art Director, **Esdaras Hartley**; Cinematographer, **James Van Trees**; Musical Director, **Leo F. Forbstein**; Dialogue Director, **Frank McDonald**.

RUNNING TIME: 62 min.

STORY: Having lost his job at one hotel, William Gargan decides to promote girlfriend Patricia Ellis' brother, Erik Rhodes, as an international chef to the Ritz Hotel. Gargan acts as Rhodes' manager. Gargen is unaware that the delicious dinner he had at Ellis' house was really prepared by her mother, Bodil Rosing. Desperate for a first-rate chef, Ritz manager Berton Churchill hires Rhodes. Then, as food is to be prepared for a large gathering, Gargan learns that Rhodes cannot cook. To save Gargan and her brother, Ellis has Rosing prepare the meal, which is a great success. Churchill hires Rosing as his new chef and retains Rhodes in a new position. Gargan and Ellis plan to wed.

NOTES AND COMMENTARY: Gordon Elliott has one scene as Berton Churchill's assistant. He's present as Churchill receives a phone call from William Gargan, and then Elliott tells Churchill that he's received calls all morning inquiring if Erik Rhodes is staying at the hotel.

REVIEWS: "The comedy works the lode of its central idea for a reasonable sum of laughter." *New York Times*, 5/16/35; "Neatly contrived fable, but with the laughs bunched in the first half." *Variety*, 5/22/35.

SUMMATION: Lame comedy that not even the talented William Gargan can save.

All Talk Thrill Drama.

Night Parade

Radio Pictures (October, 1929)

ALTERNATE TITLE: *Sporting Life.*

CAST: Paula Vernoff, **Aileen Pringle**; Bobby Murray, **Hugh Trevor**; Doris, **Dorothy Gulliver**; Zelli, **Robert Ellis**; Ann Pennington, **Ann Pennington**; Tom Murray, **Lloyd Ingraham**; Sid Durham, **Lee Shumway**; Heinie, **Heinie Conklin**; Huffy, **Charles Sullivan**; Phil, Nate Slott/ Party Guest, **Gordon Elliott.**

CREDITS: Director, **Malcolm St. Clair**; Producer, **William LeBaron**; Associate Producer, **Louis Sarecky**; Screenwriters, **James Gruen** and **George O'Hara**; Editor, **Jack Kitchin**; Art Director, **Max Ree**; Cinematographer, **William Marshall**; Photographic Effects, **Lloyd Knechtel**; Sound, **Lambert E. Day.**

RUNNING TIME: 71 min.

SOURCE: Play, *Ringside* by **Hyatt Daab**, **Edward E. Paramore, Jr.** and **George Abbott**, a **Gene Buck** production.

STORY: Under a romantic spell cast by gambler Robert Ellis's paramour, Aileen Pringle, middleweight champion Hugh Trevor agrees to throw the championship fight. Trevor's manager and father, Lloyd Ingraham, discovers Trevor's duplicity and threatens to stop the fight. Realizing Pringle and Ellis have been playing him for a sucker, Trevor decides to fight to win. In a tough fight, Trevor retains the championship.

NOTES AND COMMENTARY: Sharp Elliott watchers can see Elliott in the background during the party sequence at Aileen Pringle's house. First, Elliott can be seen over Pringle's head as Trevor is having a few drinks. Then Elliott is part of the group watching Ann Pennington dance. Finally, Elliot is present when Lloyd Ingraham and Lee Shumway arrive at Pringle's house to bring Trevor home.

Dorothy Gulliver would be Elliott's love interest in his first starring feature western, *In Early Arizona* (Columbia, 1938), and would return for *Lone Star Pioneers* (Columbia, 1939). Lloyd Ingraham would make an appearance in *Savage Horde* (Republic, 1950). Lee Shumway can be seen in *Lone Star Pioneers* (Columbia, 1939), *The Law Comes to Texas* (Columbia, 1939) and *Wyoming* (Republic, 1947).

REVIEWS: "It's the old prizefight hoke, but done with showmanship written with an idea of what should click with the patron." *Variety*, 11/13/29; "Another of those fight pictures with moments of spontaneity that hardly make up for the dull dialogue." *The New York Times*, 11/14/29.

SUMMATION: Entertaining boxing melodrama buoyed by a nifty performance by Lloyd Ingraham.

Love Had Touched Them and Gone On, Then Romance Beckoned to Her.
What Would Any Woman Have Done?

A Notorious Affair

First National (April, 1930)

A First National and Vitaphone Production

CAST: Patricia Hanley, **Billie Dove**; Paul Gherardi, **Basil Rathbone**; Countess Olga Balakireff, **Kay Francis**; Sir Thomas Hanley, **Montagu Love**; Dr. Allen Pomeroy, **Kenneth Thomson**; Lord Percival Northmore, **Philip Strange**; Higgins, the Butler, **Malcolm Waite**; // Sir Thomas' Party Guest, **Gordon Elliott.**

CREDITS: Director, **Lloyd Bacon**; Screenwriter, **J. Grubb Alexander**; Editor, **Frank**

Ware; Cinematographer, **Ernest Haller**; Musical Conductor, **Leo F. Forbstein**.

SONGS: "Hark! The Herald Angels Sing" (Mendelssohn-Bartholdy and Wesley)— sung by **carolers**; "Second Movement (Andante)" from *Violin Concerto in E Minor (Op.64)* (Mendelssohn-Bartholdy)— played by **Basil Rathbone** and **Gino Corrado**; "One Hour of Love."

SOURCE: Play, *Fame* by **Audrey** and **Waverly Carter**.

RUNNING TIME: 70 min.

STORY: Surprising her friends, Billie Dove tells them she married violinist Basil Rathbone. With help from Dove and Countess Kay Francis, Rathbone becomes a famous musician. The concert schedule is too demanding, and Rathbone becomes ill. Dr. Kenneth Thomson, an old flame of Dove's, becomes Rathbone's physician. Francis takes Rathbone to a seaside resort, where his condition worsens. After an operation, Dove and Thomson take care of Rathbone. Rathbone believes Dove and Thomson are in love. Dove assures Rathbone that she loves only him, which paves the way for his recovery.

NOTES AND COMMENTARY: Gordon Elliott plays one of Montagu Love's party guests. He is first seen at a serving table in the first scene inside Love's estate. Next Elliott is in the dining room as Philip Strange toasts the absent Billie Dove.

REVIEWS: "The story is an adaptation of 'Fame,' a stage play, and offers no end of awkward witticisms and alleged epigrammatic dialogue. Rest of the photoplay runs smoothly enough, with Mr. Rathbone corralling the majority of the performing honors." *New York Times*, 4/26/30; "The quintessential 'woman's picture.'" *The Warner Bros. Story*, Hirshhorn.

SUMMATION: Okay melodrama with nice performances from Rathbone and Francis.

On ze Boulevard

Metro-Goldwyn-Mayer (June, 1927)

CAST: Gaston Pasqual, **Lew Cody**; Musette, **Renee Adoree**; Ribot, **Anton Vaverka**; Gaby de Silva, **Dorothy Sebastian**; Count de Guissac, **Roy D'Arcy**.

CREDITS: Director, **Harry Millarde**; Story, **F. Hugh Herbert** and **Florence Ryerson**; Screenwriters, **Richard Shayer** and **Scott Darling**; Titles, **Joe Farnham** and **Earl Baldwin**; Editor, **George Hively**; Art Directors, **Cedric Gibbons** and **Frederic Hope**; Cinematographer, **Andre Barlatier** and **William Daniels**; Wardrobe, **Rene Hubert**.

RUNNING TIME: 47 min.

STORY: While gambling, Lew Cody becomes a big winner and becomes a big spender. Cody's girlfriend, Renee Adoree, wants Cody to be sensible with his winnings. Crooks try to fleece Cody, but Adoree is able to thwart the crooks' plans.

NOTES AND COMMENTARY: One source credits Gordon Elliott as appearing as a diner at the race track.

REVIEW: "It is loaded with laughs." *Variety*, 7/13/27.

SUMMATION: This film was not available for viewing by the author.

Once a Sinner

Fox (January, 1931)

ALTERNATE TITLE: *Luxury*.

CAST: Diana Barry, **Dorothy Mackaill**; Tommy Mason, **Joel McCrea**; Richard Kent, **John Halliday**; Serge Ratoff, **C. Henry Gordon**; Kitty King, **Ilka Chase**; Hope Patterson, **Sally Blane**; Marie, **Nadia Faro**; Mrs. Mason, **Clara Blandick**; Mrs. Nolan, **Myra Hampton**; James Brent, **George Brent**// Dance Extra, **Gordon Elliott**.

CREDITS: Director, **Guthrie McClintic**; Screenwriter, **George Middleton**; Editor, **Ralph Dietrich**, Cinematographer, **Arthur L. Todd**.

RUNNING TIME: 71 min.

STORY: Dorothy Mackaill, a woman with a sordid past, falls in love with inventor Joel McCrea. Before they marry, Mackaill attempts to tell McCrea of her past, but he refuses to listen. They are living a blissful life in the country when McCrea decides they must move to the city to raise money for his inventions. McCrea learns of Mackaill's past and their marriage is almost destroyed, until he realizes he still loves her.

NOTES AND COMMENTARY: According to one source, Gordon Elliott is a dance extra in this film.

REVIEWS: "Endowed with compelling photography, smooth dialogue and several clever performances." *New York Times*, 1/17/31; "Very adult and slow moving screen story." *Variety*, 1/21/31.

SUMMATION: This film was not available for viewing by the author.

Here He Is, Folks. The Prince of Charmers, in a Production of Romantic Songs and Merriment.

One Hour with You

Paramount (March, 1932)

An Ernst Lubitsch production

CAST: Dr. Andre Bertier, **Maurice Chevalier**; Colette Bertier, **Jeanette MacDonald**; Mitzi Oliver, **Genevieve Tobin**; Adolph, **Charles Ruggles**; Professor Olivier, **Roland Young**; Mlle. Martel, **Josephine Dunn**; Detective, **Richard Carle**; Mitzi's Maid, **Barbara Leonard**; Police Commissioner, **George Barbier**// Party Guest, **Gordon Elliott.**

CREDITS: Directed, **Ernst Lubitsch**; Assistant Director, **George Cukor**; Cinematographer, **Victor Milner**; Gowns, **Travis Banton**; Interpolated Music, **Richard A. Whiting.**

SONGS: "Police Number" (Robin) — talked by **George Barbier** and **male chorus**; "What a Little Thing Like a Wedding Ring Can Do" (Robin and Straus) — sung by **Maurice Chevalier** and **Jeanette MacDonald**; "We Will Always Be Sweethearts" (Robin and Straus) — sung by **Jeanette MacDonald**; "Three Times a Day" (Robin and Straus) — sung by **Genevieve Tobin** and **Maurice Chevalier**; "One Hour with You" (Robin and Whiting) — sung by **Donald Novis, Genevieve Tobin, Maurice Chevalier, Charlie Ruggles** and **Jeanette MacDonald**; "Oh That Mitzi" (Robin and Straus) — sung by **Maurice Chevalier**; "We Will Always Be Sweethearts" (reprise) — sung by **Jeanette MacDonald** and **Maurice Chevalier**; "What Would You Do?" (Robin and Straus) — sung by **Maurice Chevalier.**

COLOR: Although primarily filmed in black and white, some indoor and daytime scenes are tinted yellow, while outdoor nighttime scenes are tinted blue.

RUNNING TIME: 80 min.

SOURCE: Play by **Lothar Schmidt.**

STORY: Into the happy married life of Maurice Chevalier and Jeanette MacDonald comes MacDonald's best friend, Genevieve Tobin. Although married to Roland Young, Tobin wants to add Chevalier to her list of conquests. Tobin is successful in making MacDonald believe Chevalier has been having affairs. MacDonald tells Chevalier to leave the house, a decision she immediately regrets. Chevalier spends the night with Tobin, which gets Young the information he needs to begin divorce proceedings. After Chevalier had left the house, MacDonald allowed Chevalier's best friend, Charlie Ruggles, to kiss her. Both finally admit their indiscretions to each other, and the couple stays together.

NOTES AND COMMENTARY: Gordon Elliott is a guest at a party held in the home of Chevalier and MacDonald. He can be seen dancing four times, first behind Chevalier and Josephine Dunn, then behind Chevalier and Tobin, next behind Chevalier and MacDonald, and finally behind the butler when Chevalier is on the patio.

REVIEWS: "Filled with scintillating wit of the Parisian variety." *New York Times*, 3/24/32; "A decidedly risqué comedy, a joyous success." *The Paramount Story*, Eames.

SUMMATION: A delightful, engaging musical comedy.

They're Screen Sweethearts Now ... and Scream Mates in This Daffy Laugh-Littered Comedy Hit!

Page Miss Glory

Warner Bros. (July 1935)

A Cosmopolitan Production

CAST: Loretta, **Marion Davies**; Click Wiley, **Pat O'Brien**; Bingo Nelson, **Dick Powell**; Gladys, **Mary Astor**; Ed Olson, **Frank McHugh**; Slattery, **Lyle Talbot**; Petey, **Allen Jenkins**; Blackie, **Barton McLane**; Betty, **Patsy Kelly**; Bonner, **Hobart Cavanaugh**; Mr. Freischutz, **Joseph Cawthorn**; Mr. Hamburgher, **Al Shean**; Yates, **Berton Churchill**; Mrs. Glory, **Helen Lowell**; Beauty Shop Operator, **Mary Treen**; Kimball, **Harry Beresford**; Metz, **Gavin Gordon**; Nick Papadopolis, **Lionel Stander**; Detective, **Joseph Crehan**// Reporter, **Gordon Elliott**.

CREDITS: Director, **Mervyn LeRoy**; Screenwriters, **Delmer Daves** and **Robert Lord**; Editor, **William Clemens**; Art Director, **Robert M. Haas**; Cinematographer, **George Folsey**; Costumes, **Orry-Kelly**; Musical Director, **Leo F. Forbstein**.

SONG: "Page Miss Glory" (Dubin and Warren)— sung by **orchestra leader**; "Page Miss Glory" (reprise)— sung by **Dick Powell**.

RUNNING TIME: 93 min.

SOURCE: Play by **Joseph Schrank** and **Phillip Dunning**.

STORY: To win a radio contest, promoter Pat O'Brien enters a photograph of a nonexistent person that he calls Miss Glory. O'Brien's entry wins, and reporters clamor for an interview. Daredevil aviator Dick Powell falls in love with the picture. O'Brien is forced to pass off Marion Davies, a chambermaid at O'Brien's hotel, as Miss Glory. Powell and Davies meet and immediately plan to marry. Hoodlums Barton McLane and Allen Jenkins kidnap Davies. Powell rescues Davies. Davies renounces her fame and fortune to be Powell's wife.

NOTES AND COMMENTARY: Gordon Elliott can be seen in four scenes as a reporter. First, Elliott is in the center of the scene as the reporters are badgering Pat O' Brien about interviewing Miss Glory; then Elliott bursts into O'Brien's hotel suite with other reporters to meet Miss Glory. Next, Elliott is one of the reporters pushed out of O'Brien's suite after the interview with Marion Davies; and finally, Elliott is present when O'Brien promises to produce Davies from a locked steamer trunk, only to find Allen Jenkins inside.

REVIEWS: "Good comedy entry." *Variety*, 9/4/35; "Some of *Page Miss Glory* is funny, some of it is not and a lot is speed and noise." *New York Times*, 8/29/35.

SUMMATION: A neat, entertaining comedy about deceptive publicity stunts.

It's the Cookies! You'll Go Crazy with Laughter at Eddie's Clowning Adventures in a Bakery Full of Beauties!

Palmy Days

United Artists (October, 1931)

Howard Productions; An Edward Sutherland production

CAST: Eddie Simpson, **Eddie Cantor**; Helen Martin, **Charlotte Greenwood**; Joan Clark, **Barbara Weeks**; Mr. Clark, **Spencer Charters**: Steve, **Paul Page**; Yolando, **Charles Middleton**; Joe, **George Raft**; Henchman, Harry Woods// Guest at Clark's Party, **Gordon Elliott**.

CREDITS: Director, **A. Edward Sutherland**; Producer, **Samuel Goldwyn**; Screenwriters, **Eddie Cantor, Morrie Ryskind, David Freedman** and **Keene Thompson**; Editor, **Sherman Todd**; Art Directors, **Richard Day** and **Willy Pogany**; Cinematographer, **Gregg Toland**;

Costumes, **Alice O'Neill**; Sound, **Vinton Vernon**; Musical Director, **Alfred Newman**; Choreographer, **Busby Berkeley**.

SONGS: "Bend Down, Sister" (Akst and Conrad)— sung by **Charlotte Greenwood**, and danced by **chorus**; "Jingle Bells" (Pierpont)— sung by **Charlotte Greenwood**; "Falling in Love Again"— sung by **Charlotte Greenwood**; "There's Nothing Too Good for My Baby" (Akst and Davis)— sung by **Eddie Cantor**; "Yes, Yes, My Baby Said Yes, Yes" (Akst and Conrad)— sung by **Eddie Cantor**, and danced by **chorus** (reprised by **Eddie Cantor** and **Charlotte Greenwood**).

RUNNING TIME: 77 min.

STORY: Phony psychic Charles Middleton advises bakery factory owner Spencer Charters to hire an efficiency expert, and tells Charlotte Greenwood, an employee of Charters, that the love of her life will come to her at the factory. Middleton sends his stooge, Eddie Cantor, to meet Greenwood, but Cantor doesn't want to marry Greenwood. Escaping her clutches, Cantor ends up in Charters' office and is hired as the efficiency expert. Middleton wants the $25,000 in Charters' safe, and he and his henchmen attempt to steal it. Through the efforts of Cantor and Greenwood, Middleton's efforts are thwarted. Cantor and Greenwood decide to marry.

NOTES AND COMMENTARY: Gordon Elliott plays a guest at Spencer Charters' party. As Cantor comes to the party, he and Elliott walk past each other. Then Cantor tries to tell Charters of Middleton's duplicity, and Elliott is at Charters' right arm. Elliott can be seen in the middle of the scene as Charters attempts to announce his daughter's engagement. When Cantor tries to show Charters the money in a loaf of bread, Elliott is in the scene.

REVIEWS: "Heavily hoked but made funny throughout whether for laughs or melodrama. Children will certainly like it." *Variety*, 9/29/31; "It's hokey and jokey but it never stops pleasing." *The Motion Picture Guide*, Nash and Ross.

SUMMATION: Very amusing musical comedy, with Eddie Cantor in top form.

Dorothy Mackaill Is Better Than Ever in This Story of a Noble Marriage Experiment That Went Wrong!

Party Husband

First National Pictures (April, 1931)

CAST: Laura, **Dorothy Mackaill**; Jay, **James Rennie**; Kate, **Dorothy Peterson**; Pat, **Joe Donahue**; Purcell, **Donald Cook**; Mrs. Duell, **Helen Ware**; Renard, **Paul Porcasi**; Bee Canfield, **Mary Doran**// Wedding Guest, **Gordon Elliott**.

CREDITS: Director, **Clarence Badger**; Screenwriter, **Charles Kenyon**; Editor, **Frank Ware**; Art Director, **John J. Hughes**; Cinematographer, **Sid Hickox**; Wardrobe, **Earl Luick**; Musical Conductor, **David Mendoza**.

RUNNING TIME: 73 min.

SOURCE: Novel, *Party Husband* by **Geoffrey Barnes**.

STORY: On their wedding day, Dorothy Mackaill and James Rennie declare they will have an open, modern marriage. Both Mackaill and Rennie are career-oriented and have friends of the opposite sex that they see late into the evening. Rennie has a one-night affair with Dorothy Peterson, and Mackaill pretends to have an affair with her employer, Donald Cook. Their actions almost ruin their marriage, but Mackaill's wise mother, Helen Ware, brings the couple back together.

NOTES AND COMMENTARY: Gordon Elliott has a brief role as a wedding guest. First, Elliott can be seen on the right side of the table at the wedding supper. Then Elliott is seen throwing rice at Mackaill and Rennie as they leave for their honeymoon. Finally, Elliott is prominent in the scene as the couple drive off.

REVIEWS: "A feeble attempt at sophisticated drawing room comedy-drama." *Variety*, 5/20/31; "Over talkative screenplay rammed home its point about the sanctity of the marriage vow and Badger directed competently." *The Warner Bros. Story*, Hirshhorn.

SUMMATION: Mildly amusing comedy-drama of a modern marriage experiment, thanks to Helen Ware's delightful performance.

Passion Song

Excellent Pictures (October, 1928)

CAST: Elaine Van Ryn, **Gertrude Olmstead**; John Van Ryn, **Noah Beery**; Keith Brooke, **Gordon Elliott**; Ulambo, **Blue Washington**.

CREDITS: Director, **Harry O. Hoyt**; Screenwriter, **Elizabeth Hayter**; Titles, **Camille Collins**; Editor, **Leonard Wheeler**; Cinematographer, **Andre Barlatier**.

RUNNING TIME: 60 min.

SOURCE: *Paid with Tears* by **Francis Fenton**.

STORY: Noah Beery, who became rich in South Africa, returns to England with his wife, Gertrude Olmstead. An old friend, Gordon Elliott, visits them. Elliott and Olmstead fall in love, but Olmstead remains faithful to Beery. Elliott goes back to Africa and becomes a bum. Blue Washington, an enemy of Beery's, starts an uprising. Berry comes to Africa to stop Washington. Washington kills Beery, and now Elliott and Olmstead can renew their romance.

NOTES AND COMMENTARY: Gordon Elliott receives third billing in this one, and ends up with leading lady Gertrude Olmstead.

Noah Beery would be featured in the Bill Elliott-Tex Ritter western feature *The Devil's Trail* (Columbia, 1942).

REVIEW: "Too weak for anything but the grinds or on a double bill." *Variety*, 3/20/29.

SUMMATION: This film was not available for viewing by the author.

These Blondes Pull No Punches in the Clinches When It Comes to The Payoff.

The Payoff

Warner Bros. (November, 1935)

A First National Picture

ALTERNATE TITLE: *The Real McCoy*.

CAST: Joe McCoy, **James Dunn**; Maxine, **Claire Dodd**; Connie, **Patricia Ellis**; Marty, **Alan Dinehart**; Harvey, **Joseph Crehan**; Jimmy, **Frankie Darro**; Gorman, **Frank Sheridan**; Beetles Davis, **Eddie Shubert**; Mike, **Al Hill**; Nick, **Paul Porcasi**; Hotel Desk Clerk, **George Humbert**//Maxine's Escort, **Gordon Elliott**.

CREDITS: Director, **Robert Florey**; Story, **George Bricker**; Screenwriter, **George Bricker** and **Joel Sayre**; Editor, **Harold McLernon**; Art Director, **Carl Jules Weyl**; Cinematographer, **Arthur L. Todd**; Gowns, **Orry-Kelly**; Musical Director, **Leo F. Forbstein**.

RUNNING TIME: 64 min.

STORY: Sportswriter James Dunn is promoted to sports columnist and makes an enemy of mobster Alan Dinehart. When traveling on the sports circuit, Dunn's wife, Claire Dodd, visits Dinehart's casino and the two become romantically involved. Dinehart is using Dodd to control Dunn's column. Dunn gives in to Dinehart to prevent Dodd from leaving him but loses his job. Dinehart dumps Dodd, since she's of no further use to him. Fellow sportswriter Patricia Ellis, who's in love with Dunn, and jockey Frankie Darro help Dunn write a story resulting in Dinehart's arrest. When Dinehart is released on bail, Dodd kills him and then commits suicide. Dunn realizes that he loves Ellis.

NOTES AND COMMENTARY: Gordon Elliott escorts Claire Dodd to Alan Dinehart's casino and introduces her to the thrill of gambling. His part ends when Dodd goes into Dinehart's office.

REVIEWS: "Unauthentic, but entertaining."

The Warner Bros. Story, Hirshhorn; "*The Payoff* is better than average James Dunn material and will get by with the family trade." *Variety*, 11/13/35.

SUMMATION: Quite good little "B" melodrama about corruption in the sports world, with a dynamic performance by James Dunn.

There Was a Sour Note in Love's Old Sweet Song!
The Boys Now Offer Happy Divorce!... Painless Alimony!... Separations That Satisfy! Why Worry?...
Trade Your Used Husband for a New Model! See Bert and Bob Now!

Peach-O-Reno

Radio Picture (December, 1931)

CAST: Wattles, **Bert Wheeler**; Swift, **Robert Woolsey**; Prudence, **Dorothy Lee**; Pansy, **Zelma O'Neal**; Joe Bruno, **Joseph Cawthorne**; Aggie Bruno, **Cora Witherspoon**; Judge Jackson, **Sam Hardy**; Crosby, **Mitchell Harris**; the Secretary, **Arthur Hoyt**; the Vamp, **Josephine Whittell**// Courtroom Spectator, **Gordon Elliott**.

CREDITS: Director, **William A. Seiter**; Producer, **William LeBaron**; Story, **Tim Whelan**; Screenwriters, **Ralph Spence, Eddie Welch** and **Tim Whelan**; Editor, **Jack Kitchin**; Art Director/Costumes, **Max Ree**; Cinematography, **Jack MacKenzie**; Sound, **George D. Ellis**; Supervisor, **John E. Burch**.

SONG: "From Niagara Falls to Reno" (Whiting, Akst and Clarke)—sung and danced by **Bert Wheeler** and **Dorothy Lee**.

RUNNING TIME: 63 min.

STORY: On their 25th wedding anniversary, Joseph Cawthorne and his wife, Cora Witherspoon, decide to seek a divorce in Reno, Nevada. Both go to the law film of Bert Wheeler and Robert Woolsey and become clients. Cawthorne and Witherspoon's daughters, Dorothy Lee and Zelma O'Neal, arrive to stop the divorce proceedings. In the courtroom, Cawthorne and Witherspoon decide to reunite. Wheeler and Lee fall in love, as does Woolsey and O'Neal. The two couples get married.

NOTES AND COMMENTARY: Before the start of the climactic courtroom scene, spectator Gordon Elliott can be scene talking to a beautiful young lady who is reclining on a courtroom railing. Elliott takes a look at her legs and smiles. Then Elliott can be seen seated in the courtroom, smoking a cigar and still talking to the young lady, as Wheeler and Woolsey make an appearance. Elliott joins in the applause for the two men.

REVIEWS: "Less than average on entertainment for the energetic pair [Wheeler and Woolsey]." *Variety*, 12/29/31; "The touch was hardly original, but, thanks to William Seiter's frolicsome direction, it did generate a certain amount of humor." *RKO Story*, Jewell and Harbin.

SUMMATION: Some minor enjoyment can be found in this comedy, which features a couple of very funny double-entendres.

Laughs! Throbs! Songs!

Peg o' My Heart

Metro-Goldwyn-Mayer (May, 1933)

A Robert Z. Leonard Production; A Cosmopolitan Production

CAST: Peg, **Marion Davies**; Jerry, **Onslow Stevens**; Pat, **J. Farrell MacDonald**; Ethel, **Juliette Compton**; Mrs. Chichester, **Irene Browne**; Alaric, **Tyrrell Davis**; Brent, **Alan Mowbray**; Mrs. Brent, **Doris Lloyd**; Jarvis, **Robert Greig**;

Smythe, **Nora Cecil**; Michael, **Mutt**; Terance, **Geoffrey Gill**// Fox Hunt Party Guest, **Gordon Elliott**.

CREDITS: Screenplay, **Frank R. Adams**; Adaptation, **Frances Marion**; Editor, **Margaret Booth**; Art Director, **Cedric Gibbons**; Cinematography, **George Barnes**; Gowns, **Adrian**; Musical Score, **Herbert Stothart**.

SONGS: "Sweetheart Darlin'" (Brown and Freed)—sung by **Marion Davies and chorus**; "I'll Remember You" (Stothart and Kahn)—sung by **Marion Davies and chorus**; medley ("A-Hunting We Will Go," "There Is a Tavern in the Town [Adams]," "Do You Know John Peel," "Sweetheart Darlin'"—sung by **Marion Davies and chorus**.

RUNNING TIME: 86 min.

SOURCE: Play, *Peg o' My Heart* by **J. Hartley Manners**.

STORY: Poor Irish lass Marion Davies inherits a sizable fortune on the condition she will live on an estate in England. Davies is to live with a conniving, snobbish family. Davies falls in love with her lawyer, Onslow Stevens. Finding nothing but disappointment living with the rich, Davies returns home. Stevens, realizing he's in love with Davies, follows, and the two decide to marry.

NOTES AND COMMENTARY: Gordon Elliott has the role of a fox hunting guest, and can be seen on the right as Marion Davies leads the group in song.

REVIEWS: "Marion Davies had a stab at the famous Laurette Taylor role and made a good job of it; Leonard directed for the masses and got 'em." *The M-G-M Story*, Eames; "It has charm and entertainment, even though one might hesitate to say all the characters are natural." *The New York Times*, 5/20/33.

SUMMATION: The journey may be predictable, but Marion Davies makes the trip a pleasure.

She Makes Gossip Columnists Turn Green with Envy ... and Will Your Face Be Red as This Intimate Confidante of Debutantes Spills the Low-Down on Society's Higher Upper Crust in Personal Maid's Secret.

Personal Maid's Secret

Warner Bros. (October, 1935)

ALTERNATE TITLE: *Living Up to Lizzie*.

CAST: Joan, **Margaret Lindsay**; Jimmy, **Warren Hull**; Diana, **Anita Louise**; Lizzie, **Ruth Donnelly**; Owen, **Arthur Treacher**; Kent, **Frank Albertson**; Mr. Wilton Palmer, **Henry O'Neill**; Bobby, **Ronnie Cosby**; Warren Sherrill, **Gordon Elliott**.

CREDITS: Director, **Arthur Greville Collins**; Story, **Lillian Day**; Screenwriters, **Lillie Hayward** and **F. Hugh Herbert**; Editor, **Thomas Richards**; Art Director, **Carl Jules Weyl**; Cinematographer, **Byron Haskin**; Costumes, **Orry-Kelly**; Musical Director, **Leo F. Forbstein**.

RUNNING TIME: 58 min.

STORY: Ruth Donnelly takes a job as maid and housekeeper to Margaret Lindsay and Warren Hull. Through Donnelly's suggestions, Hull's career takes off, and Hull and Lindsay begin to climb the social ladder. Lindsay's brother, Frank Albertson, falls in love with socialite Anita Louise, who is seeing a married man, Gordon Elliott. Donnelly reveals to Louise that she is really her mother and tries to convince her to stop seeing Elliott. At first resistant, Louise begins to love Donnelly, and finally realizes Albertson is the right man for her.

NOTES AND COMMENTARY: Gordon Elliott plays a married "ladykiller" who dates Anita Louise and tries to romance Margaret Lindsay. In one scene, Elliott gets to kiss Louise.

REVIEWS: "Amusing light comedy-drama notable for Ruth Donnelly's outstanding performance." *Variety*, 12/11/35; "A pleasant filler." *The Warner Bros. Story*, Hirshhorn.

SUMMATION: Ruth Donnelly is a delight in this very good comedy-drama about mother love in high society. Gordon Elliott turns in a nice performance as a "ladykiller."

Personal Maid's Secret (Warner Bros., 1935). *Top*—Anita Louise (right) becomes fond of Frank Albertson (left), to the obvious displeasure of Gordon Elliott (center). *Bottom*— Anita Louise (right) has been seeing the married Gordon Elliott (left).

It Flames with the Spirit of Youth ... Clara Bow in a Sensational Picturization of the Modern College Girl and Her Companions

Plastic Age

Commonwealth Pictures (December, 1925)

CAST: Hugh Carver, **Donald Keith**; Cynthia Day, **Clara Bow**; Mrs. Carver, **Mary Alden**; Henry Carver, **Henry B. Walthall**; Carl Peters, **Gilbert Roland**; James Henley, **David Butler**// Road House Patron, **Gordon Elliott**.

CREDITS: Director, **Wesley Ruggles**; Producer, **B.P. Schulberg**; Adaptation, **Eve Unsell** and **Frederica Sagor**; Continuity, **Wesley Ruggles** and **Eve Unsell**; Cinematographers, **Al Siegler** and **Gilbert Warrenton**.

SONG: "All Alone" (Berlin)— lyrics and sheet music are shown to the audience when Donald Keith is forced to sing the song.

Color: Tinted yellow for most scenes, and tinted blue for outdoor night scenes.

RUNNING TIME: 73 min.

SOURCE: Novel by **Percy Marks**.

STORY: Star athlete Donald Keith becomes a freshman at Prescott College, where he meets and falls in love with Clara Bow. His relationship with Bow causes Keith to suffer low grades and poor performances on the athletic field. Bow, even though in love with Keith, breaks up with him to keep him away from the party scene. Classmate Gilbert Roland, jealous of Bow's affection for Keith and Keith's athletic prowess, deliberately injures Keith in football practice. Keith starts the big game but is further injured and replaced by Roland. With his team losing, and with just a few minutes left to play, Keith recovers enough to go back into the game. With seconds left, Keith intercepts a pass and races for the winning touchdown as the game ends. Roland, realizing he's been wrong in his actions towards Keith, tells him Bow is no longer a party girl and that she still loves him. Keith and Bow get back together.

NOTES AND COMMENTARY: This is Gordon Elliott's first screen appearance. He can be seen in the roadhouse sequence as Donald Keith and Gilbert Roland fight. As the fight starts, Elliott comes into the scene from the right, watches the fight for a few moments, and then, along with several others, tries to stop the fight.

REVIEWS: "An interesting afternoon's entertainment, largely because of Clara Bow." *New York Times*, 7/19/26; "The picture holds up nicely, largely because of Bow's charming performance." *Motion Picture Guide*, Nash and Ross.

SUMMATION: Interesting college melodrama with a sexy Clara Bow.

All the Laughs You've Hungered for ... Heart-Throbs You Ached to Feel! Romance Whose Tenderness Brings a Joyous Tear.

Platinum Blonde

Columbia (October, 1931)

A Frank R. Capra Production

ALTERNATE TITLE: *Gallagher*.

CAST: Gallagher, **Loretta Young**; Stew Smith, **Robert Williams**; Ann Schuyler, **Jean Harlow**; Butler, **Halliwell Hobbs**; Grayson, **Reginald Owen**; Conroy, **Edmund Breese**; Michael Schuyler, **Donald Dillaway**; Bingy, **Walter Catlett**; Valet, **Claud Allister**; Mrs. Schuyler, **Louise Closser Hale**// Flyer, **Gordon Elliott**.

CREDITS: Director, **Frank R. Capra**; Producer, **Harry Cohn**; Screenwriters, **Harry Chandlee**, **Douglas W. Churchill**, **Robert Riskin**, **Jo Swerling** and **Dorothy Howell**; Editor, **Gene Milford**; Cinematographer, **Joseph Walker**.

RUNNING TIME: 90 min.

STORY: Star reporter Robert Williams and socialite Jean Harlow wed, to the disappointment of reporter Loretta Young, who's in love with Williams. Harlow's attempt to turn Williams into a gentleman in high society leads to divorce. Williams finally realizes Young is the woman for him, and they plan to marry.

NOTES AND COMMENTARY: Gordon Elliott, as a round-the-world flyer, has one scene with Jean Harlow. After Elliott helps Harlow on with her coat, we find that Harlow has been parading Elliott around to speak at various functions. In return, Elliott has taken a romantic interest in Harlow and would like to spend time alone with her.

REVIEWS: "A mildly successful venture on the side of light entertainment." *The New York Times*, 10/31/31; "One of the better 'newspaper' comedies." *The Motion Picture Guide*, Nash and Ross.

SUMMATION: Though a lesser Capra film, *Platinum Blonde* is still mildly interesting and amusing, with Robert Williams a standout.

It's a 10-Goal Show! How You'll Howl and Scream! When You See Joe Brown as a One-Man Team!

Polo Joe

Warner Bros. (November, 1936)

CAST: Joe Bolton, **Joe E. Brown**; Mary Hilton, **Carol Hughes**; Haywood, **Richard "Skeets" Gallagher**; Colonel Hilton, **Joe King**; Don Trumbeau, **Gordon Elliott**; Aunt Minnie, **Fay Holden**; First Hoodlum, **George E. Stone**; Mrs. Hilton, **Olive Tell**; Jack Hilton, **David Newell**; Marker, **Milton Kibbee**; Bert, **Frank Orth**; Rusty, **John Kelly**; Second Hoodlum, **Charles Foy**.

CREDITS: Director, **William McGann**; Screenwriters, **Peter Milne** and **Hugh Cummings**; Editor, **Clarence Kolster**; Art Director, **Roland Hill**; Cinematography, **L. Wm. O'Connell**; Costumes, **Orry-Kelly**; Musical Director, **Leo F. Forbstein**.

RUNNING TIME: 65 min.

STORY: To win Carol Hughes, Joe E. Brown, who is allergic to horses, declares that he is a major polo star. When Brown finally has to play, he single-handedly wins the game — and Hughes.

NOTES AND COMMENTARY: Gordon Elliott receives fifth billing and has an important role in the film. Elliott is Joe E. Brown's rival for Carol Hughes' affections. Elliott is on horseback in his initial scene as he, Carol Hughes and other cast members are introduced to Brown. At the dinner party held for Brown, Elliott is goaded into using chopsticks, only to have the food drop into his lap. Elliott is upset when Brown is picked to play in a crucial polo game instead of him. Elliott picks a highly spirited horse for Brown to ride, which backfires when Brown is able to stay in the saddle. Elliott overhears Brown admit to his valet, Richard "Skeets" Gallagher, that he can't play polo, and that they intend to stage a phony kidnapping to keep Brown from the game. Finally, Elliott is injured in the game, which allows Brown to become a star and win both the game and Hughes.

REVIEWS: "*Polo Joe* is one of the poorer of the comedian's vehicles, and Brown's followers, no matter how faithful, will be disappointed in him this time out." *Variety*, 11/11/36; "Another gigantic cliché from which no-one emerged with credit." *The Warner Bros. Story*, Hirshhorn.

SUMMATION: This is Joe E. Brown at a low ebb. The film is not very funny nor original. Gordon Elliott does a nice job as Brown's rival for Carol Hughes' affections.

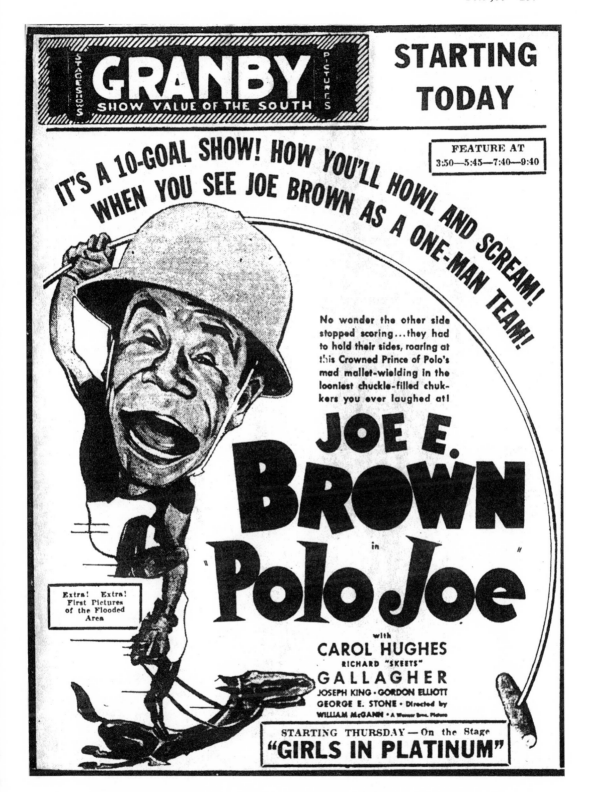

Polo Joe (Warner Bros., 1936). Elliott received fifth billing in the ad.

Back to the Type of Role That Made Him the Idol of Millions!
A Scoundrel You'll Love, with a Ravishing New Screen Sweetheart!

Private Detective 62

Warner Bros. (July, 1933)

ALTERNATE TITLES: *Man Killer* and *Private Detective*.

CAST: Free, **William Powell**; Janet, **Margaret Lindsay**; Amy, **Ruth Donnelly**; Bandor, **Gordon Westcott**; Hogan, **Arthur Hoyl**; Mrs. Burns, **Natalie Morehead**; Whitey, **James Bell**; Burns, **Hobart Cavanaugh**; Cab Driver, **Irving Bacon**// Gambler, **Gordon Elliott**.

CREDITS: Director, **Michael Curtiz**; Story, **Raoul Whitfield**; Screenplay, **Rian James**; Editor, **Harold McLernon**; Art Director, **Jack Okey**; Cinematography, **Tony Gaudio**; Gowns, **Orry-Kelly**; Dialogue Director, **Arthur Greville Collins**; Musical Conductor, **Leo F. Forbstein**.

RUNNING TIME: 67 min.

STORY: Kicked out of the French Secret Service, William Powell becomes a partner with Arthur Hoyl in a seedy private detective agency in New York. Hoyl makes a secret arrangement with gambler Gordon Westcott to financially back the agency. One of Wescott's clients, Margaret Lindsay, has become a big winner at the club, and Westcott wants Hoyl to frame Lindsay so she can't collect the money. Powell is assigned to the job. Powell meets Lindsay and the two fall in love — until she learns that Powell is a detective. Desperate, Hoyl concocts a scheme in which Lindsay believes she shot Westcott. Then a shot rings out, killing Westcott for real, and the money meant for Lindsay is stolen. Lindsay goes to Powell for help. While investigating the crime scene, an attempt is made on Powell's life. Powell's sleuthing brings him to Hoyl's minion, James Bell. Bell is forced to admit he murdered Wescott at Hoyl's direction. Powell has Hoyl arrested as Hoyl is attempting to blackmail Lindsay. Powell is reinstated in the French Secret Service. Lindsay proposes to Powell so she can travel with him. Powell joyously accepts.

NOTES AND COMMENTARY: Gordon Elliott is seen briefly at the roulette table, smoking a cigarette and watching Margaret Lindsay gamble.

REVIEWS: "*Private Detective 62* is a hearty melodrama and Mr. Powell is excellent in it." *New York Times*, 7/7/33; "There are holes in the script that a semi-truck could drive through, but Powell makes it worthwhile." *Motion Picture Guide*, Nash and Ross.

SUMMATION: A bright, sparkling melodrama with a deft performance by Powell.

She Weakened the Stronger Sex!

Private Life of Helen of Troy

First National (December, 1927)

ALTERNATE TITLE: *Helen of Troy*.

CAST: Helen, **Maria Corda**; Menelaus, **Lewis Stone**; Paris, **Ricardo Cortez**; Eteoneus, **George Fawcett**; Adraste, **Alice White**; Telemachus, **Gordon Elliott**; Ulysses, **Tom O'Brien**; Achilles, **Bert Sprotte**; Ajax, **Mario Carillo**; Malapokitoratoreadetos; **Charles Puffy**; Hector, **George Kotsonaros**; Aeneas, **Constantine Romanoff**; Sarpedon, **Emilio Borgato**; Aphrodite, **Alice Adair**; Athena, Helen **Fairweather**; Hera, **Virginia Thomas**.

CREDITS: Director, **Alexander Korda**; Producer/Adapter/Screenwriter, **Carey Wilson**; Titles, **Ralph Spence**, **Gerald Duffy** and **Casey Robinson**; Editor, **Harold Young**; Cinematographers, **Lee Garmes** and **Sid Hickox**; Costumes, **Max Ree**; Music, **Carl Edourade**.

RUNNING TIME: 87 min.

SOURCE: Book, *The Private Life of Helen of Troy* by **John Erskine**, and *The Road to Rome, a Play* by **Robert Emmett Sherwood**.

STORY: Maria Corda, who is no longer in love with her husband, Lewis Stone, decides to go with Ricardo Cortez to Sparta. Stone decides to bring Corda back to Troy. Through the use of a gigantic wooden horse, soldiers gain entrance to the city, and Stone is reunited with Corda. On their return to Troy, Corda begins to flirt with a new suitor. This time Stone is re-solved to go fishing instead of following Corda.

NOTES AND COMMENTARY: Gordon Elliott receives fifth billing in this film.

REVIEWS: "The combination of 1927 colloquialisms and ideas with the replicas of ancient settings and modes makes this film most amusing." *New York Times*, 12/10/27; "A program plum. It's well made, lively and funny." *Variety*, 12/14/27.

SUMMATION: This film was not available for viewing by the author.

"Hiding in a Glare of Light" ... He Fought the Powers of Darkness! Romantic! Daring! Glamorous!

Public Defender

RKO (August, 1931)

ALTERNATE TITLES: *Million Dollar Swindle* and *The Reckoner*.

CAST: Pike Winslow, **Richard Dix**; Barbara Gerry, **Shirley Grey**; John Kirk, **Purnell Pratt**; Rose Harmer, **Ruth Weston**; Wells, **Edmund Breese**; Charles Harmer, **Frank Sheridan**; Inspector Malcolm O'Neil, **Alan Roscoe**; Professor, **Boris Karloff**; Aunt Matilda, **Nella Walker**; Doc, **Paul Hurst**; Cyrus Pringle, **Carl Gerard**; Detective Brady, **Robert Emmet O'-Connor**, Eugene Gerry, **Phillips Smalley**// Guest at Country Club, **Gordon Elliott**.

CREDITS: Director, **J. Walter Ruben**; Producer, **William LeBaron**; Associate Producer, **Louis Sarecky**; Adaptation and Dialogue, **Bernard Schubert**; Editor, **Archie F. Marshek**; Scenery and Costumes, **Max Ree**; Cinematography, **Edward Cronjager**; Sound, **John E. Tribby**.

RUNNING TIME: 70 min.

SOURCE: Story, "The Splendid Crime" by **George Goodchild**.

STORY: Richard Dix learns that Shirley Grey's father has been unjustly convicted of a crime. Under the guise of the Reckoner, and with help from his aides, Boris Karloff and Paul Hurst, Dix reveals Purnell Pratt as the primary guilty party.

NOTES AND COMMENTARY: In one brief scene, Gordon Elliott can be seen getting up from a table at the country club as Richard Dix walks by to meet with Purnell Pratt, Frank Sheridan and Carl Gerard.

REVIEWS: "It has entertainment qualities for every class of fan." *Variety*, 8/4/31; "This is a nicely paced thriller with some fine acting by the cast." *Motion Picture Guide*, Nash and Ross.

SUMMATION: This is a first-rate, exciting crime melodrama with·fine performances by Richard Dix, Boris Karloff, Paul Hurst and Purnell Pratt.

A High Speed Romance of Today. The "Doug" You Used to Know!

Reaching for the Moon

United Artists (December, 1930)
Presented by Joseph M. Schenck
CAST: Larry Day, **Douglas Fairbanks**; Vivian Benton, **Bebe Daniels**; Roger, **Edward Everett Horton**; Horace Partington Chelmsford, **Claud Allister**; Jimmy Carrington, **Jack Mulhall**; James Benton, **Walter Walker**; Kitty, **June MacCloy**; Day's Secretary, **Helen Jerome Eddy**; Singer, **Bing Crosby**// Ship Passenger, **Gordon Elliott**.

CREDITS: Director/Screenwriter, **Edmund Goulding**; Assistant Director, **Lonnie D'Orsa**; Story, **Irving Berlin**; Additional Dialogue, **Elsie Janis**; Editors, **Lloyd Nosler** and **Hal C. Kern**; Set Decorations, **Julia Heron**; Settings, **William Cameron Menzies**; Cinematographers, **Ray June** and **Robert Planck**; Sound, **Oscar Lagerstrom** and **Theodore Reed**; Fashions, **David Cox**; Musical Director, **Alfred Newman**.

SONGS: "When the Folks High-Up Do the Mean Low-Down" (Berlin)—sung by **Bing Crosby**, **Bebe Daniels** and **June MacCloy**; "Reaching for the Moon" (Berlin).

RUNNING TIME: 90 min.

STORY: Wealthy financial tycoon Douglas Fairbanks' lifestyle consists of no alcohol, parties or women, and an early bedtime. Bebe Daniels makes a bet with one of Fairbanks' associates that she can get Fairbanks interested in her within the twenty-four-hour period before she sails for England. Daniels is successful and stands Fairbanks up on their date. Fairbanks gains access to the ship and begins pursuing Daniels. Daniels first rejects Fairbanks but then realizes she loves him. Fairbanks and Daniels wed.

NOTES AND COMMENTARY: *Reaching for the Moon* features another brief appearance by Gordon Elliott. After Douglas Fairbanks and Bebe Daniels leave the ship's bar, Elliott can be seen on the couple's left with a group of ship's passengers saying good night.

REVIEWS: "The picture is just fair." *Variety*, 1/7/31; "The script is weak, with most of the humor consisting of overused sight gags." *Motion Picture Guide*, Nash and Ross.

SUMMATION: A mildly amusing comedy with a nifty number sung by Bing Crosby, Bebe Daniels and June MacCloy.

The Picture with Everything! Breath-Taking Romance! Music! ... Melodrama!

Reckless

Metro-Goldwyn-Mayer (April, 1935)
CAST: Mona, **Jean Harlow**; Ned Riley, **William Powell**; Bob Harrison, **Franchot Tone**; Granny, **May Robson**; Smiley, **Ted Healy**; Blossom, **Nat Pendleton**; Jo, **Rosalind Russell**; Eddie, **Mickey Rooney**; Harrison, **Henry Stephenson**; Himself, **Man Mountain Dean**; Paul Mercer, **Robert Light**; Allan, **Allan Jones**; Himself, **Carl Randall**; Louise, **Louise Henry**; Dale Every, **James Ellison**; Herself, **Nina Mae McKinney**; Ralph Watson, **Leon Ames**; Gold Dust, **Farina**.

CREDITS: Director, **Victor Fleming**; Producer, **David O. Selznick**; Story, **Oliver Jeffries**; Screenplay, **P.J. Wolfson**; Editor, **Margaret Booth**; Art Directors, **Cedric Gibbons**, **Merrill Pye** and **Edwin B. Willis**; Cinematographer, **George Folsey**; Gowns, **Adrian**; Musical Conductor, **Victor Baravalle**; Choreographers, **Chester Hale** and **Carl Randall**; Synchronization, **Herbert Stothart**.

SONGS: "Reckless" (Kern and Hammerstein II)—sung by **Jean Harlow** and **Nina Mae McKinney**, and danced by **Jean Harlow** and **Rafael Storm**; "Trocadero" (Lane and Adamson)—sung by **Jean Harlow** and **Allan Jones**, and danced by **Jean Harlow** and **Carl Randall**; "Ev'rything's Been Done Before" (King, Knopf and Adamson)—sung by **Allan Jones**, and danced by **Jean Harlow**; "Reckless" (reprise)—danced by **Jean Harlow**; "Hear What My Heart Is Saying" (Lane and Adamson)—sung by **Jean Harlow**; "Reckless" (reprise)—sung by **Jean Harlow**. (Note: **Virginia Verrill** dubbed **Harlow**.)

STORY: Socialite Franchot Tone is infatuated with Broadway singer Jean Harlow. They meet, fall in love and elope. Harlow is unaware her best friend, William Powell, is in love with her and wanted to marry her but couldn't find the words. When Tone's jilted fiancée, Rosalind Russell, marries someone else, Tone realizes he really loves her and tells Russell that Harlow trapped him into marriage. This statement is overheard by Harlow and Powell. Not knowing where to go, Harlow goes to Powell's hotel suite to wait for Tone to show up. Harlow tells Powell she's pregnant and wants to remain married to Tone. A drunken Tone arrives but won't go home, so Powell gives Tone his bed. As Powell and Harlow go into the parlor, Tone commits suicide, not knowing he was to be a father. A scandal results, with Harlow and Powell accused of murder, but they are exonerated. Harlow has her baby and renounces any claim to Tone's fortune. Harlow needs to return to the stage to be able to care for her child. Bad publicity from the upper classes makes producers hesitant to star Harlow in a show. Powell raises enough money to produce a show with Harlow. On opening night, the society folks attempt to interrupt her performance, but Harlow talks to the audience and wins them over. As Harlow performs her second number, Powell proposes marriage and Harlow accepts.

NOTES AND COMMENTARY: Gordon Elliott is reported to have a role as a reporter in the film, but his scene(s) ended up on the cutting room floor. Others actors and musical numbers met the same fate.

REVIEWS: "A stale and profitless meringue of backstage routines and high society amour." *New York Times*, 4/25/35; "Haphazard backstage-meller-musical. Below par." *Variety*, 4/24/35.

SUMMATION: This not particularly distinguished M-G-M musical does manage to hold the interest due to the talents of William Powell and May Robson.

The World Will Never Know Her Name ... But It Will Always Remember Her Story!

Registered Nurse

First National Pictures (June, 1934)

CAST: Sylvia Benton, **Bebe Daniels**; Dr. Connolly, **Lyle Talbot**; Dr. Hedwig, **John Halliday**; Sadie, **Irene Franklin**; Sylvestrie, **Sidney Toler**; Jim, **Gordon Westcott**; Schloss, **Minna Gombell**; McKenna, **Beulah Bondi**; Jerry, **Vince Barnett**; Bill, **Phillip Reed**; Hammond, **Mayo Methot**; Smithy, **Renee Whitney**; Dixon, **Virginia Sale**; Dickie, **Ronnie Cosby**; Pat O' Brien, **Edward Gargan**; Interne, **Gordon Elliott**; Bonelli, **George Humbert**.

CREDITS: Director, **Robert Florey**; Screenwriters, **Lillie Hayward** and **Peter Milne**; Editor, **Jack Killifer**; Art Director, **Robert M. Haas**; Cinematographer, **Sid Hickox**; Gowns, **Orry-Kelly**; Musical Conductor, **Leo F. Forbstein**; Dialogue Director, **Arthur Greville Collins**.

RUNNING TIME: 63 min.

SOURCE: Play by **Florence Johns** and **Wilton Lackaye, Jr.**

STORY: Bebe Daniels is planning to divorce Gordon Westcott. As they're arguing in the car, Westcott loses control and the car crashes into a tree. Daniels resumes her nursing career at City Hospital in New York City. Lyle Talbot and John Halliday romantically pursue Daniels. Daniels finally tells Talbot that she's married and cannot divorce Westcott because he's violently insane. In a lucid moment, Westcott comes to the hospital in hopes an operation can be performed to restore his sanity. Westcott finds he's in the way of Daniels' happiness and commits suicide. Daniels realizes that Talbot just wants her as a romantic conquest, while

Halliday loves her and wants to marry her. Daniels decides her life will be happy with Halliday.

NOTES AND COMMENTARY: Gordon Elliott has a number of scenes with more lines of dialogue than usual at this point in his career. Elliott first tells doctors John Halliday and Lyle Talbot about Sidney Toler and his broken leg. He's present in the operating room when Toler's leg is set. Next, Elliott comes into Toler's room when wrestlers Tor Johnson and Harry Ekezian are fighting. At Minna Gombell and Edward Gargan's engagement party, Elliott, while dancing with Mayo Methot, romances her by telling of a nasty appendix operation. Finally, Elliott asks Toler why he was in Gordon Westcott's room. He then preps Westcott for his impending operation. Then he tells Halliday he couldn't stop Westcott from leaping from his window to his death.

REVIEWS: "Good acting and atmosphere cannot overcome story handicaps." *Variety*, 6/5/34.

"Highly improbable plot." *The Warner Bros. Story*, Hirshhorn.

SUMMATION: Daniels infuses this unremarkable drama of hospital life, with enough energy to get by. Elliott does fine as a sometimes bewildered interne.

A Problem of Modern Youth.

Restless Youth

Columbia (November, 1928)

CAST: Dixie Calhoun, **Marceline Day**; Bruce Neil, **Ralph Forbes**; John Neil, **Norman Trevor**; Robert Haines, **Robert Ellis**; Susan, **Mary Mabery**; George Baxter, **Gordon Elliott**.

CREDITS: Director, **Christy Cabanne**; Assistant Director, **Buddy Coleman**; Adaptation, **Howard Green**; Editor, **Ben Pivar**; Art Director, **Harrison Wiley**; Cinematographer, **Joe Walker**.

RUNNING TIME: 65 min.

SOURCE: "Restless Youth" by **Cosmo Hamilton**.

STORY: Marceline Day is expelled from college and becomes secretary to lawyer Ralph Forbes. The two fall in love and plan to marry. Forbes' father, District Attorney Norman Trevor, disapproves of the romance and persuades Day to leave Forbes. A clerk at an employment agency tries to force himself on Day, and Day kills him while defending herself. Day is arrested for murder, and Trevor tries to convict her. Forbes takes over as Day's lawyer and wins a not-guilty verdict. Day and Forbes resume their romance.

NOTES AND COMMENTARY: In his first film at Columbia Studios, Gordon Elliott receives sixth billing.

REVIEW: "Nonsense? Perhaps." *New York Times*, 1/1/29.

SUMMATION: This film was not available for viewing by the author.

Paramount's New Thriller from Sax Rohmer's Latest Mystery!

The Return of Dr. Fu Manchu

Paramount (May, 1930)

A Rowland V. Lee production; B.P. Schulberg, general manager, West Coast Productions

ALTERNATE TITLE: *New Adventures of Dr. Fu Manchu*.

CAST: Doctor Fu Manchu, **Warner Oland**; Nayland Smith, **O.P. Heggie**; Lia Eltham, **Jean Arthur**; Jack Petrie, **Neil Hamilton**; Lady Agatha Bartley, **Evelyn Hall**; Sylvester Wadsworth, **William Austin**; Lady Helen Bartley, **Margaret Fealy**; Inspector Harding, **Shayle Gardner**; Fai Lu, **Evelyn Selbie**// Wedding Guest, **Gordon Elliott**.

CREDITS: Director, **Rowland V. Lee**; Producer, **B. P. Schulberg**; Screenwriters, **Florence Ryerson** and **Lloyd Corrigan**; Cinematographer, **Archie Stout**.

RUNNING TIME: 71 min.

SOURCE: Novel, *The Return of Dr. Fu Manchu* by **Sax Rohmer**.

STORY: Warner Oland plans to murder Neil Hamilton to avenge the death of his wife and son. His plan is thwarted by the quick action of Scotland Yard Inspector O.P. Heggie.

Heggie pushes Oland and his explosive device into the Thames. Oland is presumed dead.

NOTES AND COMMENTARY: Gordon Elliott, as a wedding guest, comes to the altar as Evelyn Selbie collapses and dies.

Director Rowland V. Lee and Producer B.P. Schulberg did not receive on-screen credit.

REVIEW: "Melodramatic as the film is, it is not quite as exciting as its predecessor, *The Mysterious Fu Manchu. The New York Times*, 5/3/30.

SUMMATION: This is an interesting and above-average melodrama about the famous Dr. Fu Manchu.

Not Just a Premier — It's an Event! Don't Dare Miss Your Chance to See the New Ruth Chatterton.

The Rich Are Always with Us

First National Pictures (June, 1932)

CAST: Caroline, **Ruth Chatterton**; Julian, **George Brent**; Malbro, **Bette Davis**; Greg, **John Miljan**; Allison, **Adrienne Dore**; Davis, **John Wray**; Doctor Derwin, **Robert Warwick**; Dante, **Walter Walker**; Flo, **Virginia Hammond**; Judge Bradshaw, **Berton Churchill**// Party Guest, **Gordon Elliott**.

CREDITS: Director, **Alfred E. Green**; Screenwriter, **Austin Parker**; Editor, **George Marks**; Art Director, **Jack Okey**; Cinematographer, **Ernest Haller**; Musical Conductor, **Leo F. Forbstein**.

SONG: "What a Life, Trying to Live Without You."

RUNNING TIME: 73 min.

SOURCE: Novel, *The Rich Are Always with Us* by **E. Pettit**.

STORY: Wealthy Ruth Chatterton, married to John Miljan, is being pursued ardently by writer George Brent. Miljan is having an affair with Adrienne Dore. Chatterton's friend, Bette Davis, is in love with Brent, to no avail. Witnessing Miljan and Dore in a passionate embrace, Chatterton divorces Miljan, and Miljan marries Dore. Chatterton and Brent are in love, but Chatterton is not ready for marriage. Finally, at a party at Davis' estate, Chatterton and

Brent realize they can't live without each other. They spend the night together, which is observed by Dore. Through the efforts of Davis and Miljan, Dore is prevented from spreading gossip about the couple. Miljan and Dore leave, angry at each other. Their car leaves the road, hitting a tree, killing Dore and severely injuring Miljan. Chatterton feels an obligation to stay with Miljan through his crisis. Brent thinks Chatterton is choosing Miljan over him. To allay his fears, Chatterton immediately marries Brent and promises to come to him when Miljan has recovered.

NOTES AND COMMENTARY: Gordon Elliott is a party guest at Ruth Chatterton's estate. Elliott can be seen talking at the party, at the roulette table, at the bar and finally while dancing, when he remarks to Ruth Chatterton, "Lovely, Caroline."

REVIEWS: "It results in being mildly diverting, owing to Miss Chatterton's charming performance and the competent acting of others." *New York Times*, 5/16/32; "A moderately diverting trifle." *The Warner Bros. Story*, Hirshhorn.

SUMMATION: Thanks to Ruth Chatterton's sparkling performance, this turns out to be a very entertaining story.

*What a Cast!— And What a Story They Unfold, a Story of Marital
Love and Hate, of Drama and Comedy.*

Road to Reno

Paramount (October, 1931)

CAST: Mrs. Jackie Millet, **Lilyan Tashman**; Tom Wood, **Charles "Buddy" Rogers**; Lee Millet, **Peggy Shannon**; Jerry Kenton, **William Boyd**; Robert Millet, **Irving Pichel**; Mrs. It-Ritch, **Wynne Gibson**; Hoppie, **Richard "Skeets" Gallagher**; Jeff Millet, **Tom Douglas**; Elsie Kenton, **Judith Wood**; Mrs. Stafford Howes, **Leni Stengel**; Andre, **Emile Chautard**// Gigolo, **Gordon Elliott**.

CREDITS: Director, **Richard Wallace**; Story, **Virginia Kellogg**; Screenwriters, **Josephine Lovett** and **Brian Marlow**; Cinematographer, **Karl Struss**.

RUNNING TIME: 74 min.

STORY: Lillian Tashman decides to travel to Reno to divorce her current husband, Irving Pichel, to the displeasure of her children, Peggy Shannon and Tom Douglas. En route, Tash-man meets William Boyd and becomes attracted to him. Boyd romances both Tashman and Shannon. Feeling that Boyd will ruin the lives of Tashman and Shannon, Douglas shoots Boyd and then commits suicide. Tashman returns to Pichel, and Shannon resumes her romance with Charles "Buddy" Rogers.

NOTES AND COMMENTARY: It has been noted that Gordon Elliott plays the role of a gigolo in this production.

REVIEWS: "Plot is most artificial and hence it's a picture for the combo spots." *Variety*, 10/13/31; "A merry screen entertainment is to be expected, but it happens that the production is not a little disappointing." *New York Times*, 10/10/31.

SUMMATION: This film was not available for viewing by the author.

*Ride 'Em Cowboy!
... and Sing as You Ride!
A New Kind of Zane Gray Hero, Shooting His Way Through
Blazing Adventure ... Routing Rustlers with His Six-Guns.*

Roll Along Cowboy

20th Century–Fox (October, 1937)

A Principal Production

CAST: Randy Porter, **Smith Ballew**; Janet Blake, **Cecilia Parker**; Barry Barker, **Stanley Fields**; Mrs. Blake, **Ruth Robinson**; Danny, **Wally Albright**; Hathaway, **Frank Milan**; Fenton, **Gordon Elliott**; Shorty, **Budd Buster**; Shep, **Harry Bernard**; **Buster Fite and the Saddle Tramps**.

CREDITS: Director, **Gus Meins**; Assistant Director, **William McGaugh**; Producer, **Sol Lesser**; Screenplay, **Daniel Jarrett**; Editors, **Arthur Hilton** and **Albert Jordan**; Art Director, **Lewis J. Rachmil**; Cinematographer, **Harry Neumann**; Wardrobe, **Jerry Bos**; Sound, **Tom Carman**; Music Supervisor, **Abe Meyer**.

SONGS: "Roll Along Ride 'Em Cowboy Roll Along" (Porter and Womack) — sung by **Smith Ballew** and **chorus**; "Take Me Back to My Boots and Saddles" (Samuel, Whitcup and Powell) — sung by **Smith Ballew**; "The Old Chisholm Trail" (traditional) — sung by **Smith Ballew**; "She Tickles My Jaw" — sung by **Smith Ballew**, **Wally Albright** and **Stanley Fields**; "On the Sunny Side of the Rockies" (Ingraham and Tobias) — sung by **Smith Ballew**, with **Buster Fite and the Saddle Tramps**; "Stars Over the Desert" (Ingraham and Tobias) — sung by **Smith Ballew**; "On the Sunny Side of the Rockies" (reprise) — sung by **Smith Ballew**.

Roll Along, Cowboy (20th Century–Fox, 1937). Hero Smith Ballew (right center) has villain Gordon Elliott (right) hog-tied as Cecilia Parker (left), Budd Buster (second left) and Harry Bernard (left center) watch.

Location Filming: Iverson, California.

Running Time: 57 min.

Source: Novel, *The Dude Ranger* by **Zane Grey**.

Story: In lieu of their pay, cowhands Smith Ballew and Stanley Fields accept a lien on Ruth Robinson's ranch. In reality, Robinson's ranch has fallen on hard times. Robinson is deep in debt and is in danger of losing her ranch for back taxes. Ballew and Fields decide to help Robinson and her daughter Cecilia Parker, and suggest she sell enough cattle to pay off her debts. Saloon owner Gordon Elliott wants the Robinson ranch, and he and his men begin to rustle the cattle. Ballew and Fields arrive in time to prevent the theft. Ballew forces Elliott to buy Robinson's cattle at the top market price. Ballew decides to make the Robinson ranch his home and settle down with Parker.

Notes and Commentary: Gordon Elliott has a good role as the villain in this "B" western. In various scenes, Elliott is seen plotting to buy up all the ranches in the area; finding out that Robinson plans to sell cattle to meet back taxes; confronting Ballew when Ballew is ordering Robinson's cowhands back to the ranch, and being knocked over a table by Ballew for his troubles; plotting and then rustling Robinson's cattle; and finally being chased on horseback by Ballew, being bull-dogged from his saddle and then forced by Ballew to buy Robinson's cattle.

Roll Along Cowboy was re-released in 1948 with Wild Bill Elliott's name above the title. Smith Ballew, Cecilia Parker and Stanley Fields' names appeared below the title.

Reviews: "*Roll Along Cowboy*, despite valiant singing gymnastics by Smith Ballew, is just another cactus opus. It may appease some western devotees, but belongs on neither half of dual combo. Gordon Elliott is too polished as the rustler leader." *Variety*, 6/1/38; "Smith Ballew's second series western is none-too-good." *Western Movies*, Pitts.

SUMMATION: *Roll Along Cowboy* is a pleasant but below par western, primarily due to a lack of action. Gordon Elliott is fine as the gang leader.

Torn Between Love and Duty — Defend Her Father or Protect Her Husband!

Secret Bride

Warner Bros. (December, 1934)

ALTERNATE TITLES: *Concealment* and *His Secret Bride*.

CAST: Ruth Vincent, **Barbara Stanwyck**; Robert Sheldon, **Warren William**; Hazel Normandie, **Glenda Farrell**; Willis Martin, **Grant Mitchell**; Governor Vincent, **Arthur Byron**; Lansdale, **Henry O'Neill**; Bredeen, **Douglas Dumbrille**; Lt. Nigard, **Arthur Aylesworth**; Grosvenor, **Willard Robertson**; McPherson, **William Davidson**; Holdstock, **Russell Hicks**; Drunk in Diner, **Vince Barnett**// Vincent's Secretary, **Gordon Elliott**.

CREDITS: Director, **William Dieterle**; Screenwriters, **Tom Buckingham**, **F. Hugh Herbert** and **Mary McCall, Jr.**; Editor, **Owen Marks**; Art Director, **Anton Grot**; Cinematographer, **Ernest Haller**; Gowns, **Orry-Kelly**; Musical Conductor, **Leo F. Forbstein**; Dialogue Director, **Stanley Logan**.

RUNNING TIME: 64 min.

SOURCE: Play by **Leonard Ide**.

STORY: Attorney General Warren William and Barbara Stanwyck, daughter of Governor Arthur Byron, elope. They have to keep their marriage a secret when Byron is accused of taking a bribe. William and Stanwyck work to clear Byron. It is finally revealed that Henry O'Neill, supposedly Byron's closest friend, is behind the plot. O'Neill commits suicide. William and Stanwyck can now enjoy marriage.

NOTES AND COMMENTARY: Gordon Elliott has a brief role as Arthur Byron's secretary. First, Elliott tells Byron, "The Attorney General is not in his office, sir." Elliott leaves, then returns to hand Henry O'Neill a note, saying, "Will you telephone this number, Mr. Lansdale?"

REVIEWS: "Fast moving melodrama. Above average." *Variety*, 2/5/35; "A dashing homicide melodrama which seeks, with only minimum success, to conceal the frailties by the violence of its pace. Routine entertainment." *New York Times*, 2/2/35.

SUMMATION: Engrossing mystery drama until the weak ending.

Best Mystery Drama You've Ever Seen!

The Secret Witness

Columbia Pictures (December, 1931)

ALTERNATE TITLE: *Terror by Night*.

CAST: Lois Martin, **Una Merkel**; Arthur Jones, **William Collier, Jr.**; Bella, **Zasu Pitts**; Captain McGowan, **Purnell Pratt**; Lewis Leroy, **Ralf Harolde**; Larson, **Clyde Cook**; Tess, **June Clyde**; Gunner, **Nat Pendleton**; Jeff, **Clarence Muse**// Spectator at Crime Scene, **Gordon Elliott**.

CREDITS: Director, **Thornton Freeland**; Screenwriter, **Sam Spewack**; Editor, **Louis Sackin**.

RUNNING TIME: 66 min.

SOURCE: Novel, *Murder in the Guilded Cage* by **Sam Spewack**.

STORY: After a young woman jumps from his penthouse apartment to her death, womanizer Hooper Atcheley is found murdered. William Collier, Jr., brother of the deceased woman, is accused of the crime. Socialite Una Merkel proves Collier is innocent and that Ralf Harolde is the murderer.

NOTES AND COMMENTARY: Gordon Elliott is fleetingly seen as a spectator looking at the suicide victim.

REVIEW: "A pleasantly homicidal entertainment." *The New York Times*, 12/21/31.

SUMMATION: This interesting little murder mystery offers plenty of suspects (even a chimp comes under scrutiny).

A Thrilling Race Drama of Erin's Isle.

Shamrock Handicap

Fox Film Corporation (May, 1926)
A John Ford Production
ALTERNATE TITLE: *1732*.
CAST: Lady Sheila O'Hara, **Janet Gaynor**; Neil Ross, **Leslie Fenton**; Orville Finch, **Willard Louis**; Con O'Shea, **J. Farrell MacDonald**; Molly O'Shea, **Claire McDowell**; Sir Miles O'Hara, **Louis Payne**; Jockey Ginsburg, **George Harris**; "Chesty" Morgan, **Andy Clark**; Virus Cakes, **Ely Reynolds**// Villager, **Gordon Elliott**.
CREDITS: Director, **John Ford**; Screenwriter, **John Stone**; Titles, **Elizabeth Pickett**; Cinematographer, **George Schneiderman**; Copyright Owner and Presenter, **William Fox**.
RUNNING TIME: 66 min.
SOURCE: Story by **Peter B. Kyne**.
STORY: In danger of losing his estate in Ireland for failure to pay back taxes, Louis Payne decides to sell all his horses to Willard Louis, who's looking for race horses. Stable hand Leslie Fenton, who has dreams of becoming a top jockey, is in love with Payne's daughter, Janet Gaynor, who loves Fenton in return.

Knowing how much Gaynor loves Payne's prize horse, Dark Rosaleen, Fenton shows Rosaleen as unfit for racing, and Louis turns the horse down. Louis takes Fenton to America to develop him into a first-rate jockey. In Fenton's first major race, he's crippled in a fall. Payne brings his daughter and Rosaleen to America. Louis arranges for Rosaleen to compete in the Shamrock Handicap. The crippled Fenton rides Rosaleen to victory. Payne comes back to Ireland in triumph. Fenton and Gaynor plan to marry.

NOTES AND COMMENTARY: In his second screen appearance, Gordon Elliott can be seen briefly but to good advantage as one of the villagers welcoming Louis Payne's triumphant return to Ireland.

REVIEW: "It's as much Ford's direction as anything else that puts this one over, for he did not have a particular effective cast and his leads did not seem to get across at all." *Variety*, 7/7/26.

SUMMATION: Charming tale of Irish folk and horse racing.

What a Woman Will Do for Love!

She Couldn't Say No

Warner Bros. (February, 1930)
CAST: Winnie Harper, **Winnie Lightner**; Jerry Casey, **Chester Morris**; Iris, **Sally Eilers**; Tommy Blake, **Johnny Arthur**; Big John, **Tully Marshall**; Cora, **Louise Beavers**.

CREDITS: Director, **Lloyd Bacon**; Screenwriters, **Arthur Caesar**, **Robert Lord** and **Harvey Thew**; Cinematographer, **James Van Trees**; Sound, **Charles David Forrest**.
SONGS: "Watching My Dreams Go By"

(Dubin and Burke)—sung by **Winnie Lightner**; "That's the Way with a Woman Like Me" (Dubin and Burke)—sung by **Winnie Lightner**; "Bouncin' the Baby Around" (Dubin and Burke)—sung by **Winnie Lightner**; "Ping Pongo" (Dubin and Burke)—sung by **Winnie Lightner**; "The Poison Kiss of That Spaniard" (Dubin and Burke)—sung by **Winnie Lightner**.

RUNNING TIME: 70 min.

SOURCE: Play by **Benjamin M. Kaye**.

STORY: Cabaret singer Winnie Lightner falls in love with gangster Chester Morris who returns Lightner's love. Morris opens a night-club, which he gives to her. Morris transfers his affections to socialite Sally Eilers. Lightner becomes depressed. Morris realizes that he really loves Lightner and helps her achieve stardom. Before the two can marry, a rival gangster guns down Morris.

NOTES AND COMMENTARY: Film historians have noted that Gordon Elliott has a minor role in this production.

REVIEW: "Title and Winnie Lightner make this a good program." *Variety*, 2/19/30.

SUMMATION: This film was not available for viewing by the author.

A "Four-Star" Hit!

Silver Dollar

First National Pictures (December, 1932)

CAST: Yates Martin, **Edward G. Robinson**; Lily Owens, **Bebe Daniels**; Sarah Martin, **Aline MacMahon**; George (Mine Foreman), **DeWitt Jennings**; Colonel Stanton, **Robert Warwick**; Hamlin, **Russell Simpson**; Adams, **Harry Holman**; Jenkins, **Charles Middleton**; President Arthur, **Emmett Corrigan**; Rische, **Christian Rub**; Hook, **Lee Kohlmar**; Miners, **Wade Boteler** and **William LeMaire**// Election Party Guest, **Gordon Elliott**.

CREDITS: Director, **Alfred E. Green**; Screenplay, **Harvey Thew**; Editor, **George Marks**; Art Director, **Robert Haas**; Cinematography, **James Van Trees**; Gowns, **Orry-Kelly**; Musical Director, **Leo F. Forbstein**.

RUNNING TIME: 83 min.

SOURCE: Novel by **David Karsner**.

STORY: Storekeeper Edward G. Robinson grubstakes two miners who discover a rich silver mine, making him a wealthy man. Entering politics, Robinson is elected Lt. Governor of Colorado. In Denver, Robinson meets and falls in love with Bebe Daniels. Robinson divorces his wife, Aline MacMahon, and marries Daniels. The establishment of the gold standard devalues the worth of silver, and Robinson is left penniless. At the depths of despair, Robinson is told he will be the Postmaster in Denver. Before the appointment can come through, Robinson suffers a heart attack and dies.

NOTES AND COMMENTARY: Gordon Elliott is given no dialogue in his role of an election party guest. First, Elliott follows an entourage lead by Edward G. Robinson as they go to a balcony to celebrate Robinson's victory. Then Elliott can be seen over Robinson's right shoulder as it is announced that Robinson has the richest silver mine in Colorado.

REVIEWS: "Muddled story of Colorado silver baron, with Edward G. Robinson doing some of his best work." *Variety*, 12/27/32; "The film is directed in a straightforward, unimaginative manner by Green. *Silver Dollar* is dominated by Robinson's superb and detailed performance." *Motion Picture Guide*, Nash and Ross.

SUMMATION: Robinson's performance lifts a predictable story to above-average entertainment.

It Runs the Gamut of Glee! Rhythmic! Romantic! Laughable!

Singing Kid

Warner Bros. (April, 1936)

A First National Picture

CAST: Al Jackson, **Al Jolson**; Sybil Haines, **Sybil Jason**; Ruth Haines, **Beverly Roberts**; Davenport Rogers, **Edward Everett Horton**; Bob Carey, **Lyle Talbot**; Joe Eddy, **Allen Jenkins**; Dana Lawrence, **Claire Dodd**; Babe, **Jack Durant**; Dope, **Frank Mitchell**; Singer in Blackface, **Winifred Shaw**; Dr. May, **Joseph King**; Barney Hammond, **Wm. Davidson**; **Yacht Club Boys**; **Cab Calloway and His Band**.

CREDITS: Director, **William Keighley**; Story, **Robert Lord**; Screenwriters, **Warren Duff** and **Pat C. Flick**; Editor, **Thomas Richards**; Art Direction, **Carl Weyl**; Cinematographer, **George Barnes**; Gowns, **Orry-Kelly**; Conductor, **Leo F. Forbstein**; Orchestral Arrangements, **Ray Heindorf**; Staging of Musical Numbers, **Bobby Connolly** and **William Keighley**.

SONGS: Medley ("My Mammy" [Donaldson, Lewis and Young], "Swanee" [G. Gershwin and Caesar], "Rock-a-Bye Your Baby with a Dixie Melody" [Schwartz, Lewis and Young], "California, Here I Come" [Meyer and De-Sylva], "April Showers" [Silvers and DeSylva], "About a Quarter to Nine" [Warren and Dubin] and "Sonny Boy" [Jolson, DeSylva, Brown and Henderson])— sung by **Al Jolson**; "I Love to Singa" (Arlen and Harburg)— sung by **Al Jolson** and **Cab Calloway**; "I Love to Singa" (reprise)— sung by **Edward Everett Horton** and **Allen Jenkins**; "My How This Country Has Changed" (Arlen and Harburg)— sung by **the Yacht Club Boys**; "You Gotta Have That Hi-Di-Ho in Your Soul" (Mills and Calloway)— sung by **Cab Calloway**; "The Singiest Man in Town" (Arlen and Harburg)— sung by **Al Jolson** and **Cab Calloway**; "Save Me Sister" (Arlen and Harburg)— sung by **Al Jolson, Cab Calloway, Winifred Shaw** and **chorus**; "Here's Looking at You" (Arlen and Harburg)— sung by **Al Jolson**; "You're the Cure for All That Ails Me" (Arlen and Harburg)— sung by **Al Jolson, Sybil Jason, Edward Everett Horton** and **Allen Jenkins**; Medley ("I Love to Singa" (reprise)— sung by **Al Jolson** and **the Yacht Club Boys**, "I Want to Sing a Mammy Song" [Arlen and Harburg]— sung by **Al Jolson** and "The Sidewalks of New York" [Lawlor and Blake]— sung by **chorus**); "I Want to Singa" (reprise)— sung by **Cab Calloway** and **Al Jolson**.

RUNNING TIME: 85 min.

STORY: Broadway star Al Jolson gets in trouble with the Internal Revenue Service for underpayment of back taxes. Jolson's best friend and financial manager has been embezzling money and flees to South America with Jolson's fiancée, Claire Dodd. The incident causes Jolson to lose his voice, and he is told to rest at some secluded location. Jolson vacations in Maine, where he meets and falls in love with Beatrice Roberts. Through a misguided effort of Jolson's to help Roberts' career as a playwright, they break up. Jolson's voice returns and, as he is to make his return to the Broadway stage, Roberts realizes that she does love Jolson. She goes to New York and they reunite just before Jolson's first number.

NOTES AND COMMENTARY: It has been reported that Gordon Elliott had a role as an announcer. If so, his scene(s) ended up on the cutting room floor.

REVIEWS: "Spotty entertainment and one of Al Jolson's minor efforts for Warner Bros." *Variety*, 4/8/36; "A star vehicle if there ever was one and recommended only for Jolson fans." *1996 Movie and Video Guide*, Maltin.

SUMMATION: A tuneful but minor musical that serves as good entertainment for Jolson fans.

Lap After Lap, and Laugh After Laugh,
the Track Is 10 Laps to the Mile ... or Once Around Joe's Mouth!

6 Day Bike Rider

First National (October, 1934)

CAST: Wilfred, **Joe E. Brown**; Phyllis, **Maxine Doyle**; Clinton, **Frank McHugh**; Harry, **Gordon Westcott**; Col. Jenkins, **Arthur Aylesworth**; Mrs. Jenkins, **Lottie Williams**; Mrs. St. Clair, **Dorothy Christy**; Uncle Ezra, **Lloyd Neal**; Pop O'Hara, **William Granger**// Reporter at Race Meet, **Gordon Elliott**.

CREDITS: Director, **Lloyd Bacon**; Story/Screenplay, **Earl Baldwin**; Editor, **George Amy**; Art Director, **Anton Grot**; Cinematographer, **Warren Lynch**; Original Music, **M.K. Jerome**; Music Conductor, **Leo F. Forbstein**.

SONGS: "Asleep in the Deep" (Lamb and Petrie)— sung by **Joe E. Brown** and **chorus**; "The Very Thought of You" (Noble)— played by **Maxine Doyle**.

RUNNING TIME: 69 min.

STORY: Trick cyclist and bike racer Gordon Westcott becomes Joe E. Brown's rival for Maxine Doyle's affections. Brown decides to enter in a six-day bike race to defeat Westcott. As the race begins, Doyle finds that Westcott is married. Encountering many humorous obstacles, Brown wins the race and marries Doyle.

NOTES AND COMMENTARY: Gordon Elliott is seen but has no dialogue as a reporter covering the race. Elliott apears in three scenes.

REVIEWS: "Potentially excellent comedy idea, but poorly developed." *New York Times*, 11/3/34; "Good little comedy." *1996 Movie and Video Guide*, Maltin.

SUMMATION: Enjoyable light comedy with enough laughs to hold the interest.

Gay ... Gossipy Hilarious Hit.

Smart Woman

Radio Pictures (September, 1931)

CAST: Nancy Gibson, **Mary Astor**; Donald Gibson, **Robert Ames**; Sir Guy Harrington, **John Halliday**; Billy Ross, **Edward Everett Horton**; Peggy Preston, **Noel Francis**; Sally Ross, **Ruth Weston**; Mrs. Preston, **Gladys Gale**; Brooks, **Alfred Cross**; Mrs. Windleweaver, **Lillian Harmer**// Newspaper Reporter, **Gordon Elliott**.

CREDITS: Director, **Gregory La Cava**; Producer, **William LeBaron**; Associate Producer, **Bertram Milhauser**; Screenwriter, **Salisbury Field**; Editor, **Ann McKnight**; Art Director/Costumes, **Max Ree**; Cinematography, **Nicolas Musuraca**; Sound, **Clem Portman**.

RUNNING TIME: 68 min.

SOURCE: Play, *Nancy's Private Affair* by **Myron C. Fagan**.

STORY: Returning home from Europe, Mary Astor discovers her husband, Robert Ames, is in love with Noel Francis and wants a divorce. Astor arranges to have Francis and her mother, Gladys Gale, visit Ames and Astor's estate. Astor manages to show Ames that Francis is a gold digger and wins back her husband.

NOTES AND COMMENTARY: As Mary Astor and John Halliday are talking at the ship's rail, newspaper reporter Gordon Elliott comes aboard to interview Halliday.

REVIEWS: "This little tale is intended to entertain and in this it succeeds admirably." *New York Times*, 10/12/31; "Loopy comedy." *The RKO Story*, Jewell and Harbin.

SUMMATION: Very amusing sophisticated comedy of a wife winning back her husband.

*She Changed Her Husbands Like She Changed Her Hats! You'll Love Her ...
But ... Look Out! Her Husbands Are Jealous!*

Smarty

Warner Bros. (May, 1934)

ALTERNATE TITLE: *Hit Me Again.*

CAST: Vicki, **Joan Blondell**; Tony, **Warren William**; Vernon, **Edward Everett Horton**; George, **Frank McHugh**; Anita, **Claire Dodd**; Bonnie, **Joan Wheeler**; Edna, **Virginia Sale**; Tilford, **Leonard Carey**// Nightclub Patron, **Gordon Elliott**.

CREDITS: Director, **Robert Florey**; Screenwriters, **F. Hugh Herbert** and **Carl Erickson**; Editor, **Jack Killifer**; Art Director, **John Hughes**; Cinematographer, **George Barnes**; Gowns, **Orry-Kelly**; Musical Conductor, **Leo F. Forbstein**; Dialogue Director, **Frank McDonald**.

RUNNING TIME: 64 min.

SOURCE: Play by **F. Hugh Herbert**.

STORY: Upset at being incessantly teased by his wife, Joan Blondell, Warren William slaps her. Blondell divorces William and marries her lawyer, Edward Everett Horton. William had agreed to the divorce even though he still loved Blondell. A year later, Blondell invites William to a dinner party where she infuriates Horton, who slaps her. Blondell goes to William's apartment, where she's found in his bed by William and Horton. Blondell tells Horton he can sue her for infidelity. Blondell spends the night with William as the two get back together.

NOTES AND COMMENTARY: Look closely, and in the nightclub scene in which Joan Wheeler suggests to Warren William that she go home with him, Elliott can be seen dancing in the far background.

REVIEW: "Fairly pleasant divertissement." *Variety*, 6/26/34.

SUMMATION: Bright sparkling comedy of the battle of the sexes.

Drama Packed with Action.

Speed to Spare

Columbia (May, 1937)

ALTERNATE TITLE: *Racing Luck.*

CAST: Skids Brannigan, **Edward J. Nugent**; Tommy Morton, **Charles Quigley**; Eileen Hart, **Dorothy Wilson**; Peaches O'Brien, **Patricia Farr**; Breakaway Wilson, **Gene Morgan**; Dan Kelly, **John Gallaudet**// Steve Fellows, **Gordon Elliott**.

CREDITS: Director, **Lambert Hillyer**; Screenwriters, **Bert Granet** and **Lambert Hillyer**; Editor, **Viola Lawrence**; Cinematographer, **Benjamin H. Kline**.

RUNNING TIME: 60 min.

STORY: Brothers Edward J. Nugent and Charles Quigley are separated at birth. Both become racecar drivers. Nugent's style is to win at any cost. Quigley, while not knowing why, tries to change Nugent's racing style. Nugent retaliates by trying to win the affections of Quigley's girl, Dorothy Wilson. In a big race, Nugent is almost killed when his car crashes. Nugent realizes Quigley is his brother, and the two patch up their differences.

NOTES AND COMMENTARY: Gordon Elliott has the role of Steve Fellows in this film.

REVIEW: "Speedwagon yarns are not new, but with some spirited help via the library route, a fairly lively play of humor, romance and action has been created here." *Variety*, 6/9/37.

SUMMATION: The film was not available for viewing by the author.

Kisses for Cash! Alice Brady in a New Triumph as a Black-Mailing "Stage Mother!"

Stage Mother

Metro-Goldwyn-Mayer (September, 1933)

CAST: Kitty Lorraine, **Alice Brady**; Shirley Lorraine, **Maureen O'Sullivan**; Warren Foster, **Franchot Tone**; Lord Aylesworth, **Phillips Holmes**; Ralph Martin, **Ted Healy**; Fred Lorraine, **Russell Hardie**; Ricco, **C. Henry Gordon**; Dexter, **Alan Edwards**; Francis Nolan, **Ben Alexander**// Audience Member, **Gordon Elliott**; Guest at Dexter's Party, **Gordon Elliott**.

CREDITS: Director, **Charles R. Brabin**; Associate Producer, **Hunt Stromberg**; Screenwriters, **John Meehan** and **Bradford Ropes**; Editor, **Frank Hull**; Art Director, **Stanwood Rogers**; Interior Decorator, **Edwin B. Willis**; Cinematographer, **George Folsey**; Gowns, **Adrian**; Sound, **Douglas Shearer**; Musical Conductor, **Lou Silvers**; Dance Director, **Albertina Rasch**.

SONGS: "Any Little Girl That's a Nice Little Girl Is the Right Little Girl for Me" (Fisher)— sung by **Alice Brady** and **Ted Healy**; "When Irish Eyes Are Smiling" (Ball, Olcott and Graff Jr.)— sung by unidentified boy; "Beautiful Girl" (Brown and Freed)— sung by **Sam Ash** and **chorus**; "I'm Dancing on a Rainbow" (Brown and Freed)— sung by **Maureen O'Sullivan** and **chorus**.

RUNNING TIME: 85 min.

SOURCE: Novel by **Bradford Ropes**.

STORY: Former show business performer Alice Brady pushes her daughter, Maureen O'Sullivan, into a show business career. As O'Sullivan's career advances, Brady thwarts all suitors' advances. Brady even uses the threat of blackmail to have O'Sullivan released from a long-term contract so she can star in a Broadway show. While at out-of-town rehearsals, O'Sullivan falls in love with artist Franchot Tone. Brady comes between the two young lovers. In a desperate attempt to control her own life, O'Sullivan agrees to marry English aristocrat Phillips Holmes. In a showdown with Brady, O'Sullivan realizes she can't renounce her own mother. Finally thinking of her daughter's happiness, Brady gives O'Sullivan a letter showing that Tone is still in love with her.

NOTES AND COMMENTARY: Gordon Elliott has two roles in this film. First, Elliott is seen in the audience during the "I'm Dancing on a Rainbow" number. He's seated front left of Alice Brady. He flashes his patented smile as Maureen O'Sullivan takes a bow. Later, Elliott can be seen at Alan Edwards' party as O'Sullivan and Brady enter the apartment.

REVIEWS: "It is chiefly through Miss Brady's competent performance and Charles Brabin's experienced direction that this production succeeds in being infinitely more acceptable than most others of its type." *New York Times*, 9/30/33; "Praiseworthy." *The MGM Story*, Eames.

SUMMATION: Good melodrama, with music, of a "stage mother" and her talented daughter.

Stars of Radio — Stars of the Screen — In Warner Bros. New-Style Musicomedy!

Stars Over Broadway

Warner Bros. (November, 1935)

CAST: Al McGillevray, **Pat O'Brien**; Joan Garrett, **Jane Froman**; Jan King, **James Melton**; Nora Wyman, **Jane Muir**; Offkey Cramer, **Frank McHugh**; Freddy, **Eddie Conrad**; Minotti, **William Ricciardi**; Molly, **Marie Wilson**; Announcer, **Frank Fay**; Crane, **E.E. Clive**//Patron at Dempsey's, **Gordon Elliott**.

CREDITS: Director, **William Keighley**; Story, **Mildred Cram**; Screenwriters, **Jerry**

Wald and **Julius J. Epstein**; Additional Dialogue, **Patsy Flick**; Editor, **Bert L'Orle**; Art Director, **Carl Jules Weyl**; Cinematographer, **George Barnes**; Gowns, **Orry-Kelly**; Musical Director, **Leo F. Forbstein**; Orchestral arrangement, **Ray Heindorf**; Choreographers, **Busby Berkeley** and **Bobby Connolly**.

SONGS: "Carry Me Back to the Lone Prairie" (Robinson)— sung by **James Melton**; "Aida" (Verdi)— sung by **James Melton**; "Old Faithful / Open Up Them Perley Gates"— sung by unnamed singing group; "Sweet and Slow" (Dubin and Warren)— sung by unnamed singing group; "I'd Love to Take Orders from You" (Dubin and Warren)— sung by unnamed singing group; "You Let Me Down" (Dubin and Warren)— sung by **Jane Froman**; "Coney Island" (Dubin and Warren)— sung by unnamed singing group; "Where Am I? (Am I in Heaven?)" (Dubin and Warren)— sung by **James Melton**; "At Your Service, Madame" (Dubin and Warren)— sung by **James Melton** and **Jane Froman**; "Where Am I? (Am I in Heaven?)" (reprise)— sung by **James Melton**; "Ave Marie" (Gounod and Bach)— sung by **Jane Muir**; "Aida" (reprise)— sung by **James Melton**.

RUNNING TIME: 90 min.

STORY: Small-time promoter Pat O'Brien is ready to commit suicide until he meets singing hotel porter James Melton. O'Brien and Melton become partners, and he guides Melton to stardom via nightclubs, radio and records. Melton begins living the high life, with excessive drinking and womanizing, even to the point of seeing Jean Muir, the girl O'Brien secretly loves. Melton's conduct costs him his career, and O'Brien and Melton dissolve their partnership. O'Brien tells Muir that she has no future as a singer, and, in a daze, Muir walks in front of a taxi and is injured. O'Brien feels he is responsible for the misfortunes of Melton and Muir. O'Brien finances Melton's operatic studies in Italy and then moves to the west coast. O'Brien returns to New York for Melton's debut at the Met. Melton wants to renew his partnership with O'Brien, and Muir tells O'Brien she loves him.

NOTES AND COMMENTARY: Film historians and various movie websites claim Gordon Elliott played either a friend or a manager in this film. It looks like it could be Elliott walking around in the background at Dempsey's while Pat O'Brien is being offered a job in a pool hall.

REVIEWS: "Moderately good musical. Backstage yarn with pleasant dialog and fancy trimmings, *Stars Over Broadway* emerges as a satisfactory musical." *Variety*, 11/20/35; "A generally amiable and melodious comedy." *New York Times*, 11/14/35.

SUMMATION: This entertaining story of a singer's eventual rise to operatic stardom sports some marvelous singing by James Melton and Jane Froman.

A Picture as Great as the Man It Immortalizes.

Story of Louis Pasteur

Warner Bros. (February, 1936)
A Cosmopolitan Production
ALTERNATE TITLE: *Louis Pasteur*.

CAST: Louis Pasteur, **Paul Muni**; Marie Pasteur, **Josephine Hutchinson**; Annette Pasteur, **Anita Louise**; Dr. Jean Martel, **Donald Woods**; Dr. Charbonnet, **Fritz Leiber**; Dr. Emile Roux, Henry O'Neill; Dr. Rossignol, **Porter Hall**; Dr. Radisse, **Raymond Brown**; Dr. Zaranoff, **Akim Tamiroff**; Dr. Lister, **Halliwell Hobbes**; Dr. Pfeiffer, **Frank Reicher**; Joseph Meister, **Dickie** Moore; Mrs. Meister, **Ruth Robinson**; Napoleon III, **Walter Kingsford**; Louis Adophe Thiers, President, Republic of France, **Herbert Corthell**// Reporter, **Gordon Elliott**.

CREDITS: Director, **William Dieterle**; Story/Screenplay, **Sheridan Gibney** and **Pierre Collins**; Editor, **Ralph Dawson**; Art Director, **Robert M. Haas**; Cinematographer, Tony Gaudio; Costumes, **Milo Anderson**; Musical Director, **Leo F. Forbstein**; Dialogue Director, **Gene Lewis**.

RUNNING TIME: 87 min.

STORY: Paul Muni believes microbes cause infection, resulting in death, and that cleanliness and sterilization of instruments will improve conditions. Battling dissenters, Muni develops vaccines for anthrax and rabies. Muni also proves that antiseptic conditions will improve outcomes in surgery and childbirth. Muni is finally recognized and decorated for his accomplishments.

NOTES AND COMMENTARY: Don't blink or you'll miss Gordon Elliott as a reporter in this one. Elliott can be seen in the background on the left as Porter Hall and Fritz Leiber decide who should pass through the gate first to see the results of the anthrax test. Paul Muni enters first, then both men enter, with Elliott following.

REVIEWS: "An excellent biography, just as it is a noble photoplay." *New York Times*, 2/10/36; "Muni's dedicated, awesomely intelligent performance, and Gibney and Collings' dignified screenplay resulted in triumph for all concerned." *Warner Bros. Story*, Hirshhorn.

SUMMATION: A great picture with an extraordinary performance by Paul Muni.

He Faked Failure and Found Real Success!

A Successful Calamity

Warner Bros. (September, 1932)

CAST: Henry Wilton, **George Arliss**; Emmie, **Mary Astor**; Peggy, **Evalyn Knapp**; Connors, **Grant Mitchell**; George Struthers, **Hardie Albright**; Eddie, **William Janney**; Partington, **David Torrence**; Larry Rivers, **Randolph Scott**; John Belden, **Hale Hamilton**; Pietro, **Fortunio Bonanova**; the President, **Oscar Apfel**; Curtis, **Murray Kinnell**; Valet, **Harold Minjur**; Pauline, **Barbara Leonard**; Jane, **Eula Guy**; Barney Davis, **Leon Waycoff**; Mrs. Langstreet, **Virginia Hammond**; Lawrence, **Richard Tucker**; Butler, **Charles Coleman**; Chauffeur, **Jack Rutherford**; Lizzie, Helena Phillips// Guest at Musicale, **Gordon Elliott**.

CREDITS: Director, **John G. Adolfi**; Screenwriters, **Maude Howell**, **Julien Josephson** and **Austin Parker**; Editor, **Howard Bretherton**; Art Director, **Anton Grot**; Setting Supervisors, W & J. Sloane; Cinematographer, **James Van Trees**; Musical Conductor, **Leo F. Forbstein**.

RUNNING TIME: 73 min.

SOURCE: Play by **Clare Kummer**.

STORY: George Arliss, a financial wizard, returns home after a year's absence in the service of his country to find his family living an extravagant and busy lifestyle. To bring his family back together, Arliss tells them he's ruined financially. Arliss' ruse is successful, as his wife and children begin to work together as a family.

NOTES AND COMMENTARY: Gordon Elliott can briefly be seen as a guest in the second musicale sequence.

REVIEWS: "A lightweight comedy that stretches reality a little to keep its bright outlook." *The Motion Picture Guide*, Nash and Ross; "Another marvelous vehicle for George Arliss." *The Warner Bros. Story*, Hirshhorn.

SUMMATION: *A Successful Calamity* is a very engaging comedy with a sparkling performance by George Arliss.

Everything Is "Sunny" Now!

Sunny

First National Pictures (November, 1930)
A William A. Seiter Production

CAST: Sunny, **Marilyn Miller**; Tom Warren, **Lawrence Gray**; Jim Denning, **Joe Donahue**; Peters, **O.P. Heggie**; Weenie, **Inez Courtney**; Margaret, **Barbara Bedford**; Sue, **Judith Vosselli**; Sam, **Clyde Cook**; Wendell-Wendell, **Mackenzie Ward**// Tom's War Buddy, **Gordon Elliott**.

CREDITS: Director, **William A. Seiter**; Screenplay, **Humphrey Pearson** and **Henry McCarty**; Editor, **LeRoy Stone**; Art Director, **John J. Hughes**; Cinematographer, **Ernest Haller**; General Musical Director, **Erno Rapee**; Choreographer, **Theodore Kosloff**.

SONGS: "Oh! Didn't He Ramble" (Cole and Johnson)—sung by **Lawrence Gray** and **male chorus**; "Who?" (Harbach, Hammerstein II and Kern)—sung by **Marilyn Miller** and **Lawrence Gray**; "I Was Alone" (Harbach, Hammerstein II and Kern)—sung by **Marilyn Miller** (reprised by **Marilyn Miller**); "When We Get Our Divorce" (Harbach, Hammerstein II and Kern)—danced by **Marilyn Miller** and **Joe Donahue**; "The Hunt Dance" (Harbach, Hammerstein II and Kern)—danced by **Marilyn Miller**; "Sunny, D'Ya Love Me?" and "Two Little Love Birds" (Harbach, Hammerstein II and Kern)—orchestrations.

RUNNING TIME: 77 min.

SOURCE: Play, **Otto A. Harbach**, **Oscar Hammerstein II** and **Jerome Kern**.

STORY: To avoid marrying a man she can't stand, Marilyn Miller stows away on a ship leaving England for New York City. A passenger on the ship is Lawrence Gray, the man Miller loves. Gray is engaged to Barbara Bedford but has strong feelings for Miller. Not having a passport, Miller marries Gray's best friend, Joe Donahue, so that she can stay in the United States. After docking, Miller and Donahue get a divorce. Miller feels Gray doesn't love her and prepares to return to England. Gray finally realizes that it's Miller he loves and stops her from leaving. The two plan to wed.

NOTES AND COMMENTARY: Gordon Elliott played one of Lawrence Gray's war buddies. Elliott is seen in the opening scenes at the circus, first as the men enter the circus and then as they meet Marilyn Miller. Elliott is given one line of dialogue, "She'll have to go some to beat the old Sunny we used to know," comparing Miller to Gray's fiancée, Barbara Bedford. Elliott can be spotted when Miller is brought on deck as a stowaway, and is in the background, with hands in both front jacket pockets, as Miller dances. Elliott's last appearance is as one of the wedding guests when Miller marries Joe Donahue.

REVIEWS: "Uninspired filming of the musical comedy. Miss Miller is charming but the material is not there." *Variety*, 12/31/30; "Kosloff's choreography is a highlight in this otherwise stagy film that never comes close to showing what it was about Miller that made her a star." *The Motion Picture Guide*, Nash and Ross.

SUMMATION: Even the talented Marilyn Miller can't save this uninspired musical comedy.

Look Out for Public Swingster No. 1
He'll Mow Down Your Blues!

Swing It, Professor

Ambassador (November, 1937)

ALTERNATE TITLE: *Swing It Buddy*.

CAST: Artemis, **Pinky Tomlin**; Teddy, **Paula Stone**; Lou, **Milburn Stone**; Joan, **Mary Kornman**; Randall, **Gordon Elliott**; Toby, **Pat Gleason**; the Gentle Maniacs (**Garner, Wolf** and **Harkins**); **Four Squires (Lou Butterman, Jack W. Smith, Harry S. Powell, Glen T. Moore)**; Beaver, **Ralph Peters**; Dean, **George Cleveland**; Trustee, **Harry Depp**; Angelo, **Harry Semels**; **Four Singing Tramps (Fred Harder, Tim Clark, Art Moore, Bob Snyder)**.

CREDITS: Director, **Marshall Neilan**; Assistant Director, **Henry Spitz**; Producer, **Maurice Conn**; Associate Producer, **William Berke**; Story, **Connie Lee**; Screenwriters, **Nicholas H. Barrows** and **Robert St. Claire**; Editorial Supervisor, **Martin G. Cohn**; Editor, **Richard G. Wray**; Art Director, **E.H. Reif**; Cinematographer, **Jack Greenhalgh**; Sound, **Glen Glenn**; Musical Director, **Bakaleinikoff**.

SONGS: "An Old Fashioned Melody" (Lee, Heath and La Roux)— sung **Pinky Tomlin**, (reprise)— danced by **Paula Stone**, (reprise)— sung by **Pinky Tomlin**; "What More Could I Ask For" (Lee, Heath and La Roux)— sung by **Pinky Tomlin** and **the Four Singing Tramps**; "I'm Sorta Kinda Glad I Love You" (Lee, Heath and La Roux)— sung by **Pinky Tomlin**, (reprise)— sung by **Mary Kornman**, (reprise)— sung by **Pinky Tomlin**.

RUNNING TIME: 62 min.

STORY: Pinky Tomlin loses his position as a professor at the Music College at Brownell when he refuses to adjust to swing music. Needing work, Tomlin takes a job pretending to own and run a posh nightclub that actually belongs to gangster Milburn Stone. This subterfuge is necessary to have Paula Stone work at the club because she won't work for an underworld figure. Rival gangster Gordon Elliott wants P. Stone to work for him, and shows up at M. Stone's club to shut it down. When they hear Tomlin called "the Professor," Elliott thinks he's a notorious Chicago gangster and backs down. Later Elliott realizes his mistake and takes over the club, now actually owned by Tomlin. When Tomlin hears Elliott is holding P. Stone hostage, Tomlin bursts into the club, knocks Elliott out and wins P. Stone's hand in marriage.

NOTES AND COMMENTARY: Gordon Elliott receives fifth billing in *Swing It, Professor*, playing a nightclub-owning gangster. Elliott is first seen storming into Milburn Stone's nightclub to make trouble, but he backs down when he believes Tomlin is a Chicago crime boss. Next, Elliott and one of his henchmen plot to avoid Tomlin's takeover of the territory. Then Elliott is happy that Tomlin and his girlfriend, Mary Kornman, have come to his club. This gives Elliott the opportunity to buy Tomlin's friendship by gifting Tomlin a sizable sum of money. Then Elliott discovers that Tomlin isn't a gang boss after all, and takes over Tomlin's club, holding Paula Stone hostage. As Elliott prevents P. Stone from using the phone, Tomlin breaks in and knocks Elliott out. Cab drivers take the unconscious Elliott to jail.

REVIEWS: "Delightful comedy." *Motion Picture Guide*, Nash and Ross; "An amusing story, strung together effectively, plus good songs that are pleasantly woven into the action and a cast, which performs capably, lift this independent far above the average in the market today." *Variety*, 1/12/38.

SUMMATION: This bright, sparkling musical comedy features the talented Pinky Tomlin as a singing nightclub owner and Gordon Elliott, turning in a nice job, as an unsavory rival club owner.

Romance Roams the Jungle Night ... as Tarzan and His Glamorous Mate
Face Untold Terrors Together! Thrills Sweep the Jungle Wilds ... as Tarzan Battles
Savage Tribes and Beasts to Save the Girl He Loves!

Tarzan's Revenge

20th Century–Fox (January, 1938)

A Principal Production

CAST: Tarzan, **Glenn Morris**; Eleanor Reed, **Eleanor Holm**; Roger Reed, **George Barbier**; Ben Alleu Bey, **C. Henry Gordon**; Penny Reed, **Hedda Hopper**; Olaf Punch, **Joseph Sawyer**; Nevin Potter, **George Meeker**; Jigger, **Corbet Morris**; Koki, **John Lester Johnson**; Ben Alleu's Servant, **Frederick Clarke**// Riverboat Captain, **Gordon Elliott**.

CREDITS: Director, **D. Ross Lederman**; Assistant Director, **Wilbur McGaugh**; Producer, **Sol Lesser**; Screenwriters, **Robert Lee Johnson** and **Jay Vann**; Editor, **Eugene Milford**; Art Director, **Lewis J. Rachmil**; Cinematography, **George Meehan**; Sound, **Terry Kellum**; Wardrobe, **Jerry Bos**; Music, **Hugo Risenfeld**; Music Supervisor, **Abe Meyer**.

RUNNING TIME: 70 min.

SOURCE: Novel by **Edgar Rice Burroughs**.

STORY: On a riverboat in Africa, the rich and evil C. Henry Gordon spies Eleanor Holm. Gordon wants to add Holm to his harem. On the trek to the interior, Holm meets Glenn Morris, and the two begin to fall in love. Gordon has natives kidnap Holm and bring her to his palace. Morris eludes the natives, gains access to Gordon's palace and rescues Holm. Holm decides to stay in Africa as Morris' mate.

NOTES AND COMMENTARY: Gordon Elliott has two brief scenes as the captain of the riverboat carrying Holm and her party to the village where their safari will begin. Elliott bids Holm and her fiancé, George Meeker, good morning, and then discusses C. Henry Gordon's music and then Gordon himself. Elliott is present when Gordon's servant, Frederick Clarke, presents jewelry to Holm, which she refuses. Elliott is adequate in his part, which makes no great acting demands.

REVIEWS: "In spite of the flaws which a captious adult can pick, the youngsters seemed pleased enough with the latest adventures of their pal." *New York Times*, 1/10/38; "Strong fare for the kids and passable for adults." *Variety*, 1/12/38.

SUMMATION: The derring-do of Tarzan in the last 15 minutes is not enough to offset the tedium of the first 55.

Reach for the Sky, Stranger!
... 'Cause the Sky's the Limit for Thrills as This Sensational New Hard-Swingin', Sweet-Singin',
Trail-Blazin' Son of the West Rides into Action in His Biggest Hit Yet!

Trailin' West

Warner Bros. (October, 1936)

ALTERNATE TITLE: *On Secret Service.*

CAST: Lieut. Red Colton, **Dick Foran**; Lucy Blake, **Paula Stone**; Jefferson Duane, **Gordon Elliott**; Curley Thorne, **Addison Richards**; Abraham Lincoln, **Robert Barrat**; Colonel Douglas, **Joseph Crehan**; Lieut. Dale, **Fred Lawrence**; Happy Simpson, **Eddie Shubert**; Hawk, **Henry Otho**; Edwin H. Stanton, **Stuart Holmes**; Steve, **Milton Kibbee**; Hotel Clerk, **Carlyle Moore, Jr.**; Major Pinkerton, **Ed. Stanley**; Indian Chief, **Jim Thorpe**.

CREDITS: Director, **Noel M. Smith**; Story and Screenplay, **Anthony Coldeway**; Editor, **Frank McGee**; Art Director, **Hugh Reticker**; Cinematographers, **Sidney Hickox** and **Ted McCord**; Gowns, **Milo Anderson**.

SONGS: "Drums of Glory" — sung by **Dick**

Foran; "Moonlight Valley" — sung by **Dick Foran.**

LOCATION FILMING: Kernville, Iverson, Beale's Cut and Burro Flats, California.

RUNNING TIME: 59 min.

STORY: During the Civil War, Secret Service Agent Dick Foran is sent west to break up Confederate activity around Kent City. Foran, aided by his pal Eddie Shubert and Secret Service operative Paula Stone, discovers businessman Gordon Elliott and his partner, saloon owner Addison Richards, are behind the plots to prevent gold from reaching Union forces. After Richards is killed and Elliott is brought to justice, Foran and Stone wed.

NOTES AND COMMENTARY: Gordon Elliott, as one of the primary villains, has a good role in this Dick Foran western. Elliot appears in ten scenes: Henry Otho brings Dick Foran's credentials to Elliott; Elliott visits Army Colonel Joseph Crehan and tells Crehan that he is a Union operator, and requests the dates and routes of all gold shipments; Elliott tells Addison Richards when the next gold train goes through and to have Indians attack the train; a cavalry soldier tells Elliott that Paula Stone

went to the Army post; Elliott arrives at the army post as Foran is being court martialed; Elliott tells Crehan that Foran is an imposter, is knocked down by Foran and is thanked for his cooperation; Elliott and Richards decide to see what Stone knows, but Elliott inadvertently reveals himself a traitor resulting in a gun battle with Foran and Eddie Shubert (though Elliott and Richards get away); Elliott and Richards watch the Indians attack the gold train; Foran spies Elliott and Richards in the rocks as they watch the Cavalry rout the Indians; Foran chases Elliott and Richards, shooting Richards and bulldogging Elliott from his saddle to subdue Elliott after a short fight.

REVIEWS: "For kids, it's plenty actionful but the adults are apt to find it unbelievable. Gordon Elliott, Addison Richards and Henry Otho handle the heavy roles capably." *Variety,* 10/21/36; "A routine Foran series entry." *The Western,* Hardy.

SUMMATION: This is an average "B" western, lightning fast in execution but a little lacking, plot-wise. Gordon Elliott turns in a good job as one of the primary villains.

More Fun, More Laughs Than Convention City.

Traveling Saleslady

Warner Bros. (April, 1935)

A First National Production

CAST: Angela Twitchell, **Joan Blondell;** Claudette, **Glenda Farrell;** Pat O'Connor, **William Gargan;** Elmer, **Hugh Herbert;** Rufus Twitchell, **Grant Mitchell;** Schmidt, **Al Shean;** Mrs. Twitchell, **Ruth Donnelly;** Melton, **Johnny Arthur;** Harry, **Bert Roach;** Murdock, **Joseph Crehan;** Miss Wells, **Mary Treen;** McNeil, **James Donlan;** Freddie, **Gordon Elliott;** Burroughs, **Carroll Nye;** Mr. O'Connor, **Harry Holman;** Scoville, **Selmer Jackson.**

CREDITS: Director, **Ray Enright;** Screenwriters, **F. Hugh Herbert, Manuel Seff** and **Benny Rubin;** Editor, **Owen Marks;** Art Directors, **Anton Grot** and **Arthur Gruenberger;** Cinematographer, **George Barnes;** Gowns,

Orry-Kelly; Musical Director, **Leo F. Forbstein;** Dialogue Director, **Gene Lewis.**

RUNNING TIME: 65 min.

SOURCE: Story by **Frank Howard Clark.**

STORY: Grant Mitchell, owner of a toothpaste company, refuses to give his daughter, Joan Blondell, a job, saying a woman cannot be a businessperson. In retaliation, Blondell takes inventor Hugh Herbert's revolutionary idea of alcohol-flavored toothpaste to Al Shean's rival company. Shean gives Blondell a job selling the new product. Blondell goes head-to-head with Mitchell's top salesman, William Gargan, winning over most of his customers. At the same time, Blondell and Gargan fall in love. With Mitchell's company in financial difficulty, Blondell engineers a merger between the two companies. Blondell resigns her saleswoman job to marry Gargan.

NOTES AND COMMENTARY: Although Gordon Elliott received thirteenth billing, he's barely seen in this production. You can catch a quick glimpse when Bert Roach tells Elliott and two other delegates to the Druggists' Convention that there's a party with drinks in William Gargan's room. It seems that additional scenes with Elliott ended up on the cutting room floor, since actors receiving lesser billing or even unbilled have more prominent parts.

REVIEWS: "Snappy comedy with plenty of laughs." *Variety*, 4/3/35; "Sharp dialog and good comic performances all around." *Motion Picture Guide*, Nash and Ross.

SUMMATION: Bright comedy deftly handled by Joan Blondell.

Stars! ... Stars! ... Stars! ... In Warner Bros.' Funniest and Fastest Musical Hit!

Twenty Million Sweethearts

First National Pictures (May, 1934)

ALTERNATE TITLE: *Hot Air*.

CAST: Rush, **Pat O'Brien**; Clayton, **Dick Powell**; Peggy, **Ginger Rogers**; **the Four Mills Bros.**; **Ted Fio Rito and His Band**; Pete, **Allen Jenkins**; Sharpe, **Grant Mitchell**; Herbie, **Joseph Cawthorne**; Marge, **Joan Wheeler**; Tappan, **Henry O'Neill**; Norma Hanson's Secretary, **Johnny Arthur**; **the Three Radio Rogues** (**Jim Hollingwood, Eddie Bartell** and **Henry Taylor**)// Brass Rail Patron, **Gordon Elliott**; Nightclub Patron, **Gordon Elliott**.

CREDITS: Director, **Ray Enright**; Story, **Paul Finder Moss** and **Jerry Wald**; Screenplay, **Warren Duff** and **Harry Sauber**; Dialogue Director, **Stanley Logan**; Editor, **Clarence Kolster**; Art Director, **Esdras Hartley**; Cinematography, **Sid Hickox**; Gowns, **Orry-Kelly**; Musical Conductor, **Leo F. Forbstein**.

SONGS: Medley ("Carolina Moon" [Davis and Burke], "Marta"; "My Time Is Your Time" [Little and Dance], "Where the Blue of the Night (Meets the Gold of the Day)" [Turk, Crosby and Ahlert])— sung by **the Three Radio Rogues**; "(The Man on) the Flying Trapeze" (Leybourne)— sung by **Dick Powell**; "The Last Round-Up" (Hill)— sung by **Eddie Foster, Billy Snyder, Matt Brooks** and **Morris Goldman**, with modified lyrics; "Oh, I Heard, Yes, I Heard" (Dubin and Warren)— sung by **the Four Mills Bros.**; "Out for No Good" (Dubin and Warren)— sung by **Ginger Rogers**; "How'm I Doin'?" (Redman and Fowler)— sung by **the Four Mills Bros.**; "(The Man on) the Flying Trapeze" (reprise)— sung by **Dick Powell**; "I'll String Along with You" (Dubin and Warren)— sung by **Dick Powell**; "Fair and Warmer" (Dubin and Warren)— sung by **Dick Powell**; "Out for No Good" (reprise)— sung by **Dick Powell** and **the Four Mills Bros.**; "Fair and Warmer"— played by **Ted Fio Rito and His band**; "What Are Your Intentions" (Dubin and Warren)— played by **Ted Fio Rito and His Band**, and sung by **the Debutantes**; "I'll String Along with You" (reprise)— sung by **Dick Powell** and **Ginger Rogers**.

RUNNING TIME: 90 min.

STORY: Agent Pat O'Brien discovers singer Dick Powell waiting tables in a restaurant and decides to make him a radio star. Powell's appearance on Ginger Rogers' radio show is a success, and Powell is signed to a contract. Powell and Rogers fall in love and plan to marry. Fearing Powell's marriage will erode his popularity with his female audience, O'Brien causes the lovers to break up. Upset over O'Brien's actions, Powell leaves the program. O'Brien connives a way to bring Powell and Rogers back together and reestablishes Powell as a radio star.

NOTES AND COMMENTARY: A surprise, Gordon Elliott has two roles in this picture. First Elliott appears in an early scene when Pat O'Brien enters the Brass Rail restaurant to con money off his acquaintances. O'Brien spots Elliott and two other men. O'Brien drinks Elliott's beer. The men evade O'Brien's attempts to obtain money from them. After Dick Powell sings "(The Man on) the Flying Trapeze," Elliott and his companions leave the restaurant. Later in the film, as Ted Fio Rita and His Band play the song "Fair and Warmer," Elliott can be seen on the dance floor in the center of the scene.

REVIEWS: "A pleasant satire on radio with good performances from the stars." *The Motion Picture Guide*, Nash and Ross; "A rollicking potpourri of fun, song and romance. A happy picture." *The New York Times*, 4/27/34.

SUMMATION: Sprightly satire of the radio industry, with good songs well-performed by the stars.

The Perfect Star in Her Perfect Picture.

Two Against the World

Warner Bros. (September, 1932)

ALTERNATE TITLE: *The Higher-Ups.*

CAST: Adell Hamilton, **Constance Bennett**; David Norton, **Neil Hamilton**; Corinne Walton, **Helen Vinson**; Bob Hamilton, **Allen Vincent**; Victor Linley, **Gavin Gordon**; Courtney Hamilton, **Walter Walker**; Segall, **Roscoe Karns**; George Walton, **Alan Mowbray**; Gordon Mitchell, **Hale Hamilton**; Howard Mills, **Oscar Apfel**// Friend of Adell and Victor, **Gordon Elliott**.

CREDITS: Director, **Archie Mayo**; Screenwriter, **Sheridan Gibney**; Editor, **Bert Levy**; Art Director, **Anton Grot**; Cinematographer, **Charles Rosher**; Gowns, **Orry-Kelly**; Musical Director, **Leo F. Forbstein**.

RUNNING TIME: 71 min.

SOURCE: Novel, *A Dangerous Set* by **Marion Dix** and **Jerry Horwin**.

STORY: Socialite Constance Bennett and up-and-coming lawyer Neil Hamilton are attracted to each other. Gavin Gordon professes to be in love with Bennett but is having an affair with Bennett's sister, Helen Vinson. Mistakenly, Bennett's brother, Allen Vincent, believes Gordon has compromised Bennett. Vincent confronts Gordon and, in the process, shoots him. Bennett arrives too late to prevent the crime and becomes the "mystery woman" who is thought to be the murderer. Hamilton is forced to accept the post of special prosecutor. Vincent confesses to the crime and is found not guilty, as he defended Bennett's honor. Hamilton knows Bennett was protecting her sister, and he and Bennett plan to marry.

NOTES AND COMMENTARY: Gordon Elliott can be seen as a friend of Constance Bennett and Gavin Gordon. In his first scene Elliott escorts a young lady to the dance floor at Bennett's party, and the two dance out of camera range. Later, Elliott asks for ginger ale when he enters Gordon's apartment. Finally, in Gordon's apartment, Elliott can be seen playing roulette with Bennett, Gordon and Alan Mowbray.

REVIEWS: "Mild Constance Bennett picture." *Variety*, 8/23/32; "The dialog is as contrived as the plot. Motivations in this drama are almost nonexistent and the actors merely go through the motions." *The Motion Picture Guide*, Nash and Ross.

SUMMATION: A good drama with a courtroom background.

Past of Banker's Wife Exposed ... Couple in Suicide Pact!...
Grief-Crazed Daughter Seeks Vengeance!

Two Against the World

Warner Bros. (July, 1936)
A First National Picture
ALTERNATE TITLES: *One Fatal Hour* and *Case of Mrs. Pembroke*.
CAST: Sherry Scott, **Humphrey Bogart**; Alma Ross, **Beverly Roberts**; Edith Carstairs, **Linda Perry**; Malcolm Sims, Jr., **Carlyle Moore, Jr.**; Jim Carstairs, **Henry O'Neill**; Martha Carstairs, **Helen MacKellar**; Cora Latimer, **Claire Dodd**; Tippy Mantus, **Hobart Cavanaugh**; Dr. Leavenworth, **Harry Hayden**; Reynolds, **Robert Middlemas**; Banning, **Clay Clement**; Malcolm Sims, **Douglas Wood**; Marion Sims, **Virginia Brissac**; Miss Symonds, **Paula Stone**; Herman Mills, **Bobby Gordon**; Tommy, **Frank Orth**; Dr. Maguire, **Howard Hickman**; Sound Mixer, **Ferdinand Schumann-Heink**// News Commentator (voice only), **Gordon Elliott**.
CREDITS: Director, **William McGann**; Screenwriter, **Michael Jacoby**; Editor, **Frank McGee**; Art Director, **Esdras Hartley**; Cinematographer, **Sid Hickox**; Dialogue Director, **Irving Rapper**.
RUNNING TIME: 64 min.
SOURCE: Play, *Five Star Final* by **Louis Weitzenkorn**.

STORY: Station manager Humphrey Bogart is forced to air a twenty-year-old story in which Helen MacKeller killed her husband in self-defense. MacKeller pleads with station owner Robert Middlemas to drop the story, but Middlemas refuses. The airing of the story causes the suicide deaths of MacKeller and her husband, Henry O'Neill, and almost cancels the wedding of MacKeller's daughter, Linda Perry, to Carlyle Moore, Jr. Bogart realizes greed killed the couple and resigns from the radio station.
NOTES AND COMMENTARY: Gordon Elliott's voice is heard by Humphrey Bogart as Elliott reports the suicide deaths of Helen MacKeller and Henry O'Neill.
REVIEWS: "*Two Against the World* is too drab to get past the dual barrier." *Variety*, 7/15/36; "A lackluster screenplay and direction and performances that were equally dull, there were many more than two against this one and it died an early death." *The Warner Bros. Story*, Hirshhorn.
SUMMATION: Fairly decent drama of how an unscrupulous radio station ruins lives in two families.

An Entertainment Bombshell!
Fused with the Fireworks of Love, Life and Drama That Startle Millions into Gasping "So This Is New York!" Here Is the Type of Story That Splashes Your Newspaper with Sensational Headlines!

Two Kinds of Women

Paramount (January, 1932)
CAST: Emma Krull, **Miriam Hopkins**; Joseph Gresham, Jr., **Phillips Holmes**; Phyllis Adrian, **Wynne Gibson**; Hauser, **Stuart Erwin**; Senator Krull, **Irving Pichel**; Glassman, **Stanley Fields**; Joyce, **James Crane**; Helen, **Vivienne Osborne**; Clarissa Smith, **Josephine Dunn**; Tim Gohagen, **Robert Emmett O'Con-**nor; Murchard, **Larry Steers**; Jean, **Adrienne Ames**; Sheila, **Claire Dodd**; Babe Sevito, **Terrance Ray**; Mrs. Bowen, **June Nash**; Milt Fleisser, **Kent Taylor**; Deputy Police Commissioner, **Edwin Maxwell**; Radio Announcer, **Lindsay MacHarrie**// Dance Extra, **Gordon Elliott**.
CREDITS: Director, **William C. de Mille**;

Screenwriter, **Benjamin Glazer**; Cinematographer, **Karl Struss**.

SOURCE: Play, *This Is New York* by **Robert E. Sherwood**.

RUNNING TIME: 75 min.

STORY: Senator Irving Pichel believes New York City to be a den of iniquity. His daughter, Miriam Hopkins, accompanies him to the Big Apple. In New York, Hopkins falls in love with Phillips Holmes. Holmes is married to Wynne Gibson, whom he married while inebriated. Gibson has a boyfriend, gangster James Crane. Reporters discover Hopkins' romance with Holmes. Pichel disapproves of the liaison. Hopkins convinces Gibson to divorce Holmes without taking any money from him. Crane becomes upset and argues with Gibson. Gibson jumps from a window to her death. Hopkins and Holmes decide to marry and make New York their home.

NOTES AND COMMENTARY: Film historians state Gordon Elliott makes an appearance in this film.

REVIEWS: "Entertaining film. The tale runs along smoothly with alternate interludes of humor and drama." *New York Times*, 1/16/32; "Never a dull moment in Benjamin Glazer's script." *The Paramount Story*, Eames.

SUMMATION: The film was not available for viewing by the author.

More Desperate ... More Dangerous ... More Alluring Than the Underworld!

Upperworld

Warner Bros. (April, 1934)

ALTERNATE TITLE: *Upper World*.

CAST: Alex Stream, **Warren William**; Mrs. Stream, **Mary Astor**; Lilly, **Ginger Rogers**; Oscar, **Andy Devine**; Tommy, **Dickie Moore**; Marcus, **Ferdinand Gottschalk**; Lou, **J. Carroll Naish**; Moran, **Sidney Toler**; Banquet Toastmaker, **Henry O'Neill**; Rocklen, **Theodore Newton**; Commissioner Clark, **Robert Barrat**; Caldwell, **Robert Greig**; Kellogg, **Frank Sheridan**; Chris, **John Qualen**; Capt. Reynolds, **Willard Robertson**// Photographer at Crime Scene, **Gordon Elliott**.

CREDITS: Director, **Roy Del Ruth**; Story, **Ben Hecht**; Screenplay, **Ben Markson**; Editor, **Owen Marks**; Art Direction, **Anton Grot**; Cinematographer, **Tony Gaudio**; Gowns, **Orry-Kelly**; Musical Director, **Leo F. Forbstein**.

SONGS: "Who's Afraid of the Big Bad Wolf" (Ronell and Churchill) — sung by **Ginger Rogers** and **Warren William**, played by **Ginger Rogers**; "Shake Your Powder Puff" — sung by **Ginger Rogers**; "Fascination" (Marchetti and Manning) — played by a quintet.

RUNNING TIME: 70 min.

STORY: Feeling neglected by his socially conscious wife Mary Astor, multi-millionaire Warren William begins spending time with burlesque dancer Ginger Rogers. The initially platonic relationship finally becomes romantic. Rogers' boyfriend, J. Carroll Naish, wants Rogers to blackmail William. Rogers refuses and Naish threatens William. An argument ensues, and shots are fired. Naish kills Rogers, and in turn is killed by William. William attempts to make the deaths look like a murder-suicide. William's plan is not successful and he is arrested. William is acquitted, and William and Astor embark on a second honeymoon.

NOTES AND COMMENTARY: Gordon Elliott has only one scene in the film. He is one of a group of photographers taking pictures of the crime scene. Elliott tries to ask a question as he and his fellow photographers are ushered from the apartment.

Andy Devine would co-star with William Elliott in four big-budget westerns, *The Fabulous Texan* (Republic, 1947), *Old Los Angeles* (Republic, 1948), *The Gallant Legion* (Republic, 1948) and *The Last Bandit*.

REVIEWS: "A bit fuzzy thematically, and yet it is an interesting story with color, speed and humor." *The New York Times*, 5/25/34; "Good, literate script by Hecht puts this production above the usual run of romantic triangles turned murder-dramas." *The Motion Picture Guide*, Nash and Ross.

SUMMATION: A very good melodrama with fine acting by the principles, Warren William and Ginger Rogers in particular.

The Valley of Hunted Men

Pathé (February, 1928)
An Action Pictures Production
CAST: Tom Mallory, **Buffalo Bill, Jr.**; Dan Phillips, **Oscar Apfel**; Betty Phillips, **Kathleen Collins**; "Frenchy" Durant, **Jack Ganzhorn**; Valita, **Alma Rayford**; "Yucca" Jake, **Frank Griffith**; Frank Ellis; Beryl Roberts.
CREDITS: Director, **Richard Thorpe**; Screenwriters, **Harrington Strong** and Frank L. Inghram; Titles, **Frank L. Inghram**; Cinematographer, **Ray Ries**.
RUNNING TIME: 54 min.
SOURCE: Story, "Ride 'Em Cowboy" by **Harrington Strong**.
STORY: Revenue agent Buffalo Bill, Jr. de-

clares he can break up a gang running rum across the United States-Mexican border. Bill infiltrates the gang. One by one, Bill infuriates the outlaws to the point they chase him across the border, where they can be taken into custody.
NOTES AND COMMENTARY: Several sources list Gordon Elliott as having a small part in this picture.
REVIEW: "Excellent action story for the daily changes. Picture is action from start to finish, logical and well sustained." *Variety*, 5/2/28.
SUMMATION: This film was not available for viewing by the author.

Resist Her If You Dare! Her Charms Are Warm and Most Alluring!
Thackery's Sensational Heroine ... Bewitchingly Beautiful Becky Sharp ...
Reborn as a Modern ... The Girl of Today.

Vanity Fair

Allied Pictures Corporation (March, 1932)
A Chester M. Franklin Production
ALTERNATE TITLE: *Vanity Fair of Today*.
CAST: Becky Sharp, **Myrna Loy**; Rawdon Crawley, **Conway Tearle**; Amelia Sedley, **Barbara Kent**; George Osborne, **Walter Byron**; Dobbin, **Anthony Bushell**; Mr. Sedley, **Herbert Bunston**; Marquis of Steyne, **Montagu Love**; Mrs. Sedley, **Mary Forbes**; Joseph Sedley, **Billy Bevan**; Sir Pitt Crawley, **Lionel Belmore**; Polly, **Lilyan Irene**// Fox Hunt Participant, **Gordon Elliott**.
CREDITS: Director, **Chester M. Franklin**; Assistant Director, **Wilbur McGaugh**; Associate Producer, **M.H. Hoffman**; Screenwriter, **F. Hugh Herbert**; Editor, **Mildred Johnson**; Production Manager, **Sidney Algier**; Art Direction, **Eugene Hornbostel**; Cinematographers, **Harry Neumann** and **Tom Galligan**; Sound, **L.E. Tope**.

RUNNING TIME: 78 min.
SOURCE: Novel, *Vanity Fair* by **William Makepeace Thackeray**.
STORY: Myrna Loy, introduced to high society, uses her feminine charms to further her ambitions for wealth and position. Successful at first, her affairs with many men lead to her downfall, ultimately to live alone in squalor.
NOTES AND COMMENTARY: In the fox hunt sequence, Gordon Elliott makes a quick dismount from his horse. He then helps Myrna Loy and Barbara Kent dismount from their horses so they can assist Walter Byron, who has been thrown from his steed. Elliott has one line of dialog: "Here, get him on his side." It's all to no avail, as Byron quickly expires.
REVIEW: "The direction for this was slack, the dialog trite and the cinematography ordi-

nary." *The Motion Picture Guide*, Nash and Ross.

SUMMATION: *Vanity Fair* is a good melodrama about a fallen woman, well acted by Myrna Loy and directed by Chester M. Franklin.

Eternity Could Not Hold Him! A Mystery Drama That Will Raise Goose Pimples!

The Walking Dead

Warner Bros. (March, 1936)

CAST: John Elman, **Boris Karloff**; Nolan, **Ricardo Cortez**; Dr. Beaumont, **Edmund Gwenn**; Nancy, **Marguerite Churchill**; Jimmy, **Warren Hull**; Loder, **Barton MacLane**; Werner, **Henry O'Neill**; Judge Shaw, **Joseph King**; Prison Warden, **Addison Richards**; Blackstone, **Paul Harvey**; Merritt, **Robert Strange**; Betcha, **Eddie Acuff**; Stephen Martin; **Kenneth Harlan**; Sako, **Miki Morita**; Mrs. Shaw, **Ruth Robinson**// American Radio Announcer, **Gordon Elliott**.

CREDITS: Director, **Michael Curtiz**; Story, **Ewart Adamson** and **Joseph Fields**; Screenwriters, **Ewart Adamson, Peter Milne, Robert Andrews** and **Lillie Hayward**; Editor, **Thomas Pratt**; Art Director, **Hugh Reticker**; Cinematographer, **Hal Mohr**; Costumes, **Orry-Kelly**; Dialogue Director, **Irving Rapper**.

RUNNING TIME: 66 min.

STORY: Ex-convict Boris Karloff is framed for the murder of Judge Joseph King. Warren Hull and Marguerite Churchill are witnesses to the crime but are afraid to testify at Karloff's trial. Karloff is convicted and scheduled to be executed. Finally Hull and Churchill come forward, but lawyer Ricardo Cortez, in league with the criminal element, is able to delay matters until Karloff is electrocuted. Hull's boss, Doctor Edmund Gwenn, retrieves Karloff's body and is able to bring Karloff back to life. Karloff's death experience leaves him with the knowledge of who his enemies are. Just the presence of Karloff frightens three of the criminals into actions resulting in their deaths. Cortez and gangster Barton MacLane mortally wound Karloff but, in escaping, crash their car into a tree at a high rate of speed. With his enemies dead, Karloff also is ready to die. Karloff warns Gwenn to abandon his quest to restore life to the dead.

NOTES AND COMMENTARY: Look sharp to see Gordon Elliott report that Edmund Gwenn brought Boris Karloff back to life.

Warner Bros. could not make up their minds on how to spell Karloff's character name. In the credits it's "Elman," while in the film it's "Ellman."

REVIEWS: "Weak story and haphazardly interpolated assortment of scientific abadaba prevents Karloff from making much of a shocker out of this one." *Variety*, 3/4/36; "The best of Karloff's many 'living-dead' movies." *Motion Picture Guide*, Nash and Ross.

SUMMATION: After a promising start, the film becomes too implausible even for the diehard horror fan.

The Story of a Wife Who Failed!

Week-End Marriage

First National Pictures (July, 1932)

ALTERNATE TITLES: *Weekend Lives* and *Working Wives*.

CAST: Lola, **Loretta Young**; Ken, **Norman Foster**; Agnes, **Aline MacMahon**; Peter, **George Brent**; Doctor, **Grant Mitchell**; Shirley,

Vivienne Osborne; Connie, **Sheila Terry**; Mr. Davis, **J. Farrell MacDonald**; Mrs. Davis, **Louise Carter**; Jim, **Roscoe Karns**// Birthday Party Guest, **Gordon Elliott**; Office Worker, **Allan Lane**.

CREDITS: Director, **Thornton Freeland**; Screenwriter, **Sheridan Gibney**; Editor, **Herbert Levy**; Art Director, **Esdras Hartley**; Cinematographer, **Barney McGill**; Musical Conductor, **Leo F. Forbstein**.

RUNNING TIME: 66 min.

SOURCE: Novel by **Faith Baldwin**.

STORY: Norman Foster and Loretta Young are in love, but Foster doesn't want to marry until he becomes successful. Foster is asked to transfer from New York to Argentina. Young convinces Foster not to go, marry her and allow her to continue working. Foster loses his job, while Young becomes successful. Angry, Foster walks out on Young. Young learns Foster has become gravely ill and rushes to his side. She decides to give up her position to be with Foster.

NOTES AND COMMENTARY: Gordon Elliott shows up as a birthday party guest. Elliott arrives just ahead of Loretta Young and George Brent. He and a young lady race to the club entrance, and he says, "Hello gang. Be right with you." He hands his hat to an attendant, saying, "There you are." Elliott then looks up and asks, "How are you?"

Also in the film, unbilled, is future western star Allan Lane. Both he and Elliott would be seen in *Crooner* (First National Pictures, 1932). Elliott and Lane would both play Red Ryder for Republic in the forties. Also, Elliott and Lane would be guest stars in Roy Rogers' *Bells of Rosarita* (Republic, 1945).

REVIEWS: "The situation needs fresher writing and a less commonplace statement than it has received in this new film to make it worth listening to again." *New York Times*, 6/4/32; "The story could have been more original and the insights more profound." *The Warner Bros. Story*, Hirshhorn.

SUMMATION: An unspectacular drama about "modern" matrimony, *Week-End Marriage* barely succeeds in holding one's interest.

He Could Buy Any Girl! But He Married the One He Didn't Desire — To Spite the One He Loved!

West of Broadway

Metro-Goldwyn-Mayer (November, 1931)

CAST: Jerry, **John Gilbert**; Axel, **El Brendel**; Dot, **Lois Moran**; Anne, **Madge Evans**; Mac, **Ralph Bellamy**; Judge Barham, **Frank Conroy**; Maizie, **Gwen Lee**; Mrs. Trent, **Hedda Hopper**; Barbara, **Ruth Renick**; Wing, **Willie Fung**// Nightclub Patron, **Gordon Elliott**.

CREDITS: Director, **Harry Beaumont**; Story, **Ralph Graves** and **Bess Meredyth**; Screenwriters, **Gene Markey** and **J.K. McGuinness**; Editor, **George Hively**; Art Director, **Cedric Gibbons**; Cinematographer, **Merritt B. Gerstad**; Wardrobe, **Vivian Baer**; Sound, **Douglas Shearer**.

SONGS: "Mademoiselle from Armentieres" — sung by male chorus; "The Strawberry Roan" (Vincent and Howard) — sung by male chorus; "A Cowboy's Dream" (Bowman and Miller) — sung by male chorus.

RUNNING TIME: 68 min.

STORY: After being jilted by Madge Evans, wealthy John Gilbert marries working girl Lois Moran on the rebound. Gilbert had been drinking, and when he sobers up he tells Moran he wants a divorce. He then travels to his Arizona ranch, where he finds Moran waiting for him. Moran feels she can change Gilbert's mind about the divorce. Gilbert still insists on a divorce and gives Moran a handsome check. Moran, as she leaves, returns the check. Gilbert finally realizes Moran is the right woman for him, and she agrees to stay.

NOTES AND COMMENTARY: Gordon Elliott can be seen at a table in the background during the nightclub sequence with Gilbert, Moran, and Evans.

REVIEWS: "The result is totally unconvincing and barely coherent mass of material through which the yarn frequently double crosses itself." *Variety*, 2/2/32; "A feeble outing for former superstar Gilbert." *Motion Picture Guide*, Nash and Ross.

SUMMATION: Moderately entertaining drama of a wealthy man finding happiness with a working girl.

Double Murder! Double Action! Double Thrills!

While the Patient Slept

Warner Bros. (March, 1935)

A First National Picture; A Clue Club Picture

CAST: Sarah Keate, **Aline MacMahon**; Lance O'Leary, **Guy Kibbee**; Ross, **Lyle Talbot**; March, **Patricia Ellis**; Jackson, **Allen Jenkins**; Adolphe, **Robert Barrat**; Eustace, **Hobart Cavanaugh**; Mittie, **Dorothy Tree**; Dimuck, **Henry O'Neill**; Dr. Jay, **Russell Hicks**; Isobel, **Helen Flint**; Grondal, **Brandon Hurst**; Muldoon, **Eddie Shubert**; Richard Federie, **Walter Walker**.

CREDITS: Director, **Ray Enright**; Screenwriters, **Robert N. Lee** and **Eugene Solow**; Editor, **Owen Marks**; Art Director, **Esdras Hartley**; Cinematographer, **Arthur Edeson**; Gowns, **Orry-Kelly**; Dialogue Director, **Gene Lewis**; Musical Conductor, **Leo F. Forbstein**.

RUNNING TIME: 65 min.

SOURCE: Novel, *While the Patient Slept* by **Mignon G. Eberhart**.

STORY: On a dark, rainy night in an isolated mansion owned by wealthy Walter Walker, Robert Barrat is murdered. After the arrival of the police, the butler, Brandon Hurst, is killed. Through the efforts of nurse Aline MacMahon and police Detective Lieutenant Guy Kibbee, lawyer Henry O'Neill is revealed as the murderer.

NOTES AND COMMENTARY: The scene in which bank teller Gordon Elliott discloses the financial status of Walter Walker was deleted, as was a scene with Sam Godfrey as a medical examiner.

REVIEWS: "It's quite unsatisfactory." *The New York Times*, 3/2/35; "While the patient slept, so did the audience. An inferior thriller." *The Warner Bros. Story*, Hirshhorn.

SUMMATION: Interesting, speedy whodunit until a swift and unsatisfactory denouement.

The Gayest, Smartest, Grandest Entertainment of the Year!

Wife, Doctor and Nurse

20th Century–Fox (September, 1937)

CAST: Ina, **Loretta Young**; Dr. Judd Lewis, **Warner Baxter**; Steve, **Virginia Bruce**; Mrs. Krueger, **Jane Darwell**; Dr. Therberg, **Sidney Blackmer**; Pompout, **Maurice Cass**; Constance, **Minna Gombell**; Mrs. Cunningham, **Margaret Irving**; Bruce Thomas, **Gordon Elliott**; Glen Wylie, **Elisha Cook, Jr.**; Specialty, **Brewster Twins**; Bill, **Paul Hurst**; Dr. Hedges, **Hal K. Dawson**; Red, **George Ernest**; Nick, **Georges Renavent**; Uncle, **Spencer Charters**;

Miss Farrell, **Claire Du Brey**; Chauffeur, **Lon Chaney, Jr.**; Chef, **Charles Judels**; Delivery Man, **Stanley Fields**; Doorman, **Olin Howlin**; Supt. of Nurses, **Jan Duggan**.

CREDITS: Director, **Walter Lang**; Assistant Director, **Gene Bryant**; Producer, **Darryl F. Zanuck**; Associate Producer, **Raymond Griffith**; Screenwriters, **Kathryn Scola**, **Darrell Ware** and **Lamar Trotti**; Editor, **Walter Thompson**; Art Director, **David Hall**; Set Decorator, **Thomas Little**; Cinematographer, **Ed-**

ward **Cronjager**; Costumes, **Gwen Wakeling**; Sound, **Joseph Aiken** and **Roger Heman**; Musical Director, **Arthur Lange**.

SONG: "You Can't Have Everything" (Revel and Gordon) — sung by the **Brewster Twins**.

RUNNING TIME: 85 min.

STORY: Dr. Warner Baxter and his patient, Loretta Young, fall in love and impulsively get married. Young finds out that Baxter's assistant is Virginia Bruce. Young and Bruce have lunch, where Bruce says there has been no time for romance in their medical careers. This conversation makes Bruce realize she's really in love with Baxter, and she decides to leave his employ. Baxter's mood changes for the worse until Bruce returns. With Baxter's mood back to normal, Young thinks Baxter is in love with Bruce and decides to file for divorce. Now Baxter, normally a teetotaler, begins drinking. Young has a change of heart and returns. Baxter reverts to his normal state, needing Young for his personal life and Bruce for his professional life to be a stable, happy individual, a fact agreed upon by both Young and Bruce.

NOTES AND COMMENTARY: Gordon Elliott receives ninth billing in this comedy outing. Elliott plays a socialite who is one of Loretta Young's suitors. When Warner Baxter arrives at the High Hat nightclub, Elliott is one of the two men with Young. He shows jealousy when Baxter takes Young away from the table. Baxter brings Young back when he receives an emergency call. Elliott bids Baxter good night. Elliott and Young exchange a clearing of throats as Elliott notices the mutual attraction between Baxter and Young. In his final scene at a party, Elliott is in Young's company until Baxter arrives late and tells Young she should have married him. Elliott is very effective in his brief appearance, especially in the throat-clearing sequence.

REVIEWS: "A sparkling, cleverly written and finely directed comedy." *Variety*, 9/8/37; "The material isn't much but the direction has a light touch that gives the right tone to work." *Motion Picture Guide*, Nash and Ross.

SUMMATION: A bright little comedy sparked by neat performances by Young, Baxter and Bruce.

She Craved the Love of Her Husband's Son.

Woman Between

A Radio Picture (August, 1931)

ALTERNATE TITLE: *Madame Julie*.

CAST: Julie, **Lily Damita**; Victor, **Lester Vail**; John Whitcomb, **O.P. Heggie**; Doris, **Miriam Seegar**; Helen, **Anita Louise**; Mrs. Black, **Ruth Weston**; Buddy, **Lincoln Stedman**; Mrs. Weston, **Blanche Friderici**; Frederick Weston, **William Morris**; Barton, **Halliwell Hobbes**// Matson, **Gordon Elliott**.

CREDITS: Director, **Victor Schertzinger**; Producer, **William LeBaron**; Screenwriter, **Howard Estabrook**; Editor, **William Hamilton**; Art Director/Costumes, **Max Ree**; Cinematographer, **J. Roy Hunt**; Sound, **Hugh McDowell, Jr.**

SONG: "Close to Me" (Schertzinger) — sung by **Lily Damita**.

RUNNING TIME: 73 min.

SOURCE: Play by **Irving Kaye Davis**.

STORY: Under an assumed name, Lester Vail has fallen in love with Lily Damita, the stepmother he had never seen. Vail had been estranged from his father, O.P. Heggie. At a dinner party to celebrate Vail's return, they learn the truth. Seeing Damita despondent, Heggie plans to revitalize their marriage by turning over control of his business to Vail and spending his life with Damita. Vail asks Damita to run away with him, but she realizes Heggie is the man she truly loves.

NOTES AND COMMENTARY: Gordon Elliott can be seen dancing during the gala party sequence. Then as Lily Damita and O.P. Heggie leave the dance floor, Heggie calls to Elliott by name and says, "Congratulations. Just heard the news." Elliott replies, "Did you really?"

REVIEWS: "Nothing serious or consequential happens, and the slight humor is forced. Minor program material." *Variety*, 10/27/31; "The rather daring theme failed to ignite much of a spark." *Motion Picture Guide*, Nash and Ross.

SUMMATION: So-so soap opera story of a woman torn between the love of her husband and stepson.

At Last It Can Be Told!
The Story of the Woman Whose Sealed Lips Sealed a Man's Doom ... Who Let Him Go on Trial
Before a Jury for His Life — Because She Didn't Dare Go on Trial Before the World for Her Honor!

The Woman in Red

Warner Bros. (February, 1935)
A First National Picture
CAST: Shelby Barret, **Barbara Stanwyck**; Johnny Wyatt, **Gene Raymond**; Nicko, **Genevieve Tobin**; Eugene Fairchild, **John Eldredge**; Dan, **Phillip Reed**; Olga, **Dorothy Tree**; Clayton, **Russell Hicks**; Aunt Bettina, **Nella Walker**; Grandpa Wyatt, **Claude Gillingwater**; Mrs. Casserly, **Doris Lloyd**; Wyatt Furness, **Hale Hamilton**; Foxall, **Ed Van Sloan**; Uncle Emlen, **Brandon Hurst**// Stuart Wyatt, **Gordon Elliott**.

CREDITS: Director, **Robert Florey**; Screenwriters, **Mary C. McCall, Jr.** and **Peter Milne**; Editor, **Terry Morse**; Art Director, **Esdras Hartley**; Cinematographer, **Sol Polito**; Gowns, **Orry-Kelly**; Musical Conductor, **Leo F. Forbstein**; Dialogue Director, **Stanley Logan**.

SONG: "I Only Have Eyes for You" (Dubin and Warren) — sung by **Gene Raymond**.

RUNNING TIME: 68 min.

SOURCE: Novel, *North Shore* by **Wallace Irwin**.

STORY: Socialite Gene Raymond meets Barbara Stanwyck, both of whom work for wealthy Genevieve Tobin, and falls for her immediately. When Tobin finds Raymond has proposed to Stanwyck, she fires them both. Needing money, Stanwyck and Raymond decide to train and board horses, but they need capital to get started. Businessman John Eldredge, who loves Stanwyck, loans her the money. Eldredge asks Stanwyck to come aboard his yacht to help him swing a business deal. El-

dredge's former girlfriend, Dorothy Tree, arrives with Eldredge's potential business partner. Both have been drinking heavily. Tree accidentally falls overboard and drowns. Eldredge is accused of murder. As things look bad for Eldredge, Stanwyck comes to court to testify on his behalf, and the case is dismissed. Stanwyck thinks her marriage to Raymond is over, since the prosecution tried to paint her as an adulteress, but finds Raymond has faith in her and still loves her.

NOTES AND COMMENTARY: Gordon Elliott plays a member of Gene Raymond's family. He is first seen sitting in the spectator's box at a horse show with Raymond and Genevieve Tobin. Then Elliott is one of the men surrounding Tobin at her party, and watches her dance with Raymond. Next, Elliott is seen at a Long Island party where Stanwyck takes Tobin away from him to talk to her. Elliott also can be seen at the Hunt breakfast, and comes to the courthouse with Raymond and the rest of his family. This is one film in which Elliott can be seen periodically throughout the picture.

REVIEWS: "Not first rate entertainment of course, but a generally interesting and well acted picture." *New York Times*, 3/23/35; "Filmed from a dangerously weak screenplay, *The Woman in Red* is a success only because Stanwyck is a success." *Motion Picture Guide*, Nash and Ross.

SUMMATION: Good drama, thanks to a well-acted performance by Stanwyck. Gordon Elliott is adequate in his role.

Wonder Bar

First National Pictures (March, 1934)

CAST: Al Wonder, **Al Jolson**; Liane, **Kay Francis**; Inez, **Dolores Del Rio**; Harry, **Ricardo Cortez**; Tommy, **Dick Powell**; Simpson, **Guy Kibbee**; Mrs. Simpson, **Ruth Donnelly**; Pratt, **Hugh Herbert**; Mrs. Pratt, **Louise Fazenda**; Hal Le Roy, **Hal Le Roy**; Mitzi, **Fifi D'Orsay**; Claire, **Merna Kennedy**; Richard, **Henry O'Neill**; Captain Von Ferring, **Robert Barrat**, Mr. Renaud, **Henry Kolker**; Pete, **Spencer Charters**// Norman, **Gordon Elliott**.

CREDITS: Director, **Lloyd Bacon**; Screenplay/Adaptation, **Earl Baldwin**; Editor, **George Amy**; Art Directors, **Jack Okey** and **Willy Pogany**; Cinematographer, **Sol Polito**; Gowns, **Orry-Kelly**; Choreographer, **Busby Berkeley**; Musical Director, **Leo F. Forbstein**.

SONGS: "Welcome to My Wonder Bar / Vive La France" (Dubin and Warren)— sung by **Al Jolson**; "All Washed Up" (Warren)— instrumental; "Don't Say Good-night" (Dubin and Warren)— sung by **Dick Powell** with **chorus**, and danced by **Dolores Del Rio** and **Ricardo Cortez** with **chorus**; "You're So Divine" (Dubin and Warren)— instrumental; "Ochi Tchornya (Dark Eyes)" (traditional Russian ballad)— sung by **Al Jolson**; "Wonder Bar" (Dubin and Warren)— sung by **Dick Powell**; "Why Do I Dream Those Dreams" (Dubin and Warren)— sung by **Dick Powell**; "Tango Del Rio" (Warren)— danced by **Dolores Del Rio** and **Ricardo Cortez**; "Goin' to Heaven on a Mule" (Dubin and Warren)— sung by **Al Jolson** with **chorus**, and danced by **chorus**.

RUNNING TIME: 84 min.

SOURCE: Play by **Geza Herczeg, Karl Farkas** and **Robert Katscher**.

STORY: Dancer Dolores Del Rio is in love with her dancing partner, Ricardo Cortez. Cortez is having an affair with Kay Francis, wife of a noted banker, Henry Kolker. Café owner Al Jolson and singer Dick Powell are both in love with Del Rio. Hearing that Cortez is planning to leave with Francis for America, Del Rio, in a jealous rage, stabs Cortez. Jolson is able to cover up the crime. Francis goes back to Kolker. Del Rio and Powell plan to renew their love affair.

NOTES AND COMMENTARY: Gordon Elliott has a nice part as a gigolo who makes a pass at Louise Fazenda. First, Elliott puts his hands on Fazenda's back, and she tells Elliott her hotel room number. Next, Fazenda throws her purse at Elliott, and Elliott, after returning the purse, kisses the hands of both Fazenda and Ruth Donnelly. Finally, Elliott gives Fazenda a card with his telephone number.

Dick Jones remembered Gordon Elliott as a dress extra, with a thin mustache and slicked-back hair.

REVIEWS: "A tip top musical." *Variety*, 3/6/34; "The quintessential Warner Bros. thirties musical." *The Warner Bros. Story*, Hirshhorn.

SUMMATION: Highly entertaining musical-comedy-drama, with sparkling dialogue and a strong plot.

Working Girls

Paramount (December, 1931)

CAST: June Thorpe, **Judith Wood**; May Thorpe, **Dorothy Hall**; Boyd, **Charles** "Buddy" Rogers; Dr. Von Schrader, **Paul Lukas**; Pat Kelly, **Stuart Erwin**; Louise Adams, **Frances Dee**; Modiste, **Marjorie Gateson**; Mrs.

Adams, **Virginia Hammond**; Mrs. Johnstone, **Mary Forbes**; Lou, **Frances Moffett**; Jane, **Claire Dodd**; Loretta, **Dorothy Stickney**// Nightclub Patron, **Gordon Elliott**.

CREDITS: Director, **Dorothy Arzner**; Screenwriter, **Zoe Akins**; Cinematographer, **Harry Fischbeck**.

SONG: "Who Was Made for Who"— played by **orchestra**, and sung by **unknown singer**.

RUNNING TIME: 77 min.

SOURCE: Play, *Blind Mice* by **Vera Caspary** and **Winifred Lenihan**.

STORY: Sisters Judith Wood and Dorothy Hall come to New York City to find jobs and meet men. Hall obtains a job with Paul Lukas, who asks Hall to marry him. Hall refuses because she's in love with Charles "Buddy" Rogers. Wood begins working in a hotel tele-graph office, where she meets musician Stuart Erwin. Rogers and socialite Frances Dee become engaged, with Rogers not knowing Hall is pregnant with his child. Hall now accepts Lukas' marriage proposal. Rogers and Dee break off their engagement. Wood and Erwin are instrumental in Rogers marrying Hall. Wood meets Lukas and tells him of Hall's marriage. Lukas and Wood realize they love each other.

NOTES AND COMMENTARY: In the nightclub scene, while "Who Was Made for Who" is being sung, Gordon Elliott can be seen briefly on the dance floor.

REVIEW: "Typical 'woman's picture.'" *Motion Picture Guide*, Nash and Ross.

SUMMATION: The seamy story in this trite melodrama fails to ignite the screen.

Gay! Smart! Grand Entertainment! One of the Year's Great Pictures ... a Twinkle in Its Eye and a Catch in Its Heart!

You Can't Have Everything

20th Century–Fox (August, 1937)

CAST: Judith Wells Poe, **Alice Faye**; the Ritz Brothers, **the Ritz Brothers**; George Macrae, **Don Ameche**; Sam Gordon, **Charles Winniger**; Lulu Riley, **Louise Hovick**; David Rubinoff, **David Rubinoff**; Bevins, **Arthur Treacher**; Bobby Walker, **Tony Martin**; Evelyn Moore, **Phyllis Brooks**; Jerry, **Wally Vernon**; Specialty, **Tip, Tap and Toe**; Orchestra leader, **Louis Prima**; Romano, **George Humbert**; Mr. Whiteman, **Jed Prouty**; Blonde, **Dorothy Christy**// Lulu's Companion in Havana, **Gordon Elliott**.

CREDITS: Director, **Norman Taurog**; Assistant Director, **Jasper Blystone**; Producer, **Darryl F. Zanuck**; Associate Producer, **Laurence Schwab**; Story, **Gregory Ratoff**; Screenwriters, **Harry Tugend**, **Jack Yellen** and **Karl Tunberg**; Editor, **Hanson Fritch**; Art Director, **Duncan Cramer**; Set Decorations, **Thomas Little**; Cinematographer, **Lucien Andriot**; Costumes, **Royer**; Sound, **Arthur Von Kirbach** and **Roger Heman**; Musical Director, **David Buttolph**.

SONGS: "Santa Lucia" (Neapolitan folk song)— sung by **George Humbert** and **unknown singer**, and played by **trio** (**Frank Yaconelli**, **Nick Moro** and **unknown violinist**); "You Can't Have Everything" (Revel and Gordon)— sung by **Alice Faye**; "Chopsticks"(traditional)— played and sung by **the Ritz Brothers**; "Danse Rubinoff" (Rubinoff)— played by **David Rubinoff**; "Long Underwear" (Pokrass, Kuller and Golden)— sung and danced by **the Ritz Brothers** and **chorus**; "The Loveliness of You" (Revel and Gordon)— sung by **Tony Martin**; "Sing, Sing, Sing" (Prima)— played by **Louis Prima and His Band**; "Danger — Love at Work" (Revel and Gordon)— sung by **Alice Faye**, with **Louis Prima and His Band**; "You Can't Have Everything" (reprise)— sung by **the Ritz Brothers**, with **Louis Prima and His Band**; "Afraid to Dream" (Revel and Gordon)— sung by **Don Ameche**; "Afraid to Dream" (reprise)— sung by **Alice Faye**, **Tony Martin** and **chorus**; "Afraid to Dream" (reprise)— played by **David Rubinoff**, **Frank**

Yaconelli and band; "You Can't Have Everything" (reprise)—sung by **Alice Faye**, with **David Rubinoff**; "Please Pardon Us—We're in Love" (Revel and Gordon)—sung by **Alice Faye**; "Rhythm on the Radio" (Revel)—danced by **Tip, Tap and Toe**; "North Pole Sketch" (Revel and Gordon)—sung by **the Ritz Brothers, Tony Martin** and others, danced by **the Ritz Brothers**; "Please Pardon Us—We're in Love" (reprise)—sung by **Alice Faye, Don Ameche, Charles Winniger, the Ritz Brothers, Louise Hovick** and **Tony Martin**.

RUNNING TIME: 100 min.

STORY: Serious playwright Alice Faye, who can sing, is persuaded to take the leading role in Don Ameche's latest musical on Broadway. Ameche and Faye fall in love. Romance turns sour when Louise Hovick shows Ameche a marriage certificate and tells him they were married one night when he was drunk. Faye leaves New York but returns when she finds that her dramatic play has been rewritten as a musical comedy. Faye's anger subsides when the show becomes a hit. Ameche discovers the marriage license is invalid because he passed out before he could sign the document. Ameche and Faye are reunited.

NOTES AND COMMENTARY: Even though Gordon Elliott doesn't receive on-screen billing in this feature, his role is pivotal to the story. Elliot is seen in one scene with Louise Hovick, who went on to greater fame as Gypsy Rose Lee. Elliott is Hovick's companion in Havana and shows her a gossip column linking Don Ameche with Alice Faye. Hovick is incensed, even though she is cavorting with Elliott, and leaves immediately for New York City. Elliott is effective in his brief role.

REVIEWS: "A wild and hilarious filmusical, one of the best of the series of this type 20th Century–Fox has turned out." *Variety*, 7/28/37; "Good show-biz musical." *1996 Movie & Video Guide*, Maltin.

SUMMATION: A sparkling, tune-filled musical comedy.

Appendices

A. Elliott's Short Subject Appearances

In addition to feature films, Elliott appeared in a number of short subjects, usually released by Hal Roach/Metro-Goldwyn-Mayer or Warner Bros.

Napoleon Jr.

Fox (October, 1926)
CAST: **Frank J. Coleman**
CREDITS: Director, **Mark Sandrich**; Assistant Director, **Lesley Selander**; Screenwriters, **Edward Moran, Edward Marshall**.
NOTES AND COMMENTARY: Various sources state that Gordon Elliott has a role in this Jerry-the-Giant comedy short subject.
SUMMATION: This short feature was not available for viewing by the author.

The Boy Friend

Metro-Goldwyn-Mayer (November, 1928)
A Hal Roach Production
CAST: **Edgar Kennedy, Marion Byron, Max Davidson, Gordon Elliott, Fay Holderness**.
CREDITS: Director, **Fred L. Guiol**; Screenwriter, **Leo McCarey**; Editor, **Richard Currier**; Cinematographer, **Len Powers**.
RUNNING TIME: 21 min.
Notes and Commentary: One source indicates Gordon Elliott was featured in this short subject.
SUMMATION: This short feature was not available for viewing by the author.

Fast Work

Metro-Goldwyn-Mayer (June, 1930)
A Hal Roach Production
ALTERNATE TITLE: *The Fast Worker.*
CAST: **Charley Chase; June Marlowe; Dell Henderson; Charles K. French; Broderick O'Farrell; Pat Harmon; Gus Kerner; William Gillespie; Gordon Elliott.**
CREDITS: Director, **James W. Horne**; Screenwriters, **Leo McCarey** and **H.M. Walker**; Editor, **Richard Currier**; Music, **Leroy Shield**.
RUNNING TIME: 19 min.
STORY: Charley Chase is immediately attracted to June Marlowe. Chase meets a man who he thinks is Marlowe's father. The man turns out to be an escapee from the Insane Asylum.
NOTES AND COMMENTARY: Many sources indicate Gordon Elliott has a role in this production, but there is no mention of his character name. In a biographical sketch of Elliott for the Pasadena Community Playhouse playbill for their production of *The Young Idea* in 1932, it was noted that Elliott was under contract to the Hal Roach Studios. Elliott would appear in four comedy shorts.
REVIEW: "A laughgetter that takes front rank among two reel talkers," *Variety*, May 14, 1930.
SUMMATION: This short feature was not available for viewing by the author.

Let's Do Things

Metro-Goldwyn-Mayer (June, 1931)
A Hal Roach Production
CAST: **Thelma Todd; Zasu Pitts; George Byron; Jerry Mandy; Charlie Hall**// Music Store Customer, **Gordon Elliott.**
CREDITS: Director, **Hal Roach**; Screenwriter, **H.M. Walker**; Editor, **Richard C. Cur-**

rier; Cinematographer, **George Stevens**; Sound, **Elmer Raguse**.

RUNNING TIME: 27 min.

STORY: Thelma Todd and Zasu Pitts go on a double date with George Byron and Charlie Hall. A wild, zany time results.

NOTES AND COMMENTARY: In the opening scene, Gordon Elliott leans across a piano as Thelma Todd sings.

SUMMATION: This short feature was not available for viewing by the author.

What a Bozo

Metro-Goldwyn-Mayer (November, 1931)
A Hal Roach Production
CAST: Charley Chase, **Charley Chase**; Gay, **Gay Seabrook**; Elizabeth Van Forrester, **Elizabeth Forrester**; Waiter, **Charlie Hall**; Harry Bowen; **Sidney Bracey**// Diner, **Gordon Elliott**.
CREDITS: Director, **James Parrott**; Screenwriter, **H.M. Walker**; Music, **Leroy Shield**.
SONG: "Smile When the Raindrops Fall."
RUNNING TIME: 21 min.
NOTES AND COMMENTARY: Various sources state Gordon Elliott can be seen as a café diner.
SUMMATION: This short feature was not available for viewing by the author.

Taxi Barons

Metro-Goldwyn-Mayer (April, 1933)
A Hal Roach Production; A "Taxi Boys" short
CAST: Ben, **Ben Blue**; Billy, **Billy Gilbert**; Almeda Fowler; **Billy Bletcher**; **Eddie Baker**// Ship's Officer, **Gordon Elliott**.
CREDITS: Director, **Del Lord**; Editor, **Louis McManus**; Cinematographer, **Art Lloyd**; Sound, **James Greene**.
RUNNING TIME: 20 min.
STORY: Cab drivers Ben Blue and Billy Gilbert run afoul of a motorcycle policeman. They take refuge on a docked ship. Assuming the disguises of a baron and general, they leave the ship, but their taxi breaks down in front of an estate where the real baron and the general are guests of honor. The police arrive; the boys again make their escape but steal a police car with policemen in the car and are arrested.
NOTES AND COMMENTARY: Gordon Elliott has two scenes as a ship's officer. First, Ben Blue and Billy Gilbert get by Elliott at the gangplank and board the ship. Then Elliott helps police

officers search the ship for Blue and Gilbert.

SUMMATION: Mildly amusing but generally unfunny slapstick comedy short.

Handlebars

Metro-Goldwyn-Mayer (August, 1933)
CAST: Narrator, **Pete Smith**// Bicyclist, **Gordon Elliott**.
CREDITS: Director, **Jules White**; Producer, **Pete Smith**.
RUNNING TIME: 10 min.
STORY: The history of the bicycle is told in comedic tones dating back to 1819.
NOTES AND COMMENTARY: One source states Gordon Elliott is the bicyclist in this comedy short subject.
SUMMATION: This short feature was not available for viewing by the author.

Good Morning, Eve!

Warner Bros. (August, 1934)
CAST: Adam, **Leon Errol**; Eve, **June MacCloy**; Nero, **Vernon Dent**; Guinevere, **Maxine Doyle**// Sir Lancelot, **Gordon Elliott**.
CREDITS: Director, **Roy Mack**; Screenwriters, **Cyrus Wood, Eddie Moran** and **A. Dorian Otvos**; Editor, **Frank McGee**; Art Direction, **John Hughes**; Cinematographer, **Ray Rennahan**; Gowns, **Milo Anderson**; Music, **Cliff Hess**; Musical Conductor, **Leo F. Forbstein**; Choreographer, **Bob Vreeland**; Technicolor Color Consultant, **Natalie Kalmus**; Color by TECHNICOLOR.
SONGS: "When I Put Rhythm in the Bow" (Hess)—sung by **Vernon Dent** and quartet; "They Got There Just the Same" (Hess)—sung by **Maxine Doyle** and chorus; "Look at That Baby" (Hess)—sung by **Harry Seymour**. (Note: The title names are best guesses by the author.)
RUNNING TIME: 19 min.
STORY: The snake in the Garden of Eden temps Leon Errol and June MacCloy to take a bite of the forbidden apple. Errol and MacCloy begin a trip through history. Errol and MacCloy visit ancient Rome for a concert in Emperor Vernon Dent's gardens. In King Arthur's Camelot, Errol and MacCloy meet a heroic knight, Gordon Elliott, who engages in battle with the Black Knight. Elliott, with Errol's assistance, is victorious. Reaching the 20th Century, Errol and MacCloy hitch a plane ride to a beach filled with a cluster of bathing beauties. Errol is accosted

by a policeman and knocked unconscious. Errol awakes to find that he's been dreaming. Errol and MacCloy are staying at the Garden of Eden Nudist Colony. As they and other residents begin to undress, the police arrive and give chase.

NOTES AND COMMENTARY: In a portent of heroic things to come, Gordon Elliott takes the part of the brave knight, Sir Lancelot. Elliott battles the Black Knight and then, on horseback, brings MacCloy to King Arthur's Court. In the final scene at the nudist colony, Elliott is one of the residents who start to undress prior to the arrival of the police.

SUMMATION: This is a bright, sparkling musical comedy short with some nice puns.

Romance of the West

Warner Bros. (August, 1935)

CAST: **Phil Regan; Dorothy Dare; Henry Armetta; Mary Treen; Gordon Elliott; Joe King.**

CREDITS: Director, **Ralph Staub**; Screenwriter, **Joe Traub**; Color by TECHNICOLOR.

NOTES AND COMMENTARY: This short feature marked Gordon Elliott's fifth appearance in a western setting.

SUMMATION: This short film was not available for viewing by the author.

Romance in the Air

Warner Bros. (June, 1936)
A Broadway Brevity
CAST: **Wini Shaw; Gordon Elliott.**
CREDITS: Director, **Murray Roth**; Screenwriter, **George Bricker.**

NOTES AND COMMENTARY: One source states that Gordon Elliott appears in this short subject.

SUMMATION: This short feature was not available for viewing by the author, nor was there any substantial information.

Meet the Stars: Meet Roy Rogers

Republic (June, 1941)
Harriet Parsons Series

ALTERNATE TITLE: *Meet Roy Rogers.*

CAST: **Roy Rogers; Gene Autry; Judy Canova; Bill Elliott; George "Gabby" Hayes; Billy Gilbert; Bob Baker; Roscoe Ates; Mary Lee; "Trigger"**; Narrator, **Harriet Parsons.**

CREDITS: Director/ Producer, **Harriet Parsons**.

RUNNING TIME: 10 min.

STORY: Roy Rogers displays the station wagon and trailer he uses on his personal appearance tours, accompanied by his wife Arlene, adopted baby girl Cheryl, and his horse Trigger. Next, Rogers is shown at the Rangers' Trading Post where he sells western attire to his cowboy pals. Gene Autry, Judy Canova, Bill Elliott, George "Gabby" Hayes, Billy Gilbert, Bob Baker, Roscoe Ates and Mary Lee attend the opening.

NOTES AND COMMENTARY: Bill Elliott was on the Republic lot in 1937 in two supporting roles as Gordon Elliott. This was his first appearance as Bill at Republic. In 22 months, Elliott would be one of the mainstays at Republic, replacing Gene Autry.

Summation: This short feature was not available for viewing by the author.

Screen Snapshots: Reno's Silver Spur Awards

Columbia (January, 1951)

CAST: **Ralph Staub; John Ford; John Wayne; Harry Carey, Jr.**; Emcee, **Don Wilson// Wild Bill Elliott.**

CREDITS: Director/ Screenwriter, **Ralph Staub**.

LOCATION FILMING: Reno, Nevada.

RUNNING TIME: 9 min.

STORY: This short covers the 1951 Reno Silver Spurs Awards that went to director John Ford and actors John Wayne and Harry Carey, Jr. for their work on *Rio Grande* (Republic, 1950).

NOTES AND COMMENTARY: Wild Bill Elliott is reported to have been in Reno at the time and was captured by the camera.

SUMMATION: This short feature was not available for viewing by the author.

B. Other Elliott Film Appearances

From the use of stock footage, Elliott can be seen in the following films.

GUNS BLAZE ... when Monte goes after wanted men...!

Prince of the Plains

Republic (April, 1949)

CAST: Bat Masterson, **Monte Hale**; Sheriff Hank Hartley, **Paul Hurst**; Julie Phillips, **Shirley Davis**; Regan, **Roy Barcroft**; James Taylor, **Rory Mallinson**; Tom Owens, **Harry Lauter**; Keller, **Lane Bradford**; Sam Phillips, **George Carleton**.

CREDITS: Director, **Philip Ford**; Associate Producer, **Melville Tucker**; Screenwriters, **Louise Rousseau** and **Albert DeMond**; Editor, **Richard L. Van Enger**; Art Director, **Fred A. Ritter**; Set Decoration, **John McCarthy Jr.** and **James Redd**; Cinematography, **Bud Thackery**; Makeup, **Bob Mark**; Sound, **T.A. Carman**; Music, **Stanley Wilson**, Special Effects, **Howard** and **Theodore Lydecker**.

SONG: "Send My Mail to the Owensville Jail"— sung by **Monte Hale**.

LOCATION FILMING: Iverson, California.

RUNNING TIME: 60 min.

STORY: Monte Hale, trying to find the murderer of his parents, runs into photographer Rory Mallinson's scheme to take over Harry Lauter's bank. Hale finally forces Mallinson out into the open. Mallinson attempts to escape, but Hale bulldogs Mallinson from his horse. The two men engage in a furious fistfight on a high precipice, from which Mallinson falls to his death. Hale rides off to become a noted peace officer.

NOTES AND COMMENTARY: Scenes from two of Wild Bill Elliott's first Republic series entries were used in this Monte Hale episode. Hale was dressed to resemble Elliott, even to the point of Hale carrying two guns, which was normally out of character for him. In the sequence where Hale prevents the lynching of Harry Lauter, footage from *Man from Thunder River* (Republic, 1943) was used. Hale's chase and fight with Rory Mallinson was lifted from *Overland Mail Robbery* (Republic, 1943), with Elliott more obvious in this one, his guns reversed but turned around in the close-ups of Hale.

REVIEW: "More than passable entry in Monte Hale's series for Republic." *Western Movies*, Pitts.

SUMMATION: Entertaining Monte Hale western.

ADVENTURE ON THE ACTION TRAIL!

Outcasts of the Trail

Republic (June, 1949)

CAST: Pat Garrett, **Monte Hale**; Doc Meadowlark, **Paul Hurst**; Vinnie White, **Jeff Donnell**; Jim Judd, **Roy Barcroft**; "Ivory" White, **John Gallaudet**; Elias Dunkenscold, **Milton Parsons**; Chad White, **Tommy Ivo**; Mrs. Rysen, **Minerva Urecal**; Fred Smith, **Ted Mapes**; Horace Rysen, **George H. Lloyd**; Sheriff Wilson, **Steve Darrell**.

CREDITS: Director, **Philip Ford**; Associate Producer, **Melville Tucker**; Screenwriter, **Olive Cooper**; Editor, **Tony Martinelli**; Art Decorator, **Frank Arrigo**; Set Decorators, **John McCarthy Jr.** and **James Redd**; Cinematography, **Bud Thackery**; Makeup, **Bob Marx**; Sound, **Earl Crain Sr.**; Music, **Stanley Wilson**.

SONG: "How I Wish I Was a Kid Again"— sung by **Monte Hale**.

LOCATION FILMING: Iverson, California.

RUNNING TIME: 60 min.

STORY: On his release from prison, John Gallaudet plans to return the stolen money to its rightful owners. Gang leader Milton Parsons and henchman Roy Barcroft plan to steal the money and frame Gallaudet. Deputy Sheriff Monte Hale finds evidence implicating Barcroft and Parsons. In a chase, both bad men are killed and Gallaudet is cleared. It looks like a budding romance is looming between Hale and Gallaudet's daughter, Jeff Donnell.

NOTES AND COMMENTARY: Chase sequences are lifted from two Wild Bill Elliott Red Ryder films. The buckboard race at the beginning of the film is taken from *Colorado Pioneers* (Republic, 1945); it looks like Elliott, rather than a double, for a few seconds in this clip, as he drives a buckboard around a curve. It's interesting to note that Elliott has his two guns and holster strapped on while Hale is not carrying his pistol. The final chase in which Monte Hale and Paul Hurst bring Roy Barcroft and Milton Parsons to justice was lifted from *Vigilantes of Dodge City* (Republic, 1944).

REVIEW: "Good entry in Monte Hale's Republic series with an especially interesting plotline." *Western Movies*, Pitts.

SUMMATION: Neat Monte Hale western.

GREATEST FIGHTER OF THE LAWLESS FRONTIER

Riding with Buffalo Bill

Columbia (November, 1954)

CAST: Bill Cody, **Marshall Reed**; Reb Morgan, **Rick Vallin**; Maria Perez, **Joanne Rio**; Ruth Morgan, **Shirley Whitney**; Ace, **Jack Ingram**; Rocky Ford, **William Fawcett**; Bart, **Gregg Barton**; Jose Perez, **Ed Coch**; Elko, **Steve Ritch**; Darr, **Pierce Lyden**; King Carney, **Michael Fox**; Zeke, **Lee Roberts**.

CREDITS: Director, **Spencer G. Bennet**; Assistant Director, **Leonard Katzman**; Producer, **Sam Katzman**; Story and Screenwriter, **George H. Plympton**; Editor, **Earl Turner**; Art Director, **Paul Palmentola**; Set Decorator, **Sidney Clifford**; Cinematographer, **Ira H. Morgan**; Special Effects, **Jack Erickson**; Sound, **John Livadary**; Music Conductor, **Mischa Bakaleinikoff**; Set Continuity, **Florence Swan**; Unit Manager, **Leon Chooluck**.

LOCATION FILMING: Iverson, California.

RUNNING TIME: 234 min.

CHAPTER TITLES: Chapter 1, "The Ridin' Terror from St. Joe"; Chapter 2, "Law of the Six Gun"; Chapter 3, "Raiders from Ghost Town"; Chapter 4, "Cody to the Rescue"; Chapter 5, "Midnight Marauders"; Chapter 6, "Under the Avalanche"; Chapter 7, "Night Attack"; Chapter 8, "Trapped in the Powder Shack"; Chapter 9, "Into an Outlaw Trap"; Chapter 10, "Blast to Oblivion"; Chapter 11, "The Depths of the Earth"; Chapter 12, "The Ridin' Terror"; Chapter 13, "Trapped in the Apache Mine"; Chapter 14, "Railroad Wreckers"; Chapter 15, "Law Comes to the West."

STORY: Marshall Reed, in the guise of the Ridin' Terror, rids the territory of outlaw Michael Fox and his gang, with the help of Rick Vallin, William Fawcett and Shirley Whitney.

NOTES AND COMMENTARY: Both Marshall Reed and Rick Vallin dress as Bill Elliott from *Valley of Vanishing Men* (Columbia, 1942), and as Don Douglas from *Deadwood Dick* (Columbia, 1940) throughout the serial. Chapter endings from chapters 2, 4, 5, 7, 8, 11, 12, and 13, and footage from chapter 9, of *Valley of Vanishing Men* can be seen. In addition, footage of the raiders entering or leaving the ghost town, also from *Vanishing Men*, is used throughout the serial, a theme that is mysteriously dropped mid-way through the proceedings. Elliott and his double can only be seen from behind and in long shots.

REVIEW: "Latter day serial has little to recommend it; for genre fans only." *Western Movies*, Pitts.

SUMMATION: There's plenty of gunfire that shoots plenty of holes in this bottom-of-the-barrel cliffhanger's threadbare script. Incredibly, some action sequences were used more than once.

OUT OF THE FRONTIER'S GOLDEN AGE— THE SCREEN'S GREATEST TREASURE OF SERIAL THRILLS!

Blazing the Overland Trail

Columbia (August, 1956)

CAST: Tom Bridger, **Lee Roberts**; Ed Marr, **Dennis Moore**; Lola Martin, **Norma Brooks**; Captain Carter, **Gregg Barton**; Rance Devlin, **Don C. Harvey**; Alby, **Lee Morgan**; Bragg, **Pierce Lyden**; Carl, **Edward Coch**; Dunn, **Reed Howes**; Al, **Kermit Maynard**; Pete, **Pete Kellett**; Fergie, **Al Ferguson**// Wagon Train Member/Posse Member, **Bill Elliott**.

CREDITS: Director, **Spencer Bennet**; Assistant Director, **Gene Anderson Jr.**; Producer, **Sam Katzman**; Story/Screenplay, **George H. Plympton**; Editor, **Earl Turner**; Art Director, **Paul Palmentola**; Set Decorator, **Sidney Clifford**; Cinematography, **Ira H. Morgan**; Sound, **Ferol Redd**; Musical Conductor, **Mischa Bakaleinikoff**; Continuity, **Billy Vernon**.

LOCATION FILMING: Big Bear, San Bernardino National Forest, California.

RUNNING TIME: 239 min.

CHAPTER TITLES: Chapter 1, "Gun Emperor of the West"; Chapter 2, "Riding the Danger Trail"; Chapter 3, "The Black Raiders"; Chapter 4, "Into the Flames"; Chapter 5, "Trapped in a Runaway Wagon"; Chapter 6, "Rifles for Redskins"; Chapter 7, "Midnight Attack"; Chapter 8, "Blast at Gunsight Pass"; Chapter 9, "War at the Wagon Camp"; Chapter 10, "Buffalo Stampede"; Chapter 11, "Into the Fiery Blast"; Chapter 12, "Cave-In"; Chapter 13, "Bugle Call"; Chapter 14, "Blazing Peril"; Chapter 15, "Raiders Unmasked."

STORY: Don C. Harvey has dreams of a western empire, using outlaws and Indians to further his plans. Harvey is opposed by Army scout Lee Roberts, Pony Express agent Dennis Moore, Army Captain Gregg Barton and Norma Brooks. Undergoing many perilous situations, they put a stop to Harvey's scheme. Afterwards, Moore and Brooks find time for romance.

NOTES AND COMMENTARY: *Blazing the Overland Trail* utilizes stock footage from *The Flaming Frontier* (Universal, 1926), *End of the Trail* (Columbia, 1932) and, most prominently, Bill Elliott's second serial, *Overland with Kit Carson* (Columbia, 1939). Footage from *Overland with Kit Carson* is seen in each of the fifteen chapters, which means a bonanza for Bill Elliott watchers. Not only is Dennis Moore dressed to match Elliott's Kit Carson attire, which allows the audience to see Elliott riding, shooting and fighting in medium and long distance shots, but Elliott is seen both as wagon train and posse members. *Overland with Kit Carson* chapter endings from chapters 1, 2, 3, 4, 5, 6, 7, 8, 10, 11, 13 and 14 are utilized as either cliffhangers or other action scenes.

REVIEW: "Tacky cliffhanger, the final such film made in the U.S. and a sad finale to a grand genre." *Western Movies*, Pitts.

SUMMATION: Though fast paced and full of action, *Blazing the Overland Trail* ultimately offers an unsatisfactory story due to an incoherent and confusing script. The serial features bland heroes and villains, and an unbelievable actionless ending.

Brother, Can You Spare a Dime?

Goodtimes Enterprise (August, 1975)

CAST: **Robert Armstrong; Fred Astaire; Robert Barrat; Warner Baxter; Hank Bell; Jack Benny; Humphrey Bogart; James Cagney; Cab Calloway; Eddie Cantor; Hobart Cavanaugh; Winston Churchill; Betty Compson; Gary Cooper; Bing Crosby; Frankie Darro; Cecil B. DeMille; John Dillinger; Walt Disney; Tom Dugan; James Dunn; Dwight D. Eisenhower; Gordon Elliott; Madge Evans; Stepin Fetchit; W. C. Fields; Dick Foran; Gerald Ford; Preston Foster; Clark Gable; Janet Gaynor; Benny Goodman; Cary Grant; George Hayes; Billie Holliday; Herbert Hoover; J. Edgar Hoover; Bob Hope; Hubert H. Humphrey; Walter Huston; Lyndon Johnson; Al Jolson; Dickie Jones; John F. Kennedy; Joseph P. Kennedy; Alf Landon; Vivien Leigh; Carole Lombard; Huey Long; Joe Louis; Fredric March; Chico Marx; Groucho Marx; Harpo Marx; Grant Mitchell; Paul Muni; Fayard Nicholas; Harold Nicholas; Richard Nixon; Dick Powell; Paul Robeson; Bill Robinson; Dewey Robinson; Edward G. Robinson; Ginger Rogers; Will Rogers; Eleanor Roosevelt; Franklin D. Roosevelt; Max Schmeling; James Stewart; Shirley Temple; Harry S. Truman; Orson Welles; Wendell Wilkie; Loretta Young.**

CREDITS: Director/Screenwriter, **Philippe Mora**; Producers, **Sanford Licherson** and **David Puttnam**; Assistant to Producer, **Leontine Ruette**; Research, **Jennifer Ryan, Michael Barlow** and **Susan Winslow**; Editor, **Jeremy Thomas**; Assistant Editors, **Michael Saxton** and **Kathy Doughtery**; Sound, **Bill Rowe**; Dubbing Editor, **George Akers**; Dubbing Assistant, **Michael Taylor**; Apprentice, **Xavier Russell**.

SONGS: "Brother, Can You Spare a Dime" (Gorney and Harburg)— sung by **Rudy Vallee**; "Big Rock Candy Mountain" (McClintock); "Now's the Time to Fall in Love" (Sherman and Lewis)— sung by **Eddie Cantor**; "Ten Cents a Dance" (Etting); "In the Sweet Bye and Bye" (Webster); "Remember My Forgotten Man" (Dubin and Warren); "We're in the Money" (Dubin and Warren)— sung by **Ginger Rogers**; "There Is a Tavern in the Town" (Adams)— sung by **Rudy Vallee**; "We're Out of the Red"; "California, Here I Come" (Jolson, De Sylva and Meyer); "Nobody Knows You When You're Down and Out" (Cox); "In the Jailhouse Now" (Rodgers); "Song of the Crusades" (Whiting and Kepp)— sung by chorus; "Every Man's a King" (Long and Carazo); "Jeepers Creepers" (Warren and Mercer)— sung by **Louis Armstrong**; "We've Got Franklin D. Roosevelt Back Again" (Roosevelt Campaign Song); "You've Got to Have That Hi-Di-Ho in Your Soul" (Calloway and Mills)— sung by **Cab Calloway**; "Brother, Can You Spare a Dime" (Gorney and Harburg)— sung by **Bing Crosby**; "Dust Can't Kill Me" (Guthrie)— sung by **Woody Guthrie**; "Water Boy" (unknown)— sung by **Paul Robeson**; "Lonesome Man Blues"— sung by **Billie Holliday**; "Vigilante Man" (Guthrie)— sung by **Woody Guthrie**; "Hooray for Hollywood" (Whiting and Mercer)— sung by **Johnny Davis** and **Frances Langford**, with **the Benny Goodman Orchestra**; "Bei Mir Bist Du Schoen" (Cahn, Chaplin, Jacobs and Secunda)— sung by **the Andrews Sisters**; "(Where) the Blue of the Night (Meets the Gold of the Day)" (Turk, Crosby and Ahlert)— sung by **Bing Crosby**; "You're the Top" (Porter); "Brother, Can You Spare a Dime" (Gorney and Harburg)— sung by **Al Jolson**.

RUNNING TIME: 109 min.

STORY: This is a documentary on the Depression years leading up to the bombing of Pearl Harbor, utilizing archival footage from primarily newsreels and feature films. Topical songs are used to good advantage.

NOTES AND COMMENTARY: Gordon Elliott is seen as Wild Bill Hickok from the serial *The Great Adventures of Wild Bill Hickok* (Columbia, 1938). Elliott leads the Flaming Arrows, frontier children banded together to help Elliott defeat the Phantom Raiders, in reciting the Pledge of Allegiance. This was done to counterbalance a previous scene from *Black Legion* (Warner Bros., 1937) in which Humphrey Bogart pledges allegiance to the Klu Klux Klan. Later, during Franklin D. Roosevelt's speech against the United States' entry into war, a freeze frame shot of Elliott as Hickok is shown.

SUMMATION: An interesting, engrossing documentary of the Depression years.

Meanwhile, Back at the Ranch

Curtco & RCR Productions (May, 1977)

A Richard Patterson Film, in association with NTA

CAST: Rex Allen; Gene Autry; Don Barry; Bobby Blake; William Boyd; Johnny Mack Brown; Smiley Burnette; Buster Crabbe; Eddie Dean; Wild Bill Elliott; Hoot Gibson; Monte Hale; Raymond Hatton; Gabby Hayes; Tim Holt; Buck Jones; Tom Keene; Charles King; Allan "Rocky" Lane; Lash LaRue; Ken Maynard; Tim McCoy; George O'Brien; Tex Ritter; Roy Rogers; Al "Fuzzy" St. John; Fred Scott; Sons of the Pioneers; Charles Starrett; Bob Steele; Dub Taylor; Three Mesquiteers (Bob Livingston, Ray Corrigan and Max Terhune); Tom Tyler; John Wayne // Narrators, Pat Buttram and Ralph James.

CREDITS: Director/ Screenwriter/ Editor, Richard Patterson; Producer, Patrick Curtis; Associate Producers, Richard Stewart and Mike Mark; Associate Producer and Film Historian, Packy Smith; Assistant Editors, Sonja James and Craig Holt; Music Supervisor, Richard Theis; Title Photography, Stephen and Pamela Lovejoy; Sound Effects Editor, Alan Splet; Mixer, Ted Gormillion.

SONG: "Meanwhile Back at the Ranch" (Bricusse) — sung by Eddie Dean; "Ridin' the Old Prairie Trail" (Whitley) — sung by Ray Whitley and His Range Ramblers; "Texas Washboard Rag" — sung by Norman, Earl and Willie Phelps; "A Cowboy Sang His Song of Fate" — sung by John Wayne (Note: John Wayne's voice was dubbed, possibly by either Jack Kirk or Bill Bradbury); "Song of the Wanderer" — sung by Gene Autry and chorus; "Riding Down the Canyon" (Autry and Burnette) — sung by Gene Autry; "Oh, Susanna" (Foster) — played by Smiley Burnette, Eugene Jackson and Frankie Marvin; "You Are the One" (Tinorin) — sung by Pauline Moore; "Sing as You Work" — sung by Roy Rogers and the Sons of the Pioneers; "When the Work's All Done This Fall" (traditional) — sung by Monte Hale; "Ride Around Little Doggies" (traditional) — sung by Tex Ritter; "The Arizona Waltz" (Allen) — yodeled by Rex Allen; "Moseyin' Along" (P. Gates) — sung by Eddie Dean and Nancy Gates.

RUNNING TIME: 71 min.

STORY: A band of vicious outlaws, led by the mysterious Rattler, are terrorizing the inhabitants of Peaceful Valley. Twenty-five top lawmen are sent to bring the badmen to justice. As the badmen are being rounded up, the story turns out to be only a motion picture. But is it? The Rattler is seen once more, and he's up to no good.

NOTES AND COMMENTARY: Wild Bill Elliott can be seen in eight scenes. As Red Ryder, Elliott, using a bullwhip, lashes a chandelier to come from the second floor of a saloon to Bobby Blake's rescue as he's trying to stop Edward Cassidy from taking a shot at Elliott (*Tucson Raiders*, Republic, 1944). Then, as Ryder, Elliott comes out of a saloon to open fire at outlaws (*Sheriff of Las Vegas*, Republic, 1944). Next, Elliott, with Gabby Hayes looking on, deciphers a code message in an otherwise harmless looking note (*Tucson Raiders*). The fourth scene has Elliott receiving a phone call from Roy Rogers to come running (*Bells of Rosarita*, Republic, 1945). Then Buzzy Henry brings word to Elliott and Hayes that two ladies are being held captive; Elliott springs into action (*Calling Wild Bill Elliott*, Republic, 1943). Next, Elliott and some ranchers ride to the rescue (*Calling Wild Bill Elliott*). Then Elliott struggles with Francis Walker over a gun (*Return of Wild Bill*, Columbia, 1940). Finally, Elliott captures Roy Barcroft (*Bells of Rosarita*).

RUNNING TIME: The 2005 DVD release has a running time of 62 min.

SUMMATION: This interesting compilation

of film clips featuring various top movie cowboys makes a pretty cohesive story. It's worth watching, even for non-western film buffs.

Action Heroes of the Wild West

Film Shows, Inc. (1992)

Cast: **Roy Rogers**; **Gene Autry**; Hopalong Cassidy, **William Boyd**; Sunset Carson; **Lash LaRue**; Range Busters (Ray "Crash" Corrigan, **John "Dusty" King, Max "Alibi" Terhune**); **Eddie Dean**; Tex Ritter; Charles Starrett; Rex **Allen**; Three Mesquiteers (**John Wayne, Ray Corrigan, Max Terhune**); Wild Bill Elliott; Allan "Rocky" Lane; Jimmy Wakely; Ken May-

nard; Johnny Mack Brown; Buck Jones; Tim McCoy; Bob Steele; Buster Crabbe; Tim Holt; Whip Wilson; George Houston.

Running Time: 109 min.

Notes and Commentary: The film is a compilation of trailers and film clips from some of the top western stars. Wild Bill Elliott is featured in previews from four of his starring entries, *The San Antonio Kid* (Republic, 1944), *Vigilante Terror* (Allied Artists, 1953), *Kansas Territory* (Monogram, 1952) and *Cheyenne Wildcat* (Republic, 1944).

Summation: Great fun for those western buffs who like movie trailers.

C. Elliott Comic Books

In 1950 Bill Elliott made it into the pages of comic books with the publication of *Bill Elliott* 4-Color #278. Elliott, in the story "The Ghost of Poco Loco Ridge," exclaims, "Mister! I'm a peaceable man." With the second issue, the title was changed to *Wild Bill Elliott*. Beginning in June 1952, Elliott would be featured with Gene Autry, Roy Rogers, Johnny Mack Brown and Rex Allen in *Western Roundup*. Elliott, on his horse Stormy (Stormy Knight), rode through exciting adventures into 1956. In the past few years, Elliott would ride again in Bill Black's *Best of the West* comic magazine.

Bill Elliott

4-Color #278 (May, 1950)

1. The War on Spider Creek
2. The Ghost of Poco Loco Ridge
3. Drive to Thunder Butte

Wild Bill Elliott

#2 (November, 1950)

1. Medicine Trail
2. Robber's Roundup
3. A Race Against Odds

#3

1. (no title)
2. The Battle of the Prairie Star

#4 (April-May, 1951)

1. The Hooded Hangman
2. Express to Ruin

#5 (June-July, 1951)

1. The "Easy Money" Gents
2. Wet Paint Means Murder

#6 (August-September, 1951)

1. Twin Trouble
2. A Plumb Plain Trail

#7 (October-November, 1951)

1. Rustlers Roost
2. Oldtown Cleanup

#8 (January-March, 1952)

1. Justice of Wild Bill
2. The Ruby Robbers

#9 (July-September, 1952)

1. Mistaken Identity
2. The Big Tree Mystery

#10 (October-December, 1952)

1. The Oros Pass
2. The Strangest Trail

4-Color #472 (June, 1953)

1. The River Slaughter
2. The Robber Roundup

4-COLOR #520 (DECEMBER, 1953)

1. Death on Black Mesa
2. The Lone Wolf Killer

#13 (APRIL-JUNE, 1954)

1. The Secret of Sourdough City
2. Red River Raiders

#14 (JULY-SEPTEMBER, 1954)

1. The Treasure of the Badlands
2. The Land Rush

#15 (OCTOBER-DECEMBER, 1954)

1. The Rodeo Riders
2. The Greenback Trail

#16 (JANUARY-MARCH, 1955)

1. The Coyote Kid
2. Mustang Vengeance

#17 (APRIL-JUNE, 1955)

1. Tornado Terror
2. The Flooded Mine

4-COLOR #643 (JULY, 1955)

1. Mystery of Furnace Valley
2. Peril at Sundown

#18 (PUBLICATION DATE NOT AVAILABLE)

1. Medicine Trail (first published in Wild Bill Elliott #2)
2. El Robardo ["The Thief"]
   (this issue was released in the United
   Kingdom)

Western Roundup

#1 (JUNE, 1952)

1. The Pay-Off Bandit

#2 (FEBRUARY, 1953)

1. The Feudin' Killer

#3 (JULY-SEPTEMBER, 1953)

1. The Bullet Tip-Off

#4 (OCTOBER-DECEMBER, 1953)

1. The Teller's Hideout

Wild Bill Elliott Comics #9.

Wild Bill Elliott Comics #15.

#5 (JANUARY-MARCH, 1954)

1. Wild Bill Elliott Plays a Hunch

#6 (APRIL-JUNE, 1954)

1. A Lucky Flood

#7 (JULY-SEPTEMBER, 1954)

1. The Feather River Gang

#8 (OCTOBER-DECEMBER, 1954)

1. The Coyote

#9 (JANUARY-MARCH, 1955)

1. Dangerous Decoy (Elliott is called "William" by one of the characters)

#10 (APRIL-JUNE, 1955)

1. The Navajo Saddle

#11 (JULY-SEPTEMBER, 1955)

1. Timber Treachery

#12 (OCTOBER-DECEMBER, 1955)

1. Troubled Waters

#13 (JANUARY-MARCH, 1956)

1. Hidden Bullets

#14 (APRIL-JUNE, 1956)

1. Treasure Box Troubles

#15 (JULY-SEPTEMBER, 1956)

1. The Return of Black Don

#16 (OCTOBER-DECEMBER, 1956)

1. The Clock

#17 (JANUARY-MARCH, 1957)

1. The Phantom Rider

Best of the West

#46

1. The Clock (first published in Western Roundup # 16)

#49

1. Timber Treachery (first published in Western Roundup #11)

D. Elliott's Las Vegas Television Programs

*Shows followed by a * indicate repeat showing.   **The Long Rifle and the Tomahawk (International Television Corporation, 1964), with John Hart, was originally announced to be shown.   *** indicates the show was announced but not shown.*

The Wild Bill Elliott Show debuted on KSHO-TV on October 31, 1964, and ran through January 9, 1965. Elliott would host and introduce his starring motion pictures for most of the run.

10/31/64 — no title listed in the newspapers
11/07/64 — *Forty Niners* (Allied Artists, 1954)
11/14/64 — *Topeka* (Allied Artists, 1953)
11/21/64 — *Waco* (Monogram, 1952)
11/28/64 — *The Last Bandit* (Republic, 1949)
12/05/64 — *Sudden Danger* (Allied Artists, 1955)
12/12/64 — *Forty Niners* (Allied Artists, 1954)
12/19/64 — no title listed in the newspapers
12/26/64 — no title listed in the newspapers
01/02/65 — no title listed in the newspapers
01/09/65 — *Cheyenne Rides Again* (Victory, 1937), with Tom Tyler

The Wild Bill Elliott Show moved to KORK-TV the following week and would introduce western films on both Saturday and Sunday mornings or afternoons. None of Elliott's westerns would be shown.

01/16/65 — *Tall in the Saddle* (RKO, 1944), with John Wayne
01/17/65 — *She Wore a Yellow Ribbon* (RKO, 1949), with John Wayne
01/23/65 — *Arizona Mission*, AKA *Gun the Man Down* (United Artists, 1956), with James Arness
01/24/65 — *Roughshod* (RKO, 1949), with Robert Sterling
01/30/65 — *Man with the Gun* (United Artists, 1955), with Robert Mitchum
01/31/65 — *Return of the Bad Men* (RKO, 1948), with Randolph Scott

02/06/65 — *Valley of the Sun* (RKO, 1942), with Lucille Ball

02/07/65 — *Fort Apache* (RKO, 1948), with John Wayne

02/13/65 — *Trail Street* (RKO, 1947), with Randolph Scott

02/14/65 — *Fort Apache* (RKO, 1948), with John Wayne*

02/20/65 — *The Arizonian* (RKO, 1935), with Richard Dix

02/21/65 — *Station West* (RKO, 1948), with Dick Powell

02/27/65 — *Badman's Territory* (RKO, 1946), with Randolph Scott

02/28/65 — *Along the Great Divide* (Warner Bros., 1951), with Kirk Douglas

03/07/65 — *The Tall Stranger* (Allied Artists, 1957), with Joel McCrea

03/08/65 — *Coroner Creek* (Columbia, 1948), with Randolph Scott

03/13/65 — *Massacre at Sand Creek* (CBS-TV/ Columbia, 1956), with John Derek

03/14/65 — *Canyon Passage* (Universal, 1946), with Dana Andrews

03/20/65 — *Man from Del Rio* (United Artists, 1956), with Anthony Quinn

03/21/65 — *The Gunfighters* (Columbia, 1947), with Randolph Scott

03/27/65 — *The Halliday Brand* (United Artists, 1957), with Joseph Cotton

03/28/65 — *Texas* (Columbia, 1941), with William Holden

04/03/65 — *The Dalton Girls* (United Artists, 1957), with Merry Anders

04/04/65 — *Relentless* (Columbia, 1948), with Robert Young

04/10/65 — *Gun Duel in Durango* (United Artists, 1957), with George Montgomery

04/11/65 — *Wagonmaster* (RKO, 1950), with Ben Johnson

04/17/65 — *Gun Brothers* (United Artists, 1956), with Buster Crabbe

04/18/65 — *Gunsight Ridge* (United Artists, 1957), with Joel McCrea

04/24/65 — *Toughest Gun in Tombstone* (United Artists, 1958), with George Montgomery

04/25/65 — *Jesse James* (20th Century–Fox, 1939), with Tyrone Power

05/01/65 — *Ride Out for Revenge* (United Artists, 1957), with Rory Calhoun

05/02/65 — *The Marauders* (M-G-M, 1955), with Dan Duryea

05/08/65 — *Badlands of Dakota* (Universal, 1941), with Robert Stack

05/09/65 — *The Spoilers* (Universal, 1942), with Marlene Dietrich

05/15/65 — *Rocky Mountain* (Warner Bros., 1950), with Errol Flynn

05/16/65 — *Blood on the Moon* (RKO, 1948), with Robert Mitchum

05/22/65 — *Frontier Badmen* (Universal, 1943), with Robert Paige

05/23/65 — *Montana Belle* (RKO, 1952), with Jane Russell

05/29/65 — *The Walking Hills* (Columbia, 1949), with Randolph Scott

05/30/65 — *Devil's Canyon* (RKO, 1953), with Virginia Mayo

06/06/65 — *Slaughter Trail* (RKO, 1951), with Brian Donlevy

06/07/65 — no title listed in the newspapers

06/12/65 — no title listed in the newspapers

06/13/65 — *Return of Frank James* (20th Century–Fox, 1940), with Henry Fonda

06/19/65 — *Cattle Town* (Warner Bros., 1952), with Dennis Morgan

06/20/65 — *At Gunpoint* (Allied Artists, 1955), with Fred MacMurray

06/26/65 — *Raton Pass* (Warner Bros., 1951), with Dennis Morgan

06/27/65 — *Lone Star* (M-G-M, 1952), with Clark Gable

07/03/65 — *Annie Oakley* (RKO, 1935), with Barbara Stanwyck

07/04/65 — *The Last Outpost* (Paramount, 1951), with Ronald Reagan

07/10/65 — *The Bounty Hunter* (Warner Bros., 1954), with Randolph Scott

07/11/65 — *Run for Cover* (Paramount, 1955), with James Cagney

07/17/65 — *Tall in the Saddle* (RKO, 1944), with John Wayne*

07/18/65 — *Ambush* (M-G-M, 1949), with Robert Taylor

07/24/65 — *Barricade* (Warner Bros., 1950), with Dane Clark

07/25/65 — *Trooper Hook* (United Artists, 1957), with Joel McCrea

07/31/65 — *El Paso* (Paramount, 1948), with John Payne

08/01/65 — *Trail Street* (RKO, 1947), with Randolph Scott*

08/07/65 — *Thunder Over the Plains* (Warner Bros., 1953), with Randolph Scott

08/08/65 — *Silver Lode* (RKO, 1954), with John Payne

08/14/65 — *The Lone Ranger* (Warner Bros., 1956), with Clayton Moore

08/15/65 — *Man of the West* (United Artists, 1958), with Gary Cooper

08/21/65 — *Return of the Bad Men* (RKO, 1948), with Randolph Scott*

08/22/65 — *Outlaw's Son* (United Artists, 1957), with Dane Clark

08/28/65 — *She Wore a Yellow Ribbon* (RKO, 1949), with John Wayne*

08/29/65 — no title listed in the newspapers

09/04/65 — *Passage West* (Paramount, 1951), with John Payne

09/05/65 — *Distant Drums* (Warner Bros., 1951), with Gary Cooper

09/11/65 — *The Vanquished* (Paramount, 1953), with John Payne

09/12/65 — *The Eagle and the Hawk* (Paramount, 1950), with John Payne

09/18/65 — *She Wore a Yellow Ribbon* (RKO, 1949), with John Wayne*

09/19/65 — *Best of the Badmen* (RKO, 1951), with Robert Ryan

09/25/65 — *Station West* (RKO, 1948), with Dick Powell*

09/26/65 — *Last of the Badmen* (Allied Artists, 1957), with George Montgomery

10/02/65 — *Along the Mohawk Trail* (International Television Corporation, 1964), with John Hart

10/03/65 — *Seven Ways to Sundown* (Universal-International, 1960), with Audie Murphy

10/09/65 — *Last of the Duanes* (20th Century–Fox, 1941), with George Montgomery**

10/10/65 — *Saskatchewan* (Universal-International, 1954), with Alan Ladd

10/16/65 — *Coroner Creek* (Columbia, 1948), with Randolph Scott*

10/17/65 — *Gun for a Coward* (Universal-International, 1957), with Fred MacMurray

10/23/65 — *Along the Great Divide* (Warner Bros., 1951), with Kirk Douglas*

10/24/65 — *Hell Bent for Leather* (Universal-International, 1960), with Audie Murphy

10/30/65 — *The Big Trees* (Warner Bros., 1952), with Kirk Douglas

10/31/65 — *Last of the Fast Guns* (Universal-International, 1958), with Jock Mahoney

11/06/65 — *Carson City* (Warner Bros., 1953), with Randolph Scott

11/07/65 — no title listed in the newspapers

11/13/65 — no title listed in the newspapers

11/14/65 — no title listed in the newspapers

11/20/65 — *Mohawk* (20th Century–Fox, 1956), with Scott Brady

11/21/65 — *Horizons West* (Universal-International, 1952), with Robert Ryan

11/27/65 — *Roughshod* (RKO, 1949), with Robert Sterling*

11/28/65 — *Saga of Hemp Brown* (Universal-International, 1959), with Rory Calhoun

12/03/65 — *Wagonmaster* (RKO, 1950), with Ben Johnson*

12/04/65 — *Roughshod* (RKO, 1949), with Robert Sterling***

The Dolly Elliott Show

12/11/65 — *Blood on the Moon* (RKO, 1948), with Robert Mitchum

Beginning the following week, westerns were shown under the new title *Western Movie Time.*

E. Western Star Polls

Two motion picture trade publications, the *Motion Picture Herald* and *Boxoffice*, conducted Western Star Polls. The *Motion Picture Herald* poll ran from 1936 through 1954, while the *Boxoffice* poll covered the years 1937 through 1955. Wild Bill Elliott appeared in the *Motion Picture Herald* polls from 1940 to 1955, while only appearing in the *Boxoffice* polls from 1945 to 1953.

Motion Picture Herald Poll 1940

1. Gene Autry
2. William Boyd
3. Roy Rogers
4. George O'Brien
5. Charles Starrett
6. Johnny Mack Brown
7. Tex Ritter
8. Three Mesquiteers series
9. Smiley Burnette
10. **Bill Elliott**

Motion Picture Herald Poll 1941

1. Gene Autry
2. William Boyd
3. Roy Rogers
4. Charles Starrett
5. Smiley Burnette
6. Tim Holt
7. Johnny Mack Brown
8. Three Mesquiteers series
9. **Bill Elliott**
10. Tex Ritter

Motion Picture Herald Poll 1942

1. Gene Autry
2. Roy Rogers
3. William Boyd
4. Smiley Burnette
5. Charles Starrett
6. Johnny Mack Brown
7. **Bill Elliott**
8. Tim Holt
9. Don Barry
10. Three Mesquiteers series

Motion Picture Herald Poll 1943

1. Roy Rogers
2. William Boyd
3. Smiley Burnette
4. Gabby Hayes
5. Johnny Mack Brown
6. Tim Holt
7. Three Mesquiteers series
8. Don Barry
9. **Bill Elliott**
10. Russell Hayden

Boxoffice Poll, 1946.

Motion Picture Herald Poll 1944

1. Roy Rogers
2. William Boyd
3. Smiley Burnette
4. Gabby Hayes
5. **Bill Elliott**
6. Johnny Mack Brown
7. Don Barry
8. Charles Starrett
9. Russell Hayden
10. Tex Ritter

Motion Picture Herald Poll 1945

1. Roy Rogers
2. Gabby Hayes
3. William Boyd
4. **Bill Elliott**
5. Smiley Burnette
6. Johnny Mack Brown
7. Charles Starrett
8. Don Barry
9. Tex Ritter
10. Rod Cameron

Boxoffice Poll 1945

1. Roy Rogers
2. Gene Autry
3. William Boyd
4. Gabby Hayes
5. **Bill Elliott**
6. Johnny Mack Brown

Motion Picture Herald Poll 1946

1. Roy Rogers
2. **Bill Elliott**
3. Gene Autry
4. Gabby Hayes
5. Smiley Burnette
6. Charles Starrett
7. Johnny Mack Brown
8. Sunset Carson
9. Fuzzy Knight
10. Eddie Dean

Boxoffice Poll 1946

1. Roy Rogers
2. Gene Autry
3. Gabby Hayes
4. **Bill Elliott**
5. William Boyd
6. Smiley Burnette
7. Johnny Mack Brown
8. Ken Maynard
9. Charles Starrett
10. Sons of the Pioneers

Motion Picture Herald Poll 1947

1. Roy Rogers
2. Gene Autry
3. William Boyd
4. **Bill Elliott**
5. Gabby Hayes
6. Charles Starrett
7. Smiley Burnette
8. Johnny Mack Brown
9. Dale Evans
10. Eddie Dean

Boxoffice Poll 1947

1. Roy Rogers
2. Gene Autry
3. **Bill Elliott**
4. William Boyd
5. Gabby Hayes
6. Smiley Burnette

7. Johnny Mack Brown
8. Charles Starrett
9. Bob Nolan
10. Bob Steele

Motion Picture Herald Poll 1948

1. Roy Rogers
2. Gene Autry
3. **Bill Elliott**
4. Gabby Hayes
5. William Boyd
6. Charles Starrett
7. Tim Holt
8. Johnny Mack Brown
9. Smiley Burnette
10. Andy Devine

Boxoffice Poll 1948

1. Roy Rogers
2. Gene Autry
3. Gabby Hayes
4. **Bill Elliott**
5. William Boyd
6. Smiley Burnette
7. Tim Holt
8. Charles Starrett
9. Johnny Mack Brown
10. Leo Carrillo

Motion Picture Herald Poll 1949

1. Roy Rogers
2. Gene Autry
3. Gabby Hayes
4. Tim Holt
5. **Bill Elliott**
6. Charles Starrett
7. William Boyd
8. Johnny Mack Brown
9. Smiley Burnette
10. Andy Devine

Boxoffice Poll 1949

1. Roy Rogers
2. Gene Autry
3. Gabby Hayes
4. **Bill Elliott**
5. William Boyd
6. Andy Devine
7. Tim Holt
8. Smiley Burnette
9. Johnny Mack Brown
10. Leo Carrillo

Motion Picture Herald Poll 1950

1. Roy Rogers
2. Gene Autry
3. Gabby Hayes
4. **Bill Elliott**
5. William Boyd
6. Tim Holt
7. Charles Starrett
8. Johnny Mack Brown
9. Smiley Burnette
10. Dale Evans

Boxoffice Poll 1950

1. Roy Rogers
2. Gene Autry
3. Gabby Hayes
4. William Boyd
5. **Bill Elliott**
6. Tim Holt
7. Andy Devine
8. Smiley Burnette
9. Charles Starrett
10. Johnny Mack Brown

Motion Picture Herald Poll 1951

1. Roy Rogers
2. Gene Autry
3. Tim Holt
4. Charles Starrett
5. Rex Allen
6. **Bill Elliott**
7. Smiley Burnette
8. Allan Lane
9. Dale Evans
10. Gabby Hayes

Boxoffice Poll 1951

1. Roy Rogers
2. Gene Autry
3. Gabby Hayes
4. Tim Holt
5. Dale Evans
6. Judy Canova
7. Smiley Burnette
8. **Bill Elliott**
9. Rex Allen
10. Charles Starrett

Motion Picture Herald Poll 1952

1. Roy Rogers
2. Gene Autry
3. Rex Allen
4. **Bill Elliott**
5. Tim Holt
6. Gabby Hayes
7. Smiley Burnette
8. Dale Evans
9. Charles Starrett
10. William Boyd

Boxoffice Poll 1952

1. Roy Rogers
2. Gene Autry
3. Tim Holt
4. Dale Evans
5. **Bill Elliott**
6. Judy Canova
7. Rex Allen
8. Smiley Burnette
9. Vaughn Monroe
10. Charles Starrett

Motion Picture Herald Poll 1953

1. Roy Rogers
2. Gene Autry
3. Rex Allen
4. **Bill Elliott**
5. Allan Lane

Boxoffice Poll 1953

1. Randolph Scott
2. Roy Rogers
3. Gene Autry
4. Rod Cameron
5. George Montgomery
6. Dale Evans
7. Rex Allen
8. Tim Holt
9. **Bill Elliott**
10. Judy Canova

Motion Picture Herald Poll 1954

1. Roy Rogers
2. Gene Autry
3. Rex Allen
4. **Bill Elliott**
5. Gabby Hayes

In December 1999, Boyd Magers published his list of top cowboys of the 20th century. The top 20 were:

1. John Wayne
2. Gene Autry
3. Roy Rogers
4. Tom Mix
5. William Boyd
6. Buck Jones
7. William S. Hart
8. Ken Maynard
9. Clayton Moore
10. G.M. "Broncho Billy" Anderson
11. Randolph Scott
12. Charles Starrett
13. Bob Steele
14. Johnny Mack Brown
15. Tim McCoy
16. Audie Murphy
17. Hoot Gibson
18. **Bill Elliott**
19. Richard Boone
20. James Arness

F. Alphabetical Listing of Elliott's Starring Role Films

Across the Sierras (Columbia, February, 1941)

Bells of Rosarita (Republic, June, 1945), starring Roy Rogers

Beyond the Sacramento (Columbia, November, 1940)

Bitter Creek (Allied Artists, February, 1954)

Bordertown Gun Fighters (Republic, October, 1943)

Bullets for Bandits (Columbia, February, 1942)

California Gold Rush (Republic, February, 1946)

Calling Homicide (Allied Artists, June, 1956)

Calling Wild Bill Elliott (Republic, April, 1943)

Chain of Evidence (Allied Artists, January, 1957)

Cheyenne Wildcat (Republic, September, 1944)

Colorado Pioneers (Republic, November, 1945)

Conquest of Cheyenne (Republic, July, 1946)

Death Valley Manhunt (Republic, November, 1943)

The Devil's Trail (Columbia, May, 1942)

Dial Red 0 (Allied Artists, March, 1955)

The Fabulous Texan (Republic, November, 1947)

Fargo (Monogram, September, 1952)

Footsteps in the Night (Allied Artists, March, 1957)

The Forty-Niners (Allied Artists, May, 1954)

Frontiers of '49 (Columbia, January, 1939)

The Gallant Legion (Republic, May, 1948)

Great Adventures of Wild Bill Hickok (Columbia, June, 1938)

The Great Stagecoach Robbery (Republic, February, 1945)

Hands Across the Rockies (Columbia, June, 1941)

Hellfire (Republic, June, 1949)

Hidden Valley Outlaws (Republic, April, 1944)

The Homesteaders (Allied Artists, March, 1953)

In Early Arizona (Columbia, November, 1938)

In Old Sacramento (Republic, May, 1946)

Kansas Territory (Monogram, May, 1952)

King of Dodge City (Columbia, August, 1941)

The Last Bandit (Republic, February, 1949)

The Law Comes to Texas (Columbia, April, 1939)

Lone Star Pioneers (Columbia, March, 1939)

Lone Star Vigilantes (Columbia, January, 1942)

The Lone Texas Ranger (Republic, May, 1945)

The Longhorn (Monogram, November, 1951)

The Man from Thunder River (Republic, June, 1943)

The Man from Tumbleweeds (Columbia, June, 1940)

Marshal of Laredo (Republic, October, 1945)

Marshal of Reno (Republic, July, 1944)

Marshal of Trail City (Century Television, 1950)

The Maverick (Allied Artists, December, 1952)

Mojave Firebrand (Republic, March, 1944)

North from the Lone Star (Columbia, March, 1941)

North of the Rockies (Columbia, April, 1942)

Old Los Angeles (Republic, April, 1948)

Overland Mail Robbery (Republic, November, 1943)

Overland with Kit Carson (Columbia, August, 1939)

Phantom of the Plains (Republic, September, 1945)

Pioneers of the Frontier (Columbia, February, 1940)

Plainsman and the Lady (Republic, November, 1946)

Prairie Gunsmoke (Columbia, July, 1942)

Prairie Schooners (Columbia, November, 1940)

Rebel City (Allied Artists, May, 1953)

Return of Daniel Boone (Columbia, May, 1941)

The Return of Wild Bill (Columbia, July, 1940)

Roaring Frontiers (Columbia, October, 1941)

The San Antonio Kid (Republic, August, 1944)

Savage Horde (Republic, July, 1950)

Sheriff of Las Vegas (Republic, December, 1944)

Sheriff of Redwood Valley (Republic, March, 1946)

The Showdown (Republic, August, 1950)

Son of Davy Crockett (Columbia, July, 1941)

Sudden Danger (Allied Artists, December, 1955)

Sun Valley Cyclone (Republic, May, 1946)

Taming of the West (Columbia, October, 1939)

Topeka (Allied Artists, August, 1953)

Tucson Raiders (Republic, May, 1944)

Valley of Vanishing Men (Columbia, December, 1942)

Vengeance of the West (Columbia, August, 1942)

Vigilante Terror (Allied Artists, November, 1953)

Vigilantes of Dodge City (Republic, November, 1944)

Waco (Monogram, February, 1952)

Wagon Tracks West (Republic, October, 1943)

Wagon Wheels Westward (Republic, December, 1945)

Wildcat of Tucson (Columbia, April, 1941)

Wyoming (Republic, July, 1947)

G. Alphabetical Listing of Elliott's Supporting Role Films

All films that various historians have listed to date as featuring Bill Elliott in support are included here. Bill Elliott, billed as Gordon Elliott, has been credited with appearing in over 150 feature films and 10 short subjects. In some, Elliott's role has been documented as ending on the cutting room floor, while in a few others Elliott is nowhere to be seen, with no explanation given for his absence. In 1935, 28 films were released in which Elliott took part. Finally, in 1938, Elliott obtained the title role in *The Great Adventures of Wild Bill Hickok* (Columbia, 1938) and became a leading man in films for almost twenty years.

Alibi Ike (Warner Bros., June, 1935), with Joe E. Brown

Arizona Wildcat (Fox, November, 1927), with Tom Mix

Bachelor's Affairs (Fox, June, 1932), with Adolphe Menjou

Beyond London's Lights (FBO, March, 1928), with Adrienne Dore

Big Boy (Warner Bros., September, 1930), with Al Jolson

The Big Noise (Warner Bros., June, 1936), with Guy Kibbee

Boots and Saddles (Republic, October, 1937), with Gene Autry

Born to Love (RKO, April, 1931), with Constance Bennett

Boy of the Streets (Monogram, January, 1938), with Jackie Cooper

Bright Lights (Warner Bros., July, 1935), with Joe E. Brown

Broadway Gondolier (Warner Bros., July, 1935), with Dick Powell

Broadway Hostess (Warner Bros., December, 1935), with Winifred Shaw

Broadway Scandals (Columbia, November, 1929), with Sally O'Neil

Bullets or Ballots (Warner Bros., June, 1936), with Edward G. Robinson

— But the Flesh Is Weak (M-G-M, April, 1932), with Robert Montgomery

Case of the Black Cat (Warner Bros., October, 1936), with Ricardo Cortez

Case of the Howling Dog (Warner Bros., September, 1934), with Warren William

Case of the Velvet Claws (Warner Bros., August, 1936), with Warren William

Ceiling Zero (Warner Bros., January, 1936), with James Cagney

Children of Divorce (Paramount, April 1927), with Clara Bow

China Clipper (Warner Bros., August, 1936), with Pat O'Brien

City Streets (Paramount, April, 1931), with Gary Cooper

Cocktail Hour (Columbia, June, 1933), with Bebe Daniels

Convicted (Artclass, November, 1931), with Aileen Pringle

Crooner (First National, August, 1932), with David Manners

The Cuckoos (Radio, April, 1930), with Wheeler and Woolsey

Dance Team (Fox, January, 1932), with James Dunn

Dancing Lady (M-G-M, November, 1933), with Joan Crawford

Dangerous (Warner Bros., December, 1935), with Bette Davis

Delicious (Fox, December, 1931), with Janet Gaynor

Desirable (Warner Bros., September, 1934), with Jean Muir

Devil Dogs of the Air (Warner Bros., February, 1935), with James Cagney

Devil's Party (Universal, May, 1938), with Victor McLaglen

Dr. Monica (Warner Bros., June, 1934), with Kay Francis

Dr. Socrates (Warner Bros., October, 1935), with Paul Muni

Down the Stretch (Warner Bros., September, 1936), with Patricia Ellis

The Drop Kick (First National, 1927), with Richard Barthelmess

East Is West (Universal, October, 1930), with Lupe Velez

Final Edition (Columbia, February, 1932), with Pat O'Brien

The Firebird (Warner Bros., November, 1934), with Veree Teasdale

Five and Ten (M-G-M, June, 1931), with Marion Davies

Forbidden (Columbia, January, 1932), with Barbara Stanwyck

Friends of Mr. Sweeney (Warner Bros., July, 1934), with Charlie Ruggles

Front Page Woman (Warner Bros., July, 1935), with Bette Davis

Fugitive in the Sky (Warner Bros., November, 1936), with Jean Muir

"G" Men (Warner Bros., May, 1935), with James Cagney

Girl from 10th Avenue (Warner Bros., May, 1935), with Bette Davis

Go Into Your Dance (Warner Bros., March, 1935), with Al Jolson

God's Gift to Women (Warner Bros., April, 1931), with Frank Fay

Going Highbrow (Warner Bros., August, 1935), with Guy Kibbee

Going Wild (First National, December, 1930), with Joe E. Brown

Gold Diggers of 1933 (Warner Bros., September, 1933), with Warren William

Gold Diggers of 1935 (Warner Bros., March, 1935), with Dick Powell

The Golden Arrow (Warner Bros., May, 1936), with Bette Davis

Goose and the Gander (Warner Bros., September, 1935), with Kay Francis

The Great Divide (First National, September, 1929), with Dorothy Mackaill

Greeks Had a Word for Them (United Artists, February, 1932), with Joan Blondell

Guns of the Pecos (Warner Bros., January, 1937), with Dick Foran

Her Bodyguard (Paramount, July, 1933), with Edmund Lowe

Here Comes the Navy (Warner Bros., July, 1934), with James Cagney

Hook, Line and Sinker (Radio, December, 1930), with Wheeler and Woolsey

Housewife (Warner Bros., August, 1934), with George Brent

I Am a Thief (Warner Bros., November, 1934), with Mary Astor

I Found Stella Parrish (Warner Bros., November, 1935), with Kay Francis

I Live for Love (Warner Bros., October, 1935), with Everett Marshall

Jewel Robbery (Warner Bros., August, 1932), with William Powell

The Keyhole (Warner Bros., March, 1932), with Kay Francis

King of Hockey (Warner Bros., December, 1936), with Dick Purcell

Lady in the Morgue (Universal, April, 1938), with Preston Foster

Lady with a Past (RKO, February, 1932), with Constance Bennett

Leftover Ladies (Tiffany, October, 1931), with Claudia Dell

Letter of Introduction (Universal, August, 1938), with Adolphe Menjou

Little Giant (First National, May, 1933), with Edward G. Robinson

Living on Velvet (Warner Bros., March, 1935), with Kay Francis

Lord Byron of Broadway (M-G-M, February, 1930), with Charles Kaley

A Lost Lady (First National, September, 1934), with Barbara Stanwyck

Love Takes Flight (Grand National, November, 1937), with Bruce Cabot

Magnificent Lie (Paramount, July, 1931), with Ruth Chatterton

Man of Iron (Warner Bros., December, 1935), with Barton MacLane

Melody for Two (Warner Bros., May, 1937), with James Melton

Merrily We Go to Hell (Paramount, June, 1932), with Sylvia Sidney

Merry Frinks (First National, June, 1934), with Aline MacMahon

Merry Wives of Reno (Warner Bros., May, 1934), with Guy Kibbee

Michael O'Halloran (Republic, May, 1937), with Wynne Gibson

Midnight Court (Warner Bros., March, 1937), with Ann Dvorak

Midnight Mystery (Radio, June, 1930), with Betty Compson

Modern Hero (Warner Bros., April, 1934), with Richard Barthelmess

Moonlight on the Prairie (Warner Bros., November, 1935), with Dick Foran

Murder by an Aristocrat (Warner Bros., June, 1936), with Lyle Talbot

Murder in the Clouds (Warner Bros., December, 1934), with Lyle Talbot

Murder of Dr. Harrigan (Warner Bros., January, 1936), with Ricardo Cortez

My Lips Betray (Fox, November, 1933), with Lilian Harvey

My Weakness (Fox, September, 1933), with Lilian Harvey

Night After Night (Paramount, October, 1932), with George Raft

A Night at the Ritz (Warner Bros., February, 1935), with William Gargan

Night Parade (Radio, October, 1929), with Aileen Pringle

A Notorious Affair (First National, April, 1930), with Billie Dove

On ze Boulevard (M-G-M, June, 1927), with Lew Cody

Once a Sinner (Fox, January, 1931), with Dorothy Mackaill

One Hour with You (Paramount, March, 1932), with Maurice Chevalier

Page Miss Glory (Warner Bros., July, 1935), with Marion Davies

Palmy Days (United Artists, October, 1931), with Eddie Cantor

Party Husband (First National, April, 1931), with Dorothy Mackaill

Passion Song (Excellent, October, 1928), with Gertrude Olmstead

The Payoff (Warner Bros., November, 1938), with James Dunn

Peach-o-Reno (Radio, December, 1931), with Wheeler and Woolsey

Peg o' My Heart (M-G-M, May, 1933), with Marion Davies

Personal Maid's Secret (Warner Bros., October, 1935), with Margaret Lindsay

Plastic Age (Commonwealth, December, 1925), with Donald Keith

Platinum Blonde (Columbia, October, 1931), with Loretta Young

Polo Joe (Warner Bros., November, 1936), with Joe E. Brown

Private Detective 62 (Warner Bros., July, 1933), with William Powell

Private Life of Helen of Troy (First National, December, 1927), with Maria Corda

Public Defender (RKO, August, 1931), with Richard Dix

Reaching for the Moon (United Artists, December, 1930), with Douglas Fairbanks

Reckless (M-G-M, April, 1935), with Jean Harlow

Registered Nurse (First National, June, 1934), with Bebe Daniels

Restless Youth (Columbia, November, 1928), with Marceline Day

The Return of Dr. Fu Manchu (Paramount, May, 1930), with Warner Oland

Rich Are Always with Us (First National, June, 1932), with Ruth Chatterton

Road to Reno (Paramount, October, 1931), with Lilyan Tashman

Roll Along Cowboy (20th Century–Fox, October, 1937), with Smith Ballew

Secret Bride (Warner Bros., December, 1934), with Barbara Stanwyck

The Secret Witness (Columbia, December, 1931), with Una Merkel

Shamrock Handicap (Fox, May, 1926), with Janet Gaynor

She Couldn't Say No (Warner Bros., February, 1930), with Winnie Lightner

Silver Dollar (First National, December, 1932), with Edward G. Robinson

Singing Kid (Warner Bros., April, 1936), with Al Jolson

6 Day Bike Rider (First National, October, 1934), with Joe E. Brown

Smart Woman (Radio, August, 1931), with Mary Astor

Smarty (Warner Bros., May, 1934), with Joan Blondell

Speed to Spare (Columbia, May, 1937), with Edward J. Nugent

Stage Mother (M-G-M, September, 1933), with Alice Brady

Stars Over Broadway (Warner Bros., November, 1935), with Pat O'Brien

Story of Louis Pasteur (Warner Bros., February, 1936), with Paul Muni

A Successful Calamity (Warner Bros., September, 1932), with George Arliss

Sunny (First National, November, 1930), with Marilyn Miller

Swing It, Professor (Ambassador, November, 1937), with Pinky Tomlin

Tarzan's Revenge (20th Century–Fox, January, 1938), with Glenn Morris

Trailin' West (Warner Bros., October, 1936), with Dick Foran

Traveling Saleslady (Warner Bros., April, 1935), with Joan Blondell

Twenty Million Sweethearts (First National, May, 1934), with Pat O'Brien

Two Against the World (Warner Bros., September, 1932), with Constance Bennett

Two Against the World (Warner Bros., July, 1936), with Humphrey Bogart

Two Kinds of Women (Paramount, 1932), with Miriam Hopkins

Upperworld (Warner Bros., April, 1934), with Warren William

The Valley of Hunted Men (Pathe, February, 1928), with Buffalo Bill Jr.

Vanity Fair (Allied, March, 1932), with Myrna Loy

The Walking Dead (Warner Bros., March, 1936), with Boris Karloff

Week-End Marriage (First National, July, 1932), with Loretta Young

West of Broadway (M-G-M, November, 1931), with John Gilbert

While the Patient Slept (Warner Bros., March, 1935), with Aline MacMahon

Wife, Doctor and Nurse (20th Century–Fox, September, 1937), with Loretta Young

Woman Between (Radio, August, 1931), with Lily Damita

The Woman in Red (Warner Bros., February, 1935), with Barbara Stanwyck

Wonder Bar (First National, May, 1934), with Al Jolson

Working Girls (Paramount, December, 1931), with Judith Wood

You Can't Have Everything (20th Century–Fox, August, 1937), with Alice Faye

---

H. Chronological Listing of Elliott's Starring Role Films

Great Adventures of Wild Bill Hickok (Columbia, June, 1938)

In Early Arizona (Columbia, November, 1938)

Frontiers of '49 (Columbia, January, 1939)

Lone Star Pioneers (Columbia, March, 1939)

The Law Comes to Texas (Columbia, April, 1939)

Overland with Kit Carson (Columbia, August, 1939)

Taming of the West (Columbia, October, 1939)

Pioneers of the Frontier (Columbia, February, 1940)

The Man from Tumbleweeds (Columbia, June, 1940)

The Return of Wild Bill (Columbia, July, 1940)

Prairie Schooners (Columbia, November, 1940)

Beyond the Sacramento (Columbia, November, 1940)

Across the Sierras (Columbia, February, 1941)

North from the Lone Star (Columbia, March, 1941)

Wildcat of Tucson (Columbia, April, 1941)

Return of Daniel Boone (Columbia, May, 1941)

Hands Across the Rockies (Columbia, June, 1941)

Son of Davy Crockett (Columbia, July, 1941)

King of Dodge City (Columbia, August, 1941)

Roaring Frontiers (Columbia, October, 1941)
Lone Star Vigilantes (Columbia, January, 1942)
Bullets for Bandits (Columbia, February, 1942)
North of the Rockies (Columbia, April, 1942)
The Devil's Trail (Columbia, May, 1942)
Prairie Gunsmoke (Columbia, July, 1942)
Vengeance of the West (Columbia, August, 1942)
Valley of Vanishing Men (Columbia, December, 1942)
Calling Wild Bill Elliott (Republic, April, 1943)
The Man from Thunder River (Republic, June, 1943)
Bordertown Gun Fighters (Republic, October, 1943)
Wagon Tracks West (Republic, October, 1943)
Overland Mail Robbery (Republic, November, 1943)
Death Valley Manhunt (Republic, November, 1943)
Mojave Firebrand (Republic, March, 1944)
Hidden Valley Outlaws (Republic, April, 1944)
Tucson Raiders (Republic, May, 1944)
Marshal of Reno (Republic, July, 1944)
The San Antonio Kid (Republic, August, 1944)
Cheyenne Wildcat (Republic, September, 1944)
Vigilantes of Dodge City (Republic, November, 1944)
Sheriff of Las Vegas (Republic, December, 1944)
The Great Stagecoach Robbery (Republic, February, 1945)
The Lone Texas Ranger (Republic, May, 1945)
Bells of Rosarita (Republic, June, 1945), starring Roy Rogers
Phantom of the Plains (Republic, September, 1945)
Marshal of Laredo (Republic, October, 1945)
Colorado Pioneers (Republic, November, 1945)
Wagon Wheels Westward (Republic, December, 1945)

California Gold Rush (Republic, February, 1946)
Sheriff of Redwood Valley (Republic, March, 1946)
Sun Valley Cyclone (Republic, May, 1946)
In Old Sacramento (Republic, May, 1946)
Conquest of Cheyenne (Republic, July, 1946)
Plainsman and the Lady (Republic, November, 1946)
Wyoming (Republic, July, 1947)
The Fabulous Texan (Republic, November, 1947)
Old Los Angeles (Republic, April, 1948)
The Gallant Legion (Republic, May, 1948)
The Last Bandit (Republic, February, 1949)
Hellfire (Republic, June, 1949)
Savage Horde (Republic, July, 1950)
The Showdown (Republic, August, 1950)
Marshal of Trail City (Century Television, 1950)
The Longhorn (Monogram, November, 1951)
Waco (Monogram, February, 1952)
Kansas Territory (Monogram, May, 1952)
Fargo (Monogram, September, 1952)
The Maverick (Allied Artists, December, 1952)
The Homesteaders (Allied Artists, March, 1953)
Rebel City (Allied Artists, May, 1953)
Topeka (Allied Artists, August, 1953)
Vigilante Terror (Allied Artists, November, 1953)
Bitter Creek (Allied Artists, February, 1954)
The Forty-Niners (Allied Artists, May, 1954)
Dial Red 0 (Allied Artists, March, 1955)
Sudden Danger (Allied Artists, December, 1955)
Calling Homicide (Allied Artists, June, 1956)
Chain of Evidence (Allied Artists, January, 1957)
Footsteps in the Night (Allied Artists, March, 1957)

I. Chronological Listing of Elliott's Supporting Role Films

All films that various historians have listed to date as featuring Bill Elliott supporting roles are included here. Bill Elliott, billed as Gordon Elliott, has been credited with appearing in over 150 feature films and 10 short subjects. In some, Elliott's role has been documented as having ended up on the cutting room floor, and in a few others Elliott is nowhere to be seen — with no explanation. In 1935, 28 films were released in which Elliott took part. Finally, in 1938, Elliott obtained the title role in *The Great Adventures of Wild Bill Hickok* (Columbia, 1938) and became a leading man in films for almost twenty years.

Plastic Age (Commonwealth, December, 1925), with Donald Keith
Shamrock Handicap (Fox, May, 1926), with Janet Gaynor
Children of Divorce (Paramount, April, 1927), with Clara Bow
On ze Boulevard (M-G-M, June, 1927), with Lew Cody
The Drop Kick (First National, 1927), with Richard Barthelmess
Arizona Wildcat (Fox, November, 1927), with Tom Mix
Private Life of Helen of Troy (First National, December, 1927), with Maria Corda
Valley of Hunted Men (Pathe, February, 1928), with Buffalo Bill Jr.
Beyond London's Lights (FBO, March, 1928), with Adrienne Dore
Passion Song (Excellent, October, 1928), with Gertrude Olmstead
Restless Youth (Columbia, November, 1928), with Marceline Day
The Great Divide (First National, September, 1929), with Dorothy Mackaill

Night Parade (Radio, October, 1929), with Aileen Pringle

Broadway Scandals (Columbia, November, 1929), with Sally O'Neil

She Couldn't Say No (Warner Bros., February, 1930), with Winnie Lightner

Lord Byron of Broadway (M-G-M, February, 1930), with Charles Kaley

The Cuckoos (Radio, April, 1930), with Wheeler and Woolsey

A Notorious Affair (First National, April, 1930), with Billie Dove

The Return of Dr. Fu Manchu (Paramount, May, 1930), with Warner Oland

Midnight Mystery (Radio, June, 1930), with Betty Compson

Big Boy (Warner Bros., September, 1930), with Al Jolson

East Is West (Universal, October, 1930), with Lupe Velez

Sunny (First National, November, 1930), with Marilyn Miller

Reaching for the Moon (United Artists, December, 1930), with Douglas Fairbanks

Going Wild (First National, December, 1930), with Joe E. Brown

Hook, Line and Sinker (Radio, December, 1930), with Wheeler and Woolsey

Once a Sinner (Fox, January, 1931), with Dorothy Mackaill

City Streets (Paramount, April, 1931), with Gary Cooper

Born to Love (RKO, April, 1931), with Constance Bennett

God's Gift to Women (Warner Bros., April, 1931), with Frank Fay

Party Husband (First National, April, 1931), with Dorothy Mackaill

Five and Ten (M-G-M, June, 1931), with Marion Davies

Magnificent Lie (Paramount, July, 1931), with Ruth Chatterton

Public Defender (RKO, August, 1931), with Richard Dix

Woman Between (Radio, August, 1931), with Lily Damita

Smart Woman (Radio, August, 1931), with Mary Astor

Leftover Ladies (Tiffany, October, 1931), with Claudia Dell

Palmy Days (United Artists, October, 1931), with Eddie Cantor

Road to Reno (Paramount, October, 1931), with Lilyan Tashman

Platinum Blonde (Columbia, October, 1931), with Loretta Young

Convicted (Artclass, November, 1931), with Aileen Pringle

West of Broadway (M-G-M, November, 1931), with John Gilbert

Working Girls (Paramount, December, 1931), with Judith Wood

The Secret Witness (Columbia, December, 1931), with Una Merkel

Delicious (Fox, December, 1931), with Janet Gaynor

Peach-o-Reno (Radio, December, 1931), with Wheeler and Woolsey

Dance Team (Fox, January, 1932), with James Dunn

Forbidden (Columbia, January, 1932), with Barbara Stanwyck

Two Kinds of Women (Paramount, 1932), with Miriam Hopkins

Lady with a Past (RKO, February, 1932), with Constance Bennett

Final Edition (Columbia, February, 1932), with Pat O'Brien

Greeks Had a Word for Them (United Artists, February, 1932), with Joan Blondell

Vanity Fair (Allied, March, 1932), with Myrna Loy

The Keyhole (Warner Bros., March, 1932), with Kay Francis

One Hour with You (Paramount, March, 1932), with Maurice Chevalier

— But the Flesh Is Weak (M-G-M, April, 1932), with Robert Montgomery

Rich Are Always with Us (First National, June, 1932), with Ruth Chatterton

Bachelor's Affairs (Fox, June, 1932), with Adolphe Menjou

Merrily We Go to Hell (Paramount, June, 1932), with Sylvia Sidney

Week-End Marriage (First National, July, 1932), with Loretta Young

Jewel Robbery (Warner Bros., August, 1932), with William Powell

Crooner (First National, August, 1932), with David Manners

Two Against the World (Warner Bros., September, 1932), with Constance Bennett

A Successful Calamity (Warner Bros., September, 1932), with George Arliss

Night After Night (Paramount, October, 1932), with George Raft

Silver Dollar (First National, December, 1932), with Edward G. Robinson

Little Giant (First National, May, 1933), with Edward G. Robinson

Peg o' My Heart (M-G-M, May, 1933), with Marion Davies

Cocktail Hour (Columbia, June, 1933), with Bebe Daniels

Private Detective 62 (Warner Bros., July, 1933), with William Powell

Her Bodyguard (Paramount, July, 1933), with Edmund Lowe

Gold Diggers of 1933 (Warner Bros., September, 1933), with Warren William

My Weakness (Fox, September, 1933), with Lilian Harvey

Stage Mother (M-G-M, September, 1933), with Alice Brady

Dancing Lady (M-G-M, November, 1933), with Joan Crawford

My Lips Betray (Fox, November, 1933), with Lilian Harvey

Modern Hero (Warner Bros., April, 1934), with Richard Barthelmess

Upperworld (Warner Bros., April, 1934), with Warren William

Wonder Bar (First National, May, 1934), with Al Jolson

Twenty Million Sweethearts (First National, May, 1934), with Pat O'Brien

Merry Wives of Reno (Warner Bros., May, 1934), with Guy Kibbee

Smarty (Warner Bros., May, 1934), with Joan Blondell

Dr. Monica (Warner Bros., June, 1934), with Kay Francis

Merry Frinks (First National, June, 1934), with Aline MacMahon

Registered Nurse (First National, June, 1934), with Bebe Daniels

Here Comes the Navy (Warner Bros., July, 1934), with James Cagney

Friends of Mr. Sweeney (Warner Bros., July, 1934), with Charlie Ruggles

Housewife (Warner Bros., August, 1934), with George Brent

Desirable (Warner Bros., September, 1934), with Jean Muir

Case of the Howling Dog (Warner Bros., September, 1934), with Warren William

A Lost Lady (First National, September, 1934), with Barbara Stanwyck

6 Day Bike Rider (First National, October, 1934), with Joe E. Brown

The Firebird (Warner Bros., November, 1934), with Veree Teasdale

I Am a Thief (Warner Bros., November, 1934), with Mary Astor

Secret Bride (Warner Bros., December, 1934), with Barbara Stanwyck

Murder in the Clouds (Warner Bros., December, 1934), with Lyle Talbot

Devil Dogs of the Air (Warner Bros., February, 1935), with James Cagney

The Woman in Red (Warner Bros., February, 1935), with Barbara Stanwyck

A Night at the Ritz (Warner Bros., February, 1935), with William Gargan

Go Into Your Dance (Warner Bros., March, 1935), with Al Jolson

Living on Velvet (Warner Bros., March, 1935), with Kay Francis

While the Patient Slept (Warner Bros., March, 1935), with Aline MacMahon

Gold Diggers of 1935 (Warner Bros., March, 1935), with Dick Powell

Traveling Saleslady (Warner Bros., April, 1935), with Joan Blondell

Reckless (M-G-M, April, 1935), with Jean Harlow

"G" Men (Warner Bros., May, 1935), with James Cagney

Girl from 10th Avenue (Warner Bros., May, 1935), with Bette Davis

Alibi Ike (Warner Bros., June, 1935), with Joe E. Brown

Page Miss Glory (Warner Bros., July, 1935), with Marion Davies

Front Page Woman (Warner Bros., July, 1935), with Bette Davis

Broadway Gondolier (Warner Bros., July, 1935), with Dick Powell

Bright Lights (Warner Bros., July, 1935), with Joe E. Brown

Going Highbrow (Warner Bros., August, 1935), with Guy Kibbee

Goose and the Gander (Warner Bros., September, 1935), with Kay Francis

Personal Maid's Secret (Warner Bros., October, 1935), with Margaret Lindsay

Dr. Socrates (Warner Bros., October, 1935), with Paul Muni

I Live for Love (Warner Bros., October, 1935), with Everett Marshall

Moonlight on the Prairie (Warner Bros., November, 1935), with Dick Foran

I Found Stella Parrish (Warner Bros., November, 1935), with Kay Francis

Stars Over Broadway (Warner Bros., November, 1935), with Pat O'Brien

The Payoff (Warner Bros., November, 1935), with James Dunn

Broadway Hostess (Warner Bros., December, 1935), with Winifred Shaw

Dangerous (Warner Bros., December, 1935), with Bette Davis

Man of Iron (Warner Bros., December, 1935), with Barton MacLane

Ceiling Zero (Warner Bros., January, 1936), with James Cagney

Murder of Dr. Harrigan (Warner Bros., January, 1936), with Ricardo Cortez

Story of Louis Pasteur (Warner Bros., February, 1936), with Paul Muni

The Walking Dead (Warner Bros., March, 1936), with Boris Karloff

Singing Kid (Warner Bros., April, 1936), with Al Jolson

The Golden Arrow (Warner Bros., May, 1936), with Bette Davis

Bullets or Ballots (Warner Bros., June, 1936), with Edward G. Robinson

Murder by an Aristocrat (Warner Bros., June, 1936), with Lyle Talbot

The Big Noise (Warner Bros., June, 1936), with Guy Kibbee

Two Against the World (Warner Bros., July, 1936), with Humphrey Bogart

Case of the Velvet Claws (Warner Bros., August, 1936), with Warren William

China Clipper (Warner Bros., August, 1936), with Pat O'Brien

Down the Stretch (Warner Bros., September, 1936), with Patricia Ellis

Case of the Black Cat (Warner Bros., October, 1936), with Ricardo Cortez

Trailin' West (Warner Bros., October, 1936), with Dick Foran

Fugitive in the Sky (Warner Bros., November, 1936), with Jean Muir

Polo Joe (Warner Bros., November, 1936), with Joe E. Brown

King of Hockey (Warner Bros., December, 1936), with Dick Purcell

Guns of the Pecos (Warner Bros., January, 1937), with Dick Foran

Midnight Court (Warner Bros., March, 1937), with Ann Dvorak

Melody for Two (Warner Bros., May, 1937), with James Melton

Speed to Spare (Columbia, May 1937), with Edward J. Nugent

Michael O'Halloran (Republic, May, 1937), with Wynne Gibson

You Can't Have Everything (20th Century–Fox, August, 1937), with Alice Faye

Wife, Doctor and Nurse (20th Century–Fox, September, 1937), with Loretta Young

Boots and Saddles (Republic, October, 1937), with Gene Autry

Roll Along Cowboy (20th Century–Fox, October, 1937), with Smith Ballew

Love Takes Flight (Grand National, November, 1937), with Bruce Cabot

Swing It, Professor (Ambassador, November, 1937), with Pinky Tomlin

Tarzan's Revenge (20th Century–Fox, January, 1938), with Glenn Morris

Boy of the Streets (Monogram, January, 1938), with Jackie Cooper

Lady in the Morgue (Universal, April, 1938), with Preston Foster

Devil's Party (Universal, May, 1938), with Victor McLaglen

Letter of Introduction (Universal, August, 1938), with Adolphe Menjou

---

J. Chronological Listing of All of Elliott's Film Appearances

This appendix combines appendices A, B, H and I in one sequence, serially numbered.

1. *Plastic Age* (Commonwealth, December, 1925)
2. *Shamrock Handicap* (Fox, May, 1926)
3. *Napoleon Jr.* (Fox, October, 1926)
4. *Children of Divorce* (Paramount, April, 1927)
5. *On ze Boulevard* (M-G-M, June, 1927)
6. *The Drop Kick* (First National, 1927)
7. *Arizona Wildcat* (Fox, November, 1927)
8. *Private Life of Helen of Troy* (First National, December, 1927)
9. *Valley of Hunted Men* (Pathe, February, 1928)
10. *Beyond London's Lights* (FBO, March, 1928)
11. *Passion Song* (Excellent, October, 1928)
12. *The Boy Friend* (Metro-Goldwyn-Mayer, November, 1928)
13. *Restless Youth* (Columbia, November, 1928)
14. *The Great Divide* (First National, September, 1929)
15. *Night Parade* (Radio, October, 1929)
16. *Broadway Scandals* (Columbia, November, 1929)
17. *She Couldn't Say No* (Warner Bros., February, 1930)
18. *Lord Byron of Broadway* (M-G-M, February, 1930)
19. *The Cuckoos* (Radio, April, 1930)
20. *A Notorious Affair* (First National, April, 1930)
21. *The Return of Dr. Fu Manchu* (Paramount, May, 1930)
22. *Fast Work* (Metro-Goldwyn-Mayer, June, 1930)
23. *Midnight Mystery* (Radio, June, 1930)
24. *Big Boy* (Warner Bros., September, 1930)
25. *East Is West* (Universal, October, 1930)
26. *Sunny* (First National, November, 1930)
27. *Reaching for the Moon* (United Artists, December, 1930)
28. *Going Wild* (First National, December, 1930)
29. *Hook, Line and Sinker* (Radio, December, 1930)
30. *Once a Sinner* (Fox, January, 1931)
31. *City Streets* (Paramount, April, 1931)
32. *Born to Love* (RKO, April, 1931)
33. *God's Gift to Women* (Warner Bros., April, 1931)
34. *Party Husband* (First National, April, 1931)

35. *Five and Ten* (M-G-M, June, 1931)
36. *Let's Do Things* (Metro-Goldwyn-Mayer, June, 1931)
37. *Magnificent Lie* (Paramount, July, 1931)
38. *Public Defender* (RKO, August, 1931)
39. *Woman Between* (Radio, August, 1931)
40. *Smart Woman* (Radio, August, 1931)
41. *Leftover Ladies* (Tiffany, October, 1931)
42. *Palmy Days* (United Artists, October, 1931)
43. *Road to Reno* (Paramount, October, 1931)
44. *Platinum Blonde* (Columbia, October, 1931)
45. *Convicted* (Artclass, November, 1931)
46. *West of Broadway* (M-G-M, November, 1931)
47. *What a Bozo* (Metro-Goldwyn-Mayer, November, 1931)
48. *Working Girls* (Paramount, December, 1931)
49. *The Secret Witness* (Columbia, December, 1931)
50. *Delicious* (Fox, December, 1931)
51. *Peach-o-Reno* (Radio, December, 1931)
52. *Dance Team* (Fox, January, 1932)
53. *Forbidden* (Columbia, January, 1932)
54. *Two Kinds of Women* (Paramount, 1932)
55. *Lady with a Past* (RKO, February, 1932)
56. *Final Edition* (Columbia, February, 1932)
57. *Greeks Had a Word for Them* (United Artists, February, 1932)
58. *Vanity Fair* (Allied, March, 1932)
59. *The Keyhole* (Warner Bros., March, 1932)
60. *One Hour with You* (Paramount, March, 1932)
61. *— But the Flesh Is Weak* (M-G-M, April, 1932)
62. *Rich Are Always with Us* (First National, June, 1932)
63. *Bachelor's Affairs* (Fox, June, 1932)
64. *Merrily We Go to Hell* (Paramount, June, 1932)
65. *Week-End Marriage* (First National, July, 1932)
66. *Jewel Robbery* (Warner Bros., August, 1932)
67. *Crooner* (First National, August, 1932)
68. *Two Against the World* (Warner Bros., September, 1932)
69. *A Successful Calamity* (Warner Bros., September, 1932)
70. *Night After Night* (Paramount, October, 1932)
71. *Silver Dollar* (First National, December, 1932)
72. *Taxi Barons* (Metro-Goldwyn-Mayer, April, 1933)
73. *Little Giant* (First National, May, 1933)
74. *Peg o' My Heart* (M-G-M, May, 1933)
75. *Cocktail Hour* (Columbia, June, 1933)
76. *Private Detective 62* (Warner Bros., July, 1933)
77. *Her Bodyguard* (Paramount, July, 1933)
78. *Handlebars* (Metro-Goldwyn-Mayer, August, 1933)
79. *Gold Diggers of 1933* (Warner Bros., September, 1933)
80. *My Weakness* (Fox, September, 1933)
81. *Stage Mother* (M-G-M, September, 1933)
82. *Dancing Lady* (M-G-M, November, 1933)
83. *My Lips Betray* (Fox, November, 1933)

84. *Modern Hero* (Warner Bros., April, 1934)
85. *Upperworld* (Warner Bros., April, 1934)
86. *Wonder Bar* (First National, May, 1934)
87. *Twenty Million Sweethearts* (First National, May, 1934)
88. *Merry Wives of Reno* (Warner Bros., May, 1934)
89. *Smarty* (Warner Bros., May, 1934)
90. *Dr. Monica* (Warner Bros., June, 1934)
91. *Merry Frinks* (First National, June, 1934)
92. *Registered Nurse* (First National, June, 1934)
93. *Here Comes the Navy* (Warner Bros., July, 1934)
94. *Friends of Mr. Sweeney* (Warner Bros., July, 1934)
95. *Good Morning, Eve!* (Warner Bros., August, 1934)
96. *Housewife* (Warner Bros., August, 1934)
97. *Desirable* (Warner Bros., September, 1934)
98. *Case of the Howling Dog* (Warner Bros., September, 1934)
99. *A Lost Lady* (First National, September, 1934)
100. *6 Day Bike Rider* (First National, October, 1934)
101. *The Firebird* (Warner Bros., November, 1934)
102. *I Am a Thief* (Warner Bros., November, 1934)
103. *Secret Bride* (Warner Bros., December, 1934)
104. *Murder in the Clouds* (Warner Bros., December, 1934)
105. *Devil Dogs of the Air* (Warner Bros., February, 1935)
106. *The Woman in Red* (Warner Bros., February, 1935)
107. *A Night at the Ritz* (Warner Bros., February, 1935)
108. *Go Into Your Dance* (Warner Bros., March, 1935)
109. *Living on Velvet* (Warner Bros., March, 1935)
110. *While the Patient Slept* (Warner Bros., March, 1935)
111. *Gold Diggers of 1935* (Warner Bros., March, 1935)
112. *Traveling Saleslady* (Warner Bros., April, 1935)
113. *Reckless* (M-G-M, April, 1935)
114. *"G" Men* (Warner Bros., May, 1935)
115. *Girl from 10th Avenue* (Warner Bros., May, 1935)
116. *Alibi Ike* (Warner Bros., June, 1935)
117. *Page Miss Glory* (Warner Bros., July, 1935)
118. *Front Page Woman* (Warner Bros., July, 1935)
119. *Broadway Gondolier* (Warner Bros., July, 1935)
120. *Bright Lights* (Warner Bros., July, 1935)
121. *Going Highbrow* (Warner Bros., August, 1935)
122. *Romance of the West* (Warner Bros., August, 1935)
123. *Goose and the Gander* (Warner Bros., September, 1935)
124. *Personal Maid's Secret* (Warner Bros., October, 1935)
125. *Dr. Socrates* (Warner Bros., October, 1935)
126. *I Live for Love* (Warner Bros., October, 1935)
127. *Moonlight on the Prairie* (Warner Bros., November, 1935)
128. *I Found Stella Parrish* (Warner Bros., November, 1935)

129. *Stars Over Broadway* (Warner Bros., November, 1935)
130. *The Payoff* (Warner Bros., November, 1935)
131. *Broadway Hostess* (Warner Bros., December, 1935)
132. *Dangerous* (Warner Bros., December, 1935)
133. *Man of Iron* (Warner Bros., December, 1935)
134. *Ceiling Zero* (Warner Bros., January, 1936)
135. *Murder of Dr. Harrigan* (Warner Bros., January, 1936)
136. *Story of Louis Pasteur* (Warner Bros., February, 1936)
137. *The Walking Dead* (Warner Bros., March, 1936)
138. *Singing Kid* (Warner Bros., April, 1936)
139. *The Golden Arrow* (Warner Bros., May, 1936)
140. *Bullets or Ballots* (Warner Bros., June, 1936)
141. *Murder by an Aristocrat* (Warner Bros., June, 1936)
142. *Romance in the Air* (Warner Bros., June, 1936)
143. *The Big Noise* (Warner Bros., June, 1936)
144. *Two Against the World* (Warner Bros., July, 1936)
145. *Case of the Velvet Claws* (Warner Bros., August, 1936)
146. *China Clipper* (Warner Bros., August, 1936)
147. *Down the Stretch* (Warner Bros., September, 1936)
148. *Case of the Black Cat* (Warner Bros., October, 1936)
149. *Trailin' West* (Warner Bros., October, 1936)
150. *Fugitive in the Sky* (Warner Bros., November, 1936)
151. *Polo Joe* (Warner Bros., November, 1936)
152. *King of Hockey* (Warner Bros., December, 1936)
153. *Guns of the Pecos* (Warner Bros., January, 1937)
154. *Midnight Court* (Warner Bros., March, 1937)
155. *Melody for Two* (Warner Bros., May, 1937)
156. *Speed to Spare* (Columbia, May 1937)
157. *Michael O'Halloran* (Republic, May, 1937)
158. *You Can't Have Everything* (20th Century–Fox, August, 1937)
159. *Wife, Doctor and Nurse* (20th Century–Fox, September, 1937)
160. *Boots and Saddles* (Republic, October, 1937)
161. *Roll Along Cowboy* (20th Century–Fox, October, 1937)
162. *Love Takes Flight* (Grand National, November, 1937)
163. *Swing It, Professor* (Ambassador, November, 1937)
164. *Tarzan's Revenge* (20th Century–Fox, January, 1938)
165. *Boy of the Streets* (Monogram, January, 1938)
166. *Lady in the Morgue* (Universal, April, 1938)
167. *Devil's Party* (Universal, May, 1938)
168. *Great Adventures of Wild Bill Hickok* (Columbia, June, 1938)
169. *Letter of Introduction* (Universal, August, 1938)

170. *In Early Arizona* (Columbia, November, 1938)
171. *Frontiers of '49* (Columbia, January, 1939)
172. *Lone Star Pioneers* (Columbia, March, 1939)
173. *The Law Comes to Texas* (Columbia, April, 1939)
174. *Overland with Kit Carson* (Columbia, August, 1939)
175. *Taming of the West* (Columbia, October, 1939)
176. *Pioneers of the Frontier* (Columbia, February, 1940)
177. *The Man from Tumbleweeds* (Columbia, June, 1940)
178. *The Return of Wild Bill* (Columbia, July, 1940)
179. *Prairie Schooners* (Columbia, November, 1940)
180. *Beyond the Sacramento* (Columbia, November, 1940)
181. *Across the Sierras* (Columbia, February, 1941)
182. *North from the Lone Star* (Columbia, March, 1941)
183. *Wildcat of Tucson* (Columbia, April, 1941)
184. *Return of Daniel Boone* (Columbia, May, 1941)
185. *Hands Across the Rockies* (Columbia, June, 1941)
186. *Meet the Stars: Meet Roy Rogers* (Republic, June, 1941)
187. *Son of Davy Crockett* (Columbia, July, 1941)
188. *King of Dodge City* (Columbia, August, 1941)
189. *Roaring Frontiers* (Columbia, October, 1941)
190. *Lone Star Vigilantes* (Columbia, January, 1942)
191. *Bullets for Bandits* (Columbia, February, 1942)
192. *North of the Rockies* (Columbia, April, 1942)
193. *The Devil's Trail* (Columbia, May, 1942)
194. *Prairie Gunsmoke* (Columbia, July, 1942)
195. *Vengeance of the West* (Columbia, August, 1942)
196. *Valley of Vanishing Men* (Columbia, December, 1942)
197. *Calling Wild Bill Elliott* (Republic, April, 1943)
198. *The Man from Thunder River* (Republic, June, 1943)
199. *Bordertown Gun Fighters* (Republic, October, 1943)
200. *Wagon Tracks West* (Republic, October, 1943)
201. *Overland Mail Robbery* (Republic, November, 1943)
202. *Death Valley Manhunt* (Republic, November, 1943)
203. *Mojave Firebrand* (Republic, March, 1944)
204. *Hidden Valley Outlaws* (Republic, April, 1944)
205. *Tucson Raiders* (Republic, May, 1944)
206. *Marshal of Reno* (Republic, July, 1944)
207. *The San Antonio Kid* (Republic, August, 1944)
208. *Cheyenne Wildcat* (Republic, September, 1944)
209. *Vigilantes of Dodge City* (Republic, November, 1944)
210. *Sheriff of Las Vegas* (Republic, December, 1944)
211. *The Great Stagecoach Robbery* (Republic, February, 1945)
212. *The Lone Texas Ranger* (Republic, May, 1945)

213. *Bells of Rosarita* (Republic, June, 1945), starring Roy Rogers
214. *Phantom of the Plains* (Republic, September, 1945)
215. *Marshal of Laredo* (Republic, October, 1945)
216. *Colorado Pioneers* (Republic, November, 1945)
217. *Wagon Wheels Westward* (Republic, December, 1945)
218. *California Gold Rush* (Republic, February, 1946)
219. *Sheriff of Redwood Valley* (Republic, March, 1946)
220. *Sun Valley Cyclone* (Republic, May, 1946)
221. *In Old Sacramento* (Republic, May, 1946)
222. *Conquest of Cheyenne* (Republic, July, 1946)
223. *Plainsman and the Lady* (Republic, November, 1946)
224. *Wyoming* (Republic, July, 1947)
225. *The Fabulous Texan* (Republic, November, 1947)
226. *Old Los Angeles* (Republic, April, 1948)
227. *The Gallant Legion* (Republic, May, 1948)
228. *The Last Bandit* (Republic, February, 1949)
229. *Prince of the Plains* (Republic, April, 1949)
230. *Hellfire* (Republic, June, 1949)
231. *Outcasts of the Trail* (Republic, June, 1949)
232. *Savage Horde* (Republic, July, 1950)
233. *The Showdown* (Republic, August, 1950)
234. *Marshal of Trail City* (Century Television, 1950)
235. *Screen Snapshots: Reno's Silver Spur Awards* (Columbia, January, 1951)
236. *The Longhorn* (Monogram, November, 1951)
237. *Waco* (Monogram, February, 1952)
238. *Kansas Territory* (Monogram, May, 1952)
239. *Fargo* (Monogram, September, 1952)
240. *The Maverick* (Allied Artists, December, 1952)
241. *The Homesteaders* (Allied Artists, March, 1953)
242. *Rebel City* (Allied Artists, May, 1953)
243. *Topeka* (Allied Artists, August, 1953)
244. *Vigilante Terror* (Allied Artists, November, 1953)
245. *Bitter Creek* (Allied Artists, February, 1954)
246. *The Forty-Niners* (Allied Artists, May, 1954)
247. *Riding with Buffalo Bill* (Columbia, November, 1954)
248. *Dial Red 0* (Allied Artists, March, 1955)
249. *Sudden Danger* (Allied Artists, December, 1955)
250. *Calling Homicide* (Allied Artists, June, 1956)
251. *Blazing the Overland Trail* (Columbia, August, 1956)
252. *Chain of Evidence* (Allied Artists, January, 1957)
253. *Footsteps in the Night* (Allied Artists, March, 1957)
254. *Brother, Can You Spare a Dime?* (Goodtimes Enterprise, August, 1975)
255. *Meanwhile, Back at the Ranch* (Curtco & RCR Productions, May, 1977)
256. *Action Heroes of the Wild West* (Film Shows, Inc., 1992)

Bibliography

Books

Adams, Les, and Buck Rainey. *The Shoot-'Em-Ups.* New Rochelle, NY: Arlington House, 1978.

Barbour, Alan G. *Days of Thrills and Adventure.* Kew Gardens, NY: Screen Facts Press, 1969.

_____. *The Serials of Columbia.* Kew Gardens, NY: Screen Facts Press, 1967.

Bond, Johnny. *The Tex Ritter Story.* New York: Chappell Music Company, 1976.

Bradley, Edwin M. *The First Hollywood Sound Shorts, 1926–1931.* Jefferson, NC: McFarland, 2005.

Carman, Bob, and Dan Scapperotti. *The Western Films of Monte Hale.* Robert C. Carman, 1984.

Catalog of Copyright Entries Cumulative Series, Motion Picture 1912–1939. Washington, DC: Library of Congress, 1951.

Cline, William C. *Stroke of Fortune: Adventures of a Motion Picture Showman.* Madison, NC: Empire Publishing, 1995.

Copeland, Bobby. *Bill Elliott: The Peaceable Man.* Madison, NC: Empire Publishing, 2000.

Eames, John Douglas. *The MGM Story.* New York: Crown, 1982.

_____. *The Paramount Story.* New York: Crown, 1985.

Green, Douglas B. *Singing in the Saddle.* Nashville, TN: Country Music Foundation Press and Vanderbilt University Press, 2002.

Hardy, Phil. *The Western.* New York: William Morrow, 1983.

Harmon, Jim, and Donald F. Glut. *The Great Movie Serials.* Garden City, NY: Doubleday, 1972.

Hirshhorn, Clive. *The Universal Story.* New York: Crown, 1983.

_____. *The Warner Bros. Story.* New York: Crown, 1986.

Jewell, Richard B., with Vernon Harbin. *The RKO Story.* New York: Arlington House, 1982.

Leonard, John. *Wild Bill Elliott.* John W. Leonard, 1976.

Mathis, Jack. *Republic Confidential Vol. 2: The Play-ers.* Barrington, IL: Jack Mathis Advertising, 1992.

Miller, Don. *Hollywood Corral.* New York: Popular Library, 1975.

Nash, Jay Robert, and Stanley Ralph Ross. *The Motion Picture Guide.* Chicago: Cinebooks, 1985.

Overstreet, Robert M. *The Overstreet Comic Book Guide,* 26th edition. New York: Avon Books, 1996.

Peters, House, Jr. *Another Side of Hollywood.* Madison, NC: Empire Publishing, 2000.

Pitts, Michael R. *Western Movies.* Jefferson, NC: McFarland, 1986.

Rainey, Buck. *The Shoot-'Em-Ups Ride Again.* Metuchen, NJ: Scarecrow, 1990.

Rothel, David. *The Roy Rogers Book.* Madison, NC: Empire Publishing, 1987.

_____. *Those Great Cowboy Sidekicks.* Madison, NC: Empire Publishing, 1984.

Rutherford, John A., and Richard B. Smith III. *More Cowboy Shooting Stars.* Madison, NC: Empire Publishing, 1992.

Stier, Kenny. *The First Fifty Years of Sound Western Movie Locations (1929–1979).* Rialto, CA: Corriganville Press, 2006.

Tuska, Jon. *The Filming of the West.* Garden City, NY: Doubleday, 1976.

Variety Reviews (3 volumes). New York: Garland, 1983.

Watz, Edward. *Wheeler and Woolsey.* Jefferson, NC: McFarland, 1994.

Weiss, Ken. *To Be Continued.* New Rochelle, NY: Love's Labor Press, 2000.

Periodicals

Boxoffice (Kansas City, MO)

Boyd Magers' Serial Report (Albuquerque, NM)

Boyd Magers' Western Clippings (Albuquerque, NM)

Classic Images (Muscatine, IA)

Great Vintage Movie Ads: The American Western Film

Hit the Saddle (Kew Gardens, NY)
Movie Ads from the Past (Whiteville, NC)
Saturday's Heroes (Lubbock, TX)
Under Western Skies (Waynesville, NC)
Who's Who in Western Stars (New York, NY)
Yesterday's Saturdays (Lubbock, TX)

Newspapers

Baton Rouge Morning Advocate (Baton Rouge, LA)
The New York Times (New York, NY)
Richmond Times-Dispatch (Richmond, VA)
The Virginian-Pilot (Norfolk, VA)

Index